THE OLD TESTAMENT WORLD

THE OLD TESTAMENT WORLD

BY

MARTIN NOTH
PROFESSOR OF OLD TESTAMENT EXEGESIS
UNIVERSITY OF BONN

Translated by Victor I. Gruhn

FORTRESS PRESS PHILADELPHIA

This book is a translation of the fourth edition of *Die Welt des Alten Testaments: Einführung in die Grenzgebiete der alttestamentlichen Wissenschaft* by Martin Noth published by Alfred Töpelmann, Berlin, 1964

LIBRARY OF CONGRESS CATALOG CARD NUMBER 65-10061

SECOND PRINTING

4203 A67 1-20

PRINTED IN GREAT BRITAIN
BY R. & R. CLARK, LTD., EDINBURGH

TRANSLATOR'S FOREWORD

IN the process of translating Martin Noth's *Die Welt des Alten Testaments* for English and American readers, several things have happened of which the reader should be aware. Sentence structure naturally has had to conform to English usage. Place names have been variously spelled, according as the context seemed to call for the ancient or modern Hebrew or Arabic form. References to the German Bible, like biblical names, have been changed to accord with the English Bible. Geographical comparisons have been made to refer to more familiar sites. Measurements have been rendered both in metres and in feet. The transliteration of Hebrew and Arabic words is explained at the beginning of the respective indexes. A list of abbreviations used throughout the book—and in the field generally—is provided. References to current studies are continued to the present.

Also, parallel references to English language works are given where the original text quite understandably gives German works, for example, in translations from Babylonian or Assyrian. The warrant for such changes is to be seen in the author's introductory statement to Chapter IV to the effect that every translation is not merely a transfer of words or grammar from one language to another but actually a transfer of meaning " into the spirit of the world and age of the translator."

Gratefully do I salute those who have given special assistance in making this translation as useful as possible. Chief among these are my beloved professors George G. Cameron and George E. Mendenhall. Andrew Ehrenkreutz piloted me through the difficult seas of Arabic transliteration. I received special help on matters of geology from Franz E. Vorenkamp and on matters of geography from Douglas Crary. The text was read by my associates, Herbert Huffmon and Elizabeth von Voigtlander, and also by Dr. H. H. Rowley. The Indexes were completed by Philip Long. All of them made valuable critical suggestions.

V. I. G.

AUTHOR'S FOREWORD

From the Foreword to the First Edition

THE Old Testament has a definite geographical setting, since it came into being in a given area. It is also historically a part of the extensive, very well-documented world of the ancient Near East. Study of the Old Testament inevitably involves study of those parts of that world with which a clear connection has been established. Also, anyone, even though he is not a specialist in Old Testament study, must now be at least generally oriented on these related areas if he wants to work or converse on the Old Testament. On the other hand, these marginal areas of Old Testament study are so detailed that it is difficult to find one's way in them without specialized studies. The present volume has developed from the need to meet this problem. Its purpose is to assist in a survey of these marginal areas. It is also intended as an aid to anyone reading Old Testament scholarly works in which reference is often made to such related areas of study.

For this reason the attempt has been made to give as much concrete material as possible without overburdening the text with unnecessary details. It is self-evident that it is often difficult to decide what is important enough to include, and what in these numerous areas of study can be omitted as less important. It therefore seems impossible to satisfy equally all of the demands that one could properly make of such a book. This is true especially since this is the first attempt to make such a survey and classification. This book must present definite scholarly conclusions. In addition, unsolved problems and tentative conclusions have had to be included occasionally, along with questions still insoluble because the evidence available is limited. In such cases I have deliberately, although necessarily briefly, given a statement of various possibilities of solution. Solid scholarly training includes not only the acceptance of fixed results of research, but also orientation on still unclarified problems, as well as on the methods by which one can or must overcome them.

The actual interrelationship of the various areas treated is so great that as one studies any one of them he must repeatedly refer to the others. To meet this situation, some cross references are included. Attention is directed especially to the general index, which has been made as detailed as possible. For the areas of special concern here I have cited the basic works, such as source materials, original publications, and useful research studies, including the numerous related works in other languages, as completely as possible in order to assist anyone who wants to orient himself better on a specific area or on a given point.

M. N.

KÖNIGSBERG, PRUSSIA
February, 1940

Foreword to the Fourth Edition

THIS fourth edition represents a thorough revision of the entire book. Its viewpoint, character, and plan have not been changed essentially. It has been necessary to attempt to keep pace with the progress of research, new disclosures, and new knowledge. This is well-nigh impossible in view of the rapid strides of scholarly labours in the many areas of study under consideration here. However, materials appearing even during the process of publication have been worked into the text.

I have added a new section on trade routes of Palestine in antiquity because I consider trade links and trade relations important for understanding the historical geography of a land.

The illustrative plates which appeared in previous editions have been omitted here. There are now so many books which offer pictorial material on the history and contemporary life of Palestine and other lands of the ancient Near East, that limited illustrations would be meaningless—and numerous illustrations would change the character of the book radically.

M. N.

BONN
July, 1962

Foreword to the English Translation

THIS English translation of my book *Die Welt des Alten Testaments* is based on the German fourth edition. My forthright and hearty thanks are due to the translator, Pastor Victor I. Gruhn. He has not only undertaken the exceedingly tedious task of translating a difficult German text into English, but with uncommonly great scholarship and care he has actually brought this task to completion. If the book wins acceptance in the English-speaking world, it will be primarily due to the amazing contribution of the translator.

M. N.

BONN
August, 1965

CONTENTS

		PAGE
ABBREVIATIONS		xvii
SIGLA		xxi

PART ONE

GEOGRAPHY OF PALESTINE

CHAP.		
	Pertinent Literature	2
I.	GENERAL GEOGRAPHY	
	1. Palestine: The Name and Its Meaning	7
	2. Topography	9
	3. Size	24
	4. Climate	28
	5. Flora and Fauna	33
II.	NATURAL HISTORY	
	6. Geology	41
	7. Natural Regions	45
III.	PALESTINE AS THE ARENA OF BIBLICAL HISTORY	
	8. Biblical Geographical Terms	49
	9. Settlement	63
	10. Political Divisions	93

PART TWO

ARCHEOLOGY OF PALESTINE

I.	INTRODUCTION	
	11. Concept and History	107
	12. Literature	110
	13. Cultural Periods	111
II.	ARCHEOLOGICAL WORK	
	14. Excavation Activity	125
	15. Surface Exploration	137
	16. Archeological Finds and Literary Tradition	139

CHAP. PAGE

III. RESULTS FOR THE PERIOD OF BIBLICAL HISTORY
17. Settlements 145
18. Domestic Life 158
19. Occupations 163
20. Burial Customs 168
21. Sanctuaries 173

PART THREE

PERTINENT ASPECTS OF ANCIENT NEAR EASTERN HISTORY

Preliminary Remarks 183

I. LANDS
22. Natural Units 185
23. Trade Routes 190

II. CULTURES
24. Characteristic Features 194
25. Research on Cultures 199

III. WRITING SYSTEMS AND EXAMPLES OF ANCIENT WRITING
26. Ideographic and Syllabographic Systems 202
27. Alphabetic Writing 211

IV. LANGUAGES
28. Semitic Languages 224
29. Non-Semitic Languages 229

V. PEOPLES
30. Races in the Ancient Near East 234
31. Historical Peoples 235

VI. STATES
32. Great Powers 246
33. Small States 257
34. Cities 262

VII. DATES
35. Chronology 267
36. Chronological Synopsis of Ancient Near Eastern History 273

VIII. RELIGIONS
37. Religious Source Materials 278
38. Basic Features of Religious Outlook and Practice 280
39. The Individual Religions 287

PART FOUR

THE TEXT OF THE OLD TESTAMENT

CHAP.		PAGE
	Preliminary Remarks	301
I.	THE TRANSMISSION OF THE TEXT IN THE SYNAGOGUE	
	40. The Transmission of the Hebrew Text	303
	41. Translations into Other Languages	316
II.	THE TRANSMISSION OF THE TEXT IN THE CHRISTIAN CHURCH	
	42. The Old Testament Text in the Eastern Church (the Septuagint)	324
	43. The Old Testament Text in the National Churches of the Near East	337
	44. The Old Testament Text in the Western Church	342
III.	METHODS OF TEXTUAL CRITICAL WORK	
	45. Changes in the Original Text	349
	46. Evaluation of Textual Critical Material	355
	47. Principles of Textual Criticism of the Old Testament	358
	TIME CHART	364
	INDEX OF HEBREW AND ARAMAIC WORDS	371
	INDEX OF ARABIC WORDS	375
	INDEX OF SCRIPTURAL PASSAGES	381
	INDEX OF AUTHORS	387
	GENERAL INDEX	393

ILLUSTRATIONS

FIGURE		PAGE
1	Modern Palestine	11
2	Geological Structure	41
3	The Settlement of Palestine	65
4	Wall Construction	149
5	Temples	175
6	Area Map of the Ancient Near East	187
7	Ideographic and Syllabographic Writing	207
8	Alphabetic Writing	215
9	Samaritan Ostracon	222
10	Lachish Ostracon	223

ABBREVIATIONS

OVER and beyond the abbreviations actually appearing in this book additional ones are listed here. They are given because they will be encountered by anyone reading pertinent scholarly works. Pages noted below in parentheses refer to pages in this book on which there are additional comments on these works.

AA	=	Archäologischer Anzeiger
AAA	=	Annals of Archaeology and Anthropology
AASOR	=	Annual of the American Schools of Oriental Research (110)
AfO	=	Archiv für Orientforschung (184)
AJA	=	American Journal of Archaeology
AJSL	=	American Journal of Semitic Languages and Literatures
ANEP	=	Ancient Near Eastern Pictures Relating to the Old Testament, ed. by J. B. Pritchard (183)
ANET	=	Ancient Near Eastern Texts Relating to the Old Testament, ed. by J. B. Pritchard (183)
AO	=	Der Alte Orient
AOB	=	H. Gressmann, Altorientalische Bilder zum Alten Testament, 2nd ed., 1927 (183)
AOT	=	H. Gressmann, Altorientalische Texte zum Alten Testament, 2nd ed., 1926 (183)
APAW	=	Abhandlungen der Preussischen Akademie der Wissenschaften
ARM	=	Archives royales de Mari (225)
ATAO	=	A. Jeremias, Das Alte Testament im Lichte des Alten Orients, 4th ed., 1930 (183)
BA	=	Biblical Archaeologist (6)
BAH	=	Bibliothèque archéologique et historique (Institut Français d'archéologie de Beyrouth)
BASOR	=	Bulletin of the American Schools of Oriental Research
BBLAK	=	Beiträge zur biblischen Landes- und Altertumskunde
BH	=	Biblia Hebraica, ed. Rudolf Kittel, 3rd ed., 1937
BIES	=	Bulletin of the Israel Exploration Society (6)
BJPES	=	Bulletin of the Jewish Palestine Exploration Society (6)
BoTU	=	Die Boghazköi-Texte in Umschrift (230)
BRL	=	K. Galling, Biblisches Reallexikon, 1937 (110)
BW	=	H. Guthe, Kurzes Bibelwörterbuch, 1903

BWA(N)T	=	Beiträge zur Wissenschaft vom Alten (und Neuen) Testament
BZ	=	Biblische Zeitschrift
BZAW	=	Beiheft zur Zeitschrift für die alttestamentliche Wissenschaft
CAD	=	The Assyrian Dictionary of the Oriental Institute of the University of Chicago (225)
CIS	=	Corpus Inscriptionum Semiticarum
CT	=	Cuneiform Texts from Babylonian Tablets in the British Museum (209)
DLZ	=	Deutsche Literaturzeitung
DPV	=	Deutscher Verein zur Erforschung Palästinas (" Deutscher Palästina-Verein ") (6)
EA	=	J. A. Knudtzon, Die El-Amarna Tafeln, 1915 (208) (Transliterated text and German translation)
FF	=	Forschungen und Fortschritte
HAOG	=	A. Jeremias, Handbuch der altorientalischen Geisteskultur, 2nd ed., 1929 (183)
IEJ	=	Israel Exploration Journal (6)
JAOS	=	Journal of the American Oriental Society
JBL	=	Journal of Biblical Literature
JCS	=	Journal of Cuneiform Studies
JEA	=	Journal of Egyptian Archaeology
JNES	=	Journal of Near Eastern Studies
JPOS	=	Journal of the Palestine Oriental Society (6)
JTS	=	Journal of Theological Studies
KAH	=	Keilschrifttexte aus Assur historischen Inhalts } Included in the Series WVDOG
KAR	=	Keilschrifttexte aus Assur religiösen Inhalts } Included in the Series WVDOG
KAV	=	Keilschrifttexte aus Assur verschiedenen Inhalts } Included in the Series WVDOG
KB	=	Keilinschriftliche Bibliothek (249)
KBo	=	Keilschrifttexte aus Boghazköi (230), included in the Series WVDOG
KS I, II, III	=	A. Alt, Kleine Schriften zur Geschichte des Volkes Israel, Vols. I–III, 1953–59
KUB	=	Keilschrifturkunden aus Boghazköi (230)
LS	=	P. Thomsen, Loca Sancta I, 1907
MDOG	=	Mitteilungen der Deutschen Orient-Gesellschaft
MNDPV	=	Mitteilungen und Nachrichten des Deutschen Palästina-Vereins
MVÄG	=	Mittelungen der vorderasiatisch-ägyptischen Gesellschaft
OIC	=	Oriental Institute Communications, The Oriental Institute of the University of Chicago
OIP	=	Oriental Institute Publications, The Oriental Institute of the University of Chicago
OLZ	=	Orientalische Literaturzeitung
OTS	=	Oudtestamentische Studiën

PEF = Palestine Exploration Fund (6)
PEF Ann. = Palestine Exploration Fund, Annual (110)
PEF Qu. St. = Palestine Exploration Fund, Quarterly Statements (6)
PEQ = Palestine Exploration Quarterly (6)
PJB = Palästinajahrbuch (6)
PRU = Le palais royal d'Ugarit
PSBA = Proceedings of the Society of Biblical Archaeology
QDAP = Quarterly of the Department of Antiquities in Palestine (110)
RAC = Reallexikon für Antike und Christentum
RÄRG = Reallexikon der ägyptischen Religionsgeschichte (287)
RA = Revue d'Assyriologie
RB = Revue Biblique (6)
RE = Realencyklopädie für protestantische Theologie und Kirche, 3rd ed., 1891–1913
RGG = Die Religion in Geschichte und Gegenwart, 3rd ed., 1957–62
RLA = Reallexikon der Assyriologie (198)
RLV = Reallexikon der Vorgeschichte
SBA = Studies in Biblical Archaeology
SPAW = Sitzungsberichte der Preussischen Akademie der Wissenschaften
ThBl = Theologische Blätter
ThR = Theologische Rundschau
ThZ = Theologische Zeitschrift
VA = Vorderasiatische Abteilung der Staatlichen Museen in Berlin
VB = Vorderasiatische Bibliothek
VT = Vetus Testamentum (Journal)
WO = Die Welt des Orients
WVDOG = Wissenschaftliche Veröffentlichungen der Deutschen Orient-Gesellschaft
WZKM = Wiener Zeitschrift für die Kunde des Morgenlandes
ZA = Zeitschrift für Assyriologie
ZÄ = Zeitschrift für ägyptische Sprache und Altertumskunde
ZAW = Zeitschrift für die alttestamentliche Wissenschaft
ZDMG = Zeitschrift der Deutschen Morgenländischen Gesellschaft
ZDPV = Zeitschrift des Deutschen Palästina-Vereins (6)
ZS = Zeitschrift für Semitistik
ZThK = Zeitschrift für Theologie und Kirche

SIGLA

OUR volume uses the following sigla taken from *Biblia Hebraica*, 3rd ed., Rudolf Kittel *et al.* (*BH*). Introductory material on all of the items in the original Kittel list, together with forty-one plates of the manuscripts described, are provided in Ernst Wuerthwein, *The Text of the Old Testament: An Introduction to Kittel-Kahle's Biblia Hebraica* (Oxford: Blackwell; New York: Macmillan; 1957), translated by Peter Ackroyd.

A = Aquila   𝔄 = Arabic Version   𝔄 = Ethiopic Version
Arm = Armenian Version
𝔅 = Jacob ben Chayyim's Rabbinic Hebrew Bible published by Daniel Bomberg in 1524–25
𝔊 = Septuagint (Greek Version)

- $\mathfrak{G}^{\aleph}$ = Codex Sinaiticus
  - $\aleph^{c.\,a,\ c.\,b,\ c.\,c}$ = Correctors of the Codex Sinaiticus
- $\mathfrak{G}^{A}$ = Codex Alexandrinus
- $\mathfrak{G}^{B}$ = Codex Vaticanus
- $\mathfrak{G}^{Beatty}$ = Chester Beatty Papyri
- $\mathfrak{G}^{\Gamma}$ = Codex Rescriptus Cryptoferratensis
- $\mathfrak{G}^{C}$ = Codex Ephraimi Syrus Rescriptus
- $\mathfrak{G}^{C(om)pl}$ = Septuagint Text in Complutensian Polyglot
- $\mathfrak{G}^{Cyr}$ = Septuagint of Cyril of Alexandria
- $\mathfrak{G}^{D}$ = Codex Cottonianus (Genesis)
- $\mathfrak{G}^{E}$ = Codex Bodleianus (Genesis)
- $\mathfrak{G}^{F}$ = Codex Ambrosianus
- $\mathfrak{G}^{G}$ = Codex Colberto-Sarravianus
- $\mathfrak{G}^{\theta}$ = Codex Freer, Washington, D.C.
- $\mathfrak{G}^{h}$ = Hexaplaric Recension of the Septuagint
- $\mathfrak{G}^{(3)MSS\ (Holmes\text{-})Parsons}$ = Manuscripts in the Edition of Holmes-Parsons
- $\mathfrak{G}^{62.\ 147\ (Parsons)}$ = Minuscules 62, 147 in Holmes-Parsons
- $\mathfrak{G}^{K}$ = Codex Lipsiensis
- $\mathfrak{G}^{L}$ = Lagarde's Edition
- $\mathfrak{G}^{Luc}$ = Lucianic Recension
- $\mathfrak{G}^{M}$ = Codex Coislinianus
- $\mathfrak{G}^{N}$ = Codex Basiliano-Vaticanus
- $\mathfrak{G}^{Pap\ Lond}$ = Papyrus 37 in the British Museum
- $\mathfrak{G}^{Q}$ = Codex Marchalianus
- $\mathfrak{G}^{W}$ = Codex Atheniensis

- Θ = Theodotion
- $\mathfrak{H}^{O}$ = Hebrew Text according to Origen
- 𝔎 = Coptic Translation
- L = Codex Leningradensis
- 𝔏 = Old Latin Version (Itala) according to Sabatier
  - $\mathfrak{L}^{(\text{Berger})}$ = Old Latin Version of Berger
  - $\mathfrak{L}^{D}$ = Old Latin Version of Dold
  - $\mathfrak{L}^{h}$ = Old Latin Version in Würzburg Palimpsests
  - $\mathfrak{L}^{L}$ = Codex Lugdunensis
  - $\mathfrak{L}^{Lg}$ = Old Latin Marginal Readings of the Codex Legionensis
  - $\mathfrak{L}^{Vind}$ = Palimpsestus Vindobonensis
- 𝔐 = Masorah, Masoretic Text of the Hebrew Bible
- Mas = Masorah of the Leningrad Codex
- Mm, Mas. M = Masorah Magna
- Mp = Masorah Parva
- 𝔪 = Samaritan Pentateuch
- $\mathfrak{m}^{T}$ = Samaritan Targum
- Σ = Symmachus
- 𝔖($\mathfrak{S}^{W}$) = Peshitta (Syriac) in London Polyglot of Brian Walton
  - $\mathfrak{S}^{A}$ = Codex Ambrosianus of the Peshitta
  - $\mathfrak{S}^{Aphr}$ = Biblical Quotations of Aphraates
  - $\mathfrak{S}^{h}$ = Syrohexaplar
  - $\mathfrak{S}^{L}$ = Peshitta edited by Lee
  - $\mathfrak{S}^{U}$ = Urmia Edition
- Sah = Sahidic Version
- Sor = Soraei (Masoretes of Sura)
- 𝔗 = Targum
  - $\mathfrak{T}^{O}$ = Targum Onkelos
  - $\mathfrak{T}^{B}$ = Targum in the Bomberg Bible
  - $\mathfrak{T}^{J}$ = Targum Pseudo-Jonathan
  - $\mathfrak{T}^{JII}$ = Targum Jerusalem II
  - $\mathfrak{T}^{L}$ = Lagarde's Edition of the Targum
  - $\mathfrak{T}^{M}$ = Merx, *Chrestomathia Targumica*
  - $\mathfrak{T}^{P}$ = Palestinian Targum
  - $\mathfrak{T}^{Pr}$ = Praetorius' Edition of the Targum
  - $\mathfrak{T}^{W}$ = Targum of the London Polyglot
- 𝔙 = Vulgate
  - $\mathfrak{V}^{A}$ = Codex Amiatinus
- V(ar) = Variant Reading
  - Var^{B} = Variants of Baer's Edition
  - V(ar)^{G} = ,, ,, Ginsburg's Edition
  - V(ar)^{J} = ,, ,, Yemenite Manuscripts
  - V(ar)^{Ken} = ,, ,, Kennicott's Edition
  - V(ar)^{M} = ,, ,, Michaelis' Edition
  - V(ar)^{P} = ,, ,, Petersburg Codex

PART ONE

GEOGRAPHY OF PALESTINE

Pertinent Literature

History of the Study

MODERN scholarly study of the geography of Palestine began at the turn of the nineteenth century. Its foundations were laid by a number of daring explorers who, in spite of all difficulties and dangers, tirelessly travelled the land and systematically recorded their findings. Only the most significant of them can be named here.[1] Ulrich Jasper Seetzen, born in 1767 in the province of Oldenburg, went into the Near East in 1802, travelled through the lands on the eastern shore of the Mediterranean Sea, and lost his life in 1811 in southern Arabia under unknown circumstances. His diaries for the period from April 9, 1805 to March 23, 1809 have been published.[2] Johann Ludwig Burckhardt of Basel went to Syria in 1809, travelled through the lands between Syria and Nubia, and died suddenly in Cairo in 1817. His diaries have been published for the period from October 22, 1810 to May 9, 1812.[3] The real pioneer of scholarly and critical study of the topography of Palestine was Edward Robinson, born April 10, 1794 in Southington, Connecticut. After a thorough training in related subjects and with the help of Eli Smith, the experienced missionary in Syria, he explored Palestine intensively between Suez and Beirut from March 16 to July 8, 1838, and again travelled in southern Syria and in Palestine from March 2 to June 22, 1852. He published his findings in two scholarly works.[4] He died in New York on January 27, 1863.

Maps

Of course, careful surveying of the land for mapping purposes could not be done by individual explorers. Institutions which were

[1] Reinhold Röhricht, *Bibliotheca Geographica Palaestinae* (1890), gives a summary of all accounts of travels by pilgrims and researchers and of the literature pertaining generally to the geography of Palestine between A.D. 333 and A.D. 1878.

[2] F. Kruse (ed.), *Ulrich Jasper Seetzen's Reisen durch Syrien, Palästina, Phönicien, die Transjordan-Länder, Arabia Petraea und Unter-Ägypten* (1854–59), Vols. I–IV.

[3] Burckhardt, *Travels in Syria and the Holy Land* (1822); *Travels in Arabia* (1829).

[4] Robinson and Smith, *Biblical Researches in Palestine, Mount Sinai, and Arabia Petraea* (1841–42), Vols. I–III, presents a diary of the earlier trip in the interest of biblical geography and Robinson, Smith, *et al.*, *Later Biblical Researches in Palestine and the Adjacent Regions* (1857), presents the diary of the later one.

established in the second half of the nineteenth century for the systematic exploration of Palestine undertook this assignment. The Palestine Exploration Fund was formed in 1865 with headquarters in London. It assigned various co-workers to survey Cisjordan during 1872–75 and 1877–78, among them H. H. Kitchener, who later had a distinguished British military career culminating in the office of Secretary of State for War. The outcome of the survey was a *Map of Western Palestine*, in twenty-six sheets on a scale of 1 : 63,360, which still remains the basis of cartography for Cisjordan. An accompanying description of the area was published in a series of volumes beginning in 1881 under the general title *Survey of Western Palestine*.

The northern part of Transjordan was surveyed between 1896 and 1902 by G. Schumacher (d. 1925), a German official of the organization Württembergischer Baurat who lived in Haifa, Palestine. He was commissioned by the Deutscher Verein zur Erforschung Palästinas, an organization established in 1877 with headquarters in Leipzig. The result was a map of Transjordan published from 1908 to 1924 which comprised ten sheets on a scale of 1 : 63,360 and included cultivated Transjordan north of the Jabbok to the sources of the Jordan. *Der ʿAdschlun* (1927) by C. Steuernagel provides descriptive commentary based on Schumacher's notes and diaries.

The German " Survey Unit 27 " completed a *Map of Palestine* on the basis of these maps, as well as their own measurements, during the First World War. It has thirty-nine sheets on a scale of 1 : 50,000 and seven sheets on a scale of 1 : 25,000 and shows Cisjordan and Transjordan from the latitude of Haifa, Tiberias, and Ashtaroth in the north to the latitude of Ashkelon, Bethlehem, and Medeba in the south. It has been published by the German government surveying office in Berlin.

The southernmost part of the land, namely the area on both sides of the great rift called the Wādi el-ʿArabah (see p. 15) from the latitude of the southern end of the Dead Sea to the northern end of the Gulf of ʿAqabah and the area to the east of the Dead Sea, was repeatedly explored and surveyed by Alois Musil between 1896 and 1902. The results of these explorations are set forth in his work *Arabia Petraea*[5] and in the accompanying maps, which are on a scale of 1 : 300,000.

Shortly before the First World War, the Negeb (see p. 56) was surveyed by an Englishman, S. F. Newcombe. This survey is

[5] Musil, *Arabia Petraea* (1907–8), Vols. I–II.

the basis of the map *The Negeb or Desert South of Beersheba*, 1 : 250,000 (1921).

During the period of the British mandate a new survey of the mandated territory of Palestine and Transjordan was undertaken. This produced an outstanding map on a scale of 1 : 100,000 which has become the basic cartographic source for the study of the geography of Palestine. It uses an isohypsometric system with a twenty-five-metre contour interval. It has a special Palestine grid whose zero point is located at 33°25′ east longitude and 30°35′ north latitude. Sites are now located precisely by using the coordinates of this grid. Three-place figures give distances from this zero point in kilometres and four-place figures give one-hundred-metre distances. The part of this map which pertains to Jordan is cited as " 1 : 100,000, South Levant Series "; the Israel edition in twenty-four sheets, which simultaneously supplies modern Hebrew names, is cited as " 1 : 100,000, Palestine." The same survey produced a map with the same Palestine grid on a scale of 1 : 250,000. It appeared in two parts: three sheets as *Israel*, published by the Survey of Israel (1951), and three sheets as *The Hashemite Kingdom of the Jordan*, published by the Department of Lands and Surveys of the Jordan (1949–50).

Geographical Descriptions

From the vast literature about Palestine, varying greatly in type and value, only the most important works are selected for mention here. Among the simple descriptions of the land the monumental work of G. Ebers and H. Guthe, *Palästina in Bild und Wort: nebst der Sinai-Halbinsel und dem Lande Gosen* (1882), Vols. I–II, still deserves mention, as does H. Guthe, *Palästina: Monographien zur Erdkunde*, XXI (2nd ed., 1927), which contains numerous illustrations. Particular consideration is given to problems of the natural sciences in R. Koeppel, *Palästina, Die Landschaft in Karten und Bildern* (1930). Essentials are presented in very short form in the *Stuttgarter Biblisches Nachschlagewerk*, which includes maps, pictures, a short description of the land and a topographical concordance.

Scientific works on the historical geography of the land include George Adam Smith, *The Historical Geography of the Holy Land* (1st ed., 1894; 25th ed., 1931); F. Buhl, *Geographie des alten Palästina: Grundriss der Theologischen Wissenschaften*, II, 4 (1896); F.-M. Abel, *Géographie de la Palestine:* Part I, *Géogra-*

phie physique et historique (1933), Part II, *Géographie politique: Les villes* (1938); M. Du Buit, *Géographie de la Terre Sainte:* Vol. I, *Géographie physique,* Vol. II, *Géographie historique* (1958).

A standard atlas for the geography of Palestine is H. Guthe, *Bibelatlas* (2nd ed., 1926). It contains a great many maps on the historical geography of the land and a map of modern Palestine, drawn as accurately as possible at the time of publication. The latter, published separately as well as in the fiftieth volume of the periodical *Zeitschrift des Deutschen Palästina-Vereins*, is currently the best survey map of Palestine; it is the most reliable and at the same time the most detailed.

Among numerous illustrated works should be mentioned *64 Bilder aus dem Heiligen Lande* [" Sixty-four Pictures from the Holy Land "], published by the Württembergische Bibelanstalt, whose very fine four-colour pictures convey an unusually vivid picture of the landscape and its colours. H. Bardtke, *Zu beiden Seiten des Jordans*, presents pictures for territorial study of Palestine based on photographs taken by the author during his study journey in 1955. G. Dalman, *Hundert deutsche Fliegerbilder aus Palästina* (" Schriften des Deutschen Palästina-Instituts," 1925), Vol. II, is particularly helpful for knowledge of the structure of the land. In this work an outstanding selection of aerial photographs, taken by the Bavarian Air Corps, Wing 304, during the First World War, is presented with exact descriptions, especially for the southern part of the land. Most of the books which are published as biblical atlases supply excellent illustrations. Although these books unfortunately do not supply maps detailed enough for careful studies, they do provide more or less extensive written description and numerous good illustrations showing the land, the peoples, and the historical monuments of Palestine. See especially the Westminster Bible atlas,[6] Grollenberg's atlas,[7] the Rand McNally Bible atlas,[8] and finally the more briefly conceived volume compiled by Rowley.[9]

[6] G. Ernest Wright and Floyd V. Filson (eds.), *The Westminster Historical Atlas to the Bible*, with introductory article by W. F. Albright (Philadelphia: Westminster, 1956).

[7] L. H. Grollenberg, O.P. (ed.), *Nelson's Atlas of the Bible* (New York: Thomas Nelson & Sons, 1957). Originally published in Dutch, this work has now been published in French, German, and English.

[8] Emil G. Kraeling, *Rand McNally Bible Atlas* (New York: Rand McNally, 1956). A shorter edition, *Historical Atlas of the Holy Land*, was published in 1959.

[9] H. H. Rowley, *The Teach Yourself Bible Atlas* (English Universities, 1961).

Periodicals

The most important periodicals concerned with the study of Palestine are listed below in the order in which they began publication:

Palestine Exploration Fund Quarterly Statements (hereafter referred to as *PEF Qu. St.*), published since 1869, title changed to *Palestine Exploration Quarterly* (*PEQ*) since 1937;

Zeitschrift des Deutschen Palästina-Vereins (*ZDPV*), published since 1878;

Revue Biblique (*RB*), published since 1892 by Dominican scholars of the École pratique d'Études bibliques au Couvent St. Étienne in Jerusalem, more recently known as the École Biblique et Archéologique Française;

Palästinajahrbuch des Deutschen evangelischen Instituts für Altertumswissenschaft des heiligen Landes zu Jerusalem (*PJB*), published from 1905 to 1941;

Bulletin of the American Schools of Oriental Research (*BASOR*) published since 1919;

The Biblical Archaeologist (*BA*), published since 1938 by the American Schools of Oriental Research;

Journal of the Palestine Oriental Society (*JPOS*), published from 1921 to 1944;

Bulletin of the Jewish Palestine Exploration Society (*BJPES*), published in Hebrew since 1933, title changed first to *Bulletin of the Israel Exploration Society* (*BIES*) and then in 1962 to *Yediot*, beginning with Vol. XXVI;

Israel Exploration Journal (*IEJ*), published since 1950.

The entire scholarly literature concerning Palestine is catalogued in the large work of P. Thomsen, *Die Palästina-Literatur*, described in the subtitle as " an international bibliography, systematically arranged with an index of authors and subjects." The first volume, which catalogues the literature for 1895–1904, appeared in 1908. By 1956 the work had reached its sixth volume, dealing with the period 1935–39. Soon to be published is Volume A, which will catalogue the literature of 1878–94, closing the gap between the bibliography compiled by Röhricht cited earlier and Volume I of Thomsen's work.

CHAPTER I

GENERAL GEOGRAPHY

1. *Palestine: The Name and Its Meaning*

THE meaning of the name Palestine is anything but clear and definite.[1] In the scholarly literature of the nineteenth century, Palestine is the common yet vague title especially for Cisjordan, where most of the history of Israel took place. This usage can be traced back through Christian literature of the West. In Western pilgrim and travel literature the land of the Bible was known as Palestine. This name was used interchangeably with the biblical name Canaan and such others as *terra sancta*, " Holy Land," or *terra* (re)*promissionis*, " Promised Land "—i.e., the land promised to the Old Testament patriarchs in Gen. 12 : 7. This tradition goes back to the early church. Such influential writers as Eusebius of Caesarea and Jerome knew and used Palestine as the name of the Promised Land. The early church, however, used this name simply as a technical term taken from the official language of the Roman and, later, of the Byzantine empire, for in Greek *Palaistine* and in Latin *Palaestina* was the name of the imperial province. The old name *Judaea* (Latin) or *Ioudaia* (Greek), which had been used in accordance with earlier precedent by the Hasmonean government and that of Herod, first became the name of the Roman province established on the same soil. However, after the Jewish Revolt of A.D. 132–35, the Romans replaced the name *Judaea* with the name *Palaestina* (Latin) or *Palaistine* (Greek). Apparently the Romans found the name *Judaea* both distasteful, in view of the measures they then undertook against Jewry, and inappropriate in view of the wide expansion of Jewry beyond the narrow borders of this province. In the Roman-Byzantine period, therefore, the name Palestine had a clear and definite meaning, even if in the course of its history the borders of the province were changed occasionally. The chief part of the province of Palestine was always Cisjordan. However, portions of Transjordan always belonged to the province—at first particularly Peraea, east of the lower Jordan River and of the Dead

[1] See Martin Noth, " Zur Geschichte des Namens Palästina," *ZDPV*, LXII (1939), 125 ff.

Sea, as well as parts of the Decapolis east of the Sea of Tiberias, and from the fourth century on the southern border regions adjacent to the Wādi el-'Arabah (see p. 15). Although the province was partitioned into three parts in the fourth century (*Palaestina prima*, *secunda*, *tertia*), it remained a unit for military government under the command of a *dux*; it was this unit the early church writers had in mind when they used the name Palestine. Thus the continued use of the name Palestine in Christian literature, and the resulting modern use of this name, goes back ultimately to the official administrative terminology of the Roman-Byzantine empire.

The name itself can be traced back farther than Roman days. Naturally the Romans did not coin this name, but adopted it. It is first noted in various passages in Herodotus in the fifth century B.C., for example in Herodotus, iii.5. In this passage the inhabitants of the coast of Carmel all the way south to Gaza are " Syrians, who are called *Palaistinoi*." *Palaistinoi* naturally means " Philistines " and is the Greek for Hebrew *Pelishtim* or, more probably, Aramaic *Pelishta'in*. Greek seamen and merchants had a rather vague name for the coast of the great fifth Persian satrapy (cf. Herodotus, iii.91), namely " Syria." They distinguished between a northern " Syria " in which " Phoenicians " lived and a southern one in which " Palestinians " lived. Herodotus used the name Palestine in the accepted way but at the same time called the coastland south of Carmel " Palestinian Syria " (i.105, iii.91, and *passim*) or simply " Palestine " (vii.89). This name was very fitting. Beginning in the twelfth century B.C. the Philistines so well known from the Old Testament, and other related peoples, had lived on the coastal plain south of Carmel. These coastal inhabitants apparently still called themselves Philistines in the Persian period. Then other Greek and Roman writers, following Herodotus, also named that coastal strip Palestine (" Philistine land ")—the historian Polybius and the geographer Agatharchides in the second century B.C., among others. The Roman officials finally took up this name and called the entire province, including the interior, after the coastal strip. The port cities important to them lay on the coast, especially Caesarea, which they elevated to provincial capital. Later it was regularly called *Caesarea Palaestinae* to distinguish it from other cities of the same name. " Palestine " here was perhaps still being used basically in its original meaning, designating the coastal strip.

The name Palestine survived the Roman-Byzantine period not only in Christian usage but even in Arab and Turkish circles. Even though the Arab conquerors changed the name of the Roman-

Byzantine province *Palaestina* to *Urdunn* or " Jordan Region," they still called its western half *Filasṭīn*, or Palestine.[2]

The name Palestine was used officially during the period of the British mandate (1920–48).

The area of the modern state of Israel is often popularly referred to as Palestine.

In general, the name Palestine does not indicate specifically the historical Roman province, *Palaestina.* " Palestine " generally serves rather to designate the " Holy, Promised Land." Thus the name conventionally designates the arena of the history of the people of Israel in so far as their history took place in their cultural homeland. Of course, this definition too is unclear, for the history of Israel at times involved rather extensive areas, and then again was limited to a more confined region. The ordinary use of the name has in view approximately the area which was intended by the various promises of land to the patriarchs made in Genesis and outlined in the system of the ideal tribal boundaries recorded in Joshua, chapters 13 to 19 (see pp. 67 ff.), or approximately that territory within which the Israelite tribes settled. On this basis the name Palestine refers to the land between the Mediterranean Sea to the west and the Syro-Arabian Desert to the east, bounded on the north by the southern end of the Lebanon and Antilebanon ranges which dominate middle Syria, and on the south by approximately the latitude of the southern end of the Dead Sea, normally excluding only those parts of southern Transjordan inhabited in Old Testament times by the Ammonites and Moabites. In terms of geography this area is simply the southern third of Syria, that elongated region between the east coast of the Mediterranean Sea and the Syro-Arabian Desert. The borders cannot be exactly determined, since " Palestine " in this conventional usage is simply not a precise term.

2. *Topography*

(1) *Land Formations and Their Modern Names*

In studying modern Palestine, and certainly in studying its history, one must become acquainted with the large number of Arabic names and terms in use locally. Since there is often some uncertainty in identifying historical names and terms, colloquial ones are used in topographical studies and references. Arabic has been the native language ever since the Islamic Arabs conquered the land in the

[2] See A.-S. Marmardji, *Textes géographiques arabes sur la Palestine* (1951), pp. 160–63.

seventh century of our era and remained in control. Thus, traditional names and titles are Arabic or at least have been transmitted through Arabic. Even those place names which are pre-Arabic in origin, a considerable portion, have gone over into the Arabic language and been passed on until they are known today only in their Arabic form, which may be a garbled form of the original name. The wholesale assignment of biblical names and titles to sites began in the Middle Ages under Christian influence, particularly that of the Franciscans. This was a development as unreliable as the more recent one in which Jewish settlers adopted place names taken from the Hebrew Old Testament. Where assignment of biblical names has had official direction and sanction in modern Israel, it rests on scholarly topographical studies. Naturally, even under these circumstances there are some uncertain and premature identifications and some confusing names.[3]

The native Arabic fund of place names and titles naturally includes a number of terms for all sorts of phenomena which must become known to anyone who deals with the geography of Palestine. The most important of these terms are listed here in appropriate categories.[4] See p. 375 for our system of transliteration of Arabic words and names.

(a) *Terms for land formations*: *jebel* (pl. *jibāl*), the customary word for mountain, mountain range; *rās* (pl. *rūs*), literally head, then headland, cape, or promontory; *ẓahr* (pl. *ẓuhūr*), literally back, then ridge; *qarn* (pl. *qurūn*, dim.[5] *qurein*), literally horn, mountain horn, mountain peak; *meshref(eh)* (pl. *mashārif*, dim. *musheirifeh*), high point with view, height; *munṭār* (pl. *manāṭīr*), lookout, vantage point; *ṣakhrah* (collective *ṣakhr*), rocks, boulders; *ḥajar* (pl. *ḥijār*), individual stone; *rajm* (pl. *rujūm*, dim. *rujeim*), heaped stones, cairns; *waʿr*, stony land covered with undergrowth; *maghārah* (pl. *maghāʾir*), rock cave; *naqb* (dim. *nuqeib*), breach, narrow pass; *wādi* (pl. *widyān*), deeply cut valley (usually dry in summer); *baqʿa* (pl. *beqāʿ*, dim. *buqeiʿa*), level valley; *ghōr* (dim. *ghuweir*), lowland, low-lying plain; *sahl*, plain; *khalleh*, flat-bottomed valley; *merj* (pl. *murūj*, dim. *mureij*), pasture land;

[3] In modern Israel all identification is done in modern Hebrew. As a result sites in modern Israel are noted in this volume with their Israeli Hebrew name as well as with their Arabic name, the abbreviation "Isr." being used to indicate modern Israeli Hebrew as against biblical Hebrew.

[4] Additional material is to be found in A. Socin, "Liste arabischer Ortsappellativa," *ZDPV*, XXII (1899), 18–60.

[5] Diminutives are frequently formed from Arabic nouns, as for example, *qarn*, horn; *qurein*, little horn.

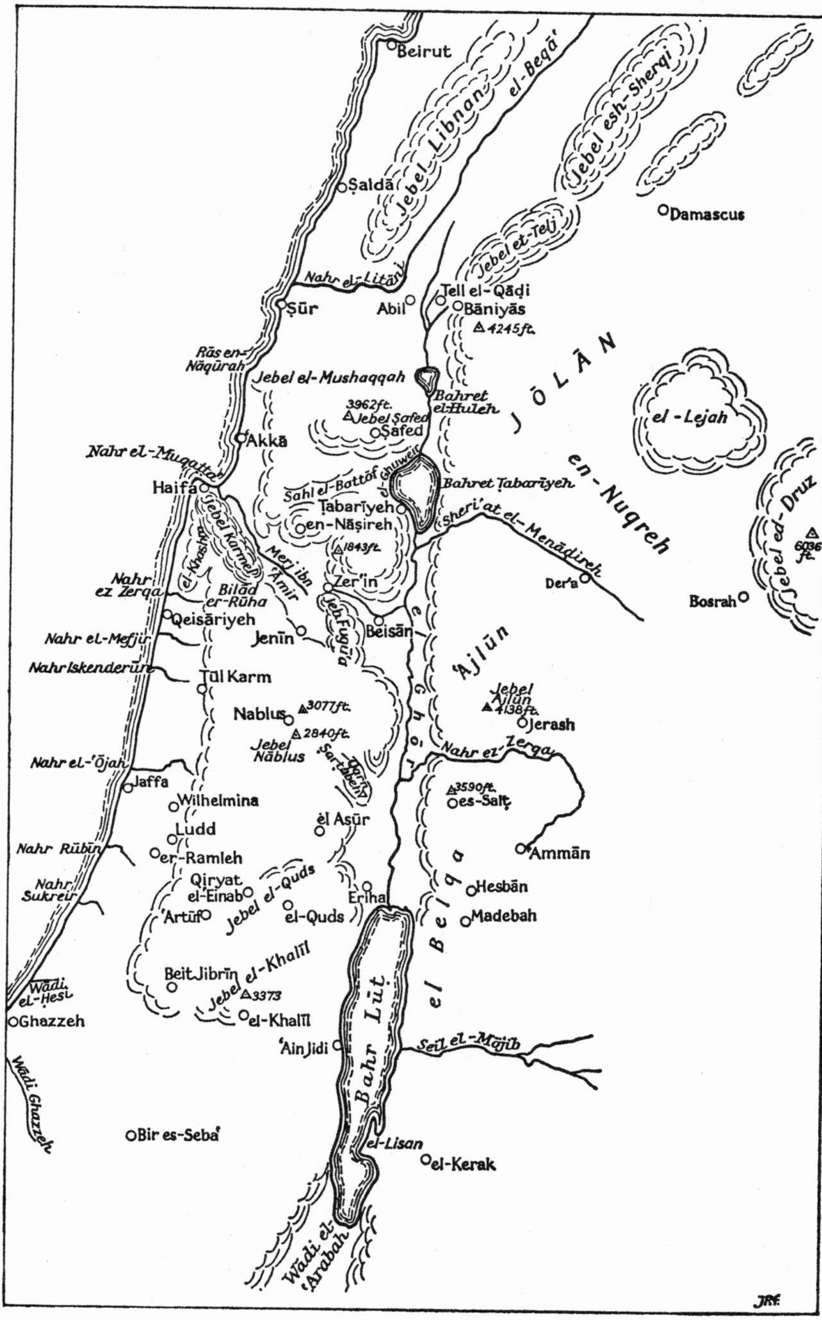

Figure 1. Modern Palestine

sabkheh (pl. *sibākh*), salty ground, flat; *raml(eh)*, sand; *rumeileh*, sandy stretch.

(b) *Terms for bodies of water*: *ʿain* (pl. *ʿoyūn*), spring; *rās el-ʿain*, fountainhead; *bir* (pl. *biyār*), underground well; *ḥammeh*, hot spring; *ḥammām*, bath at a hot spring; *seil* (pl. *suyūl*), rain trough, flash flood; *nahr*, river (perennial); *sherīʿah*, perennial watercourse; *birkeh* (pl. *burak*, dim. *bureikeh*), water reservoir, pool; *baṣṣah*, marshy ground, swamp; *baḥr(ah)*, lake, sea; *mīneh*, harbour.

(c) *Terms for structures and developed areas*: *medīneh* (pl. *medāʾin*), city; *qaryeh* (pl. *qurā*), inhabited place, village; *beit* (pl. *buyūt*), house; *qalʿah* (pl. *qilāʿ*), citadel, fort; *ḥiṣn* (pl. *huṣūn*), fortress, stronghold; *qaṣr* (pl. *quṣūr*, dim. *quṣeir*), castle (from the Latin *castrum*); *burj* (dim. *bureij*), tower; *mejdel* (pl. *mejādil*), tower, fortress (from Hebrew *mighdal*); *ṭāḥūneh* (pl. *ṭawāḥīn*), mill; *karm* (pl. *kurūm*), vineyard, planting of grape vines; *khān*, caravansary; *kenīseh* (pl. *kanāʾis*, dim. *kuneiseh*), church; *deir*, cloister; *mesjid* (pl. *mesājid*), place of worship, mosque; *jāmiʿ* (pl. *jawāmiʿ*), chief mosque in which the Islamic Friday service is held; *ḥaram*, sacred precinct; *wali*, Islamic saint, sometimes also grave of a saint; *qubbeh* (dim. *qubeibeh*), cupola, specifically the white cupola-shaped building erected over the grave of a saint; *qabr* (pl. *qubūr*), grave; *jisr* (pl. *jusūr*), dam, bridge; *qanṭarah* (pl. *qanāṭir*, dim. *quneiṭrah*), arch of a bridge, bridge; *ʿamūd* (pl. *ʿawāmīd* or *ʿimdān*), column; *khirbeh* (pl. *khurāb*), ruin site, stone ruins; *tell* (pl. *tulūl*, dim. *teleilāt*), mound, hillock composed of ancient ruins.

(2) *The Appearance of the Land*

See Figure 1.

(a) *Transjordan*.[6] As we now consider the chief features of the land of Palestine today, dealing with the area as defined above on p. 9, we will approach its border from the east. There we leave the Syro-Arabian Desert, a plateau traversed by a number of mountain chains and ridges, and having an average height of 700 metres [2,300 feet] above sea level.[7] Lack of rainfall makes cultivation of this soil impossible. Proceeding westward we note the very gradual transition to an arable region, Transjordan, for we are entering a region which receives rainfall from the Mediterranean Sea to the

[6] See Nelson Glueck, *The Other Side of the Jordan* (1940), o.p.

[7] For more detailed information on this desert see Musil, *Arabia Deserta* (New York, 1927), o.p.

west. Valleys channel winter rain water westward to the Jordan Valley and the Dead Sea.

In addition to a great many gullies and smaller ravines, three large westerly valley networks sharply divide Transjordan into sections from north to south. The southernmost is Seil el-Mōjib,[8] which flows through a gorge carved deep in the mountains and finally reaches the Dead Sea at about the middle of its eastern shore. In the Old Testament this river is called the Arnon. North and south of this valley are fertile plateaus bordered on the west by a broken mountain range, which is cut up especially on its west side by canyons. This range separates the plateaus from the Dead Sea. The area south of Seil el-Mōjib, bearing the name el-Kerak after its capital, will not be described here, since in Old Testament times it was the heart of Moabite territory. The plain north of Seil el-Mōjib has an average altitude of 700 m. [2,300 feet]; the western front range rises 100 to 200 m. [325 to 650 feet] higher. The most important town on this plain is Medeba, which is 774 m. [2,540 feet] above sea level. About 10 kilometres [6 miles] north of Medeba, east of the northern end of the Dead Sea, the plateau becomes hilly country which extends to the next major valley system to the north, that of Nahr ez-Zerqā (" Blue River ")—the Old Testament " Jabbok." The area between the valley Seil el-Mōjib and the river Nahr ez-Zerqā is called el-Belqā today. In the northern hilly part of the Belqā, the western front range rises to a peak 1,094 m. [3,590 feet] high. It is about a half-hour's walk southsouthwest of the sanctuary Nebi Ōsha' (" Prophet Hosea ") which is situated in a small depression on the mountain-side. This peak affords an extensive panorama of the Cisjordan hill country across the valley. The town of es-Salṭ is about 3 km. [2 miles] southeast of this peak, a little farther into the mountains of Transjordan. Farther to the east is the city of 'Ammān, located in the midst of the hill country of the northern Belqā on the upper course of the Nahr ez-Zerqā, which flows from there in an arc northward and then westward. 'Ammān is today the capital of the Kingdom of Jordan and the residence of its ruler.

The area called 'Ajlūn is situated between the Nahr ez-Zerqā, which flows into the Jordan about 40 km. [25 miles] north of the Dead Sea, and the next great valley network to the north, the Sherī'-at el-Menāḍireh, which empties into the Jordan a little south of the Sea of Tiberias [Galilee]. This tributary is also called the Yarmuk,

[8] It is the lower course of this valley which is called Seil el-Mōjib. Some of these valleys and rivers go by different names at various parts of their courses.

a name which is not recorded in the Old Testament, but which appears in the Mishna, in Pliny (v.74), and in other sources. The ʿAjlūn is mountainous country, rising in its southern half as high as 1,261 m. [4,138 feet] at the peak of Umm ed-Derej, which is part of Jebel ʿAjlūn, east of the city of ʿAjlūn. The ʿAjlūn is still the most heavily forested part of Palestine. Oak forests particularly are to be found here. Generally speaking, this does not mean thick forests but light woodlands; the oaks are not nearly so high as those to which we are accustomed. In the southeastern part of the ʿAjlūn is Jerash, famous for its Roman-Byzantine ruins. North of the mountainous ʿAjlūn region there is a stretch of fertile plateau country reaching up to the Sheriʿat el-Menāḍireh. The large town of Irbid is on this plateau. East of Irbid is the city of Derʿa, overlooking the Wādi ez-Zeidi, which is the upper course of Sherīʿat el-Menāḍireh. Derʿa served as a junction point while the Hejaz railroad was used.

North and northeast of the valley system of Sherīʿat el-Menāḍireh the arable country extends much more to the east toward the desert than it does farther south. Here on the eastern border of the cultivated land is Jebel ed-Drūz, called " Druse Mountain " after its inhabitants, but also called Jebel Ḥaurān. A great volcanic mass, it attains a height of 1,839 m. [6,036 feet] at the peak of Tell el-Jeina. If one counts Jebel ed-Drūz as a part of Palestine, it is the highest mountain of the land. Northwest of Jebel ed-Drūz there stretches a desolate, rugged, and sparsely settled region of lava rock called el Lejah. West of Jebel ed-Drūz and el-Lejah lies a broad, fertile plain, 500 to 600 m. [1,600 to 2,000 feet] above sea level, called en-Nuqreh, " the Hollow." Its soil is composed of crumbled lava rock. This section has its western terminus in Jōlān, an area with numerous extinct craters, which today are incorrectly called *tulūl*, " mounds " (i.e., of ruins). These craters rise above a relatively level terrain. The highest of these is the cone called " Tell " esh-Sheikha, 1,294 m. [4,245 feet] high, a few miles south of Mount Hermon.

(b) *The Jordan Valley.*[9] From north to south, Palestine is traversed by a tremendous rift, the result of a geological fault. This rift begins in North Syria, where it forms the valley of the Orontes River, now called Nahr el-ʿAṣi, continues in the depression between Lebanon and Antilebanon now called el-Beqāʿ meaning " the Depressions," and reaches its deepest part in its course through Pales-

[9] More detailed information, and particularly many illustrations, can be found in G. Wagner's *Vom Jordangraben: Landschaftsbilder eines Grabenbruchs im Trockengebiet* (reprinted from " Aus der Heimat," *Natural Science Monthly*, July–August, 1934); and in Glueck, *The River Jordan* (Philadelphia: Westminster, 1946).

tine. Southward from there it forms the Wādi el-ʿArabah or "Desert Valley," the rift between the Dead Sea and the Red Sea, and finally it enters East Africa through the present Gulf of ʿAqabah (Arabic, el-ʿAqabah) and the Red Sea. The Jordan Valley and the Dead Sea constitute the Palestinian part of the rift.

The Jordan, now called Sherīʿat el-Kebīreh ("the Great River"), has its origin in a series of springs at the southern and western edges of Mount Hermon. Next it flows through a somewhat swampy plain between Jōlān and the mountains of upper Galilee. This has now been drained, including the former lake about 6 km. [4 miles] long, called Baḥret el-Kheit or Baḥret el-Ḥūleh, 2 m. [7 feet] above sea level. South of this drained lake the Jordan cuts through a basalt barrier which lies diagonally across the Jordan rift from east to west. After overcoming this barrier, it flows on into the Sea of Tiberias, Baḥret Ṭabarīyeh, so named after the most important city, which has lain on its shores since the first century, and also called the Sea of Galilee. It is 21 km. [13 miles] long, and at its widest point, a little north of its centre, it is 12 km. [7 miles] wide. The lake is fully 200 m. [650 feet] below sea level. A small fertile alluvial plain on the western shore is called el-Ghuweir, "the Little Lowland." For the rest the lake is bordered directly on its east, west, and northwest sides by the rising mountains. Its water is clear and drinkable; the lake is full of fish.

Between the southern end of the Sea of Tiberias and the northern end of the Dead Sea, which are about 105 km. [66 miles] apart on a straight line, we find that part of the Jordan Valley which today is called simply el-Ghōr, "the Lowland." The eastern side of the Ghōr is bounded essentially by a single, rather straight, geological fault line along which the Transjordan scarp drops off into the Jordan rift. On the other side, the Cisjordan mountain plateau drops off to the Jordan rift very irregularly in various stages and levels. As a result the western edge of the Ghōr is a very broken line, repeatedly protruding and receding. Immediately south of the Sea of Tiberias the Ghōr is about 3 to 4 km. [2 miles] wide. Then about 12 km. [7 miles] farther on it opens out to the northwest. There the Jordan meets the wide, level valley of the Nahr Jālūd (Isr., Ḥarodh) or "Goliath River," which comes from the region of Jezreel. Today Beisān is in the middle of this broad opening. Tell el-Ḥiṣn, the mound of the ancient city of Beth-shan, rises opposite this town north of the deeply eroded bed of the River Jālūd. The valley becomes ever narrower south of the broad opening at Beisān. Halfway between the Sea of Tiberias and the Dead Sea, the western mountains penetrate the deepest into the Ghōr. Here at its narrowest part the Ghōr is only about 3 km. [2 miles] across. A little south of the mouth of the river Nahr ez-Zerqā a last southeasterly ridge of the mountains of Cisjordan thrusts its high landmark peak, Qarn Ṣarṭabeh, into the Ghōr. Then the mountains again recede and the widest part of the Ghōr, measuring as much as 20 km. [12 miles] from east to west, continues right down to the Dead Sea.

The soil of the great Jordan rift is composed of marine deposits which in diluvial times filled the entire area between the Sea of Tiberias and the Dead Sea. These deposits formed a level valley floor sloping gently toward the south with a moderate, continuous slope from both sides toward the centre. Through this centre the Jordan has cut its river bed, flowing along in countless little meanderings and close to the hills of Cisjordan only in the narrow central part of the rift. A narrow strip of dense tropical jungle, called ez-Zōr—and, in places, a tillable river bottom land—follows both banks of the river. Between the river bed itself and the floor of the Ghōr, a strip of deeply eroded marl 100 m. [328 feet] wide bands each side of the stream. These strips are partially flooded by the Jordan in the springtime, from the latter part of April to the beginning of May.

Lack of rainfall makes the larger southern half of the Ghōr a desert region. However, some oases are formed by occasional springs or brooks which flow from the mountains on both sides. The most significant of these oases is that of Jericho, Erīḥa, on the west bank near the southern end of the Ghōr, which is fed by springs from the edge of the western mountains. About 20 km. [12 miles] north of it is the oasis Wādi Faṣā'il. There are a number of other smaller oases, particularly in this most southern part of the Ghōr on both sides of the river. The broad valley corridor at Beisān also has a number of oases fed by springs originating at the edge of the western mountains. Only a short section of the Ghōr below the Sea of Galilee is completely arable.

The Dead Sea fills the lowest part of the great rift. Its surface is fully 390 m. [1,280 feet] below sea level. In the northern part the Dead Sea is about 400 m. [1,300 feet] deep, whereas its southern part is very shallow. This is the lowest depression anywhere on the surface of the earth. The Dead Sea is about 85 km. [55 miles] long from north to south. It is about 15 km. [10 miles] wide. South of its midpoint a peninsula, el-Lisān (" the Tongue "), projects into the Dead Sea from the eastern side. This marks the dividing line between the deep northern and the shallow southern part. On the eastern side, the cliff rises so sharply from the sea that there is not even space for a path along the shore. The hills drop off almost as abruptly at various places on the western shore. The water level varies somewhat in the course of a year, the highest level being reached sometime in June.[10] There is also greater variation over longer periods of time. For a few decades the water level rose. The small island Rajm el-Baḥr at the northern end, shown on the map of the Palestine Exploration Fund, was submerged in 1892 and remained for years about 3 m. [10 feet] under water. In recent years the water level began to drop again, so that Rajm el-Baḥr is now above the surface (see p. 30 note 27). The water of the Dead Sea has an unusually high proportion of salt and other minerals. Indeed, for some years now minerals have been industrially extracted by Jordan at the northern end and by Israel at the southern end of the lake. This high mineral content prohibits any organic life either in the lake itself or in its immediate surroundings. Hence the name " Dead Sea," *mare mortuum*,[11] which Jerome probably brought into common use, even if he did not coin it. Today in the Arabic of Jordan it is called Baḥr Lūṭ, " Sea of Lot," a reference to Genesis, chapter 19. In the modern Hebrew of Israel it again has its Old Testament name, *Yam ham-Melaḥ* (" Salt Sea ").

(c) *The Cisjordan range*. By and large this is where the history of Israel took place. This part of Palestine also has the most broken and varied topography of all. Its chief sections are now usually named after the important cities located in them. For example, the southern part, which lies west of the Dead Sea and the lower Jordan rift, is today called both Jebel el-Khalīl (el-Khalīl is the modern name of the city formerly called Hebron) and Jebel el-Quds (el-Quds, " the Sanctuary," is the Arabic name for Jerusalem). We call this part the Judean hill country (see p. 56). At a point about 5 km. [3 miles] north of el-Khalīl (Hebron), the mountains rise as high as 1,028 m. [3,373 feet]. A number of geological folds and a major geological fault toward the east have lowered the original height of the range from north to south along the watershed. Lying in the " rain shadow," this eastern slope drops off by stages toward the Dead Sea, broken in turn by numerous valleys, generally running east or eastsoutheast. " Rain shadow " is the phenomenon in which rain clouds approaching a mountain from the west deposit their water on the western slope of the mountain and on its height,

[10] *PEF Qu. St.* (1935), p. 39.
[11] Jerome's commentary on Ezek. 47 : 18 in Stummer, *Monumenta historiam et geographiam Terrae Sanctae illustrantia* (1935), I, 85.

but not on the eastern face. This side is therefore extremely low in rainfall, a desert, in which one finds only flocks belonging to nomadic Bedouin tribes, where grazing land is scarce and where cisterns are needed for water. There are spring-fed oases only in a few places. The most important is the oasis ʿAin Jidi (Isr., ʿEin Gedhi) at the middle of the western shore of the Dead Sea.

On the western side the Judean hills are bordered by a great fault, along which the mountain table has dropped to sea level. It is called the ʿArtūf fault, after the modern town of ʿArtūf (Isr., Har Tubh), a station on the railroad from Jerusalem to Jaffa, near the northern end of the fault. Thus, here in the west the Judean hills have a definite boundary, clearly visible in the landscape, into which a number of deep valleys running in a westerly direction have been cut by erosion. West of the ʿArtūf fault the sunken part of the mountain plateau forms rolling foothills, 300 to 400 m. [1,000 to 1,300 feet] high, with moderate hillocks and shallow depressions. These foothills are bordered on the west and separated from the coastal plain by another fault line extending from northnortheast to southsouthwest. The foothills increase in width toward the south. In the southern part, at the town of Beit Jibrīn (Isr., Beth Gubhrin), the foothills are about 20 km. [12 miles] wide from east to west. These foothills, the rising slope, and the top of the Judean hill country receive comparatively abundant rainfall (see p. 29). Therefore, within natural limitations, they also have relatively abundant and varied vegetation.

South of el-Khalīl, the height of the Judean hills decreases so gradually to the southwest that there is no well-defined line between the hill country and the western foothills. Nor is there in this latitude any clear line at which the eastern slope down to the Dead Sea begins. With less and less rainfall as one moves south and the distance from the Mediterranean shore increases, there is a gradual transition to steppe and desert, until the Judean hill country merges with the numerous ranges and valleys of the Sinai or Isthmus Desert. Bīr es-Sebaʿ (Isr., Be'er Shebhaʿ), the market-place for Bedouins living in the surrounding region, is at the end of the southwestern spur of the hills and is already outside of the area of settled life. In this region the soil rarely produces harvests. Only when conditions or rainfall are unusually favourable does it repay the diligence bestowed on it year in and year out by the Bedouins who cultivate it. Farther to the southwest, cultivation of the soil ceases entirely. The Negeb (southern arid region) of modern Israel extends southward from the southern end of the Judean hill country to the northern tip of the Gulf of ʿAqabah. The Negeb region is being advanced by discovery of remains of Middle Bronze Age, Iron Age, and Roman-Byzantine settlements and irrigation devices.[12]

Jebel Nāblus is a northerly continuation of Jebel el-Quds (see p. 17). Nāblus is the town which has replaced ancient Shechem. It was originally called Neapolis, meaning " New City." Jebel Nāblus is the Samaritan hill country.[13] It stretches northward to the great plain surrounded by the Cisjordanian mountains. The Judean hill country gradually merges into the Samaritan hill country without any sharp demarcation. The Samaritan, which is lower, slopes toward the north. The highest point, 1,011 m. [3,313 feet], is el-ʿAṣūr, located in the southeastern corner of the region. By comparison, even Jebel eṭ-Ṭōr and Jebel Islāmīyeh are only 868 m. [2,840 feet] and 938 m. [3,077 feet] respectively; yet these two hills, one south and the other north of Nāblus, are landmarks of the central Samaritan hill country, visible from a great distance. The northern spurs of these central hills are still lower. Jebel Karmel (Isr., Har hak-Karmel), jutting far out in the northwestern corner, is no higher than 552 m. [1,810 feet] and Jebel Fuqūʿa (Isr., Hare hag-Gilboaʿ), emerging from the northeastern corner and then bending in a semicircle in a northwesterly direction, is only 518 m. [1,697 feet] high. The western edge of the range is much less sharply defined than it is farther to the south. To be sure, even this western edge follows a definitely observable geological fault line, but the western slope is so gradual that a distinction between foothills and hill country cannot be made here as in the Judean range.

The slope is more pronounced on the eastern side, toward the Jordan rift. Here, a number of deep valleys like the Wādi el-Fārʿah, generally tending to the southeast, are cut into the slope. They separate stratified rock masses which have buckled and sunk from the highest level of the range into the Jordan rift. Since the mountain range in Samaria is not very high, its eastern slope does not lie in the " rain shadow " and therefore is not a desert like the eastern slope of the Judean hills. Generally speaking, the Samaritan hills are more rounded and rolling in contour than the Judean ones. Naturally, there are deeply eroded valleys here, too. Yet, by comparison, the Samaritan hills contain many more gently sloping valleys and more extensive level areas between the hills. This contour, together with sufficient rainfall, provides abundant crops. This

[12] W. Zimmerli, " Die landschaftliche Bearbeitung des Negeb im Altertum," *ZDPV*, LXXV (1959), 141–54.

[13] An exact detailed description of this region is found in V. Schwöbel, " Samarien das westpalästinische Mittelland," *ZDPV*, LIII (1930), 1–47, 89–135.

part of the Palestinian hill country is easily habitable and abundantly fertile.

Foothills called Bilād er-Rūḥa are on the northwestern side of the Samaritan range between the northern end of the coastal plain and the Plain of Jezreel. Rather convenient trade routes across the foothills connect the two plains, and these foothills also connect the core of the Samaritan range with the ridge Jebel Karmel (Isr., Har hak-Karmel), which juts out northnorthwest all the way to the sea. A hilly region extends from the western side of the ridge to a coastal geological fault line running parallel to the coast. On the southern side this hilly region extends into the coastal plain, its most prominent peak being el-Khashm. Hare hag-Gilboaʿ or Jebel Fuqūʿa, named for the town of Fuqūʿa on its slopes, is a spur of the Samaritan range at its northeastern corner. It separates the valley corridor at Beisān, mentioned above, from the southern part of the Plain of Jezreel. The most important town in the Samaritan hill country is the city of Nāblus, located in a broad, gentle valley on a favourable trade route running diagonally across the Samaritan hill country. Nāblus is also near the great road from north to south which follows the watershed of the Cisjordan range.

The northern third of Cisjordan is composed of hills and several lesser areas, all of which can be grouped together under the term Galilean hill country. It falls into two natural parts: lower and upper Galilee. Lower Galilee is very similar in its structure to the Samaritan hill country. It has gentle slopes and is well suited to settled life and farming, since it receives abundant rainfall. On the western side it rises gradually from a geological fault line which separates it from the coastal plain. The slope on the southern side toward the Plain of Jezreel and on the eastern side toward the upper Jordan rift is steeper and more rugged. In the centre of lower Galilee is Sahl el-Baṭṭōf (Isr., Biqʿath Beth Neṭophah), a plain lying roughly east and west. It is about 15 km. [9 miles] long and about 3 km. [2 miles] wide. The southeastern part of lower Galilee includes a region of well-rounded lava boulders, subdivided by three valley systems tending southeastward to the Jordan rift. This basalt region extends from the northern edge of the Plain of Jezreel and the Jordan rift southward to the valley of the Nahr Jālūd (Isr., Ḥarodh). In the angle between this basalt region and the rest of the lower Galilean hill country, that is, in the northeastern corner of the Plain of Jezreel, is the imposing conical mountain, Jebel eṭ-Ṭōr,[14]

[14] Another mountain of the same name is mentioned above on p. 19. The name means simply "the mountain." The Mount of Olives east of Jerusalem also bears this name.

562 m. [1,843 feet]. Near the southern end of the lower Galilean hill country is Nazareth (Arabic, en-Nāṣireh; Isr., Naṣrath), now this section's most important site. On a latitude a little north of the north end of the Sea of Tiberias a sheer mountain wall, forming the boundary of northern lower Galilee, rises to the upper Galilean mountains. The highest points of upper Galilee are immediately encountered there at Jebel Ṣafed, named for the city of Ṣafed (Isr., Ṣephath), and particularly at Jebel Jermaq, 8 km. [5 miles] from Ṣafed, whose height of 1,208 m. [3,962 feet] makes it easily the highest mountain of Cisjordan and affords an extensive panorama of Galilee and other near-by regions. Then highlands, 700 to 800 m. [2,300 to 2,600 feet] above sea level, continue to the north. Still farther north these highlands gradually diminish and finally are terminated and separated from Syrian Lebanon by the deep gorge of the River Līṭāni. This most northerly part of Galilee can scarcely be counted part of Palestine in the sense referred to above on p. 9. Approximately at the latitude of the now drained Lake Ḥūleh the ridge of Jebel el-Mushaqqaḥ runs from east to west, extending the upper Galilean hill country right to the coast of the Mediterranean Sea. From the peak of the ridge, called Rās en-Nāqūrah (Isr., Rosh han-Niqrah), the slope falls off abruptly into the sea; therefore, here on the coast this ridge forms a natural northern boundary of the land of Palestine.

(d) *The coastal plains*. Between the western limits of the mountains and the Mediterranean sea coast lie plains formed by geologically late sedimentation. This flat, undulating terrain is very productive, consisting as it does chiefly of clay and, especially in the southernmost part, of loess.[15] The sea coast is paralleled for long stretches by dunes among which two systems must be differentiated: an older one from pre-Christian times which received clay deposits during a period of moist climate and a younger one from the Christian era which is still undergoing change.[16] In the far south there are also inland dunes adjoining the dunes of the Sinai or Isthmus Desert. West of the Judean and Samaritan hill country there is a great plain which is generally called simply " the Palestinian coastal plain," though this is not a precise term. It is widest in the south, where the Sinai or Isthmus Desert imperceptibly merges into it. The town of Ghazzeh (ancient Gaza) at the inner edge of the dunes is today the chief site on the southern coastal

[15] More detailed information is found in P. Range, *Die Küstenebene Palästinas mit geologischer Übersichtskarte* (1922).
[16] Range, *ZDPV*,, LV (1932), 48 ff.

plain. Its distance from Beersheba, mentioned above, at the southwestern corner of the Judean range, is about 40 km. [25 miles] in a straight line. Farther north the distance between the port of Jaffa and the western limit of the mountains is barely 20 km. [12 miles], and in the north, at the port of Qeiṣāriyeh (Caesarea), the plain is only about 10 km. [7 miles] wide. The coastal strip west of Carmel finally has a width of only 3 km. [2 miles] or less. The sea coast is flat and without harbours, and the sea depth increases very gradually outward from the shore. As one travels north toward Jaffa an almost unbroken stretch of dunes parallels the coast. Only a few flowing coastal rivers have forced courses through it and keep the gaps open, namely, Wādi Ghazzeh just south of Ghazzeh, then to the north, Wādi el-Ḥesi, the River Sukreir, and the River Rūbīn. At Jaffa a rise in the terrain breaks the straight line of the coast. The rise juts into the sea and continues as a reef. The northern side of this rise is somewhat protected from the sea. Here tides constantly wash in deposits, forming a natural, though limited, harbour. The city of Jaffa, whose older section lies on the rise referred to, owes its origin and significance as a port city to this natural harbour.[17] Of course, for some time now Jaffa has been completely overshadowed as a port by modern Haifa (see p. 23). On the coast just north of old Jaffa is the modern city of Tel Aviv, rapidly built up by Jewish interests. Inland, southeast of Jaffa, are the rather attractive towns of Ludd (Lydda) and er-Ramleh. North of Jaffa there are further stretches of dunes along the straight, regular coast, which is broken by occasional coastal rivers. Near Jaffa is the perennial River el-ʿŌjah (Isr., Yarqon); farther on are the River Iskenderūn and the River el-Mefjir. In the northern part of the coastal plain at Qeiṣāriyeh (Caesarea) reefs jut out into the sea.[18] Although they do not form a natural harbour by themselves, an artificial harbour could be built at this place, as was done in the time of Herod. The town of Ṭūl Karm occupies an important spot in the northern part of the coastal plain. Ṭūl Karm is at the eastern edge of the plain at the broad opening of Wādi Zeimir. This same wadi under another name reaches all the way up to Nāblus (see p. 20) in the hill country. North of Qeiṣāriyeh the Nahr ez-Zerqā emerges from a swampy region into the Mediterranean Sea.[19] The northernmost very narrow part of the coastal plain begins on the

[17] This natural setting can be seen clearly in the aerial photographs in Dalman, *Hundert Fliegerbilder*, Nos. 67, 68.

[18] *Ibid.*, No. 65.

[19] There is another river called Nahr ez-Zerqā (" Blue River ") in Transjordan; see p. 16. The river here referred to is known in modern Hebrew as Nehar hat-Tanninim, or Crocodile River.

other side of this river. Around the promontory of Mount Carmel, there is only a narrow coastal strip, with just enough room for a road (and recently for a railway line).

North of the Carmel promontory there is a smaller section of coastal plain, which today is called the Plain of Acco after the old city of Acco (Arabic, ʿAkkā) which lies in the midst of it. On the coast it is bordered by gentle slopes of the Galilean hill country. Northward it reaches up to the ridge Jebel el-Mushaqqaḥ already mentioned and the promontory of Rās en-Nāqūrah (Isr., Rosh han-Niqrah). It is limited in the south by the northeastern base of the Carmel ridge. At the city of Acco this plain is about 7 km. [5 miles] wide; from south to north it decreases gradually in breadth. In the protection of the Carmel promontory a shallow bay with a very level coast reaches northward to a tongue of land jutting into the sea. At the tip of this tongue is Israeli Acco, formerly Arabic ʿAkkā, successor to the ancient city of Acco. This bay, about 15 km. [10 miles] long, in spite of its silting up is the most natural location on the Palestinian coast for the establishment of a harbour. In ancient times Acco was the port city on this bay, on the south-eastern side of the tongue of land jutting out toward the southwest where there is something of a natural harbour. Today Acco is still only a small town, while the harbour city on the bay is Haifa which lies to the south near the foot of Carmel. Extensive artificial installations were required there to create a harbour large enough for modern requirements. Haifa is currently one of the most important sites on the entire Syro-Palestinian coast. The entire coast of the Plain of Acco, including the bay, is paralleled by dunes except at the foot of Mount Carmel and again at Acco.

Southsoutheast of the Plain of Acco lies a great inland plain which is called Merj Ibn ʿĀmir in Arabic. In Israeli it is commonly called ha ʿEmeq, " the Plain." In the Old Testament (Josh. 17 : 16; Judg. 6 : 33) it was called the Plain of Jezreel after the ancient city of Jezreel situated at modern Zerʿin at its eastern end. This name, Plain of Jezreel, perhaps applied originally only to its southeastern section. The Plain of Jezreel is connected directly with the Plain of Acco by a narrow pass between the Carmel ridge and the south-western corner of the lower Galilean hill country. Again, to the east the Plain of Jezreel is directly connected with the broad valley of the River Jālūd (Ḥarodh) (see p. 15) which extends to the Jordan rift and lies between Jebel Fuqūʿa (Hare hag-Gilboaʿ), a spur of the Samaritan hill country (see p. 20), and the basalt southeastern part of the lower Galilean hill country (see p. 20). Thus we have here an opening extending from northwest to southeast entirely across the Cisjordan range. Furthermore, here the watershed between the Mediterranean Sea and the Jordan rift is only about 100 m. [328 feet] above sea level at the divide between the Plain of Jezreel draining to the Mediterranean Sea and the valley of the Nahr Jālūd (Ḥarodh) sloping toward the Jordan rift. This depression forms a distinct border between the Samaritan and the Galilean hill country. The Plain of Jezreel forms a great triangle. Its southwestern edge borders both on Bilād er-Rūḥa (see p. 20) and on the northern end of the Samaritan range; its northern edge follows the southern slope of the lower Galilean range, and its irregular eastern side goes from Mount eṭ-Ṭōr (Har Tabhor) (see p. 20) up to the western edge of Mount Fuqūʿa (Hare hag-Gilboaʿ). The plain consists of fertile alluvial soil. The town of Jenīn is at its southern end. The plain is drained by the River el-Muqaṭṭaʿ (Isr., Qishon), which flows through the narrow pass mentioned above into the southern part of the Plain of Acco and empties east of Haifa into the bay extending from Haifa to Acco.

3. *Size*

The former British mandate of Palestine (1922–48), which was limited to Cisjordan plus a long spur of land extending south to the Gulf of ʿAqabah, included an area of a little more than 26,000 square km. [10,000 square miles], or a little more than the state of Vermont, or rather less than Belgium. That southern spur of desert land occupies about 8,500 square km. [3,282 square miles]. Cisjordan [about 6,800 square miles] without that southern spur is therefore a little larger than Connecticut and Rhode Island together, or rather larger than Yorkshire. According to the census of November 18, 1931, the mandated territory included a total population of 1,035,821 people, of whom 969,268 were settled and 66,553 were nomads. [Connecticut and Rhode Island in 1930 had a population of about 2,300,000.] At that time there were 174,610 Jews in Palestine, who in great part had immigrated only after the First World War. That left about 900,000 earlier residents from the last days of Turkish rule, of whom 7 per cent were nonsedentary.[20] Of course, these figures do not represent the limits of the country's population capacity. During prosperous periods the number of

[20] These figures are derived from the official study of census data by E. Mills, *Census of Palestine, 1931* (Jerusalem, 1932).

inhabitants has probably been somewhat larger as a result of intensive use of the natural possibilities of the country, particularly in some regions now only sparsely settled. A number of sections of Cisjordan have not been permanently settled, quite apart from the southern spur recently under mandate. Such sections are the eastern slope of the Judean range and great stretches of the Ghōr.

(1) *Distances*

A tabulation of distances could help to convey a better idea of the territory involved and to show how small it really is. A person travelling southward from Jerusalem (el-Quds) on the great north–south highway along the ridge of the Judean hill country will reach el-Khalīl (Hebron) after going only 37 km. [23 miles]. After going 45 km. [28 miles] farther in a southwesterly direction, he will reach Beersheba and will already be on the southern steppe,[21] outside the area of exclusively sedentary life. Further travel of 330 km. [206 miles] would take him, first southsouthwest and then westsouthwest, between the mountain ranges and over the sand stretches of the Sinai or Isthmus Desert to Suez (Suweis) and, thus, to the border between Asia and Africa. On the other hand, travelling 67 km. [43 miles] north on the same north–south highway from Jerusalem, first along the ridge top of the hill country and then across some moderately broad troughs of the upper valleys of westerly flowing rivers, he would reach the city of Nāblus and thus the centre of the Samaritan range. He could travel 43 km. [26 miles] more on a rather winding road over the hilltops and through the little plains of the north Samaritan hill country to Jenīn at the southernmost point of the Plain of Jezreel. From there the distance to Nazareth (en-Nāṣireh or Naṣrath) is another 30 km. [19 miles], travelling across the Plain of Jezreel and through a narrow valley in the southern part of the lower Galilean hill country. From Jerusalem to Nazareth, then, it is exactly 140 km. [88 miles] by road. From Nazareth, to reach the extreme north of the country near the sources of the Jordan, the traveller must first cover a distance of 33 km. [21 miles] through the lower Galilean hill country to Tiberias. He must then travel 29 km. [18 miles] on the former Tiberias–Damascus road along the western shore of the Sea of Tiberias and through the basalt barrier in the upper Jordan rift (see p. 15) to the Jewish village of Rosh Pinnah, southwest of Lake Ḥūleh. At this

[21] In Byzantine times the limit of settlement was pushed well south of Beersheba, as the Byzantine ruins show.

point the former road to Damascus, 105 km. [66 miles] northeast, branches off south of Lake Ḥūleh, over the Jordan "Bridge of Jacob's Daughters," called Jisr Benāt Yaʿqūb in Arabic. From Rosh Pinnah a road runs 35 km. [22 miles] along the western side of the upper Jordan valley to Meṭullah, the northernmost town of modern Israel, east of which are Tell el-Qāḍi, the mound of the ancient city of Dan, and Bāniyās, formerly Caesarea Philippi. Thus Meṭullah and Tell el-Qāḍi are 235 km. [144 miles] from Jerusalem and the distance from Tell el-Qāḍi to Beersheba, which in Old Testament terms would be "from Dan to Beersheba," is 317 km. [198 miles] by roads which follow the rough terrain. However, these two places, which somehow mark the northern and southern limits of the land, are only 240 km. [150 miles] apart in a direct line.

From Jerusalem to the port city of Jaffa to the northwest, one can go by train, travelling westward in an arc along a deep gorge for 87 km. [54 miles]. The highway, which is somewhat more direct, covers 63 km. [40 miles], first across the hill country, then down abruptly through a valley which slopes off steeply, and finally through foothills and coastal plain to Jaffa.

A highway runs east from Jerusalem around the southern end of the Mount of Olives, then by way of various valleys through the dazzling white limestone of the desert of Judea to the Jordan Valley. From that point a road turns south to the northern shore of the Dead Sea, 40 km. [25 miles] from Jerusalem, or the road forks north to Eriḥa, the town which has replaced old Jericho, 37 km. [24 miles] from Jerusalem. From Jaffa to Eriḥa, the width of central Cisjordan is exactly 70 km. [45 miles] by air. Farther southward where Cisjordan is broader, 88 air km. [55 miles] separate Ghazzeh at the inner edge of the dunes from the oasis ʿAin Jidi (ʿEin Gedhi) on the western shore of the Dead Sea. In the north, on the other hand, Haifa and Tiberias are only a little more than 50 km. [30 miles] apart, and from Meṭullah the Mediterranean coast lies only 35 km. [22 miles] to the west.

The distances in Transjordan correspond. To travel from Jerusalem to ʿAmmān, the modern capital of Jordan, one can take the old road to Jericho (Eriḥa) and from there to the Jordan bridge 9 km. [5 miles] away. From the bridge one travels 63·5 km. [40 miles], first across the eastern half of the Jordan Valley, then through a canyon to es-Salṭ (see p. 13) and finally through the hills of northern Belqā. The new direct highway is considerably shorter, running along the northern shore of the Dead Sea, past Nāʿūr to ʿAmmān. ʿAmmān is close to the eastern limits of arable land and the beginning of the Syro-Arabian Desert. About 75 km. [47 miles] south of ʻAmmān one reaches the upper part of the valley of Seil el-Mōjib (see p. 13). [From there the new modern highway continues on south to Maʻan and ʻAqabah.] The Ḥejāz railway travels along the eastern border of Transjordan's cultivated land following in general the route of the ancient pilgrim road (Derb el-Ḥajj) from Damascus to Mecca.

Going north from ʻAmmān along this same railway line one can reach the city of Derʻa on the Yarmuk (see p. 14) after exactly 100 km. [62 miles] and Damascus after 127 km. [79 miles] more. From Derʻa a spur line runs westward down the Yarmuk valley. Seventy-four km. [46 miles] down this westerly spur line one reaches Samakh at the southern end of the Sea of Tiberias; after another 87 km. [54 miles], travelling through part of the Ghōr, past Beisān, through the valley of the River Jālūd and diagonally across the Plain of Jezreel, one reaches Haifa. The overland route from Derʻa totals 100 miles. The air distance between Derʻa and Haifa is about 110 km. [68 miles]. The road running eastsoutheast from Derʻa to Boṣrah on the southwestern side of Jebel ed-Drūz covers 41 km. [25 miles].

(2) *Elevations*

Palestine is a country of great differences in elevation. These are the more striking since they occur in a relatively small space. A few examples may be cited. Although there are considerable differences in elevation, the old city of Jerusalem, situated within a hollow at the top of the Judean hill country, lies on the average 750 m. [2,460 feet] above sea level. Jericho, on the other hand, lies 250 m. [820 feet] below sea level. Therefore, the 37-km. [23-mile] highway from Jerusalem down to Jericho includes a descent of 1,000 m. [3,300 feet]; between km. 26 and 27 [just past 16 miles] it passes sea level, as indicated by a sign there. Likewise, in the 25-km. [15-mile] distance from the eastern edge of the Jordan Valley to es-Salṭ, 795 m. [2,608 feet] above sea level, the road climbs about 1,020 m. [3,346 feet]. The peak (see p. 13) just northwest of es-Salṭ is 1,094 m. [3,590 feet] above sea level, but 1,220 m. [4,000 feet] above the Jordan Valley. Between the summit of the Mount of Olives, about 815 m. [2,674 feet] above sea level, just east of Jerusalem, and the Dead Sea, 390 m. [1,280 feet] below sea level, about 20 km. [12 miles] away, there is a difference in elevation of more than 1,200 m. [3,950 feet]. Again, the peak of Mount en-Nebeh only 14 air km. [8·7 miles] from the Dead Sea northwest of Medeba (see p. 13) and

806 m. [2,644 feet] high, again rises about 1,200 m. [3,936 feet] above the level of the Dead Sea. The road from Jerusalem to Jaffa drops off no less than 450 m. [1,476 feet] in an 8-km. [5-mile] stretch between the western edge of the Judean hill country at the town of Qiryat el-ʻEinab (Isr., Qiryath Yeʻarim) where the Judean hill country and its western foothills meet. The 1,011-m. [3,316-foot] massif of el-ʻAṣūr at the southeastern corner of the Samaritan hill country (see p. 19) towers about 1,250 m. [4,100 feet] over the Jordan rift only 12 air km. [7.5 miles] away at Khirbet el-ʻŌjah el-Fōqah.

In the Samaritan hill country farther north and in lower Galilee the differences in elevation are not so extreme. Yet the mountains Jebel eṭ-Ṭōr and Jebel Islāmīyeh (see p. 19), just east of Nāblus, rise about 400 or 450 m. [1,400 or 1,500 feet] from the plain. Jebel eṭ-Ṭōr (Isr., Har Tabhor) in the northeastern corner of the Plain of Jezreel has a height of nearly 500 m. [1,640 feet] from its base.

The hill country of upper Galilee rises still more abruptly. Mount Jermaq (see p. 21) is more than 1,400 m. [4,600 feet] higher than the Sea of Tiberias just 18 km. [11.2 miles] away in a straight line.

4. *Climate*

Above and beyond the usual and easily recognizable facts about weather in Palestine, individual studies of climatic phenomena were made by the first scientific explorers of the country. More systematic and continuous observations began later. In 1895 the Deutscher Palästina-Verein (DPV) installed meteorological stations in various parts of the land. These stations conducted relatively regular observations according to a definite system. At present, systematic meteorological readings are made by various institutions.[22] For a detailed study, especially of the averages derived from the various individual observations, one is referred to the works cited. In what follows, these averages are not studied; rather, the

[22] A summary and study of previous observations, but only on the subject of precipitation, is found in H. Hilderscheid, " Die Niederschlagsverhältnisse Palästinas in alter und neuer Zeit," *ZDPV*, XXV (1902), 1–105, with numerous charts. A very thorough survey of all the meteorological phenomena on the basis of the observations at the stations of the DPV during 1896–1905, with many tabular summaries, is given in F. M. Exner, " Zum Klima von Palästina," *ZDPV*, XXXIII (1910), 107–64. Many assertions and personal observations are found scattered through Dalman, *Arbeit und Sitte in Palästina*: Vol. I, *Jahreslauf und Tageslauf* (1928). Also F.-M. Abel, *Géographie de la Palestine*, I (1933), 108 ff. gives, essentially on the basis of Exner, a more detailed survey of the climatic conditions with a number of tables. The observations at the stations of the DPV were consecutively collected and published in the *ZDPV* by P. Blanckenhorn in an annual meteorological table and an annual special table concerning rainfall.

basic features of Palestinian climate are described and illustrated by some characteristic phenomena.

Of primary importance for understanding the climate of Palestine is the fact that this country as well as the whole Mediterranean world is in a zone of subtropical climate, characterized by alternation between a dry summer and a winter rainy season. It must also be noted that extreme differences of terrain within the small area of Palestine produce great variations of climate.

Rainfall is necessary for life in the land, since—in contrast to the cultures along the river plains of the Nile or the Tigris–Euphrates system—Palestine's vegetation depends almost completely on rainfall. The winter rainy season begins with the " early rain," which normally occurs at the end of October; occasionally September brings the first downpours, or again, the beginning of the rains holds off till November. The heaviest rain falls mainly in January. The rainy season closes in May with the " late rain." Naturally, there are many variations one way or the other. Aside from the western plains, the western half of the Cisjordan range receives the heaviest rainfall of any part of the country. Here the rains blown in from the Mediterranean Sea to the west fall as " ascent rains " when moisture-bearing air is forced to higher and therefore cooler air levels where condensation takes place. Jerusalem, at the top of the Judean range, in the 108 years from 1846–47 to 1953–54 had an average rainfall of 560 millimetres [22 inches] annually.[23] Rainfall averages naturally vary. In the decade from 1896 to 1905, the average rainfall in Jerusalem was 630 mm. [25 inches].[24] In the decade from 1927 to 1936, by contrast, it was only 431·6 mm. [17 inches].[25] During this latter period the average rainfall did not once reach 560 mm. [22 inches]. From the winter of 1936–37 Jerusalem again had markedly higher rainfall running even higher than 700 mm. [28 inches].[26]

By way of comparison, Sacramento, California, has an average annual precipitation of 19·4 inches on 59 days of rain annually. The geographical situation of Sacramento has marked similarity to that of Jerusalem. This applies also to the winter rains and the summer dry season in both places, and also to the number of days of rain. In the total period of the rain season of more than six months there were not even 60 rainy days a year in Palestine during

[23] See J. Neumann, " On the Incidence of Dry and Wet Years," *IEJ*, VI (1956), 59, 60.

[24] Exner, *op. cit.*, p. 129.

[25] Rainfall tables published in *ZDPV*, LI (1928)–LXI (1938).

[26] See N. Rosenan, " One Hundred Years of Rainfall in Jerusalem," *IEJ*, V (1955), 137–53, particularly the table on p. 151.

the period of 1927–36. The winter rain does not come down as a steady shower but as isolated heavy cloudbursts; even in the rainy month of January rain normally falls on only half the days. These are days with cloudbursts rather than rainy days as we know them. This has the practical meaning that the rain falling in cloudbursts is not fully absorbed by the soil, but in great part runs off into quickly filled gullies (*widyān*). According to the observations for the ten-year period before the Second World War, the coastal plain had somewhat more rainfall than the hill country, which as noted above was well below average figures. The weather station of the DPV in the former German colony of Wilhelmina on the plain inland from Jaffa (see the general map on p. 11) showed an average precipitation of 498.3 mm. [19.6 inches] on 53.9 days of rain while Haifa on the Carmel promontory, where the mountain juts out abruptly in the sea, during the same period had average precipitation of 529·5 mm. [20·7 inches] on 64.3 days of rain. By contrast, the Zionist colony of Beth Alpha east of the watershed at the western edge of the valley corridor at Beisān had an average total of only 378.2 mm. [15 inches] in an average of 51 days of rain, although the valley corridor at Beisān on its northwestern side is not separated from the Mediterranean Sea by mountains. Other parts of the Jordan rift, particularly the great southern part, are increasingly arid, with the effects of precipitation less and less evident in the landscape, the farther one goes to the east, southeast, or south. Only on the western edge of the Transjordanian range is there still a possibility of " ascent rains " ; and thus again this region doubtless receives more rainfall, though exact observations for it have long been lacking.[27]

The beginning of the winter rain means the awakening of vegetation in the land. The " flowers of the field " appear suddenly then,

[27] A comparison of the various tables available suggests more regular rainfall conditions in the western coastal regions than in the Cisjordanian hill country, as represented at Jerusalem. According to the tables, Jerusalem showed a considerable variation in average precipitation in various ten-year periods (disregarding the striking extremes of individual rain winters). Similar substantial variations cannot be established, however, for Wilhelmina and Haifa, comparing the figures in Exner, *op. cit.*, p. 128, for the ten-year period 1896–1905 and the figures above for the ten-year period 1927–36. As to the inland regions, the figures seem to show that there is currently a decrease in precipitation. To be sure, just after the low decade 1927–36, a rise in precipitation again approached the stated average for the hundred-year period. Still, in the ten-year period 1944–53 average precipitation reached only 525 mm. [21 inches], according to Rosenan, *op. cit.*, p. 151. The current observable decline in the level of the Dead Sea (see p. 17) may be related to the decrease in rainfall; the lake's maximum level was reached at the beginning of this century. In 1915 the level of the Dead Sea was 387 m. [1,269 feet] below sea level, according to Abel, *op. cit.*, I, 167. But by 1936 the level had already sunk to 392 m. [1,286 feet] below sea level, as reported in *PEQ*, LXIX (1937), 269.

even in desert regions, and seeds sprout on the farms. On the other hand, the end of the rainy season brings with it the death of all annual growth, and only wood-producing plants can endure the summer drought.

Dew, precipitated nightly from the moisture in the air, ranks next to rain in importance. In the rainless season, dew alone moistens the ground. The steppe and desert vegetation lives essentially on dew. The deserts in the vicinity of Palestine are not sand deserts, apart from dunes that have pressed inland, but limestone regions, which lack only rainfall for a more abundant vegetation, so that the moistening by the dew continually produces desert plant growth. It snows rarely in Palestine, and then only in the hills. In general people see snow only on the high mountains of central Syria. These perpetually snow-capped mountains can be seen on the northern horizon from various points inland. From afar one can see Mount Hermon, with its age-old snow-capped head. One popular name for Mount Hermon is Jebel et-Telj, " Snow Mountain." It looms up over the sources of the Jordan to a maximum height of 2,814 m. [9,230 feet].

Temperatures vary greatly in Palestine with the location and season. The month with the lowest average temperatures is generally January; August holds the claim to being the warmest month, though in some years July is warmer. Naturally, the temperature depends in part upon altitude. Jerusalem, which is at an average height of 750 m. [2,460 feet], had an average mean temperature in January of 7·9° C. [46·2° F.] before the Second World War.[28] The corresponding figures for July and August were 23·7° C. [74·7° F.] and 23·9° C. [75° F.].[29] At Sacramento, California, the mean temperature in January (the coldest month) is 45° F.; in July (the warmest month), it is 72° F. Very seldom does the minimum in Jerusalem fall below freezing. Other lower parts of the land are warmer still. The average temperature at Wilhelmina, 40 m. [131 feet] above sea level on the coastal plain (see p. 30), in the years named was in January, 13·3° C. [55° F.]; in July, 28·0° C. [82·4° F.]; in August, 28·7° C. [83·7° F.]. Jericho, in the southern Jordan rift at 250 m. [820 feet] below sea level, has still higher average temperatures.[30]

[28] Determined from the meteorological tables for 1929 to 1937 in *ZDPV*, LIII (1930); LXI (1938).

[29] The assertion of Blanckenhorn that in 1935 August showed the very unusual mean temperature of only 18·9° C. [66° F.] rests on an error of calculation.

[30] For Jericho, recent corresponding observations are lacking. A comparison of the above figures with the summaries in Exner (*op. cit.*, pp. 118 ff.) of the mean temperature

Of still greater practical importance than these average figures are certain individual phenomena, such as the fact that the winds have a determining influence on the temperatures. On the whole, westerly winds prevail in the country; they usually spring up sometime around noon or in the early afternoon and bring with them a cooling relief always awaited in the summer. Evenings and nights in all parts of the country open to the westerly wind are bearable—even pleasant—even in the summer, particularly on the Cisjordan range with its normally more moderate temperatures. Other areas, especially the southern part of the Jordan rift and the region around the Dead Sea, both very warm, do not share in the beneficial effect of the west wind, since the high Cisjordan range shuts them off from the wind.

The east winds coming from the desert have the opposite effect. During the wintry half of the year they can be stronger than the west winds for brief periods. When they occur in the fall or in the spring they are often accompanied by a withering heat. The east wind is known in the country as *esh-Sherqīyeh*, "the east [wind]," from which the Italian *scirocco* is derived. We also call this wind the sirocco. The sultry eastern air is known as *es-Samūm*, "poison [air]." It is carried along by the east wind in autumn and spring, when it sometimes lies dead over the land. It is usually filled with fine dust which darkens the atmosphere. While the east wind is cold in the winter, the appearance in fall and spring of the sirocco, which lasts a number of days, means heat so unbearable that it oppresses and drains every form of life. The months of May and again September or October are the times of this sirocco. It should be noted that these are not the months of high average temperatures. Yet frequently the highest temperatures of the year occur in these months, since they have a number of these very hot days. On these days, even in Jerusalem, the thermometer can register as high as 40° C. [104° F.].[31] A sirocco brings still higher temperatures to other parts of the country, such as the coastal plains and the Jordan rift.[32] The spring sirocco has a striking effect. After the end of the

from 1896 to 1905 shows that very recently the average temperatures have risen, which matches the conclusion reached above on p. 30, note 27 concerning rainfall. Palestine seems therefore to be becoming more arid and warmer.

[31] The highest temperature observed in Jerusalem between 1929 and 1937 in a sirocco month was only 37·5° C. [99·5° F.] in May, 1935, and the second highest was 36·2° C. [97·1° F.] in September, 1931.

[32] Wilhelmina on the coastal plain registered a maximum temperature in May, 1929, of 46·5° C. [115·7° F.]; in May, 1935, of 44·5° C. [112·1° F.]. Whether the highest temperature of 39·7° C. [103·5° F.] for Jerusalem and 47·0° C. [116·6° F.] for Wilhelmina in June 1933 are ascribable to the sirocco remains in question.

rainy season, with one blast it makes the flowers of the field wither and disappear. The sirocco is meant whenever mention is made in the Old Testament of that wind which needs only to pass over the field in order to wither the grass and make the flowers wilt (Isa. 40:6–8; Ps. 103:15–16).

There are no storms in Palestine during the rainless summer. They come now and again during the winter rainy season, with or without rainfall, and, particularly, toward this season's end in March and April. Storms are rare in May and rarer still in June. The country can have sleet and hail in the winter half of the year and even as late as the latter rains of springtime, although this rarely occurs.

5. *Flora and Fauna*

(1) *The Plant World*

The vegetation is determined both by the fact that the land is a part of the Mediterranean world within a subtropical climatic zone and by the fact that it has areas of extremely varied altitude, rainfall, and temperature. Thus, the flora of the country is in general Mediterranean. In the southern part of the Jordan rift, however, it is almost tropical in character.[33]

[33] For a basic study see E. G. Post, *Flora of Syria, Palestine and Sinai*, ed. J. E. Dinsmore (2nd ed., 1932–33), Vols. I–II. A botanically classified list of the species appearing in Palestine, with their scientific Latin designations and where possible the Arabic name used in the land today, is provided by G. Dalman and J. E. Dinsmore, "Die Pflanzen Palästinas," *ZDPV*, XXXIV (1911), 1–38, 147–72, 185–241. A guide to the plant world of the country, with its more important species and their characteristics, is provided by P. Wurst, *Aus der Pflanzenwelt Palästinas: Leitfaden der Botanik* (Haifa, 1930).

An abundance of material is found in Dalman, *Arbeit und Sitte in Palästina*, especially I (1928), 51 ff. (the plant world before the beginning of the winter rain), 249 ff. (winter vegetation), 329 ff. (springtime plant growth); II (1932), 242 ff. (field and garden plants); IV (1935), 153 ff. (olive trees), 291 ff. (grapevines).

Flowering plants are treated by S. Killermann in "Die Blumen des heiligen Landes" ("Botanical extracts from a springtime journey through Syria and Palestine"), *Das Land der Bibel*, Vol. I, Sect. 5–6 (1915), and also in "Bestimmungstabelle der in der Palästinischen Flora besonders im Frühjahr erscheinenden höheren Pflanzen nach dem natürlichen System," *ZDPV*, XXXIX (1916), 7–93, an article which includes sixty plant pictures.

L. Rost, "Judäische Wälder," *PJB*, XXVI (1931), 111–22, discusses particularly the wooded areas. Also note in R. Koeppel, *op. cit.*, p. 49, an attempt at a forest map of Palestine. On the forests in the eastern portions of the land, see H. Bardtke, "Die Waldgebiete des jordanischen Staates," *ZDPV*, LXXII (1956), 109–22.

Nearly all descriptive works on Palestine contain surveys of its plant life. Turn to the works named here for systematic study. The material below merely summarizes what will give a better grasp of Palestinian terrain and its natural life.

First to be considered are the plants that grow wild. They are forest types. Originally the Palestinian mountains were forested regions. Yet, from the most ancient days, forests have been cut back by clearing the soil for farmland. Remnants of forests are still found in the Judean and upper Galilean hill country. The Carmel ridge and the Transjordan section of ʿAjlūn are still true forest regions. The gradual clearing of the forest land of Palestine continued until very recent times. The phases of the First World War which occurred there required wood and occasioned further ravaging of the forest lands then in existence. But as far back as we can trace its history, we cannot assume a heavy forestation of the land. The records show that even in Old Testament times there were only greater or smaller remnants of primeval forests left.

Generally speaking, the forests of Palestine are not composed of high trees. Full-grown, individual forest trees stand out conspicuously from a great distance, and larger or smaller clusters of trees are equally notable. Extensive open areas are completely covered with a growth of low trees and bushes known as the *maquis*, also called *macchia* in Italian. It consists largely of evergreen perennials growing fully as tall as a man, and is characteristic of the entire Mediterranean area. The *maquis* is found especially in the above-named forest regions of modern Palestine. Brushland of the garigué type (Provençal, *garrigue*) is also common. This is stunted, often sparse growth.

The oak is the most prevalent of the forest trees of Palestine. Various kinds of oaks make up a large proportion of the trees in all the forest formations mentioned here. In the south of the country there is the kermes oak (*quercus coccifera*; in Arabic, *ballūṭ* or *sinjan*); it has small leather-hard evergreen spiny leaves, which last through the winter. In the northern part of the land there is the aegilops or valonia oak (*quercus aegilops*; in Arabic, *mell*, *mellūl*) with large leaves which fall off in the autumn. Along with the oak, the terebinth (*pistacia terebinthus*; in Arabic, *butm̩*) is a very common tree and wood. Less common is the carob tree (*ceratonia siliqua*; in Arabic, *kharrub*), likewise evergreen. Carobs stand out as single trees with their magnificent and imposing crowns, very welcome for the shade they provide. Among the conifers only the aleppo pine (*pinus halepensis*; in Arabic, *qreish*) is important as acclimated and growing wild. Here and there these trees grow to a good height, alone as well as in groups. Then, too, they are found as part of the *maquis*. Among the *maquis* are also all sorts of deciduous shrubs, including the hawthorn (*cratae-*

gus azarolus; in Arabic, *za'rūr*) and others.

As steppe and desert growth there is the tree or bush tamarisk; (*tamarix*; in Arabic, *ṭarfa* or [*n*]*eṭel*). With its finely divided leaves it is well suited to the hot, dry climate. Among the steppe and desert bushes, the common broom (*retama roetam*; in Arabic, *retem*) must especially be named, and the Christ's thorn (*zizyphus spina Christi*; in Arabic, *sidr*), out of which, according to legend, Christ's crown of thorns was plaited. With its outspread thorny branches and its shining green leaves it often forms imposing, extensive bushes.

As to annual wild growth the land produces all sorts of meadow grasses at the beginning of the winter rainy season. At that time even the steppe regions are covered with grass growth, which serves as welcome fodder for the nomads' herds of animals. The springtime pasture lands are adorned at the same time with bright flowers of great variety[34] until, following the rainy season, the sirocco in May brings all this display to a sudden end.

Among the cultivated plants which are raised by the inhabitants of the land, the types of grain are of first importance. Essentially grain means barley (Arabic, *sha'īr*) and wheat (Arabic, *ḥinṭah*), common to the whole area. The plain en-Nuqreh (see p. 14) in northern Transjordan and the southern level part of the Belqā (see p. 13) in southern Transjordan are rich grain sections, the granaries of the land. The sowing of the winter grain follows immediately after the onset of the early rain. The summer sowing, which is done before the late rains stop, is made up mainly of the so-called durra (Arabic, *dhurah*) also known as *sorgum vulgare* or kaffircorn, of African origin. Until the recent beginning of general modernization of agriculture the strewn seed was turned under with the simple plough.[35] The grain harvest, naturally with some variation in different districts, usually takes place in May. At that time, according to ancient custom the harvested grain is brought to the highest possible level spot exposed to the wind. There during the summer it is threshed by the trampling of domestic animals or by threshing sleds and carts which are driven over it. Finally it is winnowed, that is, tossed into the air against the wind with the winnowing shovel or fork so that the wind may carry away the light chaff.

The most common fruit tree is the evergreen olive (Arabic, *zeitūn*), which has a grey, thick, often fissured trunk and small

[34] See, for example, the colourful picture in *64 Bilder aus dem Heiligen Lande* (Württembergische Bibelanstalt), p. 32.

[35] Cf. *ibid.*, p. 31 [or Wright, *Biblical Archaeology*, p. 182].

dull-green leaves. It flourishes in all elevated places of the land and particularly in the mountainous parts, and is cultivated in single plantings. From September on, the little dark olives are harvested by being knocked off the trees. The oil of the fruit is pressed out in olive presses and is put to many uses.

In all parts of the land the fig tree (Arabic, *tīn*) is grown singly as well as in more extensive orchards. It has large leaves, mostly five-lobed, which it sheds in the autumn. In May or June it produces the early figs, some of which fall off, though some are picked as they become suitable for eating. The first summer figs ripen around July; they are a soft, juicy fruit.

Combined with the fig tree one frequently finds the grape vine (Arabic, *'arish*), often indeed growing among the very branches, for usually the grapevines are left to grow freely, and they creep along the ground or climb up on the fig tree or other near-by trees. Grapevines are more demanding than olive trees and fig trees. They need moisture and the unfailing sun of Palestine. The region of Hebron on the Judean range is still well known for producing wine today, as it was long ago. Ripe bunches of grapes appear from about August until October. The ripe grapes are eaten fresh or dried. Since Islam prohibits wine drinking, in Arab regions wine is prepared by non-Moslems—for example, Christian monks.

The pomegranate (Arabic, *rummān*) is a fruit tree which usually grows singly, especially in the mountainous parts of the country. Its bright red fruit ripens in September or October. The fruit has a hard shell around a pink, juicy pulp which holds many seeds. There are also some mulberries (Arabic, *tūt*), in the lowlands; their small fruit is eaten mostly by birds.

The date palm [Arabic, *nakhl*] is also relatively rare. Single specimens are encountered in the hill country, for example near Jerusalem; sizable groves are found especially on the southern coastal plain and in the southern Jordan rift. The tree's branchless trunk, often tall and massive, has the familiar crown of long pinnate leaves. Its fruit, the date (Arabic, *belaḥ*), is eaten either fresh or dried.

Finally, the banana (Arabic, *mōz*) should be mentioned. Banana trees thrive in warm, watered places. Therefore they are usually cultivated especially at oases, for example at Jericho.

The orange (Arabic, *burdeqān*; that is, " the Portuguese fruit "), transplanted by the Portuguese from East Asia to Europe and Southwest Asia, has been introduced into the country in recent years. Great quantities of oranges are cultivated, especially on the coastal plain (" Jaffa oranges "). They are one of Palestine's chief exports. Orange groves require great care, but they provide ripe fruit from November all the way to spring. Among the other non-indigenous plants is the eucalyptus tree, called *shajaret kīna* (" quinine tree "), introduced from Australia, of high slender growth. Because eucalyptus roots draw up a great deal of water, these trees are now planted to dry out swampy areas. Scattered throughout the country, even though only recently introduced from the West Indies, is the prickly-pear cactus (Arabic, *ṣabr*, originally meaning " myrrh "), by nature a desert plant; it is planted everywhere in hedges to surround orchards and the like. Its thorny members, the " leaves," form an impenetrable thicket. Its fruit is the prickly pear. Inside its shell there is a juicy meat which is very palatable.

(2) *The Animal World*

There is also a great variety of animals in Palestine. In this country, with its greatly varied terrain, one encounters the " palaearctic," " Ethiopic," and " Indo-Mesopotamian " types.[36]

In the following only the most important types of animals will be considered briefly.

The world of wild animals includes some predatory animals. Wolves (Arabic, *dīb*) still threaten flocks of sheep and goats as they did long ago. Jackals (Arabic, *wāwi*), recognized by their nocturnal howling, and cowardly hyenas (Arabic, *Ẓab'*) serve a useful function as scavengers. Foxes (Arabic, *eḥṣeini*), too, and wild dogs (Arabic, *kalb*) appear everywhere in the land. However, some predatory animals mentioned in ancient literature, for example in the Old Testament, have now died out. Lions once roamed the forested sections of the land and kept their lairs in rocky caves; bears also lodged in the forests.

Among game animals, the land has gazelles (Arabic, *ghazāl*) and

[36] For all of them see Friedrich Simon Bodenheimer, *Die Tierwelt Palästinas* (" Das Land der Bibel " Series, Vol. III [1920], Secs. 3–4.) Palestinian animal life is treated historically by Bodenheimer in *Animal and Man in Bible Lands* (" Collection de travaux de l'académie internationale d'histoire des sciences " [Netherlands: Brill, 1960]. A summary of Latin terms and Arabic names of the animals is given by Dalman, " Arabische Vögelnamen von Palästina und Syrien," *ZDPV*, XXXVI (1913), 165–79, with a supplement *ZDPV*, XXXVII (1914), 59–60; by the same author, " Palästinische Tiernamen," *ZDPV*, XLVI (1923), 65–78. A partial treatment is given by A. Gustavs, " Streifzüge durch die Vogelwelt Palästinas," *PJB*, VIII (1912), 85–103. Palestinian bird life is described with reference to the Bible by S. R. Driver, " Birds in the Old Testament," *PEQ*, LXXXVI (1954), 5–20; LXXXVII (1955), 129–40; XC (1958), 56–58. A number of interesting individual observations are given by F. Frank, " Tierleben in Palästina," *ZDPV*, LXXV (1959), 83–88.

rabbits (Arabic, *arnab*); in the southern parts of the country the ibex (Arabic, *wa'l* or *beden*) is common, and in the caves around the Dead Sea one finds an animal similar to the marmot or ground hog (Arabic, *wabr*). Wild boars (Arabic, *khanzīr berri*) still live in the Zōr (see p. 16) along the Jordan. Other species, like red deer and antelope, belong to the Palestine of the past and have died out today.[37]

There are many different kinds of predatory birds, among them vultures (Arabic, *rakham*) that gorge themselves on the blood of carrion, which is ordinarily simply thrown out on the open field. Partridges (Arabic, *shunnar*, also *ḥajal*) and other birds are hunted. There are various kinds of snakes and lizards. With its many sunny rock and sand expanses the land offers these animals excellent cover. Until the last century crocodiles (Arabic, *timsāḥ*) were still found in the Nahr ez-Zerqā (Isr., Nehar hat-Tanninim) north of Qeiṣāriyeh (see Figure 1), which was called "Crocodile River" by classical authors. Fishing is done along the Mediterranean coast as well as in the well-stocked Sea of Tiberias.[38] Among the insects, migratory locusts (Arabic, *jerād*, plus various terms for various stages of development), now and again appear as a great scourge. When they descend on the countryside in their enormous numbers, all green plant life disappears. A locust plague was warded off by vigorous measures in March, 1928; in March, 1915, a similar plague had devastated the country.[39] Scorpions (Arabic, *'aqrab*), crablike members of the spider family whose poisonous sting is rightly feared, still live in the country as they did long ago.

Among domestic animals the work animals of the farmer (*fellāḥ*), the donkey and the ox, are of prime importance in so far as the farmer does not use modern equipment. The patient donkey (Arabic, *ḥmār*) is the bearer of all smaller burdens; it carries anyone on its back who wants to travel cross-country; it carries containers filled with water from the village well; it transports the produce of field, garden, and trees which the farmer wants to get to the city market, and performs other valuable services. The ox (Arabic, *baqar*), usually brown and ungainly, serves the farmer almost exclusively as a work animal rather than for meat, since, generally speaking, beef is not eaten. It draws the plough and helps with the threshing of grain either by being driven back and forth over the

[37] Further details about hunting and about game animals are to be found in Dalman, *Arbeit und Sitte in Palästina*, VI, 314 ff.

[38] *Ibid.*, pp. 343 ff.

[39] See John D. Whiting, "Jerusalem's Locust Plague," *National Geographic Magazine*, XXVIII (Dec., 1915) 511–50, or L. Bauer, "Die Heuschrecken Plage in Palästina," *ZDPV*, XLIX (1926), 168–71.

grain spread out on the threshing floor (thus doing with its hoofs the actual work of threshing), or by drawing the threshing sled or threshing wagon in a circle across the grain. The cow (Arabic, *baqarah*), in addition, provides milk for the farmer.[40]

The camel (Arabic, *jamal*) is present to carry large and heavy burdens.[41] The breeding of camels is undertaken by Bedouins on the steppes bordering the land to the east and south. During the earlier periods, camels were not used as beasts of burden in the settled land. They were only put to common labour when the Arab penetrated the land during the beginnings of Islam. Today one still sees them often. Large camel caravans move through the country on ancient caravan routes with long rows of camels, one tied behind the other, with a donkey in front carrying the leader,[42] and camel caravans provide trade wares of the most varied sort—harvest produce from the Transjordan granaries, pottery from Gaza, and the like. The camel serves the Bedouins as a riding animal, and camel milk (Arabic, *naqah*) is used as food.

Moreover, the horse (Arabic, *ḥṣān*; the mare, *faras*) has been known in Southwest Asia as a riding animal since the second millennium B.C. Horses are bred domestically, particularly by the Bedouins in the border regions. They are ridden especially by the Bedouins. In the settled country of late they are rapidly being displaced by the introduction of European conveyances. The horse is seldom used by the natives as a draft animal.

Finally, chickens are among the most important domestic animals. They are kept for the eggs they lay. Pigeons are also raised, mostly for meat.[43]

Flocks of sheep and goats play a particularly important role in the country. One finds them everywhere, in countless large and small flocks. They crop the grass or, particularly in the dry summer, the leaves of the undergrowth and trees. Where the forest has disappeared it will not grow again, unless it is especially protected from them. Particularly the goats, standing upright on their hind legs, over and over again chew off the young shoots of the growing woodland trees. The farmers in the settled country and the semi-nomads in the steppe regions have their flocks of sheep and goats; for the semi-nomads particularly these are a major possession. Sheep and goats flock together everywhere; therefore, since ancient times the expression " small animal " has been used to designate

40 For more about the ox see *ibid.*, pp. 160 ff.

41 *Ibid.*, pp. 147 ff.

42 See *64 Bilder aus dem Heiligen Lande, op. cit.*, p. 9.

43 See Dalman, *Arbeit . . .*, VII, 247 ff.; 256 ff.

both types of animal. In the Old Testament the word for " small animal " is *ṣōn*; modern Arabic uses the word *ghanam*. The sheep (Arabic, *kharūf*) are white as a rule. They give their owners wool for clothing, and finally their pelts; furthermore, sheep provide milk for nourishment, not to mention the festive roast and, as a particular delicacy, the fat tail of the sheep. The Arab natives certainly do not eat meat every day, but only on special occasions, such as entertaining a guest. Goats (Arabic, *meʿz*, also *ʿanzeh*) are invariably black. Bedouins make their tenting materials of goat hair; for that reason Bedouin tents are black. Goats also supply milk and meat. Moreover, goat skins are still occasionally used as containers for all sorts of fluids, though they are rapidly being replaced by European substitutes. The goatskin in made into a container by sewing shut all the openings except one; that one, reserved for pouring, can be tied shut when not in use. Thus, the entire skin is used, particularly for carrying water. It is carried on a man's back or loaded on a donkey. This is what is called a " bottle " in earlier biblical translations.[44]

[44] On small animals see *ibid.*, VI, 180 ff.

CHAPTER II

NATURAL HISTORY

6. *Geology*[1]

(1) *Geological Structure*

For the following, see Figure 2.

The rock structure of Palestine is basically formed from marine lime and chalk deposits of the Jurassic and Cretaceous periods. They were deposited in horizontal layers, one on top of the other. The lowest is the Jurassic. It is visible only in a few places on both

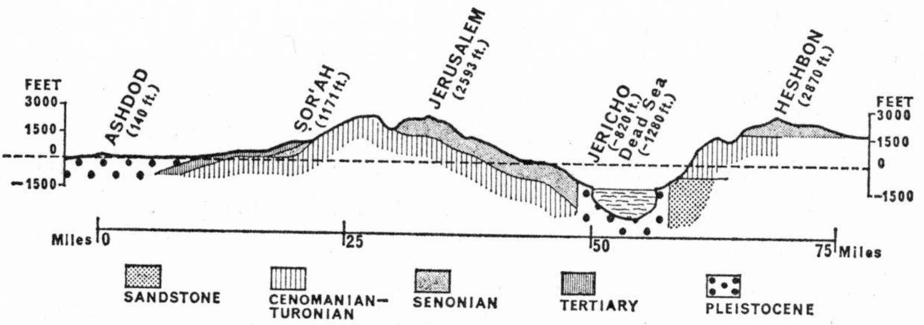

Figure 2. Geological Structure

sides of the Jordan rift. Nubian sandstone, belonging to the Lower Cretaceous, is directly above that. This too is exposed at certain places in the Jordan rift, especially at the edges of the deeply eroded valley of the Nahr ez-Zerqā (Jabbok River) and at the eastern edge of the Dead Sea. The Palestinian prominences are

[1] The findings of geological explorations in Palestine are published in very scattered fashion. A summary of the older explorations is given by M. Blanckenhorn, " Syrien, Arabien, und Mesopotamien," *Handbuch der regionalen Geologie*, V. Band, 4. Abt. (1914). A shorter summary including more recent explorations by the same author, " Geologie Palästinas nach heutiger Auffassung," *ZDPV*, LIV (1931), 3–50, gives detailed consideration to pertinent literature. More recent studies are L. Picard, *Structure and Evolution of Palestine* (Jerusalem, 1943) and for the eastern region, A. M. Quennel, *Handbook of the Geology of Jordan* (Amman, 1959). The geology of Palestine is also treated in rather detailed fashion on the basis of secondary sources by F.-M. Abel, *Géographie de la Palestine*, I (1933), 23–58, and, more briefly, by Guthe, *Palästina* (2nd ed., 1927), pp. 10–29. Particular reference should be made to the " Geologische Karte von Palästina " which Blanckenhorn has published in *ZDPV*, XXXV (1912), Table III. The explanatory text is " Kurzer Abriss der Geologie Palästinas," *ibid.*, pp. 113–139.

formed mainly of the Upper Cretaceous levels. First there is the massive Cenomanian level, on the average 600 m. [2,000 feet] thick, a hard limestone. The runoff of rain water has eroded deep, steep-walled canyons into it. The Turonian level lies above the Cenomanian level and is related to the latter. The Senonian level, the uppermost level of the Cretaceous group, lies on top of that. In extensive areas of Palestine, particularly on the eastern slope of the Judean and the Samaritan hill country, the Senonian is now the upper level of the ranges. The Senonian level is in general a dazzling white limestone which sharply reflects the rays and the radiant warmth of the sun. It is soft and forms gentle, rolling surface contours. It is frequently interspersed with layers of flint which produce sharp edges because of their hardness, while the Senonian levels above and below give meagre resistance to abrasion.

After the Cretaceous levels were deposited, there was an interruption in sedimentation, that is, in the process of forming deposits. Then a new phase of sea deposits led to the development of the Tertiary levels of which the lowest, the Eocene, is a white, occasionally grey limestone, here and there found as the upper level on the Palestinian ranges. Upon the Eocene level there follow the levels of the Oligocene, Miocene, and Pliocene with various subdivisions, all in the Tertiary period. In the mid-Pliocene epoch the first eruptions of late volcanic basalts occurred, with others at the end of the Tertiary period. They spread from northern Transjordan, Mount ed-Drūz and Jōlān, covered the entire northern third of Transjordan with a basalt level, and spread lava beyond the region of the Jordan rift north and south of the present Sea of Tiberias. The entire southeastern part of the Galilean range is covered today by a layer of basalt.

The " Quaternary " [that is, Pleistocene] alluvial deposits were laid down in a last period of sedimentation in those parts of the land which the sea again covered. Essentially these became the present plains of the land, including the Jordan rift.

The formation of the mainland by successive ocean deposits in horizontal strata would have produced a level plateau, apart from the volcanic eruptions in the northeast, if definite structural reactions, that is, disturbances and changes of the horizontal structure, had not basically modified this plateau character. Horizontal strata are most clearly preserved in Transjordan, as seen in the interior of the Syro-Arabian Desert plateau. In Cisjordan, on the other hand, there are only traces of onetime horizontal strata.

After the deposit of the Cretaceous levels there followed a period during which the ocean temporarily retreated, under lateral pressure, inducing folding and warping, that is, flexures of the horizontal strata, which occurred especially on the present eastern side of the Judean and Samaritan range, and also continued into the neighbouring region which today is called Transjordan. A new inundation of the land followed the deposit of the lowest Tertiary strata. Subsequently, between the Miocene and Pliocene periods the horizontal strata underwent tremendous block-faulting north and south. This produced the Jordan rift which became still deeper during further phases of the mountain-building process. At the same time a fault developed along the western edge of the present Cisjordan range which made it a mountain block, extending from north to south. The southeast-to-northwest faults were a later development. The most important transverse fault formed the great inland Plain of Jezreel and on its southwestern side terminated the Samaritan hill country. Subsequently, these faulted areas were inundated by the ocean and received alluvial deposits.

Water and wind continued to work as forces of attrition to mould the form of the upper layers. Thus at the top of the Cisjordan hill country the uppermost Cretaceous stratum, the Senonian level, has largely disappeared and is preserved as the top stratum only on the sunken mountain slopes and in the Transjordan hill country, which has been less disturbed by structural changes. Water, especially in earlier periods of heavier rain, carved out countless valleys in the soft limestone strata. Thus the present sharply contrasting and extremely varied form of the land came into being.

(2) *Mineral Resources*

Palestine has no abundance of mineral resources. When Deut. 8 : 9, praising the excellences of Palestine, states that its stones are iron and one can dig copper from its mountains, the assertion merely points out the contrast with the poverty of the steppe and desert. Actually Palestine is not a very productive area for minerals.[2] There are iron deposits in the Cenomanian limestone located in the southwestern corner of ʿAjlūn on the northern side of the lower course of the Jabbok. This, too, is the location of the only authentic ancient mine discovered so far on the soil of Palestine, the iron mine

[2] Blanckenhorn, *Handbuch . . .*, *op. cit.*, pp. 134 ff.; Galling, *BRL*, cols. 95 ff., under the heading *Bergbau* (" mining ") [or Nelson Glueck, *The Other Side of the Jordan* (1940), pp. 50–88].

Mughāret el-Wardeh (" the rosy cave ") south of the site of Rājib.[3] Probably not accidentally, there was a foundry near by in the Jordan Valley in which Solomon, according to I Kings 7 : 46, had the bronze fixtures cast for the temple at Jerusalem.[4] In Cisjordan copper and iron are not found at all.

The edges of the great Syrian rift and perhaps also the rift valley north of Palestine are richer in mineral resources. In ancient times the copper supply was intensively mined in the region of modern Feinān, the Punon of Num. 33 : 42–43, in the land of the Edomites on the eastern edge of the Wādi el-ʿArabah. The worked ores were smelted on the spot, as shown by discoveries at Khreibet en-Naḥās (" copper ruins ") or Khirbet es-Samrah (" brown ruins "), a little north of Feinān, and at some neighbouring places.[5] The copper-producing sites of el-Meneʿīyeh (Isr., Har Timnaʿ), which were likewise mined in ancient times, lie farther south on the western side of the Wādi el-ʿArabah, only some 30 km. [19 miles] north of the Gulf of el-ʿAqabah.[6] Then, near the northwestern shore of the Gulf of el-ʿAqabah, there are the copper deposits at Mrashrash[7] just west of Elath in modern Israel and in the Wādi el-Merāh[8] (which is now Egyptian territory). Near by, iron and copper foundries and related processing workshops have been discovered at the northern end of the Gulf of el-ʿAqabah at Tell el-Kheleifeh (see p. 166). The land of the Edomites, which repeatedly from David's time was controlled by Judah for longer or shorter periods of time, was especially valuable probably because of these mineral resources in the Wādi el-ʿArabah, as well as for the thoroughfare Edom offered to the Gulf of el-ʿAqabah and thus to the Red Sea.

On the other hand, the Beqāʿ, between Lebanon and Antilebanon, has ancient copper and iron mines. It is believed that an ancient copper mine exists near Jubb Jenīn at the southern end of the Beqāʿ on the southwestern spurs of Antilebanon.[9] It is considered improbable that there are substantial copper deposits in modern Lebanon. However, Lebanon does have iron ore deposits at several locations. At Zaḥleh on the western edge of the Beqāʿ, on the railway line from Beirut to Damascus, there are ancient iron

[3] Blanckenhorn, *Naturwissenschaftliche Studien im Toten Meer und im Jordantal* (1912), pp. 313 ff.; C. Steuernagel, *Der ʿAdschlun* (1927), p. 286.

[4] Details appear in H. Guthe, *BZAW*, XLI (1925), 96 ff.

[5] Frank, *ZDPV*, LVII (1934), 216 ff. and Plan 16.

[6] *Ibid.*, pp. 233 ff., 241 ff., and Plate XXXIX.

[7] Glueck, *AASOR*, XV (1935), 47–48 and Fig. 23 [and *The Other Side of the Jordan*, pp. 79 ff.].

[8] Frank, *op. cit.*, pp. 247–48 and Plates XLVI B, XLVII A [or Glueck, *loc. cit.*].

[9] C. F. T. Drake and R. F. Burton, *Unexplored Syria* (1872), II, 72.

foundries, where the iron ore from the ore deposit to the northeast in Wādi Ṣannīn was probably smelted.[10] These resources of the Beqāʿ, a section almost completely isolated, made this region desirable to its various neighbours and, thus, it belonged temporarily to the kingdom of David, then to the Aramean kingdom of Damascus, and still later to the kingdom of Hamath on the Orontes.[11]

Other mineral wealth of the land such as that of the Dead Sea and its surroundings can be ignored here, since in general it has been exploited only very recently and therefore has played no role in the history of the land.[12]

7. *Natural Regions*[13]

As a result of the natural conditions of geological structure working in combination with particular climatic conditions there developed in Palestine various definite natural regions whose location determined the beginnings of human history by determining the possible modes of life. This took place long before men gradually began to change the landscape by agriculture—including farming, horticulture, and animal husbandry—or by founding settlements, or by sporadic irrigation, or by any other prehistoric activities. In spite of all the radical man-wrought alterations of the landscape, we can still trace the distribution of such distinct natural regions as desert, steppe, and forest by the type and density of plant life in each. By and large the distribution accords with the amount of rainfall each region receives. In general, wherever there is less than 200 mm. [8 inches] of rainfall annually, there is desert. Regions with more annual rainfall than 500 mm. [20 inches] were originally forest regions; with 300 to 400 mm. [12 to 16 inches] of rainfall a region is a natural steppe. The limits are naturally variable.[14] We call a region a desert in which less than half of the soil is covered with plant life. A steppe is a region where soil supports more growth than a desert without having forested sections, or without showing the clear marks of earlier forestation.[15]

Palestine is bordered on the east and south by deserts, on the

[10] Blanckenhorn, *Handbuch . . .*, p. 138.
[11] Noth, *PJB*, XXXIII (1937), 44 ff.
[12] With reference to the Dead Sea resources, see Blanckenhorn. *MNDVP* (1902), pp. 65 ff.
[13] See R. Gradmann, " Palästinas Urlandschaft," *ZDPV*, LVII (1934), 161–85.
[14] Gradmann, *Die Steppen des Morgenlandes in ihrer Bedeutung für die Geschichte der menschlichen Gesittung* (1934), p. 24.
[15] *Ibid.*, p. 22.

east by the Syro-Arabian Desert and on the south by the Sinai Desert. In the east, the edge of the desert, generally speaking, matches the course of the Ḥejāz railway line. The exception is at ed-Drūz (see p. 14) where the edge of the desert is not found until some distance east of the mountain. On the southern side, the edge of the desert is near the latitude of Beersheba; only in the Jordan rift does the desert extend far to the north, to the centre of the country near the city of Beisān. That far the Ghōr (see p. 15) is desert, as is the eastern slope of the Judean range, since it is in the " rain shadow." On the eastern side of the Jordan rift and of the Wādi el-ʿArabah, on the other hand, the desert edge recedes far to the south, since the Transjordan hill country east of the Dead Sea and east of the northern half of the Wādi el-ʿArabah receives proportionally more rainfall. The Syro-Arabian Desert extends eastward into Mesopotamia, while the Sinai Desert continues through Egypt into North Africa. The deserts in the Palestine area are almost nowhere sandy deserts, but usually deserts with a thin layer of humus on calcareous soil, overgrown with all sorts of stunted, thorny desert bushes. In places there are flinty deserts almost free of vegetation, and it is similarly barren where clay soil is impregnated with salt.[16] Here and there the solitude of the desert is broken by oases, where a spring or a brook waters the soil, or by oases, where there is ground water which tree roots can reach. The shore line forest (ez-Zōr) of the Jordan is a river oasis, just as in greater measure the verdant regions along the lower Euphrates and Tigris and along the Nile are river oases in desert regions. Spring-water oases are located at various places around the Dead Sea—for example, the oasis ʿAin Jidi (Isr., ʿEin Gedhi) at the centre of the western shore.

In Palestine a rather narrow strip of steppe runs all along the edge of the desert.[17] Original steppe land is therefore not very extensive in Palestine, while on the other hand, the entire Syrian interior and Mesopotamia to the north of the line, from Damascus to Palmyra to Deir ez-Zōr (on the Euphrates) to Tekrīt (on the Tigris), is a large steppe region. These are not strictly grass steppes but, rather, brush and grass steppes (according to Gradmann), where wormwood plants (*Artemisia*), genista bushes, and all sorts of thistles and thorns grow. Here, too, occasionally there are oases, such as the oasis Jericho (see p. 16), which is within the steppe zone.

[16] Gradmann, *Die Steppen . . .*, pp. 24–25. On the division of the natural regions, cf. *ibid.*, Map 1, which also appeas ras Chart 1 in *ZDPV*, LVII (1934).

[17] On the origin and meaning of the word steppe, see *ibid.*, p. 22, and on the extent of the steppe area in the Near East, *ibid.*, Map 2.

All the rest, the high points of the Cisjordan and Transjordan hill country, together with plains surrounding or enfolded by them, were originally forest regions. It is true that by and large man is responsible for the destruction of the stands of forests, but even where every trace of the forest has disappeared, the flora still show the original forest character of the district, unless it is now regularly cultivated farm land. The thorny burnet (*poterium spinosum*; Arabic, *bellan* or *netesh*), very prevalent in former forest regions, shows this clearly. The natives gather it in great quantities as fuel, especially for lime kilns. The greatest part of the area of Palestine is natural forest land.

The distribution of the " natural regions " has had its effect on human history. The desert is not entirely devoid of people, even as it is generally not entirely lacking in vegetation. But at any given time the desert offers random habitat for only meagre groups of people and permits a half-sedentary life only in the few oases. The desert is inhabited by Bedouins (Arabic, *bedū*) who travel about with their camel herds or flocks of sheep and goats within limited areas, looking for scattered grazing sites and water holes. As a result, the desert has remained substantially unchanged in the course of time, even though the desert landscape has been somewhat changed as men have used the oases for raising crops and pasturing flocks.[18]

The steppe was important in the beginnings of human culture (concerning this see the above-mentioned works of Gradmann). Since it had what was needed for primitive agriculture, it offered a transition to settled life for men who had originally lived only as hunters and fishermen. Thus the steppe contributed to the development of the first primitive beginnings of a culture. In distinction from the desert, the steppe does reward, even though very poorly, the planting of harvest crops. Man planted the steppe before he began to uproot the forest with its superior soil. One indication that agriculture first appeared on the steppe is the fact that the grain plants which are still so necessary for human civilization were originally steppe herbs (grasses); the original wild forms of our grain types can be pointed out here and there in the Near Eastern steppe regions. Thus, the fact that there are extensive steppe regions in Syria and Mesopotamia (albeit Palestine itself has less steppe) may explain the further fact that human culture developed so much earlier in the Near East than in other parts of the inhabited earth.

[18] Abundant material about the Bedouin tribes in the Syro-Arabian Desert and their surroundings is found in M. F. von Oppenheim, *Die Beduinen*, I (1939), II (1943).

The steppe was touched and transformed by the hand of man very early, and still today steppe regions demonstrate grain cultivation and, thus, the influence of human cultural work.

The steppe itself was too poor, however, for the development of a higher culture. That required the transplanting of the culture which had begun on the steppe into more promising areas which man could learn to make useful for his purposes. When it occurred to men in river oasis regions to distribute the available water artificially, they formed irrigation cultures and extended the productive soil for human welfare. This explains the early rise of the cultural areas along the lower Euphrates and Tigris and along the Nile. On the other hand, man learned how to clear the forest and to make available for agriculture the forest areas which had abundant rainfall. Thus man pressed on into the natural forest regions of Syria and Palestine and established himself there. Understandably, it was in the natural forest regions that human activity effected by far the most striking change of appearance. Not only was the forest gradually cleared to gain farmland; beyond that, the forest was removed even where it did not crowd agriculture, in order to serve man's need for timber. As certainly as the destruction of forest land in Palestine has continued down to recent times, just so certainly must the denuding of the forest land already have started in prehistoric times. As far back as our historical records reach, the land has been poor in forest resources.

Palestine has only a narrow border region of steppe. It seems likely, therefore, that Palestine was not involved in the beginning stage of human culture. Still, Jericho, an oasis in the steppe zone, demonstrates the earliest known settled community (see p. 128). Sedentary life could develop only when men learned how to make a river oasis productive by using an irrigation system, as in the case of the Jordan, and, even more important, by clearing forest regions for agriculture. The natural forest regions were the primary location of human history and culture, as they are to the present day. In this land, which is chiefly dependent on rainfall to water the soil, only the natural forest regions receive enough rain to support the common life of large numbers of people.

CHAPTER III

PALESTINE AS THE ARENA OF BIBLICAL HISTORY

8. *Biblical Geographical Terms*

(1) *Names for the Land as a Whole*

WE are accustomed to use of the name Palestine for the land of the Bible. This usage is based on early Christian historians, as explained earlier. There was no early general name for the entire land. That is not strange because this area has neither natural boundaries nor unity. Therefore, the territory involved did not suggest a natural name. Furthermore, primitive area names are very rare indeed. Area names develop generally only after a land has become the exclusive home of a definite people and, thereby, the arena of its history. As far as we can tell, this state of affairs for Palestine was not reached until the Israelite tribes had settled the land and there had experienced an important part of their history. Even for us it is the retrospective view of this part of Israelite history which is basically the occasion for applying to this land the collective name Palestine. During Israelite times, however, there was no specific or generally used name for the country, either in Israel proper or among the peoples living around them. As the arena of Israelite history it could be called simply *Ereṣ Yiśra'el*, " the territory of the people of Israel."[1] The expression *Ereṣ Yiśra'el* does appear in the sense indicated in I Sam. 13 : 19 (in the ancient account of the history of Saul); but evidently it was not used very often. Indeed, it is not actually a name, and, besides, it is ambiguous. Israel was not only the name of the entire people but also the name of one of the two royal states that arose in the time of the kings on the territory of the people of Israel. Thus it can also mean " the territory of the state of Israel " (thus in II Kings 6: 23; Ezek. 27: 17).

In Deuteronomy and the deuteronomic literature Palestine is designated as " the land which Yahweh has sworn to your fathers

[1] Concerning giving *ereṣ* the meaning " territory of a people " see L. Rost, " Die Bezeichnungen für Land und Volk im Alten Testament," pp. 134 ff., in *Festschrift Otto Procksch* (1934), pp. 125–48.

to give you " and other similar paraphrases for the " Promised " Land.

It seems that the name Canaan (*Kena'an*) has the primary right to consideration as an old, yes, even native name for all of Palestine. Still, the name Canaan developed only secondarily in the Old Testament, and for that matter in a very vague and indefinite sense. The expression *Ereṣ Kena'an*, " the land of Canaan," and especially the gentilic name derived from it, *Kena'ani*, " Canaanite," appear rather frequently in the Old Testament. But if the later customary use of these terms was unclear and not specific, this was even more true of the original special meaning they apparently had.[2] *Ereṣ Kena'an* appears in the early narrative strata of the Pentateuch (see Gen. 42 : 5 ff. and elsewhere), apparently as a somewhat vague designation for the land of Palestine. It is used more frequently, however, in the post-exilic literature, especially by the Priestly Source in the Pentateuch. Num. 35 : 10, 14 and Josh. 22 : 10, 11 are also of this late date; in these passages the expression *Ereṣ Kena'an* refers only to Cisjordan. Of course it is debatable whether *Ereṣ Kena'an* was always understood in this limited way. (The only place where " Canaanites " are unquestionably referred to in Transjordan (Gen. 40 : 11) is unfortunately a questionable source for the word *hak-kena'ani*, as recorded here, looks very much like an explanatory gloss of the general *yoshebh ha'areṣ*.) Generally in the Old Testament, when *Kena'an* or words derived from it are used, two concepts are joined, namely, the concept of a more or less definite, limited area, and even more the concept of the bearers and the artifacts of a culture which was present in the area which the Israelite tribes settled before they occupied it, and which continued to maintain itself there. That is especially true of the word *Kena'ani*, " Canaanite," which amazingly enough was applied exclusively to the pre-Israelite and, therefore, the non-Israelite population, even when the Israelite tribes had long been settled in the " land of Canaan " and, so, to all intents and purposes, had become " Canaanites." (The concept " Canaan " is not specifically linked with the Israelites until the late reference in Isa. 19 : 18 (non-Isaianic), in which the language spoken by the Israelites is called " the language of Canaan.") The Yahwistic narrative stratum in the Pentateuch especially designates all of the population which lived

[2] Surveys of the existence and use of these designations are found in F. M. T. Böhl, " Kanaanäer und Hebräer," *BWAT*, IX (1911), 5 ff. and in B. Maisler, " Untersuchungen zur alten Geschichte und Ethnographie Syriens und Palästinas, I," *Arbeiten aus dem orientalischen Seminar der Universität Giessen*, II (1930), 59 ff.

in Palestine from pre-Israelite times on as *hak-kenaʿani* (always in the collectively understood singular). This makes it very clear that *Kenaʿan* from the outset was not an inclusive land name. More likely it referred originally to a more limited area, the one in which those older non-Israelite inhabitants were still living after the Israelite tribes were already established in the land. Thus the extension of the name " (land of) Canaan " to all of Palestine, or at least to all of Cisjordan, is secondary.

Actually, some Old Testament passages give a special meaning to the name " Canaan " or " Canaanite." According to a remark of the " compiler "[3] of the old sayings of Joshua (Josh. 5 : 1), the kings of the Canaanites lived along the sea. In II Sam. 24 : 7, " all the cities of the Hivites and Canaanites " are named in inseparable connection with the Phoenician coastal city of Tyre. In Isa. 23 : 11, within a non-Isaianic prophecy against Tyre (23 : 5–11), " Canaan " is linked with the sea—in this case, with the Phoenician coast. Also, the " kings of Canaan," called allies of Sisera in the Song of Deborah (Judg. 5 : 19), surely are to be located near the Mediterranean coast. Note also that the " Canaanites " are associated with the northernmost part of the Jordan rift. King Jabin of Hazor (Tell Waqqāṣ, southwest of Lake Ḥūleh) is called " King of Canaan " in the old prose account of the battle of Deborah. However, this is a secondary element in the narrative (Judg. 4 : 2, 23, 24). In Num. 13 : 29, the " Canaanites " are placed at the sea and at the Jordan and, likewise, in the addition to the history of Joshua's Galilean campaign in Josh. 11 : 3, reference is made to " the Canaanites in the east and in the west " (of the Galilean mountains). Probably related to this is the remark in Judg. 18 : 7, 28 which makes it appear that the uppermost part of the Jordan rift in the " time of the Judges " was still politically dependent on the " Sidonians."

This connection of the name of Canaan with the Mediterranean coast and its cities also corresponds with the extra-biblical occurrences of the name. Probably the earliest references are found in texts from Alalah (see p. 210) from the fifteenth century B.C., namely in the Idrimi inscription, line 18, and in some economic texts of level IV,[4] written *kinʾanu(m)*. These texts supply very little concrete information on the meaning of the name Canaan. Still, according to the Idrimi inscription, a Phoenician coastal city apparently lay in the " land of Canaan." The gentilic *knʿny* occurs once

[3] See Noth, *Das Buch Josua, Handbuch zum Alten Testament*, I, Sec. 7 (2nd ed., 1953), 12–13.

[4] Wiseman 48, 5; 154, 24; 181, 9.

in a text from Ugarit (311, 7) from the fourteenth century B.C. (see p. 212), which demonstrates little more than that *kn'n* appears here as a territorial name, probably applied to a specific area. Much more valuable is the appearance of the name Canaan in the Amarna letters (see pp. 207 ff.), where it appears in the form *Kinaḫḫi* or *Kinaḫna/Kinaḫni*,[5] without of course being definite as to meaning and scope. It is clear at any rate that it can indicate Phoenician regions in which there were " kings," namely city-states, that the Plain of Acco and its environs are included (Amarna Letter 8, lines 13 ff.), and that, on the other hand, even North Syrian coastal regions can apparently be called Canaan. Again (according to Amarna Letter 148, lines 41 ff.), *Ḫazura* or Hazor in the upper Jordan Valley seems to belong to *Kinaḫna*. All of this corresponds very nicely with the previously cited Old Testament references.

Less definite is the meaning of *kn'n.w* (" Canaanite ") on two stelae of Pharaoh Amenophis II from the middle of the fifteenth century B.C., and of *p.kn'n* (*p* is the Egyptian article) in Egyptian sources from the time of the nineteenth and twentieth dynasties (in this connection see p. 248), where the Palestinian and Phoenician coastal land again seems to be meant.[6]

As to indigenous Phoenician sources, *kn'n* appears as a name for Phoenicia on some coins from Laodicea (probably *Laodikeia he en Phoinike*, or Beirut on the Phoenician coast),[7] as well as in Hellenistic Greek writings.[8]

The probable original meaning of the name " Canaan " points in the same direction. In the Accadian texts from *Nuzi* (see p. 241), which date from the fifteenth and fourteenth centuries B.C., a word *kinaḫḫu* carries the meaning " red purple." Perhaps it developed from an older word for merchant, which was then especially applied to red purple merchants. Whatever the origin of this word, it has a Hurrian ending and also seems related to the name " Canaan " (see also p. 233). This suggests that Canaan was originally considered the " land of red purple merchants." The term must refer especially to the Phoenician coast, which had long been using the purple snail to dye wool.[9] Accordingly, the name Canaan originally meant a part of the Syrian coastal land (particularly Phoenicia) and therefore somewhat more, somewhat less than " Palestine."

[5] This material is compiled and arranged by Böhl, *op. cit.*, pp. 2–3; Maisler, *op. cit.*, pp. 54 ff.

[6] The passages are given in Böhl, pp. 3–4; Maisler, p. 58.

[7] See Cooke, *A Textbook of North-Semitic Inscriptions* (1903), p. 46, n. 3 and pp. 349–50.

[8] Cited in Böhl, p. 5.

[9] B. Maisler, *BASOR*, CII (1946), 7 ff.

The Israelites probably got to know the name as a term for the region of the pre-Israelite city-states on the north Palestinian coast and in the upper Jordan Valley, which was politically dependent on the coastal area. They extended the term " Canaanite " to include all of the pre-Israelite inhabitants of the land living in their environs, and finally came to call their entire homeland, or at least Cisjordan, the " land of Canaan."

There is no other ancient term for all of Palestine; non-Israelite sources use none. The Assyrians in general simply include Palestine in the names they use for Syria. Examples are " the land of *Ḫatti*," derived from the various small North Syrian states which previously had belonged to the Hittite empire (see p. 254); or " *Amurru*," derived from the term used as early as Old Babylonian times for the world in the " West." At any rate, in the eyes of the Assyrians who advanced from North Syria, Palestine was not significant enough in itself to merit a name of its own. The earliest known use of such a name is the Egyptian *rṯn*, conventionally vocalized " Retenu." It is found in texts of the Middle Kingdom, but more frequently in texts of the New Kingdom (see p. 248). Retenu can designate Palestine, at least in part, but it includes certain sections of Syria. Retenu is frequently divided into an " upper " and " lower " *rṯn* in a way which can no longer be clearly explained.[10] The term *ḏh* appearing in Egyptian texts of the New Kingdom must also be mentioned in this connection. It seems to refer to definite parts of Palestine and South Syria.[11] Of course, at no stage of the development of their meaning were *rṯn* and *ḏh* special terms for the land we mean by Palestine, because the Egyptians, like the Assyrians, never needed to give Palestine a separate name. It was only the southernmost part of Syria, as far as they were concerned. Only the land near the coast was of any particular interest to them. Indeed, only the history of Israel, most of which took place here, made Palestine a significant area.

(2) *Names for the Parts of the Land*

Though Palestine is not a geographical unit, it nevertheless consists of territories distinct from each other. As natural parts of the land, these always had their names and designations, many of

[10] See W. M. Müller, *Asien und Europa nach altägyptischen Denkmälern* (1893), pp. 143 ff., and now especially A. H. Gardiner, *Ancient Egyptian Onomastica* (1947), I, 162 ff.

[11] See Gardiner, *op. cit.*, pp. 145–46.

which are known from the Old Testament. In what follows, we assemble these territorial names and terms, excluding those which mark a given section as the location of an historical development or a political unit (concerning these see pp. 93 ff.).

(a) *The Jordan rift.* The great rift which splits Palestine from north to south is called *ha-'Arabhah* (" the desert ") in the Old Testament, and of course very correctly so. We are sure this simple designation was applied at least to the part between the Sea of Tiberias and the Dead Sea, that is, the modern Ghōr. For individual parts of this territory, the plural of this word is used, thus: *'arbhoth Yeriḥo* are " the desert regions of Jericho " and *'arbhoth Mo'abh* " the desert regions of Moab " across from Jericho—that is, the parts of the Jordan rift belonging politically to the city-state of Jericho or to the Moabite state respectively, either in the present or in the past.[12] The lower part of the Ghōr is usually called *kikkar hay-Yarden* (" the Jordan circle "; Gen. 13 : 10–11 and elsewhere) or simply *hak-kikkar* (" the circle "; Gen. 13 : 12, Neh. 3 : 22, and elsewhere). The origin and exact meaning of this term are unknown to us.

The Dead Sea is called *Yam ha-'Arabhah* (" the desert sea ") because it is located in this section, as well as *Yam ham-Melaḥ* (" the Salt Sea ") because of its natural character. The Sea of Tiberias, on the other hand, in ancient times as today was called after the most important city on its shore, and therefore did not have a geographical name. In ancient times the most important shore settlement was the fortified city of Chinnereth (in Arabic, Tell el-'Oreimeh) on the northwestern side just above the later coastal site of Capernaum, a city already attested in pre-Israelite times by the list of Thutmose III (see p. 248, n. 7) in the form *knnrt* (No. 34). It later became a border city of Naphtali (Josh. 19 : 35). As a result, the Sea of Tiberias in ancient times was called *Yam Kinnereth* (Num. 34 : 11; Josh, 12 : 3, 13 : 27). There is no traditional name in the Old Testament for the uppermost part of the Jordan rift, any more than for Lake Ḥūleh within the rift. Frequently the " Waters of Merom " in Josh. 11 : 5, 7 has been identified with Lake Ḥūleh, but this is certainly wrong, since " Merom " undoubtedly is to be identified with the modern site of Meron in Upper Galilee 5 km. [3 miles] westnorthwest of Ṣafed (Isr., Ṣephath), and the " Waters of Merom " must therefore be located in its immediate neighbourhood. Even the small productive plain of el-

[12] Concerning this and the historical situation which led to the term *'arbhoth Mo'abh*, see Noth, *ZAW*, New Series, XIX (1944), 18–19.

Ghuweir on the western side of the Sea of Tiberias had a special name in New Testament times; it was called Gennāsar. It is so named in I Macc. 11 : 67, in Josephus, and also in the Talmud. In the New Testament the derivative Gennāsaret is used (in analogy with the above-mentioned Chinnereth?). The name Gennāsar obviously is somehow connected with the word *gan*, meaning " garden." Contrary to an assumption occasionally made, it has nothing to do with the name Chinnereth. " Gennāsar " was applied not only to the plain of el-Ghuweir, as in Mark 6 : 53 and Matt. 14 : 34, but also to the Sea of Tiberias, as already in I Macc. 11 : 57 and Josephus' *Jewish Wars*, III.10.7. This is especially true in Luke 5 : 1, where *hē limnē Gennēsaret* means the Lake of Gennesareth, while otherwise the New Testament speaks of the Sea of Galilee, as in Mark 1 : 16, Matt. 4 : 18, and elsewhere, or of the Sea of Tiberias, as in John 21 : 1, a name still used today.

(b) *The Cisjordan range.* The extensive Cisjordan range naturally had different names in its different parts. The name Yehudhah (" Judah ") adhered to the southernmost part with indefinite outer limits. In all likelihood, Yehudhah was originally a territorial name and the Israelite tribe which settled in this territory was named after it, rather than the other way around as the Old Testament interprets it in the general statement on the origin of the names of the Israelite tribes.[13] The name Yehudhah itself seems derived rather from a local or territorial name than from a personal name.[14] Names like Yidh'alah (Josh. 19 : 15) are most closely related in form.[15] Then, also, the name embraced more than just the habitat of the Israelite tribe of Judah, for Hebron, which was inhabited by Calebites and not Judeans, was counted part of the " hill country of Yehudhah " (Josh. 20 : 7). It is not likely that the tribe of Judah, living in a comparatively small area (see pp. 69–70), should have given its name to the entire southern part of the Cisjordan range. On the other hand, the only one of the twelve Israelite tribes appearing in the tribal system which had its habitat in this region could very easily have received the territorial name Yehudhah to distinguish it from the rest of the tribes. In I Sam. 23 : 3,[16] in connection

[13] See also L. Waterman, *AJSL*, LV (1938), 29 ff.

[14] It is still linguistically very improbable that the divine name Yahweh (in the shortened form *Yeho* or the like, used in personal names) is contained in the name *Yehudhah*. If this were true Yehudhah would be a personal name, and at the same time would be noteworthy as the oldest attested use of Yahweh in a name. Thus Procksch translates and explains it in *Die Genesis* (3rd ed., 1924), p. 178 and *passim*.

[15] For some further place names of analogous form see W. Borée, *Die alten Ortsnamen Palästinas* (1930), p. 37.

[16] Waterman refers to this passage ,*loc. cit.*

with the old tradition of " David's rise " the name Yehudhah is clearly used as a territorial name (*bīhudhah*, i.e. " in Judah ").[17] The compound word Bethleḥem-Yehudhah (" Bethlehem in Judah "; Judg. 17 : 7, 19 : 1, 2, 18) has a close parallel in the expression Yabhesh-Gil'adh (" Jabesh in Gilead "; Judg. 21 : 8 ff., I Sam. 11 : 1, and elsewhere), where the genitive which is added to the place name indicates the territory in which the place lay. Indeed, the compound Qedhesh-Naphtali (" Kadesh in Naphtali "; Judg. 4 : 6) seems to show that a tribal name can be added to a place name as a genitive for closer identification; but it is probable that Naphtali was also originally a territorial rather than a tribal name.

If Yehudhah was originally a territorial name, then it once included the Har Yehudhah (" the hill country of Judah "), i.e., the heights of the Cisjordan range from near Bethlehem on south, past the latitude of Hebron. Judean writers sometimes speak of this region simply as ha-Har, " the Mountain " (Josh. 10 : 40, 11 : 16). Another part of Yehudhah was the Midhbar Yehudhah, " the wilderness of Judah " (Judg. 1 : 16, Ps. 63 : 1). Various sections of this wilderness received their names from towns on its fringes. This means that in these near-by wilderness areas townsmen had pasture rights for their flocks. Examples of this are Midhbar Teqoa' in II Chron. 20 : 20 and Midhbar Ziph in I Sam. 23 : 14–15.

The gentle foothills extending west of the Judean range are known in the Old Testament as *hash-shephelah*, " the Lowland," having been named from the standpoint of Israelites living in the higher hill country.

To the south, the extensive region of the semi-nomads and nomads which adjoins the Judean hill country rapidly changes from steppe to desert (see pp. 18–19). It is called *han-neghebh*, " the dry land," in the Old Testament. Naturally it has no exact borders, especially to the south.[18] The area south of the limits of settled farm land, extending to the horizon, is called simply *han-neghebh*. As a result of this the word Neghebh became the most frequently used expression in the Old Testament for the compass direction south. In late Old Testament texts, for example in Ezekiel, Job, and Ecclesiastes, as also in Palestinian Aramaic dating from after the

[17] I Sam. 23 : 3 is probably connected with the Ya'ar Ḥereth of 22 : 5b, of which we unfortunately do not know the location. The town of Qe'ilah (Tell Qīlah in the Wādi eṣ-Ṣūr, on the fault line which divides the hill country from the foothills; see p. 18) was situated in the foothills and, in contrast to the Ya'ar Ḥereth, is not counted part of Yehudhah in I Sam. 23 : 3.

[18] Concerning the fluctuation of the tradition as to limits of the Neghebh, even on the north, see Noth, *JPOS*, XV (1935), 37–38.

Old Testament period, the word *darom* is used for south.[19] Hebrew *neghebh* is regularly rendered *darom* in the Targum Onkelos.[20] Eusebius uses this word in an indefinite way, no doubt derived from the popular vernacular, for the southernmost part of the Judean range, the Idumea of Hellenistic-Roman times.[21] It probably referred originally to a more specific area, and only later became a general word for south; but this has not yet been proved.

Individual parts of the southern desert still had their own names. Thus, Midhbar Ṣin was the name for that part of the Sinai Desert which contained the spring region with the " sacred spring " of Kadesh Barnea, now called ʿAin Qedes, an area which was important in the early history of the Israelite tribes (Num. 33 : 36, 34 : 4; Josh. 15 : 3, and elsewhere).

Mount Seʿir, according to Josh. 11 : 17 and 12 : 7, was beyond Mount Ḥalaq, the " Bald Mountain " now known as Jebel Ḥalaq, north of ʿAbdeh (Isr., Abhdath) in the Negeb. Otherwise, in the Old Testament, Seʿir indicates the mountains east of Wādi el-ʿArabah inhabited by the Edomites. In the passages cited, a part of the mountains west of the Wādi el-ʿArabah seems to have the same name. It could be that, in Josh. 11 : 17 and 12 : 7, Seʿir refers to an area which just happens to have the same name as the mountains on the eastern side of the Wādi el-ʿArabah. Note that the name Seʿir appears elsewhere, as in Josh. 15 : 10, referring to a mountain near Kirjath-jearim.

The middle part of the Cisjordan range had the name Har Ephraim (" Mount Ephraim "). The name Ephraim, quite certainly, was originally the name of this very part of the Cisjordan range, or at least a portion of it, and later gave its name to the whole. Even the form of the name shows it to be the name of a place or a district. The ending *aim* repeatedly appears with geographical names[22] but

[19] In Deut. 33 : 23, where the word *darom* appears in the present text, the meaning is very nebulous and the traditional text is probably defective.

[20] See M. Burrows, " Daroma," *JPOS*, XII (1932), 142–48.

[21] See G. Beyer, *ZDPV*, LIV (1931), 246 ff.

[22] See Borée, *op. cit.*, pp. 54–55.

In II Sam. 13 : 23 the name Ephraim appears to identify Mount Baʿal Ḥaṣor more precisely. In all likelihood this is the massif el-ʿAṣur (see p. 19). Here, Ephraim is either the name of a district or of a city (in any event the ʿim in the text remains difficult); for the latter see Alt, *PJB*, XXIV (1928), 13 ff., 32 ff. In any case, this makes it seem that the name Ephraim was connected originally with the southeastern part of the Central Cisjordan range.

As a place name, Ephraim appears in the expression Yaʿar Ephraim (II Sam. 18 : 6), the term for a forest region in Transjordan. For Ephraim as a territorial name, a possible etymology could at least be proposed; see Noth, *Das Buch Josua*, *op. cit.*, p. 145.

never with personal names.[23] Again, in this case the region designated by Har Ephraim was substantially greater than the region occupied by the tribe of Ephraim (see especially I Kings 4 : 8, and also Josh. 17 : 15). Mount Ephraim embraces the Cisjordan range about from the latitude of Bethel in the south up to the Plain of Jezreel in the north. Both the northwestern and the northeastern spur of the central hill country had their own names, for they are very prominently set apart from the surrounding landscape. The spur which juts northwest right to the sea coast near Haifa had the name Har hak-Karmel, " the vineyard mountain," or simply hak-Karmel, " the vineyard," apparently for an ancient feature, later lost, of this ridge. The northeastern spur, which separates the southern part of the Plain of Jezreel from the valley corridor at Beisān (see p. 20), was called Har hag-Gilboaʿ or simply hag-Gilboaʿ (meaning unknown). Specific names are still on record for the two prominent mountains south and north of ancient Shechem; for the former, Har Gerizzim (Mount Gerizim), and for the latter, Har ʿEbal (Mount Ebal), both of unknown meaning. In Judg. 9 : 48, Har Ṣalmon is given as the name of a mountain near Shechem. Unfortunately, nothing definite can be derived from the passage as to the location of this mountain.

The Har Gaʿash of Josh. 24 : 30 would be located somewhere in the southwestern part of Mount Ephraim. But we know nothing more definite than that it lay south of the home town of Joshua, Timnath-serah, or Tibneh, east of ʿAbūd.[24] The same applies to Har Ṣemaraim, specifically noted as part of Mount Ephraim in II Chron. 13 : 4, which apparently was named for the city of Zemaraim beside it (Josh. 18 : 22). Both must be sought in the southeastern part of Mount Ephraim.

As a regional name for the northern part of the Cisjordan range we should probably understand hag-Galil, a term which appears repeatedly in the Old Testament and which may be the origin of the later name Galilee, although this is by no means certain. Thus Alt has dedicated a lengthy exposition to the " Origin of the Name of Galilee."[25] He proceeds from the frequently accepted meaning of the name hag-Galil, " the Circle," sees in the expression Gelil hag-Goyim (" the Circle of the peoples ") in Isa. 8 : 23 the original, complete form of the term for which hag-Galil is an abbreviation, and connects the term Circle of the Peoples with the city-states

[23] See Noth, *Die israelitischen Personennamen* (1928), pp. 38–39.
[24] Additional material appears in Elliger, *PJB*, XXXI (1935), 47–48.
[25] Alt, *PJB*, XXXIII (1937), 52 ff. [*KS*, II, 363 ff.]

located in the plains in a semicircle around the Galilean mountains. Thus, the name originally would have designated the coalition of city-states in the plains, as a political term, and only later would have included the Galilean mountains. The argument against that, to be sure, is that the meaning " circle " for *galil* is not proved; the feminine *gelilah*, which is usually introduced into the argument, nowhere definitely means circle, certainly not in Josh. 22 : 10–11 or Ezek. 47 : 8. On the other hand, it is only definitely recorded of one city, Kadesh (Qedes, on the hills west of the upper Jordan valley), that it was " in the Galil " (Josh. 20 : 7), and it is probable that the twenty cities " in the land of Galil " (I Kings 9 : 11–13) which were ceded by Solomon to the King of Tyre did not lie on the coastal plain, but rather in the Galilean hills. In this narrative the city of Cabul (Arabic, Kābūl) in the lower Galilean hills is expressly named. (As to the meaning of hag-Galil from II Kings 15 : 29 one can deduce only that Kol 'ereṣ Naphtali is a gloss to hag-Galil, by which a part of the Galilean hill country is meant. Isa. 9 : 1 is rather ambiguous and probably must be understood in the light of Josh. 12 : 23.) Hence it seems probable that though we can no longer clearly explain the name hag-Galil, we surmise that it originally designated a definite section and later on all of the northernmost part of the Cisjordan range.

In Josh. 20 : 7 we would then have the three parts of the Cisjordan range: hag-Galil, Har Ephraim, and Har Yehudhah listed together, within which the cities of refuge listed in this passage were distributed.

A specific name has been preserved for the imposing cone-shaped mountain in the southeastern part of the Galilean mountains at the northeastern corner of the Plain of Jezreel; it is Mount Tabor.

(c) *Lebanon.* The southern ends of the central Syrian chain of high mountains border the northern horizon of Palestine; for them the Old Testament hands down the name hal-Lebhanon (Lebanon), " the white (mountain)." (This name also appears in extra-biblical sources; see what follows.) It is probable that in passages like Deut. 1 : 7, 11 : 24 and Josh. 1 : 4 an old meaning of the name hal-Lebhanon has been preserved in deuteronomistic usage as a designation of the two high mountain ranges differentiated by the Greeks as Libanos and Antilibanos. On that basis, the designation of the depression between the two as Biqʿath hal-Lebhanon, " the Lebanon Lowland " (modern el-Beqāʿ), in Josh. 11 : 17 and 12 : 7 is understandable. Of course, the Old Testament uses a distinct name for the eastern range, namely

Ḥermon or har Ḥermon, which presumably means " (the mountain with the) towering peak." Naturally, that name applied primarily to Jebel et-Telj (see p. 31), also known as Jebel esh-Sheikh, at the southern end of this range, a mountain visible in Palestine from far off. Probably the entire chain of Antilibanos was occasionally referred to by the name Hermon, as for example in Josh. 11 : 17. According to Deut. 3 : 9, the " Sidonians " called Hermon *Siryon* and the " Amorites " called it *Senir*. In this case, too, it seems that the entire Antilebanon must be understood as Hermon; for the name Siryon appears repeatedly in texts from the new Hittite kingdom (see p. 254) along with the name Lebanon.[26] Moreover, it is probable that both high mountain chains are meant by " Lablani Šariyana." The name Saniru, or Senir, is referred to occasionally in the annals of Shalmaneser III (see p. 253), in the eighteenth year of his reign, as " lying opposite Lebanon."[27] According to the context, this certainly means some part of the Antilebanon range, though not necessarily Jebel et-Telj. In Song of Sol. 4 : 8, on the other hand, the names Senir and Hermon occur side by side and only the southern end of the Antilebanon chain seems to be understood by Hermon (likewise in the gloss in I Chron. 5 : 23).

(d) *The Cisjordan plains.* Different parts of the plains of Cisjordan had different names. The general word for plain in Hebrew is *ʿemeq*. The individual parts of the coastal plain are sometimes named for the pasture land of a town or former Canaanite city-state. For example, ʿEmeq Ayyalon (Josh. 10 : 12) is the spur of the coastal plain which once belonged to the Canaanite city of Aijalon, now called Yalo, which lay on the inner edge of the coastal plain. The numerous small plains enfolded in the hills are also properly called *ʿemeq*, as, for example, ʿEmeq Repha'im (Josh. 15 : 8 and elsewhere) southwest of Jerusalem, now called el-Baqʿa, or ʿEmeq ʿAkhor, between Jerusalem and Jericho (Josh. 15 : 7 and elsewhere), and the like.

Whenever the location was obvious to the writer, the plain intended was simply called *ha-ʿemeq*, " the plain," as in the following cases: Josh. 8 : 9, 13, the plain east of the town of ha-ʿAi, namely modern et-Tell; Judg. 1 : 34, the coastal plain west of Jerusalem; Judg. 5 : 15 and I Sam. 31 : 7, the Plain of Jezreel.

If the plains on the Mediterranean coast are considered together, they are spoken of simply as the regions *beḥoph hay-yam*, " on the

[26] See A. Gustavs, *ZAW*, New Series, I (1924), 154–55.

[27] See D. D. Luckenbill, *Ancient Records of Assyria and Babylonia*, I (1926), Arts. 663, 672.

shore of the sea," referring not only to the portions of land along the shoreline, but also to the coastal plains in general.[28]

In the expression *hay-yam*, "the sea," and occasionally also *hay-yam hag-Gadhol* "the Great Sea," the reference is plainly always to the Mediterranean Sea which lies in the west. As a result, *hay-yam* has become a general expression for "the west" (as a compass direction).

Surprisingly, the great plain between the Samaritan and Galilean hill country (see pp. 23–24) is called ʿEmeq Yizreʿel, "Plain of Jezreel" (thus probably Josh. 17 : 16; Hos. 1 : 5), after the town of Jezreel (Arabic, Zerʿīn) situated at its eastern edge. However, the name does not mean that this entire large plain ever belonged to the territory of the city of Jezreel, nor that Jezreel was ever the largest or most important city at the edge of this plain. If the name had arisen from a city's importance, one would rather have to say "the plain (or valley) of Megiddo." In truth, this expression, *Biqʿath Megiddo(n)*, does appear in very late passages (Zech. 12 : 11; II Chron. 35 : 22). Jezreel, however, was the only one of the cities on the plain which in the time of Saul and, indeed, already in the time of the Judges was in Israelite—not Canaanite—possession, and which thus belonged to the sphere of the Israelite tribes (see especially II Sam. 2 : 9). The term Plain of Jezreel consequently developed from the Israelite point of view. Possibly at one time this name referred to only a small part of the plain, which belonged to the city of Jezreel, as is probably the case in Judg. 6 : 33. Possibly the name was later extended to include the entire plain.

(e) *Transjordan*. Among the districts of Transjordan, the plateau north of the Arnon (see p. 13) is called ham-Mishor, "the level, even area," in the Old Testament (Josh. 13 : 9, 16, 17, 21; 20 : 8; elsewhere). It is just such a level area. The western front range north of the Arnon which separates this plateau from the Dead Sea is called hap-Pisgah (Num. 21 : 20, 23 : 14; Deut. 34 : 1; elsewhere), meaning perhaps "the separated part." The Old Testament (e.g., Josh. 12 : 20) uses the technical term Ashdoth hap-Pisgah, "the slopes of Pisgah," for the slope of this range down to the Dead Sea.[29] What is not clear is how the name hap-Pisgah is related to the name Har or Hare ha-ʿAbharim (meaning uncertain) which occurs in Num. 27 : 12, 33 : 47, 48, and Deut. 32 : 49. The

[28] Note especially the territories listed in Deut. 1 : 7 and Josh. 9 : 1. The term *hash-sharon* is somewhat vague. It is used repeatedly for the coastal plain or part of it as an example of a blossoming land; see Abel, *op. cit.*, I, 414 ff.

[29] See Noth, *Das Buch Josua*, *op. cit.*, pp. 60, 81.

latter name seems to have had a more inclusive meaning applying even southwards well beyond the Arnon, as shown by the place ʿIyye ha-ʿAbharim mentioned in Num. 33 : 44. Probably the name Pisgah was originally more limited in scope, and later also applied to more of the front range.[30] Har Nebho (Deut. 32 : 49, 34 : 1) is one peak in this front range. The round top, en-Nebeh, 7 km. [4 miles] northwest of Medeba preserves the name Nebo. Perhaps originally this name was applied to a more modest promontory called Rās es-Siyāghah which juts out about 1·5 km. [1 mile] to the west, which has an excellent view. It is east of the north end of the Dead Sea. Ever since the early Christian period it has been identified with the Old Testament Nebo.

Gilʿadh (Gilead) is often mentioned in the Old Testament. Gilead was centred in the foothills north of the Plain of Mishor (see p. 13) and more precisely in the region about halfway between ʿAmmān and the place where Nahr ez-Zerqā breaks out of the hills. Even today the names Jebel Jelʿad, Khirbet Jelʿad, and ʿAin Jelʿad are found south of the Nahr ez-Zerqā[31] (see p. 13). A town called Gilead is mentioned in the Old Testament (e.g., Judg. 10 : 17). This is certainly modern Khirbet Jelʿad. The area west of this town where Transjordanian Israelite clans settled is called the land of Gilead (e.g., Judg. 11 : 4 ff.). Also, the mountain range which borders this area on the east is called Har hag-Gilʿadh, " the hill country of Gilead " (Gen. 31 : 21, 23, 25). When Israelites moved into the northern end of the hill country of the ʿAjlūn, they also called this northerly area of Transjordan " Gilead," as illustrated in the name of the city of Jabesh-gilead (see p. 56). The Wādi Yābis, which flows into the Jordan southeast of Beisān, preserves the name of Jabesh. This indicates that Jabesh was on the northern edge of the ʿAjlūn hill country at the ruins of Tell el-Maqlūb. The same applies to the Hebrew compound place name Ramoth-Gilʿadh in I Kings 4 : 13 and elsewhere, which is Tell Ramith, southwest of Derʿa.[32] Furthermore, the name Gilead was applied to the entire central section of Israelite Transjordan, as is done in grouping together ham-Mishor, hag-Gilʿadh, and hab-Bashan in Josh. 20 : 8, Deut. 3 : 10, and II Kings 10 : 33. Beyond that, however, the name Gilead can even be applied to all of Israelite Transjordan, for example in Josh. 22 : 9 ff., where it is contrasted to the " Land of Canaan," meaning Cisjordan.

[30] See also Abel, *op. cit.*, I, 378 ff.

[31] See Guthe, *Kurzes Bibelwörterbuch* (1903), pp. 217–18; de Vaux, *RB*, XLVII (1938), 416–17; Noth, *PJB*, XXXVII (1941), 58 f. and *ZDPV*, LXXV (1959), 14 ff.

[32] See N. Glueck, *BASOR*, XCII (1943), 10 ff.

The plateau on both sides of Sheriʿat el-Menāḍireh, but particularly to the north (see p. 14), had its own name. It was called hab-Bashan (" the Plain "). This name once included the fruitful territory of en-Nuqreh (see p. 14), as well as the present Jōlān. The name Jōlān traces back, as does Gaulanitis, the Greek term for this area, to the city of Golan, which according to Josh. 20 : 8 was in Bashan, though its site has not been more precisely located. It is more likely that the famous oak forests of Bashan of Isa. 2 : 13, Ezek. 27 : 6, and Zech. 11 : 2 were situated in the Jōlān, which is still wooded in places, than in the Nuqreh. Mount Hauran, on the other hand, the present Jebel ed-Drūz, does not seem to be mentioned in the Old Testament. Zalmon in Ps. 68 : 14 [Heb. 68 : 15] has sometimes been identified with Mount Hauran. Yet the name Zalmon in this instance might be only a textual error; similarly, Salecah (Josh. 12 : 5, 13 : 11), named as a border of the Israelite settlement in Transjordan, apparently has no connection with the modern town of Ṣalkhad on Jebel ed-Drūz.

9. *Settlement*

1. *The Areas of the Israelite Tribes*

See Figures 1 and 3 for the modern names of districts.

We know ancient Israel only as a unit made up of individual tribes. This is true at least after the time of Israel's settlement in Palestine. In Hebrew, " tribe " is either *maṭṭeh* or *shebheṭ*. Both words originally meant staff or rod. Here staff or rod is considered originally as a symbol of rule, a sceptre. Compare " him that holds the sceptre " in Amos 1 : 5, which means that a spokesman or representative of a tribe was recognized and even legitimized by carrying a staff or rod both to represent his tribe and to exercise authority within his tribe. Thus the staff or rod became a symbol of the tribe. This alone indicates that tribes were already historically active units.

According to Old Testament tradition the tribes of Israel sprang up from one family, having descended directly from the sons of a common ancestor. These sons of a common father in turn are presented as the ancestors of the clans which made up the tribe. Actually, it was common practice in antiquity to present the origin of a people as well as the origin of a tribe in this manner. Yet this was certainly fiction or at least a great simplification of much more complicated processes. Tribes did not come into existence merely by the processes of nature. Tribes were rather the historical issue of historical events and outside forces which greatly influenced the formation of large and small human groups. The concepts of a people and of a tribe are part of human history, rather than of human reproduction.

The human societies which rest on a natural blood bond are family, extended family, and clan. The clan is the largest group within which blood relationship can still be recognized, while the tribe represents a community of clans which has arisen under the influence of historical events. The people, usually made up of a large number of tribes, is the child of great and enduring historical events. One can perhaps distinguish these concepts in this fashion, though naturally they cannot be neatly separated from each other. In Hebrew, the family is called simply *baith*, " house," meaning that community which lives together in a house or tent. For the extended family there is the expression *beth abh*, " ancestral house," that is, all those families that have come from the house of a presently known ancestor. To be sure, this expression is occasionally used vaguely in the Old Testament. At the head of the extended family is a chief, occasionally called *rosh* (" leader " or " head "), probably the person who is currently the eldest member of the line of the firstborn. The clan is called *mishpaḥah*, a word traceable to a verb which originally meant " pour out," thereby probably designating the group which is held together by natural reproduction; it is led by the assembly of elders, *zeqenim*, probably chiefs of extended families for the most part.[33]

A tribe which has not yet settled down in one area is usually a rather unstable unit. Under certain historical conditions clans join to form a tribe and then separate again to form new ties, at times in such a manner that some elements remain in the old association and separate themselves from the rest. In general, a tie to a given piece of territory, one that belongs to the tribe, that has become the basis of its natural life and in some cases of its wealth, and especially that must be maintained in the face of covetous neighbours, leads to stronger consolidation of a tribe. It cannot have been much different with the Israelite tribes. They too, as a rule, first found their enduring form on the tillable soil of Palestine. The very fact that the names of some of the Israelite tribes are derived from the territory in which they settled in Palestine (see pp. 56–62 and 69–71) shows that their conquest and settlement of

[33] Cf. A. Causse, *Du groupe ethnique à la communauté religieuse* (1937), pp. 15 ff. and R. de Vaux, *Les institutions de l'Ancien Testament*, I (1958), 17 ff.

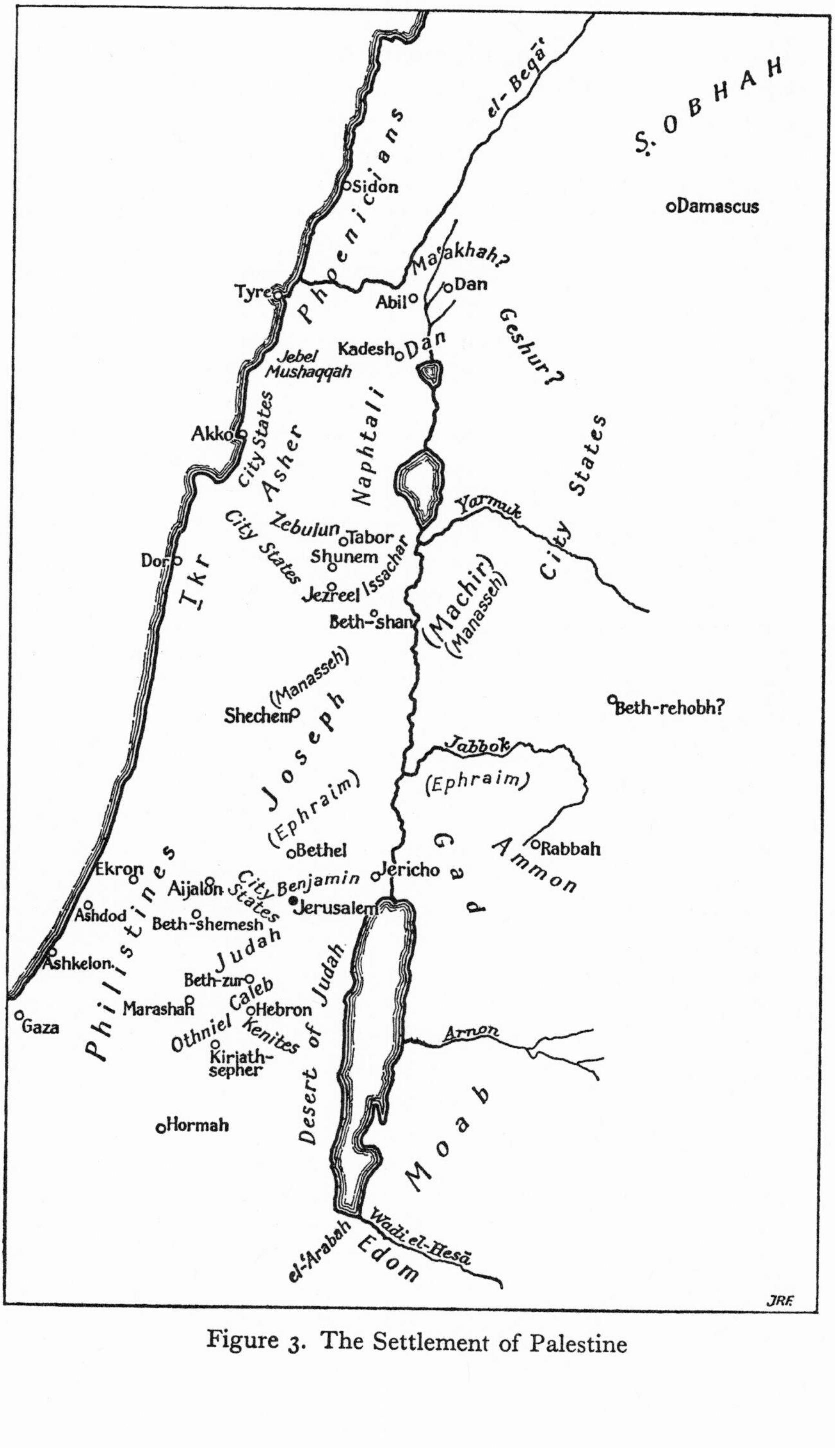

Figure 3. The Settlement of Palestine

Palestine constituted them as tribes or at least was the decisive event leading to their consolidation. We see them as historical entities only after their settling down in Palestine. It is probably not accidental that then for the first time we have definite historical traditions in the Old Testament concerning their presence, their relation to one another, and events from their life; portions of the Old Testament which narrate earlier events in an anticipatory sense occasionally give the names of the tribes. Actually, however, these early portions know only an unsegmented " Israel." Of course, there are still occasional signs in the Old Testament which point to the unstable prehistory of the tribes before they settled down. The same clan names emerge in different tribes. This fact shows how one and the same clan belonged now to one, now to another tribe, and how parts of it remained attached to one tribe or another. Thus, for example, the clan Hezron appears in the tribes of Reuben (Num. 26 : 6) and Judah (Num. 26 : 21); the clan Zerah appears not only in Judah (Num. 26 : 20) and in Simeon (Num. 26 : 13), but also among the Edomites (Gen. 36 : 13, 33) who lived south-east of Palestine.

The sources for the history and geography of the Israelite tribes in Palestine are the following: In Num. 26 : 5–51 we have an extensive list of the tribes, divided according to clans, which probably comes from the time of the Judges, i.e., the time between the occupation of the land and the appearance of forms of government. In this period, Israel existed in the form of a sacral confederation of twelve tribes with a common sanctuary as a centre. The independent significance of the twelve tribes as submembers of the whole belongs to this period.[34] Of course this list contains no statements at all about the localities of the tribes and their clans. The numbers indicating the military manpower of the individual tribes are probably secondary. In the present context, to be sure, these numbers are the point at issue, since they refer to a great census. But in order to record the circumstances of this census the later editor has used an old list of clans.

In Num. 1 : 5–15 we have before us, aside from the numbers, an old list which briefly enumerates the tribes whose representatives attended the gathering of the federation.[35]

The " Blessing of Jacob " in Gen. 49 : 3–27 is a somewhat mixed collection of poetical sayings about the individual tribes, perhaps from the time of David, but it is based on material which is doubt-

[34] For further information see Noth, *Das System der Zwölf Stämme Israels* (1930), especially, on Num. 26 : 5–50, pp. 122–32.

[35] *Ibid.*, pp. 153 ff.

less older. Here each tribe is characterized partly through praise and partly through rebuke, or mockery. The similar " Blessing of Moses " in Deut. 33 : 6–25 is a later imitation of the " Blessing of Jacob," in part dependent upon it, in part going its own way, but on the whole a less valuable source than the Blessing of Jacob. A series of old traditions about battles and victories of individual tribes or groups of tribes under the leadership of charismatic tribal heroes provides the pre-deuteronomistic form of the Book of Judges. The most important source for the geography of the tribes is " the system of the tribal borders in the Book of Joshua."[36] It is worked into the present form of Joshua, chapters 13–19, but it can be recognized without much trouble. (Scattered parts of the same system are found in Num. 34 : 3–12 and Ezek. 47 : 15–18; 48 : 1.) In its original form the scheme consisted of tabulated border points, which present rather detailed boundaries for that period.[37] With these boundaries the areas of the individual tribes became established in such a manner that all Palestine, which is to say all Cisjordan and a strip of Transjordan bordering on it, seems to be divided among the Israelite tribes.[38] This system stems again from the time of the Judges and unites in itself theory and fact. It is theory that in the time of the Judges, or at any later time, all of Palestine belonged to the Israelite tribes. Rather, " Canaanites " maintained themselves in various parts of the land; the Philistines, as well, always occupied areas adjacent to Israel (see pp. 78–79). Thus the notion that the entire land was possessed by the tribes is only claim, not fact. On the other hand, just as certainly the system proceeds from the actual occupancy of the tribes and goes beyond the tribal areas only in certain directions. Theory and fact can be separated rather easily here, using the list in Judges 1 : 21, 27–35. At least for the central and northern part of the country this list enumerates the Canaanite cities, which never came into the possession of the Israelite tribes, but which finally were drawn into the governmental system during the period of the kingdom of Israel (and Judah). Thus the " system of the tribal borders," in spite of its theoretical elements, is a historical source of the first order.

In our consideration here of the individual tribes and their territories, we follow the old traditional order and arrangement used in the lists of the sacral federation of the twelve tribes. First, there is

[36] Cf. Alt, *Sellin-Festschrift* (1927), pp. 13–24 [*KS*, I, 193–202].
[37] On these " sets of fixed border points " see Noth, *ZDPV*, LVIII (1935), 185–255.
[38] Cf. the map in Noth, *Das Buch Josua*, *op. cit.*, p. 77.

the group of six older tribes which are all traced back to Leah, the first wife of Jacob, in Gen. 39 : 31 and 30 : 24; hence the conventional term, Leah tribes. It seems likely that they settled down in Palestine earlier than the rest.[39] Three of them, the tribes traditionally listed first, Reuben, Simeon, and Levi, had almost vanished by the time for which we have historical records. Corresponding to this is the fact that in the Blessing of Jacob they are covered with reproaches and curses (Gen 49 : 3–7). The system of the tribal borders no longer provides any area of the country as a habitat for any of them. It was a later redactor of this system who first divided the originally unified tribal area in the Transjordanian Belqā, originally a unit, with an imaginary line of demarcation, ascribing the southern half thus constituted to Reuben (Josh. 13 : 15–23).[40] Not until the deuteronomistic redaction is reference made to the two and one-half Transjordanian tribes, Reuben, Gad, and half of Manasseh. The same redactor also created a tribal area for Simeon located " within Judah," simply by removing the second half of the list of sites of the first administrative district of Judah (see p. 96) and ascribing it to Simeon (Josh. 19 : 1–9). Finally, the Old Testament materials treat the tribe of Levi as identical with the Levites who are committed to the priestly office, of whom it is expressly stated that they shall have no territorial possession. Thus is removed any tendency to establish even such a theoretical tribal territory for Levi as for Reuben and Simeon. The very little old material recorded about these three tribes consists only of the appearance of their names in the enumeration of the clans of Reuben and Simeon in Num. 26 : 5–14, and in the mention of the names of Simeon and Levi in the tribal saga of Genesis, chapter 34, and in the tribal sayings of Gen. 49 : 5–7. According to the last, the tribes of Simeon and Levi once made a sudden attack on the city of Shechem; thus, they must have settled in central Palestine at one time. Simeon also appears finally in Judg. 1 : 3, 17, according to which Judah helped Simeon in the conquest of the city of Hormah (Arabic, Tell el-Mshāsh), east of Beersheba. Apparently Simeon took possession of that town from that time on. Here Simeon appears as a tribe which is no longer entirely independent. Reuben appears once again in the Song of Deborah (Judg. 5 : 15b–16), in which the tribe seems to be located in Cisjordan. Thus, there could well have been clans in Israel in the time of the Judges which traced themselves back to Reuben and Simeon, but we no longer

[39] Cf. Steuernagel, *Die Einwanderung der israelitischen Stämme in Kanaan* (1901).
[40] For details see Noth, *ZDPV*, LVIII (1935), 238–39.

know precisely where they might have lived. In view of Judg. 1 : 3, 17, one should probably look for surviving clans of Simeon primarily in the far south of the country.

Perhaps the following reconstruction is also permissible. According to the system of the tribal borders, south of Jericho on the border between Judah and Benjamin,[41] there was a rock called *ebhen bohan* (" thumb stone," Josh. 15 : 6, 18 : 17). Later *bohan* was understood as a proper noun and this Bohan was identified as a " Reubenite." If one adds that according to Josh. 15 : 7 *'Emeq 'Akhor*[42] lay near *ebhen bohan* in the region where according to Josh. 7 : 1, 5b–26 Achan, " the son of Carmi," had his tomb and probably, therefore, his abode,[43] and that according to Num. 26 : 6 Carmi was originally a Reubenite clan, one could conclude that certain remaining Reubenites lived in the northeastern corner of Judah and finally were counted as belonging to Judah, as expressly stated in Josh. 7 : 1, 17, 18.[44] Other clans which called themselves Reubenite could have been diverted into near-by southern Transjordan, so that the redactor of the system of the tribal borders could assert that the original and actual tribal territory of Reuben is to be found in the Belqā.

Judah was the most significant of the Leah tribes in the historical periods. It included the clans which settled in the northern part of Har Yehudhah and probably received its name from its residence there (see pp. 55–56). Thus it became a fixed entity only when it settled down. In the system of the tribal borders its territory seems to be vastly overextended to the west and south, but with the help of references from other parts of the Old Testament—for example, a geographical list of settlements elaborated in I Chronicles, chapters 2 and 4 concerning allotment of territory to Judean and Calebite families dating from the beginning of the period of the kingdom —the territory of the Judeans can be fairly well established.[45] In the north it reached all the way to the old city-state of Jerusalem. Note the old boundary given in Josh. 15 : 5b–10 (or 18 : 15–19), which here doubtless reflects the actual state of affairs. In the east the boundary was defined in general by the beginning of the " wilderness of Judah," which does not permit permanent settlement.

[41] For a more precise localization see Noth, *ZDPV*, LXXIII (1957), 6.

[42] For identification of *'Emeq 'Akhor* with the modern Buqei'ah northeast of the cloister of Marsaba see Noth, *ZDPV*, LXXI (1955), 52–55.

[43] Cf. Noth, *Das Buch Josua*, *op. cit.*, pp. 43 ff.

[44] Steuernagel, on the contrary, prefers to see in *ebhen bohan ben Re'ubhen* evidence for Reuben's earliest residence in Cisjordan even before Judah reached there; *op. cit.*, pp. 15, 16.

[45] On the list in I Chronicles see Noth, *ZDPV*, LV (1932), 97–124.

Only south of Jericho in the lowest part of the Jordan Valley, and perhaps here and there on the western shore of the Dead Sea, and temporarily in the Buqeiʿah northeast of Mar Sāba,[46] were there scattered Judean settlements. To the south, Hebron was already in the possession of the Calebites, as the older strata of the spy narrative in Numbers, chapters 13 and 14 show. According to them Caleb, because of his good conduct, received as a homeland the territory he had reconnoitred, including the area of Hebron, rich with grapes. Compare Josh. 14:6–15 and 15:13, 14, I Chron. 2:42 ff., and other passages. Caleb, however, according to Num. 32:12 and Josh. 14:6, 14, was a " Kenizzite " (see p. 82). Only secondary tradition made him a Judean (Num. 13:6 and elsewhere). The Judean area of occupation in the south extended to about the vicinity of the former Canaanite city-state Beth-zur (now Khirbet eṭ-Ṭubeiqah), while on the west side the rim of the mountains originally formed the boundary. Indeed, Judean families in the periods of the Judges and the Kings advanced beyond this border and established themselves in the Shephelah (see p. 56), particularly in regions which were not occupied by old Canaanite city-states. Here and there Canaanite cities certainly fell into their hands as, for example, the city of Mareshah (Tell Sandaḥanneh at Beit Jibrin; Isr., Beth Gubhrin). The Judean clan Shelah occupied these western regions, as we conclude on the basis of I Chron. 4:21 ff.; Gen. 38:5.[47]

Zebulun and Issachar were also Leah tribes, who lived along the southern edge of the Galilean mountains in historical times. (First Zebulun, then Issachar, was the old sequence, on the basis of Gen. 49:13–15, and on the basis of the original arrangement of the Yahwistic source, J, in Gen. 30:14 ff., in opposition to the later customary sequence of Issachar, Zebulun.) The wide separation of the tribes of the Leah group, the tradition concerning Simeon and Levi in Genesis, chapter 34, and the fact that the two or three first tribes of this group had disappeared by the period of tribal history of which we have records, show that the six Leah tribes had a prehistory on the soil of Palestine of which we no longer have records. They all were once active, independent entities who probably had a territorial relationship one to another. According to the border description in Josh. 19:10–16, which seems to record the true

[46] See F. M. Cross, Jr., and J. T. Milik, " Explorations in the Judaean Buqeʿah," *BASOR*, CXLII (1956), 5–17.

[47] For further detail see Noth, " Die Ansiedlung des Stammes Juda auf dem Boden Palästinas," *PJB*, XXX (1934), pp. 31–47, especially pp. 44 ff.

locations of the tribes, Zebulun lived in the lower Galilean hill country on the north side of the Plain of Jezreel near where Nazareth (en-Nāṣireh) developed in later days.

Issachar, on the other hand, occupied the hill country between the Plain of Jezreel, the plain of the River Jālūd (Isr., Ḥarodh), and the Jordan Valley north to approximately the latitude of Mount Tabor, and including the town of Jezreel (Arabic, Zerʿīn). Theoretically, the system of tribal borders in Josh. 19 : 17–23 (see 17 : 11) seems to have allotted the entire "Valley Corridor of Beisān" to Issachar, whereas in fact the region remained in possession of Canaanite city-states. Some things can still be determined with fair probability about the prehistory of the occupation of this region by Issachar.[48] In particular, the territory of the Canaanite city of Shunem, north of Jezreel (Arabic, Sōlem) on the eastern edge of the Plain of Jezreel, was later part of the area of Issachar. As the Amarna tablets show, Shunem was destroyed in the fourteenth century.[49] Thereafter, to till the city's land which had become fallow, people were used who were willing to work under the rule of neighbouring city lords, in a dependent relationship. The people who consented to the work, a people presumably not yet established, settled down and also joined the tribe of Issachar. In the part of the Blessing of Jacob in Gen. 49 : 14, apparently with reference to this particular type of occupation of the area, Issachar is disparagingly characterized as a forced labourer who condescended to bow his shoulder for the sake of the good land on which he had settled. Even the name Issachar may be related to this land occupation incident, if Issachar means "hired labourer," as it could. This name, then, may have arisen not from the tribe's description of itself, but from its neighbours' description. Moreover, this would be another example of the way the naming of a tribe results from settling in an area. It was probably by expanding from the territory of Shunem that Issachar gradually came to possess all of the hill country that later belonged to it.

The two tribes Joseph and Benjamin belonged to the group called Rachel tribes according to the old form of the twelve-tribe system. They lived in the Samaritan hill country, in the centre of the land, and, so history shows, were the most important of the tribes of Israel in the periods of the Judges and the Kings. Their borders are described in Josh. 16 : 1–17 : 13 and 18 : 12–20, in

[48] See Alt, "Neues über Palāstina aus dem Archiv Amenophis, IV," *PJB*, XX (1924), 34–41 [reprinted in *KS*, III, 158–75].

[49] *Ibid.*

virtual agreement with their actual occupation. The tribal border system theoretically extends their region east to the Jordan and west across the entire coastal plain to the Mediterranean Sea, whereas the region in fact was limited to the hill country itself. " The house of Joseph " occupied by far the largest area in the Samaritan hill country. Its territory extended from the northern rim of the hill country, which in ancient times was probably rather heavily forested, to the sanctuary of Bethel (now Burj Beitīn) and the adjoining town of Luz (now Beitīn) in the south.

Benjamin's northern border was south of the latitude of Bethel, and its southern border lay north of the latitude of Jerusalem. Its territory, therefore, formed only a relatively narrow strip, which ran from east to west across the hill country. Furthermore, the westernmost region of that strip was still occupied by the territories of the four city-states enumerated in Josh. 9 : 17 which stood in covenant relationship with Benjamin. Therefore, all that was left for the tribe of Benjamin was a mountain area along the watershed and an easterly slope into the Jordan Valley which included the territory of the former Canaanite city of Jericho. The origin of the tribe of Benjamin, limited to so narrow a region, has often been traced back to a secondary splintering off from Joseph which took place only in the country.[50] The name Benjamin, meaning " the southern " tribe,[51] which actually could refer to the Benjamite tribal area, lying—from the standpoint of Joseph—to the south, is no argument for this thesis. Neither is reference to Gen. 35 : 16–20, according to which Benjamin was the only one of all the sons of Jacob who was born on the soil of Palestine; for this latter section is not historical but etiological. Yet it is impossible to rule out this thesis completely, especially since the tradition conveyed by Joshua, chapters 2 to 9, before its present reference to all of Israel, was once an account of Benjamite occupation of the land. Therefore, this tradition assumes the independent and separate immigration of the tribe of Benjamin, but actually consists of a series of etiological sayings[52] which do not tell of a separate occupation by the tribe of

[50] Cf. O. Eissfeldt in *Festschrift Georg Beer* (1935), pp. 19–40.

[51] The name *Banū-Yamina* (" Benjaminites ") appears frequently in the Mari texts from the eighteenth century B.C. (see p. 209) as a tribal designation. For references see J. Bottero and A. Finet, *Archives royales de Mari*, XV (1954), 122. Since here the tribal designation *Banū-Simāl* also occurs in the same connection, the explanation of both names as " the Southerners " and " the Northerners " could be considered as certain. In spite of the similarity of names, one should not assume a historical connection between the *Banū-Yamina* of the Mari texts and the Benjaminites of the Old Testament, because they are very far apart in both distance and time.

[52] See Noth, *Das Buch Josua, op. cit.*, pp. 21 ff.

Benjamin but assume it as a fact. The question cannot be definitely settled with the present material. Since Benjamin already appears in the old form of the twelve-tribe system one must rather conclude that from the very beginning Benjamin was a separate body in Palestine.

" The house of Joseph " was subdivided into Manasseh and Ephraim which were counted as separate tribes in that form of the twelve-tribe system which does not include the tribe of Levi. (Manasseh was originally listed first: see Num. 26 : 29 ff., Gen. 48 : 1, 13, 14. Because of Ephraim's historical importance it was later placed first.) The system of tribal borders dealt with this situation by amending the total area of Joseph, setting apart the southern part of the Samaritan hill country, south of Shechem, as a separate area for Ephraim.[53] According to Josh. 17 : 1 ff. and Judg. 5 : 14, it would seem that the subdivisions of Joseph at first were called Machir and Ephraim (the latter again being named for the region in which it lived; see pp. 57–58). Machir later migrated to Transjordan, giving rise to the stereotyped expression " Machir, the father of Gilead " (Josh. 17 : 1, I Chron. 7 : 14, and elsewhere). Those who remained in Cisjordan who did not belong to Ephraim, for reasons unknown to us received the inclusive name Manasseh. The deuteronomistic redaction of the history then genealogically subordinated Transjordanian Machir to Cisjordanian Manasseh, designating it merely as the Transjordanian half of Manasseh, and allotted it the ʿAjlūn as territory, as well as the Jōlān and the Nuqreh (Bashan), as in Josh. 13 : 30–31. The redaction repeatedly states that this territory had already been occupied by the time the Israelite tribes advanced into Cisjordan, just as the regions of Gad and Reuben had been. Actually the tribal border system originating in the period of the Judges does not account for an Israelite tribal possession either in the ʿAjlūn and its vicinity or in the Nuqreh. Instead, it assumes Joseph as a unit, and probably also Machir and Ephraim neighbouring each other on the Samaritan hill country. Hence, the conclusion seems to be justified that only after the origin of this system—therefore only in the course of the period of the Judges—did migration take Machir, or a part of it, from the Samaritan hill country across to Transjordan, or more specifically into the area at the northern edge of the hill country of ʿAjlūn. This migration, some details of which are found in Num. 32 : 39–42, remains hazy to us. Contrary to the deuteronomistic claims, it is unlikely that this new settlement of Machir expanded

[53] See Noth, *ZDPV*, LVIII (1935), 203–4.

into the ancient city-state area of the land of Bashan.[54] On the contrary, Ephraimite clans had probably already encroached in similar fashion upon the section of the hill country of central Transjordan which lay across from them just south of the Jabbok—thus establishing themselves in the region of modern Arḍ el-ʿArḍeh—and had given this region the name Gilead[55] based on the name of the near-by hill country of Gilead and the city of Gilead (see p. 62).

Four tribes remain to be discussed which are listed in Gen. 49 : 16–21 between the Leah and Rachel groups. In Numbers, chapter 26, they conclude the list of tribes, except for Gad. In the personified tale of Gen. 29 : 31–30 : 24, these tribes do not have women of equal station ascribed to them as their tribal mothers; the meaning of this fact is not clear. At any rate, all four tribes lived somewhere on the periphery of the Israelite territory. Asher and Naphtali were in the Galilean hill country, Asher being located on the western edge, certainly no farther north than Jebel el-Mushaqqaḥ (see p. 21), and Naphtali on the eastern rim, west of the Lake of Tiberias and the upper Jordan Valley. The site, Kedesh, in the hill country northwest of Lake Ḥūleh (Arabic, Qedes), is more closely described in Judg. 4 : 6 as Qedesh Naphtali. The system of the tribal borders has tremendously overextended the area of Asher in theory (Josh. 19 : 24–31) by allotting to Asher the regions of the Plain of Acco and the whole Plain of Jezreel, together with Carmel and its approaches, all of which actually remained in the possession of Canaanite cities. The border system even proceeds to extend the area of Asher as far as Tyre and Sidon; beyond that, the system had the areas of Asher and Naphtali reach up to the interior of upper Galilee and touch one another there, which was also probably only theory.

Dan at one time lived in the northern part of the Shephelah between the Canaanite cities of Aijalon (Yālo) and Beth-shemesh (Arabic, Tell er-Rumeileh near ʿAin Shems) at Zorah (Hebrew, *Ṣorʿah*; Arabic, Ṣarʿah) and Eshtaol, and tried to settle there, as shown by Judg. 1 : 34–35, the Samson stories of Judges, chapters 13 to 16, and the narrative of Judg. 18 : 2. Since the attempt to settle failed in face of the dominance of the neighbouring Canaanite cities, according to Judges, chapter 18, Dan settled at the head of the Jordan Valley, conquered the city of Laish (Tell el-Qādi) which lay at one of the sources of the Jordan, made this its own

[54] Cf. Noth, *BBLAK*, LXVIII (1949), 2 ff.

[55] Noth, *PJB*, XXXVII (1941), 64 ff. and *ZDPV*, LXXV (1959), 30 ff.

centre, and renamed it Dan. (Compare the expression " from Dan to Beersheba.") The redactor of the geographic section of Joshua, chapters 13 to 19, tried to account for Dan's original residence in the Shephelah by utilizing the list of sites of the fifth Judean district (see p. 99) while adding the sites of Zorah and Eshtaol known from Judg. 13 : 25 and elsewhere, when he defined the area of Dan (Josh. 19 : 40–48). Yet originally this list had nothing to do with Dan. The redactor also simply omitted the description of the borders of Dan from the system of the tribal borders, which already knew Dan in its later residence in the upper Jordan Valley. This seems to have been preserved in Num. 34 : 7–11; Ezek. 47 : 15–18, 48 : 1.[56] The tribe of Dan, living far removed at the edge of the country, never played an important historical role.

Gad finally settled at the edge of the Transjordanian hill country east of the southern end of the Jordan Valley. According to Num. 32 : 1 (see also Num. 21 : 32), this tribe initially settled in the land (of the city) of Jazer (Ya'zer). According to the statements of Eusebius this Jazer was located in the basin of Wādi Kefrein and presumably more precisely on Tell 'Areimeh, 3 km. [2 miles] northwest of modern Nā'ūr.[57] Beginning from this region, the Gadites expanded their territory southward along the western edge of the southern Belqā to Seil Heidān and Seil el-Mōjib (the Arnon). In this total region the system of the tribal borders refers to an Israelite tribal region which it doubtless ascribed to the tribe of Gad. In the middle of the ninth century B.C. the Moabite king Mesha notes in his well-known inscription (see p. 219), line 10, that " the man of Gad " had been settled " since long ago . . . in the land of Ataroth " (this is Aṭṭārūs about 10 km. [6 miles] north of Seil Heidān). This is the earliest attested Transjordanian territory of Israel. We no longer know how long Gad had been settled at this location. It could have been a temporary phase when, in the period of the Judges (Judg. 3 : 12 ff.), a Moabite king once conquered the larger southern part of the Belqā and went on to occupy the Cisjordanian territory of Jericho as well. This does not exclude the possibility that the tribe of Gad lived even then not far away in upper Wādi Kefrein. Num. 21 : 27–30 is an old victory song celebrating the conquest of the city of Heshbon (modern Ḥesbān), and perhaps other cities in the Belqā, which probably refers to an actual extension of the land holdings of the tribe of Gad.

[56] See Noth, *Das Buch Josua. op. cit.*, pp. 120–21; against this view is that of Elliger, *PJB*, XXXII (1936), 34 ff.

[57] See R. Rendtorff, *ZDPV*, LXXVI (1960), 129 ff.

(2) *Other Peoples In and Around Palestine*

See Figure 3.

The Israelite tribes were never the sole occupants of the land of Palestine. As they took the land, they found it already thickly settled in certain areas by a mixed population.

Politically, this pre-Israelite population lived predominantly in many tiny kingdoms: city-states with a fortified city as centre, a " king " as ruler, and possibly a rather small ruling class dominating the population who did the work and were mainly farmers, cultivating the town lands. In addition to the Old Testament, the Amarna tablets (see pp. 207 ff.) provide a clear picture of the nature of these city-states. Note the list of conquered Canaanite kings in Josh. 12 : 13b–24, and the enumeration of unconquered city-states in Judg. 1 : 21, 27 ff., and other scattered references.[58] The pre-Israelite city-states were primarily in the parts of the country particularly favoured by nature. They were situated in the plains—in the Acco Plain, the Plain of Jezreel, and the coastal plain which extends southward from Carmel to merge with the desert of Sinai; then, too, in Transjordan, in the bountiful region on both sides of the Yarmuk. In the hilly portions of the land there was only a meagre number of city-states: in the Samaritan range, the city of Shechem; farther south, Jerusalem and the four city-states close to it, mentioned in Josh. 9: 17, still farther south, including Hebron (see especially Num. 13 : 22), as well as Kiriath-sepher (Josh. 15 : 15, 16, Judg. 1 : 11, 12).

The subject class in these city-states had certainly lived in the country for a long time; they spoke a West Semitic dialect. (Note the Canaanite glosses in the Amarna tablets, derived from the vernacular.) Later, as the Israelites became at home in the country, they took over this Canaanite language which we know as Hebrew. The ruling class, on the other hand, was a mixed group, as is seen from the names of city rulers appearing in the Amarna tablets and from the lists of names on some clay tablets found in Tell Taʿannek.[59] There, one finds next to the expected Canaanite names strikingly large numbers of Hurrian names (see pp. 233, 240–41), and also scattered Indo-Iranian names, as well as Babylonian ones.[60]

[58] On the whole matter see especially, Alt, " Die Landnahme der Israeliten in Palästina," *Leipziger Dekanats-Programm* (1925) [reprinted in *KS*, I, 89–125].

[59] Cf. A. Gustavs, " Die Personennamen in den Tontafeln von Tell Taʿannek," *ZDPV*, L (1927), 1–18; LI (1928), 169–218.

[60] Additional material is given in Noth, " Die syrisch-palästinische Bevölkerung des Zweiten Jahrtausends v. Chr. im Lichte neuer Quellen," *ZDPV*, LXV (1942), 9–67.

Through known historical movements (see pp. 255 ff.) these different elements arrived in Palestine just as they also arrived in Syria. Nevertheless, from the viewpoint of the Israelite tribes, " the Canaanites " could be considered with some justification as a definite unit, considering their manner of life, culture, and political situation as the inhabitants already occupying the land. In the Old Testament, for example in the Yahwistic (J) stratum of the Pentateuch, they are referred to as the Canaanites (on the origin of the name see pp. 50 ff.), naturally without describing them as an ethnic unit. Diverging from Old Testament usage, modern scholarship prefers to use the word Canaanite to designate the dialects of a group, namely, the oldest Semitic dialects spoken in Syria and Palestine. In addition, the word Canaanite is often used in an ethnographic sense. Both of these usages are foreign to the Old Testament. In some parts of the Old Testament, for example in the Elohistic (E) stratum in the Pentateuch, the pre-Israelite inhabitants of the land are grouped together as " Amorites," perhaps simply because the customary Accadian name for the " West " was the " Land of Amurru." Similarly, anything from this region came to be called " Amorite." The people of Syria-Palestine could have called themselves " Westerners " or " Amorites " when in Mesopotamia. Something similar happened in the use of the term " Hittites " for the pre-Israelite population (for example, by the Priestly (P) stratum in the Pentateuch: Gen. 23 : 3 ff.; 26 : 34; 27 : 46; 49 : 29, 30, and elsewhere). The term Hittite, too, comes from the Mesopotamian viewpoint and stems, at the earliest, from the Assyrians' naming Syria and Palestine " the land of Ḫatti." The Assyrian term is explained by the existence of " Late Hittite " principalities in North Syria which the Assyrians first encountered as they pressed forward toward Syria-Palestine.

The diversity of the pre-Israelite population is occasionally indicated in the Old Testament, especially in the grouping of seven traditional names—including the three names just treated—of peoples of the country, which repeatedly appears in the Old Testament, though in varying degrees of completeness and arrangement.[61] We can no longer tell what the names themselves mean, aside from those already treated, nor to what group of people they refer. Only of the Jebusites does the Old Testament say repeatedly that they are to be found in the city-state of Jerusalem (II Sam. 5 : 6 and elsewhere). But the grouping of the names together

[61] Source material is from F. M. T. Böhl, *Kanaanäer und Hebräer* (1911), pp. 63, 64.

demonstrates the extent of the diversity of the pre-Israelite population.

Also entering this world of the " Canaanites " were the Philistines, the part of the population which suddenly appeared in the land at about the same time as the Israelite tribes. The movement of the " Sea Peoples " (see p. 245) after an unsuccessful assault on Egypt had carried them into the southern part of the Palestinian coastal plain. There the Egyptians settled them in an area of Egyptian nominal control.[62] There the Philistines became the ruling class, and in five old Canaanite city kingdoms they set up centres of their own rule; their five cities were Gaza (Arabic, Ghazzeh), Ashdod (Arabic, Esdūd), Ashkalon (Arabic, ʿAsqalān), Ekron (according to the original proper vocalization, ʿAqqaron, probably Khirbet el-Muqannaʿ 20 km. [12 miles] east of Ashdod).[63] Gath was farther inland than the other cities might have been at Tell en-Najileh (Isr., Tel Negila).[64] Other " sea peoples " related to the Philistines also settled farther to the north on the coastal plain. We know this from the statement of an Egyptian official named Wen-Amun.[65] About 1100 B.C. he stated that the *Ṯkr* (vocalization unknown),[66] listed next to the Philistines among the sea peoples, were living in the city of Dor south of Mount Carmel (Arabic, Khirbet el-Burj near eṭ-Ṭanṭūrah; Isr., Dor). Other sea peoples, related to the Philistines, may also have advanced into the Plain of Jezreel and the plain of the River Jālūd (Isr., Ḥarodh) and settled there. Clear finds from the twelfth century B.C. in excavations at Beth-shan,[67] as well as the historical role of Beth-shan in the final battle of the Philistines against Saul (I Sam. 31 : 10, 12), speak for this fact. All of these sea peoples came from the eastern Mediterranean world, although neither their homeland nor the stops in their migration are definitely known to us. (Possibly one of the stops of the Philistine migration was Crete, called Caphtor in the Old Testament, in Jer. 47 : 4 and Amos 9 : 7. Compare also the *kerethi* —though more probably this means " Cretans "—which in Ezek. 25 : 16 and Zeph. 2 : 5 seems to designate the Philistines, and in I Sam. 30 : 14 designates an element of the population which occupied a part of the Negeb. The rhyming word-formation *Kerethi*

[62] See A. Alt, *ZDPV*, LXVII (1944), 1–20 [reprinted in *KS*, I, 216–30].

[63] O. J. Naveh, *IEJ*, VIII (1958), 87–100, 165–70.

[64] S. Bülow and R. A. Mitchell, *IEJ*, XI (1961), 101–10.

[65] *ANET*, pp. 25–29.

[66] Rameses III repeatedly names *Prst* (Philistines) and *Ṯkr* together as " sea peoples " conquered by him; see Breasted, *Ancient Records of Egypt*, IV, Secs. 44, 64, 403, or *ANET*, 262–63.

[67] See Alt, *PJB*, XXII (1926), 118–19 [reprinted in *KS*, I].

u-Phelethi, a term for a troop of David's used in II Sam. 8 : 18 and elsewhere, probably means "Cretans and Philistines.") The Philistines are repeatedly called "the uncircumcised" in the Old Testament, since in distinction from the Egyptians and most of the peoples of Syria and Palestine they did not practise circumcision.

Certainly, at least during the second millennium B.C. and very probably as early as the third, the Mediterranean coast from the Plain of Acco on north included the Semitic population which the Greeks called Phoenicians. The name Canaanite was originally applied especially to them (see p. 52). In the Old Testament these coastal residents are called Sidonians. This name was derived from Sidon, then the most important southern Phoenician city as seen by its Palestinian neighbours.

In a stage of historical development similar to that of the Israelite tribes were some closely related peoples which settled down east of Palestine and managed to develop states. Enumerated from south to north there were first the Edomites, whose central area was the mountains on the east side of the Wādi el-ʿArabah, south of the Wādi el-Ḥesā, which reaches the Dead Sea at its extreme southern end.[68] Their realm extended southeast up as far as the shore of el-ʿAqabah with its old port cities, ʿEṣyon Gebher (now Tell el-Kheleifeh),[69] and ʾElath, probably near modern el-ʿAqabah. We no longer know the extent of Edomite influence on the west side of the Wādi el-ʿArabah, nor when that influence began (see the editorial notes in Num. 34 : 3, Joshua 15 : 1, etc.). At any rate, in post-exilic times the Edomites pressed forward from the south against Transjordan. (Gen. 36 : 31–39 names eight Edomite kings who ruled in Transjordan before the rise of an Israelite kingdom. Thus, both the Edomites and Moabites established a central form of government earlier than the Israelites, though the Israelites made the transition to sedentary life earlier than the others.) Their ancient central area gave the Edomites valuable mineral resources (see p. 44) and control of the Gulf of el-ʿAqabah, an approach to the Red Sea. Edom was therefore important to the kings of Judah. From David on they repeatedly subjugated Edom and made it a province of the state of Judah.

The northern neighbours of the Edomites were the Moabites,

[68] On the Edomites, see F. Buhl, *Geschichte der Edomiter* (*Leipziger Dekanats-Programm*, 1893).

[69] See F. Frank, *ZDPV*, LVII (1934), 243–44. On the excavation work at this city, which disclosed amazing installations for metal working, see N. Glueck, *BASOR*, LXXI (1938), 3–17; LXXII (1938), 2–13; LXXV (1939), 8–22; LXXIX (1940), 2–18; LXXX (1940), 3–10; LXXXII (1941), 3–11.

who settled down about the twelfth century B.C. and developed a government.[70] Their area lay between the Dead Sea and the Syro-Arabian Desert, from Wādi el-Ḥesā in the south as far as the Seil el-Mōjib (Arnon) in the north. At times, they forcibly extended their area beyond the Arnon into the Belqā, and, at all events, they never completely gave up their claims to the Belqā; note Judg. 11 : 15–26 and the Mesha inscription (see p. 219), ll. 4 ff. The Moabite king Mesha apparently succeeded in returning the southern Belqā to Moab for a considerable period of time in the middle of the ninth century, the area between the Seil el-Mōjib (Arnon) and Wadi el-Wāleh together with the city of Dibon (now Dībān) having previously come under Moabite control. The Judean king Josiah at the end of the seventh century temporarily re-occupied part of it.[71]

The Ammonites lived on the eastern border of the Belqā in the region of the upper course of the Jabbok in a rather small area around their capital, Rabbath bene ʿAmmon, also called Rabbah, (now ʿAmman, the capital of Jordan). They too settled down only in the twelfth century B.C.[72] Otherwise we know relatively little about the history of the Ammonites, apart from their occasional hostile relations with their western neighbours, the Transjordanian Israelites. The Ammonites attempted to guard their borders whereever it seemed necessary by a system of fortifications, including towers and small fortresses. So far these fortifications along the Ammonite western border over against Israel have been extensively studied from the western edge of the Buqeiʿah, northwest of eṣ-Ṣuweiliḥ, running south across the heights east of modern Wādi es-Sīr and Nāʿūr.[73]

The Arameans, who had formed a considerable number of states by the time of King David, lived on the northeastern fringes of Palestine, beginning probably at about the same time as the Israelite conquest. The largest and most powerful Aramean state at that time was Aram Ṣobhah (II Sam. 8 : 3 ff., 10 : 6 ff.), whose chief

[70] See the archeological identifications of Glueck, " Explorations in Eastern Palestine, I–IV," *AASOR*, XIV (1934), 1–113; XV (1935), 1–202; XVIII–XIX (1939), 1–288; XXV–XXVIII (1951), 1–711. The known material on the Moabites and their history is collected in A. H. van Zyl, *The Moabites* (" Pretoria Oriental Series," III, 1960).

[71] See Alt, " König Josia " in Procksch, *Zahn-Festgabe* (1928), pp. 47–48.

[72] See Glueck, " Explorations in Eastern Palestine," *op. cit.* For the limited archeological material bearing on the history of the Ammonites read especially W. F. Albright, " Notes on Ammonite History," *Miscellanea Biblica* (B. Ubach, 1954), pp. 131–36.

[73] See the details in connection with the basic archeological findings of Glueck in H. Gese, *ZDPV*, LXXIV (1958), 55–64; R. Hentschke, *ZDPV*, LXXVI (1960), 103–123; G. Fohrer, *ZDPV*, LXXVI (1961), 56–71.

area seems to have been the land between Antilebanon and the Syro-Arabian Desert.[74] At the same time this state ruled the Beqā' between Lebanon and Antilebanon and exercised a sort of dominance over the Arameans living in the interior of Syria far to the north (see II Sam. 8 : 3, 10 : 16). Among the smaller Aramean states were those of Beth-Rehobh (II Sam. 10 : 6), Ma'akhah (II Sam. 10 : 6, 8), Geshur (II Sam. 15 : 8 and elsewhere), and Damascus (II Sam. 8 : 5, 6). If Beth-Rehobh is to be identified with modern Riḥāb, then Aram Beth-Reḥobh was probably a small Aramean state on the eastern edge of the 'Ajlūn, north of the region of the Ammonites. The name Ma'akhah lived on in the name of the later Israelite city Abel Beth-Ma'akhah (II Sam. 20 : 14, 15 and elsewhere). This is Ābil at the northern end of the upper Jordan Valley; later, another small Aramean city called (Beth-)Ma'akhah was founded somewhere in the vicinity of Merj'oyūn between the southern ends of Lebanon and Antilebanon. The repeated combination of the names Geshur and Ma'akhah leads one to conclude that these Aramean cities were close to one another. Therefore, one would locate Geshur at the north end of Jōlān, even without specific proof. Probably Aram-Dammeseq was originally only a small Aramean state which was formed on the site of the old city-state of Damascus. David won control of the Arameans (see II Sam. 8 : 3–8, 10 : 6–19). Then these people freed themselves again in the time of Solomon (I Kings 11 : 23–25). This freedom movement proceeded from Damascus. From then on, Damascus became the centre of a kingdom embracing a considerable part of the Arameans. This kingdom was the chief power in Syria in the ninth and eighth centuries B.C. For a long time, Syria was the most dangerous opponent of the state of Israel.[75]

Palestine adjoins desert regions in the south and southeast. For that reason it has always had to do with non-sedentary desert dwellers. From time immemorial, desert groups have tried to settle down on the cultivated land. Thus the southern and eastern borders of the settled area have always seen the process of change of non-sedentary elements to sedentary life in its various stages. For the Israelite tribes this contact with desert peoples took place particularly on the southern border of Transjordan, since, in their day, the Edomites, Moabites, Ammonites, and Arameans lived along the eastern border of the cultivated land. We know of various clans

[74] The name *Ṣobhah* seems to be linked with this region; see Noth, *PJB*, XXXIII (1937), 40 ff.

[75] On some aspects of the early history of the Arameans at the borders of and near to Palestine, see Noth, *BBLAK*, LXVIII, Sec. 1 (1949), 19 ff.

south of the tribe of Judah which, just like the then developing tribe of Judah, had come from the southern desert and sooner or later in the process of settling down merged with the tribe of Judah. The Kenizzite clan of Caleb from around Hebron, whose ancestor Caleb was later simply called a Judean, was treated above on p. 70. Southwest of Caleb, another Kenizzite clan, Othniel (Josh. 15 : 17 or Judg. 1 : 13), lived in the region of the old city of Kiriath-sepher, which they conquered and renamed Debir. This town should probably be identified with modern Khirbet Rabūḍ, 13 km. [8 miles] southwest of Hebron.[76] Kenaz was the name of a league of clans of whom (according to Gen. 36 : 11,42) parts also belonged to the Edomites. Caleb and Othniel probably changed to sedentary life very early. This is less true of the Kenites, who controlled a small area south of Hebron at the edge of the wilderness of Judah,[77] during the period of the Kingdom, and only separated themselves from the league of the non-sedentary Amalekites (see below) in the days of King Saul. They then apparently entered the league of the tribe of Judah (I Sam. 15 : 6). In the time of the Judges, according to Judg. 4 : 11,17 and 5 : 24, a Kenite, who was not a member of Israel, appeared with his tent, the dwelling of the nomad, in the north of Palestine, apparently in the Galilean hill country (4 : 17). He could not have been the only Kenite who thus lived in the land, probably as a craftsman (note the mention of a hammer in 4 : 21), without joining the Canaanites or the Israelites even though he had "separated himself" (4 : 11) far from the (rest of the) Kenites by his sojourn in Galilee. The Jerahmeelites appear next to the Kenites in I Sam. 27 : 10 and 30 : 29. Just like the Kenites, the Jerahmeelites apparently lived in the Negeb. The late genealogy of I Chron. 2 : 9,25 ff., 42 makes Jerahmeel, like Caleb, a Judean. The Jerahmeelites, therefore, of whom we otherwise know no details, finally, like the previously named groups, entered the greater whole of the tribe of Judah.

There were pure nomadic tribes only outside of Palestine itself. The tribal league of the Amalekites, apparently large, lived in the Sinai Desert to the south. In so far as the Israelite tribes lived in the southern part of Cisjordan, they were neighbours, but involved in continuous disputes (cf. Exod. 17 : 8–16, particularly v. 16). Saul still had to fight against the Amalekites (I Sam. 15 : 2 ff.); and

[76] K. Galling, *ZDPV*, LXX (1954), 135–49.

[77] The eighth Judean district (see p. 99), in which [*Zanoaḥ haq-Qayin*] "Zanoah of the Kenites" (Josh. 15 : 56–57) appears, probably embraced the area where the Kenites lived in the later part of the period of the Kings.

David, in the time of his feudal dependence on the Philistines in Ziklag, had a dispute with them (I Sam. 30 : 1 ff.). After that we no longer hear of them.

The chief pasture lands of the nomadic Midianites were farther removed, on the east side of the Gulf of el-ʿAqabah. In that region, at least in later times, there was a place known as Madian, according to the word of the geographer Ptolemy (vi. 7.2, 27), and Arabian geographers. The Midianites, who migrated on domesticated camels, occasionally raided Palestine.[78] They invaded the productive Cisjordanian plains, coming from the desert through Transjordan at harvest time to rob the produce of the land, as long as no determined resistance was offered (see especially Judg. 6 : 2 ff., 33 ff.). (It is perfectly understandable to refer, as in Judg. 6 : 3, 33 and 7 : 12, to the Midianites in connection with the Amalekites and " the people of the East," i.e., nomads of the eastern desert. However, in this narrative these others appear to be later additions to the text.) In Gen. 25 : 2, 4 the Midianites are traced back genealogically to Abraham.

The Ishmaelite nomadic tribal union is also traced back genealogically to Abraham, in Gen. 25 : 12–18. According to the statement in Gen. 25 : 8, the Ishmaelites had lived in northwestern Arabia and the Sinai Desert. We do not again find historical references to the Ishmaelites; they occur only as leaders of camel caravans passing through Palestine in the Yahwistic (J) source materials in the Joseph narrative (Gen. 37 : 25, 27–28; 39 : 1), while the Elohistic source (E), speaks of Midianites in the same connection (Gen. 37 : 28, 36).

" Arabs " are repeatedly referred to in late texts of the Old Testament, particularly in Nehemiah and Chronicles. According to Neh. 2 : 19 and 4 : 7 (Hebrew, 4 : 1), etc.,[79] the post-exilic province in the southern part of the Judean range and in the Negeb seems to have had the name Arabia in the Persian period. This name, which already appears in Neo-Assyrian royal inscriptions,[80] then suggests that the inhabitants of this province chiefly belonged to the nomadic tribes of the desert [cf. ʿArabah] bordering the settled lands, their name distinguishing them from the old inhabitants of the settled land. Originally, " Arab " seems to have been a very loosely used name for these desert nomads.

[78] On when the camel became domesticated, see both W. F. Albright, *From the Stone Age to Christianity* (1st ed., 1940), pp. 120–21 and R. Walz, *ZDMG*, New Series. XXVI (1951), 29–51; XXIX (1954), 45–87.
[79] See Alt, *PJB*, XXVII (1931), 73–74 [reprinted in *KS*, II].
[80] See E. Ebeling, *RLA*, I (1932), 125a–26.

(3) *Ancient Trade Routes*

Historical geography and the history of sedentary life require a survey of use or development of available trade routes. Since men had already begun to live in fortified settlements by the Neolithic Age (see p. 122), they must already have been aware of others beyond the limited circle of their own settlements and must rapidly have found it necessary to seek connecting links among the settlements, whether for peaceful exchange of goods or for hostile conflict and conquest. Sharply as natural factors limit the development of trade routes, especially in such rough terrain as that of Palestine, the course the rise of sedentary life took influenced the trade routes available in Palestine even more. Settlements and trade routes were in a constantly changing situation as the number of towns increased. The sites of settlements determined the choice of certain naturally preferred trade routes. On the other hand, what trade routes were available partly decided the choice of places for new settlements. Thus trade routes must be taken into account not only in studying the history of settlements, but also in studying the development of any historical process. Of course, initially there were no skilfully constructed roads, but rather customary routes, which naturally could be made more passable and convenient by clearing away minor hindrances.

Palestine had already been inhabited for millennia before the entrance of Israel and had long had its trade routes. The Israelite tribes opened up extensive areas in the hilly portions of the land for settlement, making additional trade routes necessary.

We have only a very limited idea of the road system of Palestine during the history of Israel. We are dependent on more or less accidental literary accounts and on general related conjectures, for the " roads " of the Israelite period can no longer be shown archeologically. Tracing of roadways begins only with the Roman roads (see p. 118). Even of these there are few indeed and even then they are only isolated examples of the once carefully built roadways. There are, however, many milestones and a number of road stations which serve notice of the course of the roads. This finding is significant even for the earlier period, because the Roman roads in many cases follow older roadways. However, since their roads were constructed and tended to follow as straight a course as possible, the Romans frequently chose new routes. Naturally there are no longer traces of older roads which had no milestones, even where the roads were planned and built. There were such planned roadways in the Israelite period, for the Old Testament uses another term for road besides the general term "way" (*derekh*), which can mean a road of any description, even a path beaten by constant wear. It also uses the technical term *mesillah*, which indicates a built-up roadbed, therefore a well-planned road. According to Isa. 62 : 10, to build a proper road one must prepare the way, build up the roadbed (*mesillah*), and clear it of stones, certainly only on the stretches on which the terrain required it. Cf. Isa. 40 : 3, "prepare the way, make straight a highway (*mesillah*)" and Isa. 49 : 11, according to which *mesilloth* are high, "raised up." Such roads were built not only to link important cities directly with their outposts, as in Isa. 7 : 3 and II Kings 18 : 17, but also as overland roads between cities. Thus there was a *mesillah* from Bethel to Shechem (Judg. 21 : 19). From Gibeah *mesilloth* ran to Bethel and Gibeon (Judg. 20 : 31–32). (The name Gibeon is restored here by textual conjecture. A *mesillah* is also mentioned in II Sam. 20 : 12 as near Gibeon.) The Philistine country, especially the Philistine city of Ekron, was linked with Beth-shemesh by a *mesillah* (I Sam. 6 : 12). A *mesillah* also ran from north to south through the Edomite country (Num. 20 : 19). Even widely separated large countries could be linked together by a *mesillah* (Isa. 19 : 23; cf. Isa. 11 : 16).

For its trade Palestine in ancient times was solely dependent on roads. In distinction from the great river oases of Egypt and of Mesopotamia, there was no possibility here of trade by waterways. The Jordan, between the Lake of Tiberias and the Dead Sea, was the only river of Palestine which could support boats. Yet it was not a usable trade channel because of its countless meanderings, apart from the fact that there were almost no settlements on its banks.[81] The Dead Sea could have linked the settlements along its banks, but nothing is known of any ship traffic on it during the Old Testament period. Probably the earliest such trade began with the Hellenistic period. There was such trade during the Byzantine period, since the mosaic map of Medeba shows ships on the Dead Sea.[82] We do not know of any regular Mediterranean coastal ship travel serving inland commerce during ancient times. The Mediterranean coast was important commercially only for joining distant countries. While the pharaohs controlled Palestine and Syria, they maintained bases along the coast to keep the sea route to Egypt

[81] See Noth, "Der Jordan in der alten Geschichte Palästinas," *ZDPV*, LXXII (1956), 123–48.
[82] M. Avi-Yonah, *The Madaba Mosaic Map* (1954), Plates II, III.

open.[83] According to Ezra 3 : 7, cedar was shipped from the Lebanon coast to Joppa (Arabic, Yāfa) for the reconstruction of the Jerusalem temple.[84] In the same Joppa, Jonah boarded a ship to flee to distant Tarshish (Jonah 1 : 3). The cities of the Philistines which were close to the coast could have had their connections with the coast. Later the construction of the large artificial harbour of Caesarea by Herod established a link between Palestine and the Roman world. However, for ancient Israel, with its limited possession of Mediterranean coast areas, sea commerce was never of substantial significance.

Important Palestinian land routes are treated here if they are presupposed in the Old Testament, or explicitly referred to there. Men on foot and on animals, then as now, could find their way even in trackless mountain regions. Trade with wagons necessarily made larger demands. It required constructed roads, at least in more or less difficult terrain. The *mesilloth* referred to above must have been built primarily for wagon traffic. Beginning with the Hyksos period (see p. 255), horse-drawn chariots were known in the entire ancient Near East. The kings of Israel and Judah from Solomon on had their chariot troops, for which they used the corresponding roads. In addition to chariots (*merkhabhah*), transport wagons (*'aghalah*) are also mentioned in non-military contexts. It is possible that wagons did not play a large role, since customarily people and burdens were loaded on the backs of donkeys. Still, at least for longer trips, old people, women, and children could use a wagon (*'aghalah*) (Gen. 45 : 19 ff., 46 : 5). All sorts of baggage could be loaded on an *'aghalah* (Num. 7 : 3 ff.). Even the Ark of the Covenant was transported on an *'aghalah* on occasion (I Sam. 6 : 7 ff., II Sam. 6 : 3). Amos 2 : 13 describes harvest sheaves being brought in on an *'aghalah*. While the chariot was drawn by horses, the *'aghalah* was probably generally drawn by oxen as in Num. 7 : 3 ff., I Sam. 6 : 7 ff. Even this peaceful wagon traffic requires somewhat passable roads.

Certain natural contours of Palestine in ancient times would have provided convenient north-and-south routes. The coastal plain

[83] Alt, *BBLAK* or *ZDPV*, LXVIII, No. 2 (1950), 97 ff. [reprinted in *KS*, III (1959), 107 ff.].

[84] According to I Kings 5 : 9 [Hebrew, I Kings 5 : 23], cedar and cypress were floated by sea from the Lebanon coast already for the Solomonic temple. In this connection no Palestinian port is mentioned. The chronicler mentions the harbour of Joppa (II Chron. 2 : 16; Hebrew, v. 15) for this purpose as Ezra 3 : 7 does for the later occasion. The Persian empire certainly needed the Syro-Palestinian Mediterranean coast for commerce. Note the description of the Syro-Palestinian coast in Pseudo-Skylax, dating from the Persian period: K. Galling, *ZDPV*, LXI (1938), 66–96.

offered such a possibility. There, the perennial coastal rivers, generally short, could have been forded at some spots, preferably either at their mouths, where such rivers typically flow gently through a sandy beach, or near their sources along the edge of the hills. We do not know the details of the lines followed. In the broad southern part of the coastal plain numerous possibilities existed side by side. North of the Nahr el ʿOjah (Isr., Yarqon), on the other hand, the middle part of the coastal plain had stretches of swamps and forests and offered only two possibilities, the " western line of the way of the sea," following the coast,[85] or again, a route on the eastern edge of the coastal plain, that is, along the foot of the Samaritan range.[86] Traffic going farther north into the Plain of Acco may have followed the route along the coast around the Carmel promontory, since later a Roman road followed this course. Yet the route through the low hills known to the Arabs as Bilād er-Rūha must have been more convenient. It runs through the Plain of Jezreel and down the valley of the Kishon into the Plain of Acco.

The main watershed along the top of the Cisjordanian ridge between the Mediterranean Sea and the Jordan Valley was the natural preferred line for a great north-south route. The valleys branching off east and west from the top of the range, most of them rather abrupt and deep, hindered north-and-south traffic except at the top of the mountain table. What little we know from ancient accounts indicates that in the ancient Israelite period the north-south route through the hill country followed the watershed more closely than does the corresponding modern highway. The *mesillah* from Gibeah (Tell el Fūl) to Bethel (Beitīn), according to Judg. 20 : 31, and the *mesillah* from Bethel to Shechem (Tell Balāṭah), according to Judg. 21 : 19, were doubtless sections of the main north-south road. The ancient road apparently followed a different course from the modern one; certainly it passed Bethel and continued north by way of the heights east of Wādi el-Ḥaramīyeh, while the modern one passes through the wādi. A milestone found in Yabrūd[87] indicates that the later Roman road followed this more easterly line past Bethel. At Lubban the ancient road resumed the line of the modern road. According to Judg. 21 : 19, Shiloh (Khirbet Seilūn) was east of the road and one had to leave it " south of Lebonah " (Lubban) to reach Shiloh. At Jerusalem the road apparently ran along the watershed heights west of the city, for

[85] See Maisler, *ZDPV*, LVIII (1935), 78–84.
[86] See Y. Karmon, " Geographical Influences on the Historical Routes in the Sharon Plain," *PEQ*, XCIII (1961), 43–60.
[87] No. 260 in the list of P. Thomsen (see p. 118, note 39 on this).

according to Judg. 19 : 11, 12 one had to leave the road to reach Jerusalem on the way from Bethlehem to Gibeah. On the evidence of the milestones and road stations discovered in the Judean hill country south of Bethlehem, the Roman road to Hebron, and probably also the pre-Roman road, went along the watershed west of the modern road. The most convenient way northward from Shechem was probably always across the valley of Samaria and then past Dothan (Tell Dōtān) to the southern point of the Plain of Jezreel. We have no ancient evidence at all about roads in Galilee.

Of course the Jordan Valley presented a north-south route. On both sides of the valley roads followed close to the foot of the hills. We have no evidence to guide us as to the details.

In Transjordan, first a general line was indicated for north-south traffic, which would run east of the deep valleys which cut westward to the Jordan Valley. This line, followed later by the Islamic pilgrim route and more recently by the Ḥejaz railway, led through the regions of the Edomites (cf. the *mesillah* of Num. 20 : 19), Moabites, Ammonites, and Arameans and was therefore outside the territory of Israel. In the Old Testament the description of the campaign of the four great kings in Gen. 14 : 5,6 suggests this route.

The cross roads connecting the important north-south lines were undoubtedly very valuable. These cross roads followed only those westerly valleys which were broad and open. They avoided the narrow canyons which in rainy seasons could fill rapidly with catastrophic torrential flood waters, destructive to life as well as roadbeds. The narrow valleys also offered convenient hiding places for attack by robbers and enemies. Where there were no roomy valleys people preferred the hilltops between canyons for roadways, as for the only route between the Cisjordanian hill country and the coastal plain referred to in early narratives, the " ascent " or the " descent from Beth-horon " (Josh. 10 : 10, 11). According to its name this road ran past two places called Beth-horon, Upper and Lower Beth-horon (now Beit ʻŪr el-Fōqah and Beit ʻŪr et-Taḥtah). Thus, it followed the hilltop between two canyons, Wādi Selmān to the south and Wādi ʻAin ʻArīk to the north. It began north of the Valley of Aijalon (see p. 60) near the modern village of Beit Sirah, ascended from there without great hindrances, passed Gibeon (el-Jīb), and finally reached the north-south hill country route a little north of Gibeah (Tell el-Fūl). The last section of this cross road is certainly the *mesillah* from Gibeah to Gibeon referred to in Judg. 20 : 31. (On the text of this verse see p. 85.) Farther south there certainly were several ways to get from the coastal plain into the Judean hill country. Later on the Romans had a presumably important line running from Eleutheropolis (Arabic, Beit Jibrīn; Isr., Beth Gubhrin) to Jerusalem. It ran through the broad valley Wādi es-Sant (Arabic), the Terebinth Valley [Valley of Elah] referred to in I Sam. 17 : 2, 19 and 21 : 9 [21 : 10 in Hebrew]. It then rose past the former Arab town of Beit Nettīf into the hill country region of Bethlehem. That this was an old well-used route seems probable from the fact that Rehoboam built the two fortresses of Azekah (Arabic, Tell Zakarīyeh; Isr., Kephar Zekharyah) and Soco (Arabic, Khirbet ʿAbbād) at its lower starting-point, as cited in II Chron. 11 : 7, 9. This fortification system of Rehoboam was intended in part to protect the most important approaches to the Judean hill country from hostile attack.[88]

From the very beginning, the most convenient way from the Samaritan hill country down into the coastal plain was certainly through the broad valley that moves westward from Shechem, known in its upper reaches as Wādi Nāblus and below as Wādi Zeimir. This valley reaches the coastal plain near Ṭūl Karm. Early narratives make no reference to this route. From the coastal plain just south of Carmel convenient ways ran through the Bilād er Rūḥa referred to on p. 87 into the Plain of Jezreel, reaching the region of the great east-west depression which runs from that plain to the broad valley of the Nahr Jālūd (Isr., Ḥarodh) adjoining its eastern end. This provided an easy route from the Mediterranean coast to the Jordan Valley.

Between the Cisjordan hill country and the great rift valley in the east the Old Testament notes various " ascents " [Hebrew, *maʿaleh*]. In the extreme south the " Ascent of the Scorpions " (Maʿaleh ʿAqrabbim) led from the Negeb into the Wādi el-ʿArabah. It is repeatedly mentioned as a border point (Num. 34 : 4; Josh. 15 : 3; Judg. 1 : 36). It is not easy to locate. It is probable that it was on the line known in Arabic as Naqb eṣ-Ṣafah and therefore on the line of the later Roman road from Mampsis (Kurnub) to Eiseiba (Arabic, ʿAin Ḥaṣb; Isr., Hasebah).[89] The maʿaleh haṣ-Ṣiṣ referred to in II Chron. 20 : 16, according to the context in which it appears, must have run up into the Judean hill country from somewhere in the neighbourhood of ʿAin Jidi (Isr., ʿEin Gedhi). Its course can no longer be located. It could have gone to Tekoa (now

[88] G. Beyer, *ZDPV*, LIV (1931), 111–34.

[89] On this road, see M. Harel, *IEJ*, IX (1959), 175–79; on the general Roman road system of this region, see A. Alt, *ZDPV*, LVIII (1935), 51 ff.

Khirbet Tequ'), one of the fortresses of Rehoboam according to II Chron. 11 : 6. This was scarcely a heavily travelled road. Then again the Ma'aleh Adhummim of Josh. 15 : 7 and 18 : 17, "the Ascent at the Red (Rocks)," which linked the lower Jordan rift with the hilltops at Jerusalem. This name is certainly related to the strikingly red rocks of modern Ṭal'at ed-Damm on the road between Jericho and Jerusalem. Reference to it in the old tribal border descriptions shows that it was a very old, probably pre-Israelite trade route. A route which passed modern Ṭal'at ed-Damm must have come up from the Jordan rift over the heights south of Wādi el-Qelṭ, like the older Jericho-Jerusalem highway. Then it would probably have reached the top of the Mount of Olives by way of Wādi es-Sidr. Farther north the broad Wādi el-Fār'ah was the natural line for an ascent from the Jordan rift into the heart of the Samaritan hill country. However, this ascent was by no means a straight road to Shechem. The only approach is Wādi Beidān, an extremely deep canyon, ascending from upper Wādi el-Fār'ah into the plain of Shechem. Now, this was the line of the Roman road built from Neapolis (Nāblus) to Scythopolis (Beisān).[90] It is also followed by the modern highway from Nāblus to the Jordan rift, but it is hard to believe that it was ever a natural trade route. In ancient times one would much more probably have gone from upper Wādi el-Far'āh across the not too difficult heights north of Ebal into the basin of Samaria. There one would have used the west-northwesterly road through Wādi Zeimir to reach the coastal plain. Probably there was also an ancient way through Wādi el-Khashneh, later used by the Roman road from Neapolis-Scythopolis, from the southern end of the "broad opening of Beisān" into the north Samaritan hill country. At the upper end of this valley was Bezek (now Khirbet Ibzīq), where according to I Sam. 11 : 8 Saul mustered his military forces in preparation for crossing the Jordan rift to relieve Jabesh-gilead. There were also cross roads in Galilee north of the great depression of the Jezreel Plain between the Plain of Acco and the uppermost Jordan rift valley. However, on this we have nothing in ancient writings.

We know very little about the ascents from the Jordan rift into the Transjordan hill country. The modern roads in this region are entirely construction projects and scarcely indicate natural routes. We can scarcely tell where Ma'aleh hal-Luḥit, the "Ascent of Luhith" is located. It is mentioned in Isa. 15 : 5 and Jer. 48 : 5, together with the "way of Horonaim" or the "descent of Horo-

[90] Sec. XXXI in Thomsen (cf. p. 118, note 39).

naim," as leading into the land of the Moabites. It could be in the region of the southern end of the Dead Sea and therefore far outside the Israelite territory or again somewhere near the northern end of the Dead Sea. Of course, at the northern end of the Dead Sea there were various possibilities of ascent into southern Belqā, periodically occupied by the Israelites. An ancient route could have run along the line of the later Roman road from Livias (Tell er-Rāmeh) to Esbus (Ḥesbān),[91] which reached the high Transjordan plateau south of Heshbon on the ridge which rises in stages between Wādi Hesban in the north and Wādi 'Oyūn Mūsah in the south. Perhaps the relative broad lower Wādi Kefrein a little farther north offered a possibility of entry into the Transjordan hill country. The location of the city of Betonim (Josh. 13 : 26), identical with that of modern Khirbet Baṭneh about 5 km. [3 miles] southsouthwest of es-Salṭ, seems to suggest that the once heavily travelled road from the Jordan rift through Wādi Ḥseīniyāt into the Transjordan plateau south of es-Salṭ was a route used in ancient times.[92] The Old Testament (Judg. 8 : 4 ff.) specifically mentions only the way which was presumably customary and important in ancient times. This led from Succoth (Tell Deir 'Allah) through the broad lower part of the valley of the Nahr ez-Zerqā (Jabbok) first to Penuel (Tulūl edh-Dhahab), ascended through the easily travelled Wādi Ḥejjāj to reach the plateau, and then continued in the direction of Jogbehah (now Jbeihah), mentioned in Judg. 8 : 11. Another Roman road must have climbed Wādi Ḥejjāj along approximately the same line from the Jordan rift into the Transjordan hill country.[93] The area of settlement at the northern end of the 'Ajlūn hill country certainly had its road connection with the Jordan rift south of the Lake of Tiberias, too, though we know nothing definite about its course. Perhaps the Ishmaelite caravan of Gen. 37 : 25 followed this route, coming " from Gilead " to reach Dothan (Tell Dōtān) by way of the valley of the Nahr Jālūd (Isr., Ḥarodh) and the southern tip of the Plain of Jezreel (Gen. 37 : 17). The kings of Israel with their chariotry also had to follow this line, when they set out from their capital, Samaria, to the Israelite-Aramaean battlefield at Ramoth-gilead (Tell Ramīth), as recorded in I Kings 22 : 29 and II Kings 9 : 16.

The highways to neighbouring lands were also important to

[91] Sec. XXVI in Thomsen (cf. p. 118, note 39).
[92] Outlined by T. Fast, *ZDPV*, LXXII (1956), 150; cf. Noth, *ZDPV*, LXXV (1959), 44–45.
[93] On the group of Roman milestones south of Ṣubeiḥi and the conclusions which can be drawn from them, see Noth, *ZDPV*, LXXIII (1957), 38 ff.

ancient Palestine. The shortest and natural way to Egypt ran from the southwestern corner of the Palestinian coastal plain through the Sinai Desert along the Mediterranean coast to the eastern extremity of the Nile Delta. It was already provided with the necessary well stations by the Egyptian pharaohs, particularly those of the nineteenth dynasty for their Palestinian and Syrian campaigns.[94] This is the route referred to in Exod. 13 : 17 as the "way of the land of the Philistines," from the standpoint of Egypt.

Naturally, caravan trails went south and east from Palestine through the bordering deserts on these sides. Perhaps Num. 33 : 3–49 implies such a caravan trail to the northern end of the Gulf of el-ʿAqabah, a trail which continued into northwestern Arabia.[95]

The road connections between Palestine and its northern neighbour Syria were particularly important, offering further traffic with Asia Minor or Mesopotamia. The coastal route north from the Plain of Acco offered itself for this traffic. This line had already been used a great deal in pre-Israelite times, especially by the Egyptian pharaohs—note the reliefs of Rameses II on the cliffs overhanging the Nahr el-Kelb at Beirut. The pharaohs maintained coastal fortifications here[96] which were also accessible by sea. Still, this coastal line had its natural difficulties in that the headlands of Rās en-Nāqūrah (Isr., Rosh han-Niqrah), Rās el-Abyaḍ, Rās Nahr el-Kalb, and Rās Shakkah fall off directly into the sea. These difficulties were overcome during pre-Israelite times by cutting out roadbeds from the rock, as can be shown at Rās Nahr el-Kalb. For practical purposes, the coastal road led only as far as the northern end of Lebanon; farther north, at the foot of the Nuseiriyeh Mountains, it ended in a blind alley at the mountain massif Jebel el-Aqraʿ, still heavily forested and jutting out into the sea. Through traffic had to go inland north of Lebanon through the broad plain at the mouth of the Nahr el-Kebīr to the valley of the Orontes and continue on a northerly course to the east of the Orontes. Therefore, as early as pre-Israelite times an easterly route from Palestine to the north was frequently preferred, beginning from the uppermost part of the Jordan rift. One could reach this point from all parts of Palestine on various routes. From the coastal plain the way there led across Bilād er-Rūḥa and through the Plain of Jezreel and then either through the river valley of the Nahr Jālūd (Isr., Ḥarodh), or across the not too difficult south-

[94] See A. H. Gardiner, "The Ancient Military Road between Egypt and Palestine," *JEA*, VI (1920), 99–116.

[95] Noth, *PJB*, XXXVI (1940), 5–28.

[96] Alt, *BBLAK* (*ZDPV*), LXVIII, No. 2 (1950), 97–103 [reprinted in *KS*, III, 107 ff.]

eastern part of the Galilean hill country. From the uppermost part of the Jordan rift, however, one could travel a road already used by Egyptian pharaohs and later by Assyrian and Babylonian kings with their armies. That road went through Merjʿoyūn and over low elevations into Wādi et-Teim. Following this wādi valley, which had some short difficult stretches, the way opened into the broad Beqāʿ between Lebanon and Antilebanon at modern Masnaʿ.[97] It was also possible to go northeast from the uppermost Jordan rift valley heading toward Damascus. From Damascus one could go farther northeast of Antilebanon along the inner edge of Syrian settlement. The route most preferred in ancient times for the ascent from the Jordan rift was perhaps that across the rather steep mountain ridge between the lower Yarmuk and the southern part of the Lake of Tiberias. It reached the plateau of Jōlān at modern Fīq. This Fīq in all probability is at the site of ancient Aphek, referred to in I Kings 20: 26, 30 and II Kings 13: 17. As an Israelite-Aramaean battlefield it seems to have been an important road point. It is not known whether the route was available in ancient times which has been followed since Arab times, namely the route across the Jordan bridge of Jisr Benāt Yaʿqūb (south of Lake Ḥūleh) to Jōlān and on to Quneiṭrah.

10. *Political Divisions*

(1) *The Period of Israelite Independence*

In the period of the Judges, by and large the land was divided politically between Israelite tribes and " Canaanite " city-states. The territories of the Israelite tribes, treated above on pp. 53–75, had constituted the area of the twelve-tribe federation, a sacral arrangement with a sanctuary as centre. At the same time, as a combination of the Israelite tribal segment of the population, this had some political significance. The Canaanites had lived beside some of them, politically divided into their individual small city-states. In spite of the complex manner in which Israelites here or there lived near or again among the Canaanites during the period of the Judges, probably neither friendly nor hostile relations between them were very marked, except for special situations, such as the entrance of the city of Shechem into confederation with the tribe of Manasseh. That was changed with the rise of the kingdom

[97] Noth, *ZDPV*, LXXI (1956), 61–62.

among the Israelites. At all events, the kingdom of Saul was still essentially limited to the Israelite tribes and their areas, omitting the " Canaanite " cities.[98] The description given in II Sam. 2 : 9 of the region[99] which was ruled by Ishbaal, the son and successor of King Saul, apart from the fact that Judah is missing, having gone over to David in the meantime, gives a picture of the size of the first Israelite kingdom, which in its limitation to the areas of the Israelite tribes had very complicated borders and was still very roughly defined.

David then subjected the Canaanite city-states to himself, united their territories politically with the areas of the Israelite tribes in a larger unit, and thus created an outwardly integrated state in Palestine, in which all of the internal tensions between Israelites and Canaanites still remained. The evidence for this is II Sam. 24 : 6–7, according to which the officers sent out by David for the census passed through Israelite as well as Canaanite regions on their way through the country; therefore, both now belonged to David's realm. On the other hand, it was under David that a strained relationship between the group of Israelite tribes living in the south and the central and northern tribes became a political division. This had deep roots in the past. Later on it also deeply affected the history of the period of the Kingdom. David had let himself be crowned by Judah, according to II Sam. 2 : 1–4a. That means he was crowned by the tribe of Judah, including the smaller tribes to the south (see pp. 55–57). Meanwhile, after the death of Saul the remaining tribes at first acknowledged his son, Ishbaal. Only after various disorders and after the death of Ishbaal did these tribes too make David their king (II Sam. 5 : 1–3). As a result, it was through two different constitutional acts that David received kingship over all the Israelite tribes; from then on there were two different kingdoms, even though under David and Solomon they still remained united under the royal control.

After the death of Solomon this personal union fell apart. The smaller southern kingdom bore its appropriate name " Judah "; the larger northern kingdom claimed for itself the inclusive name " Israel," on the basis of the fact that it included the majority of

[98] On this and the later developments see especially Alt, " Die Staatenbildung der Israeliten in Palästina," *Leipziger Dekanats Programm* (1930) [reprinted in *KS*, II, 1–65]. Saul seems to have attempted to subjugate only the Canaanite cities lying in the region of his own tribe of Benjamin (see II Sam. 4 : 3, 21 : 1). These are the cities which, according to Josh. 9 : 17, stood in an old covenant relationship with Benjamin.

[99] Instead of *ha-Ashuri*, *ha-Asheri* should be read, referring apparently to the Galilean hill country.

the Israelite tribes. From then on the name Israel had a double meaning. In the religious language it remained the general name of the people of the twelve tribes, including Judah. As a partner of the covenant with Yahweh, Israel remained alive as a unit above the political divisions; in the constitutional language, however, Israel became the official designation for the state of Israel as over against the state of Judah. The border between the two states was at first the border between the tribal areas of Judah and Benjamin. The Judean hill country, with parts of the Shepelah and the Negeb, constituted the territory of the state of Judah; the Samaritan and Galilean hill country, now including the areas of Canaanite city-states which lay at the fringes of these mountains, and Israelite Transjordan made up the territory of the state of Israel. Now the old Canaanite city-state of Jerusalem lay on the border between the tribes of Judah and Benjamin. David's soldiers conquered it (II Sam. 5 : 6–9) to make this city his capital (" the city of David," II Sam. 5 : 9). It was in a neutral area between his two kingdoms, Judah and Israel, and thus made it possible for David to rule both " impartially " from then on without preference for either of them.[100]

From Jerusalem, David ruled almost all of Palestine in its broadest geographical sense. Apparently only the Philistines remained independent of him. In fact, he decisively conquered even the Philistines according to II Sam. 5 : 17–25 and 8 : 1, and supplanted their hegemony in Palestine, although they continued to exist in their old political form in their five cities on the southern coastal plain. (Only the Philistine city of Gath soon thereafter lost its independence and, at least temporarily, became a part of the state of Judah; see II Chron. 11 : 8.) Still, he made the remaining neighbours dependent on him in various ways. He conquered Edom, subjected it (see II Sam. 8 : 13, emended text; cf. *BH*; I Kings 11 : 15, 16), and degraded it into a province administered by governors (II Sam. 8 : 14). Under Solomon, Edom partially regained its independence under its own kingship (I Kings 11 : 14–22, 25a, b, emended text). However, during the period of the kingdom, Edom at times became a province of the state of Judah, either in part or as a whole (see I Kings 22 : 48–50; II Kings 8 : 20–22, 14 : 7, 16 : 6). David made Moab a vassal state obliged to pay tribute through its own kings (II Sam. 8 : 2), and it remained dependent on the state of Israel until the middle of the ninth century

[100] See Alt, " Jerusalems Aufstieg," *ZDMG*, LXXIX (1925), 1–19 [reprinted in *KS*, III (1959), 246–57].

B.C., when the Moabite king, Mesha, succeeded in making Moab independent again (II Kings 3 : 4–27), and in adding a part of the Belqā as well (note the Mesha inscription described on p. 219). David subjected Ammon (II Sam. 10 : 1 ff., 12 : 26 ff.) and, taking the place of native kings, set the crown of Ammon on his own head (II Sam. 12 : 30). Apparently Ammon won its independence again soon after David or Solomon. At least, our earliest evidence comes from the middle of the ninth century in the large monolith inscription of the Assyrian king, Shalmaneser III, in which an independent king of Ammon is mentioned.[101] David set up a province for the Arameans with Damascus as its seat of government (II Sam. 8 : 6), though it is not clear which of the small Aramean states on the northeastern border of Palestine the province included. The great kingdom of Aram-Ṣobhah, at any rate, probably remained independent; after its defeat by David, it seems to have escaped by paying tribute (II Sam. 8 : 7–8; cf. 10 : 15–19). Under Solomon, a native kingdom became established in the Aramean province and laid the basis for an Aramean kingdom which soon became strong (I Kings 11 : 23–25aα).

Concerning the internal division in the states of Israel and Judah, we have a valuable document from the time of Solomon. According to I Kings 4 : 7–19, Solomon divided the state of Israel into twelve districts.[102] Each one of these districts was to provide the royal court in Jerusalem for one month a year with the needed requirements of farm produce and cattle (4 : 7; 5 : 2, 3, 7, 8). The list of districts in I Kings 4 : 8 ff. gives a picture of the extent of the Israelite state under Solomon and shows, at the same time, how the old borders between Israelite tribal regions and Canaanite city-state territories, which were now united under a single state structure, had to be considered when the districts were arranged. Some districts lay on Israelite tribal territory, as the district of the " hill country of Ephraim " (v. 8), the district of Ramoth-gilead (v. 13) in the area of Manassite new settlement at the northern edge of the Ajlūn hills, the district of Mahanaim (v. 14) in the area of new Ephraimite settlement in Transjordan south of the Jabbok, the district of Naphtali (v. 15) in northeastern Galilee, the district of Asher (v. 16) in western Galilee, the district of Issachar (v. 17) in southeastern Galilee, the district of Benjamin (v. 18), and the district of " land of Gad "[103] (v. 19a) in the Belqā. Other districts

[101] Luckenbill, *Ancient Records of Assyria and Babylonia*, I, Art. 611.

[102] See the basic work by Alt, " Israels Gaue unter Salomo," *BWAT*, XIII (1913), 1–19 [reprinted in *KS*, II, 76–89].

[103] " Gad " should be read instead of " Gilead," which stands in the text.

embraced Canaanite city-state areas, for example, the three districts of v. 9–11, the city-state regions in the coastal plain, and the district of v. 12, including the Plain of Jezreel and the plain of the River Jālūd (Isr., Ḥarodh).

For want of pertinent references, we do not know whether Solomon also similarly divided the territory of the state of Judah into twelve districts. Only in a later period do we hear of a division of Judah into districts (see pp. 98–100).

The division of the Kingdom after the death of Solomon (I Kings 12 : 1–24) signified only the separation of Israel and Judah, which had previously been politically distinct and were now held together only by a personal union. Of course, this event shifted their common border somewhat. Most of the territory of Benjamin, which under David and Solomon had belonged to " Israel," from now on belonged to Judah. (The portion of Benjamin along the Jordan Valley, including Jericho, continued with the state of Israel (see I Kings 12 : 34). In the hill country, on the other hand, the national boundary ran approximately along the northern Benjaminite border.) For Jerusalem, which continued with the Davidic dynasty in the state of Judah, and which lay on the border toward Israel and Judah, the territory of Benjamin furnished a buffer toward her now hostile northern neighbour, Israel. See I Kings 11 : 32, where by " the one tribe," just this part of Benjamin is meant, which, " for the sake of Jerusalem," should stay with the descendants of David. Thus there was a separate precinct, under the term " land of Benjamin," next to Judah and Jerusalem under the rule of the Davidic family (see Jer. 17 : 26, 32 : 44, 33 : 13).

Only once in the period of the Kingdom, as far as we know, did an Israelite king try to win back the region of Benjamin, at least in part. According to I Kings 15 : 17 ff., about 900 B.C. King Baasha of Israel, in the course of his war against King Asa of Judah, began to construct the city of Ramah (today, er-Rām), which lay in the middle of the Benjaminite region about 10 km. [6 miles] north of Jerusalem, as a border fortress. Asa, however, won the help of the Aramean king of Damascus, so that Baasha now had to defend himself against Damascus and Asa got freedom of action. Thereupon, Asa himself constructed Geba (today, Jebaʿ) about 11 km. [7 miles] northeast of Jerusalem and Mizpah (modern Tell en-Naṣbeh), 12 km. [7·5 miles] north of Jerusalem, as Judean border fortresses. Thus, from that time on the boundary between Israel and Judah crossed the watershed of the mountains north of Mizpah and then ran southeastward, probably along the course of the deeply eroded Wādi eṣ-Ṣuweinīṭ. This boundary line seems to have been maintained during the rest of the period of the kings. At any rate, at the end of the seventh century B.C., according to II Kings 23 : 8, Geba was still a northern border city of Judah. The course of the border of Israel and Judah west of the watershed cannot be as definitely fixed. The city of Kiriath-jearim (Arabic, Deir el-Azhar near el-Qiryeh), long connected with Benjamin, probably belonged to the state of Judah in the period of the Kingdom after the death of Solomon. At any rate, it was settled by Judeans, according to I Chron. 2 : 50 ff. and Josh. 18 : 14. Farther to the west in the Shephelah, according to II Chron. 11 : 10 and II Kings 14 : 11, the state of Judah possessed the Canaanite cities of Aijalon (today, Yālo) and Beth-shemesh (Arabic, Tell er-Rumeileh near the spring of 'Ain Shems). According to I Kings 4 : 9, both of these had been part of the territory of the state of Israel under David and Solomon. This means that after Solomon's death both of the southern districts of Israel (I Kings 4 : 9, 18) were taken over by Judah.

The division into twelve districts must have been maintained in Israel after the death of Solomon, even if certain changes in detail were made with regard to the territorial losses mentioned. We discover a little more from ostraca, which have been dated in the reign of Jeroboam II, found in the American excavations at Samaria, the later capital of Israel.[104] They are records of wine and oil deliveries from vineyards and olive groves which were in the king's possession as crown lands, scattered here and there in the general neighbourhood of the capital city Samaria.[105] Some of these ostraca mention a district in which the royal domain lay, and the reference to a " district " seems to imply subdivision of the province " hill country of Ephraim,"[106] and to show that the subdividing took account of the historical borders between the regions of the Israelite clans and the territories of previous city-states. The names of these districts are almost all known from the clan subdivisions of the tribe of Manasseh in Num. 26 : 30–33.

We have a valuable document on the inner division of the state of Judah in the list of sites in Josh. 15 : 21–62; 18 : 21–28 (19 : 2–7).

[104] Published by Reisner, Fisher, and Lyon, *Harvard Excavations at Samaria, 1908-1910* (1924), I, 227–46; II, Plate LV (photograph).

[105] Noth, " Das Krongut der israelitischen Könige und seine Verwaltung," *ZDPV*, L (1927), 211–44; *PJB*, XXVIII (1932), 54–67.

[106] See I Kings 4 : 8. Probably only one district (*shrq*) was outside this province in the province neighbouring it on the west, mentioned in I Kings 4 : 10, on the interior rim of the coastal plain. On this question, see also Maisler, " Der Distrikt šrq in den samarischen Ostraka," *JPOS*, XIV (1934), 96–100.

As Alt has shown,[107] these lists of sites, divided into a number of sections, refer to a complete list of the twelve districts of the state of Judah with the towns they included, dating from the reign of Josiah, king of Judah, i.e., from the last quarter of the seventh century.[108] The details of this district system show, as would be expected, that the system itself was older than the time of Josiah, but on the other hand could only be dated later than the death of Solomon, since some districts lay together, or almost together, in regions which came under Judah only after the complete separation of Israel and Judah.[109] In other respects, however, this district system is linked with old historical boundaries.

The numbering of the districts simply follows the order of their appearance in Josh. 15 : 21 ff. This order itself depends on a geographical arrangement not consistently developed.

The tenth district embraced the actual tribal area of Judah (see pp. 69–70); the ninth district, an old city-state territory which had been occupied rather early by the tribe of Judah. Those regions settled by Judeans rather early by the tribe of Judah. Those regions settled by Judeans in the Shephelah west of the hill country were included in the second and fourth districts. The region of the tribes which had settled south of Judah on the mountains (see pp. 81–82) made up the seventh and eighth districts. The eighth district seems to have enclosed the region of the Kenites (see p. 82). The sixth district, which lay south of the eighth, perhaps originally was the territory of a former Canaanite city. The first district consisted of those semi-nomadic regions of the Negeb which belonged to the state of Judah, while the third seems to have combined the territories of Canaanite city-states in the southern part of the Shephelah. The area of the former southwestern district of Israel (I Kings 4 : 9), which became Judean after the death of Solomon, was the basis of the fifth district, which was greatly extended to the northwest into the region of Jaffa (Arabic, Yāfa) by Josiah's conquests. The eleventh and twelfth districts were the tribal area of Benjamin, which previously had also belonged to Israel. The eleventh district was in the area of the city-states which were confederated with Benjamin according to Josh. 9 : 17, and now included Jerusalem. The twelfth district was in the Benjaminite tribal area east of the

[107] "Judas Gaue unter Josia," *PJB*, XXI (1925), 100–16 [reprinted in *KS*, II].

[108] F. M. Cross, Jr., and G. E. Wright, *JBL*, LXXV (1956), 202–26, basically agree on a dating in the ninth century. They propose a somewhat different division of the districts. Especially, they do not consider the fifth district treated in the following as belonging to the system.

[109] Details of the system are given in Noth, *Das Buch Josua*, *op. cit.*, pp. 14, 92 ff. 111 ff., and p. 91 (map).

watershed. This latter district was also greatly extended by conquests of Josiah. It included areas such as Benjaminite Jericho and Ephraimite Bethel which had remained in the state of Israel after the death of Solomon. The district system in its preserved form, therefore, presupposes approximately that stage in Josiah's expansion which underlies II Kings 23 : 15–18.

One sees that in Judah, too, the partition into districts was not undertaken systematically; rather, it consistently took into account the old historical divisions of the state.

(2) *The Period of Foreign Domination*

Palestine came under the control of dominant Near Eastern powers in the eighth century B.C. The Assyrian empire (see p. 201) was the first of these, and in accordance with its policy, it incorporated the conquered territory into its provincial system.[110] In 733 B.C., Tiglath-pileser III took from Israel all of the fringe areas to the north, west, and east, leaving only the Samaritan hill country in the dependent vassal state of Israel. At that time he divided the three annexed regions into three newly arranged provinces. He combined the portion of Israel on the Galilean hills with the Plain of Jezreel into a province, which received its official name, Megiddo (Assyrian, Magiddu), from the city which then became its capital.[111] The northern part of the coastal plain which until then had belonged to Israel became the province of Dor (Assyrian, Du'uru), which again, in accordance with Assyrian practice, was named after its capital. Israelite Transjordan was constituted as an Assyrian province under its old territorial name Gilead.[112] Israelite territory east of the Jordan in the eighth century probably included only the 'Ajlūn and the northern part of the Belqā, and consequently the Assyrian province of Gilead must have been limited to this area, for the northern part of Transjordan on both sides of the Yarmuk and to the north, in so far as it had ever belonged to Israel, was then under the Aramean kingdom of Damascus. With the subjection of this kingdom by Tiglath-pileser III in 732 B.C., the provinces of Qarnini and Haurina were founded. This area was

[110] On this see E. Forrer, *Die Provinzeinteilung des assyrischen Reiches* (1921), and Alt, "Das System der assyrischen Provinzen auf dem Boden des Reiches Israel," *ZDPV*, LII (1929), 220–42 [reprinted in *KS*, II, 188–205].

[111] This province seems to have been further extended during the seventh century into the Plain of Acco and at that time Acco probably replaced Megiddo as the capital. Details are given in Alt, *PJB*, XXXIII (1937), 67 ff. [reprinted in *KS*, II].

[112] The Assyrian form of the name seems to have been Gal'aza. This reading, however, is questioned. See Alt, *ZDPV*, LII (1929), 239–40 [reprinted in *KS*, II].

incorporated into the Assyrian provincial system along with other provinces taken from the previous Aramean kingdom in northern Transjordan. The province of Qarnini probably included Jōlān and Nuqreh. It, too, was named after its capital, Karnaim (now Sheikh Sa'd), as seen in Amos 6 : 13, I Macc. 5 : 26, 43, 44, and II Macc. 12 : 21, 26. On the other hand, the province of Haurina must have included the region of Jebel ed-Drūz, and probably extended from there across the Yarmuk. (The name Hauran appears in Ezek. 47 : 16, 18. It seems to refer to this very Assyrian province, for names of other Assyrian provinces occur in this context.) In 721 B.C., the Assyrian king Sargon II put an end to the truncated state of Israel and established its area as an Assyrian province, which also received the name Samaria (Assyrian, Samerina) from its capital. From then on the name Samaria, which at first applied only to the capital of the kings of Israel (Hebrew, Shomeron; note I Kings 16 : 24; now Sebaṣṭīyeh), became the name for the entire region of the hills of Ephraim. Shomeron was used in this manner in II Kings 23 : 19. From then to the present day " Samaria " has been used chiefly as a territorial name, after the Assyrian custom of naming the provinces of their kingdom after their capitals.

Following the Assyrian conquests in the last third of the eighth century the states of southern Palestine—Judah and the Philistine states in the west, and Ammon, Moab, and Edom in the east—were dependent vassal states with their own dynasties, parallel with the Assyrian provinces. This vassal relationship was interrupted only temporarily, once during the disorders that followed the death of Sargon (705 B.C.), and then during the period of the final decline and fall of Assyrian power in the last third of the seventh century. For a while an Assyrian governor was situated in the Philistine city of Ashdod.[113] Generally speaking, however, the Philistine cities were vassal areas under their own kings.

The heirs of Assyrian control in Syria and Palestine, first the Neo-Babylonian kingdom (605–539 B.C.) and then the Persian kingdom (539–333 B.C.), simply took over the Assyrian provincial system.[114] Only here and there did they expand it further. Unfortunately, we know very little about Neo-Babylonian measures in this regard. Of primary concern here is the fate of Judah. After the first defeat of Jerusalem by Nebuchadnezzar (597 B.C.), Judah became

[113] See Forrer, *op. cit.*, p. 63.

[114] The advance of the Judean king Josiah into the Assyrian province of Samaria (II Kings 23 : 19) and on into the Assyrian province of Megiddo (II Kings 23 : 29) and the province east of the Jordan was an episode which came to an end with the death of the king; Noth, *ZAW*, New Series XIX (1944), 52.

a Babylonian vassal under a new king, retaining its former borders.[115] The remaining portion of Judah lost its last shred of independence after Nebuchadnezzar's second conquest of Jerusalem (587 B.C.). The Davidic dynasty was set aside and the upper classes were led away to Babylonia, but the conquerors probably did not transplant a new upper stratum from elsewhere, as the Assyrians had done previously in Israel. Instead, the Babylonians apparently set up a provisional rule for the territory of truncated Judah. They perhaps did not make a special province of this small area, but subordinated it to the governor of the neighbouring province of Samaria, thereby setting the stage for the role which the governor and the officials of Samaria played when the post-exilic community was constituted in the former state of Judah in the beginning of the Persian period.[116]

The Persians were the first ones to intervene and set up a partially new order. Darius I (521–485 B.C.) created the well-known division of the great Persian empire into satrapies,[117] in which Palestine and Syria were joined in the great satrapy described in Herodotus iii. 91 as the "fifth." This satrapy was called *ʿabar naharā*, "Across the River"; i.e., beyond the Euphrates (so in Ezra 4 : 10 ff.; 5 : 3,6; 6 : 6,8,13; 7 : 21,25) in Standard Aramaic, the official language, especially in the western and southwestern regions of the Persian empire. In the great trilingual Persian-Babylonian-Elamite inscriptions of the Persian kings, the Babylonian text presents this name of this satrapy as Ebirnari. The Persian and Elamite texts surprisingly assign to it the name Assyria. "Assyria" as a name had here undergone a remarkable change in meaning.[118]

Within this great unit of the satrapy the individual provinces, most of them dating from Assyrian times, probably were maintained in their old condition; only in the south of Palestine did the Persians set up new provinces. Thus, under Artaxerxes I (465–424 B.C.), Judah was constituted as a separate province, and in

[115] On the events in Jerusalem and Judah during 598–97 B.C., see Noth, *ZDPV*, LXXIV (1958), 133–57.

[116] For further details see Alt, "Die Rolle Samarias bei der Entstehung des Judentums," *Festschrift Otto Procksch* (1934), pp. 5–28 [reprinted in *KS*, II (1959), 316–37].

[117] See O. Leuze, "Die Satrapieneinteilung in Syrien und im Zweistromlande von 520–320," *Schriften der Königsberger Gelehrten Gesellschaft, geisteswissenschaftliche Klasse*, Eleventh Year, Sec. 4 (1935).

[118] Note the building inscription of Darius I in the royal palace of Susa recorded in F. W. König, "Der Burgbau zu Susa," *MVÄG*, XXXV (1930), 1, Art. 6, pp. 32, 39, 43. The Persian-Elamite usage of Assyria as the name of this western satrapy was probably responsible for the name Syria assigned by the Greeks to approximately the same region. See Galling, *ZDPV*, LXI (1938), 85 ff.

445 B.C. Nehemiah was sent there (Neh. 2 : 1 ff.) as governor (Hebrew, *peḥah*; Neh. 5 : 14, emended text, and elsewhere). From the Book of Nehemiah, particularly Neh. 4: 1, 2, we discover something about the neighbouring provinces, perhaps likewise set up for the first time by the Persians.[119] The province of Ashdod lay west of Judah in the area of the former Philistine states. This province was named after its capital, which had already been a governor's seat under the Assyrians. In the east we find the province Ammon, whose area extended from the old Ammonite land (see p. 80) westward to the Jordan and, therefore, included the northern part of the Belqā. A corresponding province called Moab was probably situated east of the Dead Sea. We discover nothing about it in Nehemiah, only because it did not border on Judah. But south of Judah on the southern part of the Judean hill country and in the Negeb was the province which seems for a time to have been named Arabia (see p. 83). In the later Persian period it was apparently joined to the old Edomite land east of the Wādi el-'Arabah in a governmental unit under the name of Idumea, corresponding to " Edom."[120]

The Persian empire was overthrown by Alexander the Great. After the Battle of Issus in 333 B.C., Syria and Palestine fell under his control. After his death and the disorders which followed it, in 301 B.C., Palestine fell under the rule of the Ptolemies, whose capital was Alexandria in Egypt. We hear nothing specific about the division of Palestine in the century of Ptolemaic rule, not even from the " Zenon " papyri, the commercial papers of Apollonius, the finance minister of Ptolemy II, whose commercial transactions included Palestine, too. The Ptolemies must have made the division into *nomoi* which was customary with them.

As a result of the Battle of Paneas (today, Bāniyās at the foot of Hermon), in 198 B.C., Palestine fell to the Seleucids, whose capital was Antioch of Syria. The Seleucid kingdom was divided into " satrapies." We can no longer understand details of this process, because no consistent terminology is used. Palestine probably belonged to the satrapy called " Coele Syria and Phoenicia." The satrapies were apparently divided into " Parts " (*Merides*), which might have corresponded to the Assyrian provinces. The smallest units were the toparchies, which in Palestine (see I Macc. 11 : 28, 34), as in the time of the Ptolemies, were called *nomoi*.[121] This

[119] Alt, *PJB*, XXVII (1931), 66–74 [reprinted in *KS*, II, 338–45].
[120] Noth, *ZDPV*, LXVII (1944–45), 62–63.
[121] See E. Bikerman, *Institutions des Séleucides* (1938), pp. 197 ff.; also U. Kahrstedt, *Syrische Territorien in hellenistischer Zeit* (1926), pp. 46 ff.

division into toparchies continued within the Hasmonean state which arose from the battles of liberation of the Maccabees against Antiochus IV, Epiphanes (175–164 B.C.). Beginning with Judea, in time most of Palestine west and east of the Jordan was brought under Hasmonean rule.[122]

Finally, the period of Roman rule in Palestine began with Pompey's appearance there in 63 B.C. Originally Rome ruled through a system of vassal states and city territories. These vassal cities included the Hellenistic cities on the Mediterranean coast and the cities of the Decapolis (Matt. 4 : 25; Mark 5 : 20, 7 : 31), in Transjordan, together with one in Cisjordan, namely Scythopolis, once called Beth-shan, but today called Beisān. Under Roman rule there was a transition to provinces which began in A.D. 6 after the removal of Herod's son Archelaus. Herod's new city of Caesarea on the Mediterranean coast became the capital and residence of the procurator. The Roman provinces were divided internally according to city and colonial regions, domains, legion estates, and the like.[123]

[122] Kahrstedt, *op. cit.*, Maps IIb, IIIa.

[123] On this Roman provincial system in Palestine in its developed form, see Avi-Yonah, " Map of Roman Palestine," *QDAP*, V (1936), 139–93, and map.

PART TWO

ARCHEOLOGY OF PALESTINE

CHAPTER I

INTRODUCTION

11. *Concept and History*

WE no longer use the word archeology simply in the general sense of " study of antiquity," although this fits the basic meaning of the word. Josephus uses it in that way in his history of the people of Israel called *Archaiologia*. We now use the word rather as a technical term for the study of the material remains of a bygone culture and history, hence in a more restricted sense.[1] In this sense archeology represents a special field in the study of antiquity as a whole, parallel to research into literary sources. Hence, the archeology of Palestine means the study of remnants of its extremely varied history which are available and can be located. Human existence has left its traces from its very earliest beginnings in Palestine as everywhere else, in so far as the nature of the remains permitted their preservation through centuries and millennia. These remains include the earliest and most primitive tools of the earliest inhabitants, who lived as hunters or fishermen, and the ruins of ancient settlements, still small and simple, as well as the ruins of great architectural structures and artistic works of refined cultures. The manifold stages of the history of the land continuing up to the present are still clear to one who understands how to interpret the relics properly, even though there are missing features and though history is seen only from the standpoint of cultural development. For that reason, archeological materials are a source of information for historical research which cannot and must not be ignored, once they have been disclosed. Certainly biblical research cannot ignore the abundant conclusions of the archeology of Palestine.

Palestinian archeology has become an important auxiliary to the study of the total history of Palestine, including its biblical portion. Old Testament study can overlook Palestinian archeology all the less, since interest in biblical history first motivated archeological

[1] In the second half of the last century archeology frequently meant presentations of cultural history, which were based chiefly on literary sources, or again it meant descriptions of ancient institutions and customs important in biblical interpretation. This use should now be avoided.

work in Palestine and for a long time directed its archeological efforts. There has been interest in this land's biblical antiquities since the days of the early Christian Church, ever since Christian pilgrims began to travel this land and to hunt for the "holy" places mentioned in Old and New Testament accounts, and to link what they found on the spot with these accounts. This preliminary stage of archeological observation was essentially a matter of considering the local situation on the basis of correct or false local traditions and relating the familiar recorded incidents.

Scientific archeological work on the soil of Palestine began in the eighteen-sixties. It followed still older archeological activity in the rich cultural areas along the Nile and in Mesopotamia. It naturally began in Jerusalem, because it was hoped that remnants of a great past would be found in this city so important in history. This hope was not realized. Archeological finds are fragmentary and disconnected in Jerusalem, since it has been repeatedly destroyed and rebuilt and is still inhabited today. Thus, the finds made there could scarcely become the basis of an archeologically verified cultural history of the land, nor could they firmly establish the historical and biblical meaning of the individual finds.

Systematic archeological work began only in 1890 when Flinders Petrie, an Englishman, began to dig into a mound called Tell el-Ḥesi on the coastal plain about 25 km. [15 miles] east of Gaza to study carefully the features of the cultural strata lying one on top of another in one section of the mound and at the same time to note especially the apparently valueless small finds whose significance was not immediately clear. He paid particular attention to the earthenware pottery found in great quantities, usually shattered, which had different features in each cultural period. Thereby, Flinders Petrie introduced the study of pottery into Palestinian archeology. Pottery can always be found in abundance at the site of any ancient settlement, as a criterion for dating individual settlements and settlement levels. Pottery, whose characteristics and peculiarities change from one period to another, has remained to the present moment one of the most significant distinguishing marks for dating ancient settlements. Therefore, with the excavation on Tell el-Ḥesi the archeology of Palestine actually began to stand on its own feet. Here for the first time the work of excavation was undertaken independently, and not on the basis of biblical accounts in a search for definite finds expected and looked for at the given spot. (Of course, Tell el-Ḥesi was chosen for excavation on the erroneous assumption that it was the mound of the city of Lachish

mentioned in the Old Testament. The name Tell el-Ḥesi was supposed to be derived from Lachish. Yet this idea did not essentially affect the excavation itself.) Rather this site of ancient settlements was surveyed on the basis of whatever ancient remains it contained, even if the work was incomplete and tentative. By that fact archeological work began to free itself of dependence on the literary record and to go its own way. Its new objective was the gathering, comparison, and then explanation of archeological finds arising directly from comparison of data independent of the literary record, even though with continuing interest in the history of the land based on the literary tradition. A whole series of excavations of old mounds in different parts of Palestine, undertaken by various nations, had followed the excavation of Tell el-Ḥesi before the First World War. Excavation work began again in earnest after the war. Techniques were constantly improved. Furthermore, work was now sustained by societies and institutes of many nations. The work was almost completely interrupted by the Second World War. When once again it got under way, it did so with the support of the new state of Israel established in Palestine and its projects in antiquities.[2]

The archeology of Palestine today is a discipline in its own right. It has brought so much material to light that it is now possible to sketch a fairly detailed outline of the cultural development of the land in the millennia of its history without constant reference to transmitted literature. The picture provided by archeology naturally is not without gaps. It still needs verification and occasional correction in many details. The independent position of archeology has made it not less important for the understanding of the history of the land, especially of its biblical history. On the contrary, it now represents a relatively independent source of knowledge parallel to the literary records. In most cases it is also possible to establish a firm date for finds on purely archeological grounds and within a relatively small margin of time. Therefore, the historical significance of these finds can be determined now with far more prospect of being right than when men simply looked for some archeological find which corresponded to a literary account and did not stop to consider sufficiently the archeological stratification or the archeological interrelationships. Often enough as a result they arrived at random identifications which later proved to be false.

[2] With reference to Israel, see the survey of S. Yeivin, "A Decade of Archaeology in Israel, 1948–1958," *Publications de l'Institut historique et archéologique néerlandais de Stamboul*, VIII (1960).

12. *Literature*

The results of archeological work in Palestine are published in innumerable works and articles too numerous to list here. There are detailed publications of excavations for the great digs; a number of them are presented on pp. 125 ff. in their particular context. Series of volumes containing primarily archeological materials are, *The Annual of the Palestine Exploration Fund* (hereafter referred to as *PEF Ann.*), which has appeared so far in six volumes between 1911 and 1953; and *The Annual of the American Schools of Oriental Research* (*AASOR*) which has appeared annually since 1920. *The Quarterly of the Department of Antiquities in Palestine* (*QDAP*) was published during the British Mandate, beginning in 1931. *The Annual of the Department of Antiquities in Jordan* has been published since 1915 in Jordan. In Israel the journal *'Atiqot, The Journal of the Israel Department of Antiquities* has been published since 1955. Current preliminary reports of excavations and news of smaller investigations have appeared and continue to appear in the journals mentioned above on p. 6.

Summaries of the results of archeological work in the form of chronologically arranged descriptions of individual cultural periods on the basis of the material remains from the beginnings of civilization up to and including the Roman-Byzantine times are provided by P. Thomsen, " Palästina und seine Kultur in fünf Jahrtausenden," *Der Alte Orient*, Vol. XXX (1931), with a series of textual illustrations and plates; C. Watzinger, *Denkmäler Palästinas*, I (1933) and II (1935), likewise with abundant illustrative material; W. F. Albright, *The Archeology of Palestine* (1949, with subsequent editions and translations in other languages) in the Pelican Books series; K. Galling, *Biblisches Reallexikon, Handbuch zum Alten Testament*, First Series, I (1937), who presents and explains the finds from about 1800 B.C. to the Hellenistic-Roman period under a great number of alphabetically arranged catch words and illustrates them with many textual illustrations. Abundant archeological material is provided in G. E. Wright, *Biblical Archaeology* (1957), translated into German as *Biblische Archäologie* (1958), which presents a history of Israel based on archeology. In similar fashion the results of archeology are described in the Bible atlases, listed on p. 5. Many illustrations of excavation finds arranged as a presentation of the cultural history of Israel can be found in I. Benzinger, *Hebräische Archäologie*,[3] I (3rd ed.; Angelos-

[3] The word archeology is still used here in the sense indicated in note 1.

Lehrbücher, 1927). A whole series of archeological finds is also presented in picture form by H. Gressman, *Altorientalische Bilder zum Alten Testament* (2nd ed., 1927), with concurrent short explanations. Still more illustrative material is presented in the similarly planned work of J. B. Pritchard, *The Ancient Near East in Pictures Relating to the Old Testament*, hereafter referred to as *ANEP* (1954). A special segment of Palestinian archeological material is treated in S. A. Cook, *The Religion of Ancient Palestine in the Light of Archeology: The Schweich Lectures on Biblical Archaeology*, 1925 (1930); W. F. Albright, *Archaeology and the Religion of Israel* (2nd ed., 1946), also translated into German. A. G. Barrois, *Manuel d'archéologie biblique*, I (1939), II (1953), provides a good survey of the results of archeology in connection with the literary accounts of the Old Testament. Palestinian archeology is included in an extensive survey of the spiritual development of mankind in W. F. Albright's *From the Stone Age to Christianity: Monotheism and the Historical Process* (2nd ed., 1946) [Doubleday Anchor edition with a new introduction, 1957], translated into German under the title, *Von der Steinzeit zum Christentum* (1949) as Vol. LV of the *Sammlung Dalp*.

A short summary of the current state of the results of Palestinian archeology can be found in G. E. Wright, "The Archaeology of Palestine," in *Essays in Honor of William Foxwell Albright* (1961), pp. 73–112. Sites in modern Jordan having antiquities are shown on the "Archeological Map of the Hashemite Kingdom of the Jordan," (1949–50) 3 sheets, 1 : 250,000.

13. *Cultural Periods*

Whoever investigates the material remains of the past in a land like Palestine with its long and changing history will do well first of all to orient himself at least roughly as to what he should expect in this respect, i.e., to picture for himself how many different historical phenomena and reconstructions the land has seen one after another on its soil and what sorts of monuments and other traces each one of these different past epochs has left behind. At no time in history did Palestine live apart in isolation; at any given time, it was included in larger cultural circles, which have tied the individual lands together since primeval times in the Mediterranean area, especially in the eastern half of the area. Therefore, we

encounter all sorts of phenomena on the soil of Palestine which are well known from other lands; our previous encounters make it easier for us to interpret the diversity of the objects from the past which confront us as observers in Palestine. In what follows, we reverse the historical process to show how the individual historical periods appear in the light of archeology.

(1) *Turkish Period*

If we disregard the decades since the First World War with their extremely rapid Europeanization and Americanization of the life and culture, particularly in the larger cities—whose external marks are easily recognizable—the last significant historical epoch is the period of Turkish rule, which lasted exactly four hundred years.[4] Most of what can be seen in settlements now—or until recently—occupied naturally dates from this period, including most of the mosques[5] and Moslem burial sanctuaries[6] one sees. This is true of the present wall of the old city of Jerusalem,[7] which of course rests on more ancient foundations, and also of most of the still-used churches and foundations of the various Christian confessions, which on the whole date only from the nineteenth century. (Even the church of the Holy Sepulchre in Jerusalem in its present exterior appearance dates no farther back than 1808 when the original structure was burned.) Particularly representative structures from this period are somewhat scarce, since Palestine was only a border region of lesser importance for the Turkish state.

(2) *The Mameluke Sultans*

During the preceding period the Mameluke sultans exercised rule over Palestine from about the middle of the thirteenth century.[8] Their capitals were Cairo and Damascus. In their period, too, Palestine played only a minor role. Only a few structures remain, such as the " white mosque " in the city of er-Ramleh on the coastal plain with

[4] In the winter of 1516–17 the sultan of Ottoman Turks, Selim I, conquered Palestine; in 1917 and 1918 the British occupied the land in various stages.

[5] See as examples the illustrations in Ebers and Guthe, *Palästina* (1882), I, 92, 201, 257, 273, 303, 322; II, 152.

[6] For example see Guthe, *Palästina* (2nd ed., 1927), Figs. 68, 89 (in colour); *64 Bilder aus dem Heiligen Lande* (Württembergische Bibelanstalt), pp. 11, 15 (both in colour).

[7] Guthe, *op. cit.*, Figs. 38 (in colour), 117.

[8] For this and the following sections see R. Hartmann, *Palästina unter der Arabern 632–1516*, *Das Land der Bibel*, I (1915), 4 and the pertinent passages in P. K. Hitti, *History of Syria Including Lebanon and Palestine* (2nd ed., 1957), pp. 407 ff.

its minaret which can be seen from far off.[9] Other witnesses to the Mameluke period are the following repeatedly altered and repaired Jordan bridges: Benāt Ya'qūb[10] between Lake Ḥūleh and the Sea of Tiberias; Mujāmi[11] at the lower end of the Sea of Tiberias; and ed-Dāmyeh, now beside the mouth of the Jabbok's shifted river bed.

(3) *The Crusaders*

Palestine itself was the centre of interest in a very different manner during the next preceding period, a time of occidental rule. In A.D. 1099 Jerusalem was occupied for the first time by an army of Crusaders. In A.D. 1291 the Crusaders lost the city of Acco, their last possession on Palestinian soil, to the Mameluke sultan. This period embracing almost two hundred years left a considerable number of structures behind, though they are now for the most part in ruins.[12] Their occidental structural style makes it easy to recognize them. They have such features as early Gothic pointed arches. The Crusaders quite understandably made additions to the chief Christian sanctuary of the land, the Church of the Holy Sepulchre in Jerusalem. The remains of their activity are still evident there. Some of the occidental structures are churches like St. Anne's Church in the Old City of Jerusalem,[13] or St. John's Church in modern Sebaṣṭīyeh,[14] where the ancient city of Samaria once stood, or the Crusaders' Church in modern Kiriath-jearim (Arabic, el-Qiryeh) west of Jerusalem.[15] Some are city fortifications like the walls of Caesarea[16] and Acco.[17] Some are knights' castles or fortresses of orders, like the fortress that belonged to the Knights Templars, called Castellum Peregrinorum (" Pilgrim fortress "), now called 'Atlīt, on the coast between Caesarea and the point of Mount Carmel,[18] and the fortress Montfort (Arabic, Qal'at

[9] Illustrated by Guthe, *op. cit.*, Fig. 83 (in colour). See also the exact cross-section and vertical projection diagrams in Mayer, Pinkerfeld, *et al.*, *Some Principal Muslim Religious Buildings in Israel* (Jerusalem, 1950), Plates XIX–XXI.

[10] F.-M. Abel, *Géographie de la Palestine*, I (1933), Plate XV, 1.

[11] *Ibid.*, p. 164, Fig. 8 (diagram); *PJB*, II (1906), Plate II, 2 (photograph).

[12] The map, *Palestine of the Crusades* (published in 1938 by the *Survey of Palestine*), locates the settlements of the crusaders and their various institutions in the land. It is " a map of the country on a scale of 1 : 350,000 with historical introduction and gazeteer " (C. N. Johns).

[13] Illustrated in G. Schoene, *Jerusalem* (1961), Fig. 21.

[14] See the diagram by Ebers and Guthe, *op. cit.*, I, 269.

[15] R. de Vaux and A. M. Steve, *Fouilles à Qaryet el-'Enab Abū Gōsh* (Palestine, 1950), pp. 95 ff., Plates I, II, XII.

[16] Ebers and Guthe, *op. cit.*, II, 127, 129, 131, 133.

[17] Dalman, *Hundert Fliegerbilder*, No. 60.

[18] Ebers and Guthe, *op. cit.*, II, 119, 121, 123; Hommel-Schneller, *Durchs Gelobte Land*, Fig. 8.

el-Qurein), northeast of Acco in the West Galilean hill country,[19] which was in the possession of the Teutonic Order after 1229. The large castle Qalʿat er-Rabaḍ, visible at a distance on a knoll just west of the town of ʿAjlūn, was built in Crusader style immediately after the fall of the Crusaders. Fortresses and castles from Crusader days, reflecting the feudal knightly way of life, are to be found in many spots in the land. They were once seats of " Frankish " nobility. (Anything from the occident is called " Frankish " in Arabic-speaking countries, a practice dating back to the time of the Crusaders.) Examples are Kōkab el-Hawā, a high point between the Sea of Tiberias and Beisān, the site of the Crusader fortress Belvoir; or (Arabic) Qāqūn on the coastal plain southeast of Caesarea, the Caco of Crusader times; or the prominent height of Ṣūbah (Isr., Ṣobhah) in the Judean hill country west of Jerusalem. Hence, the Crusader period left behind numerous and characteristic signs of its life and activity in Palestine, even though the largest and strongest Crusader fortresses were built not here, but in the north, in Syria.

(4) *Arabian Rule*

The period of the Crusaders was preceded by the period of Arabian rule over Palestine, divided into successive dynasties, beginning with the Arabian conquest of the land from A.D. 634–40. First there were the Omayyads, residing in Damascus. After 750, they were followed by the Abbasids, living in Baghdad. Finally, after the second half of the tenth century, there were the Fatimids with their capital at Cairo.[20] The time of Omayyad and the early Abbasid rule was the most brilliant period of early Islamic history, while decline began under the later Abbasid rulers. The period of the latter did not leave any marks in the land worth mentioning. The magnificent structure " Dome of the Rock " (Arabic, Qubbet eṣ-Ṣakhrā) in Jerusalem[21] dates from the Omayyad period. It was erected over the rock which had been Jerusalem's sacred spot since primeval times. At first, as long as Mecca and Medinah were not yet subjected to the Omayyads, it was considered a sanctuary opposed to the spirit of these centres of Islam, but later it became and to the present moment it has remained the most important

[19] Range, " Montfort," *ZDPV*, LVIII (1935), 84–89, Figs. 8–10.

[20] I omit details of the history of these dynasties. See R. Hartmann, *op. cit.*

[21] Frequently illustrated, e.g. in Guthe, *op. cit.*, Figs. 6, 105 (interior), 107; *64 Bilder aus dem Heiligen Lande*, *op. cit.*, pp. 57, 64 (both in colour); Hommel-Schneller, Fig. 31; Dalman, *Hundert Fliegerbilder*, Nos. 5, 6 (the entire sacred precinct).

holy place of the Muslims next to those two sites. It is the most splendid monument of the early Islamic period on the soil of Palestine. Otherwise, the Omayyad period left to Palestine castles for royalty and nobility, like the desert castle Mshettah on the eastern edge of Transjordan southeast of 'Ammān[22] and the completely ruined castle at the ruins of Khirbet Mefjir in the Jordan Valley north of Jericho,[23] and the Fortress of Khirbet el-Minyeh on the northwestern shore of the Lake of Galilee.[24] The remains of an early Arabian *khān* from about the middle of the ninth century, a station on the road leading from Jerusalem into the western coastal plain, have been uncovered and identified at Kiriath-jearim (Arabic, el-Qiryeh).[25]

(5) *Byzantine Period*

The Byzantine period made a greater impact on Palestine than the Arabian one which followed, because it controlled all of life there. It reached from the time of Emperor Constantine to the Arabian conquest and can be designated as the period of the ancient Christian Church in Palestine. It is therefore characterized first of all by the church buildings, which are easily distinguished by their Byzantine style from the Crusader churches and the churches of the modern period. We are here dealing with splendid imperial buildings. Thus, Constantine had the basilica Anastasis (" the Resurrection ") built on the site of the Holy Sepulchre in Jerusalem, of which indeed only very scanty and concealed remains survive; an approximate picture of its original form can be gained from the way it is portrayed on the Byzantine geographic mosaic in the ancient Christian church of Medeba in southern Transjordan.[26] The most important monument of imperial Byzantine church architecture in Palestine, still relatively well preserved, is the Church of the Nativity in Bethlehem, an early Christian basilica, which was built by Constantine and restored and altered in some detail by Justinian.[27]

[22] Guthe, *op. cit.*, Figs. 157, 158.

[23] D. C. Baramki, *QDAP*, V (1936), 132–38; VI (1937), 157–68; VII (1938), 51–53.

[24] A. M. Schneider and O. Puttrich-Reignard, " Ein frühislamischer Bau am See Genesareth," *Palästina-Hefte des Deutschen Vereins vom Heiligen Lande*, Heft 15 (1937), and O. Puttrich-Reignard and A. M. Schneller, *op. cit.*, Heft 17–20 (1939), pp. 9–33.

[25] De Vaux and Steve, *op. cit.*, pp. 58 ff., Plates I ff.

[26] Guthe and Palmer, *Die Mosaikkarte von Madeba* (1906) with ten plates, Jerusalem on Plate VII; also M. Avi-Yonah, *The Madaba Mosaic Map* (1954), Jerusalem on Plate VII. Also see especially P. Thomsen, *Das Stadtbild Jerusalems auf der Mosaikkarte von Madeba, ZDPV*, LII (1929), 149–74, 192–219, with coloured plates, Jerusalem on Plate VI.

[27] The interior is portrayed by Guthe, *op. cit.*, Fig. 91.

The Byzantine basilica of ancient Emmaus (Roman-Byzantine Nicopolis, now called 'Amwās)[28] is still standing in ruins. So, too, is the Byzantine cloister church on Mount Nebo.[29] Only a part of the foundation of the *Theotokos* church, an octagonal structure, built at the end of the fifth century by Emperor Zeno on Gerizim, is preserved.[30] Other Byzantine structures are countless smaller parish churches all the way down to very unpretentious simple village churches. Today they lie in ruins wherever there has been no new construction on the old foundations, and are often only recognizable by their floor plans. The characteristic outline of the apse, usually at the eastern end, clearly sets them off as churches. There was the central apse and frequently two additional side apses and various possibilities of the exterior outline. Often, to our surprise, mosaic floors are found, even in simple country churches, with designs most conventional in the later Byzantine period, whose motifs are drawn frequently from the mosaic art of the Roman villas and therefore are predominantly of " secular " content, with all sorts of geometric designs, with inscriptions of their originators, and the like.[31] One still frequently encounters settlements in the border regions of the land which are characterized by Byzantine churches although they have not been regularly inhabited for a long time. The Byzantine period was the high point of the development of Palestine with reference to the extent of settlement. Finally, the synagogues of the younger type also belong in the Byzantine period. (On the synagogues of the older type see p. 118.) Only the floor plans remain, similar to those of the churches, even including the apse, without such extensive use of mosaic floors. Yet these synagogues are clearly distinguished from churches in most cases by their orientation in alignment with Jerusalem and through the presence of the customary synagogal symbols in the figures on the mosaic floors and in the relief decoration, in so far as it can be found yet in the ruins *in situ*.[32]

[28] L. H. Vincent and F.-M. Abel, *Emmaus, la Basilique et son histoire* (1932).

[29] S. Seller, " The Memorial of Moses on Mt. Nebo, I, II," *Pubblicazioni dallo Studium Biblicum Franciscanum*, No. 1 (1941).

[30] A. M. Schneider, *BBLAK*, LXVIII, No. 3 (1951), 217 ff., Figs. 2–12, Plates I-III.

[31] See, for example, A. M. Schneider, *Die Brotvermehrungskirche eṭ-Ṭabgha am Genesarethsee und ihre Mosaiken* (1934). A compilation of the mosaic floors of Palestine is available in M. Avi-Yonah, *QDAP*, II (1933), 136–81; III (1934), 26–27, 49–73, with additions to the list in the course of the following years. The church mosaic of Medeba mentioned above, with its geographic design, is an unusual if not singular instance.

[32] Note, especially for its many very good illustrations, B. Kanael, *Die Kunst der antiken Synagoge* (1961). On synagogues in general, see E. L. Sukenik, *Ancient Synagogues in Palestine and Greece, The Schweich Lectures of the British Academy, 1930* (1934).

(6) *Roman Rule*

The period of well-organized Roman rule also thoroughly left its impression on the land and its remains still can be found everywhere. Roman features continued on into the Byzantine period, which then added Christian monuments. Direct Roman rule began with the decline of the various governments of the Herods in the course of the first half of the first century after Christ. One can still see the ruins of the great Roman cities which were among the most important elements in Roman provincial rule, and which were given a considerable measure of local autonomy and often very extensive territories. We have a relatively well-preserved example of such a spaciously laid out and wealthy city with temples, theatres, forum, and colonnaded streets in the ruins of ancient Gerasa, now Jerash; in the Transjordan ʿAjlūn,[33] less extensive because it has been settled down to the present time; in Roman Philadelphia, now ʿAmmān, on the upper course of the Jabbok;[34] and in various cities in modern Ḥaurān. The aqueducts[35] which provided water for these cities, still standing in ruins here and there in Palestine, are characteristically Roman.

Roman building appears also in the remains of military structures. The Romans protected the borders of their empire—and the province of Judea was initially a border province—with lines of fortresses, which are relatively easy to recognize by their architecture; they are mostly square buildings up to about 80 m. [260 feet] on each side, frequently with square corner towers with rooms laid out along the inner walls and a room left open in the middle for a court. Thus we have such a string of fortresses, the *limes Palaestinae* (" border of Palestine "), on the southern boundary of the land running from east to west laid out in the first century of our era on the border with the Nabatean kingdom which was then still independent;[36] thus, there was the *limes Arabiae* laid out after the incorporation of the Nabatean kingdom in A.D. 106 along the entire eastern boundary of Transjordan south to the Gulf of el-ʿAqabah,[37] together with various intermediate lines for linking both

[33] Guthe, *op. cit.*, Figs. 150–55; Hommel-Schneller, Fig. 26; Dalman, *op. cit.*, Nos. 91, 92 (aerial pictures with general view). For a presentation of all of the antiquities of Gerasa, based on excavations there, see C. H. Kraeling, *Gerasa, City of the Decapolis* (1938). In Byzantine times, churches were built in Gerasa.

[34] *64 Bilder . . .*, p. 21.

[35] Guthe, Fig. 21.

[36] Particulars in Alt, "*Limes Palaestinae*," *PJB*, XXVI (1930), 43–82; XXVII (1931), 75–84.

[37] More precise information in Brunnow and von Domaszewski, *Die Provincia Arabia*, I–III (1904–09).

of these border fortification systems.[38] The network of Roman highways served chiefly military purposes. By and large it was built during the first century of Roman rule in Palestine; one encounters signs of it everywhere in the land, even though they are not very obvious.[39] The pavement of the roadbed itself still stands here and there, although most of it has naturally disappeared; curbs bordered the highways, which were 3 to 5 or even 10 m. wide [10 to 30 feet]. The substantial stone curbs are still sometimes recognizable. They were as high as 50 cm. [20 inches]. The most definite distinguishing mark of Roman roads are the milestones, stone columns, approximately 2 m. [7 feet] high, consisting of a roughly cubical base, and a round upper part with a diameter of about 60 cm. [2 feet] which frequently, although not always, has an inscription ending with a statement of the respective distance in miles from a given point of departure (*caput viae*).[40] Whenever the roads were repaired, new milestones were added to the old ones, so that frequently considerable groups of milestones stand at the same place. Finally, the way stations also belong to the road system, whether places for changing horses (*mutationes*) or places for overnight lodging (*mansiones*). Remnants of such stations are still found here and there in the countryside of the land.[41]

Signs of the Roman period are the ruins of mausoleums which are found scattered through the country. They are small rectangular structures of characteristic Roman style.

Finally, the synagogues of the older type belong to the Roman period. They have no apse. Their main entrance is on the narrow end and they are oriented in the direction of Jerusalem. They are found especially in Galilee and date from the second or third century of our era.[42] Also the ruins of the synagogue of Capernaum (Arabic, Tell Ḥūm) in their present form were part of a structure of this period rather than of the time of Jesus.[43]

[38] These lie specially in the Wādi el-ʿArabah and on both sides of it; on this see Alt, *ZDPV*, LVIII (1935), 1–59, esp. 24 (map), and "Neue Untersuchungen zum limes Palaestinae," *ZDPV*, LXXI (1955), 82–94.

[39] A compilation of the highway routes and the milestones found by that date is provided by Thomsen, *ZDPV*, XL (1917), 1–103.

[40] Illustrations of Roman milestones are given, as elsewhere, in L. H. Grollenberg, *Atlas of the Bible*, Figs. 392, 393.

[41] C. Kuhl and W. Meinhold, "Römische Strassen und Strassenstationen in der Umgebung von Jerusalem," *PJB*, XXIV (1928), 113–40; XXV (1929), 95–124.

[42] Kohl and Watzinger, *Antike Synagogen in Galiläa* (1916).

[43] Guthe, *op. cit.*, Fig. 128; *64 Bilder* . . ., p. 54; Hommel-Schneller, Fig. 14; other Galilean synagogues in Guthe, Fig. 133; Watzinger, *Denkmäler Palästinas*, II, Plate XXXV.

(7) *The Time of Herod I*

The construction work of Herod I belongs both in time and in style to the early Roman period. Yet one can single out his buildings as a particular group, because they are connected with a particular name and because we are rather well informed about them by what Josephus writes of what Herod built in Palestine. Scarcely any traces remain visible of the castle of Antonia built by Herod in Jerusalem north of the temple site;[44] but remnants of the towers of the Herodian palace in the northwest of his city near the present Jaffa gate are preserved in the present citadel,[45] and especially the fine massive squared stones in the foundation of the present walls surrounding the temple precinct, as they are still visible particularly on the " Wailing Wall,"[46] date from the Herodian building of the temple. Herod also had cities built in the land on the Roman plan. On the site of ancient Samaria he built a magnificent city in honour of the emperor with the name *Sebaste*, Greek for the Latin *Augusta*. (Derived from this is the name Sebaṣṭīyeh which is carried by the village east of the location of ancient Samaria.) Parts of the Roman city wall, the forum on the east side, and the terrace of the temple of Augustus on the top of the city hill still testify to his building activity.[47] In the city of Caesarea (Arabic, Qeiṣārīyeh), which he built on the sea coast, the ruined remains of the hippodrome theatre and harbour installations testify to his activity. The fortresses once built for him in the southeastern part of his territory now lie in ruins, together with his Herodeion on the mountain now known as Mount Ferdis, about 5 km. [3 miles] southeast of Bethlehem, where he also had his tomb constructed. Another ruin is the castle, Masada, on a very steep rock (Arabic, es-Sebbeh), on the west shore of the Dead Sea. His royal palace was built on the slope of the northern peak of this rock,[48] which after the fall of Jerusalem in A.D. 70 provided the last refuge of the revolutionary Jews. Still another ruin is the castle of Machaerus, now el-Mashnaqah at Khirbet el-Mukāwer, on the east side of the Dead Sea north of the Arnon.

[44] Particulars by Vincent, *RB*, XLII (1933), 83–113; XLVI (1937), 563–70. The *Ecce Homo* Arch, remnant of a three-section Roman street arch near Antonia, was built in the time of Hadrian.

[45] Guthe, Fig. 118 and especially Hommel-Schneller, Fig. 42 ,where the Herodian foundation can still be well distinguished from the later structures.

[46] Often illustrated, as in Guthe, Fig. 113; Hommel-Schneller, Fig. 33; *64 Bilder* . . ., p. 42; G. Schöne, *Jerusalem* (1961), Fig. 19.

[47] For the forum, see Guthe, Fig. 124 and *64 Bilder* . . ., p. 36; for the temple of Augustus, see Gressmann, *AOB*, No. 649.

[48] M. Avi-Yonah, "The Archaeological Survey of Masada, 1955–1956," *IEJ*, VII (1957), 1–60 (also reprinted as a monograph).

(8) *Hellenistic Period*

The Hellenistic period began in the Near East with the conquest of the Persian Empire by Alexander the Great between 334 and 331 B.C. Of course, the Greek world exerted a definite cultural influence on Palestine long before this event, especially on its Mediterranean coast. Politically, the Hellenistic period is concerned chiefly with the dynasties of the Diadochi that followed Alexander. Palestine belonged first to the Ptolemies, and later to the Seleucids. The Maccabean (Hasmonean) state emerged through revolt against the Seleucids. The appearance of the Romans in the east had already exerted a strong influence on Seleucid history (p. 104). Among the archeological remains of the Hellenistic period one would expect especially ruins of the plans of the Hellenistic cities. From the literary tradition we know that in that period cities were newly founded at sites of older towns and were frequently named after members of the diadoch dynasties. This is true of Ptolemais at the site of ancient Acco; Philadelphia at the site of ancient Rabbath Ammon, now called ʿAmmān; Philoteria, at the site of Khirbet Kerak (Isr., Beth Yeraḥ) at the southern end of the Lake of Galilee; and Seleucia in Jōlān, now Selūqīyeh. The Decapolis (p. 104), which included Philadelphia, was made up of newly laid out Hellenistic cities, most of them on the sites of older settlements. These Hellenistic cities have left hardly any visible traces, since Roman period structures, built right where Hellenistic ones were, have erased the Hellenistic workmanship. Excavations have here and there brought Hellenistic items to light. That applies, for example, to the outline of the Hellenistic city of Marissa, Mareshah in the Old Testament, modern Tell Sandaḥanneh, near Beit Jibrīn (Isr., Beth Gubhrin).[49] It also applies to burial places there with their famous wall paintings.[50] The same is true of Shechem (Tell Balāṭah), where the Hellenistic remains form the upper stratum of debris, since the Roman settlement was built a short distance away at the site of modern Nāblus.[51] The only substantial relic of the Hellenistic period in Palestine still open to view is the ground plan of ʿArāq el-Emir in Transjordan west of ʿAmmān, probably from the beginning of the second century B.C.[52] Hence, especially because of the building activity of the subsequent Roman period

[49] See the plan by Watzinger, *op. cit.*, Fig. 22.

[50] *Ibid.*, Figs. 56, 57.

[51] See the preliminary report of L. E. Toombs and G. E. Wright, *BASOR*, CLXI (1961), 11–54, esp. 40 ff.

[52] Particulars in Watzinger, *op. cit.*, pp. 13–17, Figs. 52, 53. [For an illustrated article on this site see also C. C. McCown, "The ʿAraq el-Emir and the Tobiads," *BA*, XX, No. 3 (September, 1957), 63–67.]

in Palestine, the signs of the important Hellenistic period have been almost entirely erased. It was during Hellenistic days that the ways of life of a new world stemming from the West began to permeate Palestinian ways, to mix with the native traditions, and to change the external appearance of the land, especially in the cities.

(9) *Ancient Near Eastern Period*

If traces of the Hellenistic period occur only under the soil then we must expect that as we go farther back we arrive at cultural periods whose remains are scarcely visible anywhere in Palestine, especially in the case of building structures. Rather, covered by debris of thousands of years, they must be exposed by excavation. We group these periods together here under the general term ancient Near Eastern period. Its characteristic was the cramped living quarters of people in confined cities, usually unbaked, sun-dried brick houses, as a rule built on a low stone foundation. From this fact it becomes clear how the remains of these settlements have lasted until now. The Hellenistic, Roman, and Byzantine periods produced extensive planned cities in which at least the public buildings were constructed entirely of stone and these planned cities, in so far as the buildings themselves are not still standing, have left great stone ruins behind—such a stone ruin in the land today is usually called a *khirbeh.* On the other hand, the closely confined groups of brick houses of those older periods, after they were abandoned, mostly sank together gradually into a uniform mass and buried the low stone foundations under their debris. Wherever, then, after the destruction of such a settlement, people started to set up homes again on the same location, they did not need to remove the remains of that older settlement, but could construct their light buildings on its levelled remains. Thus gradually layer after layer was deposited. Then, wherever some sort of strong city wall held this deposit of layers together and through the centuries protected it from falling apart and washing away with the winter rain, the remains of the ancient Near Eastern cities have been maintained in the characteristic shape of table-topped knolls of built-up debris, having distinct edges and borders. Such a land formation is now known as a *tell.* The grey colour of the accumulated rubble also helps to catch the eye. Wherever this characteristic land formation occurs, one can be fairly certain that he is looking at an ancient site with pre-Hellenistic settlement levels.

Palestinian archeology has been able to ascribe the layers of

debris deposited one after the other to various distinguishable cultural periods according to definite features. In conventional terminology, these periods are named for the use of given metals. Yet the presence or lack of these metals among the finds of the excavation is not the most important or most definite determining factor in dating the individual strata; rather, pottery is used for dating.

The Iron Age preceded the Hellenistic period. This earlier cultural period began in Palestine about 1200 B.C. It is divided into Iron I, about 1200–900 B.C., therefore about "the period of the Judges," and the time of the kingdom of David and Solomon; Iron II, about 900–600 B.C., therefore the period of the coexistence of the states of Israel and Judah; and Iron III, about 600–300 B.C., therefore the period of the Persian empire.[53]

Looking farther back in point of time, the Bronze Age is next with its various stages which one dates back to about 3100 B.C. The farther one goes back in time, the more the figures given are approximate points of reference. Dating farther back than the Bronze Age, the dates are very unrelated to neighbouring cultures in which written documents giving possibilities for reliable dating extend to the beginning of the third millennium (see pp. 203 ff.). Still farther back one is dependent on estimates, in so far as organic material found does not allow for the radiocarbon test which provides valuable results, but provides only dates with a considerable margin of uncertainty for such early periods. One distinguishes the Early Bronze Period with various subdivisions about 3100–2100 B.C.; Middle Bronze about 2100–1550 B.C., divided into Middle Bronze I, 2100–1900 B.C., and Middle Bronze II, 1900–1550 B.C.; and the Late Bronze Age, 1550–1200 B.C., divided into Late Bronze I, 1550–1400 B.C., and Late Bronze II, 1400–1200 B.C. Toward the end of the Early Bronze Age there was a development of use of potsherds for finishing pottery.

Before the Bronze Age there is the Chalcolithic Age, "the Bronze-Stone Age," from about the middle of the fifth millennium to about 3300 B.C. The Neolithic (Late Stone) Age precedes that. During the Neolithic Age, life in compact settlements is attested.

[53] Based on more recent excavation finds, Y. Aharoni and R. Amiram, *IEJ*, VIII (1958), 171–84, have proposed a somewhat different division of the Iron Age in Palestine, namely into the following phases: Israelite I, 1200–1000 B.C., the period of the Judges; Israelite II, 1000–840 B.C., the period of the kings down to and including the first construction and development of the royal capital of Samaria; and Israelite III, 840–587 B.C., the remainder of the period of the kings to the fall of the royal capital of Jerusalem.

This includes an earlier age, during which man did not yet know the art of fashioning pottery, reaching back to the eighth millennium B.C., and a later period in which men had learned to fashion pottery.[54]

Although there were some walled settlements in the pre-pottery Neolithic Age, the scattered Chalcolithic settlements do not seem to have been walled. Therefore, they are very difficult to detect. Rather they are disclosed only to exacting exploration. The subsequent Bronze Age, by contrast, was in general the period of fortified cities with strong city walls, inside of which in the course of time series of settlement strata were deposited. Thus it was primarily the settlements of the Bronze Age which left the sites of ruins in the characteristic form of the *tell.* Such tells are found especially in the parts of the land particularly favoured by nature, in the plains along the coast, in the Plain of Jezreel, in the fertile plain in the northern part of Transjordan, and also in the Jordan Valley. By contrast, there are only a few tells in the hill country. The people of the Bronze Age often chose the edges of these plains for their site. They preferred to build their cities where small spurs of the neighbouring mountains provided a raised and more secure location, while the farm land in the plain was close by. Thus, for example, the Bronze Age cities of the Plain of Jezreel do not lie in the middle of this plain itself, but are all situated along the extended southwestern edge of the plain bordering the Samaritan hill country.

In the Iron Age, on the one hand the sites of Bronze Age settlements continued to be inhabited, and thus added some Iron Age levels on top of the Bronze Age ones; at the same time, the old Bronze Age city walls were necessarily constantly improved and elevated by means of reconstructions. Without further observation, therefore, one cannot consider whether such a *tell* contains only Bronze Age, or Iron Age levels as well.

On the other hand, at the beginning of the Iron Age, or approximately at the time the Israelites were occupying territory in Palestine,[55] new settlements arose where none had been during the Bronze Age. This was particularly true of the hill country of Judah,

[54] On the current state of research in this area see the informative survey of G. E. Wright, "The Archaeology of Palestine," in *The Bible and the Ancient Near East: Essays in Honour of William Foxwell Albright*, ed. G. E. Wright (1961), pp. 73–112.

[55] Moreover, what was said above also applies to the beginning of sedentary life for the Ammonites, Moabites, and Edomites in their areas in southern Transjordan. At about the same time the Philistines settled in the southern part of the coastal plain, but established themselves in this case in older Bronze Age cities; only the Philistine city *'Aqqaron* (p. 78) seems to have been a newly founded Iron Age city. See Alt, *PJB*, XXIX (1933), 13, n. 3.

Samaria, and Galilee and of the hill country in Transjordan. Up to that time these regions had had only a few settlements. Where possible, the Iron Age cities were also situated on knolls, preferably close to a larger or smaller section of productive farm land. Yet the Bronze Age city walls were built more stoutly than the later Iron Age walls. As a result, the Iron Age walls have not withstood the ravages of time as well as the earlier ones. Therefore, generally speaking, where Iron Age cities have no Bronze Age ruins beneath them, the remains are far more scattered, the original level has been considerably erased, and there is only a meagre amount of debris present. After the protecting retaining walls had broken down and fallen apart, the winter rain had free access, and the deposited strata of debris washed away in time. In most cases, some traces remain, particularly stone wall foundations and pottery, so that at least it can be proved that an Iron Age settlement existed. These remnants are no longer obvious, but are disclosed only by careful research.

(10) *Earliest Signs of Human Existence*

Stone implements from the various stages of the Stone Age are the most ancient signs of human existence in the land. Most of these tools have been found in caves where people lived before they made the transition to construction of settlements. Therefore, in this case we are dealing exclusively with random small finds, discovered only by careful exploration.

If we scan the series of cultural periods presented here to see what archeological materials any given period left behind, we find that, allowing for unusual single monuments, the following groups of Palestinian antiquities appear most prominently: the *tulūl*[56] of fortified cities established in the Bronze Age, the planned cities and military structures of the Roman period, the Byzantine churches, and the castles and churches of the Crusaders.

[56] Plural of the Arabic word, *tell.*

CHAPTER II

ARCHEOLOGICAL WORK

14. *Excavation Activity*

ALMOST all Old Testament history fits into the period of the ancient Near East, of which all remains are covered by a layer of debris. The very latest portions of the Old Testament belong to the Hellenistic period; the writings of the New Testament fit into the early Roman period. Wherever later periods continued to build on the same site, those remnants are buried still deeper under later ruins.

The planned cities, beginning with the Hellenistic period, were designed from a different point of view; therefore, the Hellenistic-Roman cities in many cases are situated on other sites than the older settlements under discussion. The later cities needed more room and directed less attention toward defence than the Bronze Age cities, which occupied as strong locations as possible.

Only excavation can bring the buried Old Testament cities to light. A vast amount has been unearthed since Flinders Petrie completed his first systematic excavation on Tell el-Ḥesi (pp. 108–109). The most favourable object for an excavation is a *tell* such as is described on pp. 121 ff., where one settlement followed on another without interruption, and where the cultural levels deposited on top of one another have been preserved as undamaged as possible, so that the excavator can uncover them again individually and determine their various characteristics. By means of a series of such consistent excavations of strata in which parallel observations can be made concerning the peculiarity of the individual cultural periods, it has become possible to determine the characteristic details of the archeological remains of the individual periods. They are seen in the types of buildings, in the technique of constructing city walls, in the plan and architecture of the houses and the like, as well as in the characteristics of the small finds such as metal jewelry, in which the fashion changed from time to time, and especially in the products of the pottery trade, ceramics. In this field there was naturally always a common everyday ware for general use, differing little from period to period. Hand in hand with this there were always more decorative pieces in which the peculiarities of individual periods appear clearly; apart from the evident difference between handmade and wheelmade ceramics, what matters is the rather intricate individual characteristics with reference to the composition of the clay used as material, the shaping or outline of the vessels, the modelling of the handles, the treatment of the surface of the vessels with slip or polishing, and the like, as well as the decoration.

(1) *Establishing Chronology*

Paying attention to all these points has made it possible to set up a relative chronology of the cultural periods on the basis of definite characteristics. With the help of demonstrable cultural connections from the outside, import of foreign cultural products and native copies of such imported wares, it has become possible within limits to change this relative chronology into an absolute one. By itself, the Palestinian material for the earlier periods did not permit an absolute dating, particularly because there is such a lack here of inscribed finds especially from the Bronze Age, which could have served for historical assignment of the various strata; but it has been well demonstrated that during the Bronze Age the Palestinian cultural development somewhat paralleled that of Syria; indeed, Palestine-Syria constitutes a cultural unit. Nor would the Syrian material have made an absolute dating possible if Syria-Palestine had not stood in a clearly demonstrable connection with the great neighbouring cultures during the entire Bronze Age. For the Early and also the Middle Bronze Age, it is the connections with Mesopotamia and more especially Egypt which are under consideration here. The very abundant finds of inscriptions in these areas permit us to set up a well-supported relative chronology extending as far back as the middle of the third millennium. For the late Bronze Age, strikingly strong connections with the Cyprian and Cretan-Mycenean culture are available, which for these periods determine the dating of the levels in detail. With reference to the Iron Age, matters are somewhat different. Although there are certain common features for Iron Age cultural strata, still in this period certain cultural regions developed on the soil of Syria and Palestine which were coexistent but different from one another. This is connected with the historical phenomenon that in the last quarter of the second millennium new population elements settled down in the realm of the old unified Syro-Palestinian Bronze Age city culture and became consolidated into peoples in each case with their own forms of government and their own history. Thus we have, if we again disregard Syria, even in the narrow confines of Palestine a number of cultural areas coexisting which are clearly distinguishable from one another in the style of their pottery. The relatively abundant literary materials available for the Iron Age, particularly in the Old Testament, in general permit absolute dating of Iron Age cultural levels and assigning of individual cultural areas to definite peoples. In Cisjordan we encounter the cultural area of the people of Israel and adjoining that in the southern part of the coastal plain, the cultural area of the Philistines.[1] In Transjordan east of the Wādi el-ʿArabah we have the cultural area of the Edomites and east of the Dead Sea that of the Moabites,[2] while farther north in the great bend of the upper course of the Jabbok lay the cultural area of the Ammonites.[3] In the northeastern corner of Palestine in the region of the Nuqreh we should expect to find an Aramaic cultural area according to the literary records. However, so far, careful studies on the cultural history of the Iron Age have not yet been made here.

On the whole, the archeology of Palestine has been able to depict the cultural development of Palestine in the ancient oriental period. Further disclosures will augment and improve the picture.

(2) *The Excavations Themselves*

The earlier excavation projects naturally were conducted at the ruins of cities considered important and well known in the Bible, and also cities whose sites could be identified with certainty or at least with probability. This happened in the following cases. The excavations in Jerusalem which began with soundings carried through by Charles Warren from 1868 to 1870 at the temple site and subsequently continued by others. The excavations of the German society *Verein zur Erforschung Palästinas* were instituted from 1903–1905 on the mound of ancient Megiddo, Tell el-Mutesellim, under the direction of G. Schumacher. The excavations of British R. A. St. Macalister took place at Tell Jezer, the mound of

[1] Concerning "Philistine pottery," which is determined by similarities with the Mediterranean world from which the Philistines came and which disappears in the course of the tenth century with the decline of Philistine power, see Heurtley, *QDAP*, V (1936), 90–110, Figs. 1–12, and Plates LIX, LX. See also the short survey in G. E. Wright, *Biblical Archeology* (1957), pp. 94–96.

[2] Concerning Edomite and Moabite pottery see N. Glueck, "Explorations in Eastern Palestine, I, II," *AASOR*, XIV (1934), 14 ff.; XV (1935), 1246 ff., and figures.

[3] *Ibid.*, "III," *AASOR*, XVIII–XIX (1939), 151 ff., and esp. 266–67.

Gezer, from 1902 to 1905 and 1907 to 1909. The excavations of E. Sellin from 1907 to 1909 were conducted on the mound of Jericho. The American excavations on the mound of Sebaṣṭīyeh, the site of the Israelite capital of Samaria, took place from 1908 to 1910 under G. Reisner and C. S. Fisher. Excavations were begun in 1913 by E. Sellin and continued after the First World War at the site of Shechem, Tell Balāṭah. These excavations have brought to light only a small portion of the finds which the excavators had hoped for; yet instead they frequently have produced other results than had been expected. Often these results could be analysed and explained only after further developments in Palestinian archeology, which were not available to the earlier excavators. Still, these beginnings of excavation work laid the groundwork for the very productive development of Palestinian archeology which then took place in the 1920's.

Ever since Palestinian archeology has been freed from exclusive interest in the biblical history of Palestine (see p. 107), it no longer directs as much attention to sites known from the Bible, even though up to the present most excavators desire to assign a biblical name to the site where they are working, whether definite, probable, or at least possible. Palestinian archaeology is rather directed toward objects which promise important new understandings from the purely archeological point of view, especially such ruin sites as offer many archeological levels and stratification with as little disturbance as possible.[4] It is good that this is so, for only when freed from marginal interests can archeology continually increase insight into the cultural development and the history of the land. The results of interest to research on the biblical period and its history in any given case then become self-evident.

In what follows, selected excavations will be presented which illuminate specific cultural periods and their distinctive features. The following survey is limited to Palestine and omits the comparable excavations in neighbouring lands, including those on Syrian soil. In the case of the individual excavations we do not note all the results accomplished, but only those which have become particularly important for the progress of archeological research.

Jericho is the only Palestinian archeological example of a pre-pottery and pottery Neolithic town. This is an important result of the excavations carried out from 1952 to 1958 by the British School of Archaeology in Jerusalem and several other institutions under

[4] On this see H. J. Franken, *Deir 'Allā Aims and Methods* [1961].

the direction of Miss K. M. Kenyon on Tell es-Sulṭān, the site of ancient oriental Jericho.[5]

The finds so far indicate that the Chalcolithic Age was differentiated according to periods and places. Early stages of these periods are represented again on Tell es-Sulṭān in Level VIII, as shown by the British excavations in Jericho before the Second World War.[6] The same is shown in part also on Tell Fārʿah northeast of Shechem at the upper end of Wādi Fārʿah.[7] A particular type of Chalcolithic culture was found at several locations around Beersheba, resulting in the term Beersheba culture, particularly on Tell Abu Maṭar, 1·5 km. [1 mile] southeast of Beersheba. In this case men lived in early days in underground caves and only gradually transferred to construction of clay houses above ground built on stone foundations, simultaneously making notable advances in forming stone vessels, working copper, and carving ivory.[8] Somewhat more recent than the Beersheba culture, in the last phase of the Chalcolithic Age, is the culture disclosed by the excavations of the Pontifical Biblical Institute on the mounds of Teleilāt Ghassul on the eastern side of the lower extremity of the Jordan rift valley, across from Jericho.[9] Noteworthy are the fragments of frescoes found there, and only there, which had been applied to brick walls, seemingly portraying religious, mythological patterns of unknown meaning. Based on the name of this excavation site, reference is now made to a Chalcolithic Ghassulian period and to a Ghassulian culture in connection with phenomena discovered there and at similar sites.

The transition from the Chalcolithic to the Early Bronze Age is shown by studies of lower strata in Megiddo (Arabic, Tell el-Mutesellim)[10] and Beth-shan, which is the present Tell el-Ḥiṣn near Beisān.[11] The ancient large city on et-Tell, northnortheast of

[5] See the current preliminary reports of K. M. Kenyon in *PEQ*, Vol. LXXXIV (1952) ff., and the only volume of the final report published thus far, *Excavations at Jericho: The Tombs Excavated in 1952–1954* (1960). This volume does not deal with Neolithic Jericho.

[6] J. Garstang *et al.*, *Annals of Archaeology and Anthropology*, XXII (1935), 143–84; XXIII (1936), 67–90; XXIV (1937), 35–50.

[7] See the preliminary reports on the still unfinished excavation by the excavator R. de Vaux, *RB*, Vols. LIV (1947) ff.

[8] J. Perrot, *IEJ*, V (1955), 17–40, 73–84, 167–89; H. de Conteson, *IEJ*, VI (1956), 163–79, 226–38.

[9] Mallon, Koeppel, *et al.*, *Teleilāt Ghassul*, Vols. I–II (1934–40). The Pontifical Biblical Institute resumed excavations on Teleilāt Ghassul in the winter of 1959–60. Little is yet known of the results of this work.

[10] Engberg and Shipton, *Notes on the Chalcolithic and Early Bronze Age Pottery of Megiddo* (1934).

[11] Fitzgerald, "The Earliest Pottery of Beth-shan," in *Museum Journal*, XXIV (1935), pp. 5–22.

Jerusalem, is an example of the Early Bronze Age. This site was known later, in Old Testament times, as Ai (Josh. 7 : 8).[12] There are likewise numerous Early Bronze walls, levels, and graves of Jericho.[13] Comprehensive surveys of the features of the Chalcolithic Age and the Early Bronze Age, particularly their pottery, are found in W. F. Albright, *JPOS*, XV (1935), 193–234, and in G. E. Wright, *The Pottery of Palestine from the Earliest Times to the End of the Early Bronze Age* (1937). The end of the Early Bronze Age seems to have brought a sharp break in the cultural development of the land.

The American excavation completed under the leadership of W. F. Albright on Tell Beit Mirsim, fully 20 km. [12 miles] southwest of Hebron, has become pre-eminently important for the understanding of the strata of the cultures of the Middle and Late Bronze Age and their exact dating, because here the individual strata had been particularly well preserved and the stratification during the dig was observed with exemplary care; the results were published by W. F. Albright in *AASOR*, XII (1932), 1–165; XIII (1933), 55–127; XVII (1938), 1–141; XXI–XXII (1943), 1–229. The results on Tell Beit Mirsim also clarified the true significance of the Middle and Late Bronze Age finds on Tell ʿAjjūl on the coast southwest of Gaza[14] and on Tell el-Fārʿah on the Wādi Ghazzeh about 25 km. [15 miles] south of Gaza.[15] A comprehensive treatment of the pottery of the Middle Bronze Age is provided by H. Otto, "Studien Zur Keramik der mittleren Bronzezeit in Palästina," *ZDPV*, LXI (1938), 147–277, Plates IIX–XIV. The Late Bronze Age appeared as the period of Egyptian control of Palestine especially in the corresponding strata at Beth-shan, one of the centres then of Egyptian governmental power in the land.[16] Egyptian temple floor plans also came to light in the Late Bronze Age strata on Tell ed-Duweir, the ruins of the city of Lachish referred to in the Old Testament.[17] Because of the narrative of Joshua, chapter 6, excavators at Jericho have paid particular attention to

[12] J. Marquet-Krause, *Les fouilles de ʿAy (et-Tell) 1933–35* (1949), Vols. II–I.

[13] K. M. Kenyon, *op. cit.*

[14] Flinders Petrie, *Ancient Gaza*, Vols. I–IV (1931–34). The title of the publication rests on the false assumption that Tell ʿAjjūl is the site of ancient Gaza. Against this see Maisler, *ZDPV*, LVI (1933), 186–88.

[15] Flinders Petrie, *Beth-Pelet*, Vol. I (1930). The use of the name Beth-Pelet (Josh. 15 : 27; Neh. 11 : 26) rests on a false identification.

[16] A. Rowe, *The Topography and History of Beth-shan* (1930); G. M. FitzGerald, *The Four Canaanite Temples of Beth-shan*, Vols. I–II ("Publications of the Palestine Section of the Museum of the University of Pennsylvania," 1930–40).

[17] O. Tufnell, C. H. Inge, and L. Harding, *Lachish*: Vol. II, *The Fosse Temple* (1940); Vol. IV, The *Bronze Age* (1958).

Late Bronze finds. They have wanted to establish an exact archeological dating of the arrival of Israel or at least of the tribe of Benjamin.[18] Some insignificant traces of Late Bronze settlement have been found on the mound; however, there is no trace so far of a Late Bronze wall, as required by the biblical narrative. Those city walls previously claimed to be Late Bronze have since been shown to be Early Bronze.[19]

The excavation begun in the winter of 1959–60 on Tell Deir ʻAllah in the central Jordan rift valley, near where the Jabbok flows into the Jordan, promises to become important for the period of transition from Late Bronze to Early Iron.[20] The excavations at Bethel, now Beitīn, though very limited, have produced some important new information on the break between Late Bronze and the first phase of the Iron Age. The archeological remains show the latter to be culturally much simpler, even poorer and more lacking in creature comforts.[21] The history of Israel in Palestine begins with the transition to the Iron Age.

The beginnings of the Iron Age appeared some years ago at the Danish excavation at Khirbet Seilūn in the Samaritan hill country. This was Old Testament Shiloh. It represents an early Iron Age settlement, probably destroyed by the Philistines in the middle of the eleventh century.[22] Of further importance for the Iron Age is the still unfinished dig on Tell Fārʻah, where a number of Iron Age levels with Iron Age house plans have been found.[23] These strata overlie Late and Middle Bronze levels. Then there is a break in occupation with the preceding Early Bronze and Chalcolithic (see p. 129) levels beneath. The entire Iron Age, though with breaks in occupation, is also represented on the knoll of Tell el-Fūl, 6 km. [4 miles] north of ancient Jerusalem, at Gibeah of Saul, of Old Testament fame, as the American excavations there have shown.[24] The very carefully built fortification in the second stratum from the

[18] On the difficulties of basing an Israelite chronology on archeological dating at Jericho, see Noth, *PJB*, XXXIV (1938), 7–22, esp. 14 ff.

[19] K. M. Kenyon, *PEQ*, LXXXIV (1952), 62 ff.

[20] See the initial preliminary reports of H. J. Franken, *VT*, X (1960), 386–93; XI (1961), 361–72.

[21] W. F. Albright, *BASOR*, LV (1934), 23–25; LVI (1934), 2–15; LVII (1935), 27–30 and J. L. Kelso, *BASOR*, CXXXVII (1955), 5–10; CLI (1958), 3–8.

[22] H. Kjaer, "The Excavation of Shiloh, 1929," *JPOS*, X (1930), 87–174; H. Kjaer, *I det heilige Land. De Danske ugravninger i Shilo* (1931).

[23] See the preliminary reports of the excavator, de Vaux, *RB*, Vol. LIV (1947) ff. and also the comprehensive survey in U. Jochims, *ZDPV*, LXXVI (1960), 82–92.

[24] W. F. Albright, "Excavations and results at Tell el-Fūl," *AASOR*, IV (1924), 1–160; see also the report of Albright on a subsequent short dig, *BASOR*, LII (1933), 6–12 and the evaluation of the finds based on subsequent comparative material by L. A. Sinclair, *AASOR*, XXXIV–XXXV (1960), 1–52, Plates I–XXXII.

bottom proved to be noteworthy. Its first stage belongs to the end of the eleventh century B.C. It can be identified as construction of King Saul, who resided here. The lower levels of Tell Qasīleh[25] north of Tel Aviv on the right bank of the River el-ʿŌjah (Isr., Yarqon) have yielded important archeological information on the beginnings of the Iron Age. This excavation was done by B. Mazar (Maisler). Here on the coastal plain there are remains of the early period of Philistine control and culture. Of great importance are the excavations at Hazor, instituted in modern Israel under the leadership of Y. Yadin at the important city of Hazor, known from pre-Old Testament and Old Testament sources. It was called Tell Waqqāṣ by the Arabs. It is at the western edge of the uppermost Jordan rift valley, southwest of Lake Huleh. These excavations took place from 1955 to 1958.[26] In the extremely large rectangular precinct of the lower city they have disclosed Middle and Late Bronze strata and on the *tell* proper in the southern corner of the rectangle a superimposed succession of many Iron Age strata.

For the time of King Solomon, who is described as a great builder, Megiddo (Arabic, Tell el-Mutesellim) is of primary importance; here, after the Deutscher Palästina-Verein (DPV) had already dug on this location from 1903 to 1905,[27] the American excavations begun in 1926 extensively uncovered a stratum called Level IV, counting from the top, which has been shown to be Solomonic. In particular, it contains the remains of extensive installations which clearly were horse stables. They are complexes of buildings placed around a court. Each of the buildings had a paved central passageway enclosed by two rows of pillars, on both sides of which lay stalls for the horses. Stone mangers for the horses were set at intervals between the pillars.[28] We are apparently dealing here with the chariot garrisons, which, according to I Kings 9 : 15b, 17–19, Solomon had built at various fortified places in the land, among which Megiddo is expressly named. In Megiddo at least three hundred horses could be stabled in these stalls.[29]

For Iron Age II the city Samaria, now Sebaṣṭīyeh, comes into

[25] B. (Mazar) Maisler, *The Excavations at Tell Qasīleh: Preliminary Report* (1951), reprinted from *IEJ*, I (1950–51).

[26] The preliminary reports are in *IEJ*, Vols. VI–IX (195–659). Of the final reports so far the volumes on the first two campaigns have appeared. They are Y. Yadin *et al.*, *Hazor I* (1958) and *Hazor II* (1960).

[27] *Tell el-Mutesellim*, Vol. I: *The Finds of G. Schumacher*; A. Text, B. Plates (C. Steuernagel, 1908); Vol. II: *The Finds of C. Watzinger* (1929).

[28] Watzinger, *Denkmäler Palästinas*, I, Figs. 80, 81.

[29] The final excavation report on Megiddo is given in R. S. Lamon and G. M. Shipton, "Megiddo I: Seasons of 1925–1934, *Strata I-V*," *OIP*, XLII (1939); G. Loud, "Megiddo II: Seasons of 1935-1939," *OIP*, LXII (1948).

consideration first. According to I Kings 16 : 24 it was founded by King Omri as the residence of Israelite kings at the beginning of the ninth century B.C., hence about the beginning of the cultural period Iron II, and continued as that residence for fully one-hundred and fifty years. The American excavations organized there before the First World War,[30] whose results were supplemented and extended by later excavations under the direction of the Englishman, J. W. Crowfoot, in 1931–33 and 1935,[31] have, among other accomplishments, laid bare the palace of the Israelite kings, on which various kings had built, as well as parts of the wall surrounding the Iron Age acropolis.[32] On the find of ivories see pp. 162–63, on the Samaritan ostraca see p. 220. The English excavation begun in 1932 on Tell ed-Duweir (Lachish) has produced valuable results for the period of the Kingdom of Judah (Iron II).[33] The city walls with the gate installation at the south-western corner have been studied in detail. They show a destruction of these fortifications, a rapid reconstruction, and a second destruction and burning shortly thereafter. These fortunes of the city walls are probably related to the two campaigns of Nebuchadnezzar against the state of Judah in 598 B.C. and 588–87 B.C. (II Kings 24 : 10 ff.; 25 : 1 ff.). Excavation on the mound of el-Jīb, 10 km. [6 miles] northwest of old Jerusalem, began in 1956 under the direction of J. B. Pritchard and are still in progress. Results there affect primarily Iron II.[34]

Archeological evidence of the Persian Period (Iron III) is also found at Tell ed-Duweir, where a Persian palace was uncovered on top of the *tell*; in graves of Gezer and Tell el-Far'ah;[35] and in the necropolis of 'Atlīt on the Mediterranean coast south of the Carmel peak, where a Phoenician trade colony existed toward the end of the Assyrian period and during the entire Persian period.[36]

Excavations have been undertaken at Ramat Raḥel, which is

[30] Reisner, Fisher and Lyon, *Harvard Excavations at Samaria, 1908–1910*, Vols. I–II (1924).

[31] The final report is *Samaria-Sebaste*, Vol. I: *The Buildings at Samaria* by J. W. Crowfoot, K. M. Kenyon, and E. L. Sukenik (1943); Vol. II: *Early Ivories at Samaria* by J. W. and G. M. Crowfoot (1938); Vol. III: *The Objects from Samaria* by J. W. Crowfoot, G. M. Crowfoot, and K. M. Kenyon (1957).

[32] Galling, *ZDPV*, LIX (1936), 242 ff., Fig. 16.

[33] *Lachish*, Vol. III: *The Iron Age* by O. Tufnell (1953).

[34] Preliminary reports of the director are in *The University Museum Bulletin* [Philadelphia], XXI, No. 1 (1957), 3–26; XXII, No. 2 (1958), 13–24 and *BA*, XIX (1956), 66–75; XXIII (1960), 23–29.

[35] J. H. Iliffe, "A *Tell Far'a* Tomb Group Reconsidered," *QDAP*, IV (1935), 182–86; K. Galling, "Assyrische und persische Präfekten in Geser," *PJB*, XXXI (1935), 75–93.

[36] C. N. Johns, "Excavations at Pilgrim's Castle, 'Atlīt (1933)," *QDAP*, VI (1938), 121–52.

south of Israeli Jerusalem on the eastern side of the road which once led directly from Jerusalem to Bethlehem. Small finds such as jar stampings at this site have proved important for the Persian period. Work here is filling in gaps in otherwise scattered Palestinian archeological finds from the Persian period. After an initial campaign in 1954, these excavations have continued since 1959 with abundant results. So far they have disclosed remains of the late kingdom of Judah, the Persian-Hellenistic periods and the Roman and Byzantine periods.[37]

The Hellenistic period is only very scantily represented in Palestine. During the English excavations on Tell Sandaḥanneh near Beit Jibrīn (Isr., Beth Gubhrin) in the Shephelah, which is Mareshah in the Old Testament and Marissa in Hellenistic writings, the Hellenistic ground plan of the city was revealed.[38] In Samaria, Sebaṣṭīyeh, early Hellenistic remains of a city wall, immense round towers, and a fortress were found.[39] Finally, the excavation finds on Khirbet et-Ṭubeiqah, the site of Beth-zur, referred to in the Old Testament, are important for understanding the Hellenistic period. This city once again served as a fortress during the Maccabean wars. The American excavations at this ruin site brought to light the Hellenistic fortification plans in their various stages.[40] The American excavation in progress at Tell Balāṭah (Shechem) promises new archeological material on the Hellenistic period up to the end of the second century B.C. (see p. 136).

The archeological finds on the building activity of Herod and his contemporaries pertain to the post-Old Testament period. Still, they are related to the end of the history of Israel. Excavations have been undertaken of Herodian palaces and other representative buildings in Herodian Jericho on both sides of the lower course of Wādi Qelt.[41] The palace of Herod on the steep rock of Masada (Arabic, es-Sebbeh) on the western shore of the Dead Sea[42] has

[37] See especially Y. Aharoni *et al.*, *Excavations at Ramat Rahel, Seasons 1959 and 1960* (1962).

[38] Bliss-Macalister, *Excavations in Palestine during the Years 1898–1900* (1902); Watzinger, *op. cit.*, II, 12–13, Fig. 22.

[39] *Samaria-Sebaste, No. 1* (1943), pp. 24–31.

[40] O. R. Sellers, *The Citadel of Beth-Zur* (1933); also Watzinger, *op. cit.*, II, 24–25, Figs. 19–21. Excavations at Khirbet et-Ṭubeiqah were begun again in 1957 under the direction of O. R. Sellers. See the preliminary report of R. W. Funk, *BASOR*, CL (1958), 8–20.

[41] J. L. Kelso, D. C. Baramki, *et al.*, "Excavations at New Testament Jericho and Khirbet en-Nitla," *AASOR*, XXIX–XXX (1955); J. B. Pritchard, *et al.*, "The Excavation at Herodian Jericho, 1951," *AASOR*, XXXII–XXXIII (1958).

[42] *Masada, Survey and Excavations, 1955–1956* by the Hebrew University, Israel Exploration Society, Department of Antiquities (1957). This is a reprint from *IEJ*, vii (1957).

also been studied. The manuscript finds in the caves near the northwestern shore of the Dead Sea (see p. 311) resulted in the excavations at Khirbet Qumrān, which is near these caves, and also in the region of the near-by spring of ʿAin Feshkhah to the south. These excavations were made between 1951 and 1956 and in 1958 under the direction of Père R. de Vaux. They disclosed finds from Iron II, but especially of considerable material from the first century B.C. and the first century of our era.[43] There are also the excavations on the mound at the northwestern extremity of the Jezreel Plain. The Arabs called this mound Sheikh Abreiq. It contains the remains of the ancient Jewish town of Beth-shearim. Large, elaborate Jewish graves were found, dating from the end of the second to the middle of the fourth century after Christ.[44]

Still more excavations at sites mentioned in the Bible will be presented in the following paragraphs. They have not been mentioned in the previous material because they have been rather unproductive from the purely archeological point of view. As mentioned above, from 1868–1870 the Englishman, Charles Warren, studied especially the foundations of the great wall surrounding the temple site in Jerusalem.[45] In 1881 H. Guthe, by commission of DPV, undertook an excavation on the southeastern hill of Jerusalem, now outside the city, the site of the pre-Davidic and Davidic city.[46] The excavations reported by R. Weill in *La cité de David*, published in 1920, were also directed toward this southeastern hill, as were English excavations begun in 1923.[47] On the ancient archeology, topography, and history of Jerusalem there is now the comprehensive work of J. Simons, *Jerusalem in the Old Testament* (1952), as well as the still more detailed, monumental work of L. H. Vincent and A. M. Stève, *Jérusalem de l'Ancient Testament*, the first volume of which was published in 1954, followed by two others in 1956.

In Shechem, now Tell Balāṭah, E. Sellin began an excavation in 1913, which, after being interrupted by the First World War, was

[43] The preliminary reports of the director are in *RB*, LX–LXVI (1953–59).

[44] B. Mazar (Maisler), *Beth Sheʿarim, Report on the Excavations during 1936–40*, Vol. I: *The Catacombs*, I–IV (1957, Hebrew). The excavations at Beth-shearim were begun again in 1953 and are still continuing. Preliminary reports are in *IEJ* beginning with IV (1954).

[45] Warren and Conder, *Survey of Western Palestine; The Jerusalem Volume* (1884).

[46] Guthe, "Ausgrabungen bei Jerusalem," *ZDPV*, V (1882), 7–204, 271–378.

[47] Macalister and Duncan, " Excavations on the hill of Ophel, Jerusalem 1923–25," *PEF Ann.*, IV (1926); Crowfoot and Fitzgerald, "Excavations in the Tyropoeon Valley, Jerusalem 1927," *PEF Ann.*, V (1929).

undertaken again in 1926.[48] He investigated especially walls, gate plans, buildings on the acropolis, and the great temple of Shechem. In the process, levels from the Middle Bronze to the Iron Age were found. Shechem was the most important Canaanite city in the hill country of Ephraim and still played a role in various ways in the Israelite period. In 1956 excavations were begun again on Tell Balāṭah under the direction of G. E. Wright. They are still continuing.[49] In addition to the other finds these excavations disclosed material from the Hellenistic period, the last period of settlement on Tell Balāṭah.

The city of Gezer, now Tell Jezer, on the interior edge of the coastal plain southeast of Jaffa was likewise a fortified Canaanite city. According to I Kings, chapters 9 to 16, it later was annexed by the dynasty of David and was probably enlarged by Solomon as a garrison. This city was excavated in 1902–1905 and 1907–1909 under the commission of the Palestine Exploration Fund (PEF) under the direction of Macalister,[50] and in 1934 underwent another short and limited excavation.[51] In Gezer almost all cultural levels from the Chalcolithic to the Hellenistic period were encountered.

Beth-shemesh is referred to in I Sam. 6 : 12 ff., which is concerned with the return of the ark, and in various other Old Testament accounts. It is now er-Rumeileh near ʿAin Shems in the Shephelah west of Jerusalem. English excavations were conducted there in 1911 and 1912,[52] as were American excavations from 1928 to 1933.[53] This not especially large city was occupied from Middle Bronze to Iron II.

Taanach is repeatedly mentioned in the Old Testament in conjunction with Megiddo among the Canaanite cities on the southwestern edge of the Plain of Jezreel, which probably came under the control of Israel during the reign of David. This city, now Tell Taʿannek, was partly excavated by E. Sellin in 1902 and 1903 and was studied again a year later.[54] On the cuneiform

[48] E. Sellin, "Anzeiger der Ak. d. Wiss. Wien. phil.-hist. Kl.," LI (1914), 35–40, 204–207 and *ZDPV*, XLIX (1926), 229–36, 304–20, Plates XXIX–XLVI; L (1927), 205–211, 265–74, Plates VII–XII.

[49] Preliminary reports are given by G. E. Wright and L. E. Toombs in *BASOR*, CXLIV (1956), 9–20; CXLVIII (1957), 11–28; CLXI (1961), 11–54.

[50] Macalister, *The Excavation of Gezer* (1912), Vols. I–III.

[51] A. Rowe, "The 1934 Excavation of Gezer," *PEF Qu. St.*, 1935, pp. 19–33.

[52] D. Mackenzie, "The Excavations at Ain Shems 1911," *PEF Ann.*, I (1911), 41–94; "Excavations at Ain Shems," *PEF Ann.*, II (1912–13), 1–104; CLXIX (1963), 1–60.

[53] See E. Grant, *Beth Shemesh* ([Palestine], 1929); "Ain Shems Excavations, Parts I–V," *Haverford College Biblical and Kindred Studies*, Nos. 3–5, 7–8 (1931–39).

[54] See E. Sellin, *Tell Taʿannek* (1904) and *Eine Nachlese auf dem Tell Taʿannek in Palästina* (1906), identical with "Denkschr. d. Kais. Ak. d. Wiss. Wien. phil.-hist. Kl.," L, 4; LII, 3.

tablets found during this excavation see p. 207.

Old Testament Mizpah is in all probability to be found on the present Tell en-Nasḅeh, 12 km. [7 miles] north of Jerusalem on the main road leading to the north. Here between 1926 and 1935 digs were undertaken by Americans. The results of this work, which has disclosed especially Iron Age material, are now set forth in a definitive excavation publication.[55]

Since 1953 an excavation expedition under the direction of J. P. Free has been active on Tell Dōtān. This is the site of Dothan, referred to in the Old Testament narratives of Joseph and Elisha. It is 15 km. [9 miles] northnortheast of the city of Samaria on the road from Samaria to the southern extremity of the Plain of Jezreel. Walls and strata from all stages of the Bronze Age and particularly from Iron I and Iron II were found.[56]

At the site of the sanctuary of Mamre, the setting of part of the Abraham narrative, E. Mader conducted excavations from 1926 to 1928. The site is now called Ḥaram Rāmet el Khalīl and is over 3 km. [2 miles] north of modern Hebron. No definite finds from the Old Testament period have been made *in situ*. Even the *temenos* wall surrounding the consecrated area is perhaps not, as generally assumed, Herodian, but rather only Constantinian.[57] At the same time it can scarcely be doubted that Old Testament Mamre is to be located here. The final excavation report[58] also contains information on archeological finds on Jebel er-Rumeideh, probably the site of ancient Hebron on the southwestern edge of the modern city.

15. *Surface Exploration*

A thorough archeological survey of an area requires more than excavation of remains even for the ancient oriental period, largely buried under debris. Naturally, the ancient remains are not visible to the naked eye as are the monuments of more recent periods which occasionally are disclosed simply by restoration of ruins. Even so, excavation must be supplemented by a thorough searching

[55] C. C. McCown and J. C. Wampler, *Tell en-Naṣbeh Excavated under the Direction of the Late William Frederic Bade* (1947), Vols. I–II.

[56] Preliminary reports are in J. P. Free, *BASOR*, CXXXI (1953), 16–20; CXXXV (1954), 14–20; CXXXIX (1955), 3–9; CXLIII (1956), 11–17; CLII (1958), 10–18; CLVI (1959), 22–29; CLX (1960), 6–15.

[57] F. W. Deichmann in A. Kuschke, *ZDPV*, LXXVI (1960), 11, n. 5.

[58] E. Mader, *Mambre, Die Ergebnisse der Ausgrabungen im heiligen Bezirk rāmet el-halīl in Südpälastina, 1926–28* (1957); Vol. I (text), Vol. II (plates).

of the surface of the area for all remaining traces of antiquity. A prerequisite of this latter task is the exact understanding of the marks of the individual cultural periods determined by the excavator's careful study of the strata, particularly the small finds characteristic of the given period. There are ancient oriental ruin sites which are neither rewarding nor particularly suitable for excavation, because they do not have any deposit of debris worth mentioning and certainly no undamaged stratification, but rather have almost disappeared under the impact of the centuries. That is true especially of the settlements described on pp. 123–24, which were not begun until the Iron Age. These were primarily the sites in the hill country where the Israelite tribes made their transition to sedentary life. However, various remains from that ancient period, evidences of former settlement, are still scattered about on the surface, particularly potsherds, which had been everyday household utensils, and therefore have remained lying wherever people lived. Potsherds readily withstand the destructive effects of moisture. As a criterion of chronology the distinguishing marks of pottery are therefore of outstanding importance in the investigation of the surface area, since potsherds scattered about make it possible to determine the period and length of duration of a settlement there.

The investigation of a surface area is also an indispensable supplement to the business of excavation. Only a limited number of Palestine's ancient cities have been excavated as yet. At any given time this work can concentrate on only a few areas. Therefore, it is hardly likely that all available objects for excavation can be disclosed and studied even in a systematic excavation. At this point investigation of the surface area can and must enter in as a supplement. For even on a *tell* in the sense described on pp. 123–24 only the most recent level of settlement lies just below the surface and can be reached without difficulty. Hence, it is to be expected that great quantities of debris, chiefly potsherds from periods of habitation at this site, have fallen off on the sides and still lie about on the slopes of the mound, of course without any actual stratification. By a careful, thorough search of these slopes these potsherds can still be found. They do give information about the periods in which the *tell* under consideration was inhabited in the past, even if this information cannot be as exact and complete as the results of an excavation of strata, and even if the correct dating of surface pottery and other scattered finds is frequently problematical for want of the archeological setting. In such probings, success depends more on chance than on a systematic excavation. Moreover, the excavator needs such a surface-area investigation to determine in advance whether a contemplated site promises to repay the effort to be expended on it.

Surface exploration such as described above was reinstituted in 1924, and continued until 1933, with the intention to survey all the ancient settlements in Palestine. It was led primarily by A. Alt under the society Deutsches Evangelisches Institut für Altertumswissenschaft des heiligen Landes zu Jerusalem. Its valuable results were published serially by him in *PJB*.[59] W. F. Albright, as director of the American School of Oriental Research in Jerusalem, pursued the same task in the decade after World War I and published his identifications serially in *BASOR* from 1919 on.[60] Then N. Glueck completed his own general labours in Transjordan, likewise depending on surface exploration.[61] The École pratique des Études Bibliques, whose organ is *RB*, has undertaken similar researches.[62]

Surface exploration, like excavation activity, has not by any means completed its tasks. However, it has already filled in many details of the picture of the settlement of the country in the various phases of the history of the ancient Near East.

16. *Archeological Finds and Literary Tradition*

The archeology of Palestine has actually developed into an independent science, setting its own appropriate methods and goals. Nevertheless it still has the problem of connecting archeological conclusions with the literary tradition on the history of Palestine and of using these resources jointly for historical understanding. It is, of course, necessary to apply each resource properly in the process of historical research. In such research, the significance of archeology must neither be underrated nor overrated.

[59] The geographic index in *PJB*, XXX (1934), 80–103, for the volumes *PJB*, XXI (1925) to XXX, makes readily available what was achieved in this area. Since 1953 the Deutsches Evangelisches Institut has again carried on this work in the manner inaugurated by A. Alt. Its current reports appear in *ZDPV*, beginning with the 1954 issue.

[60] The topographical index in *BASOR*, L (1933), 26–36; LXXVI (1939), 15–24; and CV (1947), 16–27, serves as a guide through these labours.

[61] See the complete publication of these undertakings in N. Glueck, "Explorations in Eastern Palestine, I–IV," *AASOR*, XIV (1934), 1–114; XV (1935), 1–202; XVIII–XIX (1939), 1–288, Plates 1–22; XXV–XXVIII (1951), 1–711.

[62] De Vaux, "Nouvelles recherches dans la région de Cadès," *RB*. XLVII (1938), 89–97 and especially "Exploration de la région de Salt," *ibid.*, pp. 398–425.

(1) *Positive Influence of Archeology*

Archeology is indispensable to the literary tradition primarily in the field of topography, that is, in the establishment of the location of the places named in the literary tradition. In what follows we limit ourselves to the biblical and particularly the Old Testament tradition. Whoever wants to assign a place mentioned in the Bible to a particular location in the terrain must ascertain that on this spot, according to the evidence of the archeological remains for the period to which the literary account refers, a settlement is demonstrable, or he must at least explain why in this case one should no longer expect to find archeological remains. The simple situation is of course not often found, where the ancient name has persisted at its original spot and the corresponding archeological remains are also present, but there are several gratifying examples of it—ancient Taanach (Hebrew, Ta'anakh), whose ruins along with Bronze and Iron Age deposits to this day bear the name Tell Ta'annek, and Bethel, where the present site lies at the spot of the ancient city, inhabited according to the evidence of the archeological finds since the Middle Bronze Age, which carries the ancient name in the somewhat modified form Beitīn, and modern Ghazzeh, which still lies partly on the *tell* which conceals the deposits of the ancient city of Gaza (Hebrew, 'Azzah).[63] Frequently, the settlement has moved to another more desirable spot within the same general location while maintaining the ancient name (see p. 125). The ancient settlement can still be found in the neighbourhood of its modern successor and its exact location can be determined by archeological identification of ancient levels of debris. In these cases, too, the situation is still relatively simple. For example, ancient Jericho did not lie on the site of the modern village of Erīḥa, which has inherited the ancient name, but rather on Tell es-Sulṭān, 2·5 km. [1·5 miles] to the northeast of it. The important ancient city of Beth-shan cannot be found at the modern town of Beisān even though its name is continued here, but rather on Tell el-Ḥiṣn, some 500 m. [0·25 mile] north of it. Ancient Shechem is not on the site of the modern city of Nāblus, whose name and location are adapted from Roman Neapolis, the successor of ancient Shechem, but some 2 km. [1 mile] east of it on the *tell* at the present village of Balāṭah. Likewise, archeolcgical work has demonstrated

[63] The phonetic changes which the ancient names have undergone in connection with the repeated change of national language, from Hebrew to Aramaic to Arabic, follow definite laws. See G. Kampffmeyer, "Alte Namen im heutigen Palästina und Syrien," *ZDPV*, XV (1892), 1–33, 65–116; XVI (1893), 1–71.

that Jebusite and Davidic Jerusalem, that is, the ancient kernel of the city which was subsequently frequently enlarged from the time of Solomon on, cannot be placed inside Jerusalem's present Old City. Rather, it lay outside on the now uninhabited Southeastern Hill south of the temple site.

The solution of topographical questions is much more difficult in the numerous cases in which the ancient name of a site has not been preserved either at the ruins or anywhere about, but has been completely lost. Then only the compilation of all of the hints in the literary tradition with reference to the site, together with an exact survey of archeological finds on the ruins in the region under question, can solve the topographical problem in such a manner that every literarily attested period of settlement can be archeologically demonstrated on the ruin in question.[64]

Over and above the individual problems of topography, archeology achieves a picture of the total history of settlement of the country, which can and must be related to the literary tradition. Thus we find out, for example, by means of archeological identifications, in which parts of Palestine those Canaanite (in archeological terminology, Late Bronze Age) cities are to be found from which the Old Testament tradition repeatedly says that the Israelite tribes could not drive out the Canaanites during their conquest (Josh. 17: 16,18; Judg. 1: 27 ff., 3: 1 ff.) Likewise, archeology shows where the towns were, which were settled only in the Early Iron Age, in which the Israelites settled down after their conquest. We now know that it was essentially a coexistence—that the plains of the country were and remained in the hands of the Canaanite cities while the Israelite tribes settled down in the hills.[65] Then, too, the question how extensively and how intensively Israel occupied Transjordan must be clarified by the archeological method,[66] with which the somewhat meagre literary accounts about this process should be compared. As the examples cited show, archeological identification and research must work hand in hand with the literary tradition in any problem concerning historical occupation.

[64] Material on previous results of topographical work with reference to Palestine is found in J. Simons, *The Geographical and Topographical Texts of the Old Testament* (1959).

[65] See especially A. Alt, "Die Landnahme der Israeliten in Palästina," *Territorialgeschichtliche Studien, Leipziger Dekanats-Programm* (1925), pp. 6 ff. [reprinted in *KS*, I, 89–125].

[66] It is relevant here to cite the archeologically possible identification of the border fortifications, namely the borders of the neighbouring state of Ammon. See H. Gese, *ZDPV*, LXXIV (1958), 55–65; Rittentschke, *ZDPV*, LXXVI (1960), 103–23; G. Fohrer, *ZDPV*, LXXVII (1961), 56–71.

Archeology and interpretation of the literary tradition naturally meet in considering cultural history in the broadest sense. The literary tradition, whether narrative or prophetic, whether wisdom sayings or legal passages, contains countless references and hints on the implements of daily life, external surroundings, the stock of commodities, the furnishing of royal residences, the inventory of the temples of the land, and the like. All these things vary from time to time. They are by nature concrete expressions of civilization, which have left tangible traces behind and therefore can still be archeologically attested. In these cases archeological finds directly clarify or even express the basic meaning of descriptive statements. Details will be discussed further in Chapter III.

Finally, the appearance of archeology has also had and continues to have a positive influence on the history of scholarship. It has helped to overcome the stage of a purely literary or literary-critical view of biblical scholarship. Through its occupation with the remains of past history it has directed attention again to the concrete content of the body of written tradition and thereby to the problem of the origin and meaning of individual parts of that tradition.

(2) *Limitations of Archeology*

The significance of archeology for the understanding of history should not be exaggerated, even though all that has been said above is important and noteworthy. One must rather understand clearly what can and what cannot be expected in this respect from archeological work. Some aspects of life are better reflected in archeology, others in literary traditions. Historical events, namely the activity of historical persons and the course of individual historical events, items which form the essential content of the literary tradition, by their very nature cannot be explained by archeology, because they have not always produced tangible or visible changes in living arrangements. On the other hand even where events have produced such changes, they are not immediately recognizable or at least not unambiguous. That is especially true of Palestine. For on its soil there is an almost complete lack of inscribed finds, which can be fitted to a given archeological situation. No inscription has been found on any structure before the Hellenistic period which gives any evidence about the name of the builder. No inscribed foundation stone or foundation document has come to light. All of the structures discovered in Palestine from the ancient Near Eastern period are anonymous. Scarcely any pre-Hellenistic burial place tells who was buried there. And yet only a record, even if it is only a chiselled name or an attached inscribed line, can lead directly to understanding of historical events.

Therefore, one cannot readily describe the result of Palestinian archeology as a confirmation of the reliability of the historical tradition. As things stand it is improper to expect such a confirmation of it; yet even in scholarly articles such statements are frequently made. There are certain classes of historical events such as conquests, destructions, and occasionally the burning to ashes of fortified cities which leave archeological traces. Even in these cases, the archeological finds by themselves scarcely ever demonstrate anything about the conditions or the historical context which caused the archeologically attested destruction of a city. The definite historical significance of an archeological find is determined only by matching it to a recorded event. In most cases archeological dating is the only basis on which the actual relationship between an account and archeological finds can be understood. If such dating can actually be determined exactly, which is not the rule, in spite of all refinement of archeological methods with the precision required for an historical interpretation, and if the dating of such finds corresponds exactly with the period in which a corresponding event is described as happening, one is actually justified in combining finds and account with one another. This is particularly true when a whole series of corresponding archeological identifications at various sites can be used for confirmation. If, for example on the territory of Judah, the archeological finds showed that cities were destroyed somewhere between 700 and 600 B.C., one would have to connect this with the campaign of the Assyrian king Sennacherib in Syria and Palestine in 701 B.C., or with the campaign of King Nebuchadnezzar, of Babylon, against Judah between 589 and 587 B.C. In either case the archeological finds illustrate the recorded events and even fit a few random details into the general framework. Of course, an archeological confirmation of the literary record is not required in these cases. It would convey only indirect support of the literary record, in so far as the archeological finds do not automatically require a tie with either Sennacherib or Nebuchadnezzar, whereas only the use of literary evidence makes this tie possible.

Where the evidence leaves room for doubt and dispute as to the scope and significance of an historical event it is also very difficult and only rarely possible to reconstruct the historical incident simply on the basis of archeological identification. Just such difficulties confront one in considering the Old Testament account of the conquest of Palestine by the Israelite tribes.[67] Generally speaking, understanding of historical events is reached only from a record which mentions definite names and describes events. In no destruction of Late Bronze Age cities in Palestine, which it is chronologically plausible to ascribe to the entry of the Israelites, is any evidence furnished as to who the enemy might have been to whom the city in this special case fell victim. In periods for which we have insufficient records there are usually a number of ways to give an historical explanation of such an archeological find as the destruction of a city. One must, therefore, be very cautious in explaining a situation ascertained by means of archeology as applying to a definite historical event, without relevant written evidence.

In what follows, therefore, the products of Palestinian archeology will be treated essentially from the standpoint of cultural history.

[67] Details with reference to the Israelite conquest can be found in Noth, "Grundsätzliches zur geschichtlichen Deutung archäologischer Befunde auf dem Boden Palästinas," *PJB*, XXXIV (1938), 7–22, and in "Der Beitrag der Archäologie zur Geschichte Israels," *VT*, Suppl. VII (1960), 262–82.

CHAPTER III

RESULTS FOR THE PERIOD OF BIBLICAL HISTORY

17. *Settlements*

THERE were nomadic elements in Palestine's population in every period. They lived in tents even in settled regions. (See Judg. 4 : 17 ff.; 5 : 24; Jer. 35 : 7.) Probably too there were tent-dwellers in the " enclosures," Hebrew *ḥaṣer*, in which people lived together in the Negeb (see p. 56) and elsewhere on the border between farm-land and desert, and among which one pictures enclosures with a stone wall and thorn hedge for protection against wild animals and hostile people (see Lev. 25 : 31; Josh. 19 : 8; Neh. 11 : 25; 12 : 28 ff., and the compounds with *ḥaṣer* among the place names in the Negeb in Josh. 15 : 21b–32a).[1] There is naturally not a trace of these dwellings left. But it is also true as mentioned on p. 123 that there is hardly anything left of any part of the small Iron Age settlements in the hill country, which contained simple dwellings of sun-dried brick inside a stone wall that was built without much skill, and in which, generally speaking, we must picture the domesticated Israelite tribes as having settled.[2] Our knowledge of Iron Age dwellings is essentially limited to those formerly Canaanite Bronze Age cities which continued on into the Iron Age.

(1) *Situation of the Cities*

Various requirements were important for the location of the cities. The city needed to be readily defensible. Hence, it should be situated on a spot which was not very easy to approach, such as a knoll or a promontory. This applied above all to the cities of the Bronze Age. Here every fortified city was the centre of a city-state

[1] It seems relevant to mention here the stones still frequently seen at the outer limits of settled life in Transjordan, arranged in what look like networks of branching fences for sheep folds near which herdsmen could have set up their tents. On this see O. Eissfeldt, *FF*, XXV (1949), 8 ff., and Y. Yadin, *IEJ*, V (1955), 3–10.

[2] Many of the settlements mentioned in the long list of towns in Josh. 15 : 21–62, 18 : 21–28, and 19 : 2–7, which enumerates the towns of the territory of Judah in the period of King Josiah, must be thought of in this fashion. See Alt, *PJB*, XXI (1925), 100–17 [reprinted in *KS*, II, 276–88].

which was totally or partially independent and responsible for its own security. In the period of the states of Israel and Judah in which the central authority took over the responsibility for the protection of the government and the kings improved certain cities as fortresses,[3] protection against hostile troops was no longer the sole concern of the ordinary towns of the country and in the changed conditions of the Persian, Hellenistic, and Roman periods local fortification was in most cases completely dropped. For the period of the states of Israel and Judah, therefore, we are dealing with decentralization of settlement life, that means with an overflow of the population of a city into surrounding villages which, to begin with, still belonged to the city and are called its daughters in the Old Testament (see Num. 21 : 25, Judges 11 : 26, etc.) but gradually became independent.

The more the requirement of defensibility was disregarded, the more the other important requirements for the location of a city could be considered. For one thing in a country like Palestine there was the matter of providing the city with drinking water which could best be secured from a close and favourably situated spring. Since there is not an abundance of springs in Palestine, and, moreover, whole sections of the country are markedly short of springs, this requirement meant a considerable limitation of the free choice of sites for settlement. (See also pp. 154 ff. on this point.) Finally the nearness of arable farmland and favourable trade routes running in various directions were important for a city. Since these very requirements were not easily met, particularly in the hill country regions, the possibilities for locating cities were greatly limited. Naturally, not all of the cities of the land could provide for all these needs.

(2) *Fortification of Cities*

Fortification was one of the primary features of a city in the period we are concerned with here. In spite of all differences in details of execution, fortification was taken for granted in the entire Bronze and Iron Age, even as it was still customary in the Hellenistic and Roman Period. The walls limited the remodelling of the city. Even if people occasionally settled outside the city walls, yet the city limits were generally confined to the space within the walls.

[3] I Kings 9 : 15–19 (Solomon); II Chron. 11 : 5–12 (Rehoboam). Cf. E. Junge, "Der Wiederaufbau des Heerwesens der Reiches Juda unter Josia," *BWANT*, IV, No. 23 (1937), 6 ff.

As a result the cities were greatly restricted and their expansion was hindered. In addition, one must recall that in the ancient Near Eastern period the cities themselves were not actually the places for daily work and daily life. It was more usual for these to take place outside the city on its farm land. The cities served as a refuge from enemies and from the inclemency of the weather, also for the storage of harvest produce. Thus, the cities of the ancient Near Eastern period had a particularly limited area which, since they depended mostly on the natural conditions of their locations, as a rule remained constant through the ages, even if occasionally the Iron Age settlements claimed only a part of the area of their Bronze Age forerunners. It was not until the Hellenistic-Roman period that the city areas became more extensive. The Jerusalem of the Jebusites and of David included an area of about 400 by 100 m. [1,300 by 325 feet].[4] Bronze and Iron Age Shechem was about 230 by 150 m. [750 by 500 feet] in size. Early Bronze Jericho measured no more than 225 by 80 m. [740 by 260 feet]. Only in the Middle Bronze Age did Jericho expand to 300 by 150 m. [1,000 by 500 feet]. The important Canaanite cities on the plains of the country, most of which continued to be inhabited in the Iron Age as well, were a little larger. Taanach was about 300 by 150 m. [1,000 by 500 feet] in size, Megiddo was actually 300 by 225 m. [1,000 by 750 feet]. Middle and Late Bronze Hazor was exceptionally large, 1,100 by 650 m. [3,600 by 2,100 feet]. Iron Age Hazor again on the southern corner of the *tell* was of more normal size, 400 by 150 m. [1,300 by 500 feet]. Samaria, the capital of Israel, was 400 by 200 m. [1,300 by 650 feet] in size. Roman Sebaste which replaced it was expanded to 1,200 by 900 m. [3,900 by 3,200 feet].

The city wall consisted usually of a strong and high stone foundation and of a wall built on top of that of sun-dried bricks. This latter naturally disappeared in time. Only exceptionally has it even partially endured through the centuries as did some of the Bronze

[4] According to brief preliminary information of R. de Vaux, *RB*, LXIX (1962), 98–100, the Anglo-French excavations on the southeastern hill of Jerusalem have already demonstrated error in the previous understanding of the extent of Jebusite-Davidic Jerusalem. The portion of the wall on the eastern side of the hill, previously understood to be partly Jebusite, partly Davidic or Solomonic, has proved to be only Hellenistic. The city wall dating from Middle Bronze to Iron Age has been encountered a little farther east, namely lower on the slope of the Kidron Valley. That means also that the upper entrance of the shaft first discovered by Warren, which was planned for unhindered approach to the water of the Gihon spring, was not outside but inside the old city wall. Further study by the same expedition has shown—or perhaps confirmed—that the large southern part of the western hill across from the southeastern hill was not yet included in the city even in the Hellenistic period. In fact, it was not surrounded by the wall till the first century after Christ.

Age walls of Jericho,[5] or of the Bronze Age gate plan of Shechem. Different techniques were used in different periods in constructing the stone foundation walls. The Bronze Age and the beginning of the Iron Age showed a preference for city walls with the outside more or less battered (i.e., steeply sloping), or again a glacis extending outward at the base of a perpendicular wall to strengthen it and to prevent its collapse outward under the pressure of the piles of debris accumulating on the inside, and at the same time by broadening the lower part of the wall to foil hostile attempts to breach the wall. The mighty cyclopean glacis which surrounded Middle Bronze Age Jericho has become especially well known.[6] Especially in the Iron Age very thick walls were so arranged that a casemate wall was built on the inner and outer side, and the space between was filled up with soil and rubble. The Iron Age enclosure wall of the citadel of Gibeah of Saul, Tell el-Fūl, was constructed in this manner.[7] The cultural periods are distinctly different from one another in their fortification technique. See Figure 4. So-called cyclopean walls were constructed in the Middle and Late Bronze Age[8] by laying unhewn, frequently massive, stone blocks one on top of another and by filling up the spaces with rubble. An exception is the just-mentioned glacis of Jericho (Fig. 4 F).[9] In the first phase of the Iron Age, on the other hand, roughly hewn, irregular stones were frequently set in horizontal courses. This produced obliquely joined stones throughout in contrast to the cyclopean wall construction as seen in the wall construction of the first two stages of Gibeah of Saul[10] and the walls of the city of David at Jerusalem. Also such massive blocks were no longer used, but rather smaller irregular stones. A fine example of this type of construction is given by the Iron Age fortification of Tell Beit Mirsim.[11] At the time of Solomon, however, at least for the representative royal buildings they began to hew the stones smooth and to use these carefully

[5] Note *PEF Qu. St.* (1931), pp. 186–96, Plates II–V, and Watzinger, *Denkmäler Palästinas*, I, Figs. 57, 58.

[6] Watzinger, *op. cit.*, Fig. 57; *AOB*, No. 640.

[7] *AASOR*, IV (1924), 79, Plate XXIVa (an example of a battered wall); *AASOR*, XXXIV–XXXV (1960), Plates XXX, XXXVa.

[8] The fortification technique of the Early Bronze Age is another matter. At that time stone walls were constructed of individual, separate, strikingly low courses, as seen in J. Marquet-Krause, *Les fouilles de ʿAy (et-Tell) 1933–35* (1949), Plates IV, XXV, XXVII, showing Aion et-Tell.

[9] Note the imposing, lightly sloping cyclopean wall of Shechem in *Archäologischer Anzeiger* (1932), p. 303, Fig. 8 and the Middle Bronze Age fortification of Tell Beit Mirsim in *AASOR*, XVII (1938), Plate XVI.

[10] *AASOR*, IV (1924), 59 ff., Figs. 7–11 (shown here in Fig. 4), p. 79 Plate XXIVa; *AASOR*, XXIV–XXXV (1960), Plates XXXIII, XXXIV.

[11] *Ibid.*, XXI–XXII (1943), Plates XXXVIIIb, XXXIXa,b.

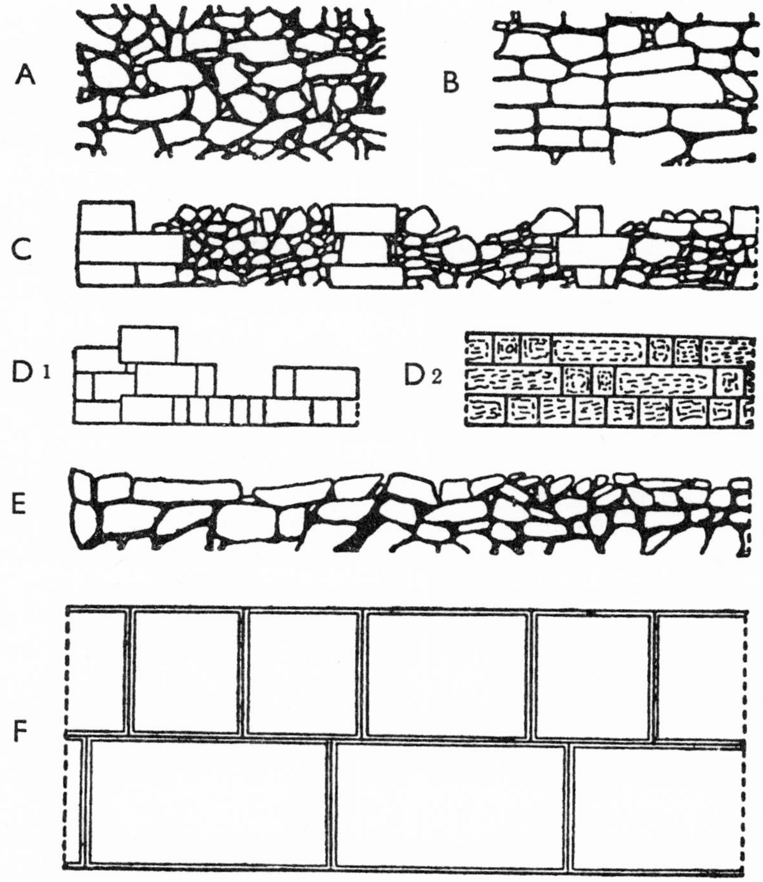

Figure 4. Wall Construction

A. Cyclopean masonry (Middle Bronze II) from the sloping wall foundation in Jericho, according to Sellin and Watzinger, *Jericho* (1913), B, 10.

B. Early Bronze Age wall section from Tell el-Fūl (second level) based on *AASOR*, IV (1924), Fig. 11.

C. Masonry of the Solomonic level of Megiddo, based on "Megiddo I," *OIP*, XLII (1939), Fig. 64.

D. (1 and 2)
Walls from the royal palace, the acropolis in Samaria from the period of the Kingdom of Israel, based on *Samaria-Sebaste*, No. 1 (1943), Plate XV, 2 and Reisner, Fisher, and Lyon, *Harvard Excavations at Samaria* (1924), II, Plate XXVIIa.

E. Hellenistic masonry of the citadel of Beth-zur, based on O. R. Sellers, *The Citadel of Beth-zur* (1933), Fig. 14.

F. A section of the Herodian exterior wall of the Jerusalem area, the "Wailing Wall."

prepared stones, not yet for the whole fortification, but at least for the wall corners and to insert them at intervals in the running wall, but they continued to use courses of irregular stones of the older style for the spaces between. Not only city walls, but also more important buildings in the cities were constructed in this manner.[12] A very refined wall technique for royal structures was used during the Iron II period. The Israelite royal palace in Samaria shows masonry of continuous smooth hewn stones.[13] The exterior walls of the acropolis of the Israelite royal city of Samaria[14] have a foundation of carefully hewn stones, which are laid as "stretchers and headers," that is, they are laid some lengthwise, some crosswise, in order to hold the wall firmly together. On the façade the stones were worked smooth, to a depressed border along the joints, the "marginal draft," while the remainder of the surface was left undressed, the "boss." During the Persian and Hellenistic periods, as far as we know, apparently the more unskilled form of wall construction in layers of roughly-shaped stones continued in Palestine.[15] Herodian and Roman architecture again for its large buildings in the cities used large, often massive, well-worked, square blocks. These stones had exactly cut edges and were likely to have a border strip and smooth surface on the façade. Note the wall around the Herodian temple (p. 119 and Fig. 4).

The sun-dried brick walls of Iron Age cities were built up on stone foundations. These walls seem to have been furnished with projections and towers, where the defenders stood. Walls and towers had battlements on top. Since there are only a few remains of the sun-dried brick fortification, we deduce this not from archeological finds, but rather from the various Assyrian portrayals of Palestinian fortified cities.[16]

The enclosures of extensive rectangular areas with walls of stamped earth, *terre pisée*, occasionally filled with reinforcing material, were an exceptional structure. They are dated to Middle Bronze II and are probably related to the appearance of the Hyksos (see p. 255) and the horse-drawn chariots that appeared with them as a new weapon. Presumably they planned these great enclosures

[12] See especially the structure of the Solomonic level of Megiddo, "Megiddo I," *OIP*, XLII (1939), Figs. 13, 60, 61, 64 (here, Fig. 4), 65.

[13] *Samaria-Sebaste*, No. 1, Plate XV, 2 (here, Fig. 4).

[14] *Ibid.*, Plate XXXII and Watzinger, *op. cit.*, Fig. 79 (here, Fig. 4).

[15] For the Hellenistic period see O. R. Sellers, *The Citadel of Beth-Zur*, Figs. 14, 17–19, as well as Fig. 4 here.

[16] *AOB*, Nos. 133–34, 141. The Palestinian cities of the Late Bronze Age were somewhat similar, as shown by the representations of Egyptian pharaohs of the New Kingdom; see pp. 248–49 and *AOB*, Nos. 94–96, 102.

for their chariot parade grounds. An example is the enclosure of the large lower city of Hazor. It seems that it was first built as such a chariot parade ground and only later in the Middle and Late Bronze Age was occupied by residential quarters. Another example in Palestine is Ashkelon (Arabic, ʿAsqalān); other examples are found in Syria and Egypt. In addition, then, older towns were also occasionally surrounded with such *terre pisée* walls for better protection, such as the town on Tell Beit Mirsim in the last stage of Middle Bronze II. Then there were the glacis, occasionally of *terre pisée*, placed about already standing city walls (see p. 148).[17]

(3) *City Gates*

The Bronze and Iron Age cities normally had no more than one or two gates. The gate structures of the Middle and Late Bronze Age cities were tower-shaped insets in the wall, consisting of several stories with a direct gate entrance, at times either side, forming two more or less extensive guard rooms, one behind the other on either side.[18] Then in the course of the Iron Age another addition with several such guard rooms was placed on the city side of the gate in front of the entrance.[19] Then again there might be only one guard room placed on the city side of the gate as in the perhaps later east gate of Shechem.[20] Outside, a ramp sloping upward, protected by bastions, was constructed at right angles with the gate entrance,[21] or the gate entrance itself made several right turns to facilitate defence.[22] Ultimately they arranged the total gate plan with the one guard room at right angles to the course of the city wall, resulting in a re-entering angle in the fortification.[23]

The gate complex with its inner chambers and with the open space before the inner side of the gate was the only extensive free space in the otherwise very compressed city of the pre-Hellenistic Age in which the city residents could assemble. (This is the space

[17] Y. Yadin, *BASOR*, CXXXVII (1955), 23–32, presents the material with the pertinent literary references.

[18] Galling, *BRL*, Cols. 523–24, Figs. 1–4; Watzinger, *op. cit.*, Fig. 19.

[19] See the gate of the fourth level of Megiddo, "Megiddo II," *OIP*, LXII (1948), Fig. 105 and the gate of Level 10 in Hazor, from which the gate of Iron Age Gezer can also be reconstructed; Y. Yadin, *IEJ*, VIII (1958), 80–86.

[20] Sellin, *ZDPV*, *XLIX* (1926), Plate XXIX. Compare with this the gate plan of Megiddo, Level 3, "Megiddo II," Fig. 104.

[21] See the gate of Megiddo IV just mentioned and the gate plan of Iron Age Lachish, "Lachish I" (1938), p. 223.

[22] See the southeast gate of Iron II in Tell Beit Mirsim, *AASOR*, XVII (1938), Plate XLVII.

[23] Note the city gate on Tell en-Naṣbeh according to McCown and Wampler, "Tell en-Naṣbeh I" (1947), p. 198 and survey map.

meant by *reḥobh sha'ar ha'ir* in II Chron. 32 : 6.) Therefore, the public life of the city took place here. "In the gate" the market was set up (II Kings 7 : 1). Legal transactions occurred "in the gate" under the direction of the "elders" of the city. This produced the expression "to judge in the gate" in Amos 5 : 12, 12, 15. Cf. Deut. 21 : 19; 25 : 7, etc.

(4) *Royal Fortresses*

The Middle and Late Bronze Age fortified cities were all seats of dynasties, residences of small, largely independent ruling families not committed to the recognition of the superior rule of any overlord.[24] Therefore, as a rule they contained a castle for the prince, a sort of acropolis, which in Hebrew was called *mighdal*, with the basic meaning "fortress." This *mighdal*, in the event that the rest of the city was already overrun by the enemy, served as the last retreat which could still be defended. (See Judg. 9 : 46 ff., Shechem; 51 ff., Thebez.) In the Iron Age, after the Canaanite city governments had disappeared, a particular acropolis would be built for the royal residences. Hence, the excavation of Tell el-Fūl, Gibeah of Saul, on the top of the hill disclosed a small, carefully built castle in the second level, which obviously was the residence of King Saul.[25] See p. 131. The Israelite capital of Samaria embraced an acropolis surrounded by a well-built fortification wall (p. 132) on the highest point of the city hill.[26] In Jerusalem, on the other hand, when Solomon set about building himself a splendid residence as centre of the great Davidic-Solomonic Kingdom, the area of the ancient Jebusite city (p. 147) proved to be too small. Therefore, Solomon built his acropolis outside the old "City of David" (see II Sam. 5 : 9) and for that matter on the knoll towering over the north side of ancient Jerusalem, which knoll originally was called Zion. This was the site of the ancient sanctuary of the city of Jerusalem. Here Solomon had his palace buildings erected, among which was the temple of Jerusalem.[27]

[24] On the origin and form of this system of government see Alt, "Die Landnahme der Israeliten in Palästina," *op. cit.*, pp. 6 ff. [reprinted in *KS*, I, 94 ff.].

[25] The floor plan of this castle can be seen in Galling, *BRL*, Col. 191 [or in W. F. Albright, *Archaeology of Palestine* (Penguin Books, 1949), Fig. 30].

[26] Galling, *ZDPV*, LIX (1936), 244 ff., Fig. 16.

[27] See I Kings, chapters 6 and 7; on the architectural history of Jerusalem, see Galling, *ZDPV*, LIV (1931), 85–90, Plate VI. On developments in the history of architecture in the capitals of Israel, see A. Alt, "Archäologische Fragen zur Baugeschichte von Jerusalem und Samaria in der israelitischen Königszeit," *Wiss. Zeitsch. der Ernst-Moritz-Arndt-Univ. Greifswald. Gesellsch.-sprachwiss.*, Reihe Nr. 1, Jahrgang V (1955–56), 33–42 [reprinted in *KS*, III, 303–325].

(5) *Houses*

The usual houses of the cities were generally sun-dried brick structures built on top of a low foundation of irregular-shaped stones. Therefore the houses have disappeared and only their floor plans can be recognized from the foundations left in place and covered with debris. In the Iron as in the Bronze Age there was the so-called courtyard house type, that is, individual rooms which were rather irregularly arranged around a small court, generally on three sides, though sometimes only on two sides.[28] The excavation on Tell Beit Mirsim with its exact observations of strata yielded considerable information on the development of house plans between Middle Bronze and Iron II.[29] Excavation on Tell Fārʿah also produced some fine ground plans of Iron Age houses.[30] The houses had flat roofs supported by wooden beams which were laid out at intervals over the individual rooms parallel with one another. These beams, in turn, were covered with sticks or small wooden laths. These again were covered with a watertight clay roof.[31] The roof was reached presumably by a wooden stairway set on the outside. It could be used for living quarters (Isa. 22 : 1) or for sleeping space, especially in the hot season of the year, as they still do. There flax could be spread to dry (Josh. 2 : 6). The roof could support an upper chamber, Hebrew *ʿaliyyah*, probably built at a corner of the roof, made of clay walls (cf. *ʿaliyyath qir* in II Kings 4 : 10) and sticks. In II Kings 4 : 10 the inventory of such an upper chamber is described—bed, table, chair, lamp—which in this case serves as a guest room. The strength of house foundations occasionally allows the conclusion that there was a complete upper storey.

Many rooms, instead of having a complete wall on the side facing the court, had only a row of pillars, whose pedestals as well as some

[28] Note the floor plans in Galling, *BRL*, Cols. 269–70.

[29] Ont his see Albright, *AASOR*, XVII (1938), 22–23, 32–33, 39–40, 63–64, with the numerous illustrations on Plates IX–XV and XVIII, and *AASOR*, XXI–XXII (1943), 19 ff., 49 ff.; Plates II–III, V–VII, XIa, XLV.

[30] de Vaux, *RB*, LXII (1955), Plate VI, and U. Jochims, *ZDPV*, LXXVI (1960), 86 ff., Figs. 4–5.

[31] Note the piece of such a roof, found fallen in at Tell Beit Mirsim, illustrated in *AASOR*, XVII (1938), Plate XVIIIb and also p. 64 in the text. Comparable to the ancient oriental house are the modern sun-dried brick houses in the southern part of the coastal plain of Palestine. They demonstrate the same roof construction attested for antiquity by the excavation finds of Tell Beit Mirsim. The usual modern house in the other parts of Palestine cannot be compared with the ancient houses, because it is formed entirely of stone and has an arched roof. On modern house forms see K. Jäger, *Das Bauernhaus in Palästina* (1912), see especially T. Canaan, "The Palestinian Arab House", *JPOS*, XII (1932), 223–47 and XIII (1933), 1–83; and finally, see G. Dalman, *Arbeit und Sitte in Palästina*, VII (1942), 1 ff. All have numerous illustrations.

lower stone parts have been preserved. Therefore, these were open halls.[32] Under Late Bronze Age houses in Bethel[33] and Tell Beit Mirsim[34] there were drainage channels made of stone paving. We do not yet know whether such drainage channels were still customary in the Iron Age.

Inside the city proper in the ancient oriental period the houses were grouped at random. There were no continuous roadways, actually no streets at all, but only occasional narrow spaces between the individual houses. But since these were not always built on a truly rectangular floor plan, there resulted simply an irregular maze of little alleys. It was only the Hellenistic period which created systematic planned cities according to the system introduced by the city builder Hippodamos of Miletus. This plan embodied a thoroughfare running through the middle of the city from gate to gate and arranged the houses on both sides in rectangular blocks (*insulae*). At the same time there were straight side streets and byroads and approximately in the middle of it all, a great market place. This plan made its appearance in the Hellenistic city plan of Marissa, Tell Sandaḥanneh.[35] Then the Roman cities of the land were designed in the form customary at the time, with main streets laid out at right angles with each other.[36]

(6) *Water Supply*

A vital problem for the cities was the water supply. Therefore, the cities showed an age-old preference for a location near a spring. As a substitute for a spring, the well (Hebrew, *be'er*) came into consideration, but underground water could not always be reached at a reasonable depth. Dependence on springs impeded the forming of settlements until the invention of cisterns (Hebrew, *bor*). It can be demonstrated that the invention occurred toward the end of the Chalcolithic Age.[37] Cisterns, usually pear-shaped, were hollowed out of the natural rock inside the city proper, but also in the country for the watering of cattle and the like. Their sides were coated with mortar to retain the water better. During the winter rainy season, water was conducted into the cisterns presumably by channels from the house roofs, the "streets," and the surroundings,

[32] See, e.g., *AASOR*, XXI–XXII (1943), Plate XLV.
[33] See Albright, *BASOR*, LVI (1934), 7; Figs. 3, 5.
[34] See *AASOR*, XVII (1938), Plate XII.
[35] See the city plan by Watzinger, *op. cit.*, II, Fig. 22.
[36] Note for example the plan of Gerasa, *ibid.*, Fig. 34.
[37] M. Dothan, *IEJ*, VII (1957), 220, 226–27; IX (1959), 17

and stored up there, to be drawn out in the dry season. Naturally, fresh spring water (Hebrew, *Maim ḥayyim*, "living water") was preferable to the stagnant cistern water. Note the figurative language in Jer. 2 : 13 and John 4 : 10 ff. Still, with sufficient cistern water they could get along without a spring.

A city which was fortunately located near a spring, but which had only a few cisterns could rest easy only in peaceful times. Naturally the spring lay outside the city wall. Springs do not flow from hilltops, where cities were built for defence. Under favourable conditions a spring rather lay below at the foot of the city mound. Hence, in the event of a siege the spring could not be reached. The besieging enemy would surely have taken care first of all that the inhabitants could not reach their source of drinking water outside the city. Therefore, as early as the Bronze Age, probably in the middle or late period, the people began to devise underground shafts and passage-ways through the solid rock in order to reach the water of the city well outside the city, unmolested by the enemy stationed outside. In Jerusalem the city spring lies on the east side at the foot of the old city hill in the Kidron Valley. It is called Gihon in the Old Testament in I Kings 1 : 33, 38, 45 and elsewhere, now 'Ain Umm ed-Derej, "Step spring," or called 'Ain Sitt Maryam, "Spring of Mary," by the Christians. It was Warren (p. 135) who discovered a shaft, which seemed to lead out of the city to this spring. Parker, an Englishman, in 1909–10 examined this shaft more closely and later H. Vincent published the facts.[38] The shaft begins about halfway up the east side of the Jerusalem city hill, but not within the line of the Bronze Age wall. Presumably it was so constructed because a shaft begun higher would have been too deep to drive, but the entrance halfway up could not readily be occupied by an enemy. From this entrance one shaft drops vertically without reaching the water. Hence, a first attempt was later given up. A stairway has been cut in the rock leading down from the entrance under the upper level. Another perpendicular shaft drops down abruptly, actually reaching the level of the spring by means of a watercourse running inward to the spring. In the event of a siege the usual overflow of the spring toward the outside was stopped up, so that the spring water welled up in this watercourse and could be drawn up from the bottom of the stairway by vessels lowered through the vertical shaft. (It has often been

[38] *Jérusalem antique* (1912), pp. 150 ff., Figs. 28–35, and Plates XVI–XVII; Vincent and Stève, *Jérusalem de l'Ancien Testament I* (1954), pp. 264 ff. and Plate LXII; Dalman, *PJB*, XIV (1918), 47 ff. and Plate II, from which *AOB*, No. 627 is taken.

conjectured that there is some connection with the development just described in the very obscure reference to *ṣinnor* in II Sam. 5 : 8, which was used in David's conquest of the Jebusite city of Jerusalem. This remains doubtful and debatable.)

A similar arrangement has been found on *Tell Jezer*, Gezer.[39] There a subterranean stairway leads downward from the very top of the city mound to the spring basin itself, so that a person did not have to draw up water through a shaft as in Jerusalem, but could take the water directly from the spring basin. The spring at the base of the city hill flows from the mouth of a natural cave, whose outer entrance was naturally blocked in times of siege. This arrangement also fits into the Bronze Age. A similar Bronze Age stairway running from the city mound down to the spring has also been found at Khirbet Belʿameh, ancient Ibleam[40] (Judg. 1: 27 and elsewhere). Khirbet Belʿameh is 1·5 km. [1 mile] south of Jenīn at the southern extremity of the Jezreel Plain.

The water tunnel of Megiddo was a very great project which was developed in the Late Bronze Age.[41] Originally the spring which flowed at the southwestern foot of the city mound could be reached only by a series of stairs from the outside. In order to bring this spring within reach from inside the city, a massive vertical shaft with peripheral stairs was sunk inside the wall. Joining it at the bottom was a steeply descending stairway, which finally became a horizontal tunnel leading to the spring. Later on in the Iron Age they dropped the floor of this tunnel deeper, to let the water run into the tunnel, after cutting off its overflow to the outside. At the same time, in place of the steps they began to extend the tunnel inward, and the vertical shaft downward to their point of intersection, so that they could draw the water directly from the top. Yet this change in arrangement was never completed. Thus, as long ago as the Bronze Age they expended tremendous efforts on amazing arrangements to secure water supply in the event of siege.

In the Iron Age people naturally used the old structures as far as possible, but also as occasion demanded constructed new accommodations of a similar sort. The city of Etam, south of Bethlehem, now Khirbet Wādi el-Khōkh, which according to II Chron. 11: 6 was remodelled into a fortress, of course had beautiful and abun-

[39] *AOB*, No. 635.

[40] See Schumacher, *PEF Qu. St.* (1910), pp. 107 ff., as well as the illustration in Vincent, *op. cit.*, Fig. 37.

[41] See the publication of R. S. Lamon, *The Megiddo Water System*, *OIP*, XXXII (1935), as well as the report of Galling, *ZDPV*, LIX (1936), 232 ff. and Fig. 10.

dant springs in its vicinity.[42] Nevertheless, in anticipation of a siege an underground stairway was constructed from the city mound to a weak spring flowing from a cave at the western foot of the mound.[43] In Lachish, now Tell ed-Duweir, which was one of the most important fortresses of the State of Judah (cf. II Chron. 11 : 9), a plan was begun in the seventh century which apparently was supposed to be like the great Late Bronze Age plan of Megiddo already discussed. It was never finished. In the southeastern part of the city a vertical shaft of large dimensions was started, but the work was broken off.[44]

The waterworks on the mound of el-Jīb fit in here. There was a deep shaft within the old city area cut into the living stone. It was rather cylindrical in form, about 10 m. [over thirty feet] in diameter, with a spiral stairway descending around the shaft wall. From its bottom one could enter a side chamber which contained ground water. There was also a stairway beginning inside the city wall and descending at a steep angle through a tunnel ending at the spring cave at the foot of the city hill. In normal times this spring was naturally reached from the outside. In wartime it could be blocked up on the outside and reached through the tunnel.[45]

Deservedly most famous of these Iron Age water supply developments, however, is the Siloam tunnel in Jerusalem.[46] According to II Chron. 32 : 30, it was constructed by King Hezekiah of Judah, at the end of the eighth century B.C. The Bronze Age shaft (p. 155) did not wholly suffice because even it could be approached only from outside the city wall. Therefore, Hezekiah had the water of the city spring diverted through a tunnel running under the entire city hill. Its terminal, of course, also was situated outside the old city wall, but at a point that could be defended rather easily, in the narrow valley on the west side of ancient Jerusalem cut off

[42] The ancient name of the city still clings to one of these springs, ʿAin ʿAṭan.

[43] Dalman, *PJB*, X (1914), 19; Kraus, *ZDPV*, LXXII (1956), 153–54.

[44] "Lachish III" (1953), pp. 158–63 and Plates XXV–XXVI. Perhaps this was planned as only a great water reservoir, a gigantic cistern.

[45] J. B. Pritchard, *BA*, XIX (1956), pp. 66–74; and especially, with its many illustrations and plans, *University Museum Bulletin* (Philadelphia), XXI, No. 1 (1957), 8–21; XXII, No. 2 (1958), 12, 18–19, 21–24; also J. B. Pritchard, *The Water System of Gibeon* ("Museum Monographs," University of Pennsylvania, 1961).

[46] Here we ignore the two conduits which took the water of the spring of Jerusalem southward along the eastern foot of the hill, the conduit discovered in 1902 by Masterman, which apparently dates back to the Bronze Age, and the conduit discovered by Schick in 1886, lying somewhat higher and running parallel to the other, probably dating from the period of the Kings of Judah. It is probable that these served only to conduct the spring water into the gardens in the Kidron Valley below Jerusalem, the "royal garden" of II Kings 25 : 4, Jer. 39 : 4, and Neh. 3 : 15. For details see Dalman, *PJB*, XIV (1918), 47 ff., and the plan in *AOB*, No. 627.

from the Kidron Valley from now on by a strong barricade wall.[47] This tunnel connects with the Bronze Age watercourse (p. 155) and travels a distance of 512·5 m. [1,679 feet] not in a straight line, but remarkably first westward, then southeastward, and finally again westward, therefore, in an S shape to its end at the southwestern foot of the city hill in the valley mentioned above, and ends in a pool which is called *Berekat hash-shelah*, "conduit pool," in Neh. 3 : 15 and *Kolymbethra tou Siloam*[48] in John 9 : 7. The tunnel has a total incline of fully 2 m. [6 feet]. It is about 60 cm. [2 feet] wide and up to 1·45 m. [4·75 feet] high. In spite of its complicated course it was begun from both ends. Its course, amazingly, was so well calculated that the workers finally met at the midpoint almost perfectly as planned. The marks of work in the tunnel themselves, the direction of blows of the pickaxes, show the fact of simultaneous work from both ends. Beside that we are advised of the same fact by the "Siloam Inscription" (p. 219), which was engraved in the tunnel wall near the lower end. It was found there in 1880 and is now located in the museum in Constantinople.

18. *Domestic Life*

Ordinary people in the ancient Near Eastern world managed their frugal life with a minimum of household furnishings. Only kings and nobles owned any lavish domestic accommodations. Average people were accustomed to squat in the still current Near Eastern fashion, even while eating, and spent the night on pelts or rugs or simply wrapped in their cloaks (see Exod. 22 : 26–27). People in the palaces and "better" houses, again, were accustomed to chairs, tables, and beds. We know this about the biblical period primarily from the narratives.[49] Moulded bronze parts have been found in an Iron Age grave from Tell el-Fārʿah, which formed the foot and corner pieces for framework of a bed and probably a chair. To serve this way, they must have had cloth stretched over

[47] See the plans in Dalman, *PJB*, XIV (1918), Plates II–III, or AOB, Nos. 626–27; see especially the thorough description and many illustrations and exact plans in Vincent and Stève, *op. cit.*, I, 269–79, Plates LXII–LXVII.

[48] The assumed name "Shiloah" is first used in Isa. 8 : 6 with the definite article and probably referred to one of the conduits mentioned in the previous note, and later to the Hezekiah tunnel and its installations. This word appears in Greek transliteration in Josephus, in the New Testament, and elsewhere and is simply the word *shelaḥ*, namely conduit, with a subsequent vocalization, something like the name *Giḥon* (see p. 155).

[49] II Kings 4 : 10. See p. 153 as well as Galling, *BRL*, Cols. 108 ff., 520 ff.

them.[50] Therefore, we are sure that there were beds and chairs. The highest development of the chair was the royal throne on which the king used to take his place for public appearances. The ornate throne of Solomon is described in I Kings 10 : 18–20. It can be better visualized by comparison with the royal throne portrayed on the almost contemporary sarcophagus of Ahiram of Byblos[51] and the royal throne on the somewhat older Megiddo ivory.[52] All these Iron Age items certainly had their origin in the Canaanite city culture of Syria and Palestine. The throne was differentiated from the ordinary chair (which resembled a stool) by its back and arm rests as well as by its massive and sumptuous style and its decoration with all sorts of portrayals of mythical figures. Solomon's throne was probably made of wood, decorated with ivory and gold inlays. Footstools went with chairs and especially thrones. The footstool (Hebrew, *haddom*) is repeatedly used figuratively in the Old Testament, especially in Psalms 110 : 1.

Lamps are added to the inventory of a well-equipped house in II Kings 4 : 10, in addition to the previously mentioned items. Lamps found in great numbers in all excavation sites are attested at least from the Middle Bronze Age on. They are simple little shallow clay bowls into which a person poured oil as fuel. Their edge was slightly pinched at one point to hold the wick fast as it extended over the edge. The development of the lamp continued with the pinched part becoming constantly more pronounced, until finally in the Hellenistic-Roman-Byzantine period the shallow clay bowl had become enclosed, except for a small hole on top for pouring in oil and an extension on the side with a separate wick hole.[53]

Every house had a hearth. It was usually in a corner and consisted of a shallow hole around the edge of which a circle of stones was set. A wood fire was lighted in the centre and cooking pots were set on the stone edge. In spite of the perishable nature of this arrangement, it is still frequently found in excavations.[54] For baking bread, which certainly regularly took place right at home, just as today, they had simply ovens which stood either in the court

[50] Watzinger, *op. cit.*, I, 110 and Fig. 44, shows a reconstruction of the bedstead.

[51] *AOB*, No. 666.

[52] *AfO*, XII (1938–39), 181, Fig. 26; *IEJ*, IX (1959), Plates A–C.

[53] See the illustrations in Galling, *BRL*, Cols. 347–48 and further details in Galling, "Die Beleuchtungsgeräte im israelitischjüdischen Kulturgebiet," *ZDPV*, XLVI (1923), 1–50, Plates I–IV. Especially for the Roman-Byzantine period, see D. C. Baramki, *BASOR*, *Supplementary Studies* 15–16 (1953), pp. 31–55.

[54] For the Bronze and Iron Age levels of Tell Beit Mirsim see *AASOR*, XVII (1938), Plates XLIX–LII and *AASOR*, XXI–XXII (1943), Plates II, VI (cross-sections). For the Late Bronze Age and Iron Age levels of Megiddo, see Watzinger, *Tell el-Mutesellim*, I (1908), Plates XII, XVI.

of the house or else outside in front of the house. The oven itself consisted of a circular hole formed of stones above which a large earthenware truncated cone was set, narrowing and open at the top. This corresponds to the modern *tannūr*.[55] The fire was set in the hole and flat cakes of dough were stuck to the inside wall of the clay cylinder and usually baked into round flat loaves of bread. We do not know whether the professional male or female bakers, Hebrew *opheh*, present at the royal courts (for Egypt see Gen. 40 : 1 ff., for Palestine, I Sam. 8 : 13) and in larger cities (note the "bakers' street" in Jerusalem in Jer. 37 : 21 and a baker in Hos. 7 : 4, 6) had more complicated forms of ovens or more refined ways of baking. Archeology attests an Iron Age *tannūr* at Megiddo shaped just like the modern one.[56] As shown by finds in Megiddo[57] and Taanach, during the Iron Age there was another very simple baking device, shaped like a slightly rounded clay platter and supported by stones. The flat cakes of dough were stuck to its convex upper side and a fire was set under it. This corresponds to the *ṣāj* used by the Bedouins today, though it is now made of iron rather than clay.[58]

The ancient houses also frequently had large round stone structures for storage of grain. These probably originally had a high-domed clay roof like the Egyptian grain silos.[59] They generally stood in the courts of the houses. Their stone foundations have frequently come to light.[60]

The supply of clay vessels needed for storing of liquids, for drinking, and for cooking must be included among household furnishings. It has already been mentioned above (pp. 108, 122, 138) that the potsherds left behind in great quantity from every ancient settlement are of great importance archeologically especially for questions of date. A compilation of the various types of clay vessels and a survey of their development from the Middle Bronze Age to the Hellenistic-Roman epoch is found in Galling, *BRL*, Cols. 314 ff., with numerous illustrations. Parallel to the usual everyday ware there were naturally show pieces which were distinctive in design and form. In addition, during the entire Bronze Age people of means were likely to have alabaster juglets, particularly for

[55] The word *tannūr* is the customary word in the Old Testament for oven. See Hos. 7 : 4, 6, 7, etc. On this read Dalman, *Arbeit und Sitte in Palästina*, IV (1935), 88 ff.

[56] See *Tell el-Mutesellim*, I (1908), Pl. XL, c. For the modern one see Dalman, *op. cit.*, Figs. 17–23.

[57] *Tell el-Mutesellim*, I, Pl. XXII B,b.

[58] See Dalman, *op. cit.*, pp. 39 ff., Figs. 9–12.

[59] See *AOB*, No. 177.

[60] See *AASOR*, XVII (1938), Plate XVIIIa, and the drawings of Plates XLIX–LII for Tell Beit Mirsim.

ointments, cosmetics, etc., imported from Egypt.[61]

The art of production of faienceware also originated in Egypt.[62] Faience vases were used as show pieces in the Middle and Late Bronze Age in Palestine. A number of faience vases are also found from an Early Iron Age level of Megiddo partly in animal shapes.[63] Moulded glass also comes from Egypt. Glass beads and the like were imported from Egypt in the Bronze and Iron Age. Glass blowing was not introduced until the Roman period and was practised especially in Phoenicia. Glass vases have frequently been found in graves of the Roman period.[64]

People used hand mills for grinding[65] the stored-up grain, which was then to be baked into bread at home. The simplest form consisted of a flat, lower millstone (Hebrew, *pelaḥ taḥtīth*), and an upper stone shaped like a rounded loaf of bread (Hebrew, *pelaḥ rekhebh*, e.g., in Judg. 9 : 53) which was rubbed back and forth on the lower one. The grain was ground between them.[66] There are also archeological examples of Iron Age upper stones in the form of a stone hopper. Grain was poured into its opening, so that it would be ground under the stone.[67] A small stone mortar with a matching stone pestle could serve the same purpose.[68] Larger stone rotating mills are frequently found in which the upper stone, which had a funnel opening, rotated around a conical top of the lower stone. During this rotation the grain was ground between them.[69] Smaller rotating stone mills of the type used today in the country probably derive from the Roman period.[70]

Decoration was included in houses and daily life, as conditions permitted, even in ancient times. Excavations give evidence of many uses of ivory, more or less artistically carved, beginning with the Chalcolithic Beersheba Culture (p. 129). There were ivory pins to hold parts of garments together, spatulas for mixing salves, combs, etc. Ivory inlays also served to decorate wooden furniture pieces, chairs, beds, boxes, and the like, beginning with the Late Bronze Age. The Iron Age inherited this fashion. I Kings 22 : 39 states that Ahab built an ivory house, of course in Samaria, and

61 See Galling, *op. cit.*, Cols. 7 ff., with illustrations.
62 *Ibid.*, Cols. 154 ff., with illustrations.
63 See Watzinger, *Tell el-Mutesellim*, II (1929), 31 ff., with illustrations.
64 For further material see Galling, *op. cit.*, Cols. 198 ff.
65 See Galling, *op. cit.*, Cols. 386 ff., with illustrations, as well as the comparable material from modern Palestine in Dalman, *op. cit.*, III (1933), 207 ff., Figs. 43 ff.
66 Ancient upper stones are illustrated in Dalman, *op. cit.*, Fig. 43; see also Watzinger, *op. cit.*, I (1908), Figs. 80, 81.
67 Galling, *op. cit.*
68 Ancient pieces of this sort are in Dalman, *Arbeit . . .*, Fig. 44.
69 *Ibid.*, Figs. 52, 53.
70 *Ibid.*, pp. 225 ff.; for the modern type, Figs. 47–51.

Amos 3 : 15 speaks of ivory houses, also likely in Samaria. The authors are referring to the costly trimming of the house furnishings. Numerous ivory inlays in relief of Egyptianizing style[71] were actually found during the more recent excavations in Samaria. Analogous pieces are known from the Assyrian royal palace in *Kalaḫ*, now Tell Nimrūd,[72] and from the Mesopotamian city of *Ḫadatu*, now *Arslan Taş*. Both of these latter groups represent Syrian booty of Assyrian kings of the eighth century. Related ivory works have been found in the palace of Canaanite Megiddo of the twelfth century.[73] Thus the ivory art of the Iron Age was derived from the Bronze Age Canaanite-Phoenician ivory carving, which had been under strong Egyptian influence.[74]

Personal ornaments consisted especially of metal art products, whether precious metals or bronze and iron are thought of. Included were necklaces,[75] earrings (Cols. 398 ff.), armbands (Cols. 30 ff.), anklets (Col. 168), and headbands (Cols. 125 ff., under the heading *Diadem*). Metal pins served to hold parts of garments together in the Bronze Age (Cols. 394 ff.). These were more and more replaced by fibulas in the Iron Age (Cols. 165 ff.). Further, they had metal mirrors with decorated handles (Cols. 493 ff.). Royal officials and noblemen, too, had their name seal in the Iron Age, i.e., a stamp seal[76] made of precious stone, faience or imitation, which was pierced so that it could be worn on a cord around the neck. The seal picture contained the name and patronym of its owner, and usually also a pictorial portrayal in Egyptianizing style. Many Iron Age seals have been found in Palestine or brought to light through excavations.[77] Frequently these stamp seals have the scarab shape popular in Egypt from early days, i.e., the large dung beetle, which was thought to bring good luck and ward off disaster. Especially in Syria and Palestine it was used as an amulet in combination with pictures and hieroglyphs which were often not under-

[71] Crowfoot, *Early Ivories from Samaria* (1938); Watzinger, ***Denkmäler Palästinas***, I, Fig. 84; Galling, *BRL*, Cols. 142 ff., with illustrations.

[72] See now R. D. Barnett, *The Nimrud Ivories in the British Museum* (1957).

[73] G. Loud, "The Megiddo Ivories," *OIP*, LII (1939).

[74] On the subject of Syro-Palestinian ivory technique and ivory art see R. D. Barnett, *A Catalogue of the Nimrud Ivories with other Examples of Ancient Near Eastern Ivories in the British Museum* (1957).

[75] Galling, *BRL*, Cols. 357 ff., with illustrations.

[76] Cylinder seals were customary in Mesopotamia. They appeared only in isolated instances in Syro-Palestine.

[77] Galling, *op. cit.*, Cols. 481 ff., with illustrations, as well as Galling, "Beschriftete Bildsiegel des ersten Jahrtausends v. Chr. vornehmlich aus Syrien und Palästina," *ZDPV*, LXIV (1914), 121–202, Plates 5–12; A. Reifenberg, *Ancient Hebrew Seals* (1950).

stood there. Scarabs designed in Egypt and native copies have been found frequently in Palestine.[78] They also had all sorts of other amulets depending on superstitious ideas.[79] The small clay images of the naked mother goddess, generally called Astarte in Palestine, should also be considered as amulets and fertility charms. Very many of them have been found in the Bronze and Iron Age levels of Palestinian cities. They appear in various fixed types.[80] These amulets were very popular among women.

19. *Occupations*

(1) *Farming*

The chief occupations in ancient Palestine were always animal husbandry and farming; the unsettled nomads were herdsmen, while the semi-nomads and the sedentary groups combined both occupations in varying proportions. Naturally, these activities have left few archeological traces. Occasionally examples have been found of the normal Iron Age long-pointed iron ploughshares with sockets for fastening them on.[81] Iron Age examples of iron sickles with handle fittings have shown up in various ways. They were used to cut the ripened grain.[82] As a threshing floor they used a level spot on which the cut grain was gathered, which was exposed to the wind needed for winnowing. Threshing did not require special structures. We know from the Old Testament tradition that later threshing was done with the help of threshing wagons or sleds. This is illustrated by the same methods of threshing still in use in the Near East.[83]

Horticulture has always occupied the attention of the settled inhabitants of Palestine. This includes the care of fig trees, olive trees, and grape vines, including preparation of oil and wine. Olive presses were necessary for extracting oil. The ripe olives were crushed in them to extract their oil. Frequently very simple devices served this purpose, namely, stone basins in the living rock, near the olive orchard. The olives were poured into them from baskets and pressed down with heavy stones so that the extracted

[78] M. Pieper, "Die Bedeutung der Skarabäen für die palästinensische Altertumskunde," *ZDPV*, LIII (1930), 185–99, Plate IX.

[79] Galling, *op. cit.*, Cols. 22 ff., with illustrations.

[80] E. Pilz, "Die weiblichen Gottheiten Kanaans," *ZDPV*, XLVII (1924), 129–68, Plate 1; J. B. Pritchard, *Palestinian Figurines in Relation to Certain Goddesses Known Through Literature* (1943).

[81] Galling, *op. cit.*, Cols. 427 ff.

[82] *Ibid.*, Cols. 475–76.

[83] Dalman, *op. cit.*, III, pp. 67 ff., Figs. 16–24.

oil collected in the stone basins.[84] In the Bronze and Iron Age cities there were devices which had a basin either cut out of a block of stone or built up for pressing olives, which had a drain into a collecting vat, likewise fashioned from a stone block.[85] Not until the Hellenistic period were "beam presses" used for pressing olives, utilizing the leverage of a beam one end of which was set into a recess in a stone post and the other end of which was weighted down with stones.[86] Those presses are Roman, which in one way or another used a threaded assembly for pressure, whether in open-air rectangular presses with a stone pier at either end or in cruciform presses attached to the house wall.[87] Traces of these are to be found here and there. Examples of olive mills are also attested only from the Roman period on. In this type a stone cylinder revolving about a perpendicular axle did the pressing over a circular lower stone. Traces of this type are also left.[88]

Wine presses (Hebrew, *yeqebh* or *gath*) were similar in construction to the simple olive presses. Grapes were pressed by trampling (Hebrew, *drk*) with the feet. Therefore, such expressions occur in the Old Testament as "pressing grapes" (Amos 9 : 13) or "to trample the wine press" (Job 24 : 11, Neh. 13 : 15, etc.). The wine press was located in the vineyard or near to it (see Isa. 5 : 2). It consisted of a trampling place hollowed in the native rock, or occasionally of rectangular construction and with a drain opening into a vat at a lower level to catch the wine. Occasionally several wine presses were arranged together. Ancient structures of this type are still frequently found there.[89]

Hunting and fishing were of minor importance in Palestine.[90] The latter was practised on the plentifully stocked Sea of Tiberias as well as along the seacoasts. The excavation at ancient Ezion-geber at the north end of the Gulf of ʿAqabah, now Tell el-Kheleifeh, has brought many copper fish hooks to light.[91] According to the record fishing with nets was also practised, yet this, of course, can no longer be proved archeologically.[92]

84 Dalman, *op. cit.*, IV, Figs. 48, 49.

85 *AOB*, No. 659; Taanach, *AASOR*, XVII (1938), 65, Plates XIXb, XXI–XXII (1943), Plate XLVIIIa: Tell Beit Mirsim.

86 On the structure at Gezer, see *AOB*, No. 637 and the details in Dalman, *op. cit.*, pp. 212 ff., 223 ff., Figs. 54–58, 65–67.

87 Dalman, *op. cit.*, pp. 216 ff., 226 ff., Figs. 68–70 [74a].

88 *Ibid.*, pp. 202 ff., Figs. 50–54, 64.

89 For details, see *ibid.*, IV, 350 ff., Figs. 95–111.

90 Particularly with reference to present conditions, see *ibid.*, VI (1939), 314 ff.

91 Glueck, *BASOR*, LXXI (1938), 5.

92 Galling, *op. cit.*, Cols. 167 ff.

(2) *Crafts*

In the well-developed culture of the Bronze and Iron Age there were professionally executed handicrafts. Pottery was important because it met a great need. In cave 4034 near Lachish (Tell ed-Duweir), a Late Bronze Age pottery workshop has been disclosed.[93] This shop with its inventory was probably also characteristic of an Iron Age pottery. In it a stone bench was found as the potter's seat, as well as a round stone with a conical hole base for the rotating wooden potter's wheel. This seems to have stood originally in a fixed depression in front of the stone bench. Also found were remnants of pigments for painting the clay vessels, as well as sea shells and smooth pebbles for polishing, and a bone stylus for making incised and dotted decorations. Finally there was also slag from the still unlocated kiln in which the clay vessels were fired.

Weaving as well as spinning were in general undertaken by women at home.[94] There was professional weaving only for finer work, such as the manufacture of *byssus*[95] (fine white linen; Hebrew, *boṣ*). Note "the house of *byssus* (fine linen) manufacture" in I Chron. 4 : 21. The only archeological remains of this handicraft are the small bored stone weights frequently found in Iron Age levels. The warp threads of the standing loom, fastened to the upper cross-beam and hanging free, were weighted at the bottom ends by these weights.[96]

In Tell Beit Mirsim, in the level of the period of the Kingdom of Judah, dye works were found.[97] These are built-up, plastered, rectangular basins. In them stood stone kettles with a small opening on top and a groove around the edge which had a drain to the inside of the kettle to return any overflowing dyestuff. Jars were also found containing lime used as a mordant for dye. The remarkably large number of loom weights indicate that weaving was a companion industry. Therefore, a settlement with a professional textile industry was situated at Tell Beit Mirsim.

Metallurgy was important for the manufacture of weapons, implements, and decorations. There were iron and copper works especially in Wādi el-ʿArabah (p. 44). The ores were smelted

[93] *Lachish IV* (1958), 91, 291–93 and Plates VIII, XCII.

[94] The modern practice in Palestine is compared with the ancient in great detail in Dalman, *op. cit.*, V (1937), 42 ff., Figs. 8 ff.

[95] Galling, *op. cit.*, Col. 122.

[96] Examples of such weights are seen in Dalman, *op. cit.*, Fig. 7.

[97] W. F. Albright, *AASOR*, XXI–XXII (1943), 55 ff., Plates XIb, LIc–d, LII–LIII; Watzinger, *Denkmäler Palästinas*, I, 101, Fig. 83; Galling, *op. cit.*, Cols. 150 ff., with illustrations.

in situ, in so far as sufficient firewood was available. In the shops, which carried on the manufacture, the metal was finally refined by smelting (Hebrew, *ṣrp*). Chalcolithic Beersheba Culture arrangements and settings for copper working have been found.[98] We also know of such workshops from Tell Jemmeh on Wādi Ghazzeh south of Gaza,[99] from the Late Bronze to Early Iron Age from Tell Qasileh,[100] from the eleventh century B.C. as especially from Iron Age Tell el-Kheleifeh at the northern end of the Gulf of el-ʿAqabah near the rich outcroppings of copper and iron.[101] Brick structures were found *in situ* with air ducts in the walls, laid out in line with the prevailing wind to fan the fire. The wood fire was set over a layer of broken limestone to provide a draft from below. Clay crucibles were found at Tell Kheleifeh. Then the refined metal was poured into forms. Middle and Late Bronze Age moulds for spear heads, axe blades, etc., have been found in Tell Beit Mirsim.[102] A clay mould for spear heads, axe blades, daggers, and sickles also came to light from Late Bronze Shechem.[103] The moulded parts were then forged with a hammer. Note Gen. 4 : 22, Hebrew *lṭš*. Beside the usual decorative pieces (p. 161) smiths finished implements for all sorts of jobs. Beside the sickles already mentioned (p. 163) they finished mattocks[104] for farmers, axes (Cols. 62 ff.), knives (Cols. 378–79), and other tools (Cols. 281 ff.) for wood working, and pickaxes (Cols. 88–89) for stone working. Naturally, weapons also were forged, such as the helmets (Cols. 279–80), spear heads (Cols. 353 ff.), daggers (Cols. 129 ff.), arrowheads (Cols. 418 ff.), swords (Cols. 472 ff.), as well as maces (Cols. 329 ff.) and metal parts of armour (Cols. 416–17). On the history and types of the different weapons in the larger context see especially H. Bonnet, *Die Waffen der Völker des alten Orients* (1926).

98 J. Perrot, *IEJ*, V (1955), 79–80.

99 Petrie, *Gerar* (1928), p. 14, Plates VI (bottom), VII, IX, XXV.

100 B. Maisler, *The Excavations at Tell Qasileh* (1951), p. 15, Fig. 3, reprinted in *IEJ*, I (1950–51), 75, Fig. 3.

101 Glueck, *BASOR*, LXXI (1938), 5 ff., particularly Figs. 2 and 3; LXXV (1939), 8 ff.; LXXIX (1940), 2 ff.; Glueck, *The Excavations of Solomon's Seaport: Ezion-Geber, Annual Report of the Board of Regents of the Smithsonian Institution for the Year Ended June 30, 1941* (1942), pp. 453–78. On ancient metal mining and metal working in the region of Wādi el-ʿArabah, particularly at Jebel el-Meneʿīyeh (Isr., Har Timnaʿ) and in Wādi el-Meneʿīyeh (see p. 44), see the report on research conducted *in situ* by B. Rothenberg, *PEQ*, XCIV (1962), 5–71. These studies have produced particularly detailed and important materials on Iron Age metal industry and also have prompted corrections in the previous explanation of the installations on Tell el-Kheleifeh.

102 *AASOR*, XVII (1938), Plate XLIII.

103 Sellin, *ZDPV*, L (1927), 210, Plate XXI; Galling, *op. cit.*, Cols. 379 ff., with illustrations.

104 Galling, *op. cit.*, Cols. 256 ff., with illustrations.

Outside of the tools referred to above, no special tools for working have been found for construction of homes (p. 153) and manufacture of various household furnishings (pp. 157 ff.). The craft of stone masonry is evident in cut stone blocks for walls (p. 150), and in the underground construction works for water supply (pp. 154 ff.) as well as elsewhere.

(3) *Trade*

Trade, that is, buying and selling, appears everywhere on a specific cultural level as a way of life. Trading was a common activity in Bronze Age city culture as well as in Iron Age settlements, where it appeared initially in a somewhat more primitive stage than in the previous Bronze Age. Weights and measures were a necessity for commerce. Cubical measures were needed for wares, for liquid and dry commodities. From the Old Testament we know the system of dry and liquid measures, their relation to each other, and their absolute value.[105] But there are only rare cases of standardized or calibrated vessels found which indicate the quantity contained. Even the few which have been determined archeologically are not intact. Containers have not as yet been definitely proved archeologically. Metal was weighed in payment for purchases much more than commodities were. Just as a number of weights are named in our literary sources, so there have been unearthed many weights, button-shaped limestone pieces, small pieces of worked metal, bearing marks and numbers, as well as with Hebrew letters and words. Unfortunately it has not yet been possible to arrive at a definite system of weights or a historical development of the system of weights by comparing the weights found with those mentioned in our literary sources.[106]

In ordinary daily life barter of farm products continued on long after money was known as a medium of exchange. At least as far back as the Late Bronze Age, Canaanite city culture recognized metal weighed out as money. It was naturally so recognized by the Israelites in the Iron Age. Since the word for silver, *keseph*, also means simply money, naturally, silver weighed out was a medium

[105] E.g., see Benzinger, *Hebräische Archäologie* (3rd ed., 1927), pp. 192–95; for great detail, see Barrois, "La métrologie dans la Bible, I," *RB*, XL (1931), 185–213 and *Manuel d'archéologie biblique*, II (1953), 247–52.

[106] Details are in Viedebantt, "Zur hebräischen phönizischen und syrischen Gewichtskunde," *ZDPV*, XLV (1922), 1–22; in Barrois, "La métrologie dans la Bible, II," *RB*, XLI (1932), 50–76 and *Manuel d'archéologie biblique*, II, 252–58; briefly, in Galling, *op. cit.*, Cols. 185 ff., with illustrations. A special problem is treated in R. B. Y. Scott, "The Shekel Sign on Stone Weights," *BASOR*, CLIII (1959), 32–35. See also *BASOR*, CLXXIII (1963), 53–63.

of exchange. The money metal in bars or "tongues" (see Josh. 7 : 21; in this case, it is gold), filled the "treasure houses" of royal palaces and of temples. Stamped money or coins are weighed pieces of metal whose correct weight was guaranteed by the impression of an official authority, king, provincial or city government. This dispensed with constant weighing. Coinage became standard in the Near East in the Persian empire, following the well-established coinage of the Lydian kingdom. The oldest Palestinian coins are probably datable to the Persian period. One should note particularly coins of the Persian province of Judah with the inscription *yhd* (i.e., Judah) and with designs copied from Attic coins which were already in use along the eastern Mediterranean coast.[107] There are Palestinian coins as well as Attic coins and coins minted by the Phoenician cities, Persian satraps, Seleucid and Ptolemaic rulers and later by the Romans. One was found in Beth-zur with the name written in Hebrew, probably of a high priest from the period of Ptolemaic rule.[108] There are Hasmonean-minted coins, generally with Hebrew-Greek inscription, Greek-inscribed coins of Herod, and then again coins inscribed in Hebrew during the days of both Jewish revolts, A.D. 66–70 and A.D. 132–135.[109]

20. *Burial Customs*

Cremation of corpses has not been customary in Palestine since the ancient Oriental period. The Old Testament recognizes cremation only as punishment for criminals who are thereby definitely excluded from the congregation of the people. (See Lev. 20 : 14; 21 : 9, and elsewhere). As a result the dead were generally buried in the ground as is quite generally practised elsewhere, and in burial places away from the dwellings. Only seldom and exceptionally were the dead in Palestine buried within occupied settlements. Thus, the grave of an old woman in Gezer within the city itself was found in the form of a pit lined with great stones,[110] and as elsewhere in the Mediterranean region, deceased children were buried in clay pots inside the settlements.[111] The custom also well-

[107] Sukenik, *JPOS*, XIV (1934), 178–82; XV (1935), 341–43, with illustrations.
[108] O. R. Sellers, *The Citadel of Beth-zur* (1933), pp. 73–74, Fig. 72.
[109] For details see G. F. Hill, *Catalogue of the Greek Coins of Palestine*, corresponding to *Catalogue of Greek Coins in the British Museum* (1914); and especially A. Reifenberg, *Ancient Jewish Coins* (2nd ed., 1947), with abundant illustrative material.
[110] *AOB*, No. 227.
[111] *AOB*, No. 228.

known in Assyria,[112] Syria,[113] and elsewhere of burying the dead under the floor of his house (the instance in I Sam. 25 : 1 is unique in the Old Testament) always was an unusual practice in Palestine. It was customary at most only for the nobility. The built-up mausoleums of the central fortress "Mittelburg" of Megiddo,[114] as well as the great burial cave in Gezer, both from the middle Bronze Age, probably are the burial places of the ruling families there. A further example is the burial place of the rulers of the city of Byblos in Lebanon on the Mediterranean from about 1,000 B.C. Rich Middle and Late Bronze Age finds were obtaineo during the excavation from this tomb. Similarly in the Books of Kings it is regularly noted that the deceased members of the family of David were buried "in the city of David." Also, among the Israelite kings their burial in their royal residence is repeatedly mentioned. (See I Kings 16 : 6, 28, and elsewhere). In the region of the old city of David in Jerusalem, long horizontal tunnels have been found, driven into the rock. There is some probability that these were the burial place of the Davidic family.[115]

The general rule was, however, to locate burial places outside the inhabited settlements. Taking the given terrain into acccount, the burial places of city inhabitants lay more or less close together in the immediate vicinity of the city. That means every city had its own necropolis. Of course, the burial sites so far located in the necropolises of the cities belonged only to the more outstanding and richer families, while the poorer people were interred outside the city in simple graves. (Note in II Kings 23 : 6, "Graves of the people" in the Kidron Valley on the east side of Jerusalem.) For, after all, the establishment of proper burial sites required a considerable expenditure. Almost nothing remains of the simple earth burials of ancient times. The history of burial customs as a result can be traced only for those more outstanding burial sites which developed different characteristic forms in different periods.[116]

Natural caves provided convenient burial places in a hilly country like Palestine.[117] Most of the later forms of burial sites

[112] Meissner, *Babylonien und Assyrien*, I (1920), 426; W. Andrae, *Das wiedererstandene Assur* (1938), pp. 14 ff., Plate IX.

[113] See the Middle Bronze graves of Rās Shamrah in *Syria*, XIX (1938), 199 ff.

[114] *AOB*, No. 217; Watzinger, *Tell el-Mutesellim*, II, 1 ff.

[115] *AOB*, No. 234; Galling, *BRL*, Col. 245 ff. Fig. 9.

[116] Galling, *BRL*, Cols. 237 ff.; Galling, "Die Nekropole von Jerusalem," *PJB*, XXXII (1936), 73–101, both with numerous illustrations.

[117] Perhaps in the Chalcolithic period the custom of burial above the ground was temporarily practised, employing megalithic stone chambers, the so-called dolmens. E.g., see *AOB*, No. 212; Watzinger, *Denkmäler Palästinas*, I, Figs. 45–46. Still, it is

developed from caves. The most important of them will be described briefly in what follows. In the Bronze Age people devised artificial caves more or less regularly hewn out of the rock with an approach by way of a shaft sunk vertically to the bottom, from which a passageway led to the burial cave.[118] Possibly stairs also led down to the cave. This approach could be filled with debris to make sure that the burial would not be disturbed. In the Iron Age then as a rule they lowered the floor in the middle of the burial chamber cut out of the rock, so that at the sides benches were left on which the dead were buried in an outstretched position. Thus, arose the type of bench tomb characteristic of the Old Testament period.[119] These were generally grave chambers cut out in a more or less rectangular form in which on three sides, excluding the entrance sides, such a bench was left standing. Therefore, three corpses could be laid out at the same time. If another burial took place, one bench at a time was cleared by placing the bones there into a common pit which was usually located in a corner of the grave chamber. The grave chambers belonged to the families and as a rule were made use of for many generations. This suggests at the same time that the thought of an individual life after death was still lacking. The bones of the deceased finally ended up simply in that common pit. Furthermore, the custom of using the bench graves for successive burials instead of single burials explains the complete lack of grave inscriptions, naming the person buried and the like. According to that well-known Old Testament expression, people were in a literal sense gathered to their fathers in the family grave.

In the Hellenistic-Roman period variations of this older manner of burial developed in adjacent places. Such variations often appeared in one and the same burial place at the same time. Ultimately the bench grave type was developed to the point that an arch vaulted over the individual bench. Thus, only a semicircular niche was carved out of the stone wall (*Bogenbankgrab*, vaulted bench tomb). This grave type was further developed so that frequently a trough-shaped depression was devised in the bench to conform to the corpse (*Bogentroggrab*, vaulted trough tomb). The

very difficult and problematical to date these dolmens. It is possible that the dolmens are a survival of a burial custom of some nomadic groups. The dolmens are found especially on the eastern edge of the Jordan rift valley, in the Transjordanian hill country, and in Galilee.

118 *AOB*, No. 215.

119 Galling, *op. cit.*, uses the term *Diwangrab* ("divan tomb") instead of bench tomb.

next significant group were the grave structures with drawer-like crypts (Hebrew, *kokhim*). In these, long, low crypts are recessed into the rock, each for a single burial. They are usually arranged in several rows, one over the other at right angles with the wall of the burial chamber. These are often extensive plans with a number of chambers behind one another and adjoining one another, all with drawer-like crypts and with a broad open vestibule as an entrance, which was occasionally furnished with emplacements of columns, squared pilasters, and the like.[120] The individual form of burial begins with the drawer-like galleries, which were closed after burial with a stone slab. Apparently repeated successive burials no longer were made in them. Therefore, grave inscriptions also appeared now in these graves. We find them, for example, together with many wall paintings, in the second century B.C., in the burial structure at Marissa, now Tell Sandaḥanneh.[121] The passage from the vestibule to the first burial chamber was built as small as possible in order to make it as easy as possible to close the burial place off. This passage-way was frequently blocked off by means of a rolling stone which could be rolled back in a channel which ran off to the side into a recess cut into the rock for this purpose.[122]

In the Hellenistic period tower-like burial monuments also appeared above the ground which were erected over or next to the subterranean burial site and made its location visible from the outside. Of this sort were the burial monuments of the Hellenistic period on the Phoenician coast at ʿAmrit.[123] Of this type also were the burial monuments in the Kidron Valley at Jerusalem which roughly date from the Herodian period, though they now carry misleading names, "tomb of Absalom" and "tomb of Zacharias."[124]

The interest in separate burial, which developed in the Hellenistic period, led to a new practice in preserving the bones of the deceased. When the time came to remove them from the burial bench or the burial trough, they were placed, not as formerly in the common pit, but rather in a special bone chest for each one, called an ossuary. The ossuaries frequently found in Palestine, dating from the first century B.C., and the first two centuries A.D., are small limestone chests with a lid, 0.5 to 1 m. [20–40 inches] long and about half as wide. Probably there were also wooden ossuaries

[120] E.g., see Watzinger, *op. cit.*, II, Fig. 62 and also the sketches in Galling, *PJB*, XXXII (1936), 85.

[121] Watzinger, *op. cit.*, II, Fig. 56.

[122] *AOB*, No. 242. Cf. Matt. 27 : 60, and Mark 16 : 3; Luke 24 : 2.

[123] *AOB*, Nos. 237–38.

[124] *AOB*, No. 240 gives the view; Watzinger, *Denkmäler Palästinas*, II, Figs. 32–33, show the plan.

which are no longer preserved. Those we have are frequently decorated by carving rosette designs and the like in theme[125] and generally have the name of the deceased engraved. They were placed in the chambers of the burial sites, occasionally in a chamber set up for this specific purpose. The inscriptions on the ossuaries form a valuable source for the supply of personal names of the New Testament period. Well-known names appear frequently, written in Hebrew-Aramaic or in Greek, among others those of Joseph and Mary and Jesus. Therefore, no further conclusions can be drawn from any given instance of the appearance of one of these names in an inscription. A burial site with a number of ossuaries in a modern southern suburb of Jerusalem, therefore in the southern vicinity of the former Hellenistic-Roman Jerusalem, which according to the evidence of a coin of Agrippa II found in it, was in use at the middle of the first century after Christ, has been declared to be the earliest monument of Christianity in the land.[126] In it an ossuary was found which had engraved on all four sides a large Greek cross together with the inscription on the lid, *Iēsous Alōth*, while another ossuary of the same burial site was inscribed with *Iēsous Iou*. Still, as was just mentioned, the appearance of the name Jesus indicates nothing and the cross was hardly used this early as a Christian symbol, but in this case perhaps simply served as decoration. Moreover, this find in south Jerusalem in modern Israel is not unusual. In the rather large necropolis near the "Dominus flevit," halfway up the western side of the Mount of Olives, which was carefully excavated and studied from 1953–55[127] similar material was produced. Here, too, on ossuaries of the first and second centuries A.D., the name Jesus appears several times on ossuaries, written in Hebrew-Aramaic, as do the names Joseph and Mary. Here also the symbol of the cross appears in various forms and styles.[128]

Sarcophagi, or coffins with lids, were never in such general use in Palestine as were ossuaries for the subsequent gathering of the bones. Wooden and stone sarcophagi were known in Egypt from the most ancient times and the rulers of the city of Byblos in Lebanon on the Mediterranean coast, which very early had par-

[125] Watzinger, *op. cit.*, II, Figs. 69–70; Galling, *op. cit.*, Cols. 405 ff., Figs. 1–4.

[126] E. L. Sukenik, "The Earliest Records of Christianity," *AJF*, LI (1947), 351–65, Plates 78–86.

[127] P. B. Bagetti and J. T. Milik, *Gli scavi del "Dominus flevit,"* Vol. I: *la necropoli del periodo romano* (1958).

[128] E. Dinkler, "Zur Geschichte des Kreuzsymbols," *ZThK*, XLVIII (1951), 148–72. He also rejects the Christian meaning of the situation referred to and ascribes a particular symbolic value to the cross already within Judaism.

ticularly close connections with Egypt, were buried in stone sarcophagi toward the end of the second and the beginning of the first millennium B.C. The most famous of them because of its art work and its inscription (see p. 213) is the sarcophagus of King Ahiram, probably of the tenth century. In Palestine itself clay sarcophagi occur, first in the twelfth century at Beth-shan and then at other places. These clay sarcophagi, anthropoid in shape, have a removable lid at the head and a stereotyped face. They represent a borrowed, foreign burial custom, perhaps under Egyptian influence, which was apparently practised in Palestine for a long time by foreign immigrants from the Mediterranean world.[129]

Later on in the Persian period the city kings in Phoenicia once again provided for their burial in anthropoid or chest-shaped stone sarcophagi, particularly in Sidon. Stone and marble sarcophagi have been found also in Sidon from the Hellenistic period with skilfully Greek relief art, such as the renowned "Alexander sarcophagus."[130] Yet stone sarcophagi with relief work did not appear in Palestine until the Roman period and then along with the other burial customs.[131] At the same time people occasionally used lead coffins with stereotyped relief pictures, just as was done in Phoenicia, from the second to the fifth century of our era.[132] Large numbers of stone and lead sarcophagi, done in relief, have been disclosed in the Jewish cemetery of Beth-shearim (see p. 135).

In all periods all sorts of gifts were left with the deceased in the grave or coffin with the assumption of a shadowy existence after death. These were articles of daily life, such as clay vases, clay lamps, ointment vases, decorations, weapons. Therefore, burial places remain an extremely important and productive source of finds for all these things for archeologists, especially if they have not been disturbed or robbed.

21. *Sanctuaries*

Many pagan temples and Jewish synagogues have been preserved in Palestine from the Roman period on. There are also

[129] On sarcophagi at Beth-shan and Tell Fār'ah, see Watzinger, *op. cit.*, I, Figs. 73–77; Galling, *BRL*, Col. 450, Figs. 1–4; on those at Lachish, Grave 570, see *Lachish IV* (1958), 131–32, 248–49, Plates XLV, 1–2, XLVI.

[130] Luckenbach, *Kunst und Geschichte*, I (9th ed., 1913), Plate I, Figs. 196–97.

[131] Examples appear in *AOB*, No. 241; Watzinger, *op. cit.*, II, Figs. 67–68, 74–75.

[132] Avi-Yonah, " Lead Coffins from Palestine," *QDAP*, IV (1935), 87–99, 138–53, Plates LV–LX; Watzinger, *op. cit.*, II, Figs. 76–79.

remains of many Byzantine Christian churches. Still, we have a very incomplete archeological understanding of Palestinian sanctuaries from the ancient Oriental period. It is certainly not easy to correctly identify sanctuaries in the excavated ground plans or other disclosed monuments. A strong desire to find temples, particularly among earlier excavators, repeatedly led to identifications of archeological finds, which afterward proved to be false or at least very problematical. We have a few definite examples of temple plans from the various stages of the Bronze Age. The sanctuary disclosed during the excavations (p. 213) on the citadel of et-Tell at Deir Dubwān belongs to the Early Bronze Age. This spot was known as Ai in Old Testament times.[133] The sanctuary there consists of an anteroom and a main room. The latter has its very small inner sanctum in a corner, cut off by a wall, with a built-up altar table, and in addition three *favissae* [pits] to catch refuse from the altar (Figure 5). Somewhat more numerous are the temple finds, from the Middle and Late Bronze Age. From this period we have in particular the temple on the acropolis of ancient Shechem.[134] It was erected in the final phase of the Middle Bronze Age. In the Late Bronze Age a new building was erected in its place, with a somewhat altered orientation, but otherwise probably following a similar plan.[135] The Middle Bronze building is a long room surrounded by a very thick wall with an open porch entrance flanked by antae.[136] The ceiling of the long room was supported by two rows of three pillars, most likely wooden, whose stone pedastals and voluted capitals have been partially recovered. In the rear half of the long room the base for the figure or the symbol of the god was found. Under it was the pit (*favissa*). On the two *maṣṣebhoth* in front of the *antae* on either side of the porch, see p. 178. This temple is shown in Figure 5. A Late Bronze Age temple with three successive building stages following one upon the other was disclosed at Tell ed-Duweir, Lachish.[137] This is a long room structure with a porch set over to the side. Wooden columns on stone bases serve as ceiling supports. A podium at the centre of the rear

[133] J. Marquet-Krause, *Les fouilles de 'Ay* (1949), Plates XCIII (including a reconstruction), XCIV; *ANEP*, No. 730.

[134] Sellin, *ZDPV*, LXIX (1926), 309 ff., Plates XXXII (floor plan), XXXVII–XLII; *ZDPV*, L (1927), 206–207, Plates XI–XII, XVII.

[135] Toombs and Wright, *BASOR*, CLXI (1961), 28–39.

[136] Cf. the Late Bronze temple of Megiddo, Level 8 in G. Loud, *Megiddo II* (1948), Fig. 402.

[137] O. Tufnell, C. H. Inge, and L. Harding, *The Fosse Temple—Lachish* (*Tell ed-Duweir*), II (1940), Plates LXVI–LXIX. The plan of the latest temple is also given in Galling, *BRL*, Cols. 513–14, Fig. 6.

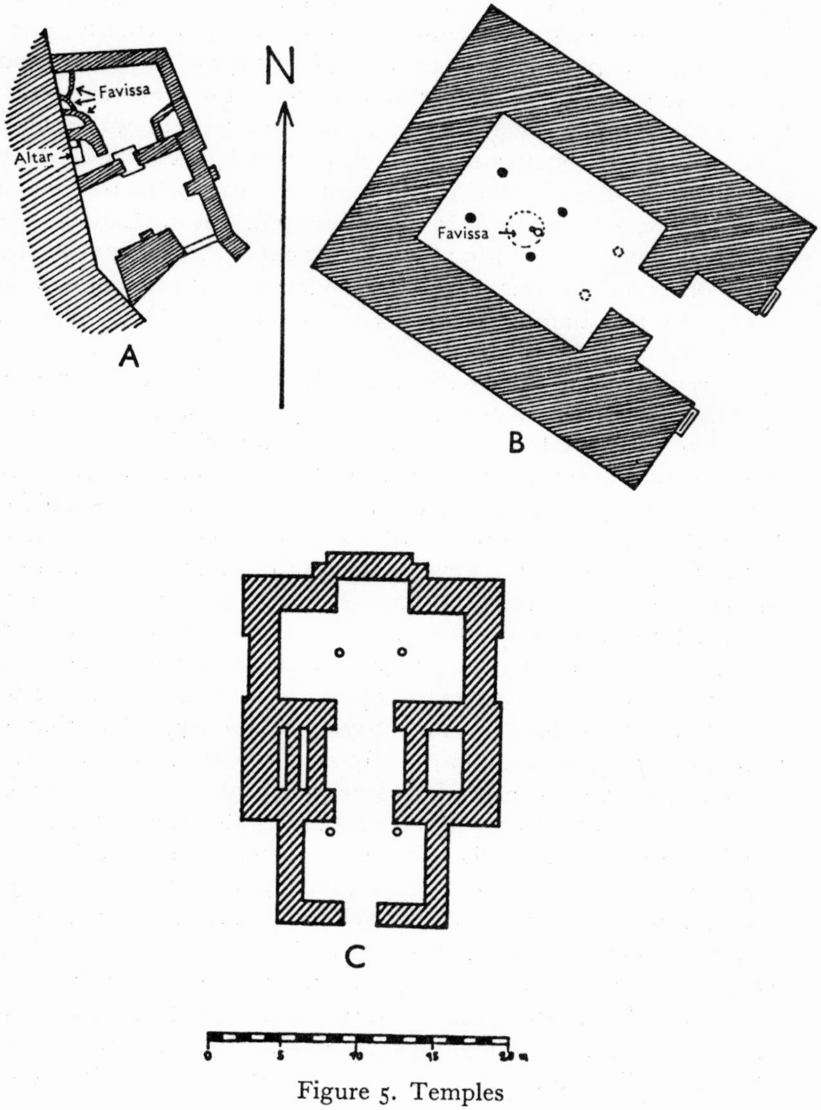

Figure 5. Temples

A. Early Bronze sanctuary of et-Tell at Deir Dubwān, J. Marquet-Krause, *Les fouilles de ʿAy* (1949), Plate XCIII.

B. Middle Bronze temple of Tell Balāṭah, Shechem, based on *ZDPV*, XLIX (1926), Plate XXXIII, and *ZDPV*, LI (1928), 119 ff.

C. Temple of Hazor in its Late Bronze form (Level 1, 6); preliminary plan based on *IEJ*, VIII (1958), 11–14, Plate VIII a; *IEJ*, IX (1959), 81–84, Plate X a-b.

wall served as an altar table and probably was used also as the stand for the figurine or symbol of the god. Particularly noteworthy is the temple which was disclosed in 1957 at the excavation of Hazor in area H near the northern corner of the great lower city. It was built already in the Middle Bronze Age, but was rebuilt three times in the course of the Late Bronze Age with apparently similar plans. Best known are the last two stages, Ib (on which Fig. 5 C is based) and Ia from the second phase of the Late Bronze Age. Especially worth noting is arrangement of three rooms behind one another on one axis, consisting apparently of an anteroom, a main room, and an inner sanctuary. This immediately reminds one of the plan of the later temple of Solomon.[138] The Late Bronze Age temples which were built in Beth-shan during the period of Egyptian domination, possibly by Egyptian officials, were of a special type.[139] While the plan from the time of Thutmose III is still very unclear, the later plans have wide rooms with a columned vestibule and a podium at the centre of the rear wall in the middle. The archeological material is still too limited to decide definitely and reliably whether there was a definite basic type of Canaanite temple, and what connections they had with the temple plans of the great neighbouring cultures. Still, in the Middle and Late Bronze temples the long room appears as a distinctive feature. The exception is the Late Bronze temples at Beth-shan, built under special circumstances. The later Syrian temple type[140] is characterized by its separate and frequently elevated innermost sanctuary. With its vestibule it consisted of three rooms, as seen already in the three-room temple of Late Bronze Hazor. It also had a forerunner in the three-room, even though not axial, temple of et-Tell.

Still more meagre is the archeological yield for the Iron Age. Not even one plan has yet been disclosed in any Iron Age level in Palestine which can be definitely described as a temple. And yet we know from the Old Testament record that there were temples in the land during this period. No trace has been found *in situ* of the temple with the sacred ark at Shiloh, now Khirbet Seilūn, which underlies I Sam. 1 : 7,9; 3 : 3,15; Jer. 7 : 14.[141] The oldest

[138] Similar to the above is the plan of a temple from the ninth century B.C., which came to light on Tell Ta'yināt in 'Amq, east of Antakya in northern Syria; C. W. McEwan, *American Journal of Archaeology*, LXI (1937), 13, Figs 4 (top), 67.

[139] Rowe and Vincent, *PEF Qu. St.* (1931), pp. 12 ff., Plates I–III (reconstruction proposals); Watzinger, *op. cit.*, I, 65 ff.; Galling, *op. cit.*, Fig. 4 (floor plan).

[140] Alt, *PJB*, XXV (1935), 83–99 [reprinted in *KS*, II, 100–15].

[141] The wall fragment south of the ruins at the site of Shiloh seemed to go back to the ancient temple of Shiloh; cf. Dalman, *PJB*, IV (1908), 12–13. Excavation has since shown that this was part of a Byzantine church; cf. Kjaer, *JPOS*, X (1930), 126 ff.

part of the Jerusalem temple which remains to this day is Herodian (pp. 119, 135). No more remains of the post-exilic temple than of Solomon's temple. Only the natural focal point of the entire sanctuary, the sacred rock itself, over which once the Holy of Holies of the temple was raised,[142] is still visible as the centre point of the Islamic Dome of the Rock (pp. 113–14). For our understanding of the Jerusalem temple we are therefore exclusively dependent on literary records, for the temple of Solomon on the detailed, but sometimes ambiguous description in I Kings, chapters 6 and 7[143] and for the post-exilic temple on Ezek. 40 : 5 to 43 : 12, and on scattered references in *Hekataios of Abdera* and in the Books of Maccabees;[144] for the Herodian temple on Josephus and Mishna tractate *Middoth*.

Not a trace has been found as yet during excavations *in situ* of the Israelite state temples in Bethel and Dan (see I Kings 12 : 29 ff., Amos 7 : 13), and Samaria (underlying Hos. 8 : 5,6). Just as little has been archeologically demonstrated so far of the temple of the god Dagon in Ashdod of Philistia, Esdūd (see I Sam. 5 : 2 ff.), or the temple of Astarte in Beth-shan. (See I Sam. 31 : 10.)

We assume that a temple was generally an integral part of the ancient Canaanite cities. However, in the Israelite period there were probably temple buildings only in the case of the amphictyonic and then of the state sanctuaries. At the same time there were numerous sanctuaries in the country. Generally, each settlement had one of them near by. They were legitimate until King Josiah of Judah carried out the centralization requirement of Deut. 12 : 13 ff. These were simply sacred places, perhaps with a surrounding wall and a minimum of furnishings. The sanctity here was linked with the site itself and its natural features, such as a sacred tree, a sacred spring, or the like. Its furnishings included primarily an altar for the presentation or burning of offerings.[145] A natural rock formation or a stone block lying there could certainly serve this purpose, on given occasions with easy modification, by carving out some steps for ascending and the like. The stone altar

[142] H. Schmidt, *Der Heilige Fels in Jerusalem* (1933).

[143] Mohlenbrink, *Der Tempel Salomos* (1932); Watzinger, *op. cit.*, I, 88 ff.; Vincent and Stève, *Jerusalem de l'Ancien Testament*, III (1956), 373–431. [Also G. E. Wright, *Biblical Archaeology* (1957), pp. 136–45; and P. L. Garber, "Reconstructing Solomon's Temple," *BA*, XIV, No. 1 (Feb., 1950).]

[144] J. Jeremias, "Hesekieltempel und Serubabeltempel," *ZAW*, New Series, XI (1934), 109 ff. [Also C. H. Howie, "The East Gate of Ezekiel's Temple Enclosure and the Solomonic Gateway of Megiddo," *BASOR*, CXVII (Feb., 1950), 13–19.]

[145] Concerning the possible altar types, see the comprehensive work of Galling, *Der Altar in den Kulturen des alten Orients* (1925).

found at formerly Arab Ṣar'ah, whose date cannot be determined,[146] underwent more thorough-going modification. It is a cubical rough-hewn stone block with steps and with its upper surface arranged with bowl-shaped holes and a drain running around it. It is most closely related to the step altars of Petra, which are very much later, though very old in type.[147] Naturally hardly anything remains of the altars presupposed in Exod. 20 : 24–26, which were constructed of heaped-up earth or uncut stones.

According to the Old Testament frequently *maṣṣebhoth* and *asherim* were also part of the furnishings of the rustic sanctuaries. The *asherim*[148] were wooden poles, which probably means trees regarded as vegetation symbols. Therefore, they have not lasted to the present. The *maṣṣebhoth* on the other hand were menhirs which seem to have been originally thought of as dwellings (as still in Gen. 28 : 22), or representatives of deity and were later understood to be memorial stones of a manifestation of God or the like (as in Gen. 28 : 18; 35 : 14) and were also later used as monuments. (See Gen. 35 : 20.) *Maṣṣebhoth* of rustic sanctuaries, which were unworked stones, have not been archeologically attested. Only worked *maṣṣebhoth* in connection with city temple sites can still be attested. Thus, in the temple site of Thutmose III at Beth-shan a low *maṣṣebhoth* was found,[149] and on both sides of the entrance of the Late Bronze temple of Shechem stones were found cut into, and the remains of flat stone uprights were found which probably once stood upright in those channels and which are probably to be interpreted as *maṣṣebhoth*.[150] These *maṣṣebhoth* from Shechem, to judge from the remains, had the form of a stone slab rounded off at the top,[151] that is, the normal form of a stela. This clarifies the connection between *maṣṣebhah* and stela. For a stela is a well-worked *maṣṣebhah*, the former usually including an inscription and a portrayal. Along with stelae with royal inscriptions and the like,[152] by the Late Bronze Age there were cultic stelae, such as the stela for the god Mekal found in the temple site dated to Thutmose III at Beth-shan,[153] bearing a hieroglyphic inscription and a portrayal consisting of native Canaanite and Egyptian elements characteristically mixed.[154]

146 *AOB*, No. 445.
147 *AOB*, Nos. 446–49, 453.
148 Galling, *BRL*, Cols. 35–36.
149 Thomsen, *AO*, XXX (1931), Plate IX.
150 Sellin, *ZDPV*, LI (1928), 119 ff., Plates VII–XII, as well as Fig. 5 B here.
151 See also Galling, *BRL*, Cols. 369–70, Fig. 3.
152 See p. 219 concerning the Mesha stela; further, see Galling, *op. cit.*, Cols. 500 ff.
153 See Watzinger, *op. cit.*, I, Fig. 71.
154 On Hellenistic portrayals one encounters a combination which is probably pre-Hellenistic, between altar and *maṣṣebhah*, in which the *maṣṣebhah* appears on the altar

The burning of incense seems to have been part of public and private cultic practice since very ancient times, likely with an apotropaic purpose. The oldest incense altars so far known, rectangular clay stands with side openings for air circulation and a bowl on top for the incense, come from the Early Bronze sanctuary of et-Tell at Deir Dubwān.[155] From Iron Age private houses various small stone altars were found, ½ to 1 m. [20–40 inches] high, rectangular in cross section, which have an upper surface measuring 20–by–20 to 30–by–30 cm. [8–by–8 to 12–by–12 inches], often having a bowl-shaped depression in the top and as a rule having "horns" in the four corners.[156] In view of their small size these items can only be incense altars which, because of the place where they were found, must have served as private censors,[157] whereas the clay object from Iron Age Taanach customarily considered an incense altar[158] was more likely a brazier for heating in the cold season of the year; cf. Jer. 36 : 22–23.

Other cultic equipment, including all sorts of bowls, bronze tripods serving as bowl stands, etc., have been found, especially in Bronze Age levels in Palestine.[159]

table or behind the altar in close connection with it. See Galling, *Der Altar*, pp. 67–68; Plate XIII, Nos. 37–47. Gressmann conjectured that the altar *maṣṣebhoth* were placed at the four corners on practical grounds, in the "horns" of the altar; cf. Galling, *BRL*, Col. 17.

[155] J. Marquet-Krause, *op. cit.*, Plates LII; LIII, No. 1506; LXV, No. 1507. It is not certain whether these objects described by the excavators as incense altars are not rather simply fire pans with bases, including the so-called incense altar of Taanach.

[156] Items from Shechem are described in Sellin, *ZDPV*, XLIX (1926), 232–33, Plate XXXIb–c; from Megiddo, in Lamon and Shipton, *Megiddo I* (1939), Fig. 31; Gezer, *AOB*, No. 444.

[157] Lohr, *Das Räucheropfer im Alten Testament, Schriften der Königsberger Gelehrten Gesellschaft, geisteswiss. Kl. IV*, 4 (1927).

[158] See Thomsen, *op. cit.*, Plate XI; Watzinger, *op. cit.*, I, Fig. 86.

[159] Galling, *BRL*, Cols. 340 ff., illus.

PART THREE

PERTINENT ASPECTS OF ANCIENT NEAR EASTERN HISTORY

Preliminary Remarks

THE Old Testament originated in the great productive world of the ancient Near East, a world of extremely varied forms and of long and complicated history, which began millennia before the time of the Old Testament. The Old Testament makes substantial and frequent reference to forms and events of this world, and Old Testament history is inseparably connected in countless ways with its *milieu*. Therefore, in order to interpret the Old Testament properly, it is necessary to understand the characteristics of the ancient Near East, its life and history.

After systematic investigation of the nature of the ancient Near East, beginning at the start, and in particular about the middle of the nineteenth century, a considerable number of specialized areas of study sprang up. Each of them is concerned with a segment of this world: its language, archeology, or history. There is so much information now available that no one person is in a position to be an expert on the whole field. Nevertheless, there is a certain basic fund of essential, certified results of the ancient Near Eastern studies which can be summarized and surveyed. The situation is such that it is possible to grasp the relation of the Old Testament to the world of the ancient Near East only by making use of these resources. While doing this it is well not only to take account of some of the chief results of ancient Near Eastern studies, but at the same time to search out the bases and sources of scholarly investigation; and therefore, actually to begin with these latter points and then proceed to the more important individual historical results, even if in the course of research itself disclosure and evaluation of sources always go hand in hand.[1]

[1] The primary [German] reference book for the more important ancient oriental textual and pictorial material is H. Gressmann, *Altorientalische Texte und Bilder zum Alten Testament*, Vols. I–II (2nd ed., 1926–27). One volume consists of texts (abbreviated *AOT*) and the other of pictures and interpretation of them (abbreviated *AOB*). Somewhat more inclusive and newer is the double work in English: *Ancient Near Eastern Texts Relating to the Old Testament*, ed. J. B. Pritchard (rev. ed., 1955), abbreviated *ANET*, and J. B. Pritchard, *The Ancient Near East in Pictures Relating to the Old Testament* (1955), abbreviated *ANEP*. Because of the texts and pictures offered, one might also refer to A. Jeremias, *Das Alte Testament in Lichte des alten Orients*, (4th ed., 1930), abbreviated *ATAO*, and A. Jeremias, *Handbuch altorientalischen Geisteskultur* (2nd ed., 1929), abbreviated *HAOG*. The first volume of a new

In general the Old Testament period extended to the time of Alexander the Great. Hellenization of the Near East entered an acute stage with him. Only here and there is it necessary to extend our consideration beyond this date.

journal on history and archeology of the entire ancient Near East appeared in 1962 under the title, *Oriens Antiquus*, probably to be abbreviated *OA*. It is published by the *Centro per le antichita e la storia dell'arte del vicino oriente* in Rome. Thus it promises to parallel the following highly respected journal. E. F. Weidner began publication of *Archiv für Keilschriftforschung* in 1923. With volume III (1926), both scope and title were enlarged in *Archiv für Orientforschung, Internationale Zeitschrift für die Wissenschaft vom vorderen Orient*. The original editor, E. F. Weidner, continues this most important journal.

CHAPTER I

I. LANDS

22. *Natural Units*[1]

(1) *The Valley of the Nile*

The northeastern corner of Africa is also part of the historical entity of the ancient Near East. More precisely this refers to the Land of the Nile which touches the Mediterranean at this northeastern corner. The Nile rises from sources in equatorial East Africa and on the highlands of Abyssinia. Then with its tributaries it crosses the Sudan, pouring its productive waters into a narrow valley confined by deserts. Below the first cataract it forms a level river valley, at first narrow but broadening out farther down and from 15 to 30 and even 50 km. [from 9 to 18 or even 30 miles] in width. Finally, in the region of the Nile Delta it expands into an extensive fertile alluvial land. We call this fertile valley ancient Egypt, based on a name coined by the Greeks. On both sides this river region is bordered by high desert plateaus, in the east by the Arabian desert, and in the west by the Libyan desert, which contains various oases. The fertility of the land, which receives only a bit of rain, depended until the construction of the Aswan dam on being regularly flooded by the water of the Nile, following the melting of snows at its sources. (Actually, the bulk of the late summer and early fall flood of the Nile is derived from the accumulation of summer rainfall on the East African plateau and the Ethiopian massif.) The Nile begins to rise perceptibly in July. It reaches its high point some time in October. At that time it covers all of the farmland in the Nile Valley proper. By about January it has again returned to its low level. At the same time the Nile is the natural commercial artery of the country.[2]

[1] Guthe, *Bibelatlas* (2nd ed., 1926), No. 5, gives a cartographic survey of the area of the ancient Near East. A substantial part is embraced in the exact, detailed map, *Syrien und Mesopotamien* in two sheets, prepared by H. H. Kiepert. It is included in the volume of M. von Oppenheim, *Vom Mittelmeer zum Persischen Golf* (1899–1900), which also contains a comprehensive survey sketch of the entire area of the ancient Near East, likewise done by H. Kiepert. With reference to what follows, note the sketch map on p. 187 which is Fig. 6. Prepared for a special purpose is *Archäologische Übersichtskarte des Alten Orients, Mit einem Katalog der wichtigsten Fundplätze* (Weimar, 1959).

[2] A survey map of Egypt and many exact detail maps are found in Karl Baedeker, *Egypt and the Sudan* (8th rev. ed., 1929).

(2) *Mesopotamia*

Mesopotamia is the counterpart to the Nile country. This is the region of the middle and lower courses of the two rivers, the Euphrates and the Tigris. These names in their present form are of Greek origin. These rivers rise not far apart in the Armenian mountains and empty into the Persian Gulf. In distant antiquity their mouths were separate. Now they are joined in the Shatt el-ʿArab, which flows through the area where river deposits have constantly extended the coast. This lower river region is also a rainless alluvial plain, watered by the two rivers. In it many arms of both rivers flow on through the vast flat swamp land. It is bordered on the southwest by the edge of the Syro-Arabian desert plateau and on the northwest by the Iranian mountains. It extends for 600 km. [373 miles] from the neighbourhood of Baghdad, the capital of present-day Iraq, downstream to the Persian Gulf. This part of Mesopotamia is *ʿIraq* proper. The nation took this as the name for the entire country, thereby considerably extending the area originally known by that name. Melting snow in the mountains leads to high water sometime between March and June. When the high-water mark is reached in April and May, extensive plains are covered by river water. But the river water can be utilized artificially for the irrigation of the land at other times too by means of canal systems between the two rivers.

Farther upstream the river beds of the Euphrates and the Tigris are widely separated and each of them, quite on its own, cuts through the northern part of the Syro-Arabian desert plateau, which is crossed by various mountain ranges. Consequently in upper Mesopotamia only the long river beds and valleys of varying width offer the possibility of settled life. In addition to the valleys of the Euphrates and the Tigris, the Khābūr and the River Belīkh, both "left bank" tributaries of the Euphrates, offer the same possibility.

This desert and steppe land between the middle courses of the Euphrates and the Tigris is now called el-Jezīreh, "the Island," and is ancient Mesopotamia, "the land between the rivers."

Northeast of the Tigris and running from the northwest to the southeast, an extensive range fringes the Iranian highlands. The front ranges rise conspicuously from the low-lying plain of Mesopotamia. These same mountains send several impressive tributaries into the "left bank" of the Tigris. They are the Great (upper) Zab, the Little (lower) Zab, and the Diyala River. The northern part of

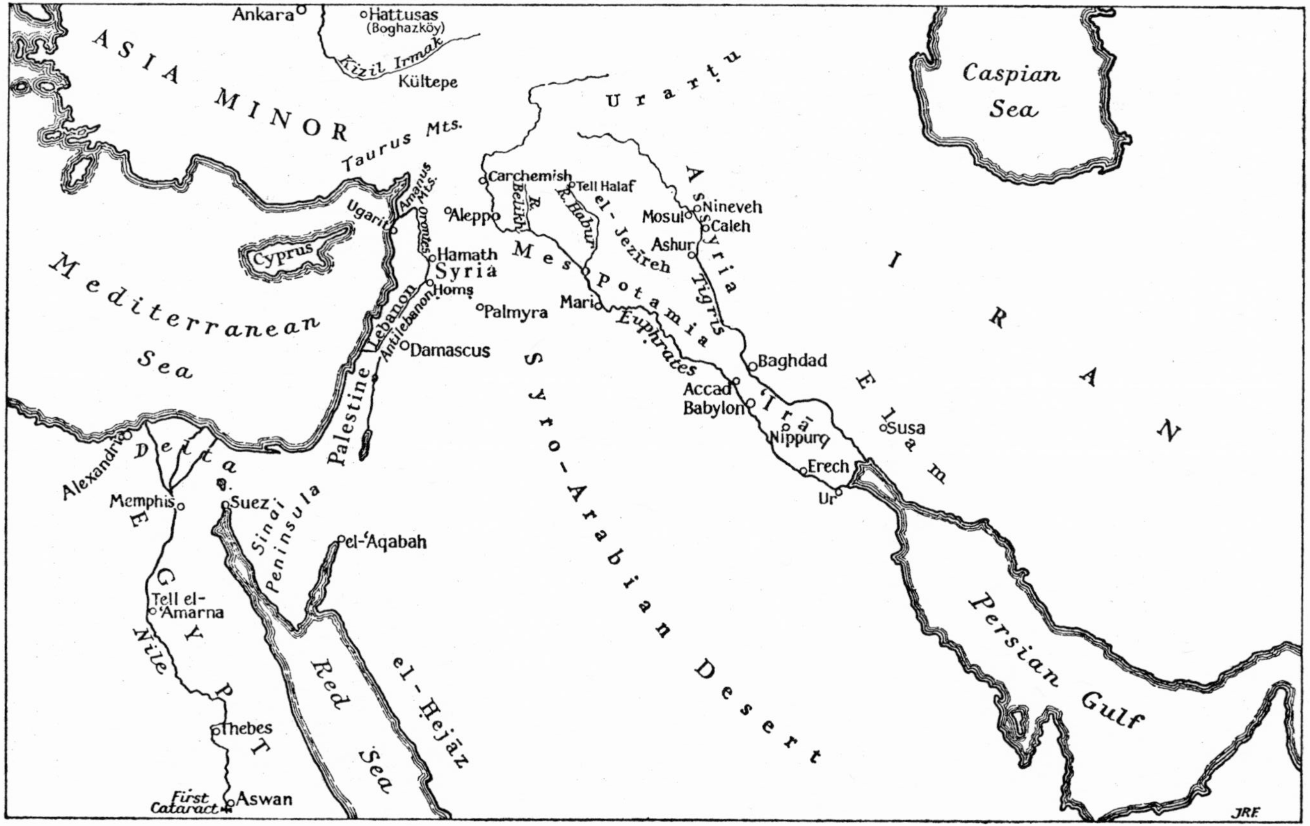

Figure 6. Area Map of the Ancient Near East

the Jezīreh is traversed by various mountain ranges and is bordered by the towering mountains of Armenia. Because of its nearness to the mountains, along this northern edge the Jezīreh has more rainfall and is better supplied with water, making it more suitable for permanent settlement. Already in ancient times it was rather thickly settled.[3]

(3) *Asia Minor*

Asia Minor forms the northwestern corner of the ancient Near East. Asia Minor is also frequently called Anatolia, a name retained by the Turks [from Byzantine days]. It is a high plateau, interspersed with steppes and deserts. This high plateau is bordered by sheer mountains which face the Black Sea in the north and the Mediterranean Sea in the south. It is traversed in a large westward bend by the Kizil Irmāk, the Halys River of the Greeks, which empties into the Black Sea. The Cilician plain lies at the northeastern corner of the eastern Mediterranean Sea and in the southeastern corner of Asia Minor. Cilicia lies outside of the southern scarp, the lofty Taurus Mountains, a name again of Greek origin. Asia Minor is bordered on the east by the massive mountains of Armenia. In the west, mountain chains running from east to west gradually taper off to the Aegean Sea.[4]

(4) *Southern Arabia*

South Arabia lies in the extreme south of the ancient Near East. This is the present land of Yemen and to the east of it is the territory of Ḥaḍramaut, the region of Wādi Ḥaḍramaut which runs eastward and then south to the Indian Ocean. This is a land which provides the possibility of settled life in contrast to the remainder of the great Arabian peninsula. Apart from the coastal regions and a number of oases in the Ḥejāz district in the southwest, as in the interior of the peninsula, it is a great desert which merges into the Syrian desert on the north. The Syrian desert in turn lies between Syria and Mesopotamia.[5]

[3] A two-part map of Mesopotamia can be found in Meissner, *Babylonien und Assyrien*, Vols. I–II (1920–25); a general map of Mesopotamia, in sections, in V Christian, *Altertumskunde des Zweistromlandes* (1938 ff.); for a map of the Jezīreh, one should consult von Oppenheim, *op. cit*.

[4] A general map and special maps on Asia Minor can be found in Baedeker, *Konstantinopel* (2nd ed., 1914).

[5] A well-detailed map of the most important part of Yemen, in three sections, can be found in C. Rathjens and H. von Wissman, *Rathjens-v. Wissmansche Südarabienreise*

(5) *Syria*

Syria, including Palestine, lies within the circle described by the lands referred to so far. This narrow land lies stretched out along the eastern coast of the Mediterranean Sea, bordered on the other side by the great Syro-Arabian desert. The coast is of primary importance for Syria. This coast, north of Carmel (p. 19), has many natural harbours, because here spurs of the inland mountains frequently extend right up to the coast forming protected bays, while generally leaving portions of rather level land of varying width inland from the coast. As a result, the necessary prerequisites for supporting human settlements along the coast were present from the very beginning.

Taken as a whole, the interior of Syria is an extensive range of mountains separating the Syro-Arabian desert plateau from the Mediterranean Sea. This range is divided lengthwise by the great rift brought about by geological forces. This rift is the northern continuation of Palestine's Jordan rift (p. 14). In the smaller southern part of this Syrian rift the Nahr el-Līṭāni flows southward. Finally it makes a right-angle bend to the west. Under the name of Nahr el-Qāsimīyeh the same river breaks through the mountains and reaches the Mediterranean Sea north of the city of Tyre. The Orontes River flows through the larger part of this Syrian rift in a northerly direction, until in northern Syria it makes a sharp bend to the southwest and empties into the Mediterranean Sea. Orontes is the Greek form of the old name. It is now known as Nahr el-ʿAṣi. Between the rift and the sea lies the western range of mountains. Beginning in the south it first consists of the Lebanon, with peaks touching 3,083 m. [10,112 feet] (pp. 59 ff.), bordered on the south by the gorge of the Nahr el-Qāsimīyeh, mentioned above, and on the north by the broad plain of the short Nahr el-Kebīr, which breaks through the mountain chain and empties into the Mediterranean Sea. North of the Lebanon, the less lofty Jebel el-Anṣārīyeh continues right on up to the lower course of the Orontes. This chain is also known as the Nuseirīyeh Mountains, named after the syncretistic sect called the Nusairi. North of the Orontes is the Amanus range which adjoins the Taurus chain and borders the Cilician plain (p. 188) on the east.

The rift is most clearly defined between Lebanon and Antilebanon, where it is called el-Beqāʿ (p. 14) and again in part on

III: Landeskundliche Ergebnisse (1934); a sectional sketch map of Ḥaḍramaut on the basis of his own travels is provided by H. Helfritz, *Vergessenes Südarabien* (1936).

the east side of Jebel el-Anṣārīyeh. In between it broadens out into a wide plain in the region of the present city of Ḥomṣ, southwest of which lies the great Lake of Ḥomṣ. At the bend of the Orontes the rift again expands into the plain called el-ʿAmq, which contains a large lake and a swampy section. North of this the rift appears again on the east side of the Amanus.

On the eastern side of the rift, only in places are there noteworthy mountains. The primary one is the counterpart of the Lebanon, called "Antilibanos" by the Greeks. Its southern prominence, rising to 2,814 m. [9,230 feet], is called Jebel esh-Sheikh or Jebel et-Telj (p. 31), while the northern main part is known as Jebel esh-Sherqi, "Eastern Mountain." Farther in the north on the eastern side of the rift we have only groups of lower mountains and chains of hills.

In contrast to the lands relying on river floods, Syria and Palestine depend on the winter rains for their livelihood. This rainfall which comes from the west diminishes constantly farther east and finally ceases almost entirely. This is responsible for a gradual transition to the Syrian desert and the gradual end of possibilities for settled life. A very productive region is at the edge of this desert. It is the great oasis of Damascus with its many gardens at the southeastern foot of the Antilebanon. Damascus is watered by the everflowing Barada River, supplied by Antilebanon. This region also has sources of underground water. Cultivated Syria is broadest in the far north where the mountains of Asia Minor and Armenia, rising to the north, send river valleys down to North Syria. The city of Aleppo, Ḥaleb, lies here in the midst of productive farmland, 110 km. [68 miles] due east of the mouth of the Orontes on the Mediterranean coast. The Euphrates lies on the other side, only 100 km. [62 miles] due east of Aleppo.[6]

23. *Trade Routes*

That Syria must be regarded as the centre of the entire ancient Near Eastern area is shown by the fact that it is in direct connec-

[6] For a general map of Syria, exclusive of Palestine, see von Oppenheim, *op. cit.* During the French mandate over Syria the entire land was carefully measured and surveyed. The magnificent new maps of Syria published by the French "Service géographique" were based on this survey. They include two maps titled "Levant." The first is drawn on a scale of 1:50,000 and published in 84 sheets. It was published from 1926–45 and includes the area of Syria as usually understood. The second is drawn on a scale of 1:200,000 in 27 sheets. It was published from 1943–45 and also includes the eastern part of modern Syria.

tion with all the other regions of the ancient Orient. Trade routes depend on not having particularly great difficulties of terrain. On the other hand, along these routes, at least at reasonable intervals, there must be enough water available for man and beast. In this respect the requirements for the great routes on which folk migrations and military campaigns could take place were naturally considerably greater than for caravan trails, where only relatively small groups travelled, where only limited amounts of drinking water were available, for men and for their pack animals, the agreeable donkeys and the camels, domesticated toward the end of the second millennium B.C. and adapted to life in arid regions (Gen. 24 : 10 ff.; 37 : 25).

The simplest connection between Syria and Egypt was by sea, from one of the numerous natural Syrian harbours to the Delta and vice versa, along the coast, inasmuch as people were still dependent upon coastal shipping for want of more developed navigation technique. Generally speaking, Palestine remained out of the picture because it had such poor harbours.

The Sinai desert was the chief hindrance to use of the overland trail from Egypt to Palestine and Syria, even though the distance was not great. From the eastern corner of the Nile Delta to the southwestern corner of Palestine's farm country, an arid stretch of about 175 km. [110 miles], broken only by small oases, had to be traversed. It was possible to gain limited relief here from water shortage by digging wells. This ultimately made even this overland route along the coast an important link between the Nile and Palestine (see p. 92).

The link between Syria and Mesopotamia was primarily by way of North Syria. From the vicinity of Aleppo to the Euphrates there was the habitable and passable section north of the salt lake at Jabbūl, which is the northern limit of the Syro-Arabian Desert. Then a person could travel down the Euphrates as far as he wanted. Or one could cross the Euphrates and reach the Tigris in the vicinity of present-day Mōṣul by traversing the similarly habitable and passable northern part of the Jezīreh through the region of the sources of the Khābūr.

A direct trail, suitable only for caravans, ran from middle Syria, near Damascus, to the middle Euphrates. It crossed the northern part of the Syrian desert, which was not too extensive. Midway along this trail an oasis was situated which was vital to this caravan trade. A settlement in this oasis became renowned under its Greek name, Palmyra. The same oasis was known already at the beginning of the second millennium B.C. under its previous name of *Tadmar* or *Tadmur*.

Asia Minor is adjacent to North Syria, though separated from it by Amanus Mountains and on the other side of Cilicia by the lofty Taurus range. Yet trade between both countries was always possible by way of the Taurus mountain passes. From the direction of eastern Asia Minor the neighbour closest and most easily reached was North Syria.

South Arabia was the most out-of-the-way of all. But even that remote land had direct connections with Syria and Palestine. For one thing, there was the coastal waterway from the northern end of the Gulf of el-ʿAqabah (p. 15) southward through the Red Sea to the South Arabian coast. On the other hand, there was the very long caravan trail travelled from primeval times. It began near Damascus in Syria, and crossed through Transjordan into northern Arabia or again from southern Palestine across the Wādi el-ʿArabah through the western Arabian territory of el-Ḥejāz, along the Red Sea, all the way down to the area of South Arabian culture. It was much later that the Ḥejāz received public attention because the cities Medinah and Mecca, prominent in Islamic history, are located here.

Syria was also the centre of the whole ancient Near Eastern area in so far as almost all lines of communication between individual regions lying on the periphery ran through Syria (and Palestine). The link between Mesopotamia and Asia Minor led most readily across the northern tip of Syria. What is more, trade between Egypt on the one side and Mesopotamia and Asia Minor on the other travelled the entire length of Palestine and Syria. That was the most important trade link that there was in the ancient Near East. On this overland route from Egypt across the Sinai desert one reached the coastal plain of Palestine and continued on north. From here on one could remain on the coastal trail, in spite of the intervening headlands, to the plain at the mouth of the River el-Kebīr (see above) in middle Syria or, for that matter, all the way to North Syria, turning inland to reach Aleppo or going on to Cilicia. To avoid the difficulties of the coastal route with its various headlands that slope right down into the sea, traders might prefer to turn inland south of Carmel on the road through the territory of Bilād er-Rūḥa (p. 20) to reach the Plain of Jezreel at Megiddo. From Megiddo and the Plain they could descend into the Jordan Valley at Beth-shan. Then again the Jordan could be reached by the path north from Megiddo by the way running north of Mount

Tabor. From the Jordan Valley one could take various ways across the Jōlān to reach Damascus with its minor caravan trail across the desert to the Euphrates via Palmyra and its major route along the eastern edge of settled Transjordan north to Aleppo. An alternative route used the Beqaʿ between Lebanon and Antilebanon to reach North Syria (see p. 93). From Aleppo on the routes already described travellers could reach either Mesopotamia or Asia Minor. From primeval times countless people in peaceful or warlike pursuits have travelled this great trade route which cuts across the western and northern part of Palestine. Here and there the way divided, offering choice of roads for which different periods had different preferences.

Even South Arabia, off the beaten path though it was, had its connections with the rest of the countries of the ancient Near East on the ways to Syria or Palestine, as indicated. Otherwise, they could get to Egypt by ship across the Red Sea. It was also possible to cross the entire Arabian peninsula on caravan trails to the Persian Gulf and ultimately to reach Mesopotamia.

CHAPTER II

CULTURES

24. *Characteristic Features*

THE monuments left behind from antiquity in the lands of the ancient Near East speak eloquently for the fact that each land in its own way was the domain of well-developed cultures from time immemorial. Each of these cultures gave its own characteristic form of expression to all areas of life from large structures to the very smallest artifacts of everyday life. Each of these cultures also had its own history, involving progressive change of cultural phenomena, though holding to certain distinctive features. These chief features will be briefly summarized here, especially those that are most evident.

(1) *Egypt*

The pyramids are a landmark of lower Egypt. The three pyramids at Gizeh, west of Cairo,[1] are the best known. There are also pyramids north and south of Gizeh on the west side of the lower Nile at the edge of the Libyan desert. They are gigantic stone structures, mostly in the smooth form of the pyramids of Gizeh, but also in step form[2] or with a bent profile.[3] They are massive royal sepulchres, built of great granite blocks and pillars. Each is linked with a mortuary temple for the cult of the dead at the edge of the Nile River bed, just below its appropriate pyramid.[4] The pyramids are frequently surrounded by smaller tombs for other members of the royal court or of the ruling class. These tombs are shaped like flat houses with various inner chambers. Such a tomb is called a *maṣṭabeh*, "stone bench."[5] The great concern for the dead which is manifested in these memorials appears again in the tombs of Upper

[1] *ANEP*, No. 765; *AOB*, No. 37; Breasted and Ranke, *Geschichte Ägyptens* (Grosse illustrierte Phaidon-Ausgabe, 1936), Figs. 4–5.

[2] *ANEP*, No. 764; Breasted and Ranke, *op. cit.*, Fig. 1.

[3] Breasted and Ranke, *op. cit.*, Fig. 2; W. S. Smith, *The Art and Architecture of Ancient Egypt* (1958), pp. 39 ff., Plate XXVa.

[4] Breasted and Ranke, *op. cit.*, Figs. 6, 7.

[5] Erman and Ranke, *Aegypten und aegyptisches Leben im Altertum* (1923), Plate XXIV, 2.

Egypt, particularly west of Luxor. They are situated at the edge of the western desert, for in Egypt the region of the setting sun was the realm of the dead. They are underground burial sites hewn out of the rock, consisting of an entrance corridor and a system of chambers. In distinction from the pyramids they are in a concealed location. These are royal tombs.[6] Their interior is most lavishly decorated with painted stucco reliefs and wall paintings, which furnish mythological portrayals and pictures drawn from daily life.[7] In the central burial chamber stood the stone[8] or wooden[9] sarcophagus, the latter frequently in human form,[10] containing the carefully embalmed mummy of the deceased.

The cult of the gods appeared prominently in the settled country itself, together with the cult of the dead on the western edge of the desert. It is seen in the temples carefully built of blocks of ashlar and therefore frequently still remaining in imposing ruins. The pylons are characteristic of the Egyptian temple sites. These pylons are pairs of broad towers which taper toward the top. They flank both sides of the main entrance. They have a flat top with a characteristically Egyptian concave quarter-rounded cornice.[11] Behind them lies the forecourt of the temple. Occasionally several pylons and courts are arranged behind one another, particularly where a temple site was enlarged and expanded. The temple proper in the rear part of the area enclosed by the wall consisted in its simplest form of a broad, columned anteroom and of the elongated inner sanctum.

The stocky columns which are so characteristic of Egypt are encountered in the temples in the colonnades surrounding the forecourts and in the anterooms. Their formal elements are derived from the papyrus plant. Either they represent stylized bundles of papyrus stems, whether closed, budding flowers[12] or with opened blooming calyxes;[13] or with only a suggestion remaining, they have been simplified into smooth round columns and have round capitals with the profile of closed[14] or open[15] papyrus flowers.

The slender obelisks, dedicated to the cult of the sun, are also characteristic of Egypt. These taper toward the top and end in a point.[16] There are also the sphinxes, reclining animal bodies with human or animal faces,[17] guarding temple entrances and

[6] *Ibid.*, Fig. 165.
[7] Breasted and Ranke, *op. cit.*, Figs. 228–29, 266.
[8] *AOB*, No. 197.
[9] Erman and Ranke, *op. cit.*, Plate XXIV, 1.
[10] *Ibid.*, Plate XXIII, 4.
[11] Breasted and Ranke, *op. cit.*, Figs. 22–25; *AOB*, No. 490.
[12] Breasted and Ranke, *op. cit.*, Figs. 13–14.
[13] *Ibid.*, Fig. 25.
[14] *Ibid.*, Fig. 15.
[15] *Ibid.*, Fig. 12.
[16] *AOB*, No. 489.
[17] *AOB*, Nos. 37, 377, 394.

processional streets. Finally the more than life size, often gigantic portrayals of standing and seated kings of the country can be found all about intact or in ruins, or as they were carved from the rock walls of the river valley in the Nile valley of Nubia.[18]

(2) *Mesopotamia*

Our heritage from the ancient civilization of Mesopotamia is not nearly so evident and impressive. Here the great architectural achievements were generally built, not from blocks of ashlar, but rather from the customary clay, sun-dried bricks which have offered much less resistance to the action of the millennia. Thus the sites of the ancient civilization look like great washed-out masses of clay,[19] and only excavation can disclose what monuments might be left.[20]

Once again the temple plans are characteristic. Especially in the cities of the south in *ʿIrāq* proper, but also farther north along the Tigris, there are remains of temple towers, called *ziqqurrātu* in ancient times. These are built-up brick terraces looking like high-towering lone mountains, rising in stages. Presumably they were understood as residences of the deities.[21] Connected with them were sanctuaries situated at the bottom of the temple towers which, again especially in the south, had the form of broad rooms placed behind a court, with a cult niche in the rear wall opposite the entrance.[22] There are examples in northern Mesopotamia of temples of the so-called *Herdhaustyp* or herdsman shelter type, namely long rooms with the inner sanctum at the narrow end, but with the entrance in one of the long sides, so that after entering the temple a person had to make a right-angle turn to face toward the inner sanctum.[23] Besides there are also long-room plans with the entrance at one end and the inner sanctum on the opposite end.[24] This combination illustrates the composite character of the civilization of Mesopotamia.

A characteristic architectural technique is the use of nail-like clay pegs of various colours. These were inserted side by side in

[18] Breasted and Ranke, *op. cit.*, Figs. 12, 16–19.

[19] For example, see R. Koldewey, *Das wieder erstehende Babylon* (2nd ed., 1925), Fig. 5; W. Andrea, *Das wieder erstandene Assur*, hereafter referred to as *Assur* (1938), Plate XXXI.

[20] See the text and plates in V. Christian, *Altertumskunde des Zweistromlandes*, I (1940).

[21] *ANEP*, Nos. 746–47, 763; *AOB*, Nos. 473, 481.

[22] *AOB*, Nos. 470 [ES], 471; Andrae, *Das Gotteshaus und die Urformen des Bauens im alten Orient*, hereafter referred to as *Die Urformen* (1930), Figs. 7, 9–10.

[23] Andrae, *Die Urformen*, Figs. 15–17.

[24] *Ibid.*, Fig. 21.

mortar to erect entire walls.[25] Again, clay knob-ended pegs, frequently painted with rosette designs, were inserted into sun-dried brick walls.[26] Later, apparently in a conscious continuation of this custom, brick walls were painted with rows of rosettes.[27] A further development, which occurs only in Mesopotamia, is the use of coloured enamelled bricks. By this means entire reliefs were portrayed on walls.[28] Related was the production of clay tiles with pictures in coloured enamel.[29] The architectural element of free standing columns is missing in the genuine architecture of ancient Mesopotamia, built as it was on brick-work technique.

A great part of the finds from Mesopotamia consists of stone slabs in relief. They are made of alabaster, gypsum, and limestone. They served as facing of the brick walls, particularly in the royal palaces on the middle Tigris, and portrayed military life, hunting scenes, and events of everyday life.[30] Stone stelae, with a semicircular round top and with portrayals of kings, also constitute a large class of finds.[31]

Composite creatures, portraying demons, executed in sculptured or relief form are distinctive and common phenomena of the civilization of ancient Mesopotamia. They are mostly combinations of the torso and legs of a lion or bull, the wings of an eagle, and the face of a man. There are also cases of snake figures used as head or tail.[32] Such creatures served as guardians of gates and were inserted in the fronts and sides of gates. Demons of composite form also are portrayed in other relief scenes.[33]

Among the human portrayals are the characteristic figures clad in garments made of pelts, which are likely shaggy sheep pelts.[34] Of course this clothing is characteristic of one definite period of antiquity. Divine figures are frequently depicted with bull-horn crowns, wearing one or more pairs of vertically arranged bull horns.[35]

(3) *Asia Minor, North Syria, and Northern Mesopotamia*

The early cultures of eastern Asia Minor, North Syria, and northern Mesopotamia share certain common features. Even though

[25] *Ibid.*, Figs. 91, 95–96.
[26] *Ibid.*, Figs. 81–82, 84, 86.
[27] *Ibid.*, Figs. 85, 87, 94.
[28] *ANEP*, Nos. 461–62; *AOB*, Nos. 371, 373, 375–76. See also the reconstruction of the Ishtar Gate of Babylon in the former State Museum in Berlin, *ANEP*, No. 460 or *AOB*, No. 372.
[29] Andrae, *Assur*, Plate I.
[30] *ANEP*, Nos. 372–75; *AOB*, Nos. 132–33, 137–38, 148–49.
[31] *ANEP*, Nos. 442–43, 447; *AOB*, Nos. 135, 144.
[32] *ANEP*, Nos. 646–47; *AOB*, Nos. 370–71, 373, 378, 381.
[33] *AOB*, Nos. 379–80, 382.
[34] *ANEP*, Nos. 18–24.
[35] *ANEP*, Nos. 514–15, 529; *AOB*, Nos. 318, 322.

these cultures are not identical any more than was the case in Mesopotamia as described above,[36] still significant traits are seen in these areas which appear again in the cultural area of the middle Tigris. These traits form a definite link with Mesopotamian cultural traditions.

In this region there are numerous fortified cities and castles with walls built on heavy irregularly-cut stone foundations. Their gate entrances are flanked by great well-worked monoliths.[37] Noteworthy is the facing of the lower part of the palace walls with low orthostats, which are upright stone slabs in relief.[38] Both human and divine figures are characterized by high conical caps and shoes with turned-up toes.[39] Their animals are portrayed with a characteristically crude form.[40] A monstrous demonic feature is prominent in the portrayal of lions with their set open jaws.[41] All sorts of composite creatures also appear, often grotesque, like the creatures with two heads, human and animal,[42] or the scorpion-bird-man.[43] Especially distinctive is the use of various animal figures, with a preference for lions, as well as composite figures, as bases for statues of deities[44] and as bases of columns which are shaped like statues of deities.[45] One base is likely to consist of a pair of lions or composite creatures.[46] The monstrous lions are frequently inset in the sides of gates as guardians of the gates. Among the symbolic figures the "winged sun" frequently appears.[47]

(4) *South Arabia*

The remains of the ancient South Arabian civilization have been explored very little so far. They apparently do not go back much farther than the first millennium B.C. Most of the monuments found so far, such as the temples with characteristic octagonal columns,

[36] A. Moortgat, *Die bildende Kunst des Alten Orients und die Bergvölker* (1933).

[37] E. Meyer, *Reich und Kultur der Chetiter* (1914), Figs. 5–7. M. von Oppenheim, *Tell Halaf*, p. 79; translated into English in 1931.

[38] E. Meyer, *op. cit.*, Figs. 62–63; von Oppenheim, *op. cit.*, Plates X, XVI ff.; *ANEP*, Nos. 654–55.

[39] *AOB*, Nos. 340, 342; Meyer, *op. cit.*, Figs. 1, 57, 60, 76; *ANEP*, No. 532.

[40] Meyer, *op. cit.*, Plates VII–VIII; von Oppenheim, Plates XVIII ff.

[41] *AOB*, No. 399 ff.

[42] Meyer, *op. cit.*, Fig. 78; *ANEP*, No. 644.

[43] M. von Oppenheim, *op. cit.*, Plate XLII (top).

[44] *AOB*, Nos. 338, 355–56 ff.

[45] M. von Oppenheim, *op. cit.*, frontispiece, Plate XIIa.

[46] *AOB*, Nos. 345, 390; *ANEP*, No. 648.

[47] *AOB*, Nos. 338, 342; von Oppenheim, *op. cit.*, Plates VIIb, XXXVIIa; *ANEP*, No. 534.

stelae, and inscribed stones[48] probably are no older than the last centuries B.C.

(5) *Syria*

Apart from North Syria, already discussed, the cultural heritage from antiquity in Syria is identical with that in Palestine (pp. 121 ff.). The monuments of those days are concealed in the mounds (*tulūl*) of the ancient cities of the land. In differing degrees they demonstrate the powerful ties between Syria (and Palestine) and the great neighbouring civilizations, whose elements appear in distinctive combinations in the culture of Syria. The Syrian coast with its cities had the liveliest ties with the outside world, namely with the Mediterranean lands. Thus the city of Byblus, now called Jbeil, on the Lebanese coast had an ancient and intensive connection with Egypt.[49] Ancient Ugarit, the present mound of Rās Shamrah, on the north Syrian coast, just opposite the eastern tip of Cyprus, had particularly close ties with Cyprus and the Creto-Mycenaean world.[50] This is shown by excavations conducted there from 1929–39 and continued after the Second World War.

On the whole, Syria and Palestine have not produced such conspicuous and well-known ancient Near Eastern monuments as those which mark the other areas.

25. *Research on Cultures*

Detailed archeological work concerned with the heritage of ancient cultures must first of all arrange the monuments and characteristic features in chronological order. From the observation of changes and developments, basic features of a cultural history of individual areas appear as well as the sequence of their

[48] Rathjens-v. Wissmann, *Rathjens-v. Wissmannsche Südarabienreise II: Vorislamische Altertümer* (1932); G. C. Thompson, *The Tombs and Moon Temple of Hureidha* (*Hadramaut*) (1944); R. L. Bowen and F. P. Albright, *Archaeological Discoveries in South Arabia* (1958); Albright, *BASOR*, CXIX (1950), 5 ff. On the current state of research in this area, see G. W. van Beek, "South Arabian History and Archeology," in *The Bible and the Ancient Near East: Essays in Honor of William Foxwell Albright* (1961), pp. 229–48.

[49] Concerning the excavations at Jbeil, see P. Montet, *Byblos et l'Égypte* (1929); M. Dunand, *Fouilles de Byblos, Vol. I: 1926–1932* (Atlas, 1937; Texts, 1939); *Vol. II: 1933–39* (Atlas, 1950; Texts, 1954).

[50] C. F.-A. Schaeffer in *Syria*, X (1929), and subsequent issues; Ugaritica I (1939); II (1949); III (1956); the preliminary summary in J. Friedrich, "Ras Schamra," *Der Alte Orient*, XXXIII (1933), Secs. 1–2.

relationship to each other. In this process sometimes there are prehistoric cultural remains which come from periods concerning which historical evidence is entirely or almost entirely lacking. In such a case the monuments from historically known periods succeed the earlier finds.

In Egypt, prehistoric, that is predynastic (on the order of the dynasties see pp. 246 ff.), Stone Age and Chalcolithic Age cultures can be demonstrated[51] which develop into the early dynastic culture toward the beginning of the third millennium B.C., upon which then follows the cultural development of the historical period proper.[52]

Prehistoric cultures of Mesopotamia are identified by the modern names of excavation sites where a certain culture was first recognized. These cultures are distinguished from one another primarily by the style and painting of their pottery and can be arranged in a definite order of periods. Thus one speaks of a "Tell Ḥalaf" culture, characterized by one specific type of monochrome pottery and again by a characteristic polychrome pottery. It is named for one of the lowest strata of Tell Ḥalaf, located in northern Mesopotamia at the head of the Khābūr River. It was excavated by von Oppenheim[53] intermittently from 1911 to 1929. This culture should probably be dated in the fifth millennium B.C.[54] It was especially prevalent in the northernmost part of Mesopotamia. In point of time the El-Obeid culture follows this, named after the little mound of Tell el-ʿObeid, about 6 km. [4 miles] northwest of the ancient city of Ur, which was situated on the right bank of the lower Euphrates. Excavation at Ur, begun in 1923 under the direction of Hall and Woolley, had as a by-product the exploration of the little original prehistoric settlement on Tell el-ʿObeid.[55] Then follows the Warkan culture in the last centuries of the fourth millennium. It is named after the German excavation of ancient Erech, now Warka, begun

[51] A. Scharff, *Grundzüge der ägyptischen Vorgeschichte*, *Morgenland*, Heft XII (1927).

[52] The manifestations and changes of this rich culture in the historical period are presented especially by A. Erman, *Ägypten und ägyptisches Leben im Altertum* (1887), revised by H. Ranke, 1923, and H. Kees, *Ägypten*, *Kulturgeschichte des Alten Orients*, I (1933) (or *Handbuch der Altertumswissenschaft*, Abt. 3, Teil 1, Bd. 3). A survey of the results of archeological work is provided by Scharff, *Ägypten*, *Handbuch der Archäologie im Rahmen des Handbuchs der Altertumswissenschaft*, ed. W. Otto, I (1939), 433–642 with the related plates in a corresponding volume.

[53] M. von Oppenheim, *Tell Halaf*, *I: Die prähistorische Funde bearbeitet von Hubert Schmidt* (1943).

[54] Tell Ḥalaf pottery is illustrated in Christian, *Altertumskunde des Zweistromlandes*, Plates XXVII ff.

[55] Pottery of this culture, which was found especially in southern Mesopotamia, is described in Christian, *op. cit.*, Plates XLVII ff.

in 1913 and still continuing after interruption during both World Wars. Warka is a short distance upstream from Ur, now on the left bank of the Euphrates. Excavation there led to the disclosure of this culture in the archaic strata of Erech IV–VI.[56] Next the Jemdet Naṣr culture follows, named after the small ruin of Jemdet Naṣr about 70 km. [40 miles] southeast of Baghdad.[57] The Jemdet Naṣr culture belongs to the two first centuries of the third millennium B.C. In this millennium it was followed by the early historical cultures of the early Sumerian and Old Accadian period and finally by the Neo-Sumerian period with its high point in the period of dominance of the third dynasty of Ur in the twenty-first and in the first half of the twentieth century B.C.[58] (see p. 250).

Of more recent date is the exploration of the prehistoric and early historical culture of Asia Minor.[59]

[56] Pottery is described in *ibid.*, Plates LV ff.

[57] On its pottery, see *ibid.*, Plates LXXIX ff.

[58] On the cultural development of the historical period see B. Meissner, *Babylonien und Assyrien*, I, II (1920, 1925) (or *Kulturgeschichtliche Bibliothek*, I, 3–4). A summary of the archeological results is given in Andrae, *Vorderasien ohne Phönikien, Palästina und Kypros, Handb. d. Arch.* (1939), pp. 643–796, with the related plates.

[59] See K. Bittel, *Grundzüge der Vor- und Frühgeschichte Kleinasiens* (1950). On the cultural patterns of the historical period see A. Goetze, *Kleinasien* in *Kulturgeschichte des Alten Orients*, III, 1 (2nd ed., 1957) or *Handbuch der Altertumswissenschaft*, Abt. 3, Teil 1, Bd. 3). Syro-Palestinian archeology is treated by C. Watzinger, *Phönikien und Palästina–Kypros, Handb. d. Arch.*, I (1939), 797–848, with plates.

CHAPTER III

WRITING SYSTEMS AND EXAMPLES OF ANCIENT WRITING

26. *Ideographic and Syllabographic Systems*

WE are dependent on ancient written historical materials in our quest for a true and complete picture of the course of history or even of its cultural processes. Material remains of life in antiquity in the ancient oriental cultural areas, though they are abundant and varied, cannot produce a history. For, not material remains, but only human speech can describe historical events involving human thought, intention, and behaviour. Nor could we present even the outline of the history of these lands or explain even in general terms the remains of its cultures if we were solely dependent on the late and sparse references of Greek historians to the history of the lands of the Near East. Rather, from the dawn of history those ancient cultures understood the art of writing and they wrote a great deal. An almost untold quantity of textual monuments has come down to us from the ancient Orient, having come to light as a result of excavations. Since we have succeeded in reading the ancient texts and understanding the inscriptions, we have at our disposal an abundance of original sources on ancient oriental history.[1]

The oldest systems of writing, which apparently arose independently, proceed from the possibility of portraying a concrete object pictorially in detail or in outline, in any given technique. Thus the word with which the object under consideration was designated could be "written" with the help of this picture. This means that not sounds but words were "written" initially. But once the given syllabic combination was associated with a given picture, the same syllable appearing in a different word or a part of a word could be written with the same picture. A very decided step forward resulted from this device. This made it possible to write a given syllable with a given sign, no matter where it occurred in the utterance. This brought about the transition from pure pictographs (picture writing) to a mixture of pictographs and phonetic script. Since many matters can be depicted in picture form and since there

[1] For this entire section, cf. J. G. Février, *Histoire de l'écriture* (2nd ed., 1959).

are also very many syllables in a language, these old scripts have many hundreds of different signs. In addition to this difficulty there was another, that the script was ambiguous from time to time. On occasion a picture can be interpreted in various ways. For example, the picture for eye stood for eye, seeing, or witness. This resulted in various syllabic values for one sign. The reverse was also true. Most syllables could be written with several signs. This came about because several pattern nouns were pronounced like the syllables for which they were substituted. [Note in English, *eye*, *I*, *aye*.] As a result, in time various reading aids were introduced into the script. Furthermore, even though it was possible to write a word in different ways, as the languages developed, frequently standard modes of writing were evolved for given words. The difficulties presented by these types of script make it understandable that writing and reading remained a skill understood only by a few "educated" people who were trained for this specific purpose, and that men who held the position of scribe belonged to a proud class. Particularly in the case of official communications kings and administrators depended on their scribes' ability and honesty in writing and reading documents.

Hieroglyphs in Egypt, cuneiform, native to Mesopotamia, and the so-called Hittite hieroglyphs are included in these difficult ancient systems of writing.

(1) *Egyptian Hieroglyphs*

Hieroglyphs[2] maintained their original pictorial form right down to the latest period (see Fig. 7). An Englishman, Th. Young, and even more a Frenchman, J. Fr. Champollion, are credited with the original decipherment.[3] Hieroglyphs merely furnished the consonantal skeleton of words, and in their step toward phonetic writing marked only the consonants. Because of the missing vowels words written in this script could not be pronounced originally. Therefore, in reading, generally the neutral vowel /e/ is introduced. The direction of writing was not fixed. One could write in vertical lines from top to bottom or in horizontal lines from either the left or the right. Since hieroglyphs have a strongly ornamental character, and the inscriptions on columns, on temple walls, and in burial chambers frequently were utilized for secondary

[2] See the lucid presentation of A. Erman, *Die Hieroglyphen, Sammlung Göschen*, DCVIII (1917) [or A. H. Gardiner, *Egyptian Grammar* (3rd ed., rev., 1957)].

[3] Erman, *op. cit.*, pp. 7 ff.

ornamental purpose, it follows that aesthetic viewpoints could determine the direction of writing; for example, writing signs were applied symmetrically on symmetrical structural parts, that is, with the directions of writing facing each other.

Along with the engraved forms of hieroglyphic writing used as late as the Roman period, from antiquity a definite book script which arose through simplification of the forms, the hieratic script, was utilized for writing with ink on papyrus. In practical use hieratic could develop a strongly cursive form, which was no longer pictorial. In the later period hieratic made a transition into the demotic script. Hieroglyphs, as well as hieratic or demotic writing, were employed only for writing the various stages of the Egyptian language. For foreign names appearing in it, as well as for the foreign and loan words that entered Egyptian, a particular orthography was utilized which probably can be ascribed to an attempt at vocalization, the so-called syllabic writing.[4]

The monuments of writing consist first of innumerable hieroglyphic inscriptions which were chiselled on the monumental structures of the land in the ashlar blocks of stone walls and the smooth level places of the columns, or were applied in various inner chambers, particularly burial chambers, on the stucco facing of the walls in flat relief, or were simply painted on. Hieroglyphic inscriptions originally were usually done in colour. Then there are the likewise very numerous papyrus scrolls, in hieratic or demotic script, which have been preserved through the millennia in the dry climate of Egypt, especially in graves. The Egyptians prepared this valuable writing material of theirs from the papyrus plant growing primarily in the swamps of the Delta. They cut its stems in strips lengthwise, then they glued these strips into pages in two layers at right angles with each other and then glued these leaves together into long "books" which could be rolled together. Finally, inscribed potsherds provided the cheapest writing material of everyday life.

The examples of writing which have come down to us fall into a number of categories.[5] Grave inscriptions form a very large part of these, whether the old pyramid texts or the inscriptions on the burial chamber walls, or finally the papyrus scrolls which were placed in the coffin with the deceased, classified generally as the Book of the Dead. These are either funerary texts proper, namely

[4] See M. Burchardt, *Die altkanaanäischen Fremdworte und Eigennamen im Ägyptischen* (1909–10); W. F. Albright, *The Vocalization of the Egyptian Syllabic Orthography* (1934).

[5] The most important of these are found translated into English throughout *ANET* by J. A. Wilson, and in *AOT*, pp. 1–107, translated into German by H. Ranke.

a variety of references to the other world, magical formulae which seemed important for understanding of the way into the other world, and the like, or mythological texts of more general content, and explanatory annotations for a variety of mythological pictures; finally, hymns to the gods, etc.

The Egyptians also possessed a literature in the narrower sense, which has become known through many papyrus finds: hymns of various types; narratives for entertainment, or instruction, or edification; further, a wisdom literature fostered and expanded from antiquity to transmit tested rules of life;[6] also lists of many phenomena common to the Egyptians, arranged by subjects;[7] and finally a variety of prophecies based on the theme of change from times of adversity to times of prosperity.[8]

Court records, accounts, and other lists originating from practical life have been found.

Historical texts are also numerous. Along with accounts of the course of life of great officials and officers of the kingdom in their tombs, we have primarily extracts from the annals of kings of the country mounted on monumental structures, particularly temples, with pictures of their military exploits and explanatory notes.[9] In their own peculiar way the kings of the Egyptian New Kingdom have repeatedly reported their conquests in foreign lands to posterity. They have portrayed themselves as striking down a host of captive enemies with the mace, while at the same moment two deities bring them enemies, bound about the neck with a long cord. These enemies are portrayed only with heads and bodies, arranged in several rows on top of one another. On each of their bodies the name of a city or location in foreign lands occupied by the pharaoh is inscribed in hieroglyphics. Thus we have a number of unusually extensive lists of Palestinian and Syrian sites which were conquered by Egyptian kings. These lists are important original sources on the ancient settlement of Syria and Palestine.[10]

[6] R. Anthes, "Lebensregeln und Lebensweisheit der alten Ägypter", *Der Alte Orient*, XXXII (1933), Sec. 2; P. Humbert, *Recherches sur les sources égyptiennes de la littérature sapientiale d'Isräel* (1929).

[7] A. H. Gardiner, *Ancient Egyptian Onomastica*, Vol. I (text), Vol. II (plates) (1947).

[8] On the entire subject see the translation of texts by Erman, *Die Literatur der Ägypter* (1923), and the description by M. Pieper, *Die ägyptische Literatur, Handbuch der Literaturwissenschaft* (1927).

[9] Collected and translated into English by J. H. Breasted, *Ancient Records of Egypt*, I–V (1906–7). An autographic reproduction of many of these texts will be found in a work begun by G. Steindorff, K. Sethe, and H. Schaefer in 1903 and still continuing: *Urkunden des aegyptischen Altertums*.

[10] Noth, "Die Wege der Pharaonenheere in Palästina und Syrien," *ZDPV*, LX (1937), 183–239; LXI (1938), 26–65, 277–304; LXIV (1941), 39–74; and on the style of depiction, *ZDPV*, LX (1937), Plate I.

(2) *Cuneiform*

The initial stages of deciphering cuneiform writing[11] were undertaken by the German, G. F. Grotefend, in 1802, with the aid of Old Persian cuneiform texts.[12] Cuneiform received its name from the fact that each individual sign of the text consists of one or more wedge-shaped lines. These have a broad head and taper down to a point (Fig. 7). The reason for this is that after older forms of simple cutting in stone or clay the customary writing material for the fully developed cuneiform writing was the clay tablet. The written signs were impressed in its soft clay with the edge of a stick or stylus. The tip of the stylus naturally made a deeper impression and thereby produced the broader head of the wedge. This wedge shape of the signs originating from clay tablets was also transferred to the numerous stone inscriptions and to the occasional inscriptions on metal sheets and tablets.[13] The oldest forerunners so far attested of cuneiform writing from the period of "Warkan Culture" (see p. 200) still show the original pictographic or pictorial nature of the cuneiform signs.[14] But already very early the tendency prevailed of engraving the pictures with straight strokes, and the wedges pressed in with the stylus naturally reproduce only straight lines. As a result the original pictures can hardly be readily recognized in the resultant cuneiform signs which often consist of complicated systems of wedges. Moreover, cuneiform writing experienced a history tending toward simplification of the cuneiform signs. The direction of writing is from left to right. In contrast to hieroglyphs the picture underlying a cuneiform sign gives both consonants and vowels of the word under consideration. Hence, the cuneiform signs with their phonetic use reproduce the total sound of a syllable including the vowel. The words written phonetically in cuneiform are therefore actually readable, which is not the case with words written phonetically in hieroglyphs because of the lacking vowels. Cuneiform remained in use right down to the last centuries B.C.

The spread of cuneiform was essentially greater than that of hieroglyphs. In the course of history, extremely varied languages were written by means of it. In the beginning it served the various

[11] See the lucid presentation by B. Meissner, *Die Keilschrift*, *Sammlung Göschen*, DCCVIII (2nd ed., 1922).

[12] *Ibid.*, pp. 7 ff.

[13] The technique of cuneiform writing and the development of the sign forms are systematically traced back to primitive forms in G. R. Driver, *Semitic Writing from Pictograph to Alphabet*, *The Schweich Lectures*, 1944 (2nd ed., 1954), pp. 1 ff.

[14] *ANEP*, No 241.

A

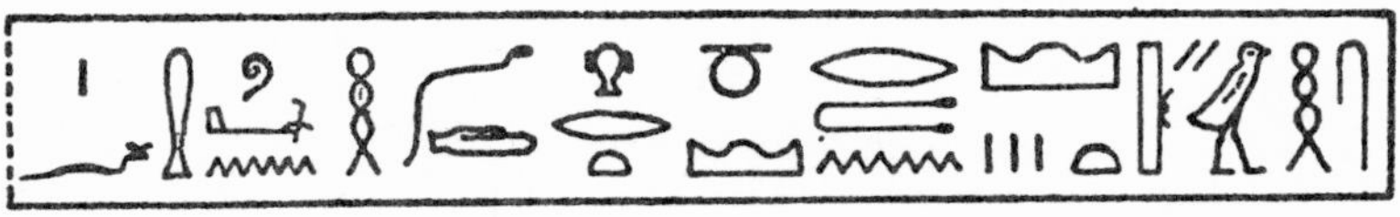

B

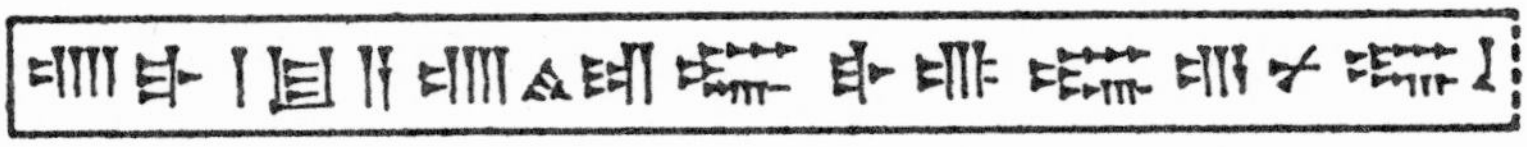

C

Figure 7. Ideographic and Syllabographic Writing

A = Egyptian hieroglyphs (to be read from right to left). Beginning of the heading of a copy of the "Palestine List" of Thutmose III, based on A. Mariette, *Karnak* (1875), Pl. XVII.
Transliteration: sḥwy h' s.wt rṯn r.t ddḥ.n ḥm.f . . .
Translation: List of the foreign lands of upper Retenu which his majesty captured . . .

B = Assyrian cuneiform (to be read from left to right). Beginning of a stone tablet inscription of Tiglath-pileser III, based on P. Rost, *Die Keilschrifttexte Tiglat-Pilesers III* (1893), II, p. 19, Pl. XXXII.
Transliteration: *e-kal* ^{m}*Tukulti-apil-e-šar-ra šarru rabu*^{u} *šarru dan-nu šar kiššati.*
Translation: Palace of Tiglath-pileser, the great king, the mighty king, the king over the totality . . .

C = " Hittite " hieroglyphs (to be read from right to left). A piece of an inscription from Carchemish on the Euphrates, based on Woolley-Lawrence, *Carchemish*, II (1921), Pl. A, 12a, b*.

languages spoken in Mesopotamia. From there its use was also transferred to Asia Minor., Further it was known in Syria and Palestine before the appearance of systems of alphabetic writing, as is shown by the cuneiform tablets found in the excavations on Tell Taʿannek (p. 137) and on Tell Balāṭah, Shechem,[15] from the beginning of the Late Bronze Age, etc. Even in Egypt at times cuneiform was known and used for the necessary correspondence with countries of southwest Asia. The latter is attested by the renowned find of clay tablets inscribed with cuneiform writing at Tell el-ʿAmārna in Upper Egypt about halfway between Cairo and

[15] The tablets from Shechem were published by Böhl in *ZDPV*, XLIX (1926), 321 ff., Plates XLIV–XLVI.

Luxor, the site of the ruins of the residence of King Akhenaten of the first half of the fourteenth century B.C. (pp. 289–90). The Amarna tablets, named after this site,[16] are the parts of the correspondence which have been recovered, which kings of south-western Asia and minor Syrian and Palestinian lords of cities conducted with the Egyptian king. Even the bits of correspondence which were sent from Egypt to those addresses, of which in a few cases the duplicate has been found in Tell el ʿAmārna, were written in cuneiform. Therefore, cuneiform was used for international correspondence, at least for a while. There must, therefore, have been in Egypt scribes who had mastered this script alongside the native hieroglyphic script. Finally, the use of cuneiform extended even to ancient Iran.

Our cuneiform heritage consists primarily of clay tablets of various sizes.[17] After they were inscribed they were frequently fired, in order to make them more durable. Hexagonal or octagonal clay prisms, inscribed on the sides, were frequently used for building records which were inserted in the foundations.[18] For monumental purposes cuneiform was transferred to stone. Stone slabs were used for cuneiform inscriptions.[19] On stone stelae (p. 197) cuneiform inscriptions were applied under the picture.[20] Obelisk-type stone monuments were furnished with pictures and cuneiform inscriptions.[21] Slabs in relief frequently simply contained running lines in cuneiform over the picture.[22] Lines were inscribed even on statues.[23] Cuneiform occurs even on metal. There are occurrences of precious metal tablets with stamped cuneiform signs for building records.[24] Bronze statues and bronze reliefs[25] had lines of cuneiform text. Cylinder seals, made of various materials, sometimes included cuneiform legends.

Cuneiform records include writings covering a wide variety of

[16] For the account of the find, see the introduction to the most important publication of the tablets in transliteration and German translation yet published, J. A. Knudtzon, *Die El-Amarna Tafeln*, *Vorderasiatische Bibliothek* (2 vols., 1915) [and also S. A. B. Mercer, *The Tell el-Amarna Tablets* (1939), Vols. I–II. See *ANET*, pp. 483–90, for selected letters and reference to editing of the translated letters. The numbering of the letters is based on Knudtzon.]

[17] For examples, note the reproductions in *ANEP*, Nos. 238–39, 245, 248 ff.; G. R. Driver, *op. cit.*, Plates I–VII, XII–XVII.

[18] E.g., see Andrae, *Assur*, Plate XV; *ANEP*, No. 247.

[19] Andrae, *op. cit.*, Plates XVI, XXXXb.

[20] *ANEP*, No. 444.

[21] *AOB*, Nos. 121–24.

[22] *ANEP*, No. 441; *AOB*, Nos. 117, 144.

[23] *ANEP*, No. 452; *AOB*, No. 325.

[24] Andrae, *op. cit.*, Plates XLVI, LIIIa–b; E. Michel, *WO*, IV (1949), Plate XIII.

[25] *ANEP*, Nos. 356 ff.; *AOB*, Nos. 126–27.

subjects. There are a great many religious texts,[26] such as myths and epics, hymns to the gods and lamentations, as well as a variety of rituals with directions for the performing of cultic acts. In addition there is an extensive omen literature, collections of spells for all sorts of occurrences of sickness and adversity. There was also a scholarly literature, primarily texts for scribal studies. There were lists to aid in learning the difficult cuneiform script, as well as lists of meanings and objects. Then there are also astrological-astronomic, as well as mathematical texts.[27] To a considerable extent these texts have become known through the discovery of the great and well-arranged library which the Assyrian king, Ashurbanipal, established in the middle of the seventh century B.C. in his capital, Nineveh, now Kuyunjik opposite Mōṣul. The treasures of this library largely ended up in London. They have been published in the great series *Cuneiform Texts from Babylonian Tablets in the British Museum*, abbreviated *CT*.

The number of legal texts uncovered is extremely large. Some are law codes, but the greater part are legal records such as contracts, legal processes, etc. There are also very many business records, including accounts of income and expenditure.

A number of royal annals provide a great deal of historical information. These annals were published as a display of royal pomp or laid down in foundation deposits. Also an extensive correspondence literature has come to light in cuneiform. This consists largely of the state correspondence of kings with their officials or of the ancient oriental rulers with one another. Historically important are also cuneiform texts containing chronologies, such as lists of annual eponyms, chronicles, and the like. A very extensive recent textual find, containing important material, deserves special mention. During the French excavations at Tell Ḥarīri at Abu'l Kemāl in the valley of the middle Euphrates, about 70 km. [40 miles] below the mouth of the Khābūr, begun in 1933 under the direction of A. Parrot and still continuing, in the royal palace of the eighteenth century B.C. archives consisting of more than 20,000 cuneiform tablets were found. Tell Ḥarīri was found to be the ruin of the ancient city of Mari. The Mari texts provide the correspondence of the rulers of Mari and their officials, as well as legal records

[26] The most important can be found in *ANET*, translated into English by W. F. Albright, A. Goetze, S. N. Kramer, T. J. Meek, A. L. Oppenheim, R. H. Pfeiffer, A. Sachs, E. A. Speiser, F. J. Stephens. For German translation, by E. Ebeling, see *AOT*, pp. 108–439.

[27] W. von Soden, "Leistung und Grenze sumerischer und babylonischer Wissenschaft," *Die Welt als Geschichte*, II (1936), 411–64, 509–57.

and business documents, and give surprisingly many insights into the history and life of that period, since the rulers of Mari carried on an amazingly extensive foreign correspondence with other rulers in Mesopotamia and Syria.[28]

A valuable textual find was also made between 1937 and 1945 during English excavations on Tell el-ʿAṭshāneh in the southern part of the Plain of el-ʿAmq about 25 km. [15 miles] eastnortheast of Antakya at the site of the ancient city of Alalaḫ. The Alalaḫ texts[29] date partly from the eighteenth and partly from the fifteenth century B.C. Apart from a few historical and religious texts they consist of legal, business, and government documents.

(3) *Hittite Hieroglyphs*

The so-called "Hittite hieroglyphs" are a pictorial script, found especially in North Syria and in southeastern Asia Minor. The southernmost site of finds is Ḥamah on the middle Orontes. They turn up in relief or incised on stone monuments and stone slabs (Fig. 7). They have also been found engraved on thin strips of lead, which apparently served as letters. This script likewise represents a mixture of ancient logographs (word pictures) and phonetic syllabic writing. It is still in the process of decipherment. So far, phonetically written proper names are the best understood part of these finds.[30] The decipherment has entered a new stage as a result of finds from the ninth or eighth century B.C., discovered on a small mound in eastern Cilicia; that is, in the extreme southeast corner of Asia Minor. The mound is called Karatepe.[31] Hittite

[28] The Mari texts are being published in autographs in the periodical *Musée du Louvre, Département des Antiquités Orientales, Textes cunéiformes* and under the separate title *Archives Royales de Mari* (abbreviated *ARM*). Already published are Vols. I by G. Dossin (1946), II by C.-F. Jean (1941), III by J. R. Kupper (1948), IV–V by Dossin (1951), VI by Kupper (1953), VII by J. Bottéro (1956), VIII by G. Boyer (1957), IX by M. Birot (1960). Parallel to each, under the same serial number, is a volume of ARM by the same scholar including transcription and French translation: I–III (1950), IV (1951), V (1952), VI (1954), VII (1957), VIII (1958), IX (1960). This series also includes the valuable volume XV by J. Bottéro et A. Finet, *Répertoire analytique des tomes I–V* (1954). It presents the contents of the first five Mari text volumes classified in many different ways.

[29] D. J. Wiseman, *The Alalakh Tablets* ("Occasional Publications of the British Institute of Archaeology at Ankara," No. 2, 1953), with a supplement. "Supplementary Copies of Alalakh Tablets," *JCS*, VIII (1954), 1–30.

[30] A comprehensive study of them is B. Hrozný, *Les inscriptions hittites hiéroglyphiques* (1933–37); see also I. J. Gelb, *Hittite Hieroglyphs* (1931) and *Hittite Hieroglyphic Monuments* (1939).

[31] On the excavations refer to H. T. Bossert, B. Alkim, *et al.*, *Karatepe Kazilari, Die Ausgrabungen auf dem Karatepe*, *Türk Tarih Kurumu Yayinlarindar* (1950), V, 9, in Turkish and German.

hieroglyphic and Phoenician inscriptions were found there which apparently present the same text, and, therefore, are bilingual texts.[32]

27. *Alphabetic Writing*

The world is indebted to the ancient Near East for the discovery of alphabetic writing, or a writing system which renders only individual speech sounds and conceives and writes every word as a formation of individual sounds. The new system vastly reduced the number of signs needed in earlier logographic (word picture) and syllabographic scripts. With alphabetic writing one generally gets along with twenty to thirty different signs to represent the various sounds of human speech. This amazing simplification again made possible a general extension of writing and reading, which from then on no longer remained a science which could be learned only by a few learned men. It could now be grasped readily by large groups of people. All of the alphabetic scripts in the entire world are derived directly or indirectly from the system of alphabetic writing which finally was adopted in the ancient Near East. Of course, the ancient oriental alphabets were still incomplete. They indicated the consonants of the words, but not the vowels, by the letters of the alphabet. In practice, this system often led to ambiguity. The Greeks were the first to create vowel signs. About 900 B.C. they borrowed the alphabet which the Phoenicians were using, but transformed the signs for laryngeal sounds, which they did not have in their language, into vowel signs. The limitation of the ancient oriental alphabetic scripts to the reproduction of the consonantal skeleton of the words reminds one of the hieroglyphic script. That suggests that there was a definite historical connection between the two. By writing very short words pictorially with only one consonant, the hieroglyphic sign actually reproduced just a single consonant, therefore, practically a letter of the alphabet. This occurred in the hieroglyphic system in scattered examples only. What was an exception in hieroglyphic writing was now made the rule in alphabetic writing. This development completed the decisive step in the history of writing.

[32] H. T. Bossert, "Die phönizisch-hethitischen Bilinguen vom Karatepe," *Oriens*, I (1948), 163–97; II (1949), 72–126. The Phoenician inscriptions which can be used to study the Hittite hieroglyphic inscriptions can be found in the original text and in German in Alt, *WO*, IV (1949), 272–87.

Syro-Palestine in the second millennium B.C. was acquainted with several attempts on the way to an alphabetic system and with several inventions of alphabetic scripts. The various ancient laborious writing systems were well known here at the centre of the ancient oriental world. Yet none of them was actually indigenous and well established. As a result, the task of writing could become a definite problem. Therefore, it is probably no accident that all sorts of experiments in writing systems were undertaken there. Finally, the important step was taken there resulting in writing by speech sounds [phonemes]. This turned out to be the best solution of the problem of writing. Indeed, phonemic writing arrived in several different but basically similar forms at the same time. If we exclude a few isolated and not yet deciphered examples of alphabetic writing,[33] there are primarily two alphabetic systems of writing which appeared in Syro-Palestine in the course of the second millennium B.C., the alphabetic cuneiform writing of Rās Shamrah and the alphabetic script which won over the world for itself. It will be advisable to proceed from the known, i.e., from the fully developed and incontestably known forms of these two writing systems, and only later to ask the question about their possible relationship and their origin.

(1) *The Alphabetic Cuneiform of Rās Shamrah*

During the excavations of Rās Shamrah (p. 178), clay tablets were immediately found written in the usual cuneiform script technique. The number of them constantly increased in the course of the excavation. Now they already constitute a considerable literature.[34]

It became evident immediately that in spite of clay tablets and cuneiform technique, this was not the old familiar cuneiform

[33] This includes, among others, the inscription on the stela from el-Bālū'ah in Moab from the twelfth century B.C., in the Egyptianizing style. See Horsfield and Vincent, *RB*, XLI (1932), 417 ff., Plates IX ff., and the inscription on p. 425, Fig. 5. Cf. *ANEP*, No. 488; *AfO*, VIII (1932–33), 265, Fig. 13. G. R. Driver, *Semitic Writing*, 1948, p. 123, considers these inscriptions the oldest known examples of south Semitic (South Arabic) script.

[34] Published in facsimile by C. Virolleaud in *Syria*, Vol. X (1929), and in the larger independent works, *La légende phénicienne de Danel* (1936), *La légende de Keret* (1936), *La déesse Anat* (1938), included within the series. *Haut-Commissariat de la République Française en Syrie at au Liban*, *Service des Antiquités*, *Bibliothèque archéologique et historique*; comprehensive treatment with transliteration of all available texts in C. H. Gordon, *Ugaritic Handbook*, *Analecta Orientalia*, XXV (1947), since expanded into three sections under the title *Ugaritic Manual*, *Analecta Orientalia*, XXXV (1955).

writing[35] but an alphabet of thirty signs, the decipherment of which was quickly accomplished.[36] Only consonants were written, except that there were three different alephs, depending on whether the aleph carries a, i, or u. The texts all date from the Late Bronze Age (p. 123). By way of contrast with the ancient cuneiform, the signs are extremely simple as they are also few in number. They were probably invented by someone thoroughly familiar with cuneiform technique and on the basis of the above-mentioned principle of alphabetic writing of consonants.[37] They wrote from left to right as the ancient cuneiform did. So far only one tablet has been found at Rās Shamrah with the reverse direction of writing.[38] The Rās Shamrah script has so far been found elsewhere only on a peculiarly formed clay tablet from Beth-shemesh in Palestine from the middle of the Late Bronze Age.[39] Once again the script runs from right to left. In spite of this isolated find from Beth-shemesh whose historical connections are unknown, so far it seems that the use of the Rās Shamrah script was local and of short duration. Parallel with it the ancient cuneiform was still in use for international trade, even in Syria and Palestine (p. 207), and from the end of the Late Bronze Age on, the Rās Shamrah script had to make way in Syria and Palestine for the prevailing alphabetic script.

(2) *The Ancient Alphabetic Script of Byblos*

The alphabetic script which was destined for the future was already complete at the beginning of the first millennium B.C. The earliest evidences of its finished form originate from the Phoenician city of Byblos, now Jbeil, and from the tenth or ninth century B.C., namely the inscription of King Yehimilk,[40] then the inscriptions on the sarcophagus and in the burial chamber of King Ahiram,[41] as

[35] There are also many texts from Rās Shamrah in the ancient ideographic syllabic cuneiform, but these do not concern us here.

[36] A sign list can be found in *Ugaritic Manual*, pp. 12–15, or among others in J. Friedrich, "Ras Shamra", *Der Alte Orient*, XXXIII (1933), Heft 1–2, 25, and in H. Bauer, *Die alphabetischen Keilschrifttexte von Ras Schamra*, *Kleine Texte für Vorlesungen und Übungen*, No. 168 (1936), p. 64. This is an edition of transliteration of the Rās Shamrah texts known up to 1935. H. Bauer himself had an important part in the decipherment of the Rās Shamrah script. *ANEP*, Nos. 261–64, shows reproduction of various texts.

[37] There are also instances at Rās Shamrah of alphabetic cuneiform being inscribed on stone and metal. See *ANEP*, Nos. 261–62.

[38] Virolleaud in *Syria*, XV (1934), 103–4.

[39] See E. Grant, *Rumeileh*, III (1934), 27, Fig. 2A(1), Plate XX (bottom); facsimile also in *AfO*, IX (1933–34), 358, Fig. 15, and *BASOR*, LII (1933), 4.

[40] Published by M. Dunand, *RB*, XXXIX (1930), 321 ff.

[41] Published by R. Dussaud in *Syria*, V (1924), 135 ff.; noted here on Fig. 8.

well as the inscriptions of Abibaal,[42] Elibaal,[43] and of Shiptibaal.[44] These inscriptions use the series of twenty-two letters of the alphabet which are also used by Hebrew. Consequently, they reproduce only consonants. The signs are rather simple linear figures. The writing runs from right to left. These Byblos inscriptions are all engraved in stone. From the eleventh century B.C. there are brief inscriptions on spear heads from el-Khaḍr near Bethlehem.[45] In addition, from the tenth or ninth century B.C. there is an inscription incised on the edge of a clay pot from Byblos,[46] and an inscription on a bronze knife from Byblos[47] as well as an inscription on a spear point from Ruweiseh in Lebanon.[48] A simple and clear line proceeds from them to the further evidences of the history of alphabetic writing in the first millennium.

(3) *The Prehistory of the Phoenician Script*

The problem of a possible prehistory of this writing system is more difficult. There are numerous inscriptions of the second millennium in which, as a rule, one can see the forerunners of this alphabet, although no one has yet succeeded in reading these inscriptions with any degree of certainty. For one thing, we have the Sinai inscriptions, which originated in the fifteenth century B.C., disclosed in 1904 and 1905 by Petrie[49] at the Egyptian mines of Ṣerābīṭ el-Khādem on the Sinai peninsula, which have been explored frequently since Petrie and augmented by new finds.[50] In addition, there are several short incised inscriptions of the late

[42] Dussaud, *Syria*, V (1924), Plate XLII; a sign list of the Ahiram and Abibaal inscription is also in *AOB*, No. 606a–b.

[43] Dussaud, *op. cit.*, VI (1925), 101 ff., Plate XXV; see also I. Benzinger, *Hebräische Archäologie* (3rd ed., 1927), Fig. 170.

[44] Published by M. Dunand, *Byblia Grammata* (1945), pp. 146 ff.; facsimile also in Driver, *op. cit.*, Plate XLV, 1. Dunand, *op. cit.*, wanted to date this inscription at the beginning of the second millennium B.C. However, the form of its letters places it definitely with the Byblos inscriptions of the tenth or ninth century B.C.

[45] J. T. Milik and Frank M. Cross, *BASOR*, CXXXIV (1954), 6–15.

[46] Dunand, *Byblia Grammata* (1945), pp. 152–53; Driver, *op. cit.*, Plate XLV, 2.

[47] See W. F. Albright, *BASOR*, LXXIII (1939), 11–12; Driver, *op. cit.*, Plate XLVII, 2.

[48] In facsimile in J. Hempel, *Die althebräische Literatur* (1930), p. 11, Fig. 6; Driver, *op. cit.*, p. 106, Fig. 55.

[49] *Researches in Sinai* (1906), pp. 129 ff.

[50] Survey of sources with references, many illustrations, and a list of signs in J. Leibovitch, *ZDMG*, New Series, IX (1930), 1 ff., Plates I–XVII; see also Driver, *op. cit.*, pp. 94 ff. A statue with "Sinai script" is reproduced in *ANEP*, No. 270 and *AOB*, No. 677. W. F. Albright proposed a suggestion in several respects new and noteworthy on the reading and meaning of these Sinai inscriptions in *BASOR*, CX (1948), 6–22.

A

B

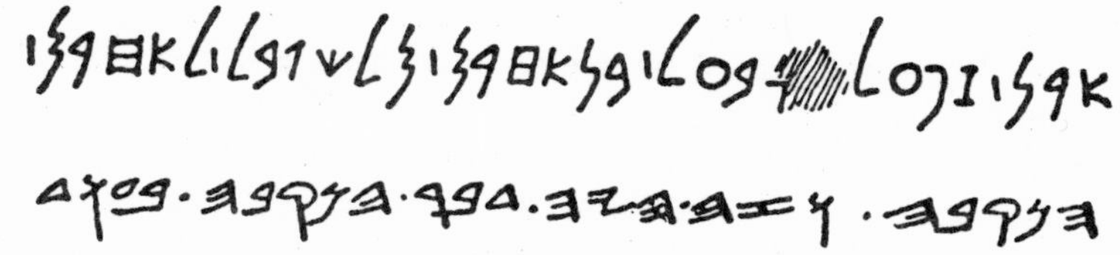

Figure 8. Alphabetic Writing

A = Beginning of the Inscription of the Ahiram Sarcophagus based on *Syria*, V (1924), p. 137.

Transcription in Hebrew:

ארן זפעל [את]בעל בן אחרם מלך גבל לאחרם

Transliteration (the original reads from right to left): ’rn zp‘l [’t]b‘l bn ’ḥrm mlk gbl l’ḥrm

Translation: coffin (which) [Itto]baal, son of Ahiram, king of Byblos (*Gebal*) had built for Ahiram.

B = Beginning of the Siloam inscription, based on *ZDPV*, IV (1881), Pls. VII, VIII.

Transcription in Hebrew:

הנקבה וזה היה דבר הנקבה בעוד

Transliteration (the original reads from right to left): . . . hnqbh wzh hyh dbr hnqbh b‘wd . . .

Translation: . . . the tunnelling, and this was the account of the tunnelling, while still . . .

Middle Bronze Age with similar signs from southwestern Palestine, at Gezer and Lachish, and central Palestine, at Shechem.[51] The signs of all these inscriptions are still strikingly pictorial (pictographic) and have only remote similarities to those of the later alphabetic script, though they seem to be alphabetic signs.

Some additional Late Bronze Age inscriptions are available from southwestern Palestine. They are not simply identical with one another as to form of script; yet, they seem to represent a link between the pictographic inscriptions of the Middle Bronze Age and the later alphabetic script.[52] These are the groups of signs incised or written with ink on an ostracon from Beth-shemesh,[53] on a potsherd from Tell el-Ḥesi,[54] on a jar from Tell ‘Ajjūl[55] as well

[51] Compiled by F. M. T. Böhl, *ZDPV*, LXI (1938), 17–25, Figs. 1–4, with sign list; LXII (1939), 163; and by Driver, *op. cit.*, pp. 98–99.

[52] Compiled by Böhl, *op. cit.*, pp. 14–17 and by Driver, *op. cit.*, pp. 99 ff.

[53] Reproduced in E. Grant, *Ain Shems Excavations*, I (1931), Plate X and in *AfO*, X (1935–36), 271.

[54] Reproduced in *AfO*, X (1935–36), 268.

[55] Petrie, *Ancient Gaza*, II (1932), Plate XXX, No. 1109.

as on various pieces of Lachish, on the underside of a crude clay bowl,[56] on a potsherd,[57] on the shoulder of a jar,[58] and finally on the underside of the lid of an incense bowl.[59] In addition, there is a gold ring from Megiddo with an inscription consisting of a few signs,[60] and from Syria the fragment of a small limestone slab from Byblos, inscribed with three lines.[61] The latter piece can be an indication that the piling up of the finds from southern Palestine (and from Sinai) is only the result of particularly intensive excavations there. Their abundance does not necessarily lead to the conclusion that the home of this alphabetic script was there in the south.

Moreover, the readings and the meanings of these Middle and Late Bronze texts, which are mostly very short, are still problematical and debated. The factual relationships and classification of these received texts into a unilinear or multilinear prehistory of alphabetic script is still uncertain. Therefore, definite assertions can hardly be proposed. Only this preliminary statement can be made, that in the second millennium B.C. in Syria and Palestine all sorts of attempts at devising an alphabetic script were made, and that a number of these trial scripts, particularly some of the Late Bronze ones, actually look like forerunners of the later linear alphabetic script.

New light has been shed on the problem of a closer connection between the cuneiform alphabetic system of Rās Shamrah and linear alphabetic writing by a find made in November 1949. A small clay tablet was brought to light on Rās Shamrah which contains a sign list of the alphabetic cuneiform system, apparently intended for school use.[62] The order of this list exactly matches the "ABC" of the linear alphabetic script. The order of signs of this alphabet was already used during the seventh century B.C. We know this because of a scribble on a stone from Lachish, Tell ed-Duweir, which provides the first five letters of the alphabet in the order found in the Hebrew alphabet.[63] This must have been the

56 *Lachish* [*Tell ed-Duweir*], IV (1958), Plates XLIII, XLIV, 3; *AfO*, X (1935–36), 388, Fig. 15.

57 *Lachish*, IV, Plate XLIV, 7.

58 *Lachish*, II (1940), Plate LI, A, No. 287; *AfO*, X, 277, Fif. 3.

59 *Lachish*, IV, Plates XLIV, 1; XLV, 4.

60 Driver, *op. cit.*, p. 102, Fig. 50.

61 Published by M. Dunand, *Mélanges Maspero*, I (1935), 567 ff.; pictured also in *BASOR*, LXIII (1936), 10, Fig. 2.

62 Published by C. H. Gordon, "The Ugaritic 'ABC'," *Orientalia*, New Series, XIX (1950), 374–76; see also O. Eissfeldt, *FF*, XXVI (1950), 217–20. This new find shows that even the fragmentary Rās Shamrah tablet, published in *RA*, XXVII (1940–1941), 34. as No. XX, contains the same alphabetic list. Therefore, it also represents such a school text.

63 *Lachish*, III (1953), Fig. 10, Plate XLVIIIb, 3.

accepted order about 900 B.C., since the alphabetic order was taken over at that time by the Greeks, together with the linear alphabet. Now the same arrangement suddenly appears as early as the fourteenth century B.C. on the Rās Shamrah tablet. Of course this provides a list of thirty signs. There is a surplus of eight signs contained in it over and above the later Canaanite-Hebrew alphabet. Five signs are scattered within the order held in common and three signs are at the very end. This latter group includes the forms of aleph with i and u and a second form of s (*samekh*). It apparently represents a special addition to the Rās Shamrah alphabet, while the other five signs seem to have been part of the basic alphabet in the fourteenth century B.C. As a result of this essential correspondence in the alphabetic order, the assumption of a connection between the cuneiform and linear alphabets, made because of the similarity of a few sign forms, is raised to certainty. The fact that the cuneiform alphabet is attested considerably earlier and that it has a somewhat fuller content need not lead to the conclusion that it is the linear alphabet which is dependent. The existence of a Late Bronze linear alphabet can also be assumed, though this has not yet been documented. This then would have motivated a man in Ugarit, acquainted with the cuneiform technique, to transfer the linear alphabet into a cuneiform alphabet, depending somewhat on the linear letter forms, but largely designing new cuneiform characters. Now the linear alphabet, on the other hand, probably had made its appearance earlier among the above-mentioned late Middle Bronze, or certainly among the Late Bronze writing experiments. This then continued on in the Canaanite-Hebrew alphabet with which we are acquainted. In this later form it was reduced to twenty-two letters, since certain characters had been combined as one, where two or more sounds previously distinguished were later undifferentiated from one another.

The linear pseudo-hieroglyphic inscriptions from Byblos from the beginning of the second millennium B.C. show that this latter possibility should be considered very seriously.[64] These ten inscriptions contain a script of about one hundred different signs.[65] Consequently it should probably be described as a syllabic script. At the same time it represents a middle position between the old writing systems of Egypt and Mesopotamia, which had developed from pictorial scripts, and the later alphabetic writing systems. Since a

[64] Dunand published these inscriptions in *Byblia Grammata* (1945), pp. 71 ff.; E. Dhorme in *Syria*, XXV (1948), 1 ff., tried to decipher them. See also Driver, *op. cit.*, pp. 91 ff.; A. Jirku, *FF*, XXVI (1950), 90 ff.; H. Schmökel, *ibid.*, 153 ff.

[65] *ANEP*, No. 287 gives a reproduction of a bronze tablet containing this script.

few of these pseudo-hieroglyphic signs show a striking similarity to the signs of the later linear letter script, consideration must be given to whether alphabetic writing was derived from the pseudo-hieroglyphic script. By contrast, if that is the case, the alphabetic Rās Shamrah script would be secondary.

Egyptian hieroglyphic writing might have inspired this entire process. The similarity of many signs of pseudo-hieroglyphic script and then of the later linear letter script with Egyptian hieroglyphs argues for this, in addition to the consideration suggested on p. 211. Of course, here we are dealing simply with a vague dependence and with the borrowing of a few signs parallel to which there are numerous newly invented signs.[66] The so-called acrophonic principle is basic to linear letter script. This means that the form of many signs was derived from outlines of objects whose names in Canaanite began with the consonant which one wanted to express with the sign. It is now clear that the fixed order of the alphabet is fairly old. It is not clear on what principle the letters were arranged in this particular order. Probably the signs were grouped together on the basis of the objects to which they originally referred.[67] Moreover, free random invention probably played a role at this point.

(4) *Later Development in Stone Inscriptions*

Following the Byblos and related inscriptions, referred to on pp. 213 ff., the further history of alphabetic writing is attested by a considerable series of inscribed objects which, if they are in a good enough state of preservation, can be read without difficulty. In the course of time various detailed distinctions developed in the form and manner of writing alphabetic characters, for instance in the manner of word division—*scriptio continua* without word division and also word division with spacing, with points or special marks. Important in this connection was the process of gradual appearance of vowel indicators in what had been a purely consonantal script. First at the end of words, then within words, certain vowels, especially long ones, were indicated by the consonants /', h, w, and y/. These consonants in this special use became known as *matres lectionis* in later Hebrew.[68]

Among inscriptions engraved in stone, we have from tenth cen-

[66] Cf. H. Bauer, "Der Ursprung des Alphabets," *Der Alte Orient*, XXXVI (1937), Heft 1–2.

[67] Cf. Driver, *op. cit.*, pp. 152 ff.

[68] F. M. Cross and D. N. Freedman, *Early Hebrew Orthography* (1952), give details on this process, which began as early as the ninth century B.C.

tury Palestine the small tablet of soft limestone from Gezer with the agricultural calendar,[69] an account of agricultural tasks which occur in the individual months. Then from the end of the eighth century there is the inscription in the Siloam tunnel (pp. 157–58) with noticeably more cursive features of the script.[70] In addition there are many more inscriptions on seals, as, for example, on the renowned Lion Seal from Megiddo.[71]

The victory stela of Israel's neighbour, King Mesha of Moab, was found at Dībān in 1868. He is referred to in II Kings 3 : 4 ff. It was inscribed with a long text and erected in the middle of the ninth century B.C.[72]

In Phoenicia itself following the Byblos inscriptions referred to, there is a larger number of Phoenician sarcophagus and votive inscriptions only from the fifth century B.C. on,[73] with an elegant slender type of script of their own.

We have a number of additional inscriptions from the interior of central and northern Syria. An inscribed stela of King Benhadad I of Aram was found at the village of el-Breij, 8 km. [5 miles] north-northeast of the citadel of Aleppo, Ḥaleb,[74] dating from the middle of the ninth century B.C. Some royal and building inscriptions were found in and around modern Zinjirli in the extreme northern part of the Syrian rift. The oldest of them is the inscription of King Kilamuwa of the ninth century B.C.[75] Of later date are some inscriptions of the eighth century.[76] The type of script used here is still fairly close to that of the old Byblos inscriptions. The stela inscription of King ZKR (Zakir ?) of Hamath and Laʿash, found

[69] *AOB*, No. 609; *ANET*, p. 320; *ANEP*, No. 272.

[70] Guthe, *ZDMG*, XXXVI (1882), 725 ff.; A Socin, *Die Siloahinschrift* (1899), reproduced in *ANEP*, No. 275. See especially Vincent and Stève, *Jérusalem de l'Ancien Testament*, I (1954), Plate LXVIII.

[71] *Tell el-Mutesellim*, I (1908), 99, Fig. 147; Watzinger, *Denkmäler Palästinas*, I (1933), Fig. 94. Other seals with inscriptions are depicted in Galling, *BRL*, Cols. 485–86, and *ZDPV*, LXIV (1941), Plates V–XII.

[72] Smend-Socin, *Die Inschrift des Königs Mesa von Moab* (1886); *AOB*, No. 120; *ANET*, p. 320; *ANEP*, No. 274.

[73] M. Lidzbarski, *Handbuch der nordsemitischen Epigraphik* (1898), pp. 416 ff., Plates III ff.; G. A. Cooke, *A Textbook of North-Semitic Inscriptions* (1903), pp. 18 ff., Plates I–II; and *Corpus Inscriptionum Semiticarum* [*CIS*], Vol. I.

[74] Published by Dunand, *Bulletin du Musée de Beyrouth*, III (1941), 65 ff. See Albright, *BASOR*, LXXXVII (1942), 23 ff.

[75] See von Luschan, *Ausgrabungen in Sendschirli*, IV, or *Mitteilungen aus den orientalischen Sammlungen der Kgl. Museen zu Berlin*, XIV (1911), 374–77 and M. Lidzbarski, *Ephemeris für semitische Epigraphik*, hereafter referred to as *Ephemeris*, III (1915), 218 ff.

[76] These, like the North Syrian inscriptions of the seventh century from Nerab southeast of Aleppo, are to be found in Lidzbarski, *Handbuch*, pp. 440 ff., Plates XXII ff., and in Cooke, *op. cit.*, pp. 159 ff., Plates V–VI.

in Afis 40 km. [25 miles] southwest of Aleppo,[77] and the stela fragments from Sefîreh 25 km. [15 miles] southeast of Aleppo[78] belong in the middle of the eighth century.

(5) *The Ostraca of Samaria and Lachish*

Alphabetic writing, in distinction from cuneiform writing, was also adaptable to writing with ink on papyrus, potsherds, and the like. Like the hieratic-demotic script in Egypt, it was actually put to this use in daily life fairly early. According to the statement of the Egyptian, Wen-Amun, as early as 1100 B.C. considerable numbers of papyrus rolls were sent from Egypt to Syria, in this case to Byblos.[79] Of course, papyrus was not preserved in the climate of Syro-Palestine, while inscribed potsherds and ostraca were. Some have been found in Palestine. The oldest are the Samaritan ostraca dating probably from the first half of the eighth century B.C., found in a room of the royal palace of Samaria, the capital of Israel.[80] The find consists of sixty-three memoranda on wine and oil deliveries from the scattered crown estates to the royal court.[81] The script (Fig. 9) of these incidental texts, each composed according to a definite plan, by royal employees or tenants, in general shows a notable skill in writing. The even greater facility and elegance of script in the ostraca of Lachish, eighteen inscribed potsherds, reflect a longer usage of writing. These were found at the beginning of 1935 during the excavations on Tell ed-Duweir, Lachish, in a room of the gate complex. They contain especially reports to the commander of the fortress of Lachish in 588 B.C., that is, in the period just before the fall of Lachish and the end of Judah by action of the troops of Nebuchadnezzar.[82] Chemical analysis shows that the potsherds were inscribed (Fig. 10) with an ink produced from gall-nut extract and soot. The ostracon from Ophel[83] (Jerusalem), very difficult to read, is dated close to the Lachish ostraca.

[77] H. Pognon, *Inscriptions sémitiques de la Syrie, de la Mésopotamie et de la région de Mossoul* (1907–8), pp. 156 ff., Plates IX–X, XXXV–XXXVI; Lidzbarski, *Ephemeris*, III, 1 ff.

[78] A. Dupont-Sommer, *Les inscriptions araméennes de Stivé* (1958).

[79] *ANET*, p. 28 [*AOT*, p. 75].

[80] See Reisner, Fisher, and Lyon, *Harvard Excavations at Samaria* (1924), I, 227–246; II, Plate LV.

[81] The text of these ostraca, too, can be found in *ZAW*, New Series, II (1925), 148–49.

[82] Edited by H. Torczyner with L. Harding, A. Lewis, and J. L. Starkey in the volume, *Lachish*, Vol. I: *The Lachish Letters* (1938); an ostracon is also depicted in *AfO*, X (1935–36), 389, Fig. 17 and *ANEP*, No. 279.

[83] Published in *PEF Ann.*, IV (1926), 182, Fig. 193.

(6) *Later Development of Alphabetic Script*

The practical and easily learned letter script finally branched out beyond Syria and Palestine. Already in the second half of the eighth century B.C. we encounter it in a number of examples of affairs of daily life in Mesopotamia.[84] About 600 B.C. a petty king, probably from the region of Philistia, addressed a petition for help to Pharaoh as shown by a papyrus found at Saqqārah in Egypt.[85] From the fifth century on, the letter script appears everywhere in the Near East along with the old-established systems of writing. It now has a very elegant form with rounded lines and nicely flourishing downstrokes often extending well below the base line. The most important and extensive finds of this type are the Elephantine papyri, disclosed in 1906–7 in Upper Egypt on the island of Elephantine in the Nile below the first cataract and in Aswan close by. They are legal records, official documents, and lists from the colony of Israelite border soldiers settled there.[86] Also from Egypt, though the exact location is unknown, and from the same period are some records on leather, which are noteworthy as examples of this writing material.[87] There are also many smaller written finds.

The so-called square letters come into common use in the Jewish community in the last centuries B.C. as a particular type of this extensively used script. It is encountered on the documents which will be treated more fully on pp. 311 ff.

The forms of letters of the late stone inscriptions tended to approximate the various types of this cursive script of the last centuries before Christ. This is true of the Palmyrene inscriptions of the first three centuries after Christ[88] and of the almost contemporary Nabatean inscriptions from Transjordan, Ḥejāz, and the Sinai peninsula.[89] Square letters occur in stone for the first time in the third century B.C. in the short inscription from ʿArāq el-Emīr east of the northern end of the Dead Sea,[90] then later at the so-called grave of Jacob in the Kidron Valley and on the border stone of Gezer,[91] as well as on numerous ossuaries (p. 171) and on

[84] Lidzbarski, "Altaramäische Urkunden aus Assur," *WVDOG*, XXXVIII (1921).

[85] Published by A. Dupont-Sommer, *Semitica*, I (1948), 43 ff. and H. L. Ginsberg, *BASOR*, CXI (1948), 24 ff.

[86] The majority of these finds are published in E. Sachau, *Aramäische Papyrus und Ostraka aus einer jüdischen Militärkolonie zu Elephantine* (1911), 75 collotype plates; text ed. A. Cowley, *Aramaic Papyri of the Fifth Century B.C.* (1923). A facsimile is in *ANEP*, No. 282. An additional portion of the Elephantine Papyri was published in E. G. Kraeling, *The Brooklyn Museum Aramaic Papyri* (1953).

[87] Driver, *Aramaic Documents of the Fifth Century B.C.* (1954; rev. ed., 1957).

[88] See Lidzbarski, *Handbuch*, II, Plates XXXVII ff.

[89] *Ibid.*, Plates XXIX ff.

[90] *AOB*, No. 608.

[91] Lidzbarski, *Handbuch*, Plate XLIII, 2–3.

the early Jewish synagogues (pp. 116–18) where it also frequently appears in mosaic on the synagogue floors.[92]

The alphabet of the South Arabian stone inscriptions is a particular offshoot of the letter script described here.[93] The later

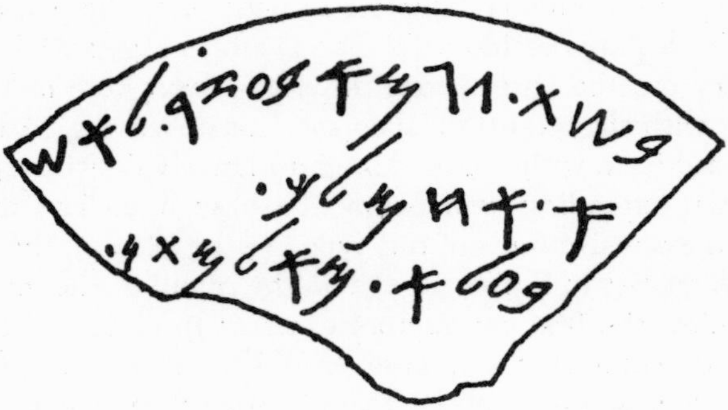

Figure 9. Samaritan Ostracon

Ostracon 28 from Samaria, based on George Andrew Reisner, *et al.*, *Harvard Excavations at Samaria* (Cambridge: Harvard Univ., 1924), I, 241.

Transcription in Hebrew:

בשת ∧ר מאבעזר לאש
א אחמלך
בעלא מאלמתן

Transliteration (the original runs from right to left):

bsht · 15 m'b'zr · l's
' · 'ḥmlk
b'l' · m'lmtn

Translation: In the year fifteen—from Abiezer—to Asa, (son of) Ahimelek. Baala from (the place) 'lmtn.

developments, such as those of Syrian and North Arabian scripts, do not need to be considered here.[94]

[92] Watzinger, *Denkmäler Palästinas*, II (1935), Fig. 49.

[93] Many examples in Mordtmann-Mittwoch, *Rathjens-v. Wissmannsche Südarabienreise*, Vol. I: *Sabäische Inschriften* (1931).

[94] Apropos of this entire section, read D. Diringer, *The Alphabet, A Key to the History of Mankind* (2nd ed., 1949).

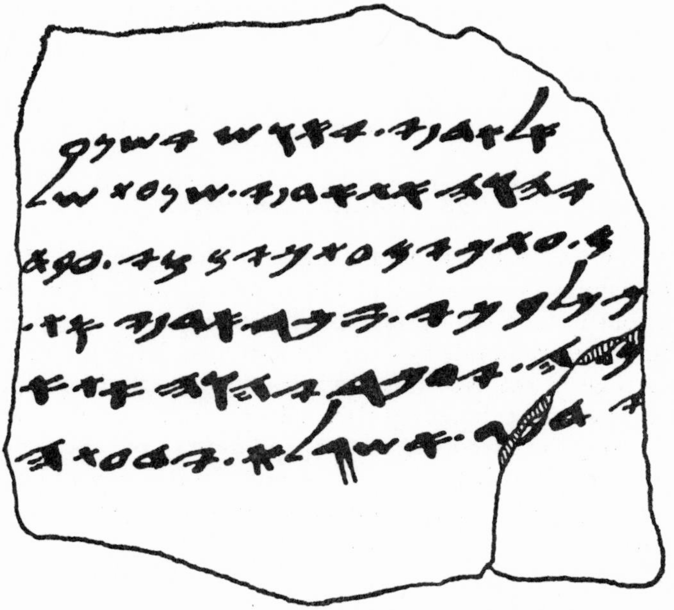

Figure 10. Lachish Ostracon

Ostracon II from Lachish based on H. Torczyner, *The Lachish Letters* (1938), pp. 34 ff.

Transcription in Hebrew:

אל אדני יאוש ישמע
יהוה את אדני שמעת של
ם עת כים עת כים מי עבד
ך כלב כי זכר אדני את
[ע]בדה יעכר יהוה את א
[ת]י דבר אשר לא ידעתה

Transliteration (the original reads from right to left):

'l 'dny y'wsh yshm'
yhwh 't'dny shm't shl
m 't kym 't kym my 'bd
k klb ky zkr 'dny 't
[']bdh y'kr yhwh 't '
[t]y dbr 'shr l' yd'th

Translation: To my lord Ya'osh: May Yahweh let my lord hear a report of peace this very day, this very day! What is your servant but a dog, that my lord has remembered his servant? May Yahweh afflict those who engage in anything of which you do not know.

CHAPTER IV

LANGUAGES

28. *Semitic Languages*

SOUTHWEST Asia is the ancient and modern home of the language family which acquired the name, Semitic, from the table of nations in Genesis, chapter 10. The word, Semitic, applies only to this language family in scholarly writings. Although there never was a time in the Near East when only Semitic languages were spoken, yet these languages were in the majority very early, at least among the native population, and most of the ancient oriental linguistic remains belong to this group. In the ancient period, we are dealing with a large number of dialects as well as with the languages to which they belong.[1]

(1) *Accadian*

We call the Semitic language which was spoken in ancient Mesopotamia "Accadian," taking this name from the city of Accad referred to in Gen. 10 : 10. Although the exact location of Accad in the central Tigris or Euphrates River area is still unknown, it was probably in the northern part of lower Mesopotamia in the general region of Baghdad. Accad was the centre of the first substantial nation of the Semitic-speaking inhabitants of Mesopotamia, to the best of our knowledge. Its name was subsequently applied especially in stereotyped expressions to the northern part of lower Mesopotamia. Occasionally, Accadian with its individual characteristics is spoken of as East Semitic to distinguish it from the other Semitic languages. In the beginning of scholarly work on this language, texts in the Assyrian dialect were studied first. As a result, scholars customarily referred to the entire language as Assyrian. Therefore, even today, we speak of Assyriology [with the broader meaning of study of Accadian]. This language was again disclosed to the scholarly world only as a result of the decipherment

[1] See the comprehensive work, C. Brockelmann, *Grundriss der vergleichenden Grammatik der semitischen Sprachen*, Vols. I–II (1908–13); the more concise work by Brockelmann, *Kurzfasste vergleichende Grammatik der semitischen Sprachen*, *Porta linguarum orientalium*, Vol. XXI (1908); and G. Bergsträsser, *Einführung in die semitischen Sprachen, Sprachproben und grammatische Skizzen* (1928).

of cuneiform, since almost all available texts in this language have come into our possession only in cuneiform scripts. Two chief dialects are distinguished, Babylonian which was at home in lower Mesopotamia, and Assyrian which was spoken farther to the north along the Tigris. Each of these dialects had a somewhat definable history with local differentiations. Accadian, which in many respects clung to original features, is marked linguistically by the loss of most of the proto-Semitic laryngeals, only /ḫ/ and in part /'/ have been retained, and by the disappearance of the half-vowels /w/ and /y/. In this respect Accadian was apparently influenced by the substratum of a non-Semitic population of Mesopotamia, whose language influenced the pronunciation of Accadian. Furthermore, Accadian has the transition of dental fricatives /ð/ [as in then], /θ/ [as in thin] and /ẓ, ḍ/ into the sibilants /z/, /š/, and /ṣ/. The old Semitic case-endings and the other short final vowels were still present. But in time their usage deteriorated. Furthermore, Accadian still has its own ancient individual verbal system.

As literature on the Accadian language, see A. Ungnad, *Grammatik des Akkadischen*, *Clavis linguarum Semiticarum*, Vol. II (3rd ed., 1949), and particularly W. von Soden, *Akkadische Grammatik*, *Analecta Orientalia*, Vol. XXXIII (1952). The language of the Mari texts (see p. 209) has received special treatment by A. Finet, *L'Accadien des Lettres de Mari*, *Académie Royale de Belgique*, *Classe des Lettres et des Sciences Morales et Politiques*, *Mémoires* 8°, T., Vol. LI, No. 1 (1956). Two extensive Accadian dictionaries are in process of publication. One is *The Assyrian Dictionary of the Oriental Institute of the University of Chicago* (abbreviated *CAD* or *Chicago Assyrian Dictionary*), published in twenty-one volumes beginning with 1956. The other is W. von Soden, *Akkadisches Handwörterbuch*, in one volume, which has appeared in fascicles since 1959. Lists of cuneiform signs are found in R. Labat, *Manuel d'épigraphie akkadienne* (1952) and, for phonetic values, in W. von Soden, *Das akkadische Syllabar*, *Analecta Orientalia*, Vol. XXVII (1948).

(2) *Canaanite*

The Semitic language which was native to Syro-Palestine in various dialects, at least from the beginning of the second millennium B.C. but perhaps considerably earlier, is best referred to as Canaanite, based on Old Testament usage of the name Canaan (see pp. 49 ff.). Its available texts have been left to us, generally speaking, in the alphabetic scripts treated on pp. 211–23. Only isolated words have been transmitted in the old cuneiform, such as the Canaanite glosses in the Amarna tablets.[2]

In the texts of Rās Shamrah we have a dialect which is called Ugaritic. Ugarit is the ancient name of the city which once lay where Rās Shamrah now is. In spite of various individual characteristics Ugaritic must be considered Canaanite. Careful investigation of this dialect is far from complete.[3] The Phoenician dialect is represented by the Phoenician inscriptions[4] (pp. 213–14, 219). Hebrew is another significant dialect of Canaanite. Being the native language of Palestine, it was adopted by the Israelite tribes after their conquest of the land. Naturally, elements of their previous language (see below) were also carried over into Hebrew, just as was the case with the Moabite of the Mesha inscription (p. 219), which is most closely related to Hebrew.[5]

Canaanite shares with Accadian the transition of the dental fricatives into sibilants (see p. 225), also a definite, even if not so radical, reduction of the number of proto-Semitic laryngeals. The phonemes /ʿ/ and /gh/ fell together into /ʿ/, at least in the written form. The two were probably still differentiated in pronunciation, as transliterations of Hebrew names seem to show. The phonemes /ḫ/ and /ḥ/ were still differentiated in Ugaritic. But alphabetic writing has only one sign for them, /ḥ/, and probably in time there was no difference in pronunciation between both consonants. As the oldest attested dialect, when compared with the other dialects, Ugaritic has a number of archaic traits. Ugaritic still retained the old case-endings and especially the short final vowels. They disappeared in the other [later] dialects. Ugaritic seems to have had an old verbal system which is still unclear in many details. In the remaining dialects it appears only in vestigial form or complicated by external influences.

(3) *Aramaic*

Tribes which called themselves Aramaic entered Syro-Palestine at the beginning of the Iron Age from the eastern steppe and

[2] Cf. F. M. T. Böhl, *Die Sprache der Amarnabriefe*, *Leipziger Semitistische Studien*, Vol. V, No. 2 (1909), Secs. 37–38.

[3] C. H. Gordon, *Ugaritic Manual*, *Analecta Orientalia*, Vol. XXXV (1955).

[4] Z. S. Harris, *A Grammar of the Phoenician Language*, *American Oriental Series*, Vol. VIII (1936); J. Friedrich, *Phönizisch-punische Grammatik*, *Analecta Orientalia*, Vol. XXXII (1950).

[5] On attested Canaanite words, apart from Ugaritic, see C.-F. Jean and J. Hoftijzer, *Dictionnaire des inscriptions sémitiques de l'ouest*, Fascicles 1–2 (1960).

formed a number of nations in the course of the first millennium B.C. Israel, as well as Ammon, Moab, and Edom were probably part of this, although they adopted the Canaanite dialects native in the places where they settled down. Farther to the north, however, in the interior of central and northern Syria, these tribes retained their old dialects. The earliest available linguistic materials, called Old Aramaic, are the alphabetic inscriptions from the interior of central and northern Syria[6] referred to on pp. 219–20. We have Aramaic only in alphabetic writing, with the exception of a few texts in old cuneiform. The decisive event in the history of Aramaic was the fact that in the sixth or fifth century B.C. it was made the official language in great parts of the Persian empire, especially in almost all of the regions of the ancient Orient which belonged to this empire. [This official language is called Imperial Aramaic.] This happened in Mesopotamia after it had prevailed as the language of international communication, particularly for trade and also as a written language in the second half of the eighth century and in the seventh century B.C. (Note the Old Aramaic records from Ashur on p. 221.) The decisive fact was that in the process of being thus established it also had been adopted as the ongoing popular language in this wide area. Imperial Aramaic is attested by the leather documents and the papyri of Elephantine in Egypt[7] (p. 221), and in Palestine by the Aramaic portions of the Book of Ezra. Vernacular Aramaic dialects which developed from Imperial Aramaic are found in the biblical Aramaic of Dan. 2–7,[8] in the Aramaic of certain texts from Khirbet Qumrān (see p. 311), in the Palestinian and Babylonian Aramaic of Rabbinic literature,[9] in the Aramaic dialect of the Palmyrene inscriptions[10] (p. 221), in certain Christian Palestinian Aramaic texts,[11] and the Nabatean[12] inscriptions (p. 221); finally, in the east Aramaic Syriac, the language of the Christian Syrians with its various

[6] See also A. Dupont-Sommer, *Les Araméens* (1949), pp. 79 ff.

[7] Cf. P. Leander, *Laut-und Formenlehre des Ägyptisch-Aramäischen* (1928).

[8] See K. Marti, *Kurzgefasste Grammatik der biblisch-aramäischen Sprache, Porta linguarum orientalium*, Vol. XVIII (3rd ed., 1925); H. L. Strack, *Grammatik des Biblisch-Aramäischen, Clavis linguarum Semiticarum*, Vol. IV (6th ed., 1921); Bauer-Leander, *Kurzegefasste biblisch-aramäische Grammatik* (1929); and for details, Bauer-Leander, *Grammatik des Biblisch-Aramäischen* (1927).

[9] See G. Dalman, *Grammatik des jüdisch-palästinischen Aramäisch* (2nd ed., 1905); also by Dalman, *Aramäisch-neuhebräisches Handwörterbuch zu Targum, Talmud und Midrasch* (3rd ed., 1939); and M. L. Margolis, *Lehrbuch der aramäischen Sprache des babylonischen Talmuds, Clavis linguarum Semiticarum*, Vol. III (1910).

[10] J. Cantineau, *Grammaire du Palmyrénien épigraphique* (1935).

[11] F. Schwally, *Idioticon des christlich-palästinischen Aramaeisch* (1893).

[12] J. Cantineau, *Le Nabatéen*, Vols. I–II (1930–32).

dialects, native primarily in upper Mesopotamia, especially in the region of the Christian Church of Edessa and spreading out from there,[13] as well as ultimately in Mandaic, the language of the sect of Mandeans in southern Mesopotamia.[14] Aramaic has been maintained as a colloquial language by a few limited groups in Antilebanon and around Lake Urmia.[15]

Aramaic shares a number of distinctive features with Canaanite. Therefore Aramaic was originally closely related to Canaanite. For this reason both dialect groups are frequently grouped together as West Semitic.[16] Aramaic shares with post-Ugaritic Canaanite of its own period the number of laryngeals in use and the dropping of short vowel endings. Nevertheless, Aramaic had its own peculiarities in vocabulary, construction of forms, and syntax, even in the earliest forms of which we know. Certain peculiarities in pronunciation are hidden in Old Aramaic by the incompleteness of the alphabet [as it omits vowels]. This script was developed in Syro-Palestine for the dialects in use there. Therefore, it was arranged for Canaanite consonants. The Arameans adopted this alphabet and adapted themselves in their early inscriptions to the Canaanite pronunciation and also adopted with the script additional Canaanite expressions from the dominant Canaanite culture.

Old Aramaic probably still had the original dental spirants. Since the alphabet had no particular sign for them, they were written with the corresponding sibilants in the old inscriptions, and, in part, still in the Elephantine papyri. Later on, /ð, θ, and ḍ/ did not become sibilants as they did in Accadian and Canaanite. Rather, they became the explosives, /d, t, and ṭ/. Original /ð/ interestingly enough appears first of all as /q/, later as /ʿ/. Making nouns emphatic or determinative by suffixing an /ā/ is noteworthy, being found in the earliest writings. Aramaic, as a widespread commercial language, adopted very many foreign words and loan words from a great variety of languages spoken in the Near East in the last centuries before Christ.

[13] Brockelmann, *Syrische Grammatik*, *Porta linguarum orientalium*, Vol. V (1938); also by Brockelmann, *Lexicon Syriacum* (2nd ed., 1928).

[14] T. Nöldeke, *Mandäische Grammatik* (1875).

[15] Bergsträsser, *Einführung*, pp. 80 ff. For Aramaic words known from writings, see the lexicon of Jean and Hoftijzer, *op. cit.*

[16] Thus, for example, in the title of the lexicon of Jean and Hoftijzer, *op. cit.*, which combines Canaanite and Aramaic words. Earlier, before Accadian was taken into account, Canaanite and Aramaic could be combined as "Northsemitic" in distinction from the "Southsemitic" Arabic dialects. This is seen in M. Lidzbarski's usage in his *Handbuch der nordsemitischen Epigraphik* (1898).

(4) *Arabic*

Arabic did not become a literary language in the ancient oriental period, since Arabic was first spoken by the Bedouin tribes of the Arabian peninsula. The forerunner of Arabic is the South Arabic of the inscriptions from the cultural areas at the southern end of the Arabian peninsula (see p. 188). The language of these inscriptions[17] is related to the Ethiopic dialects of Ethiopia. North Arabic, so-called in distinction from South Arabic, owes its expansion beyond the lands of Near Eastern culture solely to the movement of Islam. This classical Arabic, therefore, would be of no great importance for study of the ancient Orient, if it were not for the fact that the proto-Semitic phonology and morphology are retained in this language to a particularly great extent. It is for this reason that classical Arabic is fundamentally important for the understanding of, and the research into, ancient Semitic languages.[18]

Arabic in its modern dialects of different countries is the language spoken today in most of the Near East, not only by the Muslims, but also by the Eastern Christians who, in the process of time, have given up their own ancient languages in favour of Arabic.[19] A general Arabic spoken and written language has developed in the modern Arabic world in addition to the various dialects.[20]

29. *Non-Semitic Languages*

Decipherment of ancient oriental writing systems, particularly cuneiform, and disclosure of ever new written records has made it increasingly clear that especially on the fringes of the ancient Near East there was a variety of languages which have nothing to do with the Semitic family of languages. Therefore, the language atlas of the ancient Orient is extremely chequered.

[17] M. Hoefner, *Altsüdarabische Grammatik, Porta Linguarum Orientalium*, Vol. XXIV (1943).

[18] A. Socin, *Arabische Grammatik*, ed. C. Brockelmann (10th ed., 1929); G. W. Freytag, *Lexicon Arabico-Latinum*, Vols. I–IV (1830–37); also by Freytag, *ex opere majore excerptum* (1837); E. W. Lane, *Maddu-l-Kamoos, An Arabic-English Lexicon* (1863–93).

[19] On modern Palestinian Arabic, see L. Bauer, *Das palästinische Arabisch* (4th ed., 1926); L. Bauer, *Deutsch-arabisches Wörterbuch der Umgangssprache in Palästina und im Libanen* (2nd ed., 1957).

[20] H. Wehr, *Arabisches Wörterbuch für die Schriftsprache der Gegenwart* (Arabic-German), Vols. I–II (1952; 3rd ed., 1958), Supplement (1959).

(1) *Egyptian*

The Egyptian language was written in hieroglyphs. Both language and script remained limited to the Nile land, where they held a monopoly until Imperial Aramaic came into use (p. 227). Since the hieroglyphic system reproduces only consonants, an exact reproduction of the Egyptian language can no longer be given. Fortunately Coptic, the latest stage of the Egyptian language—the language of the Egyptian Christians—was written with an alphabet derived from Greek. Therefore, this late stage reproduces the language with its vowels. Looking back from this point of vantage, it is possible to formulate conclusions on the vocalization of the older Egyptian. Egyptian belongs among the "Hamitic" languages which have survived to our day in East and North Africa, a language group distantly related to the Semitic family of languages. Methodical philological study of Egyptian is linked primarily with the name of the late Berlin Egyptologist, A. Erman.[21]

(2) *Indo-European Languages*

Materials from various Indo-European languages have emerged in the north and east of the ancient Orient.

(a) *Hittite*. In 1906 H. Winckler, under commission of the society *Deutsche Orient-Gesellschaft*, uncovered a large archive of cuneiform texts during his excavations on a mound at the village of Boghazköy, east of Ankara in the interior of Asia Minor.[22] Among them were texts in Accadian, especially international treaties.[23] However, among them also were numerous texts in a language unknown until then, but written in the well-known old cuneiform. Hrozný[24] was successful in gaining understanding of this language. Research into this language has progressed from

[21] A. Erman, *Ägyptische Grammatik, Porta linguarum orientalium*, Vol. XV (4th ed., 1928); G. Roeder, *Ägyptische Grammatik, Clavis linguarum Semiticarum*, Vol. VI (2nd ed., 1926); Erman and Grapow, *Wörterbuch der ägyptischen Sprache*, Vols. I–V (1926–31); A. Gardiner, *Egyptian Grammar* (3rd rev. ed., 1957); also by Erman and Grapow, *Die Belegstellen*, Vols. I–V (1935–53), condensed in Erman and Grapow, *Ägyptisches Handwörterbuch* (1921); G. Steindorff, *Lehrbuch der koptischen Grammatik* (1951).

[22] These texts were published serially in *Keilschrifttexte aus Boghazköi* (abbreviated *KBo*) from 1916 to 1923, in *Keilschrifturkunden aus Boghazköi* (*KUB*) from 1922, and in *Die Boghazköi-Texte in Umschrift* (*BoTU*) again since 1922.

[23] E. F. Weidner, *Politische Dokumente aus Kleinasien, Die Staatsverträge in akkadischer Sprache aus dem Archiv von Boghazköi, Boghazköi Studien*, 819 Heft (1923).

[24] *Die Sprache der Hethiter, ihr Bau and Ihre Zugehörigkeit zum indogermanischen Sprachstamm* (1917).

then on through a number of detailed studies[25] based on the foundation he laid. The term "Hittite" is not found in the ancient texts, but was invented by modern students, resting on the historical connection between this language and the kingdom of *Ḫatti* in Asia Minor, with whose name again the Old Testament use of the term "Hittites" is related. "Hittite" represents the official language in this kingdom. According to its structure, "Hittite" belongs to the western group of Indo-European languages, that of the *centum*[26] languages, and has special connections with Italo-Celtic. It is completely isolated. A non-Indo-European substratum seems to make its appearance here.

(b) *Other dialects of Asia Minor and North Syria.* Among the cuneiform texts from Boghazköy there are fragments of another language, probably also Indo-European, which was probably spoken in southern Asia Minor. These texts themselves characterize it as "Luwian."[27]

The language of the "Hittite hieroglyphs" should probably also be referred to in this connection. They come from southeastern Asia Minor and North Syria (p. 210), and are later than the texts from Boghazköy. The conventional term Hittite is irrelevant and confusing when applied to them. They also are written in an Indo-European dialect.[28]

(c) *Indo-Iranian dialects.* In the first half of the second millennium B.C., certain technical terms, divine names, and personal names emerge which are of Indo-Iranian origin. They have been found in the texts of Boghazköy and elsewhere. However, there are no connected linguistic materials. Only very much later does this eastern group of Indo-European languages (*satem* languages) appear in the ancient Orient in actual linguistic materials, namely, in the Persian inscriptions from the Achaemenid kings of the

[25] See the general survey in J. Friedrich, *Hethitisch und "Kleinasiatische" Sprachen, Grundriss der indogermanischen Sprach- und Altertumskunde, Geschichte der indogermanischen Sprachwissenschaft*, Vol. II: *Die Erforschung der indogermanischen Sprachen*, Part V, No. 1 (1931); and J. Friedrich, *Kleinasiatische Sprachdenkmäler, Kleine Texte*, 163 (1932). See especially J. Friedrich, *Hethitisches Elementarbuch*, Vol. I: *Kurzefasste Grammatik* (1940), Vol. II: *Lesestücke in Transkription mit Erläuterungen und Wörterverzeichnissen* (1946), also available as *Indogermanische Bibliothek*, Vol. I: *Abt., Sammlung indogermanischer Lehr- und Handbücher, 1. Reihe: Grammatiken*, 23. Band. See also J. Friedrich, *Hethitisches Wörterbuch* (1952–54); Supplement (1957), also available as *Indogermanische Bibliothek 2. Reihe: Wörterbucher.*

[26] Concerning *centum* and *satem* languages referred to here, see *Encyclopaedia Britannica* under "Indo-European, Language Classification."

[27] Friedrich, *Hethitisch und "Kleinasiatische" Sprachen*, pp. 41–42.

[28] *Ibid.*, pp. 49 ff. [also Ignace J. Gelb, *Hittite Hieroglyphs* (1931); by the same author, *Hittite Hieroglyphic Monuments* (1939)].

second half of the sixth century B.C. on. The inscriptions of the Persian kings from Susa and various Iranian sites are frequently trilingual. In addition to the Babylonian and Elamite (see below) text there is also the Persian. For these Old Persian inscriptions a greatly simplified syllabic cuneiform system was developed from the old cuneiform script with a remarkably reduced number of signs.[29] Later on, the alphabetic writing system became the foundation for the writing of Persian (Middle Persian). This came about as a result of the dissemination of the Aramaic language everywhere in the ancient Orient.

(3) *Languages of Unknown Origin*

Other languages have been found, extensively preserved, primarily in cuneiform, whose linguistic connections are still vague. Concerning them, little more can be said than that they belong neither to the Semitic nor to the Indo-European family of languages, and also that most of them have no definitely demonstrable connections with each other.

(a) *Sumerian.* Extremely early texts from southern lower Mesopotamia have been preserved, written in an "agglutinizing" language having various dialects, called "Sumerian," after the early name of the southern part of lower Mesopotamia. Cuneiform was devised first of all for the Sumerian language, and in the sacral and learned literature Sumerian was still used as a sort of sacred language in Mesopotamia long after Accadian became the colloquial language. Sumerian-speaking inhabitants were the carriers of ancient culture in this area, which had enduring after-effects.[30]

(b) *Elamite.* A language was native east of the lowest course of the Tigris and the northern tip of the Persian Gulf, which is called Elamite after the name of this land, Elam, which also occurs repeatedly in the Old Testament. Apart from several texts in an old Elamite syllabic script, it was written with the old cuneiform script and appears in connected texts in the trilingual cuneiform inscriptions of the Achaemenids (see above) from a relatively late period, and in various cuneiform linguistic materials, too, from older periods, including inscriptions, letters, and legal records.[31]

[29] The texts are in F. H. Weissbach, *Die Keilinschriften der Achämeniden*, *Vorderasiatische Bibliothek*, Vol. III (1911).

[30] A. Poebel, *Grundzüge der sumerischen Grammatik* (1923); A Deimel, *Sumerische Grammatik* (2nd ed., 1939).

[31] E. F. König, *Corpus Inscriptionum Elamiticarum* (1926 ff.); F. Bork, *Elam*, B: *Sprache, in Reallexikon der Vorgeschichte*, III (1925), 70–83.

(c) *Hurrian.* A language was rather widely scattered in the second millennium B.C. in northern Mesopotamia and beyond, as well as in northern Syria, which first became well known through an Amarna letter.[32] It was written in the familiar ancient cuneiform script, but not in the Accadian language. Texts in ancient cuneiform and in the same language have been found in Boghazköy. Recently texts in this language have come to light at Rās Shamrah in the alphabetic Rās Shamrah script. In texts from Boghazöy this language is called Hurrian. Research in it is still in process.[33]

(d) *Kassite.* A few details are known concerning the language of people who are called *Kashshu* in Accadian. Their home was in the mountains northeast of the lower Tigris. Temporarily they played a role in the history of Mesopotamia (p. 251). What is known of their language comes from a list of words transmitted in old cuneiform and from Accadian explanations of the names of kings.[34]

(e) *Urartean. Urarṭu,* Ararat in the Old Testament, is the ancient name of the modern highlands of Armenia. A variety of inscriptions coming from this land have been found, in the vernacular, written in old cuneiform script, dating from the first half of the first millennium B.C.[35] There seems to be linguistic relationship between Urartean and Hurrian.[36]

(f) *Protohattic.* A number of materials have been found among the texts from Boghazköy from a language which apparently belonged to an older level of the linguistic history of Asia Minor than Hittite (pp. 230–31) and apparently was native among the original population of the interior of Asia Minor. In the texts from Boghazköy it is called "Hattic."[37] The term "Hattic" is actually the same as "Hittite." According to the texts from Boghazköy this term actually belongs to the pre-Indo-European original population. However, since the term "Hittite" had already been conventionally accepted as the name of the chief Indo-European language of Asia Minor, "Hattic," actually only a formal variant, was chosen for the older language, or to emphasize the difference more clearly, "Protohattic."

[32] Knudtzon, *op. cit.*, No. 24.

[33] E. A. Speiser, "Introduction to Hurrian," *AASOR*, Vol. XX (1941).

[34] On the language, see Friedrich Delitzsch, *Die Sprache der Kossäer* (1884) [also Kemal Balkan, "Kassitenstudien, Part I: Die Sprache der Kassiten," *AOS*, Vol. XXXVII].

[35] C. F. Lehmann-Haupt, *Corpus Inscriptionum Chaldicarum* (1928 ff.). Lehmann-Haupt prefers the term *Chaldisch* or *Haldian* instead of the clearer and probably better-founded term Urartean. On the language, see J. Friedrich, " Einführung ins Urartäische," *MVÄG*, Vol. XXXVII, No. 3 (1933).

[36] J. Friedrich, "Kleine Beiträge zur churritischen Grammatik," *MVÄG*, XLII, No. 2 (1939), 59 ff.

[37] J. Friedrich, *Hethitisch und "Kleinasiatische" Sprachen*, pp. 42 ff.

CHAPTER V

PEOPLES

30. *Races in the Ancient Near East*

THERE is very little evidence in the ancient Near East on which to base racial distinctions. From earliest times, countless population movements have taken place in the Near East. It is impossible to derive ancient racial distinctions from modern ones. Furthermore, by the beginning of recorded history there were no longer neatly separated types of people in the ancient Near East. Rather, the various segments of this great area were mutually interrelated. Language distinctions must not be confused with racial ones nor does insight into the array of languages and language families in the ancient Near East satisfactorily explain the existence and spread of particular races. We might expect that anthropological deductions could be based on measurement of skeletons well identified in a fixed setting of time and place, thus shedding light on the vexed question of races. Yet we have only scattered skeletal remains, rather than the connected series of data for the necessary research. Stereotyped portrayals of men in ancient art provide only a limited substitute, for we cannot measure them. In view of these factors, we cautiously state that we are dealing with the following races, which are still represented in the present population of the area.[1]

Exclusive of Negroes, who play a role only on the border of the Near East as neighbours of Egypt, we meet with members of the long-headed, dark-coloured, short-statured, Mediterranean race and specifically with its African sub-type in North Africa, including Egypt, and with its oriental sub-type in southwest Asia. The latter sub-type is usually simply called the oriental race. We also meet a dark-coloured race with round head and with flattened occipital region, which race von Luschan calls Armenoid and which could be designated simply as Southwest Asian. It seems to have appeared first of all in the northern parts of the ancient Near

[1] F. von Luschan, *Völker, Rassen, Sprachen* (1922), pp. 55 ff. [C. U. A. Kappers, *Introduction to the Anthropology of the Near East in Ancient and Recent Times* (1934)].

East, in North Syria and in the northern and northeastern front ranges. Finally, the Aryan race also had a part in the population of the ancient Near East. The fact of the occurrence of Indo-European languages in the ancient Near East can be used with caution in this connection, though the part played by the Aryan race was probably not very great, nor can this part be determined in detail.

31. *Historical Peoples*

The concept of a people is inseparable from the context of history. Peoples are united groups of human beings who appear collectively in historical activity and thereby become constituent elements in the historical process, even though they do not always belong to the same ethnic group. We have knowledge of the historical peoples of the ancient Near East in so far as we know their history from written remains. Since a people usually, though not necessarily, has a common language, a survey of the languages of the ancient Near East (cf. §§ 28–29) can also contribute to a knowledge of its peoples. Finally, a people frequently has a certain characteristic way of coining personal names, so that its members can often be identified by their names, as by some distinctive garb, or custom, or the like.

(1) *The Peoples of the Nile Country*

The Egyptians have lived in the fertile Nile land ever since prehistoric times. Their appearance is preserved for us in countless statues, reliefs, and paintings from Egypt.[2] They were always presented in profile in reliefs and in paintings. They appear as slender figures with similar features and straight noses, types such as one still meets frequently in Egypt. The men are usually beardless, but kings at least and outstanding personages wear an artificial chin beard, apparently substituting for an earlier beard fashion.

The Libyan tribes, who were related to the Egyptians and inhabited the western desert and oases bordering on Egypt, frequently menaced the civilized land along the Nile and at times also more or less peacefully established themselves on Egyptian territory. They are usually presented with their two-feathered

[2] See the many illustrations in G. Steindorff, *Die Kunst der Ägypter* (1928), in *AOB*, Nos. 1, 26 ff., and in *ANEP*, Nos. 12 ff.

headdress, with bearded cheeks and pointed chin beards, with a lock of hair on the side, as well as with their characteristic body tattooing.[3]

Egypt proper extended up the Nile to the first cataract at modern Aswan; south of it on both sides of the river lay the land of the Nubian tribes, centring in the region of the S-shaped bend of the Nile above its second cataract. The ancient Egyptians called Nubia *Kš* (Cush in the Old Testament); and the Greeks and Romans named the Nubians Ethiopians. Yet ancient Nubia must not be confused with the land or people of modern Abyssinia, situated much farther to the south. The Nubians were ethnically related to the Egyptians. Their land was important to the Egyptians as a thoroughfare to the treasures of the Sudan still farther up the Nile, where Negroes lived. The Egyptians frequently portrayed Negroes.[4] The Egyptians also portrayed the people living along the Nile south of Egypt in a generalized and certainly incorrect manner, with typical Negro faces, beardless, and with large earrings, especially in the stereotyped lists of conquests in foreign lands, described above on p. 205, by incorrectly classifying the Nubians as Negroes. The Nubians were at most very slightly related to the Negro tribes bordering them on the south.[5]

(2) *The Peoples of Mesopotamia*

Ever since primeval times Mesopotamia has been much more affected by all sorts of ethnic movements than the Nileland, which is geographically more isolated. Therefore, the population map of Mesopotamia is considerably more chequered than that of the Nileland. The great plain of the lower Tigris and Euphrates, the lower part of Mesopotamia, Iraq in the narrower sense (p. 186), is divided in old native texts into the territories of Sumer and Accad. Sumer indicates the southern, Accad the northern portion. The language established in Sumer in the oldest period is known as Sumerian, and those who spoke it are called Sumerians (p. 232). There is a striking type of male heads found in the most ancient portrayals from this southern portion of Iraq, some bearded, some beardless with very prominent, pointed noses and receding foreheads, in short, with a birdlike appearance which must be identi-

[3] *AOB*, No. 1; Steindorff, *op. cit.*, p. 277; *ANEP*, Nos. 1–2, 7–8.

[4] *ANEP*, Nos. 4, 6, 8; *AOB*, No. 1; Steindorff, *op. cit.*, p. 288; Breasted and Ranke, *Geschichte Ägyptens* (Grosse illustrierte Phaidon-Ausgabe, 1936), Plates CCLXVII, CCCIX.

[5] See Mariette, *Karnak* (1875), Plate XXVIId.

fied as Sumerian.[6] The Sumerians were probably not indigenous in lower Mesopotamia, though their origin is still undetermined. They were the bearers of a high and influential culture. The concept of order played an important role in their life and thought. Like the Egyptians in the Nile country, they attended to the regular irrigation of the alluvial land in which they lived and developed an evidently prosperous life in their cities. In their temples they worshipped cosmic and astral gods and fertility goddesses with a highly developed cult.

North of them in the land of Accad lived the people whom we call Accadians. Their name was derived from the city of Agade, which was of prime importance in the area for a time. It can be demonstrated that the Accadians lived in this region at least from the beginning of the third millennium B.C. on. Their Semitic language is also known as Accadian (p. 224).[7] They appeared on the scene of history about the middle of the third millennium. Very early they adopted essential elements of the Sumerian culture. In the course of time the Accadians achieved control. Their language became the common tongue of all of lower Mesopotamia. It is questionable that the Accadians of the third millennium were actually one single unit. Observations of the Accadian language and of the Accadian personal names of this period permit the assumption that in the course of the third millennium an essential immigration of new Semitic elements took place in Mesopotamia,[8] which is still not clearly understood.

Much more clearly understood was a new great immigration movement, which is recognizable with the beginning of the second millennium B.C., from very numerous newly-found personal names, which are clearly not Accadian, but rather West Semitic in the sense indicated on p. 228. Bearers of such names occur in lower Mesopotamia, partially, too, farther up the Tigris, but especially along the Middle Euphrates and its two tributaries, the Belīkh and the Khābūr. Particularly the Mari texts (see p. 209) have shown that this new population played a significant role in the middle Euphrates region. The Mari letters, which stem from these immigrants, also have preserved certain traces of the ancestral language of these people in various non-Accadian words, word forms, and

[6] See E. Meyer, *Sumerier und Semiten in Babylonien*, *APAW philhist. Kl.* (1906), No. 3. See also the illustrations in *AOB*, Nos. 2, 4, 44, 528, 530–31 and in *ANEP*, Nos. 18–24.

[7] A portrait of an Accadian with a slightly bridged nose, a moustache, and a cheek and chin beard is in *AOB*, No. 3.

[8] W. von Soden, *Wiener Zeitschrift für die Kunde des Morgenlandes*, LVI (1960), 185 ff.

linguistic usages found in their otherwise Old Babylonian dialect. The new arrivals had come from the Syro-Arabian desert, had established themselves in the fertile area, and had adopted the script and language of the fertile area at least for official written communication. Still, they remained in touch with their relatives at the edge of the fertile area and in the desert.[9] There is no known self-designating name of this historically important immigrant population, nor can we expect one. Various names have been proposed for them. Th. Bauer in his *Die Ostkanaanäer* (1926), because he considered their personal names especially Canaanite, proposed the name, "East Canaanite." Generally, especially in scholarly works in the English language, these people are called Amorites, based on the Accadian name *Amurru* for the "Land in the West" (see p. 53). Probably the one name is as unsatisfactory as the other. Peculiarities of their personal names just as the few recognizable traces of their ancestral language indicate that we could recognize in them the first heralds of that population element who later appear on the Euphrates and in Syro-Palestine as Arameans, that we could therefore call them Proto-Arameans.[10] Portrayals of Mari people have been found on wall paintings in the royal palace on Tell Ḥarīri (see p. 251). Some are shown beardless, some heavily bearded, often with their heads covered with a high cap, with long hooked noses and rather large mouths.[11]

In the first half of the second millennium, in the course of historical events those peoples were formed which from then on played their historical role under the names of Assyrians and Babylonians. With the first dynasty of Babylon (see p. 250) the city of Babylon became a political centre in lower Mesopotamia. This brought the Babylonians into history, and from then on they can properly be described as a people. The various older elements of lower Mesopotamia were merged into this people: the Sumerians of the cities in the south, the Accadians living north of them, and the recently arrived "Proto-Arameans," whose peculiarities in name construction and language were lost in time. In language the Accadians prevailed, for Babylonian in its various stages (old, middle, late Babylonian) is a further development of Accadian. In the area of

[9] J.-R. Kupper, *Les nomades en Mésopotamie au temps des rois de Mari* (Bibliothèque de la Faculté de Philosophie et Lettres de l'Université de Liège, 1957), Fasc. CXLII.

[10] Noth, *Die Ursprünge des alten Israel im Lichte neuer Quellen*, *Arbeitsgemeinschaft für Forschung des Landes Nordrhein-Westfalen*, *Geisteswissenschaften*, Heft 94 (1961).

[11] A. Parrot, *Mission archéologique de Mari: Le palais, Peintures murales* (1958), Frontispiece, Figs. 18–19, 70–71, Plates V–VI, VIII ff., XIX, XXIII, and others.

religion and cult, namely in world view, the old Sumerian traditions continued in force.[12] Once again in the late period of the history of the Babylonian tribes from the Syro-Arabian desert achieved importance in Babylon, becoming one more ingredient in the Babylonian population. These were the Chaldeans.[13] They were probably part of the Aramean family of peoples. In the first half of the first millennium B.C. they settled west of the mouth of the Euphrates and the northern end of the Persian Gulf. In the seventh century B.C. they played a historically important role in Babylonia (p. 225).

The ethnic relationships farther up the Tigris River were different from those in lower Mesopotamia. This difference obtained in the limited area on both banks of this river from near modern Mosul on downstream, and on the east side of the Tigris to the foothills of the Iranian front range, an area from which proceeded the most powerful and lasting influences on the ancient Near Eastern history; for here the Assyrians lived. They spoke a dialect of Accadian and were an off-shoot from the Accadians, who established themselves along the middle Tigris. From the Accadians living farther south, the Assyrians absorbed essential elements of the old Sumerian culture. However, as a folk unit they were of different composition from the Babylonians in the south, among whom the Sumerians were absorbed. Once again, among the Assyrians the Accadian element was probably permeated by a pre-Assyrian population of the middle Tigris region and by a variety of ethnic elements moving in from time to time.[14] These admixtures were obviously elements from the near-by Iranian front range, as well as Hurrians whom we recognize by their distinct language (p. 233). Peoples of both sorts kept merging with the Assyrians, likely already in the third but certainly during the second millennium. This particular composition is definitely related with the fact that, in distinction from the Babylonians, the Assyrians were extremely aggressive and warlike. As conquerors they were the most powerful people known in the ancient Orient before the Persians. The Assyrian type with great aquiline noses, rich well-groomed hair, long, likewise well-groomed full beards, and

[12] *ANEP*, No. 454 and *AOB*, No. 142 show Babylonians with carefully groomed hair and beards.

[13] The Old Testament in Hebrew uses the original name for them, *Kaśdim*. Since there is a phonetic law in Accadian according to which sibilants immediately preceding dentals change into "l," *Kaldu* and related names exhibit the secondary accadianized form of the name.

[14] Von Soden, *Der Aufstieg des Assyrerreichs als geschichtliches Problem*. *Der Alte Orient*, Vol. XXXVII (1937), Secs. 1–2.

muscular bodies is well known to us from countless portrayals, particularly from the first half of the first millennium.[15]

Attention must be given to the Hurrians, in addition to their presence among the Assyrian ethnic complex, to which reference has been made. For as shown by the spread of their language and their personal names, the Hurrians also played a role as an independent people in upper Mesopotamia and even beyond in North Syria and eastern Asia Minor.[16] These Hurrians are still frequently confused with the "Subarians" known from the records of Mesopotamia, and have even been called "Subarians."[17] Actually the cuneiform tradition from most ancient times mentions a land Subartu in the north of Babylonia. Particularly in omen texts *Subartu* means nothing more than "the northern regions" where the inhabitants are called "Subarians," even then an ancient ethnic name. However, according to the personal names preserved these "Subarians" were scarcely Hurrians. It is more likely that they belonged to a group of mountain peoples on the border of Mesopotamia and must therefore be distinguished from the Hurrians who historically were much more important.[18] There is indeed no evidence that they called themselves Hurrians. However, their widely-used language is named "Hurrian" in the texts from Boghazköy. Further, the Egyptians of the second half of the second millennium knew a people in Southwest Asia which they named *Ḫr*,[19] from which the Egyptians then derived a completely generalized and vague name for the neighbouring Asiatic region.[20] Finally, the Hebrew Old Testament knows the Hurrians in the form *Ḥori* (Old Testament, Horites) as an element in the pre-Israelite population of Palestine, without, of course, having a knowledge of the actual homeland and expansion of the *Ḥori* in Southwest Asia, since at best only scattered segments of them reached Palestine. The Hurrians, who were the bearers of the Hurrian language (p. 233), seem to enter the picture primarily as bearers of the particular culture described on pp. 197–98. The Hurrians did not

[15] *AOB*, No. 5, pp. 116 ff., pp. 130 ff.; *ANEP*, Nos. 366 ff.

[16] A. Götze, *Hethiter, Churriter, und Assyrer* (Oslo: Instituttet for sammenlignende Kulturforskning, 1936), Series A, XVII.

[17] See especially A. Ungnad in his book, *Subartu* (1936), in which much material is presented concerning both the language and the repository of names of persons and deities characteristic of the Hurrians.

[18] See especially I. G. Gelb, *Hurrians and Subarians, Studies in Ancient Oriental Civilization*, No. XXII (1944).

[19] Examples in M. Burchardt, *Die altkanaanäischen Fremdworte und Eigennamen im Ägyptischen*, II, p. 38, No. 732.

[20] W. M. Müller, *Asien und Europa nach alt-ägyptischen Denkmälern* (1893), pp. 148 ff.

belong to the oldest circle of ancient Near Eastern peoples. They were immigrants, appearing in their central area in northern Mesopotamia about the beginning of the second millennium B.C. Perhaps they penetrated into upper Mesopotamia and the regions beyond from the eastern and northeastern mountains bordering the Near East.

It is a significant fact that we find a ruling class of Indo-Iranian origin among the Hurrians. This class does not seem to have been connected everywhere with the appearance of the Hurrians. Thus, the American excavations have uncovered an old city on the mound of Jorghan Tepe southwest of modern Kirkuk in the region east of the Tigris, southeast of the original land of the Assyrians, which in the second millennium bore the name Nuzi.[21] In this period it was inhabited by Hurrians, as shown by the numerous cuneiform tablets found written in the Accadian language, but without evidence of Indo-Iranian nobles. We also are not certain whether the Indo-Iranian nobility among the Mesopotamian Hurrians immigrated with them, or whether only later they assumed control over them. The only thing certain is that these Indo-Iranians were present there during the second millennium. This we know, first from clearly Indo-Iranian personal names which appear in the circle of these Hurrians, then also from special Indo-Iranian gods, who were worshipped there. These gods appear as witnesses to an oath in a covenant found among the texts from Boghazköy.[22] Finally, we know this from a series of technical expressions which emerge from them, such as the designation of the military *élite* by the term *maryannu*, which is attested in Accadian and Egyptian texts.[23]

A work found among the texts from Boghazköy concerning the care of race horses is important above all for this latter point. This text, which contains a number of Indo-Iranian technical terms, was compiled by a man named Kikkuli, originating from the region of the Mesopotamian Hurrians.[24] This is direct evidence that the Hurrians, that is, their Indo-Iranian element, trained the horse for riding and driving. On the other hand, the horse as an animal seems to have been known already in the third millennium. Still, these same Hurrians were involved in the spread of skilled horsemanship, of increasing importance in the entire Near East,

[21] Cf. V. Christian, *Altertumskunde des Zweistromlandes*, I, 27–28.

[22] Cf. E. F. Weidner, *Politische Dokumente aus Kleinasien* (1923), No. 1, Rs. Z. 55–56.

[23] Cf. Burchardt, *op. cit.*, p. 25, No. 470.

[24] Cf. A. Kammenhuber, *Philologische Untersuchungen zu den "Pferdetexten" aus dem Keilschriftarchiv von Boghazköy*, *Münchner Studien zur Sprachwissenschaft*, II (1952), 47–120.

particularly for the conduct of war, from the middle of the second millennium on.[25]

It is also necessary to think of certain peoples whose homeland was at the edge of Mesopotamia, but who periodically more or less decisively influenced the history of Mesopotamia. The Elamites[26] had been very close neighbours of Babylonia ever since primeval times. They lived on the northern and northeastern side of the Persian Gulf extending into the Iranian front range. They had a distinct language (p. 232) with its own names for persons and deities. They often gave the Babylonians trouble and held their own as neighbours to the Babylonians. Thus, Elamite still appears among the three languages of the Persian Achaemenid kings.

As neighbours of Babylonia other peoples from the Iranian border mountains and from the interior of Iran north of Elam began to play a decisive role in the ancient Near Eastern history. In the second millennium B.C. there were above all the Cassites with a language of which only vestiges remain (see p. 233) and with characteristic personal names, who were important in the history of Babylonia.

On the Armenian highlands north of Mesopotamia we have the Urarteans, whose language is known (p. 233). They appeared historically in the first half of the first millennium B.C.[27] Of their prehistory nothing is known.

In the second half of the seventh century B.C. it was the Medes and, in the second half of the sixth century B.C., the Persians who operated from Iran to play a decisive role in the history and destiny of the ancient Near East.

(3) *Hittites*

The Hittites lived in Asia Minor during the second millennium B.C. Linguistic evidence (pp. 230–33) shows that we are dealing again with a ruling class speaking an Indo-European language, ruling over a non-Indo-European earlier population. To this antecedent population the name Hittite really belongs; for what fragments of their language are transmitted are designated as

[25] M. Mayrhofer, "Zu den arischen Sprachresten in Vorderasien," *Die Sprache*, V (1959), 77–95, is a careful study of Indo-Iranian names and language elements in the ancient Near East and at the same time a caution against rash theses and conclusions.

[26] *ANEP*, Nos. 25, 30, 168, 204.

[27] The Armenians, users of an Indo-European language, later occupied the same area. The name Armenia, indeed, is not derived from those we call the Armenians, but from the area itself, where it is already attested in the third millennium. Cf. H. A. Rigg, *JAOS*, LVII (1937), 416 ff.

"(Proto-)Hattic." Therefore, they gave the name to the whole population. The ruling class on the contrary made their own language prevail, at least for all official matters and to a large degree also for the religion. After the disappearance of the Hittites from History about 1200 B.C. other Indo-European elements, such as the Phrygians, established themselves in inner Asia Minor. Yet at the same time Asia Minor withdrew into the background in the great history of the ancient Near East for the time being and became significant again only in the Persian and Hellenistic periods. In the fringe mountains of Asia Minor through these historic changes the ancient indigenous peoples maintained themselves without achieving historic significance.

(4) *Peoples of Syria and Palestine*

The ethnic conditions in Syria and Palestine are complex. Here one decidedly cannot speak of definite peoples until the end of the Bronze Age. It is no accident that to this day no ethnic name has been handed down which was native in this area. Such a name is found neither in an indigenous record nor in the accounts of their powerful neighbours. All of the more comprehensive names for Syria-Palestine or parts of it, as well as the names for its inhabitants, have proved to be references to governments or names of smaller groups. These names later were broadened in their use and thereby simultaneously lost definiteness and clarity. None of these terms is a genuine Syro-Palestinian ethnic name.[28] Because this area contained many geographic contrasts and communication difficulties, it strongly fostered the separate life of even the smallest groups. Therefore, the individual groups did not combine into greater units in the course of events. In fact, such larger units were not even taken seriously. Only language built a definite bond of unity in the historical period. The different dialects of Canaanite (pp. 225–26) were spoken in great parts of this area. Yet, even that was true only to a limited extent. It does not furnish strong support for the idea of an original ethnic unity of the Syro-Palestinian population. In northern Syria Hurrian is also attested as a spoken language by the discoveries of Rās Shamrah. The study of the old place names of the land[29] also shows that in the whole area, but especially in northern and middle Syria, non-Canaanite and indeed

[28] Cf. A. Alt, "Völker und Staaten Syriens im frühen Altertum," *Der Alte Orient*, Vol. XXXIV (1936), Sec. 4 [reprinted in *KS*, III, 20–48].
[29] Cf. Alt, *op. cit.*, pp. 9 ff., 25 ff.

non-Semitic place names were very common. The early founders of these settlements, therefore, to a great extent were not Canaanites but, more likely, related to some of the indigenous population of Asia Minor. (The appearance of "Hittite" hieroglyphic inscriptions in northern Syria and in middle Syria in Hamath as late as the first millennium B.C. indicates the presence of individual elements which spoke a distinctly Indo-European language.) The use of Canaanite subsequently extended beyond its original territory, gradually being adopted by a number of folk elements whose origin was not Canaanite. This came about perhaps because it was the language of communication used in the great commercial centres on the Phoenician coast and partly, too, because of the practical Canaanite alphabetic form of writing. Thus, the use of the Canaanite language does not supply strong evidence to explain conditions in the Syro-Palestinian population back in very early times. This population must have been rather mixed, especially since Syria-Palestine was on a great trade route (p. 189). Beyond that, the geographic features isolated the ethnically related groups. The population of the coastal cities, particularly in central Syria, seem to be the earliest observable historical entity. Indeed, precisely as residents of port cities they were not likely homogeneous. But communication was easily possible between them by means of the coastal ship traffic. They also had a mutual interest in the sea as well as in the other inhabitants of the eastern Mediterranean area. Thus their mutual interests might have made a definite bond between them, even though we do not hear much from them of common actions.

This division of Syro-Palestine into small units was altered from about 1200 B.C. by the appearance in the interior of Syro-Palestine of the Aramaic-speaking tribes from the eastern desert. They developed individual ethnic units after they had settled down. The behaviour of these units then deeply affected the history of Syria and Palestine until they fell victims to foreign conquerors from the eighth century B.C. Such peoples in the south, on the east side of the great Syrian rift were the Edomites, Moabites, and Ammonites, and west of the rift, the Israelites; of these at least the Israelites and Moabites demonstrably adopted the Canaanite dialect. These peoples occupied extensive land areas both east and west of the rift which had not been settled previously; the previous inhabitants of various ethnic origins gradually were assimilated into ethnic units.

While the population of the coastal cities remained essentially unchanged, tribes known as Aramean in the more limited sense established themselves in the interior of central and northern Syria, primarily in sparsely settled places. They not only maintained their traditional Aramaic language but apparently also remained aware of their ethnic unity. For even where they divided themselves into several state structures (pp. 80–81), the names of these states maintained the common designation Aram. The Old Testament mentions Aram-Naḥaraim, Aram-Zobah, Aram-Beth-Rehob, and Aram-Damascus. In the first centuries of the first millennium B.C. we also notice a number of attempts to unite all the Arameans politically. On the stela found at Aleppo (cf. p. 219) Ben-Hadad, probably identical with the Ben-Hadad referred to in I Kings 15 : 18 ff., who resided in Damascus, called himself "king of Aram" as the Old Testament does. Some of the older inhabitants maintained their identity either next to or among the Arameans, such as those who continued to use "Hittite hieroglyphic writing," though others were merged with the Arameans.

The successful appearance, on the Palestinian coast, of the Philistines and the "Sea Peoples" related to them, about 1200 B.C., did not serve to form an ethnic group. These elements came from the direction of the Mediterranean Sea from some unknown place and probably by different but no longer demonstrable routes. They established themselves as a presumably very small ruling class over the "Canaanite" population in the Palestinian coastal plain as well as in the Plain of Jezreel and apparently soon merged with this prior population. The "language of Ashdod" which was spoken in Nehemiah's times in old Philistia (Neh. 13 : 24) was, however, probably not the one time Philistine language, but rather a Canaanite dialect.

CHAPTER VI

STATES

32. *Great Powers*

EACH of the peoples of the ancient Near East developed an individual governmental structure, even as all historical peoples of the world have done. These governmental structures provide the setting for the troubled history of the ancient Near East.[1]

(1) *The Egyptian State*[2]

The late-Egyptian priest, Manetho, in his work *Aigyptiaka Hypomnemata* written at the beginning of the third century B.C. and preserved in fragments by Josephus and others, compiled what he knew of the millennia-long Egyptian history. Following his system, Egyptian history is divided into royal reigns and arranged further into thirty dynasties down to the time of the conquest of Alexander the Great. On the whole these thirty dynasties can be related to the ancient authentic tradition. Moreover, on the basis of certain chief periods and high points of the Egyptian history, one speaks of the Old Kingdom (abbreviated OK), Middle Kingdom (MK), and New Kingdom (NK); also of the Late Period and the Ptolemaic Period.

[1] On ancient Near Eastern history as a whole, see E. Meyer, *Geschichte des Altertums*, Vol. I, Part 1 (5th ed.; H. E. Stier, 1925); I, 2 (4th ed., 1921); II, 1 (2nd ed., 1928); II, 2 (2nd ed., 1931); III (2nd ed., 1937). See also *The Cambridge Ancient History*, a comprehensive portrayal of history written by many authors, Vols. I–III (1923 ff.). For a limited time span, see F. Bilabel, *Geschichte Vorderasiens und Ägyptens; vom 16.–11. Jhr. v. Chr., Bibliothek der klassischen Altertumswissenschaft*, Vol. III (1927). Finally for brief summaries, see A. Scharff and A. Moortgat, *Ägypten und Vorderasien im Altertum* (1950), which presents world history in single narratives, and, not including Egypt, R. Kittel, *Die Völker des vorderen Orients*, *Propyläen-Weltgeschichte*, I (1931), 409–568; L. Delaporte, *Geschichte der Babylonier, Assyrer, Perser und Phöniker*, *Geschichte der führenden Völker*, III (1933), 175–333.

[2] Concerning the history of Egypt, see James H. Breasted, *History of Egypt* (rev. ed.; New York: Scribner, 1942); John A. Wilson, *The Culture of Ancient Egypt* (1951); Georg Steindorff and Keith C. Seele, *When Egypt Ruled the East* (rev. ed., 1951); W. S. Smith, *The Art and Architecture of Ancient Egypt* (1958); H. Junker, *Geschichte der Ägypter*, *Geschichte der führenden Völker*, III (1933), 1–174. The historical Egyptian sources are presented in English translation by James H. Breasted, *Ancient Records of Egypt*, Vols. I–V (1906–7), o.p.

According to Manetho, at the beginning of the third millennium, probably in the twenty-ninth century, a certain Menes began the order of kings of the first dynasty. He united the rule over all Egypt in his hands. What preceded this can only be surmised on the basis of reconstructions.[3] Certainly there was an earlier kingdom of Lower Egypt in the Delta and of Upper Egypt along the Nile Valley, for the division into Lower and Upper Egypt continued on in a variety of formal matters throughout the history of Egypt. For example, Pharaoh[4] wore a double crown, the crown of Lower and Upper Egypt. The first great period of Egyptian history was one of strictly centralized and precisely ordered government by officials of the Old Kingdom. It developed in the middle of the third millennium, namely from the third to the sixth dynasty. Its high point in the time of the fourth and fifth dynasties. It was the time of the famous pyramid builders: Djoser in the third dynasty, Khufu and Khafre in the fourth dynasty. After a period of decline called the First Intermediate Period, the Middle Kingdom, the time of the twelfth dynasty[5] followed (about 1991–1788 B.C.) It was the classical period of Egyptian literature and art. The form of the state to be sure had been changed rather essentially; powerful and self-confident provincial rulers had developed out of the administrative officials of the Old Kingdom in the time of decline. They had transformed their position into a hereditary dominion and from then on in the Middle Kingdom they stood next to the crown as great fief holders. The pharaohs themselves of the eleventh and probably also the twelfth dynasty had been originally Upper Egyptian feudal lords before they assumed control over a newly-united Egypt. With the intrusion of a foreign rule over Egypt, known as the Second Intermediate Period (pp. 255–257), the twelfth dynasty was terminated together with the Middle Kingdom. The Desecration Texts date from the eighteenth century B.C., the end of the twelfth dynasty, when the control of Pharaohs was no longer very secure. They are hieratic texts written on potsherds or clay figurines. They enumerate all the possible actual or potential enemies or dangers facing the Egyptian

[3] Cf. K. Sethe, *Urgeschichte und älteste Religion der Ägypter*, *Abhandlungen für die Kunde des Morgenlandes*, Vol. XVIII, No. 4 (1930).

[4] The royal title, "Pharaoh," in this normal form borrowed from the Old Testament or rather from its Greek translation, means "Great House" (Egyptian pr-ˤ) or the government, including the ruler.

[5] From the eleventh dynasty on, it became customary that the same names were repeated frequently for rulers of the same dynasty. In the eleventh dynasty the pharaohs were named mostly Intef or Mentuhotep; in the twelfth dynasty, Amenemhet and Sesostris.

kingdom. The potsherds or figurines bearing these texts were then shattered to produce a magical effect. Among others the texts bear hostile places and powers from Egypt's neighbouring lands, namely from Nubia and Syro-Palestine. Thereby these records provide certain valuable information on the conditions then pertaining in these neighbouring lands and are especially revealing for Middle Bronze Syro-Palestine.[6]

The time of the New Kingdom was the period of the Egyptian Empire, that means of the extension of the Egyptian control not only over Nubia in the south, but also over a great part of Syria, at times over all Syria. Again it was Upper Egyptian feudal lords who about 1570 B.C. removed foreign control in Egypt and in consequence occupied Syria also, to which the foreign conquerors had withdrawn. We next observe the eighteenth dynasty, the dynasty of the different Amenophises and Thutmoses.[7] After its decline and fall the nineteenth dynasty rose in which the pharaonic names Seti and Rameses appeared, with which the restoration of the Egyptian Empire was linked. The pharaohs of the eighteenth dynasty were able to extend Egyptian control as far as North Syria. The pharaohs of the nineteenth dynasty were able to restore this control at least in the southern half of Syria and Palestine. Particularly Rameses II, with his extremely long reign (1290–1223 B.C.), represented the might of the nineteenth dynasty; he was at the same time in all probability the so-called pharaoh of the Oppression (Exod. 1 : 8 ff.). Through great military successes the eighteenth and nineteenth dynasties had established their rule, and the New Kingdom was above all a mighty military state. In addition, the outstanding temples of the land became rich during this period, and their hierarchies won power through gifts of the pharaohs. Military leaders and priests in the time following oppressed and weakened the kingdom and loosened the structure of the state. The twentieth dynasty in the twelfth century, whose pharaohs again were almost all called Rameses, was already a time of beginning decline.

With the beginning of the twenty-first dynasty, for the first time a high priest of the priesthood of Amon-Re (p. 289) ascended the

[6] The texts are published in K. Sethe, *Die Ächtung feindlicher Fürsten, Völker and Dinge auf altägyptischen Tongefässscherben des Mittleren Reiches*, *Abh. d. Preuss. Ak. d. Wiss.* (1926), *Phil.-hist. Kl.*, No. 5; and in G. Posener, *Princes et pays d'Asie et de Nubie*, *Textes hiératiques sur des figurines d'envoûtement du moyen empire* (1940).

[7] The most illustrious pharaoh of this dynasty was Thutmose III (1490–1436 B.C.), who undertook a famous campaign against Palestine and several military expeditions through all of Syria, and who listed his conquests in these and other lands as described on p. 205. His record is generally called the Thutmose list.

throne of pharaoh. Under the following pharaohs these priests were the chief power in the state. With the twenty-second dynasty (935–745 B.C.) a number of Libyan military leaders came to the throne, among whom the name Shishak frequently appeared.[8] With the twenty-fifth dynasty in 714 B.C. Nubian rulers took over the kingship in Egypt.[9] A temporary restoration of ancient Egypt was finally attempted by the provincial rulers of the Delta city of Sais, who ruled Egypt as the twenty-sixth dynasty (663–525 B.C.) and in whose number belong Necho, referred to in II Kings 23 : 29 ff., Amasis, encountered in the Greek tradition, as well as several named Psammetichus. With the conquest of Egypt by the Persian king, Cambyses, in 525 B.C. the old Egyptian history ended, for the Macedonian dynasty of the Ptolemies, successors of Alexander the Great (323–30 B.C.), again controlled a divided Egypt, but was still a foreign rule.

(2) *The States of Mesopotamia*

Mesopotamia had a much more complicated development of ethnic groups than did Egypt (pp. 236 ff.). As a result, Mesopotamian history was much more characterized by troubled coexistence and succession of distinctly different states. Expansion toward North Syria was a common tendency for all the more significant states of Mesopotamia, for Syria was rich in timber and mineral resources. The same expansion continued toward the Mediterranean Sea and then on toward southeastern Asia Minor, as well as toward the rest of Syria.[10]

(a) *The states of southern Mesopotamia.* At the beginning, during the fourth and on into the third millennium B.C., the Sumerian city-states existed next to one another in the far south (see p. 264), ruled by priest-kings. This cluster of states had a sacral centre in

[8] Shishak, the founder of the dynasty, undertook the campaign in Palestine mentioned in I Kings 14 : 25–28. He is called *Shushaq* as written, or *Shishaq* as read, in the Hebrew Old Testament.

[9] II Kings 19 : 9 gives to the third and last ruler of this dynasty, Tirhakah, the anticipatory title "King of Cush (Ethiopia)"; for in the year 701 B.C. dealt with there, Tirhakah was not yet king but only general of the Ethiopian pharaoh of Egypt. [Recent findings even suggest that in 701 B.C. Tirhakah might have been only ten years old.]

[10] *The Keilinschriftliche Bibliothek* (abbreviated *KB*), Vols. I–III (1889–92) presents in transliteration and German translation the long-known historic cuneiform sources for the history of states of Mesopotamia. In addition to the works referred to on p. 246 on specific problems, note the pertinent and often very detailed historical articles in *Reallexikon der Assyriologie* (abbreviated *RLA*), Vols. I (1932), II (1938), III ff. (1957 ff.), and in popularized form, B. Meissner, *Könige Babyloniens und Assyriens* (1926).

the temple of the god, Enlil, or Ellil, in the city of Nippur, now Niffer, about 150 km. [93 miles] southeast of Baghdad. Temporarily one or another of these states achieved the mastery over neighbouring states or over larger areas or even over the whole, and also undertook campaigns into the neighbouring lands. Then about the twenty-fourth century, the Accadian-speaking Semitic part temporarily achieved the mastery from their centre in the north of this area. At that time a certain Sargon established the kingdom of Accad with the city of Accad (p. 224) as centre, and from there ruled essentially all of Mesopotamia. A number of rulers then succeeded him over a period of more than one hundred and fifty years dynasty of Accad. Finally the Sumerian city-states regained control. Particularly in the rulers of the third dynasty of Ur, in the twenty-first and the first half of the twentieth century B.C., they again produced significant representatives of Sumerian might. Subsequently the kings who laid claim to the rule of all southern Mesopotamia called themselves "Kings of Sumer and Accad."[11]

In the following period it is characteristic of the states in southern Mesopotamia that they did not develop from the indigenous inhabitants of the land, but from newly-appearing, immigrant or invading elements. In the nineteenth century B.C. the "West Semitic" elements, who were discussed above, established their rule over lower Mesopotamia at a number of centres, but especially in a governmental unit with the city of Babylon as centre. Here Babylon appeared historically for the first time, but soon became the centre of the entire area, producing the all-inclusive and enduring name Babylonia. The Old Babylonian Kingdom which resulted at times extended its power far out over the neighbouring lands. The sixth king of this "first dynasty of Babylon" was Hammurabi (1728–1686 B.C.).[12] He established the pre-eminence of the Old Babylonian Kingdom by his victories over King Rim-Sin of Larsa, an important Old Sumerian control centre and over King Zimri-Lim of Mari. He is well known because of his Law Code which he had drawn up for his well-ordered kingdom,[13] and who together

[11] The cuneiform sources for this oldest period are found in F. Thureau-Dangin, *Die sumerischen und akkadischen Königsinschriften*, *Vorderasiatische Bibliothek*, Vol. I, No. 1 (1907).

[12] In a recent sketch of chronology of the ancient Near East, Hammurabi is dated 1704–1662 B.C.; E. F. Weidner, *AfO*, XV (1945–51), 98 ff. Others prefer an earlier date for the Hammurabi dynasty (see p. 270). [For the basis of the dates used in the text see M. B. Rowton, "*Ṭuppu and the Date of Hammurabi*," *JNES*, X (1951), 184–204.]

[13] *Codex Hammurabi* translated into German in *AOT*, pp. 380–410; [in English, *ANET*, pp. 163–80].

with his officials earnestly cared for the affairs of his kingdom as his correspondence indicates.[14] The Old Babylonian Kingdom was destroyed in 1550 B.C. by an expedition of the Hittites against the city of Babylon. The Cassites had previously controlled certain parts of the land from their eastern mountain homeland. Now after the Hittite raid the Cassites assumed full control. They ruled Babylonia from then until the twelfth century B.C. After an extended period full of fluctuations, which was characterized by trouble caused by the Assyrians as well as by outright Assyrian rule, another powerful state arose in Babylonia. This was the Chaldeans, once again an immigrant element which took over the rule (p. 214). In the time of the decline of the Assyrian might, Nabopolassar the Chaldean in 625 B.C. founded the Neo-Babylonian kingdom which soon inherited the eclipsed Assyrian hegemony in large parts of southwestern Asia.[15] Nebuchadnezzar, the son of Nabopolassar, was the most important ruler of this short-lived kingdom. In 539 B.C. Babylon was conquered by the Persian Cyrus. With that began the Persian rule which was finally broken by Alexander the Great. After his death the Macedonian house of Seleucus took control over the Fertile Crescent.

(b) *The Middle Euphrates.* Temporarily a political role was played by the region of the Middle Euphrates from near where the river leaves the northern mountains to where the river valley narrows below Abu'l-Kemāl near the modern border of Syria and Iraq. This state of affairs is first recognizable soon after the beginning of the second millennium. The city of Mari was situated in the Middle Euphrates region. It was a royal capital in the second half of the eighteenth century B.C. and the centre of a rather important state, because of its position on the Euphrates waterway between lower Mesopotamia and Syria. Between 1933 and 1939 the royal palace of Mari was excavated.[16] In the palace was found the royal archive with over 20,000 cuneiform tablets (see p. 209). These inscriptions are very important because they throw a bright light upon the historical situation of the time. In some respects they have a direct bearing on the Old Testament (see

[14] Cf. A. Ungnad, *Babylonische Briefe aus der Zeit der Hammurabi-Dynastie*, *Vorderasiatische Bibl.*, Vol. VI (1914) [in English, L. W. King, *The Letters and Inscriptions of Hammurabi*, Vols. I–III (1898–1900)].

[15] The historic texts are presented in S. Langdon, *Die neubabylonischen Königsinschriften*, *Vorderasiatische Bibl.*, Vol. IV (1912) and in D. J. Wiseman, *Chronicles of Chaldaean Kings* [626–556 B.C.] in the British Museum (1956), for those parts of the Babylonian chronicle pertaining to the Neo-Babylonian period.

[16] The final excavation report is in A. Parrot, *Mission archéologique de Mari*, Vol. II; *Le palais* or *BAH*, Vols. LXVIII (1958), LXIX (1958), LXX (1959).

pp. 71, 293). The state of Mari had a great, even if temporary significance. These considerations have secured an important place in ancient Near Eastern history for Mari. Mari was ruled after about 1750 B.C. by Yagitlim and Yaḫdunlim. After a time of Assyrian rule under King Shamshi-Adad, who had his son, Yasmah-Adad sit in Mari as regent, local rule was assumed by Zimrilim, a contemporary of King Hammurabi of Babylon, who finally conquered him. Thus the state of Mari became part of the Babylonian Empire in 1695 B.C. Later, in the same region on the Middle Euphrates, the kingdom of Ḫana existed temporarily. It was, however, of less importance. Toward the end of the second and during the first half of the first millennium B.C. the Middle Euphrates was one of the chief regions of Aramean settlement. Even though no great Aramean state was established there, the Arameans of the Middle Euphrates temporarily did play a significant role in the struggle of the great powers for control.

(c) *Assyria.*[17] Assyria first appeared historically after the time of the Kingdom of Accad (p. 250) to whose sphere of influence it had belonged. In the nineteenth and eighteenth centuries B.C. we have an old Assyrian kingdom, insignificant as yet, which with varying success maintained itself against the nearly contemporary Old Babylonian Kingdom. Among its kings a Sargon I (Assyr.: *Sarru-kin*) appears about 1750 B.C. who named himself after Sargon of Accad (p. 250). His adoption of this name shows that he laid claim to lower Mesopotamia. Soon thereafter, "West Semites" seized control in Assyria, too (see p. 238). Under the "West Semitic" king Shamshi-Adad I and his son, Ishme-Dagan, temporarily the state of Mari was under Assyrian control. Assyrian clay tablets, known as the Cappadocian Tablets, which were found on the mound of Kültepe in eastern Asia Minor near Kayseri, have

[17] D. D. Luckenbill, *Ancient Records of Assyria and Babylonia*, Vol. II: *Historical Records of Assyria* (1927), gives the Assyrian historical cuneiform sources in English. They are also presented in transliteration and German translation from the older period down to the thirteenth century B.C. by Ebeling, Meissner, and Weidner, *Die Inschriften der altassyrischen Könige, Altorientalische Bibliothek*, Vol. I (1926) and E. Weidner, "Die Inschriften Tukulti-Ninurtas I. und seiner Nachfolger," *AfO*, Beiheft 12 (1959), the continuation of the incomplete *Altorientalische Bibliothek*. For the later period, collections of inscriptions of individual rulers are available in transliteration and translation; Amiaud-Scheil, *Les inscriptions de Salmanasar II* [now referred to as Shalmaneser III] *roi d'Assyrie (860–824)* (1890); P. Rost, *Die Keilinschrifttexte Tiglat-Pilesers III*, Bd. I–II (1893); H. Winckler, *Die Keilinschrifttexte Sargons*, Bd. I–II (1889); M. Streck, *Assurbanipal und die letzten assyrischen Könige bis zum Untergange Niniveh's*, Bd. I–III, *Vorderasiatische Bibl.*, VII (1916); Th. Bauer, *Das Inschriftenwerk Assurbanipals*, I–II, *Assyriologische Bibliothek*, new series I–II (1933).

shown that about 1800 B.C. the Assyrians occupied trade colonies[18] there, and that her political influence might have been felt that far from Mesopotamia. Because of this distant influence the control of the state of Mari must have been important to the Assyrians. After that, however, it was again the Assyrians themselves who took in their own hands the development of their power. After a long period of insignificance, during which other powers in Mesopotamia played the first role, the Middle Assyrian Kingdom arose in the fourteenth and thirteenth centuries. Then after a time of decline, this kingdom was reconstituted about 1100 B.C. Among the kings of this state some of the royal names appear which are better known from the later New Assyrian period, such as Ashur-uballit (I), Adad-nirari (I), Shalmaneser (I), Tiglath-pileser (I).

Assyria rose to the high point of its power at the time of the New Assyrian Kingdom. In that period the Assyrians succeeded in subjecting all of Mesopotamia, including Babylonia, and the border regions. They also extended their rule over a part of Asia Minor, over all Syria, and for a while even over Egypt. Through their practice of deportations the Assyrians tried to uproot the conquered indigenous peoples and deliberately mix them with one another. They devised a well-ordered system of provinces for their constantly increasing kingdom, whose governors functioned one after the other in an established sequence as eponym of the year within the framework of the individual royal reigns.[19] The rise of the Neo-Assyrian Kingdom had already begun in the ninth century B.C. under the kings Ashurnasirpal II (884–859) and Shalmaneser III (850–824) who energetically advanced as far as Middle Syria without being able to establish lasting control there. Then the succession of the great Assyrian conquerors began with Tiglath-pileser III (745–727).[20] They conquered Syria and Palestine, as well as other lands, and undertook frequent campaigns there. They include Shalmaneser V (727–722), Sargon II (722–705), Sennacherib (705–681), and Esarhaddon (681–669) who undertook several campaigns against Egypt and occupied the Delta and the old royal city of Memphis (pp. 263–64). Thereby the final goal of

[18] Cf. B. Landsberger, "Assyrische Handelskolonien in Kleinasien aus dem dritten Jahrtausend," *Der Alte Orient*, Vol. XXIV, No. 4 (1925). The title of this article rests on a chronology since revised.

[19] Cf. E. Forrer, *Die Provinzeinteilung des assyrischen Reiches* (1921); A. Ungnad, "Eponymen," *RLA*, II (1938), 412–57.

[20] As king of Babylonia Tiglath-pileser bore the throne name *Pūlu* which appears in II Kings 15 : 19, while elsewhere in the Old Testament the name Tiglath-pileser is also used. The customary form of most Neo-Assyrian royal names is borrowed from the Old Testament or rather its Greek translation.

Assyrian expansion, the overthrow of Egypt, the last remaining ancient oriental power of that time, was brought very close. Esarhaddon's son and successor, Ashurbanipal (669–631), could indeed still garrison the Upper Egyptian royal city of Thebes (p. 264), but under him the Egyptian adventure soon came to an end, and the decline of the Assyrian might began. This came to a swift conclusion under his successors. In 612 the Assyrian capital city of Nineveh fell to the attack of the combined Medes and Neo-Babylonians. Even a vestigial Assyrian state in northwestern Mesopotamia came to its end after a few years. In Mesopotamia and in Syro-Palestine the Neo-Babylonian "empire" (p. 251) then succeeded the Assyrian kingdom.

(3) *The Hittite State*

From the middle of the second millennium until the thirteenth century B.C., Asia Minor was ruled by a government consisting of "Hittite" overlords controlling an established population. The Hittites have left a number of historical records.[21] There are detailed Hittite royal annals.[22] The treaties of the Hittite Kingdom with other powers customarily had historical introductions.[23]

After a period of coexistent Hittite city-states in Asia Minor, the Hittite Kingdom was established in the first half of the second millennium by King Labarnas, who firmly bound the coexistent little states together into a unit. Under his successors, Hattusilis I and Mursilis I, the expansions toward North Syria took place, which were significant and very natural for the Hittite Kingdom. Through a sudden campaign Mursilis I, moreover, brought the Old Babylonian Kingdom to an end about the middle of the sixteenth century (p. 251). Toward the end of the fifteenth century the real growth of the power of the Hittite Kingdom began. The following royal names occur frequently: Tudhaliyas (Tidal, Gen. 14 : 1, 9), Hattusilis, Arnuwandas. The most significant rulers, under whom the expansion of the Hittite might in Syria and Mesopotamia succeeded, were Suppiluliumas (until about 1350 B.C.), Mursilis II

21 Cf. J. Friedrich, "Aus dem hethitischen Schrifttum, Part I: Historische Texte usw.," *Der Alte Orient*, Vol. XXIV (1925), Sec. 3.

22 Note especially A. Götze, "Die Annalen des Muršiliš," *MVÄG*, Vol. XXXVIII (1933).

23 Cf. J. Friedrich, "Staatsverträge des Hatti-Reiches in hethitischer Sprache," *MVÄG*, Vol. XXXI (1926), Sec. 1; XXXIV (1929), Sec. 1; also E. F. Weidner, "Politische Dokumente aus Kleinasien" ["The State Treaties in the Accadian Language from the Archive of Boghazköy"], *Boghaz-köi-Studien*, Vols. VIII–IX (1923).

(about 1353–1325), Muwatallis (about 1315–1285), Hattusilis III (about 1280–1260).[24]

The invasion of "Sea Peoples" who came from elsewhere in the Mediterranean world[25] brought the Hittite Kingdom to a sudden end about 1200 B.C.

(4) *Hyksos Control*

The period between the Middle Kingdom and the New Kingdom in Egypt was a period of foreign rule exercised by a ruling class which brought the Delta and a part of Upper Egypt under their control. Rulers arose among them who were regarded as pharaohs in Egypt. These rulers were called "Hyksos" by Manetho (p. 246), according to an excerpt in Josephus, *Contra Apionem*, I, 14, vv. 73–90. Manetho erroneously and vaguely explains this name as "Shepherd Kings," although it is actually derived from Egyptian, *ḥqꜣ.w ḫsꜣ.wt*, meaning "Rulers of Foreign Lands." It seems that these rulers held this title and that in Egypt they combined it with their pharaonic titulary in the Egyptian manner. Somehow, between 1700 B.C. and 1580 B.C., the Hyksos rulers controlled not only Egypt but also parts of Syro-Palestine. That is indicated by the location of their capital, Avaris, at the very edge of Egypt in the northeastern Delta, now Ṣān el-Ḥagar. It is also shown by the fact that after their expulsion from Egypt by the first pharaoh of the eighteenth dynasty (see p. 248), they withdrew to Palestine and Syria, where they were harassed by the pharaohs of the New Kingdom. In time the pharaohs pressed their campaigns on into North Syria and to the Euphrates. The advance of the pharaohs to North Syria was probably simply the attempt to replace Hyksos influence as far as possible. Unfortunately we have only very meagre information concerning the Hyksos influence, since this is the first instance in the history of the ancient Orient of partial joining of several cultural areas of the ancient Orient under one control. The records are scanty because the Hyksos rulers left hardly any monuments of their own. Those we have reflect only their character as Egyptian pharaohs.[26] There is no definite answer as to how the Hyksos achieved their control in Egypt, whether by a

[24] The exact dates for the reigns of the Hittite kings are still very uncertain and debated. [For a king list and statement on Hittite chronology, see O. R. Gurney, *The Hittites*, pp. 216–17.]

[25] Cf. the statement of Rameses III in Breasted, *Ancient Records of Egypt*, Vol. IV, Sec. 64.

[26] K. Galling, "Hyksosherrschaft und Hyksoskultur," *ZDPV*, LXII (1939), 89–115.

great military attack on the fertile land of the Nile or rather by the process of gradual infiltration of southwest Asian elements into the Nile Delta, where they in time were able to achieve control over Lower Egypt and then temporarily over Upper Egypt, too.[27] The ethnic origin and composition of the "Hyksos" remains problematical. The known names of Hyksos kings do not present us with conclusive evidence. Probably they should not be taken as an ethnic unit. Rather, Semitic-speaking elements from southwestern Asia seem to be joined with other elements, presumably especially Hurrians (see p. 239). Nor can the extent of their control in Syro-Palestine be clearly defined. The assumption that they had a very large kingdom embracing all of Syro-Palestine in addition to Egypt has against it the consideration that the contemporary southwestern Asian sources do not show any evidence of any such tremendous phenomenon. On the other hand, the assumption has much in its favour that the great *terre pisée* walled enclosures, contemporary with the Hyksos, described on p. 150, from the second phase of the Middle Bronze Age, can be traced back to the Hyksos, since the Hyksos seem to have introduced the military use of horse-drawn chariots. However, these walled enclosures have been found not only in Lower Egypt and Palestine, but also in middle and northern Syria, in Sefīnet Nūḥ, 22 km. [14 miles] southwest of Ḥomṣ, at el-Meshrefeh, the site of ancient Qaṭna, 18 km. [11 miles] northeast of Ḥomṣ, and at Carchemish on the Euphrates, about 100 km. [62 miles] northeast of Aleppo.[28] Were the "Hyksos" as we know them from Egypt, a warrior caste, perhaps of mixed ethnic background, which established power centres in Egypt and Palestine, as well as in middle and northern Syria, without giving rise to a great unified kingdom? After the expulsion of the Hyksos from Egypt and the Egyptian conquest of Syro-Palestine it seems a remnant of either the Hyksos kingdom or of the various Hyksos power centres maintained itself as a state beyond the Euphrates in upper Mesopotamia. This state continued from the beginning of the fifteenth to the middle of the fourteenth century. We know that the pharaohs in attacking the Hyksos did not press on earnestly across the Euphrates. This kingdom called Mitanni then remained as a neighbour of the Egyptians. It is well known from the Amarna letters, where King Tushratta of Mitanni appears, sending several messages to Pharaoh, as well as from the texts of Boghazköy. The

[27] Preference for the latter is seen in A. Alt, "Die Herkunft der Hyksos in neuer Sicht," *Berichte üb. d. Verh. der Sächs. Ak. d. Wiss. zu Leipzig, Phil.-hist. Kl.*, Vol. CI, No. 6 (1954) [reprinted in *KS*, III (1959), 72–98].

[28] Details are given in the article by Y. Yadin, *op. cit.*

population of Mitanni was predominantly Hurrian. A letter of Tushratta is written in the Hurrian language. (See also p. 233.) However, the Mitannian royal names show that the ruling class was Indo-Iranian. Based on this, it could be imagined that the Hyksos ruling class was made up of similar folk elements, although we have no direct evidences for this assumption. This would, however, explain the striking and yet inexplicable fact that, after the Hyksos period, we find an upper class in Syria and Palestine in which especially Hurrian as well as Indo-Iranian names are not uncommon.[29]

The historical significance of the Hyksos dominance cannot be minimized in spite of its relatively short duration. Certainly the Hyksos were not identical with the Israelites in Egypt, as Josephus, *op. cit.*, contends and as has been supposed from time to time in somewhat modified form until recently. However, it seems that Hyksos control joined the various regions of the ancient Near East with one another and brought them into an historical relationship which was never again entirely lost. Moreover, it was possibly the Hyksos who extended the training and use of horses for military technique over the entire ancient Near East as far as Egypt. Thus they would have inaugurated this new type of warfare which at the same time had significant consequences in the social structure of the people in that they were followed by the appearance of a privileged military class of chariot warriors. At any rate we are confronted by all of these phenomena in the ancient Near East immediately after the Hyksos period. We find Syria and Palestine strewn with minute governmental units whose centre in each case was headquarters for charioteers.[30] These were the Canaanites with their "iron chariots" which were found in the land before the Israelites, according to the Old Testament (Josh. 17 : 16; Judg. 1 : 19; 4 : 3). Accordingly they might have been the remnants of Hyksos chariotry.

33. *Small States*

Even the great powers of the ancient Near East grew from small states and, depending on historical factors, at times declined again

[29] Note the personal names appearing in the Amarna letters as in A. Gustavs, "Die Personennamen in den Tontafeln von Tell Ta'annek," *ZDPV*, L (1927), 1–18; LI (1928), 169–218; and in Noth, "Die syrisch-palästinische Bevölkerung des zweiten Jahrtausends v. Chr. im Lichte neuer Quellen," *ZDPV*, LXV (1942), 9–67; and by the same authors, "Die Herrenschicht von Ugarit im 15./14. Jrh. v. Chr.," *loc. cit.*, pp. 144–64.

[30] A. Alt, "Die Landnahme der Israeliten in Palästina," *Leipziger Dekanats-Programm* (1925), pp. 6 ff. [reprinted in *KS*, I, 94 ff.; and above, pp. 65–66].

to the level of small states. A number of small states on the periphery of the ancient Near East were from time to time historically important to their immediate neighbours; for example, Nubia, south of Egypt, or Elam, east of southern Mesopotamia, or the state of Urartu, north of Assyria. Because of their central location (p. 189), the small states of Syro-Palestine became important in the history of the great powers of the ancient Near East from the twelfth century B.C. until they were incorporated by the Assyrians into their empire, thenceforward to remain subject to successive empires.

The Edomites, Moabites, and Ammonites living in the south on the eastern side of the great Syrian rift, each had a kingdom, probably from the time they took their territory, at any rate well before the Israelites made the transition from their old, original formation of the sacral federation of tribes to the development of fixed forms of government. (See Gen. 36 : 31–39; Num. 20 : 14; 22 : 4 ff.; Judg. 11 : 12–14; 28; I Sam. 12 : 12.) Yet the kingdoms of Edom, Moab, and Ammon did not produce significant historical developments.

Israel had the Philistines of the southern coastal plain as their neighbours on the other side. Probably as long as they were situated there, beginning about 1200 B.C. they had their five principalities (p. 78), which seem to have been linked with each other by means of a sort of federation, in which one of the five princes at a time presided.[31] After their attempt to subject all of Cisjordan had been finally crushed by David, the Philistines hardly played a historically active role even in their own very limited region.

The kingdom of Saul probably did not last long. Following it a rather large kingdom arose under David on the territory of the tribes of Israel. To his double kingdom over the two states, Israel and Judah, whose coexistence depended on the peculiar way in which David became king, David was able to annex a number of foreign provinces and dependent border states (p. 94), so that he was actually lord of all Palestine in the largest sense, as well as over a part of southern Syria. However, this great state fell apart under Solomon, gradually lost its outposts, and after the death of Solomon the two parts, Israel and Judah, separated from one another and continued on as little independent kingdoms.

We find more significant forms of government which lasted

[31] According to the Old Testament the Philistine princes held the special title *seren*. Its connection with Greek *tyrannos* has been suggested.

longer in central Syria. Here especially the kingdom of Damascus, which was newly founded at the time of Solomon (I Kings 11 : 23, 24), succeeded in joining older Aramean states (cf. II Sam. 10 : 8) under one central kingdom (cf. I Kings 20 : 1) and in forming the Aramean kingdom of Damascus, which ruled over the settled region east of Antilebanon as well as the Beqāʿ between Lebanon and Antilebanon. From that point this kingdom probably temporarily extended its influence farther to the north.[32] This Aramean kingdom in the ninth century B.C. not only gave the neighbouring state of Israel a difficult time, but especially in this period had a place of authority among the Syro-Palestinian states, until the power of this kingdom was broken by a campaign of the Assyrian king, Adadnirari III, to whom Damascus capitulated. This kingdom continued to exist, but was finally eliminated in 732 B.C. by Tiglath-pileser III.

The Aramean kingdom of Damascus was apparently removed from its hegemony by the kingdom of Hamath about 800 B.C. Hamath, known today as Ḥamah, on the middle Orontes, was probably an unassuming city-state at first, whose kingdom, however, succeeded in persuading a number of other independent states, especially those with Aramaic populations, to join with it. The ZKR inscription (p. 219) shows that a king of Hamath was also master of the North Syrian land of Laʿash about the middle of the eighth century B.C. Similarly, the kings of Hamath must have subjected other regions in central and northern Syria in one way or another. Here, as in the case of Aramean control of Damascus, we are dealing with one of those Syrian forms of government which externally look like a unit, but internally consist of individual, relatively independent parts, some of which were still ruled by their own dynasties, though all were subordinate to a central kingdom.[33] These federated states, which were similar in structure to the kingdom of David, naturally were relatively unstable structures, whose existence was dependent on the real power of the central kingdom and on the total contemporary political situation. The kingdom of Hamath, which arrived at its zenith after 800 B.C., following the downfall of Damascus, was already eliminated by the Assyrians in two stages in 738 and 720 B.C. (See II Kings 18 : 34; 19 : 13; Isa. 10 : 9; Jer. 49 : 23; Amos 6 : 2.)

There was a similar federated state of modest proportions in

[32] Cf. the inscription of the "Aramean king" Barhadad (Benhadad) found at el-Breij at Aleppo and referred to on p. 219.

[33] A. Alt, "Die syrische Staatenwelt vor dem Einbruch der Assyrer," *ZDMG*, New Series, XIII (1934), 233–58 [reprinted in *KS*, III, 214–32].

North Syria about the middle of the eighth century B.C. It was known by the name of its capital, Arpad, now Tell Rifʿat (II Kings 18 : 34; 19 : 13; Isa. 10 : 9; Jer. 49 : 23) and also by the name Bīt-Agusi, most likely for its dynasty. The inscriptions from Sefīreh (p. 220) shed some light on its structure and its internal situation.[34] The state of Arpad was liquidated by Tiglath-pileser III in 740 B.C.

There were still more small states in northern Syria, southeastern Asia Minor, and western Mesopotamia which sprang up there after the destruction of the Hittite kingdom and which certainly had an Aramean population or upper class. They were all transformed into Assyrian provinces in the ninth and the eighth centuries. Here they are tabulated in so far as they appear in the Old Testament or are noteworthy for other reasons.[35]

The state of Queh was situated on the Cilician plain (p. 188). Solomon obtained horses for his force of chariots from it. *Miq-Quweh* ["from Quweh"] should be read twice instead of *miqweh* in I Kings 10 : 28. The name of this land appears in the ZKR inscription, a: 6, as *Qwh*. In the mountainous country at the eastern edge of the Cilician plain across the right bank of the Ceyhan River, the ancient Pyramus was the capital of the apparently ephemeral domain of King Azitawadda, the "king of the Danunians," on the hill now called Karatepe. This domain seems to belong in the ninth century B.C. It has become important as a result of the Hittite hieroglyphic and Phoenician inscriptions, which it has left behind on Karatepe (see p. 210).

The state of Ya'di with its capital of Sam'al, now known as Zinjirli, was located on the other side of Mount Amanus in the extreme northern part of the Syrian rift.[36] The old Aramaic inscriptions referred to on pp. 219 and 227 came from this region.

The ancient city of Carchemish, together with its territory, was located farther to the east on the right bank of the Euphrates at an important river crossing. Its site is inside Turkey north of the Syrian border village of Jerāblus. It is the chief site for finds of "Hittite hieroglyphic" inscriptions.[37] Isa. 10 : 9 alludes to the overthrow of this city-state by the Assyrians.

[34] Noth, *ZDPV*, LXXVII (1961), 128–38.

[35] Cf. E. Forrer, *Die Provinzeinteilung des assyrischen Reiches* (1921), pp. 56 ff., 70 ff., 103 ff.

[36] On the German excavations there, consult the publication *Ausgrabungen in Sendschirli*, I–V, *Mitteilungen aus den orientalischen Sammlungen der Kgl. Museen zu Berlin*, XI–XV (1893–1943).

[37] On the excavations there, see D. G. Hogarth, *Carchemish I* (1914); L. Woolley, *Carchemish II* (1921); L. Woolley and R. D. Barnett, *Carchemish* III (1952).

A little farther down the Euphrates on its left bank the city of *Til-Barsip*, known today as Tell Aḥmar,[38] was the centre of a state which is called *Bit-Adini* in the Assyrian sources. In Ezek. 27 : 23 it is called *'Edhen*. In II Kings 19 : 12 its inhabitants are called *benē 'Edhen*. It remains doubtful whether *Beth 'Edhen* in Amos 1 : 5 is related to this.

Gozan, Haran, and Rezeph are also mentioned in II Kings 19 : 12 as states subjected to the Assyrians. They were previously centres of independent minor states in northern Mesopotamia which were enveloped rather early in the growing Assyrian empire. Moving from west to east we have first Haran (note also Gen. 11 : 31; 12 : 5; 27 : 43), on the upper reaches of the River Belīkh (p. 187), called *Ḫarrānu* in Assyrian and known as *Carrhae* in Roman days. Then comes Gozan (note also II Kings 17 : 6; 18 : 11), the city on ancient Tell Ḥalaf (p. 200), called *Guzana* in Assyrian, at the time when a minor Aramean king had his capital there. Finally there is Rezeph, called *Raṣappa* in Assyrian, which Forrer, *op. cit.*, p. 15, would locate in the present-day Beled Sinjār.

The Old Testament also mentions a Calno or Calneh in Isa. 10 : 9; Amos 6 : 2; and in Zech. 9 : 1 refers to a Hadrach. These were the chief cities of two North Syrian states, which were included in the federation of the kingdom of Hamath in the last stage of their history before they were absorbed in the Assyrian Empire. They lay south of the North Syrian minor state of *Ḫattina*, later called Unqi by the Assyrians, which was situated in the Plain of el-'Amq. Calno, *Kullâni* in Assyrian, was perhaps on the sea, along Jebel el-Anṣārīyeh; Hadrach, the *ḤZRK* of the ZKR inscription, *Ḫatarikka* in Assyrian, was apparently the chief city of the land of La'ash (p. 259), inland southwest of Aleppo. The city of *Alalaḫ* on Tell el-'Aṭshāneh was situated in the part of the Plain of el-'Amq referred to above. During the entire Bronze Age it served as a rather important control centre for the entire plain and its opening through the lower Orontes Valley to the Mediterranean Sea. *Alalaḫ*[39] was the capital of the land of *Mukiš*. In the course of the fifteenth century B.C. there was a certain king of Idrimi in *Alalaḫ* who left a statue with a long cuneiform inscription.[40] In addition,

[38] On the excavations there, consult Thureau-Dangin and Dunand, *Til-Barsip* (1936).

[39] On excavations there, see L. Woolley, *Alalakh* (1955), and the popular account, L. Woolley, *A Forgotten Kingdom* (1953), also translated into German.

[40] S. Smith, *The Statue of Idri-mi, Occasional Publications of the British Institute of Archaeology in Ankara*, No. 1 (1949); a reproduction of the statue is in *ANEP*, No. 452.

the *Alalaḫ* cuneiform inscriptions from the eighteenth and the fifteenth century B.C. were found on Tell el-ʿAṭshāneh. They were referred to on p. 210.

With the decline of the Seleucid kingdom many small states were again formed in southwestern Asia from the second to the first century B.C. The rise of the Hasmonean state in Palestine fits into this framework.

34. *Cities*

The Mediterranean coastal cities were political units, that is, independent city-states, during the entire course of ancient Near Eastern history. Even after they were loosely incorporated into the empires of the late first millennium B.C., they still maintained their independence to all intents and purposes. Their beginnings extend well back into the dawn of the historical period. The most important of them, figuring from south to north, were:

(1) The island city of Tyre, now called Ṣūr, which Alexander the Great had joined to the mainland by a causeway in order to conquer it in 332 B.C. This causeway is still in existence, though now covered by sand dunes.

(2) Sidon, now Ṣaida.

(3) A city probably called Beeroth, where Beirut now stands. As a result of continuous occupation, all three are without remains worthy of mention from the ancient oriental period (except for the necropolis of Sidon with its sarcophagi referred to on p. 173, part of which dates back to the pre-Hellenistic period).

(4) Byblos, originally called *Gubla*, Gebal in the Old Testament, now known as Jbeil. (On the excavation see p. 199.)

(5) Presumably an ancient Near Eastern city of uncertain name in the region of present-day Ṭarablus, the Tripoli of the Persian-Hellenistic-Roman period.

(6) The island city of Arvad, also mentioned in the Old Testament, now called Ruad.

(7) Ugarit, now called Rās Shamrah (on its excavations see p. 199), which remained in existence no later than the end of the Bronze Age.

These were rich commonwealths, usually headed by a king. Ugarit, the last-mentioned city, occupied a sizable territory in the Late Bronze Age. It played a significant role in the circle of the

Syro-Palestinian states and of neighbouring powers, especially the Hittite kingdom and Egypt. Abundant information on this is found in the texts of the royal archives. They are written partly in alphabetic Ugaritic and partly in ancient cuneiform in other languages. They were found during the excavation of the Ugaritic royal palace conducted after the Second World War. They are published in the series: *Le palais royal d'Ugarit*, abbreviated *PRU*.[41]

There were additional politically independent city-states in the prehistoric period and at the beginning of the historical period in Egypt, Mesopotamia, and Asia Minor. They were beginnings of political bodies. They were also found in Syria and Palestine in the Late Bronze Age, namely in the period between the end of the Hyksos power structure and the rise of larger forms of government at the beginning of the Iron Age. These were the headquarters of charioteers, to be found in great numbers all over the land. They likely owned their independent existence to the inner structure of Hyksos power (p. 256). Of course, as established cities they were usually older. Their beginnings extend back to the remote and unknown past. However, in the Late Bronze Age they once more played a politically independent role. Apart from Palestine (cf. pp. 76–77) the most important of them were in central Syria: Kadesh on the Orontes,[42] at Tell Nebi Mend, south of present-day Ḥomṣ, Qaṭna,[43] now called el-Meshrefeh, northeast of Ḥomṣ; in northern Syria, the great cities which were in time subjected to the late Hittite kingdom, Aleppo, known in ancient times particularly as *Ḫalab*, now known as Ḥaleb, as well as the city of Carchemish on the Euphrates (p. 260).

The greatest and most imposing ancient oriental cities were the capitals of the rulers of empires.

The Egyptian pharaohs of the Old Kingdom resided at Memphis, known still by the Greek version of its name. This city was situated a little south of present-day Cairo at the southern point of the Delta, therefore approximately at the border between Upper and Lower Egypt, the two halves of the kingdom united by the pharaohs. West of Memphis they erected their famous pyramids at

[41] *PRU*, Vol. II: Ch. Virolleaud, *Textes en cunéiformes alphabétiques des archives est, ouest et centrales* (1957); *PRU*, Vol. III: J. Nougayrol, *Textes accadiens et hourrites des archives est, ouest et centrales* (1955); *PRU*, Vol. IV: J. Nougayrol, *Textes accadiens des archives sud*, *Archives internationales* (1956).

[42] On a partial excavation, see M. Pézard, *Qadesh* [*Haut Commissariat de la République Française en Syrie et au Liban*, *Service des Antiquités*, *Bibliothèque archéologique et historique*, XV (1931)].

[43] On the excavations, consult the reports of Du Mesnil in *Syria*, Vol. VII (1926), as well as later editions.

the edge of the desert. Even the pharaohs of the twelfth dynasty in the Middle Kingdom, who came from Upper Egypt, removed the capital of their kingdom to ancient, favourably situated Memphis, after their predecessors of the eleventh dynasty had maintained their seat in Upper Egypt. There are very few remaining ruins from Memphis.[44]

By contrast the pharaohs of the New Kingdom, particularly during the eighteenth dynasty, made the city of Thebes in Upper Egypt their capital. This customarily used name also comes by way of the Greeks, as noted in the phrase, " hundred-gated Thebes." Of course the pharaohs of the eleventh dynasty, who came from near by, had already resided here. The great temple complexes are the chief remains of this capital. They are situated on the eastern side of the Nile at the modern village of Karnak, northeast of the city of Luxor and in Luxor itself, as well as on the opposite western side, where the mortuary temples are. On the western side in a desert valley the underground graves of the pharaohs, together with the graves of high-ranking officials and others,[45] still testify to that great past. The removal of the royal residence from Thebes to the site of Tell el-ʿAmārna proved to be a fleeting episode (p. 289).

Pharaohs to whom the relations with Palestine and Syria were important had their residence in the northeastern part of the Delta, where the military road to Palestine left Egypt. This was true of the Hyksos rulers with their capital of Avaris (p. 255) and then again particularly of Rameses II of the nineteenth dynasty, who had the city of Rameses built in the Delta as his residence (Exod. 1 : 11).[46] This was in the vicinity of the mound of Ṣān el-Ḥagar[47] and of the town of Qantīr, 20 km. [12 miles] farther south.

The Macedonian foundation of Alexandria in the northwestern Delta on the Mediterranean became the capital of the land under the Ptolemies.

In southern Mesopotamia primary interest centres in the ancient Sumerian cities. Of these, Ur and Erech are mentioned in the Old Testament. Ur (Gen. 11 : 28, 31; 15 : 7; Neh. 9 : 7) was made famous by the American and British excavations there.[48] Erech

[44] In addition to Baedeker, *Egypt and the Sudan*, pp. 147 ff., see A. Hermann, *Führer durch die Altertümer von Memphis und Sakkara* (1938).

[45] See Baedeker, *op. cit.*, pp. 259 ff.

[46] *Die Deltaresidenz der Ramessiden*, *Festschrift für Friedrich Zucker* (1954), pp. 3–13 [reprinted in *KS*, III, 176–85].

[47] On the excavations there, see P. Montet, *Les nouvelles fouilles de Tanis* (1933).

[48] C. L. Woolley, *Excavations at Ur* (1954), also available in German.

(see p. 200 concerning excavations there) occurs in Gen. 10 : 10. Erech was also historically important and was already a very large city in very early days.

The city of Accad (Gen. 10 : 10), the centre of the kingdom of Accad (p. 250), lasted a short time and was not very important. Furthermore, it has not yet been identified archeologically.

The city of Babylon became increasingly important. In Accadian it was *Bâb-ili*, taken to mean "Gate of God"; in the Old Testament this became Babel. It was made the centre of the land by the Old Babylonian rulers and remained so until Alexander the Great. The finds *in situ*[49] have not produced anything worth mentioning for the Old Babylonian period.[50] Generally speaking, they go back only to the Assyrian king, Esarhaddon, who, as overlord of Babylonia, had the city rebuilt, following its destruction by his father, Sennacherib, or even only to the Neo-Babylonian king, Nebuchadnezzar, who rebuilt his capital magnificently and lavishly. The Seleucids later established their own foundation at Seleucia, north of Babylon on the Tigris at Tell ʿOmar. Seleucia became the administrative headquarters of the land in place of Babylon. At the same time the Seleucid rulers resided in Antioch in North Syria on the lower Orontes, a city now known as Antakya. It seems that all traces of this city from the Seleucid period have disappeared.

Temporarily the city of Mari on the middle Euphrates played a role as a royal residence. (The city and the excavations there are referred to on pp. 209–10, 251–52.)

Initially the city of Ashur, now called Qalʿat Sherqāt, on the right bank of the Tigris, was the capital of Assyria. The kings of the Old and Middle Assyrian kingdom built their palaces there. Even when later kings built other residences for themselves, Ashur remained the ancient holy city of the kingdom with the temple of the national god, Ashur. The German excavations on Qalʿat Sherqāt have uncovered remains from the extended period of Assyrian history, all the way back to the beginning of the second millennium B.C., including palaces, temples, walls, and gates.[51]

49 For a survey of the German excavations, see R. Koldewey, *Das wieder erstehende Babylon* (4th ed., 1925). The literary records on the buildings of this city are collected in E. Unger, *Babylon, die Heilige Stadt* (1931). Note also the article by E. Unger on Babylon in *RLA*, I (1932), 330–69. See also the popular presentation of A. Parrot, "Babylon and the Old Testament," *Studies in Biblical Archeology*, Vol. VIII (1958).

50 Even the stela with the Code of Hammurabi (p. 250), which had been set up in Babylon, was found in the winter of 1901–2, not in Babylon, but in the Elamite capital, Susa. It had been taken there by the Elamites as booty.

51 For a survey, see W. Andrae, *Das wiedererstandene Assur* (1938) and the article by E. Unger, "*Aššur*" in *RLA*, I (1932), 170–95.

In the Neo-Assyrian period the kings resided a little farther up the Tigris. Kings of the ninth century B.C., especially Ashurnasirpal II (p. 253), established their capital at the city of Kalah (Gen. 10 : 11), in Accadian *Kalaḫ* or *Kalḫu*, on the left bank of the Tigris at the mouth of its tributary, the Upper *Zāb*. Later kings also built there. The ruin site is known as Tell Nimrūd. It bears the name of Nimrod, found in Gen. 10 : 8. It has been studied repeatedly since the middle of the nineteenth century.[52] Productive English excavations are still being undertaken there.[53]

King Sargon II built himself a new capital at the end of the eighth century B.C. at modern Khorsabad, northeast of Mōṣul a short distance from the left bank of the Tigris. He called it *Dūr-Šarrukîn*, "Sargon's Fortress,' applying his own name to it.[54]

His successor, Sennacherib, preferred the city of Nineveh on the left bank of the Tigris, opposite Mōṣul, as his residence. Previous Old, Middle, and Neo-Assyrian kings had built here. This location had also been developed in the prehistoric and early historic periods.[55] Nineveh then remained the capital of the Assyrian kingdom until its end. The capture of Nineveh by the Medes and the Neo-Babylonians in 612 B.C. practically marked the end of the Neo-Assyrian kingdom.

The royal city of the Hittites in Asia Minor during the time of the Hittite empire was Hattusas. Its ruins are at modern Boghazköy, east of Ankara, on the other side of the Kizil Irmak. The society *Deutsche Orient-Gesellschaft* has been making excavations there ever since 1906.[56]

[52] V. Christian, *Altertumskunde des Zweistromlandes*, I, 15 ff., Plate II.

[53] Current reports are in the journal *Iraq*, Vols. XII ff. (1950 ff.).

[54] Christian, *op. cit.*, Plate I.

[55] For archeological research at the very extensive ruin site of Nineveh within which the villages of Kuyunjuk and Nebi Yūnis are situated, see Christian, *op. cit.*, pp. 16 ff., Plates III–IV, and A. Parrot, "Ninive et l'Ancien Testament," *CAB*, Vol. III (1953), available in English as "Nineveh and the Old Testament," *Studies in Biblical Archaeology*, Vol. III (1955).

[56] K. Bittel, *Die Ruinen von Boghazköy, der Haupstadt des Hethiterreiches* (1937).

CHAPTER VII

DATES

35. *Chronology*

IT is impossible to present or even to name here the profusion of often very difficult studies on the many problems of ancient oriental chronology. Rather, only a rapid survey will be given as to what this chronology is based on. From this survey one should be able to assess the certainty and reliability of periods and dates given for characters and events in ancient oriental history.[1]

(1) *Relative Chronology*

We have a number of documents from the ancient Near East which present exact figures for the course of a state's history, in addition to general references to the progress of historical events. These documents are chiefly king lists giving the length of royal reigns. For the first five dynasties we have the fragmentary Palermo Stone[2] and some other fragmentary stone inscriptions,[3] which taken together give a consecutive account divided into regnal periods. In addition, the Turin Papyrus,[4] also very fragmentary, a list of kings extending from the Old Kingdom into the New Kingdom, gives the length of their reigns. Finally there is Manetho's list of kings and dynasties (see p. 246), which S. Julius Africanus borrowed from Manetho and which ancient Christian historians then transmitted on the basis of Africanus.[5] Though the ancient documents are only fragments and details of Manetho's trustworthiness remain doubtful, to say the least, particularly in his figures, yet

[1] On scholarly chronology as a whole, see F. K. Ginzel, *Handbuch der mathematischen und technischen Chronologie*, I–III (1906–14), as well as W. Kubitschek, *Grundriss der antiken Zeitrechnung*, *Handbuch der Altertumswissenschaft*, I, 7 (1927). A survey of more recent literature on ancient Near Eastern chronology and a tabular collection of its results is given by E. F. Campbell in *The Bible and the Ancient Near East, Essays in Honor of William Foxwell Albright* (1961), pp. 214–24.

[2] Breasted, *Ancient Records of Egypt*, Vol. I, Secs. 76 ff.

[3] L. Borchardt, *Die Annalen und die zeitliche Festlegung des alten Reiches der ägyptischen Geschichte* (1917), pp. 21 ff.

[4] *Ibid.*, Plates IV–VI.

[5] H. Gelzer, *Sextus Julius Africanus*, I (1880), 191 ff. In Manetho's list and probably also on the Palermo Stone the order of pharaohs begins with mythical kings and continues with the order of definitely historical pharaohs.

the succession of Egyptian pharaohs is essentially accepted. However, with reference to the exact figures of years given by Manetho, a number of uncertainties remain, since his figures differ from available original records of individual pharaohs. Their figures allow us to accept only a minimum of the regnal years tabulated by Manetho.

We have a number of king lists from Mesopotamia, too. There are some from Babylonia, arranged by individual dynasties, giving the duration of reigns, here, too, frequently introduced by numbers of mythical rulers.[6] In addition, there are various annal type tabulations, not linked with royal reigns, such as the fragmentary Babylonian Chronicle.[7]

Aside from the problem of the reliability of the figures given, at times doubtful themselves, there remains the fact that in the king lists dynasties are arranged consecutively which apparently at times were ruling contemporaneously in different places.

The excavations at Ashur (p. 265) have added various valuable chronological lists to the previously known portions about Assyria. These have produced not only king lists, but also enumerations of the Assyrian *līmu*, the official years of the eponyms, high officials for whom it was the custom to name the individual years of a king's reign.[8] These *līmu* lists apply to the period of the Middle and Neo-Assyrian kingdom. The Assyrian king list from Khorsabad,[9] which came to light some years ago, is a particularly important chronological document, which lists the Assyrian kings with their regnal years from the earliest period to the eighth century B.C.

Unfortunately corresponding portions of native records are still lacking for the Hittite kingdom.[10] Therefore, Hittite chronology is still poorly grounded.

For Israel we have statements apparently based on records, giving the length of regnal periods of the kings of Israel and Judah from the death of Solomon to the end of the states of Israel and

[6] See *AOT*, pp. 331 ff., as well as H. Zimmern, "Die altbabylonischen vor- (und nach-) sintflutlichen Könige nach neuen Quellen," *ZDMG*, New Series, III (1924), 19 ff.

[7] *AOT*, pp. 359 ff., 362 ff.; also D. J. Wiseman, *Chronicles of Chaldaean Kings* (626–556 B.C.) in the British Museum (1956).

[8] A. Ungnad, "Eponymen," *RLA*, II (1938), 412–57.

[9] Published by A. Poebel in *JNES*, I (1942), 247–306, 460–92; II (1943), 56–90. Note also E. F. Weidner, "Bemerkungen zur Königsliste von Chorsābād," *AfO*, XV (1945–51), 85–102.

[10] Cf. three articles by A. Goetze, "The Problem of Chronology and Early Hittite History," *BASOR*, CXXII (1951), 18–25; "Alalaḫ and Hittite Chronology," *BASOR*, CXLVI (1957), 20–26; and "On the Chronology of the Second Millennium," *JCS*, XI (1957), 53–61, 63–73.

Judah.[11] These appear in the deuteronomistic setting of the Books of Kings. These statements form the hard core of Old Testament chronology. There are no exact references to dates based on records for other Old Testament periods. Generally speaking, the Old Testament does permit one to estimate the course of Israel's history for the period before the death of Solomon, but not to give even approximate dates with certainty for any individual event. In the Book of Ezekiel we have a few more dates for the exilic period after the first Jewish deportation. Then Old Testament chronological references stop. Only in Ezra and Nehemiah are there a few more interrelated dates. Once again, the post-canonical literature in the Books of Maccabees and in Josephus provides the elements of a self-contained, continuous relative chronology for the late Maccabean, Hasmonean period.

(2) *Synchronisms*

The chronologies of the individual ancient oriental regions can be related to one another by various cross-references. This reinforces the given chronologies and occasionally supplements them where they are deficient. Interrelated incidents and dates, that is, contemporaneous events, or synchronisms, can be established from the historical connections between given areas. Such connections substantially strengthen and secure the structure of relative chronology. In this process we are dealing with synchronistic original records from the ancient period, as well as with actual synchronisms indirectly attested by the historical tradition.

We have original synchronistic records for two distinct regions, both in Mesopotamia and in the Old Testament. These are lists which continuously relate royal succession periods of two neighbouring lands to each other, probably because for practical considerations such as trade from time to time they wanted to be able handily to translate into their own dating system the dates of neighbouring lands, based on regnal years. We have such synchronistic lists of Babylonian and Assyrian kings.[12] The Babylonian Chronicle (p. 268) also contains much synchronistic material. In the Old Testament in the Deuteronomistic framework of the

[11] J. Begrich, *Die Chronologie der Könige von Israel und Juda und die Quellen des Rahmens der Königsbücher* (1929); E. R. Thiele, *The Mysterious Numbers of the Hebrew Kings, A Reconstruction of the Chronology of the Kingdoms of Israel and Judah* (1951).

[12] E. F. Weidner, "Die Könige von Assyrien, Neue chronologische Dokumente aus Assur," *MVÄG*, XXVI, No. 2 (1921), 2 ff.

Books of Kings, again apparently on the basis of documents in addition to the regnal years of the kings', current synchronisms are given in the order of kings of Israel and Judah. The lists of royal regnal years and the synchronisms in both cases in all probability are derived from official sources and not one from the other. Therefore, this parallel placement makes it possible to control both lists thoroughly. Naturally, each of these synchronistic original records applies to only a very limited portion of the ancient Near Eastern world. In addition, each applies to a rather short period of time.

The class of actual synchronisms attested by historical tradition is also of great practical significance for chronology. Even though these frequently cannot lead to dates exact to the year, still they produced approximate synchronisms of characters and events in the most widely separated areas of the ancient Orient. I shall give only a few examples. The Mari texts (p. 209) have produced a very important synchronism of this sort. According to them King Zimrilim was a contemporary of the well-known Hammurabi of Babylon. Yet Zimrilim had ascended the throne of his father after a period of Assyrian rule over Mari under the Assyrian king, Shamshi-Adad I. The partial contemporaneity of Hammurabi and Shamshi-Adad I is given still more concretely by a previously known source,[13] according to which Shamshi-Adad I was still reigning in the tenth year of Hammurabi. This synchronism required a revision of the entire chronology of southwestern Asia for the first half of the second millennium B.C., and also for the third millennium. Since Shamshi-Adad I of Assyria belongs in a later period than was usually assumed previously, on the basis of the king list of Khorsabad[14] (p. 268), Hammurabi and the entire first dynasty of Babylon must be dated considerably later. Therefore, all datings from before the Mari texts and the king list of Khorsabad became known have been shown to be erroneous and certainly considerably too high. Incontestable synchronisms are given by the official diplomatic correspondence of the Amarna tablets. Here sequences of kings of eighteenth-dynasty Egypt, Cassite Babylon, early Middle Assyria, Mitanni, and the Hittite kingdom are given. The conflicts between Egyptians and Hittites in Syria in the thirteenth century B.C. provide further Egyptian-Hittite synchronisms. The conflict between the Hittites and Mitanni on the other border yield corresponding synchronisms. For evi-

[13] F. Thureau-Dangin, *RA*, XXXIV (1937), 138.

[14] E. Weidner, *AfO*, XV (1945–51), 100, based on new sources, assigns the regnal years of Shamshi-Adad I as 1727 B.C.–1695 B.C.

dence note the state treaties of Boghazköy. So far Hittite chronology has to be built essentially on such synchronisms, for lack of its own chronological sources. The encroachments of Neo-Assyrian kings on Syro-Palestine and even on Egypt again produced synchronisms with Egypt, as, for example, when in their annals the Assyrian kings, Esarhaddon and Ashurbanipal, repeatedly mention the contemporary Egyptian pharaoh, *Tarqū*, or Tirhaka, of the twenty-fifth dynasty. The Old Testament royal chronology also fits at this point as an important connecting link. On the one hand it is firmly related at various points with the very well-preserved Neo-Assyrian chronology and thereby securely fits into the ancient oriental relative chronology. Such incidents are the tribute of the Israelite king, Jehu, to Shalmaneser III in his eighteenth year;[15] the tribute of King Menahem of Israel (II Kings 15 : 19–20) to Tiglath-pileser III in his eighth year;[16] the fall of Samaria (II Kings 17 : 6) in the first year of Sargon;[17] the siege of Jerusalem by Sennacherib (II Kings 18 : 13–16) on his third campaign.[18] On the other hand it established connections with Egyptian history, such as the campaign in Palestine of Pharaoh Shishak I of the twenty-second dynasty in the fifth year of Rehoboam (I Kings 14 : 25–28) and the death of King Josiah of Judah (II Kings 23 : 29) in battle against Pharaoh Necho of the twenty-sixth dynasty.

The end of the Neo-Babylonian kingdom and the end of the twenty-sixth dynasty in Egypt are linked with events in the history and chronology of the Persian kingdom. Finally, ancient oriental history also gets an indirect connection with the chronology of the Greek historians through the history of the Persian empire.

The examples cited show that the genuine synchronisms are related to the later phases of ancient Near Eastern history. Archeological synchronization of the earlier periods is basically possible, namely establishment that events are contemporary with each other on the basis of corresponding archeological finds from various cultural areas. This requires the presupposition that given characteristic phenomena, such as a certain technique and style of painting pottery or an individual style in the manufacture of metal jewelry items appeared at the same time in various areas and probably with some dependence of one on the other. It is clear that such synchronization can be treated only with great caution and care. More favourable is the rare occasion in which at any point

15 Luckenbill, *Ancient Records of Assyria and Babylonia*, Vol. I, Sec. 672.

16 *Ibid.*, Vol. I, Sec. 815, and Vol. II, Sec. 1198.

17 *Ibid.*, Vol. II, Sec. 4.

18 *Ibid.*, Vol. II, Sec. 240. Additional material and details can be found in Begrich, *op. cit.*, pp. 94 ff.; Thiele, *op. cit.*, *passim*.

in a datable archeological level imported ware from another cultural area or native imitation of it can be disclosed, from which an approximate contemporaneous dating can be concluded. Finally, archeology has the possibility of showing contemporaneity, leading to absolute dates, by use of the radio carbon test (p. 122) with a reasonable margin of error.

(3) *Eras*

Toward the end of the ancient oriental period under varying circumstances the change was made from basing dates on regnal years or eponyms to simply counting years from a fixed date. While Ptolemaic Egypt continued to date according to royal years, in the neighbouring realm the Seleucids introduced an era whose epoch or initial point was the harvest of 312 B.C. Dating proceeded from this era for hundreds of years in southwest Asia. Then in the Roman period cities which were granted the right of self government also had their individual eras. Thus the Hellenistic cities in Syro-Palestine which had autonomy bestowed by Pompey, had a Pompeian era beginning in 64 B.C. or 63 B.C. Later, Roman provinces such as Provincia Arabia also received particular eras.[19] The era from which the dating began in any given case was not usually specifically stated, so that then one must determine it from the context as to event and date.

(4) *Absolute Chronology*

Generally speaking, the relative chronology of the ancient Near East is sound. However, it is weak in some spots because solid traditions are lacking and exact confirmation is missing. Astronomical confirmations can convert a relative chronology into an absolute chronology, specifically, a system of dates related to our calendar. For example, there were dated observations in Egypt on the heliacal rising of Sirius immediately before sunrise, which determined the Egyptian calendar. In Babylonia there were dated observations on the morning rising of Venus, and the like. There are accounts of unusual phenomena observed at given times, such as eclipses of the sun or of the moon. When astronomical tables are related to such ancient astral observations, astronomically exact dates are the result.[20]

[19] Details on this can be found in Ginzel, *op. cit.*, III, 43 ff.

[20] See T. von Oppolzer, *Kanon der Finsternisse* (1887) on eclipses of the sun and of the moon from 1207 B.C. to A.D. 2163; see also F. K. Ginzel, *Spezieller Kanon der*

Briefly the results are as follows:[21] There is, of course, an astronomical dating for the Egyptian Old Kingdom, based on a record. Yet this leaves various possibilities open and therefore the evaluations still vary considerably from one another. On the other hand, a particular astronomical dating during the Egyptian Middle Kingdom is fixed within a very narrow margin. The bases for establishing a date in the Old Babylonian Kingdom (Hammurabi) were given on p. 270. By relating these to given astronomical observations it becomes possible to make an approach to absolute chronology. Unfortunately there are several parallel possibilities. As a result, the dating of the Hammurabi dynasty is still debated. The chronology of previous periods of Mesopotamia and also of the earlier Hittite kingdom depends on this. For the Egyptian New Kingdom there are again astronomical possibilities of dating which allow for a margin, even if rather small. Most firmly established is the chronology of the Neo-Assyrian period. The eclipse of the sun which the Assyrian eponym canon C^b reports for the time of King Ashur-dan III[22] is astronomically established as being June 15, 763 B.C.[23] One can figure backwards from that point of the basis of the eponym canon. The chronology of the period of kings in Israel has also been established by this Neo-Assyrian chronology. Generally speaking, so has the late Egyptian chronology. Then follows the chronology of succeeding periods, which is known to the very year, having been established by Ptolemaic Greek astronomical studies.[24]

36. *Chronological Synopsis of Ancient Near Eastern History*

During the initial periods of ancient Near Eastern history the component cultural areas led a substantially separate existence and usually made aggressive attempts only on their closest

Sonnen- und Mondfinsternisse für das Ländergebiet der klassischen Altertumswissenschaften und den Zeitraum von 900 v. Chr. bis 600 n. Chr. (1899); P. V. Neugebauer, *Tafeln zur astronomischen Chronologie, zum Gebrauch für Historiker, Philologen, und Astronomen*, Vols. I–III (1912–22); and P. V. Neugebauer, *Spezieller Kanon der Sonnenfinsternisse für Vorderasien und Ägypten für die Zeit von 900 v. Chr. bis 4200 v. Chr., Astronomische Abhandlungen, Erg.-Heft*, Vol. VIII, No. 4 (1931).

21 Cf. E. Meyer, *Die ältere Chronologie Babyloniens, Assyriens und Ägyptens* (1925; 2nd ed., 1931).

22 Ungnad, *RLA*, II, 430, 432.

23 Ginzel, *Spezieller Kanon . . .*, pp. 243 ff.

24 On absolute chronology of the Late Babylonian period see Richard A. Parker and Waldo H. Dubberstein, *Babylonian Chronology, 626 B.C.–A.D 75* (Providence: Brown Univ., 1956).

neighbours, like those of Egypt on the Syrian coast and southern Palestine-Syria, or the powers of Mesopotamia on North Syria. The formation of the power structure of the Hyksos in the eighteenth century B.C. initiated a general ancient Near Eastern history in which nearly all regions of the ancient Near East were directly or indirectly involved. Admittedly, we do not know the particulars of these early developments, because there are no literary traditions to substantiate them. Parallel with the Hyksos power structure there were the then small Assyrian kingdom, the Old Babylonian kingdom of Hammurabi's dynasty, and the old Hittite kingdom. About the middle of the sixteenth century B.C. the Hittites of Asia Minor made what looks, for want of evidence, like a completely unprovoked attack on the Old Babylonian kingdom, bringing it to an end. These states must have had relations with the Hyksos domain in Egypt and Syro-Palestine, though there is no evidence to support this.[25]

After the fall of the Hyksos a remnant of its power structure was left in the Mesopotamian state of Mitanni, while eighteenth-dynasty Egypt filled the gap left by the collapse of Hyksos power in Palestine during the sixteenth and fifteenth centuries.

After a temporary period of decline, the pharaohs of the nineteenth dynasty at the end of the fourteenth century and during the thirteenth century wanted to reconstitute Egyptian control over Palestine-Syria. In the attempt, they encountered the advancing might of the later Hittite kingdom pressing on Syria from the north. The encounter resulted in the indecisive Egyptian-Hittite battle at Kadesh on the Orontes in central Syria in the fifth year of Rameses II, about 1285 B.C., and in the conclusion of a treaty between Rameses II and the Hittite king, Hattusilis III,[26] as a result of which Syria was divided roughly in the middle into a southern Egyptian and a northern Hittite sphere of influence. In the Hittite sphere of influence in Syria there were then some small vassal states of the Hittite kings, such as the state of Amurru in the valley of the Nahr el-Kebīr. This state had appeared already in the Amarna tablets. The Hittite kings concluded various treaties with it in the fourteenth and thirteenth centuries. The texts of these treaties were found at Boghazköy.

On the other side the Hittites had already in the fourteenth century B.C. brought the state of Mitanni in Mesopotamia, "the last remnant of the Hyksos power structure," under their control.

[25] Cf. A. Alt, *ZDPV*, LXX (1954), 130–34.
[26] G. Roeder, "Ägypter und Hethiter," *Der Alte Orient*, Vol. XX (1919).

Mitanni finally collapsed under the double pressure of the Hittite kingdom on the one side and the rising Middle Assyrian state on the other.

About 1200 B.C. Egyptian power finally declined; the Hittite empire suddenly disappeared following the invasion of the "Sea Peoples"; on the other side Assyria was not yet reaching out in earnest beyond Mesopotamia; even Babylonia having been ruled for centuries by Cassite kings was then insignificant as an international force. These circumstances left Syria and Palestine to themselves. At that moment numerous small states were coming into being, among which was Israel, just then making its bid for historical identity. Its world at this time consisted of the small Syro-Palestinian states. (The encroachment of a foreign power on the Syro-Palestinian enclave in this period, for example the campaign of Pharaoh Shishak against Palestine, was only a passing episode without significant results.)

The resurgence of the Neo-Assyrian kingdom in the ninth and, after a lapse, in the eighth century B.C. changed all this and brought about an advance of the Assyrians against Syria and Palestine. The Egyptians were still the antagonists of the Assyrians, somewhere in the background. In spite of the weakness of Egypt during this period, the Syro-Palestinian states looked to her for support in their battle against the advancing Assyrians. The outcome was vacillation of the small states between voluntary subjection to the Assyrians, invincible as they were, and opposition with the hope of Egyptian help. Such vacillation is prominently reflected in Old Testament prophecy of the eighth century. At any rate, the historical result was that Egyptian help disappointed them and that the Syro-Palestinian lands became transformed either into Assyrian provinces, like the state of Israel in 733 B.C. and 721 B.C., or at least into Assyrian vassal states, like the state of Judah in 733 B.C. Thus Assyria became the first of the ancient Near Eastern empires which ruled almost all of the ancient Near East. In the second quarter of the seventh century, Assyria temporarily even occupied a part of Egypt.

The short-lived interlude of Neo-Babylonian rule began in 612 B.C. when Nineveh fell to the united Medes and Neo-Babylonians. Therewith the Assyrian kingdom came to a sudden end, in spite of the help of an Egyptian ally, Pharaoh Necho, of the twenty-sixth dynasty. Apparently he now feared the newly rising powers more than weakened Assyria, which only a short time before had been the chief enemy of Egypt. Syria and Palestine on the contrary, having been under the yoke of Assyria, took their stand on the side of the opponents of Assyria and thus resisted Pharaoh Necho. The conflict between the Judean king Josiah and Necho at Megiddo (II Kings 23 : 29; II Chron. 35 : 20 ff.) fits into this context, clarified only by the discovery of a part of the Babylonian Chronicle.[27] Then the Neo-Babylonian kingdom succeeded Assyrian control in Babylonia, on the Euphrates, and after the decisive victory over the Egyptians at Carchemish in 605 B.C., even in Syro-Palestine. Egypt remained independent. The Medes became the heirs of Assyrian rule in the Assyrian home land and in the mountains to the north and to the east. The best-known historical activity of the Neo-Babylonian kingdom was the removal of the state of Judah and the destruction of Jerusalem in 587 B.C. In 539 B.C. Babylon was subjected to the Persians under Cyrus, who in the meanwhile had taken over from the Medes. This gave the Persians control over Syro-Palestine. In 525 B.C. under Cambyses they even conquered Egypt. Thus they won the rule over the entire ancient Near East until Alexander the Great in 334 B.C. to 331 B.C. subjugated the entire Persian empire.

After Alexander's death, his empire fell apart into various domains of his successors (*diadochi*). Egypt fell to the Macedonian dynasty of the Ptolemies, southwestern Asia to the Seleucids. As late as 198 B.C., the Ptolemies still occupied neighbouring Palestine and Phoenicia, but finally they lost it to the Seleucids. While the Ptolemies in Egypt maintained themselves until their land was occupied by the Romans in 30 B.C., the gradual decline of the Seleucid kingdom had already set in during the second century B.C., brought about by the rise of the Romans in the second and first centuries, when they gradually took control of this area.

The Historical Chronology of the Ancient Near East appended to this book attempts to present a survey of ancient Near Eastern history. In addition, lists of Egyptian pharaohs can be found in Breasted and Ranke, *Geschichte Ägyptens*, 1911 ed., pp. 445 ff.; 1936 ed., pp. 325 ff. [English edition: Breasted, *History of Egypt* (rev. ed., 1942), pp. 597–601]; in Erman and Ranke, *Ägypten und ägyptisches Leben im Altertum* (1923), pp. 658 ff.; in selection also in Scharff-Moortgat, *Ägypten und Vorderasien im Altertum* (1950), pp. 191 ff. King lists of the kingdoms of Mesopotamia, particularly for Babylonia and Assyria, are provided in L. Delaporte, *Geschichte der führenden Völker*, III (1933), 336 ff. and E. F. Weidner, "Die

[27] C. J. Gadd, *The Fall of Nineveh* (1923); D. J. Wiseman, *Chronicles of Chaldaean Kings* (626–556 B.C.) in the British Museum (1956).

Könige von Assyrien," *MVÄG*, XXVI, No. 2 (1921), 61 ff. Note the remarks on p. 250 in connection with the dates given in both of the last-named works. The latest lists of the earlier Babylonian kings, the Assyrian kings, and the Hittite kings are presented by E. F. Weidner in *AfO*, XV (1945–51), 98–102. Also see P. van der Meer, *The Chronology of Ancient Western Asia and Egypt* (1955).

CHAPTER VIII

RELIGIONS

37. *Religious Source Materials*

THE history of religions of the ancient Near East supplies the background for the Old Testament. It reaches into many areas of study, complicated by an abundance of phenomena and developments. A presentation of these would have to range wide and treat an abundance of material. Here we can only introduce the chief features and make reference to the literature.

The religious source materials are partly literary, partly archeological. The religious literary texts are hymns and prayers to the individual gods, which were recorded for cultic use, a variety of procedural notes for cultic celebrations, and mythical narratives for recitation at particular festivals of the gods. There are also incantation texts to ward off demons bringing adversity and illness, and omen texts based on a divination craft, which listed specific portents. Incantation and omen texts occur especially in Mesopotamia; actually, they belong to the field of magic rather than that of religion. Finally there are also texts for the dead like grave inscriptions with religious contents, and engraved or written instructions placed in the grave with the deceased for his journey into the other world, as particularly in Egypt. Yet even the texts which are not specifically religious, like royal inscriptions, laws, treaties, epics, narratives, fables, etc. usually contain some material affecting the history of religion, names of deities, oath formulas, references to various cults, etc.

The most important religious texts can be found in translation in various collections, in addition to the periodicals *ANET* and *AOT*, such as the following: Lehmann-Haas, *Textbuch zur Religionsgeschichte* (2nd ed., 1922), containing Egyptian texts by H. Grapow, Babylonian-Assyrian texts by B. Landsberger, and Hittite texts by H. Zimmern. On the ancient Orient there are two volumes in the series *Religionsgeschichtliches Lesebuch*, edited by A. Bertholet, Vol. X, H. Kees, *Ägypten* (2nd ed., 1928) and Vol. XVII, A. Bertholet, *Die Religion des Alten Testaments* (2nd ed., 1932). The series *Religiöse Stimmen der Völker*, edited by W.

Otto, contains G. Roeder, *Urkunden zur Religion des alten Ägypten* (1915) and A. Ungnad, *Die Religion der Babylonier und Assyrer* (1921). In addition, one should note many individual text publications and special articles. [An inexpensive paperback, but very useful edition of translated Sumero-Accadian and Ugaritic religious texts, is Isaac Mendelsohn (ed.), *Religions of the Ancient Near East*, Vol. IV in the "Library of Religion" series (1955).]

The importance of the archeological as well as literary sources for the understanding of the history of ancient religions has become recognized in increasing degree in recent decades. This is true of the remains of ancient cultic structures, such as temples, and cultic equipment, such as altars, also of the many representations of deities in sculpture or relief and imitations of them in miniatures, as well as on coins, then too of the portrayal of mythical events, cultic scenes, of images of divine symbols, etc. A wealth of illustrative material on the history of ancient oriental religions is provided by the periodicals *ANEP* and *AOB*. Then there is *Bilderatlas zur Religionsgeschichte*, edited by H. Haas, including Parts 2–4; H. Bonnet, *Ägyptische Religion* (1924), Part 5; H. Zimmern, *Religion der Hethiter* (1925), Part 6; B. Landsberger, *Babylonisch-Assyrische Religion* (1925), Part 7; and G. Karo, *Religion des ägäischen Kreises* (1925). Especially for Palestine we have a history of religions (including the Roman period) based on the archeological material in S. A. Cook, *The Religion of Ancient Palestine in the Light of Archaeology, The Schweich Lectures, 1925* (1930), which contains a wealth of illustrative material; and for the older periods, W. F. Albright, *Archaeology and the Religion of Israel* (2nd ed.; Baltimore: Johns Hopkins, 1946).

The religions and cults of the individual areas and periods can be grasped by careful individual work based on these sources. Then they can be composed into a general historical presentation of religions. Naturally, any individual can treat and present only limited, related areas at any one time in scholarly fashion. Yet for a general history of religion, which also includes the area of the ancient oriental religions, one should see the thorough presentation of Chantepie de la Saussaye, *Lehrbuch der Religionsgeschichte*, edited by A. Bertholet and E. Lehmann, Vols. I–II (4th ed., 1925), with a number of collaborators including O. Lange for Egypt and F. Jeremias for the Semitic peoples of southwest Asia. Then there are the brief Tiele-Söderblom, *Kompendium der Religionsgeschichte* (6th ed., 1931); the survey, G. Mensching, *Allgemeine Religionsgeschichte* (2nd ed., 1949); and F. Heiler,

Erscheinungsformen und Wesen der Religion, Die Religionen der Menschheit, Vol. I (1961).

Many native cults and rites, such as those practised among the still unsettled tribes of southwest Asia, have persisted through the ages with great tenacity and have had a definite part in the background of the religions of ancient oriental civilized countries. They comprise the material of W. R. Smith's classic, *Lectures on the Religion of the Semites*, edited by S. A. Cook (3rd ed., 1927). Cf. also J. Wellhausen, *Reste arabischen Heidentums* (2nd ed., 1927).

38. *Basic Features of Religious Outlook and Practice*

Certain common features in the historical background of religions are noticed throughout the entire ancient Near East in spite of different arrangement of details and names. They will be presented here briefly.

Apparently one of the oldest religious concepts in the ancient Near East is belief in a great female deity, a universal mother of all life, particularly of human and animal life, who embodied fertility as such in herself. A young god was frequently associated with her of the type of the so-called dying and rising gods, who represented the quickly blooming and fading vegetation, so striking in the Near East. He appears mostly as the beloved of the great goddess, suddenly loses his life in one way or another, is mourned by the goddess, but finally awakes to life anew. This divine couple appears in Mesopotamia under the names of Ishtar and Tammuz. The late records in Asia Minor describe this couple under the names *Magna Mater* (Cybele) and Attis. In Egypt the originally separate deities Isis and Osiris assumed the role of this pair of gods. Syro-Palestine used the names Ashtart, Asherah, ʿAnat for the great mother goddess, while the youthful god did not have a generally accepted name as far as we can see. Here and there he seems to have been worshipped under the name of Eshmun. The later Hellenistic records give him the title of majesty, "Adonis,"[1] which corresponds to Hebrew *adhon*, "Lord." Everywhere life and fertility were worshipped as divine in this pair. The cults directed toward the mother goddess or toward this divine pair probably played a great role and deeply affected the life and activity of the people. The general fertility and vitality in nature were magically produced

[1] W. W. Graf Baudissin, *Adonis und Esmun* (1911).

and continually renewed in these deities through definite rites, running through a regular cycle in the natural course of a year. Sacral sexual intercourse was a prominent part of these rites, in which the divine propagation of life was portrayed. It was consummated by priests and priestesses as well as by special "devoted" persons at the sanctuaries who are also described in the Old Testament under the titles, *qedheshim* or *qedheshoth*. The thought arose in connection with these cults of renewal of life that man, too, could come to life again after his bodily death and for that matter through being included magically in the dying and rising of the youthful god. There was the belief in Mesopotamia that a person deceased could be transformed by magical phrases into Tammuz, so that he could then share in a being brought to new life. The Egyptian ritual for the dead particularly recognizes the transformation of the deceased person into Osiris.

The great cosmic gods, the heavenly and astral gods, who were worshipped everywhere in the ancient Orient, were additional members of the circle of the universal deities. By the heavens originally they understood quite generally the great vault of air over the earth, which was conceived to be an area just as habitable as the earth. These heavens were the domain of the winds and clouds in which divine beings held sway who could be either beneficial or devastating. The stars which for their part pursue their courses in this realm were considered as deities because of the apparently eternal regularity of their movements. As deities the stars became guarantors of universal order, and frequently guarantors of justice as well. With the progress of reflection the divine powers of the earth, the underworld, and the deep were frequently joined to the cosmic might of the heavens.

The numerous localized divine beings played a great role alongside these universal gods. They had a particular practical significance especially for cultic activity. We are acquainted with such divine beings particularly in Syro-Palestine. The Old Testament lumps them together under the concept of the "Baals of the Canaanites." They were thought of as living in sacred trees or springs, on mountain tops, or in sacred rocks. They were "owners" (Hebrew, *ba'alim*) of these through a materially conceived sanctity of designated localities. These *numina*, which originally frequently did not even have a proper name and which were titled only by the word *ba'al* with any imaginable specific attribute, at first actually did not have a separate identity and originally were not gods at all, but either beneficial or dread spirits, which in the limited surroundings of their dwelling either provided the fertility of the land or wrought sinister, demonic consequences. They were provided with offerings as gifts at their sacred places, which were thought of as their abodes and which did not necessarily require a particular inventory except the sacred tree, rock, or the like, and perhaps at least an implied enclosure of the consecrated precinct. The offerings for these spirits, which were primarily thought of as food, were simply deposited; in a more advanced stage of conception they were transposed into a sort of "immaterial" state by being burned up, in order to ascend as a "burnt offering" (cf. Judg. 6 : 17–21; 13 : 15–20). Even though this phenomenon of locally related divine beings is known to us especially from Syro-Palestine, still it doubtless occurred in every area in which we study ancient oriental religion.

Deities related to persons appear alongside of *numina* related to places. A particular link between a deity and a given group of people is involved. The connection between place and deity was more prevalent in well-settled, civilized regions; the personal tie, on the other hand, appeared pre-eminently among tribes not yet sedentary. Note that non-sedentary groups tend to have a warmer sense of human ties than is customary with inhabitants of civilized lands. This phenomenon is seen in cults of tribal gods. These cults had their roots in the area of non-sedentary life. Still, they frequently continued on after the transition to sedentary life in the settled land had taken place. The tribal god was conceived of in human terms in a patriarchal society such as we observe in the ancient Orient at the beginning of times which can be roughly described as historical. In a very primeval stage the deity was still regarded as being a blood relative of the tribe. In very ancient personal names he was simply called "ancestor," "tribal brother," "relative." He was viewed as the lord, leader, and judge of the tribe. In line with this a tribe had just one single actual tribal god, who claimed the cultic supremacy in the circle of the members of the tribe. Therefore, there was a henotheistic tendency in these cults. These cults of tribal gods also must have had a vague local connection. Yet in this case this connection was not deeply rooted and as the areas of migration and settlement shifted, the cult centres had to do the same. The personal tie became particularly evident whenever the deities were named father gods, conforming to the human form which they probably had originally before they became venerated by their offspring. A. Alt[2] has traced this situa-

[2] "Der Gott der Väter," *BWANT*, Vol. III, No. 12 (1929) [reprinted in *KS*, Vol. I].

tion in which a deity was titled "god of X" at two spots in the realm of ancient oriental religion, namely once in the patriarchal narratives of the Old Testament and a second time in the area of Syro-Palestinian culture during the Hellenistic-Roman period. This type of cult, which naturally has left only random literary or inscribed evidence, presumably expanded more generally in the ancient oriental world, particularly among those who had not yet become sedentary. The particular phenomenon of the community sacrifice (Hebrew, *shelem*), connected with a sacrificial meal, was likely native to all these tribal cults. Basic to this type of sacrifice was the thought of eating in common with the deity and of mysterious union between deity and tribal members brought about by the common partaking of the sacred sacrificial animal.

We find a combination of a local and personal tie in the cults of certain city gods. These cults played a significant role in the ancient Orient from primeval times. Such city gods were the *genii loci* of the city settlements and their territories, but at the same time they were the divine lords of the historical communities of the city dwellers and as such the guardians of the urban community, its fortunes, and its affairs. The city deities were accorded urban houses, or temples, just like the city dwellers. By nature the temple is primarily part of the city. Its basic forms were originally copies of city dwellings, especially of the palace of the city king. Naturally, in time it developed and was arranged in a manner corresponding to its peculiar nature. In the old areas of city culture, particularly in southern Mesopotamia and Egypt, city gods played an important role from primeval times.

In all of this we are dealing with ideas which occur not only in the ancient Orient, but everywhere in the history of religion. It is a process frequently observed in the ancient Orient and common in the history of religions, that various divine beings were identified with one another in the historical process and merged with one another in the cultic worship, that especially deities from the various mentioned categories were united with one another, whether in the course of a change in the religion produced by historical developments, such as comminglings of populations, or whether by conscious priestly or "theological" deliberation. In this process the most varied possibilities are conceivable and have certainly occurred, even though it is not possible to trace these processes everywhere. Thus, almost any local *numen*, because of its share in divine activity, could ascend into the circle of the great universal deities and be identified in his cult with the god of the heavens. For example, in Syro-Palestine a "Baal of the heavens" was known already from primeval times.[3] Cosmic deities could at the same time take over the role of city gods because they had a famous cultic site in a given city, as frequently happened in Mesopotamia. Tribal gods were united at local cultic centres with the *numina* native there, as their worshippers became newly sedentary in the regions dominated by these settled *numina*. The abundance of deities of various classes in a given region led to priestly speculations on the relations of these deities to one another. Thus they frequently arrived at developed ideas of a pantheon with a whole hierarchy of divine beings, in which these were brought into relations of kinship with one another, in which there was a "father of the gods," or also a "king of the gods," or a "lord of the gods." Such speculations then occasionally were carried on to the point that many deities could be absorbed in one great deity. A hymn to the moon god given the Sumerian name *Nanna(r)* is known from Mesopotamia, in which he is not only exalted as "ruler of the gods," but at the same time is addressed with the names of various other gods and therefore identified with them.[4] Similarly in an Egyptian hymn to the god Amon, he is praised, not only as the first of all gods, but even beyond this, other gods are designated as "forms" of him.[5] Again, some gods were united with one another in such a way that their names appeared as various epithets of one given god. Deliberation and intent were involved in this entire process. The abundance of divine beings held its own for the practical divine worship of the peoples along with the abundance of cultic sites.

The will and activity of the deities was generally conceived in human fashion. Even their external form was mostly conceived in human terms. Only demons and spirits of lower rank appeared in the frequently seen total or partial animal form. They were frequently represented as guardian forces in the form of fantastic composite creatures (see p. 197) at the entrances of temples and palaces. Theriomorphic beings of similar type were figured to be the serving attendants of great deities. Particularly in the sphere of North Syria–Asia Minor–Mesopotamia, frequently an anthropomorphic deity was accompanied by a given animal, and in such a manner that the deity was shown standing on the specified animal or on a pair of these animals, as, for example, on the well-known

[3] O. Eissfeldt, *ZAW*, New Series, XVI (1939), 3 ff.
[4] *AOT*, p. 241 [*ANET*, pp. 385–86, reprinted in I. Mendelsohn, *op. cit.*, pp. 160–62].
[5] *ANET*, pp. 368–69.

rock reliefs of Maltaya on the upper reaches of the Euphrates and Yazylykaya at Boghazköy in Asia Minor.[6] Therefore, even the "golden calf" recorded in the Old Testament was certainly not thought of originally as an image of deity, but only as the pedestal of a deity, in this case not depicted, but rather conceived as invisibly standing on it. Egypt alone had a large number of deities in animal form from primeval time. This tendency persisted throughout the entire history of the religion of Egypt. In fact, in the late period it again came into the foreground rather prominently. At all events, even here they spoke of the activity of these animal deities as of human activity and were accustomed to portray them at least partially in human form, and in such a manner that the human body had only an animal head.[7]

People were created by the gods to serve them, so it was said.[8] They were devoted to the fulfilment of the requirements of the gods as to care and services. They did not recognize a well-defined border between the world of the gods and that of men. Particularly the great ones of the earth, meaning kings and rulers, in whom the human society which they controlled was represented or even embodied, had a close relationship to the world of the divine. The views on this were of course varied in the various areas of the ancient Orient.[9] It is scarcely right to assume a general and unanimous ancient oriental view of the divinity of kingship and of the individual kings.[10] It is true that in Egypt the pharaohs were actually called sons of the sun god Re and incarnations of the god Horus in their official title formula. They were also very prominently described as bodily sons of a goddess. Yet these remarks do not apply in the same manner to Mesopotamia, either for the old Sumerian city rulers or even properly for the Babylonian and Assyrian kings, who were regarded as divinely called and commissioned, and as special confidants of the gods, but not as divine beings. Nor can divinity of kingship be demonstrated for Syro-Palestine, except where specifically Egyptian ideas penetrated during the period of Egyptian control in the Late Bronze Age. At any event, it was a customary concept in the Near East that rulers on earth were close to the sphere of the gods. In the course of a persistent

[6] *AOB*, Nos. 335, 337–38; *ANEP*, Nos. 522, 530–31, 534, and especially No. 537.

[7] E.g., *AOB*, Nos. 299, 302–3; *ANEP*, Nos. 553, 558, 565, 572.

[8] Cf. the excellent study of C. J. Gadd, *Ideas of Divine Rule in the Ancient Near East, The Schweich Lectures 1945* (1948).

[9] Cf. Henri Frankfort, *Kingship and the Gods: A Study of Ancient Near Eastern Religion as the Integration of Society and Nature* (Chicago: Univ. of Chicago, 1948).

[10] As particularly in I. Engnell, *Studies in Divine Kingship in the Ancient Near East* (1943).

"democratization" running through the long history of the ancient Near East, assertions which initially were made only of kings were transferred first to other prominent persons and then to all men.

The cult of the gods at the sacred places[11] was a complex phenomenon in which various elements were united one with another. At first the cult served to care for the gods, who required this. Therefore, people placed particularly food and drink as offerings for gods at their places. The burning of these offerings, hence the presentation of burnt offerings, was not customary either in Egypt or Mesopotamia. Even in Syro-Palestine the food offerings were frequently simply placed at the local cultic centres for the service of the gods. It could be that the burning of the offerings was native particularly to the non-sedentary elements, who presented their offering from the animals of their flock, not only roasting these herd animals at the fire but for the gods, burning them to ashes, for naturally they presented to their gods as food what was also customary as food among men. In the settled lands the produce of civilization likewise constituted the normal "food offerings" just as among the nomadic herdsmen it was the animals of the flock (cf. Gen. 4 : 2b–4a). In "community sacrifice" the human participants in the sacrifice also participated in the sacred meal. Only a portion of the material sacrificed was presented to the deity. The rest was consumed in a sacrificial meal. Thus the meal constituted and energized the community. These matters were originally so powerful and unquestioned basically that the service of the gods in the cults also had the objective of strengthening or even actually making possible the benevolent activity of the gods through feeding and strengthening them. By this process the cultus won the significance of a productive activity. This productive activity also included given cultic celebrations in which the beneficent action of the gods desired by men was portrayed and directly brought about by virtue of an original idea of an automatically operating analogy between cultic and divine action. The close connection between the divine and the human sphere once more becomes particularly clear at this point. The cultically active priest according to extensively held ancient oriental thought completed the divine action in given ceremonials. Thus somehow in the cult the battle and victory of a god over powers hostile to the gods and threatening life were "played" and therewith realized. At this point especially the "sacred marriage," referred to on pp. 280-81, fits in; for it should not only depict but

[11] In the temples of the lands, the deities were "represented" by statues and also by symbols; cf. K.-H. Bernhard, *Gott und Bild* (1956).

directly complete the life-developing and life-giving activity of the gods.

Thus we may hope to clarify the close connection which usually obtained in the ancient Near East between cult and myth. Myth deals with the interactivity of divine figures, particularly with battles and victories. Especially the universal, cosmic deities appear in myth to carry out the drama of the cosmic forces in the great natural phenomena. However, these were not presentations of poetic fantasy, but presentations of events in the divine world, which were produced in the cultic celebrations. The cosmic powers were personified in myth, even as they were presented in the cult by the human cultic persons, so that mytho-cultic action would activate the gods. Therefore the myths related the "drama" to be produced in the cult. On occasions the greatly elaborated myths were simply recited at cultic ceremonials, as in the case with the Babylonian creation myth *Enuma elish* recited at the Babylonian New Year's Festival in spring. Naturally, ultimately mythical materials could also be poetically expanded. The mythical personification of cosmic phenomena, particularly of those which continually recurred in the natural process, actually defied comparison with mortal experience. This led to such unusual concepts as that of the birth of the sun god from the queen of the heavens daily at dawn and of his entry into the realm of the dead every evening; or of the constantly alternating death and resurrection of deities representing vegetation.

39. *The Individual Religions*

(1) *Egypt*

Numerous monuments and literary evidences describe Egyptian religion. There is the detailed, well-illustrated book of A. Erman, *Die Religion der Ägypter, ihr Werden und Vergehen in vier Jahrtausenden* (1934); also the section, "Die Religion" in Erman-Ranke, *Ägypten und ägyptisches Leben im Altertum* (1923); S. Morenz, *Ägyptische Religion, Die Religionen der Menschheit*, Vol. VIII (1960); very good material and many illustrations are found in the reference work, H. Bonnet, *Reallexikon der ägyptischen Religionsgeschichte* (1952), abbreviated *RÄRG*.

There were age-old local cults in the individual cities of Egypt. At these sites the many gods conceived and depicted in the form of animals or plants were worshipped. Even such an object as a wooden post could be thought of as a deity. Yet theriomorphic deities played a particularly great role. An animal image depicted the deity. The priest wore the corresponding animal mask in the cult and thereby represented the deity. Given specimens of the species of animal in question were regarded as sacred and untouchable, and later this was extended to include the entire species. Particularly well known are the sacred bulls, the Apis bull as the figure of the god Ptah of Memphis and the Menvis bull as the figure of the god Atum of Heliopolis.[12] A gigantic burial structure was found at Memphis for deceased sacred Apis bulls. Parallel with these original fetishistic cults there were the cults of universal-cosmic deities, which seem to have been native primarily in the Delta and perhaps had a primeval connection with similar southwestern Asiatic cults.[13] These cosmic deities, which were originally imagined not in animal form but in human form and which were included with others in the priestly-theological system of the Ennead "the nine," of Heliopolis, of course withdrew almost from view as far as cultic practice was concerned in the historical periods; they continued to play a role only as *di otiosi* in the traditional conceptions. The sole exception was the Heliopolitan sun god Re, who at one point in history achieved supreme importance in Egyptian religion.

Among the known phenomena of Egyptian religion one feature became very characteristic. It powerfully influenced the development of Egyptian religion in the historical period. This was the official status of that religion within the rigidly autocratic Egyptian state. The pharaoh was basically the priest in the Egyptian cult, even when the cultic activities were actually performed by royally appointed priests. However, as officially depicted, the pharaoh is repeatedly shown as personally sacrificing to the gods. On the other hand the pharaoh himself is called god. The title, "the good god," is an integral part of the titulary of the pharaoh (see p. 285). Therefore the changing dynasties and pharaohs also exercised a substantial influence on the development of the cult. Thus the cosmic sun god Re achieved his great significance through one Egyptian dynasty. The pharaohs of the fifth dynasty in the Old Kingdom originated from the priests of the Re temple in Heliopolis, which was situated in the Delta north of modern Cairo. This same city is mentioned in the Old Testament under its old name of *'ōn*. They elevated the cult of their god Re to the central state cult, erecting for him sun temples and those great obelisks,[14] which serve as

[12] *AOB*, Nos. 544, 547; *ANEP*, No. 570. [13] H. Stock, *WO*, III (1948), 140.
[14] *AOB*, No. 492; H. Bonnet, *RÄRG*, Fig. 175.

tokens of the sun god, and thereby founded the supremacy of the sun god Re for all time in the Egyptian cult, which clung very conservatively to all tradition. Then in the course of time many other gods were identified with him in such a manner that their names were united with the name of Re in compound divine names. Later on, again in connection with the history of the dynasties of pharaohs, the god Amon rose to the position of supreme might. He was originally depicted as a ram and had an ancient seat in the Upper Egyptian city of Thebes (p. 264). Previous to this the pharaohs of the eleventh dynasty had resided in Thebes and worshipped Amon there. The pharaohs of the twelfth dynasty also, coming from Thebes, had continued the Amon cult, even though they returned their palace to time-honoured Memphis. In the New Kingdom the pharaohs elevated Thebes, the city of the god Amon, as their capital. At that time Amon became the chief national god; his name from then on was linked with that of the previous national god Re, as Amon-Re. In this Egyptian Empire period he achieved tremendous power. Gigantic temple complexes were built for him in Thebes. Rich gifts made the property of his cult very great in land and other goods. His priesthood brought his cult to extraordinary influence. Only for a short period was the position of Amon-Re endangered and disputed, once more from the official side, namely during the reign of Pharaoh Amenophis IV of the eighteenth dynasty, the "theologian" on the throne; for he wanted to replace the great number of the traditional Egyptian cults, including the great Amon-Re cult, with the sole cult of the solar disc, called *Aten* in Egyptian. In the name of the cult of the sun disc Amenophis IV undertook his campaign against the ancient gods of the land, especially against Amon-Re, who had then become so powerful. In the ancient inscriptions the hated name of Amon was scratched out. The king replaced his own name, which contained the divine name Amon, with the new name Akhenaten (Ikhnaton), meaning "favoured by the solar disc." Finally the king left the capital of Thebes, the chief abode of the Amon-Re cult, and built himself a new capital farther down the Nile on the right bank, which he called Akhet-aten, or "the horizon of the solar disc." Its ruins are at modern Tell el-ʿAmārna. In this new capital a freer manner of living and style of art immediately developed, known as "Amarna culture" and distinct from the old traditions. A great hymn to the solar disc as the universal provider and sustainer of life is referred back to Akhenaten.[15] In all likelihood the author of

[15] *AOT*, pp. 15–18; *ANET*, pp. 369–71.

Psalm 104 was acquainted with this hymn. The cultic measures of Akhenaten did not last long. The force of tradition showed itself as superior to the will of the king. Aman-Re and the royal city of Thebes resumed their old traditional position soon after the death of Akhenaten, under the rule of one of his stepsons who changed his name from Tut-ankh-aten to Tut-ankh-aman. This change in itself indicates a basic return to the old way.

The service of the dead played a very substantial role in connection with the religion of Egypt.[16] It was said first of the divine pharaohs, then also of the nobles surrounding the king or important in the state, and finally of all men, that after their death they went into "the West," into the realm of the dead which was located in the region of the setting sun. There they continued to exist as "blessed ones" under the rule of Osiris as the lord in this realm. Everything had to be done on earth to facilitate the passage for the deceased into this realm and their maintenance there. Tombs were erected at the western edge of the Nile Valley for kings and nobles. There were the pyramids at Memphis for kings of the Old and the Middle Kingdom. Beginning in the New Kingdom there were the great underground burial places at Thebes, hidden and where possible protected against grave robbers. All of the objects required for daily life were placed in the grave for the future service of the deceased. The bodies of the deceased were protected before burial by embalming. In this process the internal organs were removed and deposited separately in jars for organs, called canopic jars. In the temples for the dead which were connected with each of the royal tombs at given places in the burial compounds of the nobility a cult of the dead was observed, which provided for the feeding of the "blessed." Endowments were set up to maintain them. The necessary information was placed with the deceased at their burial in order to instruct them on their journey into "the West" and to give them the required incantations to overcome all sorts of dangers and difficulties on their way. These "texts for the dead" were inscribed in the pyramids and underground burial places, the so-called pyramid texts; or they were applied to the stone or wooden coffins with a variety of painted drawings, the "coffin texts"; or they were placed in the coffin, recorded on a papyrus roll, the "Book of the Dead." The expensiveness of these provisions made such a careful service of the dead possible only for kings and the great and rich people of the realm,

[16] Cf. the section "Die Toten" in Erman and Ranke, *Ägypten und ägyptisches Leben, op. cit.*

while the masses of the people had to content themselves with a simple burial in the earth.

(2) *Mesopotamia*

The history of religion in Mesopotamia was considerably more complicated than it was in Egypt, as the historical phenomena on the soil of Mesopotamia were also more extremely varied. However, there was a certain continuity in Mesopotamia too, and certain continuous individual features.[17]

In Mesopotamia we see initially a number of local cults in the ancient Sumerian city-states. The temples of the gods stood on high terraces within the city areas, the forerunners of the famous temple towers of Mesopotamia. The cosmic and astral function played a considerable role even in these from primeval times. The Sumerians very early systematized the world of their deities because of their interest in proper "Order" and distinguished the realms of activity of the individual divine powers from one another. Anu was designated as god of the heavens, Enlil as god of the earth, Ea as god of the deep. The sun and moon were gods who were worshipped under various names. The great mother goddess was also known by various names. The cult of the god Enlil or Ellil played a central role at least for a time in the city of Nippur.[18] This god was called lord of the gods and ruler of the Sumerian city-states. The Sumerian pantheon with its cults remained influential in following times in all of Mesopotamia, long after other peoples and forms of government had been in control of affairs in this realm. In part the ancient Sumerian divine names were maintained. Sumerian remained a sacred language for a long time, long after it ceased to be used colloquially. The Sumerian ideas of the divine sphere were maintained.

In connection with the organization of states given cults were favoured. Thus it happened that the cult of the city god of Babylon gained a significant position which later persisted. This was brought about during the period of the first dynasty of Babylon in the Old Babylonian Kingdom, through which for a time Babylon became

[17] On Mesopotamia, we have the very comprehensive, though dated work of M. Jastrow, *Die Religion Babyloniens und Assyriens*, Vols. I–II (1905–12), with a picture map. Then there is the excellent work of E. Dhorme, *Les religions de Babylonie et d'Assyrie* in the collection "Mana" 1: *Les anciennes religions orientales*, II (1949), 1–330. Sections pertaining to religion will be found in B. Meissner, *Babylonien und Assyrien*, II (1925), 1–282.

[18] F. Nötscher, *Ellil in Sumer and Akkad* (1927).

the political centre of all Mesopotamia. The god of Babylon was called Marduk. His name appears in Jer. 50 : 2 in the derivative form, Merodach. (See also Isa. 39 : 1.) He was a manifestation of the sun god. Just as Enlil was once referred to simply as "the Lord," so now Marduk received the Babylonian honorary title, Bēl, or "Lord." He appears under this title in Isa. 46 : 1; Jer. 50 : 2; 51 : 44. He was worshipped as king of gods and men. Every year in spring at the beginning of the new year the festival of his enthronement was celebrated in his cult. This took place at a special New Year's Festival House (Accadian, *bīt akītum*), situated outside of the city. At this time he always inherited the rule of the world anew. On a day of this great festival they festively recited the great Babylonian Creation Epic, called *Enuma elish* because of its opening words. This epic praises Marduk as the victor over the chaotic powers of the deep in the battle of creation, and as the creator of the world and of men.[19] For the Assyrians[20] the god, Ashur, stood at the head of the gods, as the national god of the kingdom of Assyria. He had his great ancient cultic abode in the city of Asshur, the ancient Assyrian royal city. As Ashur's name indicates, he was likely the ancient tribal or ethnic god of the Assyrians. One can only ask whether in this case the divine name or the ethnic name was primary. The god Ashur mounted ever higher in importance with the historical growth of Assyrian might. The great rulers and conquerors on the Assyrian throne described themselves as called and installed by him, and ascribed their many victories to his superior might. What Marduk was to the Babylonians, Ashur was to the Assyrians. Thus a coronation festival was celebrated for Ashur, too, on the analogy of the Babylonian celebration, at least in the Neo-Assyrian period. In Ashur, too, this took place in a New Year's Festival House, situated outside the city. There was a variety of significant and distinguished cults of various gods at specific great cultic centres in Mesopotamia in addition to these official cults. Nabu's temple was at Borsippa, south of Babylon, which is Birs Nimrūd. He was worshipped particularly as the god of the art of writing and of learning. His name is mentioned in Isa. 46 : 1 in the form Nebo. Sippar, which is now Abu Habba of Babylon, was the headquarters of the cult of the sun god with the Semitic name Shamash. The moon god, Sin, once had his most important temples in the ancient Sumerian city of Ur, near

[19] Translation in *ANET*, pp. 60–72; in I. Mendelsohn, *op. cit.*, pp. 17–46; in German, in *AOT*, pp. 108–29.

[20] Cf. H. Hirsch, "Untersuchungen zur altassyrischen Religion," *AfO*, Suppl. 13–14 (1961).

to the original mouth of the Euphrates (see p. 264) and later in the city of Haran, mentioned in the Old Testament, located in western Mesopotamia on the Nahr Belīkh. Ishtar, the great goddess of motherhood and of love, was known on the basis of important centres of her cult as Ishtar of Arbailu, in the region east of the Tigris and as Ishtar of Nineveh across from Mōsul. The god Dagan had an important cultic centre in Terqa, now Tell ʿAshārah on the Middle Euphrates above Mari.

Divination and sorcery played a very substantial role in Mesopotamia in all periods. Divination had a highly developed system of omens behind it. Whole series of such omen texts have been found. Hepatoscopy, or inspection of livers, was very common, obtained by deducing omens from given observations of the liver of newly slaughtered animals. Priests of a given kind, called *bārū*, "seers," were particularly expert in the technique of divination. Sorcery was practised with incantation formulas, which were provided for all possible cases of adversity and illness. It was again an important priestly function to know these incantation formulas exactly and to apply them properly. Divination and sorcery were particularly important for daily life in Mesopotamia, since people lived in constant fear of malevolent powers, of dangerous spirits, and of demons.

(3) *Syro-Palestine*

The picture of the history of religions in ancient Syro-Palestine is very chequered. The sources of this history are very scattered, varied, and of varying antiquity. Particularly W. W. Graf Baudissin[21] formerly devoted a number of detailed studies to this multiform phenomenon, such as the book about Adonis and Eshmun, referred to on p. 280. Since then, the alphabetic cuneiform texts of Rās Shamrah (pp. 212–13) have come to light, which can scarcely be valued too highly. They represent not only the oldest documentary material worthy of mention on the history of religion from Syro-Palestine, in the copies found dating from the beginning of the fourteenth century B.C., but they are, in fact, the only extensive direct evidence of Canaanite religion from before the Hellenistic period, which consists of connected, specifically religious texts. On this basis "Canaanite" can mean the entire Bronze Age world of Syro-Palestine which continued to have a strong influence on into

[21] For a comprehensive study with quotation of a very abundant literature, see Baudissin, *Kyrios*, edited by O. Eissfeldt, Vol. III (1929).

the Iron Age. The great importance of this amazing find lies in the fact that it has offered us first-hand sources for the area in the history of religions within which the Old Testament later arose. These texts, which are written in a script at first unknown (pp. 216–17) and in a particular dialect of Canaanite, now known as Ugaritic, were very quickly deciphered after they were discovered. Yet the interpretation of them, as to language and content, is still extremely problematical, in spite of all of the research already devoted to them. It is not even clear yet with what to connect these apparently rhythmical texts. On the whole these narratives have mythical contents. Still, it has not yet been clarified how they were related with Ugaritic cultic practice, even though this relation must be definitely assumed. Are these passages for festive recital at cultic festivals? Or are they cultic dramas which were presented on given occasions by different players? In line with this we do not yet have a satisfactory historical overview of the religious materials derived from Rās Shamrah, describing its significance in relation to the Canaanite religion of Syro-Palestine.[22] Supreme in the Ugaritic pantheon is El (simply meaning God). He remains in the background in our texts.[23] In the foreground is Baal,[24] perhaps at the expense of the more ancient El. As the provider of fertility and blessing he fits among the embodiments of natural life-giving and life-threatening powers. His antagonist is Mot (*mt*, or Mot, was Death). In battle with Mot a drama unfolds of the death and resurrection of Baal, representing the dwindling and return of vegetation. Additional divine figures at Ugarit are "River" and "Sea," the goddesses Asherah and ʿAnat. The sun and moon and dawn are cosmic deities, as well as others. The great mountain north of Ugarit, now called Mount el-aqraʿ, was regarded as a divine dwelling place, the home of Baal Zaphon (*bʿl ṣpn*). One could assume that all of this gives us a typical picture of cultic life in a Bronze Age Syro-Palestinian city-state.

There were also many local cultic centres in Syro-Palestine. The great urban communities, such as the Phoenician coastal cities, had their particular city gods. In Tyre they worshipped the god, Melcart (mlqrt), meaning the "king of the city," whose name appears in an inscription for the first time on the recently discovered stela

[22] A preliminary study is J. Gray, "The Legacy of Canaan, the Ras Shamra Texts and their Relevance to the Old Testament," *VT*, Suppl. V (1957).

[23] O. Eissfeldt, "El im ugaritischen Pantheon," *Ber. üb. d. Verh. d. Sächs. Ak. d. Wiss. zu Leipzig, phil.-hist. Kl.*, Vol. XCIX, No. 4 (1951); A. S. Kappelrud, *Baal in the Ras Shamra Texts* (1952); M. H. Pope, "El in the Ugaritic Texts," *VT*, Suppl. II (1955).

[24] A. S. Kappelrud, *op. cit.*

of Benhadad I (p. 219). Byblos had a female city deity, repeatedly called *bʿlt gbl*, the "lady of Gebal, or Byblos" in inscriptions. In Ugarit the excavations have disclosed a Baal temple and a Dagon temple. There were temples of the god Dagon in Ashdod and Gaza according to Judg. 16 : 23 and I Sam. 5 : 2 ff. The Philistines certainly borrowed their Dagon cult from older Canaanite tradition. This god Dagon is certainly identical with *Dagan* from the middle Euphrates (p. 293), who was originally brought to Syro-Palestine by immigrants. This situation might serve as one of many examples of how the numerous population elements which settled down in time in Syro-Palestine introduced their gods in the urban and local sanctuaries of the country. Syro-Palestine was predestined by its situation and function as a thoroughfare to become an area of a multiple syncretism in its religious development. In the period of Egyptian supremacy in the Late Bronze Age the official Egyptian cult made inroads in Syro-Palestine, as Egyptian temples were built and cults of Egyptian gods were introduced at the centres of Egyptian government.[25] Yet the rather foreign Egyptian religion does not seem to have left any very substantial signs in the history of religion in Syro-Palestine, over and beyond the period of its official role.[26]

(4) *Hittite, Hurrian, and Persian Religion*

Hittite texts, such as lists of gods, rituals, descriptions of statues of gods, and prayers, as well as random archeological finds in Asia Minor, provide some light on the religion of the Hittites of Asia Minor.[27] They seem to have had a goddess at the centre of their state religion, the "sun goddess of the city of Arinna," who was the highest national deity. In addition to her, a weather god was also worshipped in the capital. So far we do not know the name of either one.

A weather god, Teshub, and his consort, the goddess Hepa, seem to have been the most important deities among the Hurrians. Very few details are known on this subject. The Indo-Iranian elements among the Hurrians (pp. 241–42) had brought some deities with them. At any rate, Indo-Iranian deities, such as Indra and

[25] A. Alt, *ZDPV*, LXVII (1944–45), 1 ff. [reprinted in *KS*, Vol. I, 216 ff.].

[26] In connection with this and the following section, one should note the comprehensive presentation of R. Dussaud, *Les religions des Hittites et des Hourrites, des Phéniciens et des Syriens*, in the collection "Mana," 1, *op. cit.*, II, 331–414.

[27] A. Goetze, *Kleinasien*, *Kulturgeschichte des alten Orients*, *III*, I (2nd ed., 1957), 130–71; source materials in *ANET* and *ANEP*.

Varuna, occur among the divine treaty guarantors in the state treaties between the Hittite Kingdom and the state of Mitanni, found in the archive from Boghazköy. Apparently, therefore, they were deities worshipped in the Mitanni state.

The religions of the Hittites and the Hurrians did not play a substantial role in the immediate environment of the Old Testament. On the other hand, the religion of the Persians became significant for the Old Testament at one stage in history. Ancient Iran at first had simple shepherd and farmer cults.[28] Zarathustra lived among them, though just when is not quite clear. His ethical, eschatological faith led to the establishment of a very vigorous original religion based on a marked dualism of "good" and "evil." It is frequently assumed that the first great Achaemenid kings of the sixth and fifth centuries B.C. were already Zarathustrians. That is still not definite. Previously it was a rather common assumption that Zarathustrian Persian religion and its world view had strongly influenced the Old Testament in the post-exilic period. This assumption has found only limited support and is even more questionable for the post-canonical period of Judaism. Yet in another respect Persia was certainly important for post-exilic Israel in the religious-cultic respect. The previous oriental empires had required acknowledgment of their national gods from their subject and dependent peoples and had forced the cults of these gods on all their subjects (II Kings 16 : 10–16), even though this did not imply suppression of the indigenous cults. On the other hand, the Persian Kingdom did not force on the conquered peoples an official national cult, the cult of the ancient Iranian god, Ahuramazda, worshipped by the Achaemenids as their supreme lord, who also was pre-eminent in the religion of Zarathustra. The Persian Kingdom not only tolerated the native cults, but even furthered them and where necessary re-established them. This basic policy of cultic support, which was also to the advantage of the post-exilic reconstruction of the cult of Jerusalem, then remained customary in the empire of Alexander and in the Hellenistic states. Even worship of rulers, which continued to increase in importance, was limited at least in principle to voluntary and spontaneous recognition by religious communities in these states. The interference of the Seleucid, Antiochus IV, Epiphanes, with the Jerusalem cult in December, 168 B.C., led to the plundering of the temple, to the introduction of a new cult in this very temple in place of the

[28] These are excellently presented in H. S. Nyberg, "Die Religionen des alten Iran," *MVÄG*, Vol. XLIII (1938).

traditional cult, and to suppression of the particular religious and ritual practices of the Jerusalem cultic community, bringing on the Maccabean revolt. Yet, even this interference came about with the understanding of groups in Jerusalem and was rather an act of despotic caprice than an expression of basic religious policy.

PART FOUR

THE TEXT OF THE OLD TESTAMENT

Preliminary Remarks

THE text of a sacred scripture comes to us as the result of a historical process. This textual history is part of the history of the use and influence of the scripture involved. The textual history unfolds within the life of the religion or church which uses that scripture. In this textual process there are always two distinct concerns of varying importance. The first concern is contemporary, namely, that textual clarification shall give answers to the pressing religious questions of the day and establish and confirm important items of faith. The second concern is basic to all religious communities which depend on sacred scripture, namely, to maintain the correct, original content and meaning of the scripture, and to understand it constantly in this original form, so that modern faith is warranted by the basis of that faith found in the scripture. As a result of the first concern, concepts of past ages are understood in a new or altered light, even to the point that occasionally a new wording creeps into the transmitted text. As a result of the second, there is interest in guarding the traditional wording faithfully and understanding it properly, a process which, whether conscious or not, whether partial or far-reaching, is always a kind of "learned" work on the transmitted text.

It is natural that both concerns develop, particularly when translation of a sacred scripture into another language is involved. For no translation, whether into a language closely related or into one totally unrelated, can simply mechanically translate the original text, because no language consists solely of words. Rather, language always has a progressively developing distinctive character. Thus every translation is necessarily, to a certain extent, a transfer of the original text into the spirit of the world and age of the translator. On the other hand, it will always have the intent to convey the contents of the original as faithfully as possible in its new linguistic form; therefore, for its part it will be a scholarly undertaking.

These general considerations apply also to the textual transmission of the Old Testament. One can certainly say that in so far as we are able to survey and reconstruct its textual history, there has stood constantly in the foreground the interest in true and exact maintenance of the transmitted wording and, in the case of translations, in the conscientious reproduction of the original text, since its content constitutes God's revelation in history. Yet one should not overlook the fact that the transmission of the Old Testament text is a historical process which has been closely related to developments in church history and the history of religions, that in particular the important events in the textual history were all essentially related to such developments. One can, therefore, treat the textual history of the Old Testament realistically only within the framework of church history and the history of religions; one must also always have these relationships in mind when considering individual textual problems, in order to be able to make realistic judgments. Thus, in what follows, particular attention will be directed to these relationships.

The Old Testament is sacred scripture for Judaism and Christianity. Therefore, it has had a textual history within the synagogue, including the Samaritan community, and within the Christian church with its various confessions. This history extends down to the present day and will continue. Of course, here we are observing textual history not for its own sake, but in order to extract from a knowledge of that history the criteria for a method in textual criticism. Therefore it is necessary to pursue the textual history only to that point where the different textual witnesses have assumed a definite and fixed form, attested to us in a host of extant manuscripts, beyond which the further textual history is no longer a problem.[1]

[1] On the textual history of the Old Testament, see R. Kittel, *Über die Notwendigkeit und Möglichkeit einer neuen Ausgabe der Hebräischen Bibel* (1902). For a noteworthy treatment, including recent materials, see E. Würthwein, *Der Text des Alten Testaments* (1952) [translated into English by Peter Ackroyd as *The Text of the Old Testament* (Oxford: Blackwell, 1957)]. It is an introduction to the use of Rudolf Kittel's *Biblia Hebraica*. It has forty plates, most of them specimens of manuscripts. Another valuable work is Bleddyn J. Roberts, *The Old Testament Texts and Versions* (Naperville, Ill.: Allenson, 1951). Then there are the introductions to the Old Testament, complete, including detailed studies, such as C. Steuernagel, *Lehrbuch der Einleitung in das Alte Testament* (1912) pp. 19–85; Robert H. Pfeiffer, *Introduction to the Old Testament* (rev. ed.; New York: Harper; London: Black, 1948), pp. 71–126; O. Eissfeldt, *Einleitung in das Alte Testament* (2nd ed., 1956), pp. 823–75. A readily understood introduction, which also includes the textual history of the New Testament, is available in the book of O. Paret, *Die Bibel, ihre Überlieferung in Druck und Schrift* (2nd ed., n.d.), which is particularly valuable because of its very numerous illustrations of manuscripts.

CHAPTER I

THE TRANSMISSION OF THE TEXT IN THE SYNAGOGUE

40. *The Transmission of the Hebrew Text*

(1) *The Masoretic Text*

THE Hebrew text of the Old Testament, in the form in which we now read it in our printed editions with vowels and accents, dates only from the ninth and tenth centuries A.D.[1] The oldest complete manuscripts of the Hebrew Old Testament which we have date from the same time. It is the Masoretic text, called *masorah* in Hebrew, meaning "tradition." This is the text as it was most carefully fixed at that time at Tiberias in Galilee, one of the centres of Synagogal textual learning. Naturally, this Masoretic text (designated in *BH* by 𝔐) had a prehistory and historical parallels which will be described below and which have been considerably illuminated in recent decades, particularly by the discoveries and researches of Kahle[2] and by the recent discovery of manuscripts. Apart from numerous Hebrew manuscripts in the libraries of Europe and America, such as those in the public library at Leningrad which Kahle has studied, it is manuscripts found over a half-century ago in the *genizah* (a "chamber" where unusable scriptural texts were hidden instead of being destroyed) of the synagogue of Old Cairo, as also the recent finds of manuscripts in caves at the northwestern edge of the Dead Sea which, because of the great antiquity of the material which has come to light, have provided valuable documents on the pre-Masoretic history of the Old Testament text.

First of all, it is advisable to observe more closely the fixed and well-known Masoretic text as a whole. From the end of the eighth to the beginning of the tenth century A.D.,[3] there were two learned

[1] Basic to this entire chapter is *Biblia Hebraica*, edited by Rudolf Kittel with A. Alt, O. Eissfeldt, *et al.* (3rd ed., 1937). It is abbreviated *BH* here. A new edition is now in preparation.

[2] P. Kahle, "Masoreten des Ostens," *BWAT*, XV (1913); "Masoreten des Westens, I, *BWAT*, II, 8 (1927) and . . . II," *BWANT*, III, 14 (1930); *The Cairo Geniza* (2nd ed., 1959).

[3] Kahle, "Masoreten des Westens, I," *op. cit.*, p. 39.

families in Tiberias, Ben Asher and Ben Naphtali. They began with the received consonantal text and the traditional reading of that text. They worked for several generations on the final fixing of the text, including its vocalization and clarity. This work is closely related to the rise of the Jewish sect of the Karaites in the eighth century A.D. They originated in Babylonia, increased greatly in Asia Minor, and then also in eastern Europe. Remnants of them still exist today.[4] The name Karaites is derived from Hebrew *Qara'im*, meaning "adherents of the Scriptures." This group rejected rabbinic-talmudic tradition and scriptural interpretation. As authority they accepted only literal interpretation of the sacred Scripture itself. Therefore, they had a special interest in establishing the exact wording of the text. This concern proceeded to affect the adherents of the rabbinic-talmudic tradition, the rabbinists (from the Hebrew, *rabbanim*), so that among them, too, work on the biblical text received new impetus and led to the fixing of the Masoretic text. The families of Ben Asher and Ben Naphtali were probably not Karaites but rather rabbinists.

The Ben Asher and Ben Naphtali schools then fixed the reading and consequently the meaning of the traditional consonantal text, with the help of a detailed system of vowel signs and accents, developed *ad hoc*, which has long been called the "Tiberian" system. It established too the consonantal text itself, by means of a host of notations. By means of short marginal notes parallel with the text (*Masora parva; BH: Mp*), they draw attention to all of the conspicuous and noteworthy phenomena of the text, including *Ketib* and *Qere*, singular or rare words and forms.[5] They wrote down longer commentaries (*Masora magna; BH: Mm* or *Mas. M*) partly in the margins surrounding the text (Plate II), called the *Masora marginalis* (enumerations of noteworthy forms, etc.), and partly at the end of the books, called the *Masora finalis*, giving statements on the number of consonants and sentences of a book. The Masoretes have also enumerated certain critical notes on the transmitted consonantal text. On dogmatic grounds they have at times insisted on a "corrected" consonantal textual basis for the *reading*, as over against the transmitted consonantal text which was itself not modified, but handed on unchanged. Such cases are called *tiqqun sopherim* (abbreviated *Tiq Soph* in *BH*), meaning "a correction of the scribal scholars" (cf., e.g., Gen. 18 : 22). At

[4] V. Ryssel, *RE*, X (1901), 54–70. [See also *Karaites* in Schaff-Herzog Encyclopedia.]
[5] In the third edition of *BH*, the marginal Masora is set down beside the text. A ist of the abbreviations used in the marginal Masora is given in *BH*, pp. xxxiv–xxxix.

times, by inserting so-called *puncta extraordinaria* (Hebrew, *niqqudot*) over a word or a part of a word, they apparently expressed a doubt about the correct transmission of the consonants of the word (see Gen. 16 : 5, 18 : 9, etc.). Under the catchword *sebir* (*BH: seb*), meaning "what would be expected," they have occasionally noted in connection with a transmitted word that, even though it has not been changed to another word, it still should be understood as the other word (cf., e.g., Gen. 49 : 13).[6]

A treatise of a certain Mishael ben Uzziel,[7] probably drafted in the tenth century A.D., tells us about the differences in the details of the work of the Ben Asher family and the Ben Naphtali family. These differences are minute in nature and are almost entirely negligible for the understanding of the text. Among other things they deal with the system of placement of *methegh*. Yet on the basis of that treatise it is possible to classify the Tiberian pointed manuscripts which we have received. It has been demonstrated on that basis that in the later Middle Ages a *textus receptus* was developed which joined various individual features of the Ben Naphtali textual treatment (e.g., in the placement of *methegh*), to the basic Ben Asher textual treatment. Therefore, it was a composite text. This composite text was published in the printed editions of the Hebrew Old Testament beginning with the fifteenth century and continuing until recent years. Even the first two editions of the *Biblia Hebraica* use this composite text, because their text is based on the edition of the Venetian printer Daniel Bomberg printed in 1524–25 (called 𝔅 in all editions of *BH*), which reproduces the work of Jacob ben Hayyim.

The pure text of the Ben Asher family was traced by Kahle and is now provided in the third edition of the *Biblia Hebraica*, published in 1937. About A.D. 1200, the great authority of Maimonides[8] was largely responsible for the establishment of this text as the authoritative Hebrew biblical text for synagogue use. On the whole this text is also the basis of the later *textus receptus*. This text was attested by Kahle and produced in the third edition of *BH*. Kahle himself collaborated in the work in *BH* on the Masoretic text. The Ben Asher text survived, particularly in the

[6] The Masoretic material on the textual notations from manuscripts known in his time was collected by C. D. Ginsburg, *The Massorah Compiled from Manuscripts*, Vols. I–V (1880–1905). Note also the summary by Ginsburg, *Introduction to the Massoretico-critical Edition of the Hebrew Bible* (1897).

[7] Cf. Kahle, "Masoreten des Westens," *op. cit.*, II, pp. 60 ff.; *BH*, pp. vi–viii.

[8] On Maimonides, in German see *RE*, XII (1903), 80–84 or *RGG* (3rd ed., 1960), Cols. 611–12. [In English, see Schaff-Herzog Encyclopedia.]

famous model codex,[9] preserved until recently in the synagogue of the Sephardim (western Jews) in Aleppo in North Syria. It is now preserved in Israeli Jerusalem.[10] Its colophon, or final statement, was copied, translated, and commented on in Kahle, "Masoreten des Westens."[11] This colophon indicated that it was written as a consonantal text in the beginning of the tenth century by a well-known scribe and that shortly thereafter it was pointed and provided with the Masorah by the last famous member of the family of Ben Asher himself, by Aaron ben Mosheh ben Asher. Concerning its later fortunes, see Kahle.[12] In the middle of the eleventh century it was owned by the Karaite synagogue of Jerusalem, then by the Karaite synagogue in Cairo, and finally reached Aleppo.

There is a model codex of the prophets [Former and Latter] now located in the Karaite synagogue of Cairo. According to its colophon (translated by Kahle)[13] it was written by Mosheh ben Asher himself in A.D. 895. He was the father of Aaron, who was referred to above. It represents a somewhat earlier stage in the Masoretic work of the Ben Asher family than the Codex of Aleppo (cited in *BH* under *siglum* C, for *cairensis*). Furthermore, there is a London Pentateuch codex (Ms Or 4445), which repeatedly cites Aaron ben Asher in marginal notes, apparently as still living.[14]

Other manuscripts of the tenth century to the twelfth century provide the genuine text of the Ben Asher family, as is shown by comparison with the model codices. In this group Manuscript B 19A of the public library of Leningrad, written in A.D. 1008, is particularly important, because it contains not a part, but the entire Old Testament, and because, according to its colophon,[15] it was prepared in Cairo from model codices of Aaron ben Mosheh ben Asher. Since the model codex of Aleppo was inaccessible,[16] this manuscript, cited with the *siglum* L, for Leningradensis, was used as the basis of the new [third] edition of Kittel's *Biblia Hebraica*.

The Masoretic work also occupied itself with the division of

[9] In previous times there were other model codices of this type. One of them was *Codex Hillel* (*BH: Hill* or *MS Hill*). Written about A.D. 600, it was repeatedly cited later by scholars, though it has not survived. Another was the *Codex Severi Hebraicus* (*BH: Sev*).

[10] [*IEJ*, XI (1961), 86 reports that it survived the fire of the Synagogue of Aleppo of 1947 almost intact.]

[11] Kahle, *op. cit.*, I, 1 ff.

[12] *Ibid.*, pp. 7 ff.

[13] *Ibid.*, pp. 15–16.

[14] *Ibid.*, pp. 17–18.

[15] *Ibid.*, pp. 66–67.

[16] *IEJ*, XI (1961), 86 says it is preserved almost intact. Cf. *BH*, p. vi. This codex is now being studied at the Hebrew University for the new Hebrew Bible in the process of publication there.

the Books of the Old Testament. The Talmudic period was already acquainted with the division of the text into sentences (verses), even though there was no universally accepted plan. In the Masoretic texts verse division is fixed by the accent system, even apart from the double point (*soph pasuq*), "end of the verse"), as a verse separator, which not all of the manuscripts have (L has it) The numbering of the verses did not come into use until the sixteenth century in printed editions, together with chapter headings (see below).

The division of the text into connected sections for synagogal reading of the text considerably antedated the Masoretic work. (At this point I mention only the things that occur in *BH*, therefore in L.) For this purpose in Palestine they first of all divided the Pentateuch into a series of *Sedharim*. The singular is *Sedher*, meaning Order or Sequence. Subsequently they also extended this division to the remaining parts of the Old Testament. In L the beginnings of the *sedharim* are marked by ס̇ (s) placed at the margin and numbered in sequence in individual books (Joshua, Judges, Psalms—this *sedharim* division has no relationship to the division of Psalms into the traditional five books, of which L, moreover, does not take account—Job, Proverbs, Daniel, Ezra-Nehemiah, Chronicles). In Babylonia instead of these they used a division of the Pentateuch into *parashoth* (*parashah* means section), which are usually longer than the Sedarim and which were later adopted in Palestine, too. In L the beginnings of these *parashoth* are indicated by פרש (*prš*) placed in the margin.

Even apart from the requirements of liturgical reading, the text was divided into paragraphs, except in the Psalms which were already sufficiently divided. These divisions were likewise called *parashoth* and were in use already at the time of the Mishna. Larger divisions were indicated by beginning a new line, smaller ones by leaving a blank space in the line.[17] Later on, instead of this they simply left a small blank space and in it inserted פ (meaning *petuḥa* or "open" [section]) for larger divisions, or ס (meaning *setuma*, or "closed" [section]) for smaller divisions. It is also this way in L.[18]

The Masoretic text knew nothing about our divisions into chapters. It was borrowed from the Christian Vulgate only in the

[17] This is also the case in the recently discovered Isaiah scroll from Qumran (see below).

[18] Arrangement of poetic texts by rows was already recognized in the manuscripts of the Talmudic period. Yet the format of the poetic portions in *BH* comes from the hand of the compilers, not from traditional usage.

fourteenth century A.D. With this then came the division of the Books of Samuel, Kings, and Chronicles into two parts. The same tendencies later brought the assignment of numbers to the verses.

(2) *Prehistory of the Masoretic Text* (*Palestinian and Babylonian Pointing*)

There was a long prehistory to our Masoretic text.[19] Generally speaking, we do well to assume that the consonantal text which we now read was already fixed in its final form about A.D. 100. From then on it was recopied with meticulous accuracy. Biblical quotations in rabbinic literature already presuppose this text. The same applies to some of the translations which were made in the second century A.D. (pp. 322–23). Naturally that does not mean that slightly divergent text forms did not continue in use and were not recopied. Indeed as late as the twelfth century A.D. a scholastic living in England, named Odo, seems to have known a Hebrew text of the Old Testament, which exhibited not only a pre-Masoretic vocalization system, but also a divergent consonantal text from the Masoretic text.[20] Yet such cases are apparently side shoots independent of the actual line of textual transmission.

The prehistory of the Masoretic text deals particularly with the pointing. The researches of Kahle have shown that the success of the textual edition of the Ben Asher family was only their victory over various other available systems. Even the textual edition of the Ben Naphtali family was crowded out by Ben Asher, though both were very closely related, contemporary, and even from the same city of Tiberias. Of course, Ben Naphtali[21] on its part was recopied for a considerable period and later penetrated into the *textus receptus* in various points (p. 305).

The Tiberian pointing system, used by both of these textual editions, was just the substitute for an older, less complete, supralinear pointing system, in which all of the signs which indicate the vowels are placed over the consonants. This system may be observed in a number of manuscripts of the sixth to the ninth century A.D., which include partly fragments of biblical texts,

[19] On new manuscript finds of this order see A. Diez Macho, *VT*, Suppl. IV (1957), pp. 27–46. [20] Cited in *BH* as *V(ar)*. Cf. J. Fischer, *BZAW*, LXVI (1936), 198–206.

[21] On the peculiarities of the Ben Naphtali text and the remaining manuscripts which provide its text, including the *Codex Reuchlinianus*, a codex of the Prophets, written in A.D. 1105, and now in Karlsruhe, see Kahle, "Masoreten des Westens," II, *op. cit.*, 45*–68*. The (once existent) Erfurt manuscripts, of which three are cited in *BH* as $Var^{E\ 1,2,3}$, are among the Ben Naphtali manuscripts leading up to the *textus receptus*. Details are in Kahle, *op. cit.*, pp. 54*–56* and Plate XIII.

partly biblical portions written according to a certain abbreviation system, and partly liturgical texts.[22] Even the Palestinian Pentateuch targum[23] is still frequently available in manuscripts with this "Palestinian" pointing.[24] The supralinear Palestinian pointing system was related to the Samaritan pointing system which seems to have originated in the fifth century A.D. in dependence on the pointing of Syriac texts appearing at that time.[25] This Palestinian system was still incomplete in its designation of vowels. Therefore, it was later replaced by the Tiberian system, fashioned with more mature deliberation. Textual variants from Palestinian pointed manuscripts are cited in *BH* with V(ar)^{pal}.

The victory of the textual edition of the Ben Ashers, including the Tiberian pointing system, signified at the same time the crowding out of the editions of the biblical text, which had been made for centuries in Babylonia, likewise a centre of Jewish settlement and learning in post-Christian days. The Babylonian scribal scholars are called "the Masoretes of the East" (*BH: Or*) in distinction from the Palestinian scholars, or "the Masoretes of the West" (*BH: Occ*). Another supralinear pointing system likely related to the Palestinian one, was in use in Babylonia. It was elaborated and developed in the course of time so that one distinguishes an older "simple" from a later "complicated" Babylonian pointing. In various details the Babylonian pointing requires a somewhat different pronunciation of Hebrew from the Tiberian. For example, it seems to be as unaware of the doubled, explosive, and fricative pronunciations of the six stop consonants *b,g,d,k,p,t* as the early Palestinian system. Rather, it presupposes the simple fricative pronunciation of undoubled *b,g,d,k,p,t.* From this one may conclude that the Tiberian system on the whole follows the orally transmitted pronunciation of Hebrew, though in some details it is probably artificially constructed.

In *Masoreten des Ostens* (1913), Kahle edited and published manuscripts with Babylonian pointing which to a considerable extent come from the previously mentioned *genizah* of the synagogue of Old Cairo. In the periodical *ZAW*, he provided a list of biblical fragments available with Babylonian pointing.[26] An even more complete list appears in *BH*.[27] In his list, Kahle marks

[22] *Ibid.*, I, 23–36, 77–89, 1*–66*, X = כא and Plates I–XVI; *ibid.*, II, 14*–45*, 66–95 and Plates VII–XI.

[23] *Ibid.*, II, 1*–13*, 1–65; Macho, *VT*, Suppl. VII (1960), pp. 222–45.

[24] Kahle, *op. cit.*, II, Plates, I, VI.

[25] *Ibid.*, I, 51 ff.

[26] *ZAW*; New Series, V (1928), 113–37 and Plates I–LXX.

[27] Kittel (ed.), *BH*, pp. xxx–xxxiii.

manuscripts *E* which come from about the seventh century A.D. and have simpler [*einfacher*] pointing. Those from the eighth and ninth centuries with more complicated [*komplizierter*] pointing, he marks *K*. By adding the letter *a*, *b*, or *c* he indicates whether the fragment under consideration comes from the *Torah*, the *Nebhiim*, or the *Kethubhim*, respectively. Thus, the manuscripts are cited in *BH* as Ea 1, etc. Moreover, there were various Masoretic schools in Babylonia, among which were those at Nehardea and Sura. The Masoretes of the latter school (Soraei) are cited in *BH* under *siglum Sor*.

Not only was the Babylonian biblical text crowded out finally by the Western type, so that for about a thousand years it was essentially missing until the finds of most recent decades; but even in the late manuscripts pointed in Babylonian fashion the Tiberian Masoretic system had already penetrated. As a result they remain only partial witnesses to Babylonian textual transmission. For example, this is the case with the famous Petersburg Prophet Codex, written in A.D. 916 and published in a great facsimile edition by H. L. Strack.[28] In *BH* its variants are cited under the *siglum* $V(ar)^{P}$.

The great old collections of variants in the Hebrew biblical text have lost in importance as a result of the recent possibility of penetrating into the prehistory and history of the Masoretic work. For on the whole these collections simply compare late Middle Age manuscripts with the *textus receptus*.[29] The same is true of older editions of the Hebrew text.[30]

(3) *The Consonantal Text*

The consonantal text behind the Masoretic work was probably finally fixed about A.D. 100, probably in the form in which we still read it. The fall of Jerusalem in A.D. 70 terminated the entire temple cult. The rabbinic Synagogue then constituted rallied around the transmitted sacred scriptures, gave them a final, binding form in canon and text, and devoted great care to their preservation. The recently found pre-Masoretic biblical texts, which go back to the sixth century A.D., provide only a few variants from

[28] *Prophetarum posteriorum Codex Babylonicus Petropolitanus* (Petersburg, 1876).

[29] B. Kennicott, *Vetus Testamentum Hebraicum cum variis lectionibus* (1776–88), cited in *BH* as $MS(S)^{Ken}$ or $V(ar)^{Ken}$; G. B. de Rossi, *Variae lectiones Veteris Testamenti* (1784–88).

[30] Cited in *BH* as Var^{B}, $V(ar)^{F}$, $V(ar)^{G}$, $V(ar)^{J}$, $V(ar)^{M}$, $V(ar)^{S}$, and $V(ar)^{W}$. See *BH*, p. xxviii

the consonantal text worth mentioning. Like the abundance of Middle Age Hebrew manuscripts, they revert to the previously fixed consonantal text. Most of the variants are of an orthographic nature and are insignificant formal differences. However, as a matter of course it is likely that the consonantal text fixed about A.D. 100 was not simply identical with the original text. Rather it represented a textual edition behind which lay a long textual transmission with various changes and distortions of the original text.

The manuscripts found in the caves at the Dead Sea provide a glimpse into a portion of the prehistory of the Hebrew consonantal text. In the summer of 1947, large jars with manuscript scrolls were found by Bedouins in a cave near the foot of the cliff near the northwestern end of the Dead Sea, near the ruin site called Khirbet Qumrān. Some of the scrolls then came into the possession of the Syriac cloister of St. Mark in Jerusalem and some into the possession of the Hebrew University in Jerusalem.[31] Four scrolls that came into Syriac hands were transferred to the American Schools of Oriental Research for publication. Three of the four scrolls were published under the title, *The Dead Sea Scrolls of St. Mark's Monastery*, edited by Millar Burrows: Vol. I, *The Isaiah Manuscript and the Habakkuk Commentary* (1950); Vol. II, Part 2, *Plates and Transcription of the Manual of Discipline* (1951). After this part of the find had been sold to the Hebrew University of Jerusalem, the fourth scroll was also partially published by N. Avigad and Y. Yadin as *A Genesis Apocryphon, A Scroll from the Wilderness of Judea* (1956). The three scrolls which initially came into the possession of the Hebrew University at Jerusalem have appeared under the title אוצר המגילות הגנוזות ("Oṣar ham-Megilloth hag-Genuzoth"), edited by E. L. Sukenik (1954).

Subsequent manuscript finds were made in other caves in the same region. Also small manuscript fragments came to light subsequently during the investigation in 1949 of the first cave of finds, "Cave I," which are preserved in the Palestine Archeological Museum in the Jordanian section of Jerusalem. They include fragments from Genesis, Exodus, Leviticus, Numbers, Deuteronomy, Judges, and others.[32] Manuscript finds were also made in some

[31] [A survey of the accounts of this discovery may be found in many sources, among them Frank M. Cross, Jr., *The Ancient Library of Qumrān* (New York: Doubleday, 1958), Chapter I.]

[32] They are published as *Qumrān Cave I, Discoveries in the Judean Desert*, Vol. I (1955), edited by D. Barthélemy and J. T. Milik with contributions by R. de Vaux, G. M. Crowfoot, H. J. Plenderleith, and G. L. Harding and Vol. III (1961), *Les petites grottes de Qumrān*, edited by R. de Vaux, M. Baillet, and J. T. Milik.

further caves in the surrounding Khirbet Qumrān, including some biblical texts, especially from Cave IV and Cave XI, both very close to the ruin Khirbet Qumrān. Only random samples of the texts found there have been published as yet. A preliminary survey of the manuscript fragments found in the caves referred to is found in the periodical *RB*.[33, 34]

There are various names for the manuscripts found. Originally they were called the manuscripts from the Dead Sea, as they still are in some circles. However, this name is general and inaccurate. For a while, especially in the English-language literature, they were strangely named "the manuscripts from 'Ain Feshkhah," for the spring of 'Ain Feshkhah, which is a few miles south of the caves, below the prominent headland of Rās Feshkhah. It is becoming more and more customary to name them after the ruin site of Khirbet Qumrān, in the immediate region of the caves where they were found, on a marl terrace at the foot of the cliff overlooking the shoreline at the northwestern end of the Dead Sea. It is quite proper to do so, for the people of Khirbet Qumrān were apparently the owners of the manuscripts hidden in the neighbouring caves. The following system is becoming customary to designate the individual parts of this great complex of finds. The letter *Q* indicates all of the manuscript find of the region of Khirbet Qumrān. Before the *Q* is given the number of the cave in which the portion in question came to light, and following the *Q* the content of the manuscript in question is designated with a *siglum* (mark of identification). Several manuscripts from the same cave with the same content are distinguished from one another by small index letters. For example *1QIsa*[a] means the manuscript of the Book of Isaiah found in the first cave in the surroundings of Khirbet Qumrān, which is the first of the two manuscripts of Isaiah (*a* and *b*) from this cave. The designation *1QpHab* means the manuscript found in the first cave of Khirbet Qumrān of the so-called "Habakkuk Commentary," in Hebrew *pesher Habaqqūq*

[33] *RB*, LXIII (1956), 49–67.

[34] In the winter of 1951–52 there was another fortunate manuscript find in an almost inaccessible cave at the edge of steep Wādi Murabba'āt, about 18 km. [11 miles] southsouthwest of Khirbet Qumrān and about 25 km. [15 miles] southeast of Jerusalem, not far from the west coast of the Dead Sea. There is no direct historical connection between the Murabba'āt scrolls and those from Qumrān. However, fragments of biblical texts were found at Murabba'āt, too, dating to the first half of the second century A.D. Represented are the Pentateuch and Isaiah, but especially extensive fragments of a manuscript of the minor prophets. They were published by P. Benoît, J. T. Milik, and R. de Vaux, with contributions from G. M. Crowfoot, E. Crowfoot, and A. Grohmann, as *Discoveries in the Judean Desert*, Vol. II (1961), *Les grottes de Murabba'āt, Texte et Planches*.

("interpretation of Habakkuk"). The designation *4QSam*[b] refers to the Samuel manuscript (mentioned above because of its antiquity) which was discovered in the fourth cave of Khirbet Qumrān and which was the second of two Samuel manuscripts discovered at the same spot. The individual passages of the manuscripts are then exactly designated by their column in Roman numerals and their line in Arabic numerals.[35]

The manuscript find from Qumrān is important from various viewpoints. It has already produced a phenomenal scholarly literature. Some of the more important general works are cited here.[36] The manuscripts from Qumrān were part of the library of a sectarian Jewish group which had its foundation at Khirbet Qumrān and which in all probability if not identical with the Essenes referred to by Josephus, Pliny the Elder, and Philo of Alexandria, were then at least closely related to them. This library contained copies of the text of Old Testament books, such as the two great Isaiah manuscripts from Cave I, the one complete, the other no longer complete, and copies of non-biblical literary works, which were religious writings of special interest to the group. The commentaries on Old Testament books occupy a mid-position. In these the text of the given Old Testament book is cited in short passages. Following each there is a paragraph of explanation, *pesher*. The best example is the Habakkuk Commentary on Habakkuk I and II from Cave I. These are almost exclusively parchment manuscripts, made of treated leather strips, sewn together. Only a few papyri have been found. The parchment manuscripts were copied in adjoining columns and rolled together in scrolls. Most of the non-biblical writings are also composed in the Hebrew language. Only a few are in Aramaic. Most of the manuscripts are written in Hebrew square letters (see p. 221). Only a little of the writing, such as the small fragments of manuscripts of the Books of Leviticus and Numbers from Cave I, is written in a type of Old Hebrew script, which reminds one of the ostraca of Lachish (see p. 220).

There has been considerable debate on the question of the date of the Qumrān manuscripts. Distinctions in style of the script

[35] The texts from the cave in Wādi Murabba'āt are cited with the *siglum* Mur. Mur 88 is the manuscript of the minor prophets referred to above.

[36] Millar Burrows, *The Dead Sea Scrolls* (New York: Viking, 1955) and *More Light on the Dead Sea Scrolls* (New York: Viking, 1958); Cross, *The Ancient Library of Qumrān and Modern Biblical Studies* (New York: Doubleday, 1961); A. Dupont-Sommer, *Les écrits esséniens découverts près de la mer Morte* (1959) [available in English as *The Essene Writings from Qumrān*, trans. G. Vermes (Oxford: Blackwell, 1962)]; H. Bardtke, *Die Handschriftenfunde am Toten Meer* (1952, 1958).

show that not all of the manuscripts are contemporary. Still, all of them can apparently be fitted within approximate time limits. Quite properly there was an immediate effort to date the manuscripts paleographically, even though there is a scarcity of comparative datable material. In the initial attempts at dating the Nash Papyrus, published years ago and now located at Cambridge,[37] played a role. W. F. Albright had dated it as probably from the second half of the second century B.C. in a thoroughgoing study.[38] The script of the Nash Papyrus proved to be very close to that of the Qumrān manuscripts. Then the beginning of the Jewish Revolt of A.D. 66 to A.D. 70 was accepted as almost certainly the *terminus ad quem* for the manuscripts, though with some dispute. The jars of Cave I in which some of the manuscripts were found had their counterparts in some found in the ruins of Khirbet Qumrān. The excavations of Khirbet Qumrān (see p. 135) have also shown that the level of the ruins under consideration was settled only to the beginning of the Jewish Revolt. It is altogether probable that the people of Khirbet Qumrān, members of that Essene sect, hid the treasures of their library before the chaos of the revolt. However, we must still answer the question as to how old the individual manuscripts were when they were hidden in the caves. Drawing up even a relative chronology for the various manuscripts and manuscript fragments depends on many difficult individual observations. Therefore, it is rather difficult, occasionally involving not a unilinear development, but rather a coexistence of particular manuscript types,[39] for example, formal book style characters, or more or less cursive characters. Attention must be given also to the coexistence of Hebrew-Aramaic square characters and Old Hebrew characters. It is not self-evident that manuscripts written in the latter script must be considered old. The possibility must always be considered that the Torah (Pentateuch) continued to be copied in the Old Hebrew characters while normally the Hebrew-Aramaic square characters were in general use. In some manuscripts otherwise written in Hebrew square letters the name of God, *yhwh*, or the word God appears in old Hebrew characters. Among the manuscripts written in square characters, one fragmentary manuscript of the Books of Samuel seems to be particularly old. It is the First Book of Samuel from Cave IV, which F. M. Cross, Jr., dates to

[37] First published by S. A. Cook in *PSBA*, XXV (1905), 34–56.

[38] *JBL*, LVI (1937), 145–76.

[39] For a complete discussion, see Cross, "*The Bible and the Near East,*" in *Essays in Honor of William Foxwell Albright* (1961), pp. 133–202.

the last quarter of the third century B.C.[40] Also old is the likewise fragmentary Jeremiah manuscript from Cave IV, which seems to be only slightly more recent and which Cross ascribes to about 200 B.C. If that is correct, the Qumrān manuscripts probably were written over a time span of more than two centuries.

In this connection the copies of Old Testament books are interesting, as are the commentaries, since these also literally cite the Old Testament text under discussion. They represent Old Testament texts which are many centuries older than any previously known manuscripts containing Hebrew Old Testament textual material. Therefore, the Qumrān manuscripts provide insights into the pre-Masoretic early history of the Old Testament text. They provide a purely consonantal text, still lacking all pointing [for vowels or accents]. They make considerable, if not consistent, use of the *matres lectionis* for the indication of vowels. They still contain elements of an older pre-Masoretic Hebrew. They also interestingly disclose some scribal customs of older copyists of biblical texts, such as word dividers, line composition, paragraphs, and spacing.[41] As far as the wording of the text is concerned, there are fewer variations from the later Masoretic text than one might have expected. Nevertheless, they have numerous variants and thereby introduce one to the stage of the consonantal text before this was definitely fixed about A.D. 100. Occasionally these variants agree with ancient translations of the Old Testament, particularly with the Septuagint. The place of the various Qumrān manuscripts in the pre-Masoretic textual history still requires thorough study.

(4) *The Samaritan Pentateuch*

The Samaritan community centred at Shechem, with its sanctuary on Gerizim (John 4 : 20–21), separated from the Jerusalem cultic community, possibly toward the end of the Persian period. The Samaritans retained the previously canonized Torah (Pentateuch) as a sacred scripture. Therefore, there is a textual transmission of the Hebrew Pentateuch also from within the Samaritan community. The text was edited by von Gall, working from late medieval manuscripts which are located in various libraries of Europe and America.[42] There are still older Pentateuch manuscripts in the possession of the only remaining, sadly shrunken

[40] "The Oldest Manuscript from Qumrān," *JBL*, LXXIV (1955), 147–72.

[41] Thoroughly discussed in M. Martin, *The Scribal Character of the Dead Sea Scrolls*, Vols. I–II (1958).

[42] A. von Gall, *Der Hebräische Pentateuch der Samaritaner* (1914–18).

Samaritan community in Nablus, the successor of ancient Shechem.[43] It has particularly a Pentateuch scroll, well guarded, not exactly datable, but asserted to be older than the Masoretic manuscripts referred to on p. 305.[44] The Samaritan manuscripts are written in a book script[45] independently derived from the old Hebrew alphabet (p. 219). Parallel to this book script there was and is an underlying Samaritan lapidary script, to be seen in the Samaritan stone inscriptions from the Christian era in Palestine and, furthermore, a Samaritan cursive script[46] used for ordinary communication. The Samaritan Pentateuch manuscripts are unvocalized on the whole, have an independently developed punctuation system, and even their own system of *Parashah* division (see pp. 307 ff.).

The several thousand variants which the Samaritan Pentateuch text (*BH siglum:* ࠔ) shows in comparison with the Masoretic text are in great part of an orthographic nature, or they concern details. Actual variants rest in part upon dogmatic corrections. Therefore, there is a remarkably small number of actually important variants for which a source independent from 𝔐 can be assumed. (The figures in Genesis, chapters 5 and 11, are examples of the types of variants to be expected. See the apparatus in *BH*.) Therefore, one must ask whether the pre-Masoretic rabbinic and the Samaritan history of the consonantal text in the Pentateuch truly developed independently, even after the cultic separation of the communities. Hence, the agreement of the two text recensions cannot be assumed without further investigation to trace back to the time before that separation. A certain group of medieval Masoretic manuscripts agrees with the text of *Samaritanus* in many details.[47] This fact could indicate continuing relations from both sides between the textual traditions.

41. *Translations into Other Languages*

(1) *Translations into Aramaic* (*the Targums*)

Aramaic became the official language of the Persian Empire for southwestern Asia. Increasingly, Aramaic also became an exten-

[43] On this community see Kahle, "Die Samaritaner im Jahre 1909," *PJB*, XXVI (1930), 89–103 and J. Jeremias, "Die Passahfeiger der Samaritaner," *BZAW*, Vol. LIX (1932).

[44] Kahle has reported on its history in *BZAW*, XXXIII (1918), 247–60.

[45] Examples in M. Gaster, *The Samaritans*, *The Schweich Lectures 1923* (1925), Plates VII–XIV. See also Goettsberger, *Einleitung*, Plate III, 3.

[46] Examples in Gaster, *op. cit.*, Plates VI, XV.

[47] J. Hempel, *ZAW*, New Series, XI (1934), 254–74, has admirably demonstrated this agreement, using Deuteronomy as an example.

sive colloquial language (see pp. 226–27) spoken by the post-exilic community in Palestine and in great portions of the diaspora. Thus, Hebrew gradually was limited to the role of sacred and learned language. In conformity with these developments it became necessary to render the Hebrew text read in synagogue worship in the generally understood Aramaic language. This rendering, called *targem* in Hebrew-Aramaic, was done by an interpreter, called a [*me*]*turgemān*[*a*] in Hebrew-Aramaic, which has given us our word "dragoman." From this point of view it is understandable that these oral and originally impromptu renderings turned out differently on different occasions. Furthermore, various well-established expressions in the religious language, such as anthropomorphisms in statements about God, were subsequently forbidden out of awe for the Holy. In this oral interpretation these expressions were avoided and replaced by paraphrases. Finally, ancient formulations and names, particularly geographic names, which could not be understood without further explanation, were replaced for clarification by "modern" terms. Furthermore, various clarifying additions were made. Indeed, these interpretations were not supposed to be exact translations in the sense that they made the original text unnecessary. This original text continued to be read as it had been. The interpretation simply made it understandable to all.

Naturally definite fixed traditions for the wording of these interpretations soon grew up. Finally this wording was also fixed in writing. Thus the Aramaic Targums arose. (Hebrew-Aramaic *targūm*[*ā*] means "translation.") Either the Targum was added to the Hebrew original, verse by verse, in the manuscripts used for synagogue reading, or entire manuscripts were prepared for the Aramaic Targum exclusively. It is likely that the Pentateuch Targum was the first to be put in writing in view of the importance of the Torah (Pentateuch) for synagogue reading. Actually the treasures of the *genizah* of the synagogue of Old Cairo (see p. 303) have presented us with remains of an old Palestinian Pentateuch Targum.[48] The remains of manuscripts found there show that it was still in use in the seventh to ninth century A.D. in Palestine. However, it was naturally put in writing centuries earlier (cited in *BH* as $\mathfrak{T}^{P}$). The remnants found come from seven different Targum manuscripts. The double appearance of two Old Testament sections in two of the accidentally found manuscript fragments shows at once that the wordings of the Targum were strikingly divergent

[48] Kahle, "Masoreten des Westens," *op. cit.*, II (1930), 1–65, Plates I–VI.

in the different manuscripts. Recently another version of the Palestinian Pentateuch Targum has been found.[49] The Targum's origin in oral usage easily explains the fact that it became fixed in various forms.

From that standpoint it is also understandable that the Targum continued to develop, as particularly its basic feature of paraphrasing and explaining the original text continued to develop, and this additional material continued to be set in writing. In this sense the so-called *Targum Yerushalmi II*,[50] also called the *Fragment Targum* (*BH*: 𝕿^{II}), is a further development and enlargement of the old Palestinian Pentateuch Targum.

A variety of Targum material on the Prophets and *Kethubim* in the rabbinic tradition is also available. It is of similar origin and type to the Pentateuch Targum just described.[51]

Subsequently, at least the Targums on the Pentateuch and on the prophets were redacted by unifying the more or less spontaneously developed Targumic material. In this redacted form they were declared normative. The official Pentateuch Targum of the later days is customarily called *Targum Onkelos* (*BH*: 𝕿^{O}). This is a questionable name, since it seems to rest only on a misunderstood rabbinic tradition concerning the Greek translator Aquila (see p. 322), reproducing his name in the form Onkelos. The Targum Onkelos comes from the Palestinian Targum tradition, but was edited in the fourth or fifth century A.D. in Babylonia by learned scribes, remaining fixed thereafter. Substantially it presupposes the Hebrew Masoretic text. It later became regarded so highly that it was provided with a Babylonian Masorah, as though itself a sacred text.[52] Although the Targum Onkelos was described as the official Pentateuch Targum, the Old Pentateuch Targum was still used in the seventh to the ninth century A.D. in Palestine. In addition to this, approximately at the same time, the Targum Pseudo-Jonathan was formed in Palestine.[53] It com-

[49] Macho, *VT*, Suppl. VII (1960), pp. 222–45.

[50] M. Ginsburger (ed.), *Das Fragmententargum, Targum jeruschalmi zum Pentateuch* (1899).

[51] A variety of material on the prophets in Babylonian pointing and tradition was published, along with the material on the Pentateuch, in A. Merx, *Chrestomathia Targumica, Porta linguarum orientalium*, Vol. VIII (1888), called 𝕿^{M} in *BH*. Material on individual books is in F. Practorius, *Das Targum zu Josua in jemenischer Überlieferung* (1899) and *Targum zum Buch der Richter in jemenischer Überlieferung* (1900), called 𝕿^{Pr} in *BH*. The material on the *Kethubhim* is in P. de Lagarde, *Hagiographa Chaldaice* (1873), called 𝕿^{L} in *BH*.

[52] A. Berliner (ed.), *Targum Onkelos herausgegeben und erläutert*, Vols I–II (1884).

[53] The name Targum (Pseudo) Jonathan rests on a false interpretation of the abbreviation ת״י which rather means *Targum Yerushalmi*, or Jerusalem Targum.

bined the official Targum Onkelos with the old, traditional native Pentateuch Targum of Palestine. Therefore, this *Targum Yerushalmi I* (Targum Pseudo-Jonathan) translation is particularly rich in explanatory material.[54]

The Targum on the prophets was also redacted. In this official form it was transmitted under the name Targum Jonathan.[55] It was probably established at about the same time as Targum Onkelos. It was regarded as authoritative in Palestine and Babylonia.

The Targum was published in the form customary in the late medieval period (*BH*: $\mathfrak{T}^{B}$) in the Hebrew Bible published by Bomberg at Venice in 1524 and 1525 (see p. 305). The Targums also appeared in assorted forms in the great polyglot editions of the sixteenth and seventeenth centuries. These were multilingual biblical editions which printed the original text paralleled by the various ancient translations in the textual forms then available.[56]

The Samaritans also had a rendering of their Hebrew Pentateuch in Palestinian colloquial Aramaic, which means a Samaritan Targum (*BH*: ɯ^{T}), which likewise was set in writing in distinctly variant versions. At any rate, the transmitted texts and the received manuscripts and manuscript fragments of the Samaritan Pentateuch Targum demonstrate striking deviations from one another.[57]

(2) *Translations into Greek*

A translation of the Old Testament text into Greek became increasingly necessary, for synagogal reading as well as for private use among the Greek-speaking diaspora of Mediterranean lands as understanding of Hebrew became completely lost. Up to this point, the translations of the Old Testament into Aramaic and into Greek manifest parallel phenomena. Yet we cannot simply

As a result one should distinguish this Targum as *Targum Yerushalmi I* from the *older* Fragment Targum, *Targum Yerushalmi II.*

54 Ginsburger (ed.), *Pseudo-Jonathan* (1903).

55 Targum Jonathan (*BH*:$\mathfrak{T}^{L}$) was edited by P. de Lagarde, *Prophetae Chaldaice* (1872) on the basis of *Codex Reuchlinianus* (see p. 308), which contains it. A page of *Codex Reuchlinianus* is provided in facsimile in B. Stade, *Geschichte des Volkes Israel,* Vol. I (1887), f. p. 32. Here the Targum follows the Hebrew text verse by verse. See A. Sperber, *ZAW*, New Series, IV (1927), 267–88.

56 The Targum text of the most comprehensive of these polyglot editions, the so-called *London Polyglot,* was edited by Brian Walton (1654–57). Also known as the Walton Polyglot, it is cited in *BH* under the *siglum* $\mathfrak{T}^{W}$.

57 Details in Kahle, *ZA*, XVI (1901), 79–101; *ZA* XVII (1902), 1–22; and *ZDMG*, LXI (1907), 909–12.

compare the translation in Greek with the Aramaic Targum, calling it "the Greek Targum."[58] The reason for this is that the situation was different among those whose language was Greek from that among those whose language was Aramaic. Aramaic was closely related to Hebrew. Therefore, among Aramaic users the original text of the Old Testament was probably foreign, but not completely incomprehensible. There were also still enough people who were in the position to undertake the oral transfer of the text read in Hebrew in the synagogal service into the Aramaic vernacular without being dependent on a written translation in Aramaic. Things were quite different in the Greek-speaking diaspora. For it seems that in the Hellenistic period there were hardly any people who even knew how to read Hebrew correctly. Therefore, Hebrew texts were transliterated in Greek characters, apparently for synagogal reading of the Hebrew original which was maintained. These could be pronounced mechanically even if neither the reader nor the hearer could understand Hebrew correctly or well. For Wutz is probably right when he asserts that the fragments of Greek transliterations of the Hebrew Old Testament text, dating from the Christian era (see also p. 330), revert to transliteration texts which owed their origin not to a later learned pastime, but rather to the practical need of making the Hebrew original legible, or at least of fixing the pronunciation of the consonantal text.[59] He is also probably right in his assertion that this requirement was first laid down among the diaspora synagogues in a Greek-speaking area during the Hellenistic period.

Now if such an aid as transliteration was necessary even for the simple reading of the Hebrew text, a translation into Greek was all the more necessary in order to understand the text correctly. If the Hebrew text read in the synagogal service could be provided in the language understood by all, that would not impede private scriptural study. In view of the way in which understanding of Hebrew quickly decreased in the Greek-language area, one could hardly expect such random, freely declaimed transpositions of the Hebrew text into Greek as there were among those who spoke Aramaic. The Aramaic transpositions initially took on many shapes and only considerably later assumed the written form of the various versions which we know as the Aramaic Targums. Among those who spoke Greek, we must rather assume written translations from the very beginning. These were not transposi-

[58] As is done by A. Sperber, *OLZ*, Vol. XXXII (1929), Cols. 533–40.
[59] F. Wutz, *BWAT*, New Series, Vol. IX (1925–33), particularly pp. 123 ff.

tions and interpretations of the scantily understood Hebrew text, but exact-as-possible renderings of the original; translations in the true sense of the word.

Initially the Torah (Pentateuch) was translated into Greek. This was done in about the third century B.C. in Alexandria, Egypt, which was not only the capital of the Ptolemaic kingdom (p. 264) but also the seat of the largest and most important Greek-speaking diaspora community. The translation of the remaining parts of the Old Testament took place somewhat later. The Pseudepigraphic Letter of Aristeas[60] narrates a legend about the origin of this translation, which apparently intends to indicate that the correctness and authority of one specific Greek translation disseminated in Alexandria about 100 B.C., when the Letter of Aristeas was written, was accepted as original and valid.[61] For this purpose the story is told that seventy-two scholars, who were called to Alexandria from Jerusalem by King Ptolemy II, Philadelphus, completed the work of translation at the same moment after seventy-two days and agreed perfectly down to individual words, so that from then on this wording was binding. It was this legend that gave the Alexandrian Greek translation of the Old Testament the name of "the (translation of the) Seventy," or the "Septuaginta." Already in the Early Christian Church it was cited as *οἱ ο'*, meaning "the Seventy" (note Origen on pp. 330 ff.). On the whole we know only that part of the history of the transmission of the Septuagint which took place within the sphere of the Christian Church (§ 42).

Still, there are two documents on the pre-Christian history of the Septuagint among the other numerous sensational papyrus finds of recent years for which we are indebted to the soil of Egypt.

In 1917, R. Harris obtained pieces of mummy wrapping from Egypt for the John Rylands Library in Manchester. These mummy wrappings consisted of used leaves of papyrus glued together and piled on top of one another in a mass. It turned out that these included some scraps of an inscribed papyrus scroll dated to the middle of the second century B.C. on the basis of its type of script, with fragmentary pieces of the Greek translation of Deuteronomy.

[60] The Greek text is edited in P. Wendland, *Aristeae ad Philocratem epistula* (1900); in H. B. Swete, *An Introduction to the Old Testament in Greek* (1900), pp. 499–574; with translation and short commentary by P. Wendland in E. Kautzsch, *Die Apokryphen und Pseudepigraphen des Alten Testaments* (1900), II, 1–31; and in R. H. Charles, *The Apocrypha and Pseudepigrapha of the Old Testament in English* (1913), II, 83–122. [A recent edition and translation is Moses Hadas, *Aristeas' Epistle* (1951).]

[61] Cf. Kahle, *The Cairo Geniza* (2nd ed., 1959), pp. 209 ff.

See Plate IIIA. They include Deut. 23 : 24; 24 : 3; 25 : 1–3; 26 : 12, 17–19; 27 : 15; 28 : 31–33; and two very small pieces not yet placed. It is naturally not known how much of the Pentateuch the complete scroll originally contained.[62]

In addition, from about the same time there is Papyrus Fouad 266, owned by the *Société Égyptienne de Papyrologie,* which contains parts of the Greek translation of Deut. 31 : 28; 32 : 7.[63] These papyrus fragments written in beautiful clear script are exceedingly important, not only as the only evidences of the pre-Christian Septuagint, separated from the completion of the translation of the Pentateuch by only one century, but also because they provide the same translation text on the whole which we find used subsequently in the Christian Septuagint.

The Septuagint was accepted by the Christian Church as the form of the Old Testament in accepted usage, from whose text the church derived its scriptural references. After this happened the Septuagint fell into disrepute in the synagogue. As a result other translations of the Old Testament were made for the requirements of the Greek-speaking, Jewish diaspora communities. Particularly important was the translation of Aquila (*BH: A*), a Greek converted to Judaism. About the middle of the second century A.D., he translated the Old Testament into Greek very literally; in fact, so literally that he used very grotesque distortions of the Greek language in the interest of being literal. Actually he accomplished only a transposition of Hebrew into Greek words. Yet, precisely because of this literalness his translation was highly respected in Judaism. Once again, the *genizah* of the synagogue of Old Cairo has provided fragments of Aquila's translation from the sixth century A.D.[64] Moreover, Origen later used Aquila for his textual critical work on the Septuagint. As a result, there are extracts from Aquila's translation within the remaining fragments of this work (see pp. 330 ff.).

[62] These fragments, which had also been inscribed with other writings on their free reverse side, before they were used as mummy wrapping, now are called Rylands Greek Papyrus 458 and have been published by C. H. Roberts, *Two Biblical Papyri in the John Rylands Library* (Manchester, 1936).

[63] Published by W. D. Waddell in the *Journal of Theological Studies*, XLV (1944), 158–61, Papyrus Fouad is noteworthy for the fact that it contains the divine name in Hebrew script, entered by a hand other than that of the scribe of the Greek text, who apparently was not equipped to write the Hebrew *tetragrammaton* [four consonants in *Yahweh*], and therefore left spaces at the appropriate spots. Rylands Greek Papyrus 458 does not contain an example of the divine name.

[64] See F. C. Burkitt, *Fragments of the Books of Kings according to the Translation of Aquila* (1897) and C. Taylor, *Hebrew-Greek Cairo Genizah Palimpsests from the Taylor-Schechter Collection* (1901).

Theodotion's revision of the Septuagint (*BH*: Θ), likewise comes from the middle of the second century A.D. According to early Christian tradition he also was a Greek converted to Judaism. Yet his Septuagint revision was also treasured in the Early Church. The Book of Daniel appears in Theodotion's translation in most of the Christian Septuagint manuscripts. Otherwise we have only fragments of this translation and also only in connection with the textual work of Origen.

We know least of all about the person and translation efforts of Symmachus (*BH*: Σ). At the beginning of the third century A.D. he translated the Old Testament into good Greek. According to early Christian tradition he also was a converted Jew. Origen used his translation, too. As a result, some traces of it remain.[65] When Hellenistic Judaism disappeared long ago these Greek translations of the Old Testament made specifically for Jews lost their reason for existence. Therefore, they have almost completely disappeared.

(3) *A Possible Syriac Translation*

According to Josephus, in the first half of the first century A.D., in a small Parthian dependency called Adiabene on the eastern side of the middle Tigris, the ruling house became converted to Judaism and had close dealings with Jerusalem.[66] In this region an East Aramaic dialect was spoken and it is possible that these rulers at that time had at least the Torah translated in their East Aramaic dialect for themselves and their subjects, while the Targums were being produced in the West Aramaic language. The translation of the Old Testament produced for the Syriac Church in East Aramaic Syriac (see pp. 337 ff.) manifests evident relationships with a preliminary stage of the Palestinian Pentateuch Targum.[67] This fact suggests that there was at least a partial Jewish translation of the Old Testament in East Aramaic or Syriac.

65 The Samaritans also had a Greek translation of their Pentateuch, which Origen repeatedly cited as *Samareitikon*. Fragments of this were found in Egypt in a manuscript from the fourth century A.D. See P. Glaue and A. Rahlfs, *Fragmente einer griechischen Übersetzung des Samaritanischen Pentateuchs*, *Mitteilungen des Septuaginta-Unternehmens*, Vol. II (1911).

66 Josephus, *Antiquities* (ed. Niese), XX_2, 1 ff. in Secs. 17 ff.

67 A. Vööbus, *Peschitta und Targumim des Pentateuch*, *Neues Licht zur Frage der Herkunft der Peschitta aus dem altpalästinischem Targum* (1958); A. Baumstark, *BZ*, XIX (1931), 257 ff.

CHAPTER II

THE TRANSMISSION OF THE TEXT IN THE CHRISTIAN CHURCH

42. *The Old Testament Text in the Eastern Church (the Septuagint)*

AFTER the decline and rapid disappearance of the Jewish Christian element in the Primitive Church, Greek was used as the language of the church. In the further development of the history of the church, Greek remained the language of the state church in the eastern half of the Mediterranean world, as it remains to this day the language of the Bible and liturgy of the remnants of that church. Therefore, the Early Church also read the Old Testament in this language, placing beside it the New Testament in its original Greek form. Still, the Eastern Church did not create its own translation of the Old Testament in its Greek language. Rather, it adopted the only Greek translation available in the first century A.D., the Alexandrian translation or Septuagint (see pp. 321 ff.), produced for the Greek-speaking, Jewish diaspora community. Even later, the church did not replace the Septuagint version with one of its own for general purposes. Therefore, the history of the Old Testament text in the Eastern Church is simply the history of the Septuagint (*BH*: 𝔊). The converse is also true, that the history of the Septuagint in so far as we are acquainted with it is almost exclusively its history within the Eastern Church, with very few exceptions (see p. 322). The direct significance this gave the Septuagint for the Eastern Church, and the indirect significance it had for the other ancient and medieval churches (see pp. 337–48) explains the fact that it was very frequently copied together with the New Testament and that there are numerous manuscripts on hand to this day.[1] Even R. Holmes and J. Parsons, *Vetus Testamentum Graecum cum variis lectionibus* (1798–1827) in their collection of variants of the Septuagint (*BH*: 𝔊 (Holmes-Parsons)) compared 311 manuscripts which are simply numbered there. In the great manuscript list of Rahlfs, there are about 2,000

[1] On this Old and New Testament Greek Bible, its prehistory and its continued use, cf. F. G. Kenyon, *The Text of the Greek Bible* (2nd ed., 1948).

numbers, though this includes small fragments and manuscripts of individual books.[2] The oldest of the manuscripts consists of deposits of papyrus leaves and the most impressive of them are great parchment codices.[3] Copies on paper first appeared in the Middle Ages. Manuscripts are distinguished by types of script: those written in "capital letters," known as majuscules or uncials, customary until the early Middle Ages; those in cursive script known as minuscules, beginning in the ninth century A.D.

(1) *Septuagint Manuscripts*

Until recently the oldest Christian Septuagint manuscripts were papyrus fragments from the third century A.D.[4] Now there are larger, more extensive papyrus manuscripts, some of which extend back to the second century A.D. A few decades ago papyri appeared in trade in antiquities in Cairo which probably come from the ruins of a Christian church or a Christian cloister in the Fayyum, southwest of Cairo. A considerable number of them were acquired by an Englishman, Chester Beatty, while others of them ended up in America. Nevertheless, the entire find is customarily called simply the Chester Beatty Papyri (*BH*: 𝔊 *Beatty*).[5] They include substantial parts of twelve manuscripts in all, which date in part from the second, in part from the third and fourth centuries A.D. A large part of the New Testament is included in these manuscripts; of the Old Testament there are substantial parts of Genesis, Numbers, Deuteronomy, Isaiah, Jeremiah, Ezekiel, Esther, Daniel, and Sirach.

The oldest of our great parchment manuscripts date to the fourth century A.D. Codex Vaticanus, Codex Sinaiticus, and Codex Alexandrinus are the oldest and best known of them. The first two date from the fourth century. Codex Vaticanus, called *Cod. Vat. Gr.* 1209, or 𝔊B in *BH*, or elsewhere designated simply with the letter *B*, except for a few gaps contains the whole Greek Bible

[2] A. Rahlfs, *Verzeichnis der griechischen Handschriften des Alten Testaments*, *Nachr. v. d. Kgl. Ges. d. Wiss. zu Göttingen*, *Phil.-hist. Kl.* (1914), Supplement.

[3] Details on the nature of the manuscripts are found in Knopf, Lietzmann, and Weinel, *Einführung in das Neue Testament* (5th ed., 1949), pp. 26 ff.

[4] Cf. Bleddyn J. Roberts, *The Old Testament Texts and Versions* (Naperville, Ill.: Allenson, 1951), pp. 146–47.

[5] These texts are published in F. G. Kenyon, *The Chester Beatty Biblical Papyri*, Vols. I–III (1933–37). One segment of the portions of this find which are in America is published in A. C. Johnson, H. S. Gehman, and E. H. Kase, *The John H. Scheide Biblical Papyri: Ezekiel*, "Princeton University Studies in Papyrology," Vol. III (1938).

text.[6] Missing in the Old Testament are the sections Gen. 1 : 1—46 : 28, and Pss. 105 : 27—137 : 6. These sections were completed in the manuscript as late as the fifteenth century in the Vatican. The Book of Daniel appears in the Theodotion text (see p. 323). The origin of the manuscript (Egypt?) is not definitely known.

Tischendorf discovered part of Codex Sinaiticus in May 1844, and the rest in 1859 at the Monastery of St. Catherine on Mt. Sinai.[7] The forty-three leaves discovered in 1844 were deposited in the Library of Leipzig University. They are referred to as Codex Friderico-Augustanus and classified as *Cod. Gr.* 1. The rest were deposited in the Czar's Public Library in St. Petersburg and were transferred by sale from there to London in 1933, abbreviated *Brit. Mus. Add.* 43, 725. The codex was incomplete, even originally. Now only portions remain of what the original once contained of the Old Testament.[8] The New Testament text is provided in its entirety. Codex Sinaiticus was subsequently corrected by several hands, designated by *c(orrector) a, b, c* (*BH* : 𝔊$^{\aleph\ \text{c.a.}}$ etc.). This codex probably originated in Egypt or in Caesarea, Palestine.

Codex Alexandrinus (*BH* : 𝔊^{A}, otherwise indicated simply with the letter *A*) is located in the British Museum in London (classified as *Royal MSID V–VIII*). It dates from about the middle of the fifth century A.D., probably from Egypt. Its name originates from its having belonged to the library of the Patriarchate of Alexandria during the Middle Ages. It contains almost the entire Bible. The only substantial lacks in the Old Testament are the sections I Sam. 12 : 17—14 : 9 and Pss. 49 : 20—79 : 11 (according to the Septuagint enumeration); the Book of Daniel is the Theodotion text.[9]

Of the remaining Septuagint manuscripts the only ones which will be briefly described here are those which are customarily re-

[6] Description of the manuscript appears in A. Rahlfs, *op. cit.*, pp. 258 ff.; a facsimile edition of the entire manuscript in *Codices e Vaticanis selecti phototypice expressi*, IV, *Bibliorum SS Graecorum Codex Vaticanus gr. 1209* (1904–7).

[7] Indicated in *BH* by 𝔊$^{\aleph}$, and in the Septuagint edition of Swete by ℵ; H. B. Swete, *The Old Testament in Greek According to the Septuagint*, Vols. I–III (1887–94). Rahlfs, *op. cit.*, uses *S*, as do A. E. Brooke and N. McLean, *The Old Testament in Greek* (Cambridge, 1906–).

[8] Of the Pentateuch, only Gen. 23 : 19—24 : 46 and Num. 5 : 26—7 : 20 remain with gaps in both of these portions. The codex also includes, I Chron. 9 : 27—19 : 17; Ezra-Neh., beginning at Ezra 9 : 9; Esther, Tobit, Judith, with gaps; I and IV Maccabees, Isaiah, Jeremiah, Lam. 1 : 1—2 : 20; Joel-Malachi, Psalms, Proverbs, Ecclesiastes, Song of Solomon, Wisdom of Solomon, Sirach, and Job. For commentary, see Rahlfs, *op. cit.*, pp. 96, 226 ff. A facsimile edition is H. and K. Lake, *Codex Sinaiticus . . . Now Reproduced in Facsimile from Photographs* (1922). [The most recent discussion is in Milne and Skeat, *Scribes and Correctors of the Codex Sinaiticus* (London, 1938).]

[9] Commentary on the manuscript is in Rahlfs, *op. cit.*, pp. 114 ff. A facsimile edition is *The Codex Alexandrinus, Royal MS I D V–VIII in Reduced Photographic Facsimile*, Parts I–III (1909–36).

ferred to in the textual critical apparatus of *BH*. On the remaining ones see Rahlfs.

It is debatable whether the portions of a papyrus book from Egypt, designated in BH as $\mathfrak{G}^{\text{Pap Lond}}$, and by Rahlfs and Swete as *U*, belong in the fourth century A.D. or later.[10] They contain Pss. 10 : 2—18 : 6, 20 : 14—34 : 6, and are now located in the British Museum in London (classified as Pap. 37).

Codex Colberto-Sarravianus (*BH* : $\mathfrak{G}^{G}$, otherwise simply *G*) comes from the fourth to fifth century A.D.[11] It is now located partly in the University Library at Leyden (classified as *Voss. graec. in qu.* 8) and partly in Paris (classified as *Bibl. Nat. Grec.* 17), with one leaf in the Public Library at Leningrad (classified as *Cod. Gr.* 3). It contains Genesis, chapter 31 to Judges, chapter 21, with a good many gaps.

Codex Ambrosianus (*BH:* $\mathfrak{G}^{F}$: otherwise, simply *F*), located at Milan in the Biblioteca Ambrosiana (classified as *A 147 inf.*), dates from the fifth century A.D. and contains Genesis, chapter 31 to Joshua, chapter 12, with many gaps.[12]

The one Codex Freer (*BH*: $\mathfrak{G}^{\Theta}$, Brooke and McLean: Θ, Ralfs: *W*) likewise belongs to the fifth century. It contains Deuteronomy and Joshua except for gaps.[13]

Codex Ephraemi Syri Rescriptus (*BH*: $\mathfrak{G}^{C}$; otherwise, generally referred to as *C*) is a palimpsest manuscript, now located in Paris (*Bibl. Nat. Grec.* 9).[14] A palimpsest is a reused codex whose initial text has been erased. Codex $\mathfrak{G}^{C}$ also preserves the New Testament.[15] In the Middle Ages it was reused for copying the Greek translation of works of the Syriac theologian, Ephraem, hence its name.[16] Originally it was a Greek manuscript of the fifth century A.D., whose erased text could still be recovered. From the Old Testament there are parts of Job, Proverbs, Ecclesiastes, Song of Solomon, Wisdom of Solomon, and Sirach.

Codex Cottonianus Geneseos, which contains the Septuagint text of Genesis in fragments and belongs to the fifth or sixth century A.D., must not be confused with the well-known *D* manuscript of the New Testament, although this Septuagint manuscript,

[10] Cf. Rahlfs, *op. cit.*, pp. 111–12.

[11] *Ibid.*, pp. 94–95, 195, 221.

[12] *Ibid.*, p. 125.

[13] Cf. *ibid.*, p. 312. There is another somewhat later Codex Freer in Washington (known as Washington Smithsonian Institution Freer Gallery I) containing portions of Psalms. See Roberts, *op. cit.*, p. 158.

[14] Rahlfs, *op. cit.*, pp. 193–94.

[15] Cf. Knopf, Lietzmann, and Weinel, *op. cit.*, pp. 36–37.

[16] See *RGG* (3rd ed., 1958), Vol. I, Col. 522. [In English, see Schaff-Herzog Encyclopedia.]

too, is generally designed by *D* (*BH*: $\mathfrak{G}^{D}$).[17] Most of the fragments of this manuscript, damaged by fire in 1731, are located in the British Museum in London (classified as *Cott. Otho B.* VI). Some are also at the Baptist College in Bristol.

Codex Marchalianus (*BH*: $\mathfrak{G}^{Q}$, or quite generally *Q*), located in the Vatican Library, dating from the sixth century (classified as *Vat. gr.* 2125), contains all of the prophetic Scriptures.[18]

Codex Coislinianus[2] (*BH*: $\mathfrak{G}^{M}$, otherwise known as *M*) is a seventh-century manuscript, now deposited at Paris (classified as *Bibl. Nat. Coisl.* 1).[19] It contains Genesis, chapter 1 to I Kings 8, although with substantial gaps in the material.

Tischendorf brought back a manuscript from the monastery of Mar Saba southeast of Jerusalem in 1844 and 1859.[20] It is designated as $\mathfrak{G}^{K}$ in *BH* and otherwise known as *K*. Its biblical text dates from the seventh or eighth century. In A.D. 885–86 it was reused for Arabic texts. From Tischendorf's estate, part of it went to the Leipzig University Library (classified as *Cod. Lipsiensis*, or *Gr.* 2 [*Tischendorf* II]) and part to the Czar's Public Library at St. Petersburg (*Gr.* 26). Except for sizable gaps it contains Numbers to Judges.

There is an eighth-century Septuagint manuscript, in part at the Vatican (*Vat. gr.* 2106 [*Basil* 145]) and in part at Venice (*Biblioteca Naz. Marciana Gr.* 1), which contains the entire Old Testament apart from Psalms, but with sizable portions lost. Rahlfs refers to it as *V*, as a whole, while previously the two separate parts were referred to respectively as Codex Basiliano-Vaticanus (*N*, or $\mathfrak{G}^{N}$ in *BH*) and Codex Venetus (*V*, or $\mathfrak{G}^{V}$).

The palimpsest manuscript Codex Rescriptus Cryptoferratensis is designated as $\mathfrak{G}^{\Gamma}$ in *BH* (Swete: Γ; Rahlfs: 393).[21] It was reused in the thirteenth century. The first partially restored text contained an eighth-century Septuagint copy of the prophets. It is now located at Grottaferrata in the Albanian mountains (classified as *A XV*). Four leaves now deposited in the Vatican (*Vat. gr.* 1658) are part of the same manuscript.

Codex Bodleianus Geneseos came from the ninth or tenth century.[22] Tischendorf brought back portions in 1853 and 1859, presumably from Mount Sinai. As its name suggests, it is located in the Bodleian Library at Oxford (classified as *Auct. T. inf.* 2, 1).

[17] Rahlfs, *op. cit.*, pp. 36–37, 107–8.
[18] *Ibid.*, p. 273.
[19] *Ibid.*, pp. 183–84.
[20] *Ibid.*, pp. 96 ff., 222.
[21] *Ibid.*, pp. 75, 264.
[22] *Ibid.*, pp. 41, 105, 163–64, 223. Designations are *BH*: $\mathfrak{G}^{E}$; Swete and Brooke and McLean: *E*; Rahlfs: 509.

However, one leaf in the Cambridge University Library (*Add.* 1879, 7), sixteen leaves in the British Museum at London (*Add.* 20002), and one hundred forty-six leaves in the Leningrad Public Library (*Gr.* 62) are all part of the same manuscript. Therefore, this is not simply a Genesis manuscript but a codex whose remaining portions include Gen. 1 : 1 to I Kings 16 : 28, with a number of gaps.

Additional Septuagint manuscripts are cited in the apparatus of *BH*, either with further index letters, derived from the system of notation in the work of Brooke and McLean, or with index numbers derived from the enumeration of manuscripts in Holmes and Parsons.[23]

Codex Atheniensis, indexed $\mathfrak{G}^{W}$, belongs to the first group (Brooke and McLean: *W*; Rahlfs: 314).[24] It is a thirteenth-century manuscript at Athens (*Nat.-Bibl.* 44), including the historical books Esther, Judith, and Tobit.

(2) *Recensions of the Septuagint*

Septuagint research has the important task of arranging the abundance of available manuscripts in families and groups, whether it serves as part of the Bible of the Eastern Church or as a witness to the Old Testament text. As the Christian Church accepted the Alexandrian translation, it apparently consisted of a tradition with numerous variants, which were partly due to inadvertent textual errors, partly to intentional changes for stylistic or dogmatic reasons. This is demonstrated by the Old Testament citations contained in the New Testament, which frequently differ from the Septuagint text transmitted to us. This divergence into multiple variants probably rather increased than decreased in the first Christian centuries. In order to put an end to the textual confusion which resulted from this, various attempts to revise and to fix the Septuagint text conclusively were made in the third century and at the beginning of the fourth century A.D. This means that definite authoritative textual recensions were made. According to a statement by Jerome, in his lifetime in Egypt the Septuagint was read, following the recension of Hesychius.[25] In the region between Constantinople and Antioch, the recension of the martyr Lucian was

[23] A synopsis of the various systems of notation is given in Rahlfs, *op. cit.*, pp. 335 ff.

[24] Rahlfs, p. 6.

[25] In his preface to the Books of Chronicles, Migne, *Patrologia Latina*, Book XXVIII, Cols. 1392–93. This statement is given in Goettsberger, *Einleitung*, p. 444, n. 1.

used. In Palestine at the same time, they were using the Septuagint text form as drafted by Origen and disseminated by Pamphilus and Eusebius.

The textual critical work of Origen was a great learned opus. His aim was not simply to devise recensions of the Septuagint text as transmitted, but rather to compare it with the Hebrew original and to bring it into agreement with the Hebrew. Thus he hoped to void Judaism's charge that the church depended on an inexact and garbled translation of the Old Testament. To accomplish this in the middle of the third century A.D. at Caesarea, Palestine, Origen formed the extensive opus of the Tetrapla and Hexapla, meaning the fourfold and sixfold work. In the former, he placed the later translations of Aquila, Theodotion, and Symmachus (see p. 322) in columns parallel to the Septuagint text for comparison. In the latter he introduced the Hebrew text of the Old Testament in two forms, producing six parallel columns: (1) the Hebrew original in Hebrew consonants; (2) a transliteration of the Hebrew text in Greek letters;[26] (3) the text of Aquila; (4) the text of Symmachus; (5) the Septuagint text; and (6) the text of Theodotion.[27] It is noteworthy that he occasionally used additional textual witnesses.[28] On the basis of this combination, Origen revised the Septuagint text, using Aristarchus's symbols, customary in Alexandrian philological studies. These symbols were introduced by Aristarchus at the end of the third century B.C. He noted additions of the Septuagint text in comparison with the Hebrew text with a prefixed obelos (—, ÷, or the like; *BH*: *ob*). Items missing in the Septuagint in comparison with the original text he usually added, following the text of Theodotion. He marked these additions with an asterisk ([*] or the like; *BH*: *ast.*). At the end of any such portion marked by an obelos or an asterisk, he placed a metobolos (ɣ or the like). Moreover, where necessary, he inverted the words of the Septuagint text to conform with the original text and placed variant read-

[26] See p. 320 concerning the introduction of such transliterated texts. Certainly in this column Origen followed a transmitted transliteration.

[27] It is usually assumed that the Tetrapla is a later, improved extract from the larger work of the Hexapla; namely, that in the Tetrapla, Origen used only the most important columns for his purpose. Yet Procksch, "Tetraplarische Studien," *ZAW*, New Series, XII (1935), 240–69 and XIII (1936), 61–90, as well as others, attempts to prove that the Tetrapla which gives only the comparison of the Greek translations is an earlier, still less developed stage of Origen's work while the Hexapla, which also utilizes the Hebrew text, represents a later more complete stage. A definite decision can hardly be reached in this matter.

[28] Thus a "fifth" (*Quinta; BH*: *E'*) and "sixth" (*Sexta*) Greek translation of the Old Testament are referred to in various ways in hexaplaric notations. So, too, are others, including the *Samareitikon* (see p. 323 n. 65). Very little is definitely known as yet about the origin of these.

ings of the original text with an asterisk next to the transmitted Septuagint reading, marked with an obelos. Otherwise he simply corrected the transmitted Septuagint text to conform with the original text without a word. As a result his work produced a new Septuagint recension which is customarily called hexaplaric (*BH*: 𝔊ʰ, *Orig.* or *Hex.*).

This gigantic learned work, which contained an abundance of textual critical work, was understandably seldom, if ever, copied as a whole. Therefore, it is no longer available. Only small fragments are known to us. Beneath later writings, G. Mercati discovered fragments of the Hexapla in a minuscule of the tenth century A.D. on a parchment palimpsest manuscript of Milan.[29] The Mercati Fragments include parts of Psalms 17, 27–31, 34, 35, 45, 48, 88, according to Septuagint listing. As the only remains of the Hexapla transmission they are very important and occupy the five last columns, not including the Hebrew consonantal text.[30]

Additional hexaplaric material is available. The Septuagint column of the Hexapla was circulated by itself for ecclesiastical use from Caesarea, Palestine, in the beginning of the fourth century A.D. by Pamphilus and Eusebius. As a result it is available in part to our day. Thus Codex $\mathfrak{G}^{G}$ (p. 327) provides the hexaplaric text with the symbols of Aristarchus. The Codices $\mathfrak{G}^{M}$ and $\mathfrak{G}^{Q}$ (p. 328) also contain many hexaplaric readings, at least in marginal notes (*marginalia*; cited by M^{mg} and the like). In addition, there are also a number of minuscules with a hexaplaric text or hexaplaric marginal readings.[31] Furthermore, the hexaplaric Septuagint text was translated into Syriac in A.D. 616–17 by the Syriac bishop Paul of Tella maintaining the symbols of Aristarchus. This Syro-hexaplaric text (*BH*: $\mathfrak{C}^{h}$) is found especially in a ninth-century Milan manuscript (*Ambr. C.* 313) containing the second

[29] Classified as *Bible. Ambr.* o.39; see Rahlfs, *op. cit.*, Index, pp. 130–31. Mercati described it in *Atti d. R. Accademia delle Scienze di Torino*, XXXI (1895–96), 655–76. A specimen of these Mercati Fragments was published by A. Ceriani in *R. Istituto Lombardo di Scienze e lettere, Rendiconti*, II, No. 29 (1896), 406–8. E. Klostermann has reproduced this specimen in *ZAW*, XVI (1896), 336–37. It consists of Ps. 46 : 1–4 according to Septuagint listing, Psalm 45). Small specimens based on this are also given in Steuernagle, *Einleitung*, pp. 52–53; Goettsberger, *Einleitung*, p. 438. Part I of the final publication of the Mercati Fragments has now appeared: *Psalterii Hexapli Reliquiae cura et Studio Johannis Cardinal Mercati editae in Bybliotheca Vaticana, I* (1958) in the series: *Codices ex Ecclesiasticis Italiae Bybliothecis delecti phototypice expressi jussu Pii XII, Pont. Max., consilio et studio Procuratorium Bybliothecae Vaticanae*, Vol. VIII.

[30] On the Hebrew text found in Greek transliteration in the fragments (*BH*: $\mathfrak{H}^{o}$), see A. Pretzl, *BZ*, XX (1932), 4–22.

[31] Procksch, *op. cit.*, p. 240.

part of the Old Testament,[32] also in a number of manuscripts of individual Bible books in very fragmentary form.[33]

The *Recensio Luciana* (*BH*: $\mathfrak{G}^{Luc}$),[34] traceable to Lucian of Antioch,[35] martyred in 312 A.D., was among the remaining Septuagint recensions referred to by Jerome (see p. 329). It was considered authoritative in the imperial capital of Constantinople, widely distributed in ecclesiastical usage, and of basic importance to the textual form which was subsequently generally accepted in the Eastern Church. P. de Lagarde, in his edition, *Librorum Veteris Testamenti canonicorum pars prior Graece*, 1883 (*BH*: $\mathfrak{G}^{L}$), wished to present the Lucianic text; however, it proved that his text was not solely based on Lucianic manuscripts.

Jerome's ascription of one Septuagint recension to a certain Hesychius is unclear. It is not certain that this Hesychius is identical with the Egyptian Bishop Hesychius, martyred in A.D. 311.[36] It could be expected that the Hesychianic recension was based on the Egyptian textual tradition. It is difficult to relate this recension to any one group of manuscripts.

The geographical distribution of given textual recensions can be determined especially on the basis of texts of biblical citations among the church fathers. Thus, the biblical citations in the numerous exegetical-homiletical works of the patriarch Cyril of Alexandria[37] of the first half of the fifth century A.D., cited in *BH* as $\mathfrak{G}^{Cyr}$, testify to the text form in use in Egypt and have close relationships to $\mathfrak{G}^{B}$. At the same time, the biblical citations in the exegetical works of his contemporary, Bishop Theodoret of Cyrrhus,[38] of the school of Antioch attest the text of Antioch, as do others.

The custom arose in the Byzantine period of gathering the expositions of the classical church fathers on individual Scripture

[32] Reproduced lithographically by A. M. Ceriani, *Monumenta sacra et profana*, Vol. VII (1874).

[33] Presented in A. Baumstark, *Geschichte der syrischen Literatur* (1922), p. 186, n. 12. The hexaplaric textual material known in his time is assembled in F. Field, *Origenis Hexaplorum quae supersunt* (1875). Fragments of the Septuagint column of the Tetrapla are also found in manuscripts and marginal readings of manuscripts. Yet the difference between hexaplaric and tetraplaric texts is confusing and not yet completely understood.

[34] *BH* (1st ed., 1905–7) and *BH* (2nd ed., 1920) classify it as $\mathfrak{G}_{\mathfrak{L}}$.

[35] See *RE*, XI (1902), 654 ff. and *RGG* (3rd ed., 1960), III, Cols. 463–64. [Schaff-Herzog Encyclopedia, VII, 53–54, in English.]

[36] Concerning Hesychius, see *RE*, VIII (1910), 18 and *RGG*, III, Col. 299. [See Schaff-Herzog Encyclopedia for references in English.]

[37] *RE*, IV (1898), 377 ff. and *RGG*, III, Cols. 1894–95 [Schaff-Herzog Encyclopedia, III, 333–34].

[38] See [Schaff-Herzog Encyclopedia, XI, 323–25]; *RE*, XIX (1907), 609 ff.; *RGG*, V (1931), Cols. 1109–10.

passages into catenas or "chain commentaries," in which authoritative expositions were recorded in serial fashion for consecutively quoted biblical passages.[39] A large catena on the historical books of the Bible was published in 1772–73 by Nicephorus (called Catena Nicephori; cited in the first and second editions of *BH* as $\mathfrak{G}^{N}$), based on a manuscript in Athens.[40] Rahlfs (see p. 336) has developed a separate "catena recension" of the text of the Septuagint from the biblical passages in a number of catena manuscripts, in addition to the older recensions previously mentioned.

Relating the individual manuscripts to given recensions and groups is extremely important for the classification of the material. Yet such a grouping is hindered by the fact that the manuscripts in the various biblical books sometimes follow more than one recension and that the various recensions influenced one another. As a result, scarcely anywhere is there a given recension in pure form. Rather, to a considerable extent we must contend with mixed texts in the manuscripts. Those portions of the Chester Beatty find (see above) which were written well before all of the Septuagint recensions of which we know, are particularly essential for the question as to the original Septuagint text which lies behind all of these recensions. Naturally, these too do not actually provide the original Septuagint text. Rather they only represent a relatively early stage in the history of the Septuagint text in its native land of Egypt. Since the most recent discoveries (see p. 336), there is reason to hope that further papyrus finds will bring us still closer to the original text of the Septuagint.

(3) *The Character and Content of the Septuagint*

In spite of everything said, the available material does permit one to reconstruct a hypothetical original text in general terms and to make some assertions about the type and technique of this Alexandrian translation. For one thing it has turned out that the translation in the different biblical books and even in individual parts of the same book is sometimes so different that one must assume several translators.[41] Furthermore, it must be considered that the Septuagint is not only a translation into the Greek language, but also a transposition of the content of Old Testament

[39] See [Schaff-Herzog Encyclopedia, II, 451–53] and *RE*, III (1897), 754 ff.
[40] *Nat.-Bibl.*, 43; see Rahlfs, *op. cit.*, Index, p. 6.
[41] See J. Herrmann and F. Baumgärtel, "Beiträge zur Entstehungsgeschichte der Septuaginta," *BWAT*, New Series, Vol. V (1923).

revelation into the spirit and into the thought pattern of Hellenistic Judaism. On the other hand, the thesis of Wutz has not proved true, to the effect that the translation into Greek was not prepared on the basis of the Hebrew consonantal text, but of a Greek transliterated text (p. 320), and that the differences between 𝔊 and 𝔐 were based chiefly on the ambiguity or misunderstanding of this transliterated text.[42] Wutz, on the basis of his thesis of translation from a transcribed text cleverly reconstructs the Hebrew original text, operating from the Septuagint.[43] Yet not even his way of reconstruction commends this thesis of his to us.

The 𝔊 differs substantially from 𝔐 in contents and arrangement of the books. The 𝔊 seems preferable partly in Greek translations of those scriptures with a Hebrew-Aramaic original which were not accepted in the canon of the synagogue, partly as to books coming from Hellenistic Judaism and originally written in Greek. The 𝔊 differs substantially from 𝔐 in its arrangement of books, as 𝔊 classifies books as historical, poetical, or prophetic. Particularly in following this plan, the Septuagint has abolished the third chief division of the Hebrew Old Testament, the *Kethubim*, and reassigned its books to designated places. The same was done with the books which are new in the Septuagint.[44] Thus, the Septuagint has inserted the Book of Ruth in the division "Historical books," following Judges. Furthermore, the two Books of Chronicles[45] follow the four Books of Kings.[46] Then comes the apocryphal[47] Book of I Ezra, followed by II Ezra, which is Ezra-Nehemiah in 𝔐, and Esther. The Books of Judith and Tobit,[48] together with the four books of Maccabees, all of them missing in

[42] Wutz, "Die Transkriptionen von der Septuaginta bis zu Hieronymus," *BWAT*, New Series, Vol. IX (1925–33).

[43] In his comprehensive book, Wutz, *Systematische Wege von der Septuaginta zum hebräischen Urtext* I (1937).

[44] Details, including variations in compass and arrangement in the history of textual transmissions of the Septuagint, will be found in H. B. Swete, *An Introduction to the Old Testament in Greek* (1900), pp. 197 ff.

[45] Chronicles, which 𝔊 has divided into two books, is called *Paraleipomena* in the Septuagint and the Vulgate. Therefore, one may find it cited as I and II Par.

[46] The Septuagint, which divides [the Hebrew] Samuel and Kings into two Books each, also with good reason renames Samuel a "Book of Kings." Thus it arrives at the four Books of Kings. Since this enumeration was transferred to the Vulgate (see pp. 345 ff.), it is frequently used by Roman Catholic authors, whose I and II Kings therefore correspond to I and II Samuel and whose III and IV Kings correspond to I and II Kings.

[47] On the word apocryphal see p. 347.

[48] Esther, Judith, and Tobit also frequently appear at the end of the order of "poetical books" in Septuagint tradition.

$\mathfrak{M}$, conclude this division.[49] Psalms[50] begins the order of poetical books, usually followed by Proverbs, Ecclesiastes, Song of Solomon, Job, as well as the books of the Wisdom of Solomon and Sirach, missing in $\mathfrak{M}$.[51] In the division, Prophetical Books, the Septuagint has first the "minor prophets," with the longer books of Hosea, Amos, and Micah at the head. Then come the "major prophets," Isaiah, Jeremiah, Ezekiel, together with the Book of Daniel. Not only Lamentations (*Threnoi*), but also the apocryphal Books of Baruch and the Epistle of Jeremiah are attached to the Book of Jeremiah. Also the apocryphal Scriptures of Susanna and Bel and the Dragon are joined with Daniel.

In the Septuagint manuscripts, which have no division into verses, certain divisions into related sections, as well as pericopes for reading are found, varying greatly in detail. In the ancient manuscripts, which generally simply provide the continuous text, these sections were already marked in the margins by signs or other notations, though some of these were by later hands. In $\mathfrak{G}^{A}$ the beginnings of the sections are even indicated by particular initials. Some ancient manuscripts also set poetical passages apart into poetical verse lines. Even individual sections occasionally have captions giving contents.[52] The division into chapters and verses to which we are accustomed was, however, taken over only from the Vulgate (see p. 347).

(4) *Printed Editions of the Septuagint*

The earliest printed editions of the Septuagint will be mentioned next. The Septuagint appeared in print in the polyglot editions of the sixteenth and seventeenth centuries (see p. 319) such as the earliest of them arranged in 1514 to 1517 by Cardinal F. Ximenes, the Complutensian Polyglot, Complutum being the Latin name of the Spanish city of Alcalá. Its Septuagint text (*BH*: $\mathfrak{G}^{C(om)pl}$) rests on late minuscules. The same applies to the edition of the Septuagint printed at the press of Aldus at Venice in 1518, called *Aldina* (*BH*: $\mathfrak{G}^{Vn}$). On the other hand, the basic source of the *Editio Sixtina* of the Septuagint (1586–87), sponsored

[49] I–IV Maccabees also sometimes appear at the end of the Septuagint.

[50] In $\mathfrak{G}^{A}$ and other manuscripts, following Psalms is another book of "Odes," a collection of poetical portions from both Old and New Testaments.

[51] The Hebrew original to the Wisdom Book of Jesus Sirach, which was not adopted in $\mathfrak{M}$ and naturally appears only in Greek translation in $\mathfrak{G}$, has to a considerable extent been rediscovered. See R. Smend, *Die Weisheit des Jesus Sirach hebräisch und deutsch* (1906). In late manuscripts, occasionally the Psalms of Solomon are also found after Sirach.

[52] Details on this in Swete, *op. cit.*, pp. 342 ff.

by Pope Sixtus V, was the ancient Codex Vaticanus ($\mathfrak{G}^{B}$).

Today the following Septuagint editions must be considered. First, H. B. Swete, *The Old Testament in Greek According to the Septuagint,* was published in three volumes between 1887 and 1894, with a number of later editions. It prints $\mathfrak{G}^{B}$, except that wherever the text is missing $\mathfrak{G}^{A}$ is used. In its textual critical apparatus the significant variants of the most important majuscules are noted. The large Cambridge edition by A. E. Brooke and N. McLean, *The Old Testament in Greek* (Vols. I, 1–4 and II, 1–4, including II Ezra, published between 1906 and 1935, are available thus far), likewise is based primarily on $\mathfrak{G}^{B}$, completed when necessary by $\mathfrak{G}^{A}$, but in its very comprehensive textual critical apparatus the work provides all of the variants of the majuscules and a number of minuscules, in addition to the variant material from the translations derived from the Septuagint (cf. pp. 337–48). The text editions of A. Rahlfs follow a different principle. For the great Septuagint project of the *Göttinger Akademie der Wissenschaften,* he has devoted himself for decades exclusively to his work on the Septuagint. Similarly the great edition,[53] as well as the completed hand edition, *Septuaginta,* edited by Rahlfs (2 vols., 1935), provides not simply the text of a given manuscript, but rather a critical Septuagint text constructed from the "earliest" means at hand, as close as possible to the "original text," which naturally, practically speaking, agrees with the text of our oldest and best manuscripts, particularly $\mathfrak{G}^{B}$. Rahlfs did not merely assemble the variants of a number of manuscripts; rather, he observed all of the variant material and wherever possible arranged it in groups which are indicated in the apparatus with cursive capital letters. The most important of these are the group of hexaplaric, Origenistic manuscripts (*O*), that of Lucianic (*L*) manuscripts, and that of the manuscripts of the so-called "Catena Recension" (*C*); on the last, see p. 333.

Indispensable for study of the Septuagint and research into the problem of the relation between the Septuagint text and the Hebrew text is the work of E. Hatch and H. A. Redpath, *A Concordance to the Septuagint* (2 vols., 1897; with supplement, 1906),

[53] *Septuaginta Vetus Testamentum Graecum, Auctoritate Societatis Litterarum Gottensis editum* (published thus far are: Vol. IX, 1: *Maccabaeorum liber I,* by W. Kappler (1936); Vol. IX, 2: *Maccabaeorum liber II,* by Kappler and R. Hanhart (1959); Vol. IX, 3: *Maccabaeorum liber III,* by Hanhart (1960); Vol. X, *Psalmi cum Odis,* by Rahlfs (1931); Vol. XIII: *Duodecim prophetae,* by J. Ziegler (1943); Vol. XIV, *Isaias,* by Ziegler (1939); Vol. XV: *Jeremias, Baruch, Threni, Epistula Jeremiae,* by Ziegler (1957); Vol. XVI, 1: *Ezechiel,* by Ziegler (1957); Vol. XVI, 2: *Susanna, Daniel, Bel et Draco,* by Ziegler (1954).

which lists all of the words of the Septuagint and their Hebrew equivalents.

43. *The Old Testament Text in the National Churches of the Near East*

A number of separate churches developed around the edges of the Greek-speaking eastern state church. In time they not only separated, or were excluded from the main church as heretics, but in distinction from the church of the empire, which regarded itself as ecumenical, they constituted themselves as national churches. As this happened they either provided themselves with translations in these languages, or continued to use and conserve already available translations. Since these national churches had withdrawn from the church of the empire, they usually based these translations on the recognized Greek biblical text of the church of the empire, the Septuagint. From the point of view of textual history these are in general translations derived from the Septuagint. Therefore, in textual criticism they rank only as attestation for the Septuagint text used in the church of the empire. These translations were in part not limited to the canon of the Septuagint which was finally fixed in the church of the empire, which was already more extensive than the Hebrew canon (p. 334). Rather, these translations contained a number of other scriptures, particularly apocalyptic in nature, which the church of the empire had excluded from its canon. They consisted chiefly of the so-called Pseudepigrapha of the Old Testament,[54] which are therefore transmitted chiefly in Near Eastern language, even if they are traceable to Greek and occasionally to older origins.

(1) *Translations into Syriac*

The oldest and most important of these translations into Near Eastern languages is the translation into Syriac, which was given a name which still clings to it, namely Peshitto or Peshitta; Syriac *peshiṭtā* most likely means "the simple or common [translation]" (*BH*: 𝔖). Its origin is unknown. Furthermore, there is no critical edition of its text.[55]

[54] Translated in R. H. Charles, *The Apocrypha and Pseudepigrapha of the Old Testament in English*, Vol. II (1913) and E. Kautzsch, *Die Apocryphen und Pseudepigraphen des Alten Testament*, Vol. II (1900).

[55] For a thorough study of its history and character, see L. Haefeli, *Die Peschitta des Alten Testaments, Alttestamentliche Abhandlungen*, Vol. XI, 1 (1927). A critical

As early as second century A.D., Christianity got a firm foothold in the city of Edessa in northwestern Mesopotamia, now called Urfa.[56] About A.D. 200 even the ruling house of Edessa was converted to Christianity, though this dynasty was soon removed by the Romans. Thus the first instance of a "state church" occurred here on a small scale. Christianity then continued to spread from Edessa as a centre and the East Aramaic dialect of Edessa became the basis of the Syriac ecclesiastical language. The Peshitta also probably originated in Edessa, probably even in the second century A.D. It is the work of several translators, and likely was prepared progressively over a long period of time. It has unquestionable connections with the textual transmission of the Septuagint, which is exactly what one would expect with its Christian origin.[57] On the other hand, of course, and this is what constitutes its individuality and its particular value for textual criticism, it demonstrates clear connection with the Hebrew text, particularly in its Palestinian tradition. That is explained by the fact that it could be related to a Jewish translation of at least individual parts of the Hebrew Old Testament in an East Aramaic dialect (see p. 323).[58]

The split of the Syriac Church from the imperial church, based on doctrinal differences, took place about the middle of the fifth century. With this came a further Syriac division into West Syriac Jacobites and East Syriac Nestorians. When this occurred, the textual tradition of the Peshitta divided into two branches. Particularly, the Nestorians continued to have a long, significant, and troubled history, both during the Sassanid kingdom and after it.

Among the Peshitta manuscripts extant, the most important because of its age, compass, and state of preservation is the West Syriac Codex Ambrosianus (*BH*: $\mathfrak{S}^A$), coming from the sixth or seventh century.[59]

Only biblical quotations of Syriac theologians trace back to the

text edition is now being prepared by the Peshitta Commission of the International Organization for the Study of the Old Testament.

56 Harnack, *Die Mission und Ausbreitung des Christentums* (4th ed., 1924), pp. 678 ff. and E. Kirsten, "Edessa," *RAC*, Vol. IV (1958), Cols. 552–97.

57 For example, see J. Hänel, "Die aussermasorethischen Übereinstimmungen zwischen der Septuaginta und der Peschitta in der Genesis," *BZAW*, Vol. XX (1911).

58 For further study of this question consult the work of A. Vööbus referred to on p. 323.

59 Milano, *Bibl. Amb. B 21 inf.*; details on it are given in Haefeli, *op. cit.*, pp. 75 ff. The text was published lithographically by A. M. Ceriani, *Translatio Syra Pescitto Veteris Testamenti* (1876–83). Additional Jacobite manuscripts and the Nestorian Peshitta manuscripts are enumerated and described in Haefeli, *op. cit.*, pp. 74 ff.

time before the Jacobite-Nestorian split. That applies, for example, to the quotations, frequently inexact, in the letters ("homilies") of the Syriac bishop Aphraates[60] of the beginning of the fourth century A.D., cited as $\mathfrak{G}^{\text{Aphr}}$ in *BH*. The quotations in the commentaries and homilies of Ephraem[61] also extend back to the middle of the fourth century, which means to the period before the dogmatic split.

The printed editions of the Peshitta are unfortunately of little value. The Peshitta of the Old Testament was printed initially on the basis of late, accidentally available manuscripts in the Paris Polyglot (1629–45). The London Polyglot (see p. 319) simply derived its Peshitta text (*BH*: $\mathfrak{G}$ or $\mathfrak{G}^{\text{W}}$) from the Paris Polyglot in more imperfect form and did nothing but fill in its gaps on the basis of late manuscripts. Subsequently S. Lee simply had this Polyglot text printed in his Peshitta edition, *Vetus Testamentum Syriace* (published by the London Bible Society, 1823), produced for missionary purposes (*BH*: $\mathfrak{G}^{\text{L}}$). While the printed editions mentioned so far substantially follow Jacobite manuscripts, the Peshitta edition of Urmia, *Vetus Testamentum Syriace et Neosyriace*, also published for missionary purposes in 1852 by American missionaries, was based on Nestorian textual tradition. The same applies to the Peshitta edition of Mosul, arranged by Dominicans between 1887 and 1891. Printed editions of individual Bible books, particularly Psalms, are indexed by Haefeli, *op. cit.*, pp. 70 ff.

Of course, the efforts of Syriac Christians in behalf of the Syriac biblical text did not conclude with the rise of the Peshitta. Primarily in various West Syriac circles, even later the Syriac biblical text was given final form on the basis of the Septuagint, the biblical text of the imperial Church. Naturally that applies first of all to the Syriac-speaking Christians who remained dogmatically and hierarchically in the imperial church, the so-called Melchites, who lived primarily in Palestine and Syria. In addition to their own Christian literature in the so-called Syro-Palestinian dialect, they also had a biblical translation in this dialect, coming from the fifth or sixth century, which agreed with the hexaplaric textual form of the Septuagint as used in Palestine (see pp. 331–32), but also used the Peshitta. Unfortunately only small fragments of this so-called Syro-Palestinian or Jerusalem translation have been found.[62]

[60] Cf. *RE*, I (1896), 611–12; *RGG*, Col. 146; Haefeli, *op. cit.*, pp. 88–89 [English in Schaff-Herzog Encyclopedia].

[61] *RGG*, Col. 522 and Haefeli, *op. cit.*, pp. 89–90.

[62] See especially Goettsberger, *op. cit.*, p. 467, n. 2.

The Jacobites as neighbours of the imperial church also were concerned with adjusting the Syriac biblical text to the Septuagint. About A.D. 500 Bishop Philoxenes of Mabug in North Syria (now known as Membij, northeast of Aleppo) in addition to a translation of the New Testament had at least parts of the Old Testament translated. This is known as the Philoxeniana, which depended on the Lucianic text of the Septuagint (p. 332), native to near-by Antioch, as well as on the Peshitta. We have a few small fragments of it.[63]

Finally in this connection we must also mention the exact translation of the hexaplaric text into Syriac, using the Aristarchic signs (*BH*: $\mathfrak{G}^{h}$) referred to above.

(2) *Translation into Armenian*

The separation of the Armenian Church from the imperial Church began in the fifth century A.D. Since the nearest neighbour of the Armenian Church was the Syriac Church, the statement of Moses of Chorene, an Armenian historian of the fifth century, sounds plausible. He states that the first Armenian Bible, probably at the beginning of the fifth century, was a translation from the Peshitta. The translation into Armenian of which manuscripts are still on hand (*BH*: *Arm*)[64] is ascribed to Mesrob[65] in the tradition. This translation, which became authoritative in the Armenian Church, was based on the Hexaplaric Septuagint text.

(3) *Translation into Gothic*

Bishop Ulfila, who died in A.D. 383 in Constantinople, made the translation of the Bible into Gothic for the Visigoths, neighbours of the Eastern Church, who had been converted to Christianity. This translation has become famous as a Gothic linguistic monument. There are extensive fragments of the Gospels in this translation in the well-known Codex Argenteus of the University Library of Upsala. However, there are only very meagre fragments of the Old Testament portion. Nevertheless, these show that, as one would expect, the Lucianic textual form of the Septuagint, authoritative in Constantinople, was the basis of this translation.

[63] See Baumstark, *op. cit.*, pp. 144–45.

[64] Concerning editions of it see Goettsberger, *op. cit.*, p. 476, n. 1 and Pfeiffer, *Introduction*, pp. 118–19.

[65] Cf. *RE*, XII (1903), 659–61 and *RGG*, Vol. IV, Col. 884 [Schaff-Herzog Encyclopedia].

(4) *Translations into Arabic*

Already in Byzantine days there were Christianized Arabic tribes along the eastern borders of the empire, who were loosely joined to the empire and provided its border guard against the tribes of the desert. Yet we do not know of any biblical translations into Arabic from this period. These rather come from the needs of the Christians of those lands of the Near East, who in the seventh century A.D. came under the rule of the Arab world, expanding tremendously under Islam. Among these people Arabic became progressively the vernacular language. In these areas then translations were made into Arabic, based on biblical textual forms which had previously been used locally. These Arabic translations (labelled 𝔄 in *BH* as a whole) are therefore rather late and by no means a unit.[66]

(5) *Translations into Coptic*

Coptic, the latest linguistic offshoot from ancient Egyptian, was the language of the Christians of Egypt. Since Egypt was Christianized rather early and extensively,[67] the beginnings of the translation into Coptic go back to the third century A.D. Naturally, these translations were based on the Septuagint textual form, which was commonly used in Egypt. As a result they are important testimonies for us as to the Greek biblical text which was read in Egypt in the early Christian centuries. After the separation of the Monophysitic Coptic Church from the imperial Church in the fifth century, the Coptic translations became the authoritative biblical texts in the Coptic Church. Coptic split up into a considerable number of regionally divided dialects. Correspondingly, there were a number of Coptic translations (grouped together in *BH* under the *siglum* 𝔎). Best known are the translations in the Sahidic and Bohairic dialect. Because of its antiquity (about A.D. 300) the Sahidic translation (*BH*: *Sah*) is important. Sahidic is the Coptic dialect of Upper Egypt, receiving its name from the Arabic term for Upper Egypt: eṣ-Ṣaʿid, namely "the Highland." Furthermore, Bohairic is the Coptic dialect of the Delta, receiving its name from the Arabic term for a Lower Egyptian province: el-Buḥeirah, namely "the one at the Sea." The Lower Egyptian Bohairic translation is

[66] Editions and literature are listed in Goettsberger, *op. cit.*, p. 478.

[67] See Harnack, *Die Mission und Ausbreitung des Christentums* (4th ed., 1924), pp. 705 ff.

attested by the available translations only for a later period (seventh century A.D.?).[68]

(6) *Translation into Ethiopic*

Christianity was introduced in the northern part of modern Abyssinia, in the kingdom of Aksum, already in the fourth century by missionaries from Syria and very quickly established as the state religion. The Bible was also translated into Ethiopic not much later, and very possibly based on the Lucianic Septuagint textual form accepted in Syria. Of course this cannot be definitely proved, since the Ethiopic Bible was subsequently poorly transmitted and as a result was repeatedly redacted, and since the earliest available manuscripts of the Ethiopic translation (*BH*: 𝔄) go back no farther than the thirteenth century.[69]

The noteworthy textual variants of all of these Near Eastern translations of the Old Testament produced from the Septuagint are entered in the textual critical apparatus in the large Septuagint editions.[70]

44. *The Old Testament Text in the Western Church*

In the very beginning Christendom still made use of the Greek language, even in the western half of the Roman Empire, particularly in Rome itself. However, since Latin, the general popular language in this region, was spoken by Christian congregations, need arose of translating the Bible into this language. Subsequently, the more important the Latin-speaking church became as it passed through a considerable history, the more the Latin biblical translation and its history gained in prominence.[71]

(1) *The Old Latin Translations* (*Vetus Latina*)

In the nature of the case it is quite understandable that the earliest translations into Latin are based on the Septuagint, the

[68] Editions and literature on the Coptic translations are listed in Goettsberger, *op. cit.*, pp. 472–73; Roberts, *op. cit.*, pp. 230 ff.

[69] Editions and literature in Goettsberger, *op. cit.*, pp. 473–74 and Pfeiffer, *op. cit.*, p. 116, n. 31.

[70] Especially in Brooke and McLean, *op. cit.*, and in the large edition of Rahlfs (see p. 336).

[71] For a thorough treatment of this subject, see F. Stummer, *Einführung in die lateinische Bibel* (1928).

accepted biblical text in the influential Eastern Church of that time. Since these translations came into being fairly early, from the textual critical viewpoint they are important indirect evidence for a fairly old Septuagint text, antedating the Septuagint recensions of the third or fourth century A.D. The existence of a Latin translation in the second half of the second century A.D. is attested by the statements of early church historians, first for North Africa. This was the region in which Latin was probably first used as the language of Christian worship and literature. The historians also refer to a Latin translation in use during the same period in southern Gaul. By the beginning of the third century the use of a Latin biblical translation at Rome can also be attested.

Unfortunately we know far too little of these Old Latin translations. Since they were later superseded by the Vulgate, there are very few manuscript remains of them. The first great learned work on the material available from Old Latin biblical translations had to collect its text largely from biblical quotations of early church writers who used Latin.[72] From these it could recover only a fragmentary text, while only certain parts could be based on manuscript materials. In the meanwhile a considerable amount of manuscript material of the Old Latin translations has come to light. Yet even this falls far short of yielding a complete text and does not promise success in the renewed attempt to achieve Sabatier's goal, namely, to reconstruct the Old Latin biblical text from all available quotations of early church Latin writers by means of current learned research.[73] The more important manuscripts which are used in the textual critical apparatus of *BH* include, first, a manuscript from the fifth century which contains larger and smaller fragments of the Old Latin translation of the prophets (and the Gospels). In the fifteenth century it was cut up and used for book bindings in the Cathedral Library at Constance, thus scattering it to the winds. Still the fragments could be partially put together again.[74] Codex Lugdunensis (*BH*: $\mathfrak{L}^{L}$) belongs to the sixth century. It is now in the Library of Lyons (*MS. No.* 54). It contains all of Numbers, Deuteronomy, and Joshua, and various fragments

[72] P. Sabatier, *Bibliorum sacrorum latinae versiones antiquae seu vetus italica*, Vols. I–III (1739–49; 2nd ed., 1751), cited in *BH* as $\mathfrak{L}$.

[73] This is the aim of the great work, *Vetus Latina—Die Reste der altlateinischen Bibel nach Petrus Sabatier neu gesammelt und herausgegeben von der Erzabtei Beuron*, Vols. I ff. (1949).

[74] They were published by A. Dold, *Konstanzer alt-lateinische Propheten- und Evangelienbruchstücke mit Glossen* (1923), cited in *BH* as $\mathfrak{L}^{D}$.

of Genesis, Exodus, Leviticus, and Judges.[75] Rather extensive fragments of the Pentateuch, as well as of the prophets, are also contained in the under-writing found on a palimpsest manuscript at Würzburg (*Cod. membr. No.* 64), also dating to the sixth century.[76] A palimpsest manuscript from Vienna (*Cod. Vind. lat.* 17) contains some Old Latin fragments from Genesis, as well as from First and Second Samuel.[77]

In addition, the Old Latin translations—or at least marginal notations based on them—are occasionally found in Vulgate manuscripts of some of the books of the Bible. Although the Codex Complutensis from the ninth or tenth century, now located at Madrid (*Univ Bibl. MS. No.* 31), generally contains the Vulgate text, some of its books, for example, Ruth, Tobit, and the Books of Maccabees, appear in the Old Latin translation.[78] Another Vulgate manuscript, Codex Gothicus Legionensis, in the St. Isidore Chapter Library at León since A.D. 960, contains large and small fragments of the Old Latin text of the Books of Kings, of Tobit, and of Baruch in its margins.[79]

The remaining available manuscripts on the Old Latin translations are listed and described by Stummer.[80] Unusual readings from these texts are entered in the large Septuagint editions of Brooke and McLean and of Rahlfs.

There is not enough Old Testament manuscript material available to prove how many were the Old Latin translations to which repeated references are made by early church writers, particularly Augustine. One could easily imagine that the different regions which used Latin as a Church language, North Africa, Gaul, and Italy, each had their own biblical translation, or at least read the Old Latin in their own individual textual form. For the New Testament, where the manuscript sources are more abundant, a North African text and an Italian text can be distinguished. On the basis of a statement by Augustine[81] the latter is called *Itala*; correspondingly the former is called *Afra*. Naturally, there were both of these

[75] Published by U. Robert, *Pentateuchi versio latina antiquissima e codice Lugdunensi* (1881) and *Heptateuchi partis posterioris versio latina antiquissima e codice Lugdunensi* (1900).

[76] Published by E. Ranke, *Par palimpsestorum Wirceburgensium, Antiquissimae Veteris Testamenti Versionis Latinae Fragmenta* (1871), cited in *BH* as $\mathfrak{L}^{h}$.

[77] Published by J. Belsheim, *Palimpsestus Vindobonensis antiquissima Veteris Testamenti translationis latinae fragmenta* (1885), cited in *BH* as $\mathfrak{L}^{Vind}$.

[78] See S. Berger, *Notices et Extraits des Manuscrits de la Bibliothèque Nationale et autres Bibliothèques*, XXXIV (1893), 119 ff.

[79] Published by C. Vercellone, *Variae Lectiones Vulgate Latinae Bibliorum editionis*, Vols. I–II (1860–64), cited in *BH* $\mathfrak{L}^{Lg}$.

[80] Stummer, *op. cit.*, pp. 33 ff.

[81] Given by Stummer, *ibid.*, p. 56.

textual forms for the Old Testament, too, but the material available is too limited for a corresponding grouping of the manuscripts.

(2) *The Vulgate*

The Vulgate, the "commonly distributed" translation as it has been called especially since the Council of Trent, had a somewhat official aspect even in its conception. It was a pope, Damasus I, 366–84, who gave the occasion for its existence, as he commissioned the learned and well-travelled monk, Jerome of Stridon in Dalmatia in A.D. 383, then living in Rome, to revise the Old Latin translations in the interest of improving and unifying the numerous textual forms in circulation. The first Old Testament book Jerome revised was the psalter of the Vetus Latina, using Septuagint manuscripts whose type is no longer known to us. Thus arose a new Latin textual form of the psalter which, because it was adopted into the use of the liturgy of the city of Rome and is still used today in St. Peter's Church, is called Psalterium Romanum.[82] After the death of his patron, when Jerome went to the Near East and stayed in Bethlehem, he once more improved this text of the Psalms on the basis of the hexaplaric Septuagint manuscripts with which he became acquainted there. He even adopted the Aristarchic signs in this new text of Psalms. Since this text of Psalms became accepted first of all in Gaul, it was called Psalterium Gallicanum. According to his own statement, Jerome revised the entire Old Testament in similar fashion. However, outside of the psalter, only the Book of Job is available in manuscripts of this revision. Finally, Jerome once again revised the Latin Old Testament at Bethlehem on the basis of the Hebrew text, which he knew substantially in the form of the later Masoretic text. It was not actually an entirely independent new translation based on the original. For he drew on the traditional Old Latin text as he had previously done, and was guided not only by the original and explanation of it by Jewish scholars whom he knew, but also by the Septuagint and the translations of Aquila, Theodotion, and Symmachus. This work was concluded in A.D. 405. It was the basis of the Vulgate.[83]

Jerome's Latin biblical translation (*BH*: 𝔙), which subsequently

[82] The traditional derivation of the *Psalterium Romanum* of Jerome has been debated. Cf. Bleddyn J. Roberts, *op. cit.*, pp. 248–49.

[83] On the nature of this translation, see the thorough treatment in Stummer, *op. cit.*, pp. 90 ff. The biblical quotations appearing in Jerome's exegetical writings, etc., are cited in *BH* as *Hie(r)*.

became accepted in the Roman Catholic Church, contained the text as defined by Jerome for most of the Old Testament books. Only the psalter was maintained in the form of the Psalterium Gallicanum, while the translation of Psalms done by Jerome with reference to the Hebrew text, the *Psalterium juxta Hebraeos*, not adopted in ecclesiastical usage, continued to be handed down by itself in manuscripts. The Vulgate maintained the Old Latin version of various "apocryphal" books which Jerome had not included in his translation because they were not in the Hebrew Old Testament. In spite of several initial conflicts, the translation efforts of Jerome in time won their own way in the church. Naturally, the Old Latin translations were not wholly superseded, as is shown by the fact that in the Vulgate manuscripts, occasionally individual books appear in this earlier textual form (see p. 344), or at least the Old Latin translations are also given in the margins of the manuscripts of the Vulgate; particularly, elements of the Old Latin translations again penetrated into the Vulgate text itself. Thus confusion arose in the text all over again. This, then, gave occasion to further efforts at revising the text of the Vulgate, such as are linked with the names of Cassiodorus, the secretary of Theodoric the Great, and of Alcuin, the friend of Charlemagne. It has been conjectured that Codex Amiatinus (*BH*: $\mathfrak{V}^{A}$) textually demonstrates the revision of Cassiodorus. This is an eighth-century manuscript now located in Florence.[84] The Examplar Parisiense[85] is linked with Alcuin's revision. It was created in Paris in the thirteenth century as a model manuscript. It is known because of a number of thirteenth- and fourteenth-century manuscripts. It also was important for the further history of the biblical text (see p. 347).

Subsequently, the Council of Trent in its fourth session on April 8, 1546 declared that the Vulgate text was the authoritative Latin textual form for the Roman Church, by means of its decree *De Usu et editione sacrorum librorum*. This once more resulted in the need of fixing this text authentically for the future. Thus by papal appointment the Vulgata Sixtina came into being. It was published in 1590 under Sixtus V, 1585–90. Since it proved to be insufficient, immediately thereafter under Clement VIII, 1592–1605, the Vulgata Clementina appeared in three successive revised editions of 1592, 1593, and 1598. The latter form of the Vulgate afterwards continued to be accepted. Recent Vulgate editions are

[84] See Stummer, *op. cit.*, p. 131.

[85] See *ibid.*, pp. 149 ff.

based on it.[86] In 1907 the pope assigned to the Benedictine order "*restitutio primiformis textus Hieronymianae bibliorum versionis.*" As a result of their efforts, a revised Vulgate text is now appearing with a textual critical apparatus, making use of the available manuscript tradition.[87]

In compass and arrangement of books, the Vulgate follows not the Hebrew original but the Septuagint (see pp. 334–35), since it is basically only a revision of the Old Latin biblical translations based on the Septuagint. Missing are only a few books which are not generally attested even in the manuscript tradition of the Septuagint, such as the Odes, the Psalms of Solomon, the Epistle of Jeremiah, the Books of Susanna and Bel and the Dragon, as well as Third and Fourth Maccabees. Apart from a few lesser changes, the Vulgate differs from the Septuagint in the order of the books, since the Vulgate follows the Hebrew text in placing the major prophets before the minor prophets and in arranging the minor prophets. Furthermore, the Vulgate shifts Third Ezra,[88] together with the apocalyptic Fourth Ezra it contains, to the very end of the Bible like an appendix.

Luther in his German Bible adhered closely to the order of the Books in the Vulgate, except that in his arrangement he omitted those books from the main part of the Old Testament which are not in the Hebrew Old Testament, assembling them as an appendix to the Old Testament, "The Apocryphal Books." He left out Third and Fourth Ezra altogether. However, he did include various portions from the Septuagint, his "Additions to Esther," and the additions to Daniel which are also included in the Vulgate, namely, "The Prayer of Azariah" and "The Song of the Three Men in the Fiery Furnace." Also included in Luther's additions to Daniel are the small books: "History of Susanna and Daniel," corresponding to *Sus.* in 𝔊, and "Concerning Bel of Babylon" and "Concerning the Dragon of Babylon," which together correspond to *Bel et Draco* in 𝔊.

The division of biblical books into the chapters still in use arose in the Vulgate. It traces back to Cardinal Stephen Langton, later Archbishop of Canterbury. At the beginning of the thirteenth

[86] This is true of the two editions of M. Hetzenauer, the large edition, *Biblia Sacra Vulgatae editionis* (1906) and the pocket edition, *Biblia Sacra secundum Vulgatam Clementinam* (1922—).

[87] *Biblia Sacra juxta Latinam Vulgatam versionem ad codicum fidem . .. edita*, Vols. I ff. (1926—). H. Quentin is the reviser of the first volumes to appear.

[88] This is First Ezra in 𝔊. First and Second Ezra in 𝔄 are together Second Ezra in 𝔊, and are Ezra plus Nehemiah in 𝔐.

century, he was a teacher in Paris. His division was adopted in the Exemplar Parisiense of the Vulgate. From there it came into general use in the Vulgate. Then in the fourteenth century it became adopted in the Hebrew Bibles (see p. 307). Through the polyglots of the sixteenth and seventeenth centuries, it made its way into the other translations of the Old Testament. Just the other way around, the division into verses proceeded from the Masoretic text (see p. 307) through the polyglots to the other translations of the Old Testament. Naturally, there have always been certain variations in divisions into chapters and verses in the various lines of tradition.

CHAPTER III

METHODS OF TEXTUAL CRITICAL WORK

45. *Changes in the Original Text*

TEXTUAL criticism of the Old Testament receives its assigned task for one thing from the fact that we have no original for any Old Testament book or even any abstract very close to it in point of time. Rather the manuscripts of the complete Hebrew text which we have are many centuries later than even the latest Old Testament Scriptures. Also there is a large gap in time even when we assume that the consonantal text transmitted from these Scriptures was fixed about A.D. 100 and from that date was transmitted unchanged (p. 308). Finally, even the most recently found copies of parts of the Old Testament are still separated from the originals by a considerable period of time. It must therefore be taken into account that the Old Testament books have shared the common lot of all literary works copied in manuscript form. Namely, in the course of copying manuscripts a variety of errors and changes has altered the original text. A glance at passages appearing more than once in the Old Testament shows that this is actually the case: Second Samuel, chapter 22, is the same as Psalm 18, and Second Kings, chapters 18 to 20 is the same as Isaiah, chapters 36 to 39; note also the sections of the Books of Samuel and of Kings which are literally repeated in Chronicles. The parallel passages have many textual variations in details, even though naturally their texts were continually adjusted to one another. Thus the basic text, which originally was literally identical, subsequently was changed and altered in many details. What, then, is the "Original Text" of the Old Testament? Is it possible to reconstruct the "Original Text" after setting aside the errors and changes definitely contained in the transmitted texts?

It is a primary, methodically necessary principle that whoever assumes a subsequent change of the text at a given spot must be able to give an explanation how the error probably occurred. Therefore, it is indispensable for every effort at textual criticism to know the possible sources of errors. These fall into two groups:

unintentional, accidental textual alterations and intentional textual changes.

(1) *Accidental Changes*

In the group of textual errors which occurred accidentally,[1] naturally there is always a possibility of individual cases which cannot be classified, for in the field of copyist's slips, certainly the irrational element of chance plays a considerable part. None the less a methodical textual criticism can take that possibility into account only in a very exceptional instance, unless it desires to surrender itself to pure caprice in the area where there are no fixed rules. When we have a text before us which probably manifests various distortions as over against the "Original" which we cannot control, we may not be able to set up a strict requirement for reconstructing the "Original Text," but we can attempt to approach the "Original," by removing those textual errors which have come about by definite, recurrent reasons for textual distortion. In this process we must consider, first, the types of error which occur whenever any manuscript is copied, and, second, the errors most probable in copying Hebrew script.

(a) *Errors which appear in any manuscript copy.* Letters which look alike are frequently exchanged during copying. In order to be able to demonstrate this phenomenon in a concrete case, one must be thoroughly familiar with the styles of script in which the literary work under consideration was written or copied. In the portions of the Old Testament which go back to pre-exilic days, such errors could have come about when the material was still being copied in Old Hebrew characters, like those in the ostraca of Samaria and Lachish (see p. 220). (This script, which had become time honoured in the meanwhile, seems to have been used in the post-exilic period, too, for the copying of the Old Testament canon or at least for given parts of it; see p. 313.) In the writing style of the ostraca of Lachish (see Figure 10) the confusion of such letters as *n* with *k* or ʿ with *d*, or ʾ with *t* was natural, particularly if one of these letters was written unclearly. Of the later square Aramaic characters in which the later portions of the Old Testament were written, and into which the earlier portions were copied, *d* and *r*, or *h* and *ḥ* were almost identical, and *y* and *w* among other pairs could easily be confused.[2]

[1] See the large collection of material by F. Delitzsch, *Die Lese- und Schreibfehler im Alten Testament* (1920).

[2] Examples in Delitzsch, *op. cit.*, pp. 103 ff. In the manuscripts from the Dead Sea (see pp. 311 ff.), written in square letters, *y* can hardly be distinguished from *w*.

Too often it also happens, particularly in the process of mechanical thoughtless copying, that the order of the letters is accidentally transposed. One example among many is the word occurring in I Chron. 11 : 33, though not entirely correctly vocalized *hbḥrmy* or "the (man) of Bahurim," which in the parallel passage in II Sam. 23 : 31, because of transposed letters, is distorted into *hbrḥmy*. Naturally, letters of similar appearance, which are not distinctly contrasted in the copy at hand, will be particularly easily transposed. This phenomenon can apply just as readily to entire groups of letters, or even to entire words.

Furthermore, a letter which actually occurs twice in succession can accidentally be written only once. This phenomenon is called haplography, "writing singly," abbreviated *haplogr.* in *BH*.[3] For instance, *lpdwt l*[4] *lʿm* in II Sam. 7 : 23 appears erroneously in the parallel passage, I Chron. 17 : 21, as *lpdwt l ʿm*. This omission can occur with letters which are only similar and with entire groups of letters or entire words.

The counterpart of haplography is dittography (abbreviated *dittogr.*), which means accidentally writing twice one letter, one group of letters, or one word. Thus in Jer. 7 : 25 we have the word *ym*[5] in an unusual connection, which is all the more noteworthy since it is regularly missing elsewhere in the same stereotyped expression which occurs repeatedly in Jeremiah (29 : 19; 35 : 15; 44 : 4). Closer examination shows that this *ym* is only the accidental repetition of the last two consonants of the immediately preceding word *hnbyʾym*.

A very frequent mistake in copying rests on homoeoteleuton, abbreviated *homoeotel.* in *BH*. This is the omission of an entire passage between two similar words or at least between words *ending* with the same letters (whence the name). An example can clarify this easily. Second Kings 23 : 16 originally had the following text: *wayyiqqaḥ eth-haʿaṣamoth min-haqebharim wayyisroph ʿal-hammizbeaḥ wayeṭammeʾhu kidhebhar yhwh asher qaraʾ ish haʾelohim* (*baʿamodh yarabhʿam beḥagh ʿal-hammizbeaḥ wayyiphen wayyissaʾ eth-ʿeynaw ʿal qebher ish haʾelohim*) *asher qaraʾ et-haddebharim haʾelleh.* "And he [Josiah] took the bones out of the tombs, and burned them on the altar, and defiled it, according to the word of the Lord which the man of God proclaimed (when Jeroboam stood at the altar during the festival.

[3] Rudolph Kittel (ed.), *Biblia Hebraica*, abbr. *BH* (3rd ed., 1937).
[4] The introduction of the *mater lectionis* (לוֹ) came about only later.
[5] The introduction of the *mater lectionis* (יוֹם) occurred later.

Then he turned and directed his eyes toward the tomb of the man of God) who said these things." The words in parentheses, which are missing in the Hebrew text, must have been there originally, since without them the last relative clause hangs in mid-air and since they are necessary for the continuity of the narrative. Fortunately they are found in 𝔊 whose master copy still contained them. They were erroneously omitted by a copyist because they end with the expression *ish ha'elohim* which also appears immediately before them. When the copyist had written the first *ish ha'elohim* and wanted to continue, by a lapse in his observation (generally noted in the apparatus of *BH* as *aberratio oculi*) he caught sight of the second *ish ha'elohim* and continued to write on from that point, omitting the entire part between. Omission by homoeoteleuton can also occur when two words or groups of words are only similar in form, without being identical. For example, in the Hebrew text underlying the Septuagint of Jer. 27 : 10, a homoeoteleuton is produced by the similar words *'dmtkm* and *'bdtm*, the portion between them having been overlooked either by an earlier copyist of the Hebrew text or by the translator of the Septuagint. See *BH* on this point. Omission occasioned by homoeoarchy, the counterpart of homoeoteleuton, occurs more rarely. This is the loss of a passage which *begins* in a manner identical with or similar to the following portion of the text.

(b) *Errors peculiarly due to the nature of Hebrew script.* The Old Testament was copied first of all as a pure consonantal text until about the fifth century A.D. when an initial, still incomplete vocalization system was introduced (see p. 308). Only the hint of the vowels, particularly in word final position, was introduced rather early by means of the *matres lectionis* which are consonants used as vowel letters. This is demonstrated once again by the ostraca of Lachish (see the example in Figure 10) and also by the recently discovered Dead Sea manuscripts. It is quite evident that a group of consonants by itself written without vowels is frequently capable of various readings and meanings. Yet this fact must not be exaggerated in the case of the textual transmission of the Old Testament, for on the whole the later Masoretic vocalization simply rests on an old, never disconnected tradition, as can be demonstrated by the history of the language. Therefore, the ambiguity of an unvocalized text is not particularly great, since the context conveys the meaning of the individual words. As a rule one cannot read the Old Testament consonantal text in any very different manner from that in which the Masoretes finally vocalized it. Moreover, every textual critic simply sets aside the later vocalization and takes a good look at the pure consonantal text. Therefore, an error in vocalization in the transmitted text must not be viewed as a textual error in the exact sense. Only where an erroneous reading has influenced the consonantal text is it important for textual criticism. That applies naturally only in a limited sense to the *matres lectionis*, which, it is true, are externally a part of the consonantal text but actually are a rather early, though initially a very slowly developed element of the vocalizing of the text. Therefore, the textual critic must substantially disregard them and erroneous placements of the *matres lectionis* are only to be observed as textual errors of a secondary nature. The original lack of vocalization is important only in cases in which a misunderstanding of the text led to a misrepresentation of the pure consonantal skeleton of a word. Thus, for example, we have the word *w'ltw* in I Kings 10 : 5 which was vocalized by the Masoretes as a singular (ועֹלָתוֹ) *we'olatho*, but originally was probably intended as a plural (ועֹלֹתָו) *we'olothaw*. In the parallel passage, II Chron. 9 : 4, this word was definitely וְעֹלוֹתָו (*we'olothaw*), adding the *mater lectionis* (ו). Then the one w (ו) was mistaken for y (י) (see p. 350) and was taken to be part of the consonantal structure of the word. An entirely different and here meaningless word results, וַעֲלִיָּתוֹ (*wa'aliyyāthō*).

The Hebrew script is characterized by limited separation of words. This is incorrectly described as *scriptio continuus*, meaning writing without separation of words. The old alphabetic script even separated words from one another by means of a vertical line or dot (see Figures 8, 9, and 10). However, the later Aramaic script of the Persian period and the resultant Hebrew square letters gave up this word separator and as a rule left only a small intervening space between the individual words. Examples are the papyri of Elephantine (see p. 221) and the Qumrān Old Testament manuscripts. Naturally, this intervening space could be omitted, thus removing any separation of words. The missing word separation combined with any uncertainty produced by unwritten vowels could lead to misinterpretations and textual corruptions. Yet this factor of uncertainty must not be exaggerated since usually the context clearly indicates how one should separate the words. In Isa. 2 : 20 a word which occurs only this one time, לחפרפרות, *lḥprprwt*[6] is erroneously divided into the unintelligible *laḥpor perōth*. The

[6] Θ still presupposes the original text and transcribes it *pharpharōth*.

other way around, one now reads a word in Num. 23:10 as *ūmispar*, which is an erroneous combination of the words *umi sapar*, which the *parallelismus membrorum* requires in this line of verse, a reading which ש preserves.

(2) *Intentional Changes*

Intentional textual changes are usually not so easily recognized in the traditional text, since they generally have not left any irregularities in the text which might point to them. Such changes could be of a formal nature intended to smooth out an awkward expression or to replace an expression difficult to understand with a more customary one. They could also have dogmatic grounds and be intended to remove or modify a passage considered disagreeable from the standpoint of religion or custom. Such changes, even if they were produced rather late in the process of manuscript copying of the texts, are not a concern of pure textual criticism but rather of literary criticism. In the larger sense, however, some of these textual changes should be considered here.

That is true of explanatory glosses inserted in the text.[7] One usually thinks of them as having been written between the lines or in the margin. Then, as the glossed text was copied, they were simply drawn into the continuous text, either intentionally or accidentally. Often they are revealed only by the very deficient way they dovetail with the syntactic context. They are also recognizable because they subsequently "explain" the text or a word in the text in a sense which clearly contradicts the meaning of the original text. For example, when the words *eth melekh Ashur* are placed at the end of Isa. 7 : 17, it is true they convey to the preceding prophetic warning a meaning which is not factually wrong, but they reveal themselves as an explanatory gloss because they completely fail to dovetail with the context of the sentence. On the other hand, the words *hi 'Bethel* stand in the text of Joshua 18 : 13 to explain the preceding *Luz* and to identify it as the well-known site of Bethel. Here, the placing of these words, which should actually be with the first *Luzah*, already reveals them as a gloss, probably once written in the margin and then drawn into the continuous text at an awkward spot. In this case the note is also factually erroneous,

[7] Glosses and abbreviations in the Hebrew text of the Old Testament have been collected and classified by G. R. Driver. See his works, *Glosses in the Hebrew Text of the Old Testament*, *Orientalia et Biblica Lovaniensia*, I (1957), 123–61 and "Abbreviations in the Masoretic Text, I," *Annual of the Hebrew University Bible Project* (1960), pp. 112–31.

since in the time of the Judges the site of Luz was still distinguished from the sanctuary, Bethel (see Josh. 16 : 2), and only later, in the sense of the gloss, was this site also given the name of Bethel.

Probably we also have caption glosses in the Old Testament.[8] In these marginal notes, the word from the text which they should explain is repeated at the head of the note as a caption. Subsequently both the note and the caption have been drawn into the continuous text. Only in this manner can one explain the unusual text at the beginning of II Kings 9 : 4, where the young "son of the prophets" of verse one is simply designated as *hanna'ar*, "the young man" in the original text. Apparently a commentator wanted to note distinctly that by the "young man" in verse four the "prophet" of verse one was meant. Therefore, he placed *hanna'ar* as a caption in the margin and added the explanatory gloss *hannabhi'* ["the prophet"]. During subsequent copying this caption gloss was drawn into the text, giving rise to the linguistically impossible combination *hanna'ar hanna'ar hannabhi'* of the present text.[9]

Finally it seems that certain common words or names were abbreviated and that here and there later these abbreviations were wrongly analysed. Such a case could be involved in Isa. 7 : 10. Here probably the name, *Yesha'yahu*, was abbreviated as Y', which would be conceivable in the Book of Isaiah. Later this name was misinterpreted as an abbreviation for the divine name *Yahweh*, even though what follows is the speech not of God but of the prophet.

46. *Evaluation of Textual Critical Material*

Textual criticism is not limited to conjectures and surmises in efforts to remove textual errors and textual changes which have crept in. Rather, the entire abundant material of Old Testament textual transmission is at our disposal, requiring careful consideration. The material available from manuscript transmission of the Hebrew text by the synagogue naturally provides us with only the wording of the Old Testament as fixed by the Masoretes. Even what has become known from pre-Masoretic manuscripts (see pp. 308 ff.) on the whole contains the same consonantal text probably

[8] J. Herrmann, "Stichwortglossen im Alten Testament," *OLZ*, XIV (1911), Cols. 200–4; "Stichwortglossen im Buche Ezechiel," *OLZ*, XI (1908), Cols. 280–82.

[9] A very complicated case of a caption gloss is involved in Josh. 17 : 11, according to G. Dahl, *JBL*, LIII (1934), 381–83; see also Noth, *Das Buch Josua* (2nd ed., 1953), p. 98.

fixed about A.D. 100. The manuscripts from Qumrān (see pp. 311 ff.) have taken us beyond this period of synagogue textual transmission, but so far only with parts of the Old Testament. The Qumrān texts are relatively close to the Masoretic text, and in any case come from a period in which the textual transmission of the Old Testament had already passed through a rather long initial stage. Yet it is precisely the fortunes of the text in this initial stage which form the textual critical problem. For the Pentateuch we have still Samaritanus as a special Hebrew textual witness which, however, is known only from rather recent manuscripts, the history of whose transmission is a problem in itself. Yet in relation to the Hebrew Pentateuch text, Samaritanus can be taken into account as a relatively independent line of textual transmission. Its textual variations must always be tested for the extent to which they reflect Samaritan textual changes, or ancient variants of the Hebrew Pentateuch.

We get behind the resultant Hebrew text for the entire Old Testament with the help of those translations which had a Hebrew textual source which was older than our present Hebrew text. For this purpose the Septuagint comes under consideration before all others, since it was derived from a Hebrew text of the third and second centuries B.C. Then from that point on it went its own way with all of its later offshoots and translations. At least in the case of the Pentateuch, the basis of the Peshitta gives independent testimony on the Hebrew source as known in either the first century B.C. or the first century A.D. (see pp. 323 and 338). Yet it is difficult to say in detail, in the case of the Peshitta, how far it reflects the Hebrew text or again only the Septuagint text in the relatively early form of the second century A.D. Naturally, the Targumic material is also a direct witness to the Hebrew text, though this material was fixed in writing substantially later than A.D. 100. Therefore, in general, it presupposes the later (Masoretic) consonantal text and indicates only exceptional evidence of being based on a parallel variant source. The Vulgate, on the contrary, must be viewed with great caution as a witness to any Hebrew source (see p. 345). Even as a witness, it attests only a Hebrew text which was in circulation substantially later than A.D. 100. Therefore, apart from the problematical character of details in treating the Peshitta as a first-hand translation, when considering the Hebrew text of the last pre-Christian centuries, we are dependent essentially on the great line of Septuagint transmission, which also plays a considerable part in the textual criticism of the Old Testament. Subsequent translations are naturally of secondary importance. The "Original Text" of the Septuagint has not been preserved either. It is also known that the Septuagint was repeatedly approximated to the later forms of the Hebrew text and also suffered various other textual changes. Therefore, the possibility exists that here and there the original Septuagint text is preserved only in one of the later translations. In such a case the original Septuagint could have represented its Hebrew source accurately and this source could have provided a more nearly original text than the Hebrew consonantal text transmitted to us. Nevertheless, one must allow for the fact that in any remotely derived translation of the Septuagint a reading will be indirectly attested, which is not only older than all other textual material for the passage in question, but even perhaps represents the "Original Text" at this point. In this situation naturally those derived translations of the Septuagint are particularly important which trace back to the days before the great Septuagint recensions known to us (see pp. 329 ff.) and before the use of a broader manuscript transmission of the Septuagint text as we know it. There are especially the Sahidic translation (see p. 341), the Old Latin translation in so far as it is preserved, and finally the Peshitta, important in this respect also, wherever it is dependent on the Septuagint.

An accurate use of the translations of the Old Testament for textual critical work must constantly take their particular natures closely into account. Each of these translations is first of all an entity in itself and must be understood from the standpoint of the views and requirements of the circle for which it was made. Furthermore, each of these translations—or where a translation comes from several hands, each of the translators—employs a particular translation technique, which one must know in order to be able to determine correctly concerning the nature of the translation in any given case. This means that one must read every translation in its given context before one can properly evaluate its textual critical witness on a given passage. This is the risk involved in using the textual critical apparatus of *BH*, which at any given point can provide only single words or groups of words from the translations, so that the character of each translation as a whole of a peculiar sort will remain unnoticed. Actually one should understand these textual critical notes as only references and always refer to the translation in question in order to read it in its context.

When we find a variation in a translation from the traditional Hebrew text, our first question will naturally be whether this variation is based on the peculiar nature of the given translation—whether it rests on the limited nature of the available means of expression in the language of the given translator or on the stylistic aims as well as the religious or ethical views of the translator. If these questions are answered in the negative, the further question is raised whether the variation has been brought about by a textual error or a textual corruption within the given translation. For, naturally, in the process of copying manuscripts of every translation the same or corresponding sources of errors come into consideration. Only when this question, too, has been decided in the negative does the question of the relation of the textual variation to the source of the translation have its turn. In the case of first-hand translations this means a relation to the Hebrew source. At this point there is the possibility, as with every process of translation, that the translator has misunderstood his source and therefore translated it wrong. Only if this, too, gives insufficient explanation for the variation in question, must we conclude that the translator has used a different basic text from the one transmitted to us. That is, we see in the variant translation evidence for an actual textual variant. Then it becomes necessary to retranslate the text of the variant translation into the source text, for which process again an exact knowledge of the style and technique of the translation in question is a necessary part. For the retranslation from the Septuagint into Hebrew we have the technical assistance of the Septuagint concordance of Hatch and Redpath (see p. 336). For the lexical relationship between the Syriac of the Peshitta and the Old Testament Hebrew of the psalter we have L. Techen, "Syrisch-Hebräisches Glossar zu den Psalmen nach der Peschitta."[10] Finally there is the question which of the two variants of the basic text constituted in this manner represents the "Original Text," or at least is close to the "Original Text." At this point, however, we enter the realm of the basic questions of Old Testament textual criticism.

47. *Principles of Textual Criticism of the Old Testament*

The goal of textual criticism is the closest possible approach to the "Original Text" of the Old Testament, keeping in mind the caution noted earlier (see p. 349). By "Original Text" in this area of textual criticism we have in mind, generally speaking, the hypothetical textual form of the Old Testament which the Palestinian

[10] *ZAW*, XVII (1897), 129–71, 280–331.

canon produced as it was taking shape in individual parts of the Old Testament from about the fourth century B.C., which at the same time fixed the traditional wording. Of course there is reason for assuming that this canon also faithfully assimilated very much older portions, even the pre-exilic ones which entered into it, to a considerable extent in their original wording, thus rendering the prophetic sayings approximately in the form in which they were probably recorded by the students of the prophets. Yet questions on the prehistory of the portions united in the canon, on their relationship to original notes and sketches, and on the possible alterations even in wording on the way leading from the initial fixing in writing to the last formulation as it later appeared in the context of the canon—these are the concern of exegesis and literary criticism, not of textual criticism. Certain methodical principles apply to textual criticism understood in this sense, in spite of the many viewpoints pertinent to it, which should not be ignored.[11]

(1) *The Masoretic Text the Basis of Criticism*

Always and everywhere the traditional Hebrew text is the basic starting-point for all textual work on the Old Testament. The few Old Testament portions which were originally in Aramaic are to be included here. The Masoretic text is the text of the canon in its original language, continually recopied in a straight line. All translations, even if they are very old, represent only offshoots. Indeed, every process of translation is a great source of errors since no translation can mechanically reproduce the original exactly, entirely apart from all misunderstandings and mistakes of the translator. In addition, it has been demonstrated in detail over and over again that 𝔐 rests on a rather careful guarding of a text which had become canonical. The Pentateuch as found in the Hebrew Samaritanus, though it is not a translation, cannot begin to compare with it. This principle does not mean that the wording of 𝔐 must be maintained at all costs as the original wording, since it cannot be doubted at all that it, too, contains mistakes and corruptions. It does, however, mean that in any scholarly work every variation from 𝔐 must be noted and substantiated, even if this variation follows a variant of the Hebrew text attested by textual evidence

[11] Cf. the basic, even if occasionally debatable, studies by H. S. Nyberg, "Das textkritische Problem des Alten Testaments am Hoseabuche demonstriert," *ZAW*, New Series, XI (1934), 241–54 or Nyberg's *Studien zum Hoseabuche, zugleich ein Beitrag zur Klärung des Problems der alttestamentlichen Textkritik* (Uppsala Universitets Årsskrift, 1935–36).

from some other quarter, and certainly if the variation depends on a pure conjecture on the part of a modern commentator.[12] Again, variants of other textual witnesses in works which are not particularly textual-critical in their make up can be passed over in silence. Even a variation from the Masoretic vocalization and pointing must be noted each time, even if these textual elements have less weight as a tradition than the consonantal text.

(2) *The More Difficult Reading Preferred*

If we have textual variants under consideration in any passage at all, such as on the one hand 𝔐, and on the other hand a Hebrew text inferred from 𝔊, after careful evaluation of the possibilities listed on pp. 357–58, then for the decision as to which variant represents the "Original Text" or is closer to the "Original Text," the principle is authoritative that the *lectio difficilior* is to be preferred. It must be assumed that in the course of the textual history clarifications or simplifications of more difficult manners of expression, took place, that current words replaced uncommon or obsolete ones, etc., rather than assuming that more difficult expressions would have been substituted for simple ones. Therefore, the text with the uncommon expression is considered the older or "more original." Naturally, the principle of *lectio difficilior* does not mean that every imaginable oddity and obscurity of a transmitted text must be snatched up as original.[13] It does mean, however, that in an unusual passage all possibilities for explanation must first be attempted and exhausted before one proceeds to the conclusion that the text is corrupt in this passage (*BH*: *crrp*, *corr*, standing for corruption), and therefore a more understandable textual form should be assumed to be more original, which again would give the illuminating explanation of the error that had occurred in the text.

Above all, linguistic possibilities for explanation must be attempted first. The living Hebrew language was more wealthy in vocabulary, word meanings, and word forms than the later tradition and explanation of the Old Testament text would let us know

[12] Part of this proof must be an explanation of the origin of the assumed textual error in 𝔐. Wherever there is no room for textual critical notes, a notation, *text. em.*, meaning *textus emendatus*, is sufficient.

[13] In the case treated on pp. 351–52, dealing with the corruption in II Kings 23 : 16, the textual form attested by 𝔊 is the smoother and therefore the "easier" one. None the less, in this case we must not cling to 𝔐 as the *lectio difficilior*, for 𝔐 provides no reading at all here, but rather an apparent textual error.

readily, and we must often contend with words and meanings in Old Testament Hebrew which were later forgotten. Particularly careful and deliberate use of related languages can still help to convey them to us.[14] In this manner many an apparently obscure passage can be explained beautifully in its context and in its original, concrete, and specific wording without any textual alteration.

The principle of the preference of the *lectio difficilior* applies, within the limits indicated, not only with reference to proved ancient textual variants but particularly with reference to all "simplifying" textual emendations of modern commentaries.

(3) *Free Conjecture*

It must be definitely assumed that the "Original Text" of the Old Testament canon has been corrupted by a variety of errors at a time to which no remaining textual witness extends, not even the Septuagint translation which came into being very early; furthermore, we must assume that a number of original readings which had been maintained for some time were not assimilated either in 𝔐 or in any of the translations. Therefore, there is basically the right of free conjecture (*BH*: *conj.*), which means an assumption about the original wording which is not supported by any available old textual witness. It is evident that in the practical use of this basic right there is a pressing necessity to practise extreme caution! All other possibilities of explanation of a textual passage must be put forward and exhausted before textual corruption is definitely assumed. Likewise, here where every ancient tradition is missing, the textual process which led to the assumed corruption must be particularly carefully clarified. Often it is easier to attest the defectiveness of a textual passage with great certainty than to propose a clarifying assumption about the original text of this passage. Such conjectures demonstrate very different grades of possibility or probability.

Of course, there are textual conjectures whose correctness is simply evident. In such cases it is also permissible to assume even uncommon processes of textual corruption. In this category, for example, I would treat the conjecture of A. Bertholet,[15] on Ps. 2 : 11–12 according to which both of the last words of verse 11

[14] Cf. L. Kopf, "Arabische Etymologien und Parallelen zum Bibelwörterbuch," *VT*, IX (1959), 247–87.

[15] *ZAW*, XXVIII (1908), 58–59.

and both of the first words of verse 12 must be inverted, so that, ignoring the *mater lectionis* and the vocalization and the word division, the more original text reads *nashequ bheraghlaw bire'adhah*, "kiss his feet with trembling." This reading gives the best restoration from the arrangement of obscure words in the given passage presupposed even by the reading in 𝔊. This not only renders a good meaning but also restores the *parallelismus membrorum* to the best effect. One will then probably have to assume, somewhat differently from Bertholet, that the consonantal text of this passage was once written in rather narrow columns and that in the process of mechanical copying two columns were accidentally exchanged in their order.

(4) *Consideration of Metre*

If there was rhythmically formed speech in Hebrew—and this fact is not to be doubted at all—then with the portions of this form involving chiefly the prophetic sayings, the Psalms, and the wisdom passages, the metre cannot be ignored in textual criticism. Rather the verse form must be considered in all efforts to reconstitute the "Original Text" of these portions. This produces at the same time the basic right to explain a text as corrupt because of the damaged metre (*BH*: *mtr cs* or *m c*, standing for *metri causa*) and by means of consideration of the metre to attempt its improvement. On the other hand, the practical exercise of this basic right is difficult, because even the question of the bases of Hebrew metre is still debated.[16] Many details have not yet been clarified,[17] for example, the very important question for textual criticism to what extent rhythm, whose very nature is regularity, allowed mixed metres in Hebrew. (Mixed metre means a variation in the number of beats in the individual lines of verse.) Perhaps in this question one must distinguish between the more strict "Song" and the freer spoken "Saying." At any rate, one can scarcely

[16] J. Ley, *Grundzüge des Rhythmus, des Vers- und Strophenbaues in der hebräischen Poesie* (1875); *Leitfaden der Metrik der hebräischen Poesie* (1887); E. Sievers, *Metrische Studien I: Studien zur hebräischen Metrik, Abh. d. phil.-hist. Kl. d. Kgl. Sächs. Ges. d. Wiss.*, XXI (1901), No. 1; J. W. Rothstein, *Grundzüge des hebräischen Rhythmus und seiner Formenbildung* (1909); on the other hand, S. Mowinkel, "Zum Problem der hebräischen Metrik," *Festschrift für Alfred Bertholet* (1950), pp. 379–94; F. Forst, "Die Kennezeichen der hebräischen Poesie," *Theologische Rundschau*, New Series XXI (1953), 97–121; S. Segert, "Problems of Hebrew Prosody," *VT*, Suppl. VII, (1960), pp. 283–91.

[17] An exact knowledge of early Hebrew pronunication of words is essential for exact metrical analysis of early Hebrew poetry. However, this pronunciation is known only in broad outline. In details it can only be reconstructed hypothetically.

consider it possible that there was a very arbitrary variation in rhythm; one must rather look for definite reasons for such a variation in a given instance.

Frequently, however, one discovers that an irregularity in the metrical construction of a "poetical" piece goes hand in hand with an actual disturbance of the meaning, and that the reconstruction of the expected metrical form of a verse brings order into its contents as well. I take a random example. In Amos 3 : 3–6 we have verses with 3 plus 2 beats, based on the system of Sievers. On this basis, verse 5a has one beat too many. At the same time, in this verse the word פַּח (*paḥ*) is not in place, since the bird trap is not mentioned until the next line, while this verse deals with the [*moqesh*] "throw stick or snare." If one removes the word פַּח (*paḥ*) in verse 5a, *mtr cs*, because it found its way in accidentally from verse 5b, then metre and content are in order at the same time. In addition, it must be mentioned that 𝔊 did not yet have this word in verse 5a in its source. If that is true, then one is basically justified in removing or introducing a word or its equivalent, *mtr cs*, even when the textual corruption revealed by the disturbance of the metre by chance has not caused any offence against the meaning, and no ancient textual witness provides a witness. On the same metrical grounds in verse 4b one could consider the superfluous מִמְּעֹנָתוֹ (*mimme'onathō*) secondary, even though in this case no further convincing arguments can be adduced. It must be stressed, however, that all textual operations based on metre require the utmost care and caution.

ANCIENT NEAR EASTERN CHRONOLOGY

Egypt	*Syria-Palestine*	*Mesopotamia*	*Asia Minor*
Prehistoric Cultures	Chalcolithic Period	Halafian Culture, *c.* 2nd half of the 5th millennium	
		Obeidian Culture, *c.* 1st half of the 4th millennium	
	Early Canaanite Culture, Early Bronze Age, *c.* 3300–2100	Warkan Culture, *c.* 2nd half of the 4th millennium	
Early Dynastic Period, 1st and 2nd dyn., *c.* 2850–2650		Jemdet Nasr Culture, *c.* 3000–2800	
Old Kingdom, 3rd–6th dyn., pyramid builders, *c.* 2650–2200		Early Sumerian city states, middle of the third millennium	
		Dynasty of Accad, *c.* 2300–2100	
		Sargon of Accad, *c.* 2300–2250	
First Intermediate Period:	Middle Canaanite Period,	Late Sumerian city states, *c.* 2100–1850	
9th and 10th dyn., 2200–2050	Middle Bronze Age, *c.* 2100–1550		
11th dyn., capital at Thebes, *c.* 2050–1991			
Middle Kingdom, 12th dyn., 1991–1788		"West Semitic" rulers gain control:	
		1 dyn. of Babylon, *c.* 1830–1550	
		Yagitlim and Yahdunlim of Mari	
		Shamshi-Adad I of Assyria, 1749–1717	
		Zimrilim of Mari	
Second Intermediate Period:		Hammurabi of Babylon, 1728–1686	
13th–16th dyn., 1788–*c.* 1570		Beginning of Cassite rule in Babylonia, *c.* 1700	Early Hittite Kingdom, *c.* 1700–1500
Hyksos rule, *c.* 1670–1570			

Egypt	*Syria-Palestine*	*Assyria-Babylonia*	*Asia Minor*
New Kingdom, 18th and 19th dyn., *c.* 1570–1200	Late Bronze Age, *c.* 1550–1200		
	Late Canaanite period		
18th dyn., *c.* 1570–1345	Rās Shamrah texts		
Thutmose III, 1502–1448	Egyptian control of Palestine: Amarna period, 1400–1360		
Amenophis III, 1413–1377			
Amenophis IV, 1377–1360			
19th dyn., *c.* 1340–1200		Middle Assyrian Kingdom, *c.* 1300–1100	Late Hittite kings:
Rameses II, 1290–1223	Tribes of Israel occupy Palestine		Suppiluliumas, *c.* 1350
Merneptah, 1223–1210			Mursilis II, *c.* 1325
Appearance of the Sea Peoples	Appearance of the Sea Peoples		Hattusilis III, *c.* 1250
20th dyn., *c.* 1200–1085	Beginning of the Iron Age		End of the Hittite kingdom, *c.* 1200
Rameses III, 1197–1165			
		End of Cassite rule in Babylonia, *c.* 1150	
	Formation of the state in Israel, *c.* 1000	Various native dynasties in Babylonia	
	Saul		
	David		
	Solomon		
22nd dyn., Libyan, *c.* 935–745	Division of the Personal Union, Israel-Judah, 926		
Shishak I, *c.* 935–915			

Egypt	*Palestine*	*Assyria*	*Iran*
Shishak I, *c.* 935–915	Parallel states of Israel and Judah		
		Neo Assyrian kingdom:	
		Ashurnasirpal II, 884–859	
	Ahab of Israel, 871–852	Shalmaneser III, 859–824	
	Battle of Qarqar, 853		
	Jehu of Israel, 845–818		
	Tribute of Jehu to Shalmaneser III, 842		
		Adadnirari III, 810–782	
		Ashurdan III, 771–754	
	Menahem of Israel, 746–737	Tiglathpileser III, 745–727	
	Tribute of Menahem to Tiglathpileser III, 738		
	Ahaz of Judah, 742–725		
	Syro-Ephraimite war and first catastrophe of Israel, 733		
		Shalmaneser V, 727–722	
		Sargon II, 722–705	Median kingdom, *c.* 715–550
Late period	End of Israel, 721		
25th dyn., Nubian, 714–663	Hezekiah of Judah, 725–697		
		Sennacherib, 705–681	
	Sennacherib's campaign in Palestine, 701		Achaemenid rule in Persia, beginning *c.* 700
		Esarhaddon, 681–669	
26th dyn., Saite, 663–525		Ashurbanipal, 669–631	
	Josiah of Judah, 639–609		

Egypt	*Syria-Palestine*	*Mesopotamia*	*Iran*
		Neo Babylonian kingdom, founded by Nabopolassar, 626–604	
		Fall of Nineveh, 612	
Necho, 609–593	Clash of Necho and Josiah at Megiddo, 609		
		Nebuchadnezzar II, 604–562	
	Fall of Jerusalem and end of Judah, 587		
			Cyrus II, the Achaemenid, conquers Media, *c.* 550
		Cyrus II conquers Babylon and the Neo Babylonian Empire, 539	
Cambyses, the son of Cyrus II, 529–522, conquers Egypt in 525			
	Persian Empire lasts until 334–331		
	Alexander the Great conquers the Persian Empire, 334–331		
	Death of Alexander the Great and beginning of the rule of the Successors (Diadochi), 323		
Ptolemaic kingdom, 323–30	Seleucid kingdom, 312–64		

INDEXES

INDEX OF HEBREW AND ARAMAIC WORDS

Transliterated words are listed here. Old Testament names which are spelled as in the English Bible appear in the General Index.

This transliteration is an attempt to render the consonants as clearly as possible in this English edition. Wherever possible, one English consonant represents one Hebrew consonant; exceptions are *sh*, *bh*, *dh*, *ph*, *th*, *gh*, and *kh*, which represent single Hebrew consonants. The text does not reflect distinctions in length of vowels. Definite articles are omitted, except in the construct chain (e.g., *ḥoph hay-yam*, 'the shore of the sea'). Proper nouns are capitalized.

Words are listed in the order of the Latin alphabet. This arrangement does not take ' (*aleph*) and ʿ (*ʿayin*) into account. Their consonantal value is not commonly recognized in English. Consonants with diacritical marks (e.g., *ṭ*) are listed with the corresponding consonants without such marks. Initial *aleph* is not recorded in this transliteration. Initial *aleph* is to be assumed in words which begin with vowels here. Anyone interested in study of Hebrew consonants where they differ from English ones will best refer to a Hebrew grammar.

ʿAbhar Nahara, 102
ʿAbhdath, 57
Abhel Beth Maʿakhah, 81, Fig. 3
adhon, 280
ʿaghalah, 86
ʿAi, 60, 130, 174
ʿAkko, 23, Fig. 3
ʿaliyyah, 153
ʿAqqaron, 78, 123
ʿarabhah, 54, 83
Aram Beth Reḥobh, 81, 245 (*see also* Beth Reḥobh)
Aram Dammaseq, 81, 245
Aram Naharaim, 245
Aram Ṣobhah, 80, 96, 245 (*see also* Ṣobhah)
ʿArbhoth Moʿabh, 54
ʿArbhoth Yeriḥo, 54
Ashdoth hap-Pisgah, 61
ha-Asheri, 94
ha-Ashuri, 94
ʿAzzah, 140

baʿal, 281
Baʿal Ḥaṣor, 57
baith, 64
Bashan, 62, 63
be'er, 154
Be'er Shebhaʿ, 18
berekhath hash-shelaḥ, 158
beth abh, 64
Beth ʿEdhen, 261
Beth Gubhrin, 18, 70, 89, 120, 134
Beth Maʿakhah, 81
Beth Reḥobh, 81, Fig. 3
Beth Yeraḥ, 120
Bethleḥem Yehudhah, 56
Biqʿath Beth Neṭophah, 20
Biqʿath hal-Lebhanon, 59
Biqʿath Megiddo(n), 61
bor, 154
boṣ, 165

darom, 57
derekh, 85
Dor, 78
drk, 164

ebhen bohan, 69
ʿEdhen, 261
ʿEin Gedhi, 18, 26, 46, 89
ʿemeq, 60
ha-ʿEmeq, 23, 60
ʿEmeq Akhor, 60, 69
ʿEmeq Ayyalon, 60
ʿEmeq Repha'im, 60
ʿEmeq Yizreʿel, 61
Ephraim, 57
Ereṣ Kenaʿan, 49, 50
Ereṣ Naphtali, 59
Ereṣ Yisraʿel, 49
ʿEṣyon Gebher, 79

galil, 58, 59
gath, 164
Gelil hag-Goyim, 58
gelilah, 59
genizah, 303, 309, 317, 322
Geshur, 81, Fig. 3
Giḥon, 155, 158

Gil'adh, 62
Gilboa', 58
Golan, 63

hadhom, 159
har, 56 (*see also* General Index, *s.v.* Mount; Arabic Index, *s.v.* Jebel)
Har(e) ha-'Abharim, 61
Har Ephraim, 57-59
Har Ga'ash, 58
Har Gerizzim, 58
Har hag-Gil'adh, 62
Har hag-Gilboa', 19, 20, 23-24, 58
Har Ḥermon, 60
Har hak-Karmel, 19, 20, 58
Har Nebho, 62
Har Ṣalmon, 58
Har Ṣemaraim, 58
Har Tabhor, 24, 28, 59 (*see also* General Index, *s.v.* Tabor)
Har Timna', 44
Har Tubh, 18
Har Yehudhah, 56, 59, 69
Ḥarodh, 15, 20, 23-24, 71, 78, 89, 91-92, 97
Ḥaṣebhah, 89
ḥaṣer, 145
Ḥermon, 60
ḥoph hay-yam, 60
Ḥori, 240

'Iyye ha-'Abharim, 62

Karmel, 58
Kasdim, 239
Kephar Zekharyah, 89
Kena'an(i), 49-51
Kerethi (u-Phelethi), 78, 79
keseph, 167
kethubhim, 334
Kikkar (ha-Yarden), 54
Kinnereth, 54
Kokhim, 171

Laish, 74
Lebhanon, 59
lṭsh, 166

Ma'akhah, 81, Fig. 3
ma'aleh, 89
Ma'aleh Adhummim, 90
Ma'aleh 'Aqrabbim, 89
Ma'aleh hal-Luḥith, 90
Ma'aleh haṣ-Ṣiṣ, 89
maim ḥayyim, 155
masorah, 303
maṭṭeh, 63
merkhabhah, 86
mesillah, 85-88
Meṭullah, 26
meturgeman, 317
Midhbar Ṣin, 57
Midhbar Tekoa', 56
Midhbar Yehudhah, 56
Midhbar Ziph, 56
mighdal, 12, 152
mishor, 61, 62
mishpaḥah, 64

Naṣrath, 21, 25
neghebh, 56-57, 94, 99 (*see also* General Index, *s.v.* Negeb)
Nehar hat-Tanninim, 22, 38
niqqudhoth, 305

on, 288
opheh, 160

parashah, 307, 316
peḥah, 103
pelaḥ taḥtith (rekhebh), 161
Pelishtim, 8
pesher, 312, 313-15
petuḥa, 307
Pisgah, 61, 62

qara'im, 304
Qedhesh Naphtali, 56, 74
qedheshim, qedheshoth, 281
Qe'ilah, 56
Qenaz, 70
Qiryath Ye'arim, 28 (*see also* General Index, *s.v.* Kiriath-jearim)
Qishon, 24
Quweh, 206

Rabbath bene 'Ammon (Rabbah), 80, 120, Fig. 3
Ramoth Gil'adh, 62
reḥobh sha'ar ha'ir, 152
rosh, 64
Rosh han-Niqrah, 21, 23, 92
Rosh Pinnah, 25, 26

Salkhah, 63
sebhir, 305
sedher, 307
Se'ir, 57
Ṣemaraim, 58
Senir, 60
Ṣephath, 21, 54
seren, 258
sethuma, 307
shebheṭ, 63
shelaḥ, 158
shelem, 283

Shomeron, 101
Shrq, 98
ṣinnor, 156
Siryon, 60
Ṣobhah, 81, Fig. 3
Ṣobhah II, 114
ṣon, 40
soph pasuq, 307
Ṣor'ah, 74, Fig. 2
Ṣrp, 166

Ta'anakh, 140
Tabhor; *see* Har Tabhor
tannur, 160
targem, targum, turgeman, 317
tiqqun sopherim, 304

Ya'ar Ephraim, 57
Ya'ar Ḥerath, 56
Yabhesh Gil'adh, 56, 62
Yahweh, 55
yam, 61
Yam ha-'Arabhah, 54
Yam Kinnereth, 54
Yam ham-Melaḥ, 17, 54
Yarqon, 22, 87, 132
Ya'zer, 75
Yehudhah, 55, 56
yeqebh, 164
yhd, 168
Yidh'alah, 55

zeqenim, 64

INDEX OF ARABIC WORDS

Included in this list of Arabic words are the few Turkish words which are used here.

The transliteration follows customary norms for rendering Arabic words in English. The emphatic consonants (*ẓ, ḍ, ṭ, ṣ*) indicated by a dot placed below them, are to be pronounced farther back on the palate than consonants not so marked. The consonant *q* falls into the same grouping in that it is to be pronounced farther back than the corresponding non-emphatic *k*. The symbols (*dh, th, gh, kh, sh*) represent fricative consonants, each of which is a single Arabic consonant. The *dh* and *th* distinguish between the voiced and voiceless English *th* as in *then* and *thin* respectively. The ' and ʻ correspond to Hebrew *aleph* and *ʻayin*. The latter is a characteristic Semitic language sound produced by expulsion of air from the contracted larynx. The *ḥ* is a fricative. The *kh* resembles German *ch* as in *ach*. Final *h* is a silent letter, reproduced for orthographic purposes.

Word stress falls as close to the end of a word as possible. The stress is on the nearest long vowel to the end of a word or on a short vowel followed by two or more consonants. Words without any long vowels or combinations of a short vowel followed by two consonants are stressed on the initial syllable.

In the transliteration Arabic definite articles are bound by a hyphen to the nouns they modify. The definite article is *el-*. This article is assimilated to any following consonant which is pronounced roughly in the same place as *l* itself, as are dentals, alveolars, and sibilants.

The words are arranged according to the English alphabet. In this arrangement the articles, the consonants ' and ʻ, and diacritical points and marks are not taken into account. Initial ' is omitted in the transliteration.

ʻAbdeh, 57
Ābil, 81, Figs. 1 & 3
Abu Habbah, 292
ʻAbūd, 58
Abu'l Kemal, 209, 251
Āfis, 220
ʻain, ʻoyūn, 12
ʻAin ʻAṭān, 157
ʻAin Feshkhah, 135, 312
ʻAin Ḥaṣb, 89
ʻAin Jelʻad, 62
ʻAin Jidi, 18, 26, 46, Fig. 1
ʻAin Qedes, 57
ʻAin Shems, 74, 98, 136
ʻAin Sitt Maryam, 155
ʻAin Umm ed-Derej, 155
ʻAjlūn, 13, 14, 34, 43, 62, 73, 81, 91, 96, 100, 114, 117, Fig. 1
ʻAkkā, 23, Fig. 1
ʻAmmān, 13, 26, 27, 62, 80, 115, 117, 120, Fig. 1
el-ʻAmq, 190, 210, 261
ʻAmrit, 171
ʻamūd, ʻawāmīd, ʻimdan, 12
ʻAmwās, 116
Antakya, 210, 265
ʻanzeh, 40
el-ʻAqabah, 15, 24, 44, 79, 83, 92, 117, 164, 166, 192, Fig. 6
ʻaqrab, 38
ʻArāq el-Emīr, 120, 221
ʻArḍ el-ʻArḍeh, 74
ʻarīsh, 36
arnab, 38
Arslan Tas, 162
ʻArtūf, 18, Fig. 1
ʻAsqalān, 78, 151
el-ʻAsūr, 19, 28, 57, Fig. 1
ʻAtlīt, 113, 133
ʻAṭṭārūs, 75

baḥr(ah), 12
Baḥr Lūṭ, 17, Fig. 1
Baḥret el-Ḥūleh, 15, 21, 25-26, 51, 54, 74, 93, 113, Fig. 1
Baḥret el-Kheiṭ, 15

Baḥret Ṭabarīyeh, 15, Fig. 1
Balāṭah; *see* Tell Balāṭah
ballūṭ, 34
el-Bālū'ah, 212
Bāniyās, 26, 103, Fig. 1
baq'a, beqa', buqei'a, 10
el-Baq'a, 60
baqar(ah), 38, 39
baṣṣah, 12
beden, 38
bedū, 47
Beisān, 15-16, 20, 27, 30, 46, 58, 62, 71, 90, 104, 114, 129, 140, Fig. 1
beit, buyūt, 12
Beit Jibrīn, 18, 70, 89, 120, 134, Fig. 1
Beit Nettīf, 88
Beit Sīrah, 88
Beit 'Ūr el-Fōqah, 88
Beit 'Ūr et-Taḥtah, 88
Beitīn, 72, 87, 131, 140
belaḥ, 36
Beled Sinjār, 261
el-Belqā, 13, 26, 35, 68-69, 75, 80-81, 90, 96, 100, 103, Fig. 1
el-Beqā', 14, 44-45, 59, 93, 189, 193, 259, Figs. 1 & 3
Bilād er-Rūḥa, 20, 24, 87, 89, 92, 192, Fig. 1
bīr, biyār, 12
Bīr es-Seba', 18, 22, 25, 26, 46, 68, 75, 129, Fig. 1
birkeh, burak, bureikeh, 12
Birs Nimrūd, 292
Boṣrah, 27, Fig. 1
el-Breij, 219, 259
el-Buḥeirah, 341
burdeqān, 36
burj, bureij, 12
el-Burj, 78
Burj Beitīn, 72
buṭm, 34

deir, 12
Deir el-Azhar, 98
Deir Dubwān, 174, 179, Fig. 5
Deir-ez-Zōr, 46
Der'a, 14, 27, 62, Fig. 1
Derb el-Ḥajj, 27
dhurah, 35
dīb, 37
Dībān, 80, 219

eḥṣeini, 37
Erīḥa, 16, 26, 140, Fig. 1
Esdūd, 78, 177
ethel, 35

faras, 39
Faynūm, 325
Feinan, 44
fellāḥ, 38
Filasṭīn, 9
Fīq, 93
Fuqū'a, 20

ghanam, 40
ghazāl, 37
Ghazzeh, 21, 22, 26, 78, 140, Fig. 1
ghōr, ghuweir, 10
el-Ghōr, 15-16, 25, 27, 46, 54, Fig. 1
el-Ghuweir, 15, 55, Fig. 1
Gīzeh, 194

Ḥaḍramaut, 188, 189
ḥajal, 38
ḥajar, ḥijār, 10
Ḥalab, Ḥaleb, 190, 219, 263
Ḥamāh, 210, 259
ḥammām, 12
ḥammeh, 12
ḥaram, 12
Ḥaram Rāmet el-Khalīl, 137
Ḥauran, 117
el-Ḥejāz, 188, 192, 221, Fig. 6
Ḥesbān, 75, 91, Fig. 1
ḥinṭah, 35
ḥiṣn, ḥuṣūn, 12
ḥmār, 38
Ḥomṣ, 190, 256, 263, Fig. 6
ḥṣān, 39
Ḥūleh; *see* Baḥret el-Ḥūleh

'Irāq, 186, 196, 236, Fig. 6
Irbid, 14

Jabbūl, 191
jamal, 39
jāmi', jawami', 12
Jbeihah, 91
Jbeil, 199, 213, 262
Jeba', 97
jebel, jibāl, 10 (*see also* General Index, *s.v.* Mount ; Hebrew Index, *s.v.* har)
Jebel 'Ajlūn, 14, Fig. 1
Jebel el-Anṣārīyeh, 189-90, 261
Jebel el-Aqra', 92, 294
Jebel ed-Drūz, 14, 27, 42, 46, 63, 101, Fig. 1
Jebel Ferdis, 119
Jebel Fuqū'a, 19, 20, 23-24, Fig. 1
Jebel Ḥalāq, 57
Jebel Ḥaurān, 14
Jebel Islāmīyeh, 19, 28
Jebel Jel'ad, 62
Jebel Jermaq, 21, 28
Jebel Karmel, 19-20, 23, Fig. 1
Jebel el-Khalīl, 17, Fig. 1
Jebel Libnān, Fig. 1

Jebel el-Mushaqqaḥ, 21, 23, 74, Figs. 1 & 3
Jebel Nāblus, 19, Fig. 1
Jebel el-Quds, 17, 19, Fig. 1
Jebel er-Rūmeideh, 137
Jebel Ṣafed, 21, Fig. 1
Jebel esh-Sheikh, 60, 190
Jebel esh-Sherqi, 190, Fig. 1
Jebel et-Telj, 31, 60, 190, Fig. 1
Jebel eṭ-Ṭōr (I), 19-20, 28
Jebel eṭ-Ṭōr (II), 20, 24, 28
Jebel eṭ-Ṭōr (III), 20
Jel'ad; *see* 'Ain-, Jebel-, Khirbet- (*see also* General Index, *s.v.* Gilead)
Jenīn, 24-25, 156, Fig. 1
Jerāblus, 260
jerād, 38
Jerash, 14, 117, Fig. 1
el-Jezīreh, 186, 188, 191, Fig. 6
el-Jīb, 88, 133, 157
jisr, jusūr, 12
Jisr Benāt Ya'qūb, 26, 93
Jisr ed-Dāmyeh, 113
Jisr el-Majāmi', 113
Jōlān, 14, 42, 63, 73, 81, 93, 101, 120, 193, Fig. 1
Jubb Jenīn, 44

Kābūl, 59
Kalb, 37
karm, kurūm, 12
Karnak, 264, Fig. 7
kenīseh, kenā'is, kuneiseh, 12
el-Kerah, 13, Fig. 1
Khābūr, 186, 191, 200, 209, Fig 6
el-Khaḍr, 214
el-Khalīl, 18, 25, Fig. 1
khalleh, 10
khān, 12, 115
khanzīr berri, 38
Kharrūb, 34
kharūf, 40
el-Khashm, 20, Fig. 1
khirbeh, khurāb, 12, 121
Khirbet 'Abbād, 89
Khirbet Baṭneh, 91
Khirbet Bel'ameh, 156
Khirbet el-Burj, 78
Khirbet Ibziq, 90
Khirbet Jel'ad, 62
Khirbet Kerak, 120
Khirbet Mefjir, 115
Khirbet el-Minyeh, 115
Khirbet el-Mukāwer, 119
Khirbet el-Muqanna', 78
Khirbet el-'Ōjah el-Fōqah, 28
Khirbet Qumrān, 135, 227, 311-15
Khirbet Rabūḍ, 82
Khirbet es-Samrah, 44
Khirbet Seilūn, 87, 131, 176
Khirbet Teqū', 90
Khirbet eṭ-Ṭubeiqah, 70, 134
Khirbet Wādi el-Khōkh, 156
Khorsābād, 266, 268, 270
Khreibet en-Naḥās, 44
Kirkuk, 241
Kizil Irmak, 188, 266, Fig. 6
Kōkab el-Hawā, 114
Kül Tepe, 252, Fig. 6
Kurnub, 89
Kuyunjuk, 209, 266

el-Lejah, 14, Fig. 1
el-Lisān, 16, Fig. 1
Lubban, 87
Ludd, 22, Fig. 1

Ma'an, 27
maghārah, maghā'ir, 10
Maghāret el-Wardeh, 44
Maltāya, 285
Mār Sāba, 69-70, 328
el-Mashnaqah, 109
Maṣna', 93
maṣṭabeh, 194
medīneh, medā'in, 12
Meirōn, 54
mejdel, mejādil, 12
mell, mellūl, 34
Membij, 340
el-Mene'īyeh, 44
merj, murūj, mureij, 10
Merj ibn 'Āmir, 23, Fig. 1
Merj'oyūn, 81, 93
meshref(eh), mashārif, musheirifeh, 10
el-Meshrefeh, 256, 263
mesjid, mesājid, 12
me'z, 40
mīneh, 12
mōz, 36
Mrashrash, 44
Mshettah, 115
munṭār, manāṭīr, 10

Nāblus, 19-20, 22, 25, 28, 90, 120, 140, 316, Fig. 1
nahr, 12 (*see also* General Index, *s.v.* River)
Nahr el-'Āṣi, 14, 189
Nahr Belīkh, 186, 261, 293, Fig. 6
Nahr Diyālah, 186
Nahr Iskenderūn, 22, Fig. 1
Nahr Jālūd, 15, 20, 23-24, 27, 71, 78, 89, 91-92, 97
Nahr el-Kebīr, 92, 189, 192, 274
Nahr Līṭāni, 21, 189, Fig. 1
Nahr el-Mefjir, 22, Fig. 1
Nahr el-Muqaṭṭa', 24, Fig. 1

Nahr el-Ōjah, 22, 87, 132, Fig. 1
Nahr el-Qāsimīyeh, 189
Nahr Rūbīn, 22, Fig. 1
Nahr Sukreir, 22, Fig. 1
Nahr ez-Zerbā (II), 22, 38, Fig. 1
Nahr ez-Zerqā (I), 13, 16, 22, 41, 62, 91, Fig. 1
nakhl, 36
nāqah, 39
naqb, nuqeib, 10
Naqb eṣ-Ṣafa, 89
en-Nāṣireh (Nāsreh), 21, 25, 71, Fig. 1
Nā'ūr, 26, 75, 80
en-Nebeh, 27
Nebi Ōsha', 13
Nebi Yūnis, 266
Nerab, 219
netesh, 47
nethel, 35
Niffer, 250
Nimrūd; *see* Tell Nimrūd
en-Nuqreh, 14, 35, 63, 73, 101, 127, Fig. 1

qabr, qubūr, 12
qal'ah, qilā', 12
Qal'at el-Qurein, 113
Qal'at er-Rabaḍ, 114
Qal'at Sherqāt, 265
qanṭarah, qanāṭir, quneiṭrah, 12
Qantīr, 264
Qaqūn, 114
qarn, qurūn, qurein, 10
Qarn Ṣarṭabeh, 16, Fig. 1
qaryeh, qurā, 12
qaṣr, quṣūr, quṣeir, 12
Qedes, 59, 74
Qeiṣārīyeh, 22, 38, 119, Fig. 1
el-Qiryeh, Qiryat el-'Einab, 28, 98, 113, 115, Fig. 1
Qreish, 34
qubbeh, qubeibeh, 12
Qubbet eṣ-Ṣakhrā, 114
el-Quds, 17, 25, Fig. 1
Quneiṭrah, 93

Rājib, 44
rajm, rujūm, rujeim, 10
Rajm el-Baḥr, 17
rakham, 38
er-Rām, 97
raml(eh), rumeileh, 12
er-Ramleh, 22, 112, Fig. 1
rās, rūs, 10
rās el-'ain, 12
Rās el-Abyaḍ, 92
Rās Feshkhah, 312
Rās Nahr el-Kalb, 92
Rās en-Nāqūrah, 21, 23, 92, Fig. 1
Rās Shakkah, 92
Rās Shamrah, 169, 199, 212-13, 216, 218, 226, 233, 243, 262, 293-94, 365
Rās es-Siyāghah, 62
retem, 35
Riḥāb, 81
Ruād, 262
er-Rumeileh, 136
rummān, 36
Ruweiseh, 214

sabkheh, sibākh, 12
ṣabr, 37
Ṣafed, 21, 54, Fig. 1
sahl, 10
Sahl el-Battōf, 20, Fig. 1
eṣ-Ṣa'id, 341
Ṣaidā, 262, Fig. 1
ṣāj, 160
ṣakhrah, ṣakhr, 10
Ṣalkhad, 63
es-Salṭ, 13, 26-27, 91, Fig. 1
Samakh, 27
es-Samūm, 32
Ṣān el-Ḥagar, 255, 264
Saqqārah, 221
Sar'ah, 74, 178
Sebaṣṭīyeh, 101, 113, 119, 128, 132-34
es-Sebbeh, 119, 134
Sefinet Nūḥ, 256
Sefīreh, 220, 260
seil, suyūl, 12
Seil Heidān, 75
Seil el-Mōjib, 13, 27, 75, 80, Fig. 1
Selūqiyeh, 120
Ṣerābīṭ el-Khādem, 214
sha'ir, 35
shajaret kīna, 37
Shaṭṭ el-'Arab, 186
Sheikh Abreiq, 135
Sheikh Sa'd, 101
sherī'ah, 12
Sherī'at el-Kebīreh, 15
Sherī'at el-Menāḍireh, 13-14, 63, Fig. 1
esh-Sherqīyeh, 32
shunnār, 38
sidr, 35
sinjān, 34
Sōlem, 71
Ṣūbah, 114
Ṣubeiḥi, 91
Ṣūr, 262, Fig. 1
eṣ-Ṣuweiliḥ, 80
Suweis (Suez), 2, 25, Fig. 6

Ṭabarīyeh, 15, Fig. 1
eṭ-Ṭābghah, 116
ṭaḥuneh, ṭāwaḥīn, 12
Ṭal'at ed-Damm, 90

tannūr, 160
eṭ-Ṭanṭūrah, 78
Ṭarāblus, 262
ṭarfa, 35
Tekrīt, 46
Teleilāt Ghassūl, 129
tell, tulūl, tuleil, teleilāt, 12, 14, 121, 123-125, 138, 199
et-Tell, 60, 129, 174, 179, Fig. 5
Tell Abu Maṭar, 129
Tell Aḥmar, 261
Tell 'Ajjūl, 130, 215
Tell el-'Amārna, 207-8, 264, 289, Fig. 6
Tell 'Areimeh, 75
Tell 'Asharah, 293
Tell- el-'Aṭshānah, 210, 261-62
Tell Balāṭah, 87, 120, 128, 134-36, 140, 207, Fig. 5
Tell Beit Mirsim, 130, 148, 151, 153-54, 159-60, 164-66
Tell Deir 'Allah, 91, 131
Tell Dōtān, 88, 91, 137
Tell ed-Duweir, 130, 133, 157, 165, 174, 216, 220
Tell Far'ah, 129, 131, 153, 173
Tell el-Far'ah, 130, 133, 158
Tell el-Fūl, 87-88, 131, 148, 152, Fig. 4
Tell Ḥalaf, 200, 261, Fig. 6
Tell Ḥarīri, 209, 238
Tell el-Ḥesi, 108-9, 125, 215
Tell el-Hiṣn, 15, 129, 140
Tell Ḥūm, 118
Tell el-Jeina, 14
Tell Jemmeh, 166
Tell Jezer, 127, 136, 156
Tell el-Kheleifeh, 44, 79, 164, 166
Tell el-Maqlūb, 62
Tell el-Mshāsh, 68
Tell el-Mutesellim, 127, 129, 132, 160
Tell en-Najīleh, 78
Tell en-Naṣbeh, 97, 137, 151
Tell Nebi Mend, 263
Tell Nimrūd, 162, 266
Tell el-'Obeid, 200
Tell 'Omar, 265
Tell el-'Oreimeh, 54
Tell el-Qādi, 26, 74, Fig. 1
Tell Qasīleh, 132, 166
Tell Qīlah, 56
Tell er-Rāmeh, 91
Tell Rāmīth, 62, 91
Tell Rif'āt, 260
Tell er-Rumeileh, 74, 98
Tell Sandaḥanneh, 70, 120, 134, 154, 171
Tell esh-Sheikha, 14
Tell es-Sulṭān, 129, 140
Tell Ta'annek, 76, 136, 140, 207, 257
Tell Ta'yīnāt, 176
Tell Waqqāṣ, 51, 132
Tell Zakarīyeh, 89
Tibneh, 58
timsāḥ, 38
tīn, 36
Ṭūl Karm, 22, 89, Fig. 1
Tulūl edh-Dhahab, 91
tūt, 36

Umm ed-Derej, 13
Urdunn, 9
Urfa, 338

wabr, 38
wādi, widyān, 10, 30
Wādi 'Ain 'Arīk, 88
Wādi el-'Arabah, 3, 8, 14, 44, 46, 57, 79, 89, 103, 118, 127, 165, 192, Figs. 1 & 3
Wādi Beidān, 90
Wādi Fār'ah, 19, 90, 129
Wādi Faṣā'il, 16
Wādi Ghazzeh, 22, 130, 166, Fig. 1
Wādi Ḥaḍramaut, 188
Wādi el-Ḥaramīyeh, 87
Wādi Ḥejjāj, 91
Wādi el-Ḥesā, 79, 80, Fig. 3
Wādi Ḥesbān, 91
Wādi el-Ḥesi, 22, Fig. 1
Wādi Ḥseinīyāt, 91
Wādi Kefrein, 75, 91
Wādi el-Khashneh, 90
Wādi el-Merāḥ, 44
Wādi Murabba'at, 313
Wādi Nāblus, 89
Wādi 'Oyūn Mūsa, 91
Wādi Qelt, 90, 134
Wādi Ṣannīn, 45
Wādi es-Sanṭ, 89
Wādi Selmān, 88, 90
Wādi es-Sidr, 90
Wādi es-Sīr, 80
Wādi eṣ-Ṣūr, 56
Wādi eṣ-Ṣuweinīṭ, 98
Wādi et-Teim, 93
Wādi el-Wāleh, 80
Wādi Yābis, 62
Wādi ez-Zeidi, 14
Wādi Zeimir, 22, 89, 90
wa'l, 38
wali, 12
wa'r, 10
Warka, 201
wāwi, 37

Yabrūd, 87
Yāfa (Jaffa), 22, 26, 28, 86, 99, Fig. 1

Yālo, 60, 74, 98
Yemen, 188
Yorghan Tepe, 241

Ẓabʿ, 37
Zaḥleh, 44
ẓahr, ẓuhūr, 10
zaʿrūr, 35
zeitūn, 35
Zerʿin, 23, 61, 71, Fig. 1
Zinjirli, 219, 260
ez-Zōr, 16, 38, 46

INDEX OF SCRIPTURAL PASSAGES

OLD TESTAMENT

Genesis
1 328
1: 1 329
1: 1-46: 28 326
4: 2b-4a 286
4: 22 166
10 224
10: 8 266
10: 10 . . . . 224, 265
10: 11 266
11: 28, 31 264
11: 31 261
12: 5 261
12: 7 7
13: 10-11 54
13: 12 54
14: 1, 9 254
14: 5, 6 88
15: 7 264
16: 5 305
18: 9 305
18: 22 304
19 17
23: 3 ff. 77
23: 19–24: 46 . . . 326 n. 8
24: 10 ff. 191
25: 2, 4 83
25: 8 83
25: 12-18 83
26: 34 77
27: 43 261
27: 46 77
28: 18 178
28: 22 178
29: 31–30: 24 74
30: 14 ff. 70
30: 24 68
31 327
31: 21, 23, 25 62
34 . . . . . 68, 70
35: 14 178
35: 16-20 72
35: 20 178
36: 11, 42 82
36: 13, 33 66
36: 31-39 . . . . 79, 258
37: 17 91
37: 25 . . . . 91, 191
37: 25, 27-28 83
37: 28, 36 83

Genesis—*contd.*
38: 5 70
39: 1 83
39: 31 68
40: 1 ff. 160
40: 11 50
42: 5 ff. 50
45: 19 ff. 86
46: 5 86
48: 1, 13, 14 73
49: 3-7 68
49: 3-27 66
49: 5-7 68
49: 13 305
49: 13-15 70
49: 14 71
49: 16-21 74
49: 29, 30 77

Exodus
1: 8 ff. 248
1: 11 264
13: 17 92
17: 8-16 82
20: 24-26 178
22: 26-27 158

Leviticus
20: 14 168
21: 9 168
25: 31 145

Numbers
1: 5-15 66
5: 26 = 7: 20 . . . 326 n. 8
7: 3 ff. 86
13: 6 70
13: 22 76
13: 29 51
20: 14 258
20: 19 . . . . 85, 88
21: 20 61
21: 25 146
21: 27-30 75
21: 32 75
22: 1 ff. 258
23: 10 354
23: 14 61
26 74
26: 5 50
26: 5-14 68
26: 5-51 66
26: 6 . . . . . 66, 69

Numbers—*contd.*
26: 13 66
26: 20 66
26: 21 66
26: 29 ff. 73
26: 30-33 98
27: 12 61
32: 1. 75
32: 12 70
32: 39-42 73
33: 3-49 92
33: 36 57
33: 42-43 44
33: 44 62
33: 47, 48 61
34: 3. 79
34: 3-12 67
34: 4. . . . . 57, 89
34: 7-11 75
34: 11 54
35: 10, 14 50

Deuteronomy
1: 7 . . . . 59, 61 n. 28
3: 9 60
3: 10. 62
8: 9 43
11: 24 59
12: 13 ff. 177
21: 19 152
23: 24 322
24: 3. 322
25: 1-3 322
25: 7. 152
26: 12, 17-19 322
27: 15 322
28: 31-33 322
31: 28 322
32: 7. 322
32: 49 . . . . 61, 62
33: 6-25 67
33: 23 . . . . 57 n. 19
34: 1. . . . . 61, 62

Joshua
1: 4 59
2: 6 153
2-9 72
5: 1 51
7: 1, 5b-26 69
7: 1, 17, 18 69
7: 8 130
7: 21. 168
8: 9, 13 60
9: 1 . . . . 61 n. 28
9: 17 . . 72, 76, 94 n. 98, 99
10: 10, 11 88
10: 12 60
10: 40 56
11: 3. 51
11: 5, 7 54

Joshua—*contd.*
11: 16 56
11: 17 . . . . 57, 59, 60
12 327
12: 3. 54
12: 5. 63
12: 7. . . . . 57, 59
12: 13b-24 76
12: 20 61
12: 23 59
13-19 . . . . 9, 67, 75
13: 9, 16, 17, 21 61
13: 11 63
13: 15-23 68
13: 26 91
13: 27 54
13: 30-31 73
14: 6, 14 70
14: 6-15 70
15: 1. 79
15: 3. . . . . 57, 89
15: 5b-10 69
15: 6. 69
15: 7. . . . . 60, 69, 90
15: 8. 60
15: 10 57
15: 13, 14 70
15: 15, 16 76
15: 17 82
15: 21 ff. 99
15: 21-62 . . . . 98, 145 n. 2
15: 21b-32a 145
15: 27 . . . . 130 n. 15
15: 56-57 . . . . 82 n. 77
16: 1–17: 13 71
16: 2. 355
17: 1. 73
17: 1 ff. 73
17: 11 . . . . 71, 355 n. 9
17: 15 58
17: 16 . . . . 23, 61, 257
17: 16, 18 141
18: 12-20 71
18: 13 354
18: 14 98
18: 15-19 69
18: 17 . . . . 69, 90
18: 21-28 . . . . 98, 145 n. 2
18: 22 58
19: 1-9 68
19: 2-7 . . . . 98, 145 n. 2
19: 8. 145
19: 10-16 70
19: 15 55
19: 17-23 71
19: 24-31 74
19: 35 54
19: 40-48 75
20: 7. . . . . 55, 59

Joshua—*contd.*
20: 8. . . . 61, 62, 63
22: 9 ff. 62
22: 10-11 . . . 50, 59
24: 30 58
Judges
1: 3, 17 . . . 68, 69
1: 11, 12 76
1: 13. 82
1: 16. 56
1: 19. 257
1: 21, 27 ff. 76
1: 21, 27-35 67
1: 27. 156
1: 27 ff. 141
1: 34. 60
1: 34-35 74
1: 36. 89
3: 1 ff. 141
3: 12 ff. 75
4: 2, 23, 24 51
4: 3 257
4: 6 . . . . 56, 74
4: 11. 82
4: 11, 17 82
4: 17 ff. 145
4: 21. 82
5: 14. 73
5: 15. 60
5: 15b-16 68
5: 19. 51
5: 24. . . . 82, 145
6: 2 ff., 33 ff. 83
6: 3, 33 83
6: 17-21 282
6: 33. . . . 23, 61
7: 12. 83
8: 4 ff. 91
8: 11. 91
9: 46 ff. 152
9: 48. 58
9: 51 ff. 152
9: 53. 161
10: 17 62
11: 4 ff. 62
11: 12-14, 28 258
11: 15-26 80
11: 26 146
13-16 74
13: 15-20 282
13: 25 75
16: 23 295
17: 7. 56
18 74
18: 2. 74
18: 7, 28 51
19: 1, 2, 18 56
19: 11-12 87
20: 31 . . . 87, 88

Judges—*contd.*
20: 31-32 85
21 327
21: 8 ff. 56
21: 19 . . . 85, 87
I Samuel
1: 7, 9 176
3: 3, 15 176
5: 2 ff. . . . 177, 295
6: 7 ff. 86
6: 12. 85
6: 12 ff. 136
8: 13. 160
11: 1. 56
11: 8. 90
12: 12 258
12: 17 = 14: 9 326
13: 19 49
15: 2 ff. 82
15: 6 82
17: 2, 19 89
21: 9. 89
23: 3. 55
25: 1. 169
27: 10 82
30: 1 ff. 83
30: 14 78
30: 29 82
31: 7. 60
31: 10 177
31: 10, 12 78
II Samuel
2: 1-4a 94
2: 9 . . . . 61, 94
4: 3 . . . . 94 n. 98
5: 1-3 94
5: 6 77
5: 6-9 95
5: 8 156
5: 9 . . . . 95, 152
5: 17-25 95
6: 3 86
7: 23. 351
8: 1 95
8: 2 95
8: 3 ff. . . . 80, 81
8: 3-8 81
8: 5, 6 81
8: 6 96
8: 7-8 96
8: 13. 95
8: 14. 95
8: 18. 79
10: 1 ff. 96
10: 6 ff. . . . 80, 81
10: 6, 8 81
10: 6-19 81
10: 8. 259
10: 15-19 96

II Samuel—*contd.*
10: 16 81
12: 26 ff. 96
12: 30 96
13: 23 . . . . 57 n. 22
15: 8. 81
18: 6. . . . . 57 n. 22
20: 12 85
20: 14, 15 81
21: 1. . . . . 94 n. 98
22 349
23: 31 351
24: 6-7 94
24: 7. 51
I Kings
1: 33, 38, 45 155
4: 7 96
4: 7-19 96
4: 8 . . . . 58, 98 n. 106
4: 8 ff. 96
4: 9 . . . . . 98, 99
4: 9, 18 98
4: 10. . . . . 98 n. 106
4: 13. 62
5: 2, 3, 7, 8 96
5: 9 . . . . . 86 n. 84
5: 23. . . . . 86 n. 84
6-7 . . . . 152 n. 27, 177
7: 46. 44
8 328
9: 11-13 59
9: 15-19 . . . . 146 n. 3
9: 15b, 17-19 132
9-16 136
10: 5. 353
10: 18-20 159
10: 28 260
11: 14-22, 25a, b . . . 95
11: 15, 16 95
11: 23, 24 259
11: 23-25 81
11: 23-25a 96
11: 32 97
12: 1-24 97
12: 29 ff. 177
12: 34 97
14: 25-28 . . . 249 n. 8, 271
15: 17 ff. 97
15: 18 ff. 245
16: 6, 28 169
16: 24 . . . . 101, 133
16: 28 329
20: 1. 259
20: 26, 30 93
22: 29 91
22: 39 161
22: 48-50 95
II Kings
3: 4-27 96
II Kings—*contd.*
3: 4 ff. 219
4: 10. . 153, 158 n. 49, 159
6: 23. 49
7: 1 152
8: 20-22 95
9: 4 355
9: 16. 91
10: 33 62
13: 17 93
14: 7. 95
14: 11 98
15: 19 . . . . 253 n. 20
15: 19-20 271
15: 29 59
16: 6. 95
16: 10-16 296
17: 6. . . . . 261, 271
18: 11 . . . . . **261**
18: 13-16 271
18: 17 85
18: 20 349
18: 34 . . . . 259, 260
19: 9. . . . . 249 n. 9
19: 12 261
19: 13 . . . . 259, 260
23: 6. 169
23: 8. 98
23: 15-18 100
23: 16 . . . 351, 360 n. 13
23: 19 . . . 101, 101 n. 114
23: 29 . . 101 n. 114, 271, 276
23: 29 ff. 249
24: 10 ff. 133
25: 1 ff. 133
25: 4. . . . . 157 n. 46
I Chronicles
2-4 69
2: 9, 25 ff., 42 82
2: 42 ff. 70
2: 50 ff. 98
4: 21. . . . . 70, 165
5: 23. 60
7: 14. 73
9: 27 = 19: 17 . . . 326 n. 8
11: 33 351
17: 21 351
II Chronicles
2: 16. . . . . 86 n. 84
9: 4 353
11: 5-12 . . . . 146 n. 3
11: 6. . . . . 90, 156
11: 7, 9 89
11: 8. 95
11: 9. 157
11: 10 98
13: 4. 58
20: 16 89
20: 20 56

II Chronicles—*contd.*
32: 6. 152
32: 30 157
35: 20 ff. 276
35: 22 61
Ezra
3: 7 86
4: 10 ff. 102
5: 3, 6 102
6: 6, 8, 13 102
7: 21, 25 102
9: 9 . . . . 326 n. 8
Nehemiah
2: 1 ff. 103
2: 19. 83
3: 15. . . . 157 n. 46, 158
3: 22. 54
4: 1, 2 103
4: 7 83
5: 14. 103
9: 7 264
11: 25 145
11: 26 . . . . 130 n. 15
12: 28 ff. 145
13: 15 164
13: 24 245
Job
24: 11 164
Psalms
2: 11-12 361
10: 2=18: 6 327
17 331
18 349
20: 14=34: 6 327
27-31 331
34 331
35 331
45 . . . . . 331 n. 29
46: 1-4 . . . . 331 n. 29
48 331
49: 20=79: 11 326
63: 1. 56
68: 14 63
88 331
103: 15-16 33
104 289
105: 27–137: 6 326
110: 1 159
Song of Solomon
4: 8 60
Isaiah
2: 13. 63
2: 20. 353
5: 2 164
7: 3 85
7: 10. 355
7: 17. 354
8: 6 . . . . . 158 n. 48
8: 23. 58
Isaiah—*contd.*
9: 1 59
10: 9. . . . 259, 260, 261
11: 16 85
15: 5 90
19: 18 50
19: 23 85
22: 1. 153
23: 5-11 51
23: 11 51
36-39 349
39: 1. 292
40: 3. 85
40: 6-8 33
46: 1. 292
49: 11 85
62: 10 85
Jeremiah
2: 13. 155
7: 14. 176
7: 25. 351
17: 26 97
27: 10 352
29: 19 351
32: 44 97
33: 13 97
35: 7. 145
35: 15 351
36: 22-23 179
37: 21 160
39: 4. . . . . 157 n. 46
44: 4. 351
47: 4. 78
48: 5. 90
49: 23 . . . . 259, 260
50: 2. 292
51: 44 292
Lamentations
1: 1–2: 20 . . . . 326 n. 8
Ezekiel
25: 16 78
27: 6. 63
27: 17 49
27: 23 261
40: 5–43: 12 177
47: 8. 59
47: 15-18 . . . . 67, 75
47: 16, 18 101
47: 18 . . . . 17 n. 11
48: 1. . . . . 67, 75
Hosea
1: 5 61
7: 4, 6 160
7: 4, 6, 7 . . . . 160 n. 55
8: 5, 6 177
Amos
1: 5 . . . . . 63, 261
2: 13. 86
3: 3-6 363

Amos—*contd.*
3: 15 162
5: 12, 15 152
6: 2 . . . . . 259, 261
6: 13 101
7: 13 177
9: 7 78
9: 13 164

Jonah
1: 3 86

Zephaniah
2: 5 78

Zechariah
9: 1 261
11: 2 63
12: 11 61

NEW TESTAMENT

Matthew
4: 18 55
4: 25 104
14: 34 55
27: 60 . . . . 171 n. 122

Mark
1: 16 55
5: 20 104
6: 53 55
7: 31 104
16: 3 . . . . 171 n. 122

Luke
5: 1 55
24: 2 . . . . 171 n. 122

John
4: 10 ff. 155
4: 20-21 315
9: 7 158
21: 1 55

Hebrews
4: 1 83
21: 10 89
68: 15 63

APOCRYPHA

I Maccabees
5: 26, 43, 44 101
11: 28, 34 103
11: 57 55

I Maccabees—*contd.*
11: 67 55

II Maccabees
12: 21, 26 101

INDEX OF AUTHORS

(*See also* the General Index)

Abel, F. M., 4, 28, 30, 41, 62, 113, 116
Africanus, S. Julius, 267
Agatharchides, 8
Aharon, Y., 122, 134
Albright, F. P , 199
Alkim, B., 210
Amiaud (Amiaud-Scheil), 252
Amiram, R., 122
Andrae, W., 169, 196, 201, 208, 265
Anthes, R., 205
Avi-Yonah, M., 85, 104, 115-16, 119, 173
Avigad, N., 311

Baedeker, K., 185, 188, 264
Bagetti, P. B., 172
Baillet, M., 311
Balkan, Kemal, 233
Baramki, D. C., 115, 134, 159
Bardtke, H., 5, 33, 313
Barnett, R. D., 162, 260
Barrois, A. G., 111, 167
Barthélemy, D., 311
Baudissin, W. W. Graf, 280, 293
Bauer, H., 213, 218
Bauer, L., 38, 229
Bauer, Th., 238, 252
Baumgärtel, F., 333
Baumstark, A., 323, 332, 340
Begrich, J., 269, 271
Belsheim, J., 344
ben Asher, Aaron ben Mosheh, 306
Benoît, P., 312
Benzinger, I., 110, 167
Berger, S., 344
Bergsträsser, G., 224, 228
Berliner, A., 318
Bernhard, K. H., 286
Bertholet, A., 278-79, 361-62
Beyer, G., 57, 89
Bikerman, E., 103
Bilabel, F., 246
Birot, M., 210
Bittel, K., 201, 266
Blanckenhorn, P., 28, 31, 41, 43-45
Bliss (Bliss-Macalister), 134
Bodenheimer, F. S., 37
Böhl, F. M. T., 50, 52, 77, 207, 215, 226
Bonnet, H., 166, 279, 287-88
Borchardt, L., 267
Borée, W., 55, 57
Bork, F., 232
Bossert, H. T., 210-11
Bottero, J., 72, 210
Bowen, R. L., 199
Boyer, G., 210
Breasted, 78, 194-96, 205, 236, 246, 255, 267, 276 (*see also* Ranke)
Brockelmann, C., 224, 228-29
Brooke, A. E., 326-29, 336, 342, 344
Brunnow (Brunnow & Domaszewski), 117
Buhl, F., 4, 79
Bülow, J., 78
Burchardt, M., 204, 240-41
Burkitt, F. C., 322
Burrows, M., 57, 311, 313
Burton, R. F., 44

Campbell, E. F., 267
Canaan, T., 153
Cantineau, J., 227
Causse, A., 64
Ceriani, A. M., 331-32, 338
Charles, R. H., 321, 337
Christian, V., 196, 200, 241, 266
Conder, 135
Cook, S. A., 111, 279-80, 314
Cooke, 52, 219
Cowley, A., 221
Cross, F. M., Jr., 99, 214, 218, 311, 313-14
Crowfoot, E., 312
Crowfoot, G. M., 133, 162, 311-12
Crowfoot, J. W., 133

Dahl, G., 355
Dalman, G., 5, 22, 28, 33, 37-39, 113-14, 117, 153, 157-58, 160-61, 163-65, 176, 227
de Conteson, H., 129
Deichmann, F. W., 137
Deimel, A., 232
de Lagarde, P., 318-19, 332
Delaporte, L., 246, 276
de la Saussaye, Chantepie, 279
Delitzach, F., 233, 350
de Rossi, G. B., 310
de Vaux, R., 64, 115, 129, 131, 135, 139, 147, 153, 311-12
Dhorme, E., 217, 291
Dinkler, E., 172
Dinsmore, J. E., 33

Diringer, D., 222
Dold, A., 343
Domaszewski (Brunnow & Domaszewski), 117
Dossin, G., 210
Dothan, M., 154
Drake, C. F. T., 44
Driver, G. R., 206, 208, 212, 354
Driver, S. R., 37, 214-18, 221
Du Buit, M., 5
Du Mesnil, 263
Dunand, M., 199, 213-14, 216-17, 219, 261
Dupont-Sommer, A., 220-21, 227, 313
Dussaud, R., 213-14, 295

Ebeling, E., 83, 209, 252
Ebers, G., 4, 112-13
Eissfeldt, O., 72, 145, 216, 284, 293-94, 302
Elliger, 58
Engberg, 129
Engnell, I., 285
Erman, A., 230, 287
Exner, F. M., 28, 30

Fast, T., 91
Février, J. G., 202
Field, F., 332
Filson, Floyd V., 5
Finet, A., 72, 210, 225
Fischer, J., 308
Fisher, C. S., 128, 220
Fitzgerald, G. M., 129, 130, 135
Fohrer, G., 80, 141, 253, 260-61
Forrer, E., 100, 101
Forst, F., 362
Frank, F., 37, 44, 79
Franken, H. J., 128, 131
Frankfort, H., 285
Free, J. P., 137
Freedman, D. N., 218
Freytag, G. W., 229
Friedrich, J., 199, 213, 226, 231, 233, 254
Funk, R. W., 134

Gadd, C. J., 276, 285
Galling, K., 82, 86, 102, 110, 133, 151-53, 156, 158-59, 161-65, 169-74, 176-79, 219, 255
Gardiner, A. H., 53, 92, 203, 205, 230
Garstang, J., 129
Gaster, M., 316
Gelb, I. J., 210, 231, 240
Gelzer, H., 267
Gese, H., 80, 141
Ginsberg, H. L., 221
Ginsburg, C. D., 305
Ginsburger, M., 318
Ginzel, F. K., 167, 272, 273
Glaue, P., 323
Glueck, Nelson, 12, 14, 43-44, 62, 79-80, 127, 139, 164, 166
Goettsberger, 316, 329, 331, 339, 341-42
Goetze, A., 201, 209, 240, 254, 268, 295
Gordon, C. H., 212, 216, 226
Gradmann, R., 45, 46, 47
Grant, E., 213, 215
Grapow, H., 230, 278
Gray, J., 294
Gressman, H., 111, 119, 179, 183
Grohmann, A., 312
Grollenberg, L. H., 5, 118
Gurney, O. R., 255
Gustavs, A., 37, 60, 76, 257
Guthe, H., 4-5, 41, 44, 62, 112-15, 117-19, 135, 185, 219

Haas, H., 278, 279
Hadas, Moses, 321
Haefeli, L., 337-39
Hall (Hall & Woolley), 200
Hänel, J., 338
Hanhart, R., 336
Harding, L., 130, 174, 220, 311
Harel, M., 89
Harnack, A., 338, 341
Harris, R., 321
Harris, Z. S., 226
Hartmann, R., 112, 114
Hatch, E., 336, 358
Heiler, F., 279
Helfritz, H., 189
Hempel, J., 214, 316
Hentschke, R., 80
Hermann, A., 264
Herodotus, 8, 102
Herrmann, J., 333, 355
Hetzenauer, M., 347
Heurtley, 127
Hilderscheid, H., 28
Hill, G. F., 168
Hirsch, H., 292
Hitti, P. K., 112
Hoefner, M., 229
Hoftijzer, J., 226, 228
Hogarth, D. G., 260
Holmes, R., 324, 329
Hommel (Hommel-Schneller), 113-14, 117, 119
Horsfield (Horsfield & Vincent, R. B.), 212
Howie, C. H., 177
Hrozný, B., 210, 230
Humbert, P., 205

Iliffe, J. H., 133
Inge, C. H., 130, 174

Jäger, K., 153
Jastrow, M., 291
Jean, C. F., 210, 226, 228
Jeremias, J., 177, 183
Jirku, A., 217
Jochims, U., 131, 153
Johns, C. N., 113, 133
Johnson, A. C., 325
Junker, H., 246

Kahrstedt, U., 103, 104
Kammenhuber, A., 241
Kampffmeyer, G., 140
Kanael, B., 116
Kappelrud, A. S., 294
Kappers, C. U. A., 234
Kappler, W., 336
Karmon, Y., 87
Karo, G., 279
Kase, E. H., 325
Kautzsch, E., 337
Kees, H., 200, 278
Kelso, J. L., 131, 134
Kennicott, B., 310
Kenyon, F. G., 324, 325
Kenyon, K. M., 129-31, 133
Kiepert, H. H., 185
Killermann, S., 33
King, L. W., 251
Kirsten, E., 338
Kittel, R., 246, 302, 309, 351
Kjaer, H., 131, 176
Klostermann, E., 131
Knopf (Knopf, Lietzmann & Weinel), 325, 327
Knudtzon, J. A., 208, 233
Koeppel, R., 4, 33, 129
Kohl, 118
Koldewey, R., 196, 265
König, E. F., 232
Kopf, L., 361
Kraeling, C. H., 117
Kraeling, Emil G., 5, 221
Kramer, S. N., 209
Krause, 157
Kruse, F., 2
Kubitschek, W., 267
Kuhl, C., 118
Kupper, J. R., 210, 238
Kuschke, A., 137

Labat, R., 225
Lake, H., 326
Lake, K., 326
Lamon, R. S., 132, 156, 179
Landsberger, B., 253, 278-79
Lane, E. W., 229
Langdon, S., 251
Lange, O., 279
Lawrence (Woolley-Lawrence), Fig. 7
Leander, P., 227
Lee, S., 339
Lehmann, E., 278, 279
Lehmann-Haupt, C. F., 233
Leibovitch, J., 214
Leuze, O., 102
Lewis, A., 220
Ley, J., 362
Lidzbarski, M., 219, 221, 228
Lietzmann (Knopf, Lietzmann & Weinel), 325, 327
Lohr, 179
Loud, G., 132, 162
Luckenbach, 173
Luckenbill, D. D., 60, 96, 252, 271

Macalister, 136
Macalister (Macalister-Bliss), 134
Macalister (Macalister & Duncan), 135
Macho, A. Diez, 308, 309, 318
Mackenzie, D., 136
Mader, E., 137
Maisler, B., 50, 52, 87, 98, 132, 135, 166
Mallon, 129
Margolis, M. L., 227
Mariette, A., 236, Fig. 7
Marmardji, A. S., 9
Marquet (Marquet-Krause, J.), 130, 148, 174, 179, Fig. 5
Marti, K., 227
Martin, M., 315
Masterman, 157
Mayer (Mayer, Pinkerfeld, *et al.*), 113
Mayrhofer, M., 242
McCown, C. C., 120, 137, 151
McLean, N., 326-29, 336, 342, 344
Meek, T. J., 209
Meinhold, W., 118
Meissner, B., 169, 188, 201, 206, 249, 252, 291
Mendelsohn, I., 279, 284, 292
Mensching, G., 279
Mercati, G., 331
Mercer, S. A. B., 208
Merx, A., 318
Meyer, E., 198, 237, 246, 273
Michel, E., 208
Migne, 329
Milik, J. T., 172, 214, 311-12
Mills, E., 24
Mitchell, R. A., 78
Mohlenbrink, 177
Montet, P., 199, 264
Moortgat, A., 198, 246, 276
Mordtmann-Mittwoch, 222
Morenz, S., 287
Mowinkel, S., 362
Müller, W. M., 53, 240

Naveh, O. J., 78
Neugebauer, P. V., 273
Neumann, J., 29
Newcombe, S. F., 3
Nöldeke, T., 228
Noth, M., 51, 54, 56-58, 61, 66-69, 72-76, 81, 85, 92-93, 98-99, 101-3, 131, 144, 238, 257, 260, 355
Nötscher, F., 291
Nougayrol, J., 263
Nyberg, H. S., 296, 359

Oppenheim, A. L., 209
Otto, H., 130, 200, 279

Palmer (Guthe & Palmer), 115
Paret, O., 302
Parker, R. A., 155, 273
Parrot, A., 209, 238, 251, 265-66
Parsons, J., 324, 329
Perrot, J., 129, 166
Pézard, M., 263
Pfeiffer, R. H., 209, 302, 340, 342
Picard, L., 41
Pieper, M., 163, 205
Pilz, E., 163
Plenderleith, H. J., 311
Poebel, A., 232, 268
Pognon, H., 220
Polybius, 8
Pope, M. H., 294
Posener, G., 248
Post, E. G., 33
Praetorius, F., 318
Pretzl, A., 331
Pritchard, J. B., 111, 133-34, 157, 163, 183
Procksch, 330, 331
Ptolemy, 83
Puttrich (Puttrich-Reignard, O.), 115

Quennel, A. M., 41
Quentin, H., 347

Rahlfs, A., 323-29, 333, 336, 344
Range, P., 21, 114
Ranke (Breasted & Ranke), 194-96, 200, 204, 236, 276, 287, 290, 344
Rathjens, C., 188, 199
Redpath, H. A., 336, 358
Reifenberg, A., 162, 168
Reignard, O. (Puttrich-Reignard), 115
Reisner (Reisner, Fisher & Lyon), 98, 133, 149, 220
Reisner, G., 128, 220, Fig. 9
Rendtorff, R., 75
Rigg, H. A., 242
Rittentschke, 141
Robert, U., 344
Roberts, Bleddyn J., 302, 325, 327, 342, 345
Roberts, C. H., 322
Roeder, G., 274
Röhricht, Reinhold, 2, 6
Roseman, N., 29, 30
Rost, L., 33, 49, Fig. 7
Rost, P., 207, 252
Rothenberg, B., 166
Rothstein, J. W., 362
Rowe, A., 130, 136, 176
Rowley, H. H., 5
Rowton, M. B., 250
Ryssel, V., 304

Sabatier, P., 343
Sachau, E., 221
Sachs, A., 209
St. Macalister, R. A., 127
Schaefer, H., 205
Schaffer, A., 199
Scharff, A., 200, 246, 276
Scheil (Amiaud-Scheil), 252
Schick, 157
Schmidt, H., 177
Schmökel, H., 217
Schneider, A. M., 115, 116
Schneller, A. M., 115
Schoene, G., 113, 119
Schwally, F., 227
Schwöbel, V., 19
Scott, R. B. Y., 167
Seele, K. C., 246
Segert, S., 362
Seller, S., 116, 134, 149
Sellers, O. R., 150, 168
Sellin, E., 128, 135-36, 151, 166, 174, 178-79, Fig. 4
Sethe, K., 205, 247-48
Shipton, G. M., 129, 132, 179
Sievers, E., 362, 363
Simons, J., 135, 141
Sinclair, L. A., 131
Smend, R., 219, 335
Smith, George Adam, 4
Smith, S., 261
Smith, W. R., 280
Smith, W. S., 246
Socin, A., 10, 219, 229
Söderblom (Tiele-Söderblom), 279
Speiser, E. A., 209, 233
Sperber, A., 319, 320
Stade, B., 319
Starkey, J. L., 220
Steindorff, G., 205, 230, 235-36, 246
Stephens, F. J., 209
Steuernagel, C., 3, 44, 68, 69, 302
Stève, A. M., 135, 158, 177, 219

Stock, H., 288
Strack, H. L., 227, 310
Streck, M., 252
Stummer, F., 342, 344-45
Sukenik, E. L., 116, 133, 168, 172, 311
Swete, H. B., 321, 326-28, 334-36

Techen, L., 358
Thiele, E. R., 269, 271
Thompson, G. C., 199
Thomsen, P., 6, 87, 90-91, 110, 115, 117, 178-79
Thureau-Dangin, F., 250, 261, 270
Tiele (Tiele-Söderblom), 279
Toombs, L. E., 120, 136, 174
Torczyner, H., 220, 223
Tufnell, O., 130, 133, 174

Unger, E., 265
Ungnad, A., 225, 240, 251, 253, 268, 273, 279

van Beek, G. W., 199
van der Meer, P., 277
van Zyl, A. H., 80
Vercellone, C., 344
Vermes, G., 313
Viedebantt, 167
Vincent, L. H., 116, 135, 155-56, 158
Vincent, R. B., 119, 176-77, 212, 219
Virolleaud, C., 212-13, 263
von Gall, A., 315
von Luschan, 219, 234
von Oppenheim, M. F., 47, 185, 188, 190, 198, 200
von Oppolzer, T., 272
von Soden, W., 209, 225, 237, 239
von Wissman, H., 188, 199
Vööbus, A., 323, 338

Waddell, W. D., 322
Walz, R., 83
Wampler, J. C., 137, 151
Warren, Charles, 127, 135, 147, 155
Waterman, L., 55
Watzinger, C., 110, 118, 120, 132, 134, 148, 150-51, 154, 159, 161-62, 165, 169, 171-73, 176-78, 201, 219, 222, Fig. 4
Wehr, H., 229
Weidner, E. F., 184, 230, 241, 250, 252, 254, 268-70, 276-77
Weill, R., 135
Weinel (Knopf, Lietzmann & Weinel), 325, 327
Weissbach, F. H., 232
Wellhausen, J., 280
Wendland, P., 321
Whiting, J. D., 38
Wilson, J. A., 204, 246
Winckler, H., 230, 252
Wiseman, D. J., 51, 210, 251, 268, 276
Woolley (Hall & Woolley), 200
Woolley, C. L., 264
Woolley, L., 260, 261
Woolley (Woolley-Lawrence), Fig. 7
Wright, G. Ernest, 5, 35, 99, 110-11, 123, 127, 130, 136, 174, 177
Wurst, P., 33
Würthwein, E., 302
Wutz, F., 320, 334

Yadin, Y., 132, 145, 151, 256, 311
Yeivin, S., 109

Ziegler, J., 336
Zimmerli, W., 19
Zimmern, H., 268, 278-79

GENERAL INDEX

Abbasids, 114
Abbreviations in the Hebrew Text, 354-55
Abibaal inscription, 214
'Absalom's Tomb', 171
Abyssinia, 185, 236, 342
Accad, 224, 236, 250, 252, 265, 364, Fig. 6
Accadian (language), 77, 224-25, 230, 237-39, 241, 254
Accadians, 237
Acco (plain), 23-24, 52, 74, 76, 79, 87, 90, 92, 100, 113-14, 120
Achaemenids, 231-32, 242, 296, 366-67
Achan, 69
Acropolis, 133, 136, 150, 152, 174, Fig. 4
Adadnirari I, 253
Adadnirari III, 259, 366
Adiabene, 323
Adonis, 280
Afra, 344
Ahab, 161, 366
Ahiram Sarcophagus (inscription), 159, 173, 213, Fig. 8
Ahuramazda, 296
Ai, 130, 174
Aijalon, 60, 74, 88, 98, Fig. 3
Akhenaten (Amenophis IV), 208, 289-90, 365
Akhetaten, 289
Aksum, 342
Alabaster, 160, 197
Alalah texts, 51, 210, 262
Albright, W. F., 80, 83, 110-11, 130-31, 139, 153-54, 165, 204, 209, 214, 279, 314
Alcuin, 346
Aldina, 335
Aleppo, 190-93, 219, 245, 256, 259, 261, 263, 306, 340, Fig. 6
Aleppo Codex, 306
Aleppo Pine, 34
Alexander the Great, 103, 120, 184, 246, 249, 251, 262, 265, 276, 296, 367
Alexandria, 103, 264, 321, 326, Fig. 6
Alluvium, 42-43, 185-86
Alphabet, 211-17
Alt, Albrecht, 58, 67, 76, 78, 80, 83, 86, 89, 92, 94-96, 99-100, 102-3, 117-18, 123, 139, 141, 145, 152, 176, 211, 243, 256-57, 259, 274, 282, 295
Altar, 174, 176-78, 279, Fig. 5
Amalekites, 82
Amanus, 189-90, 192, 260, Fig. 6
Amarna Tablets, 52, 71, 76, 207-8, 226, 233, 256, 270, 274, 365
Amasis, 249
Amenemhet, 247
Amenophis, 248
Amenophis II, 52
Amenophis IV (Akhenaten), 289, 365
Ammon(ites), 9, 80-81, 88, 96, 101, 103, 123, 127, 227, 244, 258, Fig. 3
Amon, 284, 289
Amon-Re, 248, 289, 290
Amorites, 60, 77, 238
Amulet, 162-63
Amurru, 53, 77, 238, 274
Anat, 280, 294
Anatolia, 188
Animal husbandry, 45, 163
Ankara, 230, 266, Fig. 6
Annals, 205, 209, 268
Antilebanon, 44, 59-60, 81, 93, 189, 228, 259, Fig. 6
Antioch, 103, 265, 329, 332, 340
Antiochus IV, 104, 296
Antonia, 119
Anu, 291
Aphraates, 339
Apis, 288
Apocrypha, 334, 346-47
Apollonius, 103
Apses, 116, 118
Aqueducts, 117
Aquila, 318, 322, 330, 345
Arabia, Arabs, 8, 83, 92, 103, 114-15, 198, 272
Arabic (language), 9-12, 229, 341
Aramaic (language), 56, 102, 219, 226-28, 230, 232, 244-45, 259-60, 313, 316-19, 320, 323
Aramaic, Imperial, 102, 227, 230
Arameans, 80-81, 88, 96, 100, 238-39, 244-45, 252, 259
Ararat, 233
Arbailu, 293
Archelaus, 104
Arinna, 295
Aristarchus, Aristarchic signs, 330-31, 340, 345
Aristeas' Letter, 321
Ark, 86, 136, 176
Armenia, 186, 188, 233, 242, 340

Armenian translation, 340
Armenoid race, 234
Arnon, 13, 61, 62, 75, 80, 119, Fig. 3
Arnuwandas, 254
Arpad, 260
Artaxerxes I, 102
'Artuf Rift, 18
Arvad, 262
Asa, 97
Ascent, 88, 89-90
Ashdod, 78, 101, 103, 177, Figs. 2 & 3
Ashdod, language of, 245
Asher, 74, 96, Fig. 3
Asherah, 280, 294
Asheroth, 178
Ashkelon, 78, 151, Fig. 3
Ashur (city), 265, 268, 292, Fig. 6
Ashur (deity), 265, 292
Ashurbanapal, 209, 252, 254, 271, 366
Ashurdan III, 273, 366
Ashurnasirpal II, 253, 266, 366
Ashuruballit I, 253
Asia Minor, 188, 192-93, 197-98, 201, 207, 230-31, 233, 240, 242-43, 249, 252-54, 260, 263, 266, 274, 280, 284, 295, 304, 364-67
Assyria, 100, 102, 169, 252-54, 259, 261, 265-66, 268-69, 270, 275-76, 292, 364-65, 366, Fig. 6
Assyrian (language), 224-25
Assyrians, 53, 102, 238-39, 251-54, 261, 268, 270-71, 273, 274-75, 292
Astarte, 163, 177, 280
Asterisk, 330
Aswan, 185, 221, 236, Fig. 6
Ataroth, 75
Aten, 289
Attis, 280
Atum, 288
Augustine, 344
Avaris, 255, 264
Azekah, 89
Azitawadda, 260

Baal, 281, 294
Baal Zaphon, 294
Baalat Gebal, 295
Baasha, 97
Babel, 265
Babylon, 197, 238-39, 250, 265, 270, 291-292, 364, 367, Fig. 6
Babylonia, 102, 239, 250-52, 253, 265, 268-69, 270, 273, 275-76, 304, 309, 318-319, 365, 367
Babylonian (language), 76, 102, 225, 232
Babylonians, 238-39, 275, 292
Baghdad, 114, 186, 201, 224, 250, Fig. 6
Baker, 160
Banana, 36
Barada River, 190
Barley, 35
Bārū, 293
Baruch, 335
Basalt, 15, 20, 42
Bashan, 63, 73
Battlements, 150
Bauer, Hans, 213, 218
Bear, 37
Beards, 235, 236-38
Beatty, Chester, 325, 333
Bed, 153, 158, 161
Bedouin, 18, 39-40, 47, 229, 311
Beeroth, 262
Beersheba, 18, 22, 25-26, 46, 68, 75, 129, Fig. 1
Beirut, 2, 44, 52, 92, 262, Fig. 1
Bel, *bēl*, 292
Bel and the Dragon, 335, 347
Ben Asher, 304, 305, 308, 309
Ben Hayyim, Jacob, 305
Ben Naphtali, 304, 305, 308
Benhadad I, 219, 245, 259, 295
Benjamin, 68, 71-73, 94-99, Fig. 3
Beth Alpha, 30
Beth Horon, 88
Beth-pelet, 130
Beth-shan, 15, 78, 104, 129-30, 140, 173, 176-78, 192, Fig. 3
Beth-shearim, 135, 173
Beth-shemesh, 74, 85, 98, 136, 213, 215, Fig. 3
Beth-zur, 70, 134, 150, 168, Figs. 3 & 4
Bethel, 58, 72, 85, 87, 100, 131, 140, 154, 177, 354-55, Fig. 3
Bethlehem, 56, 88-89, 345
Betonim, 91
Bezek, 90
Bilingual texts, 211
Birds, 38
Bīt-Adini, 261
Bīt-Agusi, 260
Bīt-Akītum, 292
Boghazköy, 230-31, 233, 240-41, 254, 256, 266, 271, 274, 285, Fig. 6
Bohairic Translation, 341
Bohan, 69
Bomberg, Daniel, 305, 319
Book of the Dead, 204, 290
Borsippa, 292
Boss, 150
'Bottle', 40
Brazier, 179
Bread, 160
Bricks, 197
Bronze Age, 122-24, 126, 129-32, 144, 146, 147-48, 150-51, 153, 156, 165-66, 167-68, 170, 364-65, Fig. 5
Building records, 208

Burckhardt, J. L., 2
Burial inscriptions, 170-71, 204, 278
Burnet, thorny, 47
Burnt offering, 282, 286
Byblos, 159, 169, 172, 199, 213-14, 216-17, 220, 262
Byssus, 165
Byzantine Period, 25, 115-16

Cabul, 59
Cactus, 37
Caesarea Palaestinae, 8, 22, 104, 113-14, 119, 326, 330-31
Caesarea Philippi, 26
Cairo, 112, 114, 194, 207, 263, 288, 303, 306, 309, 317, 322, 325
Caleb, Calebites, 55, 69, 70, 82, Fig. 3
Calendar, agricultural of Gezer, 219
Calf, golden, 285
Calno, Kalneh, *Kullāni*, 261
Cambyses, 249, 276, 367
Camel, 39, 47, 83, 191
Canaan, 7, 49-52, 62
Canaanite (language), 50, 52-53, 75, 136, 225-26, 243-45, 293-94
Canaanites, 49-51, 67, 76-79, 82, 93-95, 99, 141, 245, 257, 281, 293-94, 364-65
Canon of the Old Testament, 350, 359
Canopic jars, 290
Cap, conical, 198
Capernaum, 54, 118
Caphtor, 78
Cappadocian tablets, 252
Caravans, 39, 83, 91-92, 191-93
Carchemish, 256, 260, 263, 276, Figs. 6 & 7
Carmel, 8, 22-23, 34, 74, 76, 113, 189, 192
Carmi, 69
Carob tree, 34
Carrhae, 261
Carrion, 38
Cassiodorus, 346
Cassite (language), 233
Cassites, 242, 251, 270, 275, 364-65
Castellum peregrinorum (pilgrim castle), 113
Castle, Roman, 117
Catchword glosses, 354-55
Catenas, 333, 336
Cattle, 39
Cave burial, 169-70
Cedar, 86
Cenomanian, 41-43, Fig. 2
Ceramics, 108, 122, 125-27, 130, 138, 200
Ceyhan River, 260
Chair, 153, 158-59, 161
Chalcolithic, 122-23, 129-30, 154, 200, 364
Chaldeans, 239, 251
Champollion, J. Fr., 203
Chapter divisions, 307-8, 335, 347-48
Chickens, 39
'Christ's thorn', 35
Chronology, 126-27, 199, 267-77, 314, 364-67
Church of the Nativity, 115
Church of the Holy Sepulchre, 112-13, 115
Churches, Byzantine, 115-16, 124, 174, 176
Churches, Crusader, 113, 124
Cilician Plain, 188-89, 260
Circumcision, 79
Cisterns, 17, 154
Cities, Bronze Age, 123-25, 145, 151-52
Cities, Hellenistic, 120, 125, 134, 154
Cities, Iron Age, 123-24, 145, 151
Cities, Roman, 117-19, 124-25
City-states, 52, 59, 61, 69, 71, 76-78, 93-96, 145, 262, Fig. 3
Clan, 62-64, 66, 98
Clay pegs, 196
Clay pots (*see* Ceramics), 160, 165, 173
Clay prisms, 208
Clay tablets, 206, 208, 212, 251
Coastal plain, Palestinian, 17, 21-24, 26, 32, 60-61, 76, 87
Codex Alexandrinus, 325-26, 336
Codex Ambrosianus (Peshitta), 338
Codex Ambrosianus (Septuagint), 327
Codex Amiatinus, 346
Codex Argenteus, 340
Codex Atheniensis, 329
Codex Basiliano-Vaticanus, 328
Codex Bodleianus Geneseos, 328
Codex Cairensis, 306
Codex Coislinianus, 328, 331
Codex Colberto-Sarravianus, 327, 331
Codex Complutensis, 344
Codex Cottonionus Geneseos, 327
Codex Ephraemi Syri rescriptus, 327
Codex Freer, 327
Codex Hammurabi, 250, 265
Codex Hillel, 306
Codex Legionensis, 344
Codex Leningradensis, 306
Codex Lipsiensis, 328
Codex Lugdunensis, 343
Codex Marchalianus, 328, 331
Codex rescriptus Cryptoferratensis, 328
Codex Reuchlinianus, 308, 319
Codex Severi Hebraicus, 306
Codex Sinaiticus, 325-26
Codex Vaticanus, 325, 332, 336
Codex Venetus, 328
Coele Syria, 103
Coffin texts, 291
Coins, 168, 279

Columns, Egyptian, 195, 203
Columns, North Syrian, 198
Columns, South Arabian, 198
Comb, 161
'Commentaries', 361 (*see also* Hebrew Index, *s.v.* pesher)
Composite creatures, 197-98, 284
Conjecture, 361
Constantine, 115
Copper, 43-44, 166
Coptic, 230, 341-42
Cornice, 195
Coronation festival, 292
Covenant, 95
Creation epic, Babylonian, 292
Cremation, 168
Cretaceous Period, 41-43
Crete, 78, 126
Crocodile, 38
Cross (symbol), 172
Crusaders, 113-14
Crypts, 171
Cult of rulers, 296
Cuneiform, 206-10, 212-13, 220, 225, 229-30, 232, Fig. 7
Cuneiform literature, 208, 212
Cush, 236, 249
Cybele, 280
Cylindrical stone, 171
Cypress, 86
Cyprus, 126, 199, Fig. 6
Cyril of Alexandria, 332
Cyrus, 251, 276, 367

Dagan, 293
Dagon, 177, 295
Damascus, 25-27, 44, 46, 81, 93, 96-97, 100, 112, 114, 190, 192-93, 259, Figs. 1, 3, & 6
Damasus I, 345
Dan (city), 26, 75, 177, Fig. 3
Dan (tribe), 74-75, Fig. 3
Danuni, 260
Darius I, 102
Date palm, 36
'Daughters' of a city, 146
David, 44, 66, 79-81, 83, 94-98, 102, 122, 135-36, 147-48, 258, 365
Dead Sea, 8, 13, 15-16, 26-27, 30, 32, 38, 41, 45-46, 54, 61, 70, 79-80, 85, 90
Dead Sea caves, 135, 303, 311-15
Debir, 82
Decapolis, 104, 120
Deities, ancestral, 282
Deities, astral, 281, 291
Deities, city, 283-84, 294
Deities, cosmic, 237, 281, 284, 287-88, 291, 294
Deities, dying and rising, 280
Deities, female, 280
Deities, local, 281
Deities, theriomorphic, 197-98, 284-85, 288
Deities, vegetation, 280, 287
Delta, 185, 191, 247, 253, 255-56, 263-64, 341, Fig. 6
Demons, 197-98, 293
Demotic, 204
Desert, 31, 35, 45-47, 54, 81-83, 186
Desert, Arabian, 185
Desert, Isthmus, 18, 21, 25
Desert, Judean, 26, 56, 69, 82, Fig. 3
Desert, Libyan, 185, 194
Desert, Sinai, 18, 21, 25, 46, 56-57, 76, 83, 92, 191-92
Desert, Syro-Arabian, 9, 26, 42, 46, 80-81, 186, 189, 191, 238-39, Figs. 3 & 6
Deutscher Verein zur Erforschung Palästinas (DPV), 3, 28, 30, 132, 135
Dew, 31
Dibon, 80
Dittography, 351
Divination, 293
Djoser, 247
Dog, 37
Dolmen, 169
Dome of the Rock, 114, 177
Dominus flevit, 172
Donkey, 38-39, 86, 191
Dor, 78, 100, Fig. 3
Dothan, 88, 91
Drains, 154
Drama, cultic, 287, 294
Dunes, 21-23, 26, 31
Dūr Šarrukīn, 266
Durra, 35
Dye works, 165
Dynasties, Egyptian, 200, 246-49, 267-68, 364-66

Ea, 291
Ebal, 58, 90
Ecce Homo Span, 119
Eclipse of sun, 272-73
Edessa, 338
Edom(ite), 44, 57, 66, 79, 81-82, 85, 88, 95, 101, 103, 123, 127, 227, 244, 258, Fig. 3
Egypt, 46, 92, 126, 160-61, 172, 185, 191-196, 199-200, 207-8, 220-21, 234-36, 246-47, 253-56, 263-64, 270-73, 275-76, 278, 280, 284-85, 287-90, 321, 326-27, 329, 332-33, 341, 364-67, Fig. 6
Egyptian (language), 203-5, 230, 255, 341
Egyptian literature, 205
Egyptians, 53, 78, 203-5, 235-36, 240, 270
Eiseiba, 89

Ekron, 78, 85, Fig. 3
El, 294
Elam(ites), 232, 242, 258, 265, Fig. 6
Elamite (language), 102, 232, 242
Elath, 44, 79
Elephantine, 221-22, 227, 353
Eleutheropolis, 89
Elibaal (inscription), 214
Ellil, Enlil, 250, 291, 292
Elohist, 77, 83
Embalming, 290
Emendation, 360-61
Emmaus, 116
Enamel pictures, 197
Enamelled bricks, 197
Enuma ēliš, 287, 292
Eocene, 42
Ephraem, 327, 339
Ephraim, 57, 73-74, 96, 98, 101, 366, Fig. 3
Eponyms, 209, 253, 268, 272-73
Eras (epochs), 272
Erech, 200-1, 264-65, Fig. 6
Erfurt manuscripts, 308
Erman, A., 194-95, 200, 203, 205, 230, 276, 287, 290
Esarhaddon, 253, 265, 271, 366
Esbus, 91
Eshtaol, 74-75
Esmun, *Esmun*, 280, 293
Essenes, 313-14
Etam, 156
Ethiopia, 236, 249
Ethiopic (language), 229, 342
Eucalyptus tree, 37
Euphrates, 46, 48, 102, 186, 190-91, 193, 200, 209, 224, 236, 238, 251-52, 255-56, 260, 265, Figs. 6 & 7
Eusebius, 7, 57, 75, 330-31
Excavations, 121, 124-37, 200
Exemplar Parisiense, 346, 348
Ezion-geber, 79, 164

Faïence, 161-62
Family, 64
Farming (agriculture), 45, 163-64
Fatimids, 114
Favissa pits, 174, Fig. 5
Fibula, 162
Fig tree, 36, 163
Fish, fishing, 15, 38, 164
Fleece clothing, 197
Flexures, 43
Flint, 42, 46
Flowers, 30, 32-33, 35
Food offerings, 286
Footstool, 159
Forest, 14, 33-34, 37, 39, 45-48
Fortifications, 113-14, 117-18, 123, 146-152
Fortresses, 119, 146-51, 152, 157
Foundry, 44
Fox, 37
Fresco, 129

Gad, 68, 73, 75, 96, Fig. 3
Galilee, 20, 28, 51, 54, 58, 70, 74, 88, 96, 100, 118
Garigue, 34
Gate, 151, 197, 198
Gath, 78, 95
Gaza, 8, 21, 39, 78, 108, 130, 140, 166, Fig. 3
Gazelle, 37
Geba, 97-98
Gebal, 262
Genista, 46
Genizah, 303, 309, 317, 322
Gennesaret, 55
Gerasa, 117, 154
Gerizim, 58, 116, 315
Gezer, 128, 133, 136, 156, 164, 168, 215, 219, 221
Gibeah, 85, 87-88, 131, 148, 152
Gibeon, 85, 88
Gilead, 56, 62, 73-74, 91, 100
Glass, 161
Glosses, 354-55
Goat, 40
Gods, *see* Deities
Golan, 63
Gold, 168
Gothic translation, 340
Gozan, *Guzana*, 261
Grain, 35, 47
Granary, 160
Grape, 33, 36, 163, 164
Grass, 35, 47
Grave, 169-73, 194-95, 204 (*see also* Tomb)
'Grave of Jacob', 221
Grave sanctuaries, 194, 290
Graves of children, 168
Graves of David's descendants, 169
Greek Bible translations, 315, 319-37
Grotefend, G. F., 206
Gubla (Gebal), 262

Habakkuk Commentary, 312-13
Hadatu, 162
Hadrach, *Hatarikka*, 261
Haifa, 22-24, 26-27, 30, 58, Fig. 1
Hail, 33
Ḫalab, 263

Halafian culture, 364
Halys, 188
Hamath, 45, 210, 219, 244, 259, 261, Fig. 6
Hammurabi, 250, 270, 273-74, 364

Ḫana, 252
Haplography, 351
Haran, *Ḫarrānu*, 261, 293
Hasmoneans, 104, 120, 168, 262, 269
Ḫatti, land and kingdom of, 53, 77, 231, 254, 274
Hattic (language), 233, 243
Ḫattina, 261
Hattusas, 266, Fig. 6
Hattusilis I, 254
Hattusilis III, 255, 274, 365
Hauran (mountain), *Ḫaurina*, 63, 100, 101, 117
Hawthorn, 34
Hazor, 51-52, 132, 147, 151, 176, Fig. 5
Headbands, 162
Hearth, 159
Hebrew (language), 76, 226, 313, 317, 320, 322, 358, 360, 362
Hebron, 17, 25, 36, 55, 56, 70, 76, 82, 88, 130, 137, Fig. 3
Hejaz train, 14, 27, 46, 88
Hekataios of Abdera, 177
Heliopolis, 288
Henotheism, 282
Ḫepa, 295
Hermon, 14, 31, 60, 103
Herod, 22, 117, 119, 134, 150, 168, 177, Fig. 4
Herodeion, 119
Heshbon, 75, 91, Fig. 2
Hesychius, 329, 332
Hexapla, 330-31, 336, 340
Hezekiah, 157
Hezron, 66
Hieratic, 204
Hieroglyphs, Egyptian, 162, 178, 203-5, 208, 210-11, 218, 230, Fig. 7
Hippodamos of Miletus, 154
Hittite, 210-11, 231, 233, 242, 245, 260, Fig. 7
Hittite (language), 230-31, 233
Hittites, 53, 60, 77, 231, 242-43, 251, 254-55, 260, 266, 268, 270-71, 275, 295-97, 364-65
Hivites, 51
Homoeoarchy, 352
Homoeoteleuton, 351-52
Horites, 240
Hormah, 68, Fig. 3
Horned crown, 197
Horns of the altar, 179
Horonaim, 90-91
Horse, 39, 132, 241, 256-57, 260
Horus, 285
House, 153-54
Huleh, Lake (*see* Arabic Index, *s.v.* *Baḥret el Ḥuleh*)
Hunt, 164
Hurrian (language), 76, 233, 240, 243, 256-57
Hurrians, 239-41, 256-57, 295-97
Hyena, 37
Hyksos, 150, 255-57, 263-64, 274, 364

Ibleam, 156
Idrimi inscription, 51, 261
Idumea, 57, 103
Implements, 165-66
Incantations, 209, 293
Incense altar, 179
Indo-European languages, 230-32, 235, 242, 244
Indo-Iranian (language), 76, 231-32, 241, 257
Indo-Iranians, 241, 257, 295
Indra, 295
Ink, 204, 215, 220
Intef, 247
Inundation, 43
Iraq, 186, 196
Iran, 186, 208, 239, 296, 366-67, Fig. 6
Iron, 43-44, 166
Iron Age, 122, 126, 217, 131-33, 145-48, 150-53, 156, 159, 167, 170, 176, 179, 365
Irrigation, 45, 48, 186, 237
Isaiah Scroll, 311
Ishbaal, 94
Ishmaelites, 83
Ishme-Dagan, 252
Ishtar, 280, 293
Ishtar gate, 197
Isis, 280
Israel, 9, 10, 26, 49, 67, 93, 94-100, 101, 122, 146, 258, 259, 268-69, 270, 271, 275, 365, 366
Issachar, 70-71, 96, Fig. 3
Issus, 103
Itala, 344
Ittobaal, Fig. 8
Ivory, 133, 159, 161-62

Jabbok, 13, 41, 43, 74, 80, 91, 96, 113, 117, Fig. 3
Jabesh-Gilead, 56, 62
Jabin, 51
Jackal, 37
Jacobites, 338-40
Jaffa, 18, 22, 26, 28, 30, 37, 86, 99, Fig. 1
Jahwist, 50, 77, 83
Jazer, 75
Jebusites, 77, 147
Jehu, 271, 366
Jemdet Naṣr culture, 201
Jerahmeelites, 82

Jericho, 16, 26-27, 31, 36, 46, 48, 54, 60, 69, 72, 75, 90, 97, 100, 115, 128-30, 134, 140, 147, Figs. 2, 3 & 4
Jeroboam II, 98
Jerome, 7, 17, 329, 332, 345-46
Jerusalem, 17, 25-30, 32, 36, 60, 69, 72, 76-77, 87-90, 95-97, 99, 101-2, 108, 112, 113, 114, 116, 119, 127, 134, 141, 147-148, 152, 155-56, 157, 169, 220, 271, 276, 296-97, 306, 310, 321, 323, 367, Figs. 2, 3 & 4
Jerusalem translation, 339
Jesus Sirach, 335
Jewelry, 162
Jezreel, 15, 23, 61, 71, Fig. 3
Jezreel, Plain of, 20, 24-25, 27-28, 43, 58-61, 71, 74, 76, 78, 87-92, 97, 100, 123, 135-36, 192, 245
Jogbehah, 91
Jonah, 86
Jordan, 15, 26, 46, 48, 51, 62, 85
Jordan Valley, 13, 14-17, 24-27, 30-33, 36, 41-44, 46, 51-55, 70-72, 74-75, 81, 87-88, 90, 123, 129, 189, 192-93
Joseph, 71-73, Fig. 3
Josephus, 55, 107, 119, 158, 177, 246, 255, 257, 269, 313, 323
Joshua, 51, 58
Josiah, 80, 99-101, 145-46, 177, 271, 276, 366-67
Judah (state), 44, 67, 79, 89, 94-102, 122, 146, 258, 268-69, 270, 275-76, 365-67
Judah (tribe), 55-56, 66, 68, 69-70, 82, 94-95, 99, Fig. 3
Judea, 7, 17-18, 55
Judith, 334
Jura, 41
Justinian, 115

Kadesh (Kadesh-Barnea), 57, 139
Kadesh (in Naphtali or Galilee), 56, 59, 74, Fig. 3
Kadesh (on the Orontes), 263, 274
Kahle, P., 303, 305-6, 309, 316-17, 319, 321
Kalaḫ, *Kalḫu*, 162, 266, Fig. 6
Karaites, 304, 306
Karatepe, 210, 260
Ḳarnaim, 101
Kayseri, 252
Kenites, 82, 99, Fig. 3
Kenizzites, 70, 82
Khafre, 247
Khufu, 247
Kidron Valley, 155, 158, 169, 171, 221
Kîkkuli, 241
Kilamuwa, 219
Kingship, 249
Kiriath-jearim, 57, 98, 113, 115
Kiriath-sepher, 76, 82, Fig. 3
Kishon, 87
Kitchener, H. H., 3
Kizil Irmak, 266, Fig. 6
Kültepe, 252, Fig. 6

La'ash, 219, 259, 261
Labarnas, 254
Lachish, 108, 130, 133, 151, 157, 165, 173-174, 215-16, 220, Fig. 10
Lamp, 153, 159, 173
Langton, Stephen, 347
Larsa, 250
Laryngeal, 211, 225-26, 228
Latin Bible translations, 342-48
Lava, 14, 20
Leah tribes, 68-71, 74
Lebanon, 21, 44, 59-60, 81, 87, 92-93, 189, 214, 259, Fig. 6
Lectio difficilior, 360-61
Letter inversion (transposition), 351
Letter of Jeremias, 335, 347
Letters, 209, 251
Levi, 68, 70, 73
Libyans, 235, 249, 365
Limes Arabiae, 117
Limes Palaestinae, 117
Lion, 37
Locust, 38
Lucian, 329, 332, 336
Luther Bible, 347
Luwian, 231
Luxor, 195, 208, 264
Luz, 72, 354
Lydda, 22

Maccabeans, 104, 120, 269, 297
Macchia, 34
Machaerus, 119
Machir, 73, Fig. 3
Mahanaim, 96
Maimonides, 305
Majuscules, 325, 336
Mamelukes, 112-13
Mampsis, 89
Mamre, 137
Manasseh, 68, 73, 93, 96, Fig. 3
Mandaic, 228
Manetho, 246-47, 255, 267-68
Manuscripts of the Hebrew Text, 307-15, 325, 349
Marduk, 292
Mareshah, Marissa, 70, 120, 134, 154, 171, Fig. 3
Marginal draft, 150
Mari, 209, 237-38, 250-53, 364, Fig. 6
Marriage, sacral, 281, 286
Maryannu, 241
Masada, 119, 134

Masorah, 303, 318
Masoretes, masoretic text, 303-10, 315-316, 318, 348, 352, 355-56, 359-60
Maṣṣebah, 174, 178
Matres lectionis, 218, 315, 351-53, 362
Mausoleum, 118, 169
Measures, 167
Mecca, 27, 114, 192
Medeba, 13, 27, 62, 115
Medes, 242, 254, 266, 275-76, 366
Medinah, 114, 192
Mediterranean race, 234
Megiddo, 61, 100, 127, 129, 132, 136, 147, 150-51, 156-57, 162, 169, 179, 192, 216, 276, Fig. 4
Mekal, 178
Melcart, 294
Melkites, 339
Memphis, 253, 263-64, 288, Fig. 6
Menahem, 271, 366
Menes, 247
Mentuhotep, 247
Mercati fragments, 331
Merodach, 292
Merom, 54
Mesha, 75, 96
Mesha Inscription, 75, 80, 96, 219, 226
Mesopotamia, 46, 92, 108, 126, 186, 192-193, 196-98, 200, 207, 220, 224, 227-28, 232-33, 236-42, 249-54, 256, 260-61, 264-65, 268-69, 274-75, 278, 280, 284-285, 291-93, 338, 364-67, Fig. 6
Mesrob, 340
Metal work, 162, 165-66
Metobolos, 330
Metre, poetic, 362
Midianites, 83
Milestones, Roman, 84, 88, 91, 118
Mill, 161
Minaret, 113
Minerals, 17, 43-45, 249
Mines, 43
Minuscules, 325, 335-36
Miocene era, 42
Mirror, 162
Mishael ben Uzziel, 305
Mitanni, 256-57, 270, 274-75, 296
Mizpah, 97, 137
Mnevis, 288
Moabites, 9, 13, 54, 75, 79-81, 88, 91, 95-96, 101, 103, 123, 127, 212, 219, 226-27, 244, 258, Fig. 3
Model codex, 306
Money, 167
Monolith, 198
Montfort, 113
Monument, 111, 171, 178, 194, 196, 208, 210
Moon, eclipse of, 272
Mortar, 161
Mortuary temple, 194, 264
Mosaic, 115-16
Mosaic map of Medeba, 85, 115
Moses of Chorene, 340
Mosque, 112
Mosul, 191, 209, 239, 266, 293, 339, Fig. 6
Mot, 294
Mother goddess, 280
Moulds, 166
Mount (*see* Arabic Index, *s.v.* Jebel; Hebrew Index, *s.v.* Nar)
Mukish, 261
Mummy wrapping, 321
Mursilis I and II, 254, 365
Musil, Alois, 3, 12
Muwatallis, 255
Myths, 205, 209, 278, 287, 292

Nabatean (language), 221, 227
Nabateans, 117
Nabopolassar, 251, 367
Nabu, 292
Naming of sites, 128, 141, 200
Nanna(r), 284
Naphtali, 54, 56, 74, 96, Fig. 3
Nash Papyrus, 314
Nazareth, 21, 25, 71
Neapolis, 19, 90, 140
Nebo (deity), 292
Nebo (mountain), 62, 116
Nebuchadnezzar, 101, 102, 133, 143, 220, 251, 265, 367
Necho, 249, 271, 275-76, 367
Necropolis, 168-73
Negeb, 3, 18, 56, 78, 82-83, 89, 95, 99, 103, 145
Negroes, 234, 236
Nehardea, 310
Nehemiah, 103, 245
Neo-Babylonian Kingdom, 101, 251, 254, 265-66, 271, 275
Neolithic Period, 84, 122-23, 128
Nestorians, 338-39
New Year's Festival, 292
Nicephorus, 333
Nicopolis, 116
Nile, 46, 48, 108, 185, 194, 196, 234, 247, 264
Nineveh, 209, 254, 266, 275, 293, 367, Fig. 6
Nippur, 250, 291, Fig. 6
Nomadic tribes, 24, 35, 56, 82, 145 (*see also* Bedouin)
Nubia, 2, 196, 236, 247, 249, 258, 366
Nuseiriyeh Mountains, 189
Nuzu, 241

Oak, 14, 34, 63
Oases, 16-18, 26, 36, 46-48, 185, 188, 190-91, 235
Obeidian Culture, 364
Obelisks, 195, 288
Obelos, 330
Occupation (conquest), 64, 66-75, 141, 144
Odes, 335, 347
Odo, 307
Offerings, 282, 286
Oil, 36, 98, 159, 163-64, 220
Oligocene, 42
Olives, 33, 35, 36, 163-64
Olives, Mount of, 20, 26-27, 90
Omayyads, 114
Omens, 209, 240, 278, 293
Omri, 133
Orange, 36
Oriental race, 234
Origen, 322-23, 330-31, 336
Ornaments, 162, 166, 173
Orontes, 14, 92, 189-90, 210, 259, 261, 263, 265, 274, Fig. 6
Orthostats, 198
Osiris, 280-81, 290
Ossuaries, 171-72, 221
Ostraca, Beth-shemesh, 215
Ostraca, Lachish, 220, 313, 350, 352, Fig. 10
Ostraca, Ophel, 220
Ostraca, Samaritan, 98, 133, 220, 350, Fig. 9
Othniel, 82, Fig. 3
Oven, 159-60

Palermo stone, 267
Palestine, name, 7-9, 49, 53
Palestine Exploration Fund (PEF), 3, 17, 110
'Palestine List', 249, Fig. 7
Palimpsest, 327, 331, 344
Palimpsestus Vindobonensis, 344
Palmyra, 46, 191, 193, Fig. 6
Palmyrene (language), 221, 227
Pamphilus, 330-31
Paneas, 103
Papyrus, 195, 204, 220-21, 227, 321, 325, 333, 353
Papyrus, Nash, 314
Papyrus Fouad, 322
Parashoth, 307, 316
Parchment manuscripts, 325
Partridge, 38
Pasture land, 35
Paul of Tella, 331
Penuel, 91
Peoples, 63-67, 234-35
Perea, 7
Persia, 101-103, 122, 227, 242, 249, 251, 271, 276, 295-97, 316, 367
Persian (language), 102, 231-32
Persian Gulf, 186, 193, 232, 239, Fig. 6
Personal names, 231, 235, 237, 240
Peshitta, 337-40, 356-58
Petersburg Prophet Codex, 310
Petra, 178
Petrie, Flinders, 108, 125, 130, 166, 214-15
Pharaoh, 205, 247-49, 255-56, 264, 267-268, 271, 275, 285, 288
Philadelphia, 117, 120
Philistines, 8, 67, 78-79, 83, 85, 95, 101, 123, 127, 131, 245, 258, Fig. 3
Philo of Alexandria, 313
Philoteria, 120
Philoxeniana, 340
Phoenician (language), 219, 226
Phoenicians, 8, 51, 79, 211, 244, 260, Fig. 3
Phonetic script, 202, 206, 210, 212, 219
Phrygians, 243
Pictographic (ideographic) script, 202, 206, Fig. 7
Pins, 161-62
Pisgah, 61 = 62
Pliny the Elder, 14, 313
Pliocene, 42
Plow, 35, 38, 163
Pointing systems, 304-5, 308-10
Polyglots, 319, 335, 339, 348
Pomegranate tree, 36
Pompeii, 104, 272
Population figures, 24
Potsherds, 122, 138, 204, 215, 220 (*see also* Ostraca)
Pottery, 165, 200 (*see also* Ceramics)
Precipitation, 17, 20, 28-33, 35, 45
Predatory animals, 37
Predatory birds, 38
Prehistory, 122-23, 200-1, 364
Presses, olive, 164
Prickly pear cactus, 37
Priestly Source, 50, 77
Procurator, 104
Prostitution, sacral (*see* Marriage, sacral)
Proto-Arameans, 238
Protohattic (language), 233, 243
Provinces, 75, 95, 98, 100, 102, 103
Provinces, Assyrian, 100-2, 253, 260, 275
Provinces, Roman, 7, 8, 104, 272
Psalms of Solomon, 335, 347
Psalterium Gallicanum, 345-46
Psalterium juxta Hebraeos, 346
Psalterium Romanum, 345
Psammetichus, 249
Pseudepigrapha of the Old Testament, 337

'Pseudohieroglyphic' Writing, 218
Ptah, 288
Ptolemais, 120
Ptolemies, 103, 120, 249, 264, 272, 276, 321, 367
Ptolemy II, 103, 321
Pūlu (Pul), 253
Punon, 44
Pylon, 195
Pyramid texts, 204, 290
Pyramids, 194, 247, 263, 290, 364
Pyramus, 260

Qatna, 256, 263
Quaternary (Pleistocene) era, 42, Fig. 2
Queh, 260
Quinta, 330
Qumrān (Khirbet Qumrān), 227, 311, 312-15, 353, 356

Rabbath Ammon, 80
Rabbinites, 304
Rabbit, 38
Rachel tribes, 71-74
Radio carbon test, 122
Rainfall, 29-33, 35, 45
Ramah, 97
Ramoth-gilead, 62, 91, 96
Rameses, 248
Rameses II, 92, 248, 264, 274, 365
Rameses III, 78, 255, 365
Re, 285, 288-89
Rehoboam, 89-90, 271
Relief sculpture, 173, 195, 197, 204, 210, 235
Retenu, 53, Fig. 7
Reuben, 66, 68-69, 73
Rezeph, *Raṣappa*, 261
Rhythm, 362-63
Rim-Sin, 250
River (*see* Arabic Index, *s.v.* Nahr)
Robinson, Edward, 2
Roof, 153
Rosette, 197
Royal domain, 96, 220

Sacrifice, community, 283, 286
Sahidic Translation, 341, 357
Sais, 249
Sam'al, 260
Samareitikon, 323, 330
Samaria (city), 91, 98, 101-2, 113, 119, 128, 132-34, 147, 150, 152, 161-62, 177, 220, 271, Fig. 4
Samaria (state), 19-20, 71-72, 88, 90, 101-2
Samaritans, 315, 319, 323
Samaritanus, Samaritan Pentateuch, 315-316, 319, 354, 356, 359
Sandstone, 41, Fig. 2
Sarcophagi, 172-73, 195, 213, 219
Sarcophagus, 'Alexander', 173
Sargon I, 252
Sargon II, 101, 252-53, 266, 271, 366
Sargon of Accad, 250, 252, 364
Satrapy, 8, 102-3
Saul, 49, 61, 78, 82, 90, 94, 131-32, 148, 152, 258, 365
Scarab, 163
Schumacher, Gottlieb, 3, 127, 132, 156
Scorpion, 38
Scorpion ascent, 89
Scorpion-bird-man, 198
Scribes, 203, 208
Scriptio Continua, 218, 353
Scythopolis, 90, 104
Sea Peoples, 78, 244-45, 255, 275, 365
Seal (stamp), 162, 219
Sebaste, 119, 147
Sedarim, 307
Seetzen, U. J., 2
Seleucia, 120, 265
Seleucids, 103, 120, 251, 262, 272, 276, 296, 367
Selim I, 112
Semitic, 224-30, 292, 364
Senir, 60
Sennacherib, 143, 253, 265, 271, 366
Senon, 41-43, Fig. 2
Sephardim, 306
Septuagint, 315, 321-45, 347, 352, 356-358, 361, 363
Septuagint manuscripts, 325-29
Septuagint recensions, 329-33, 357
Sesostris, 247
Seti, 248
Sexta, 330
Shalmaneser I, 253
Shalmaneser II, 252
Shalmaneser III, 60, 96, 253, 271, 366
Shalmaneser V, 253, 366
Shamash, 292
Shamshi-Adad I, 252, 270, 364
Sharon, 61
Shechem, 19, 58, 68, 73, 76, 85, 87-90, 93, 120, 128-29, 134-36, 140, 147, 151-52, 166, 174, 178-79, 207, 215, 315-16, Figs. 3 & 5
Sheep and goats, 18, 35, 39-40, 47, 56
Shelah, 70, 131
Shephelah, 56, 70, 74-75, 95, 98-99, 134, 136
Shiloh, 87, 176
Shishak, 275
Shishak I, 249, 271, 275, 365-66
Shoes, upturned, 198
Shrq, 98
Shunem, 71, Fig. 3

Sickle, 163, 166
Sidon, 74, 173, 262, Fig. 3
Sidonians, 51, 60, 79
Siloam, 158
Siloam Inscription, 158, 219, Fig. 8
Siloam tunnel, 157, 219
Silver, 167
Simeon, 66, 68-69, 70
Sin, 292
Sinai (peninsula), 214, 221, 326, Fig. 6
Sinai Inscriptions, 214
Sippar, 292
Siptibaal (inscription), 214
Sirocco, 32, 35
Siryon, 60
Sisera, 51
Smith, Eli, 2
Smiths (metal workers), 166
Snakes, 38
Snow, 31
Soco, 89
Solomon, 59, 81, 86, 94-95, 96-100, 122, 132, 136, 141, 146, 148, 152, 159, 176-77, 258-60, 268-69, 365, Fig. 4
South Arabia, 188, 192-93, 198-99, 222, 229
Southwest Asian race, 234
Sphinx, 195
Spinning, 165
Spring, 146, 154-58, 177
Square letters (Aramaic), 221, 313-14, 350, 353
Statues, 208, 214
Stela, 178, 197, 199, 208, 219
Steppe, 18, 35, 45-48, 186
Stone Age, 124, 200
Storms, 33
Streets, 154, 196
Streets, Roman, 117-18
Subartu, Subarians, 240
Succoth, 91
Sudan, 185, 236
Suez, Fig. 6
Sumerian (language), 232, 236
Sumerians, 236-38, 249-50, 264, 291-92, 364
Suppiluliumas, 254, 365
Sura, 310
Susa, 102, 232, 265, Fig. 6
Susanna, 335, 347
Syllabic writing, 202, 204, 210, Fig. 7
Symmachus, 323, 330, 345
Synagogues, 116, 118, 173, 222
Synchronisms, 269-72
Syria, 8, 9, 102, 126, 189-93, 197-99, 205, 210-11, 220-26, 231, 233, 240, 243, 245, 247-49, 253-61, 263-64, 270-72, 274-76, 280-81, 284-85, 293-95, 338-40, 364-67, Fig. 6
Syriac, 227, 323, 331, 337-40, 358
Syro-Hexaplaric Text, 331, 339-40
Syro-Palestinian Translation, 339

Taanach, 136, 140, 147, 160, 164, 179 (*see* Tell Ta'annek, Arabic Index)
Tables, 153, 158
Tabor, Mount, 71, 193, Fig. 3
Tadmar, *Tadmur*, 192
Tamarisks, 35
Tammuz, 280-81
Targum Jerushalmi, 318-19
Targum Jonathan, 318-19
Targum Onkelos, 57, 318-19
Targum Pseudo-Jonathan, 318-19
Targums, 309, 316-20, 323, 356
Tarqu, 271
Taurus, 188-89, 192, Fig. 6
Tekoa, 89
Tel Aviv, 22, 132
Tell Ḥalaf culture, 198, 200
Tel Neqila, 78
Temperatures, 31
Temple towers, 195-96, 291
Temples, 173-79, 279, 283, Fig. 5
Temples, Bronze Age, 174, 176, Fig. 5
Temples, Egyptian, 195, 203, 288
Temples, Iron Age, 174, 176
Temples, of Jerusalem, 117, 119, 127, 135, 152, 176-77
Temples, Mesopotamian, 196
Temples, South Arabian, 198
Tent, 40, 145
Terebinth, 34
Terqa, 293
Terre pisée, 150-51, 256
Tertiary, 41, 42, Fig. 2
Teshub, 295
Tetrapla, 330, 332
Textual errors, 349-54, 358
Textus receptus, 305, 308, 310
Thebes, 254, 264, 289-90, 364, Fig. 6
Thebez, 152
Theodoret of Cyrrhos, 332
Theodotion, 323, 326, 330, 345
Theotokos Church, 116
Threshing, 35, 38-39, 163
Throne, 159
Thutmose, 248
Thutmose III, 54, 176, 178, 248, 365, Fig. 7
Thutmose List, 248, Fig. 7 (*see also* 'Palestine List')
Tiberias, 15, 25-26, 303-4
Tiberias, Sea of, 15, 25, 27-28, 38, 54-55, 74, 91, 93, 113, 164
Tideal, 154
Tiglath-pileser I, 253
Tiglath-pileser III, 100, 252-53, 259-60, 271, Fig. 7

Tigris, 46, 48, 186, 191, 196-98, 224-25, 232-33, 236, 239, 265-66, 323, Fig. 6
Til Barsip, 261
Timnath-Serah, 58
Tirhaka, 249, 271
Tischendorf, K. v., 326, 328
Ṭkr, 78, Fig. 3
Tobit, 334
Tomb, 170-71
Toparchy, 103
Topography, 140-41
Towers, 150
Transcriptions, Greek, 320, 330, 334
Transjordan, 12-14, 26, 42, 61-63, 80, 88, 91, 123, 192
Transport wagon, 86
Tribe, 61, 63-75, 81-83, 93-94, 282, 365
Tripoli, 262
Tudḫaliyas, 254
Tukulti-Ninurta, 252
Turin Papyrus, 267
Turks, 112
Turonian, 42, Fig. 2
Tushratta, 256
Tut-ankh-Amn, 290
Tyre, 51, 59, 74, 189, 262, 294, Fig. 3

Ugarit, 52, 199, 226, 262-63, 294-95, Fig. 6
Ugaritic (language), 226, 263
Ulfila, 340
Uncials, 325
Unqi, 261
Upper chamber, 153
Ur, 200, 264, 292, Fig. 6
Urartean (language), 233
Urarteans, 242, 258
Urarṭu, 233, 258, Fig. 6
Urfa, 338
Urmia, Lake, 228, 339

Varuna, 296
Verse divisions, 307, 335, 348
Vetus Latina, 342-45, 357
Vowel writing, 203, 206, 211
Vulgata Sixtina, 335, 346
Vulgate, 334-35, 344-48, 356
Vulture, 38

Wailing wall, 119, Fig. 4
Walls, 123, 146-50, 197, Fig. 4
Walton, Brian, 319
War chariots, 150, 256-57
Warkan culture, 200, 206, 364
Water, 'Living', 155
Waterways, 85
Way stations, Roman, 84, 118
Weapons, 165-66, 173
Weaving, 165
Weights, 167
Well, 154, 191
Wen Amun, 78, 220
Wheat, 35
Wild boars, 38
Wilhelmina, 30-32, Fig. 1
Wind, 32-33
Wine, 98, 163-64, 220
Winged sun disk, 198
Winnowing, 35, 163
Wisdom Literature, 205
Wolf, 37
Wormwood, 46

Ximenes, F., 335

Ya'di, 260
Yagitlim, 252, 364
Yaḫdunlim, 252, 364
Yarmuk, 13, 27, 76, 93, 100-1, Fig. 3
Yasmaḫ-Adad, 252
Yazilikaya (Yazylykaya), 285
Yehimilk, 213
Young, Th., 203

Zab, 186, 266
Zarathustra, 296
Zebulun, 70-71, Fig. 3
Zeno, 116
Zenon papyri, 103
Zerah, 66
Ziklag, 83
Zimrilim, 250, 252, 270, 364
Zinjirli, 219, 260
Zion, 152
Ziqqurātu, 196
Zkr (Zakir) Inscription, 219, 259-61
Zorah, 74, 75